D0934743

COUNTRY AND MIDWESTERN

MARK GUARINO

COUNTRY & MIDWESTERN

CHICAGO
IN THE **HISTORY** *OF*
COUNTRY
MUSIC
✶ AND THE ✶
FOLK
REVIVAL

The University of Chicago Press
Chicago and London

Publication of this book has been aided by a grant from the Neil Harris Endowment Fund, which honors the innovative scholarship of Neil Harris, the Preston and Sterling Morton Professor Emeritus of History and Art History at the University of Chicago. The fund is supported by contributions from the students, colleagues, and friends of Neil Harris.

The University of Chicago Press, Chicago 60637
The University of Chicago Press, Ltd., London
© 2023 by Mark Guarino; foreword © 2023 by Robert William Fulks
Published 2023
Printed in the United States of America

32 31 30 29 28 27 26 25 24 23   2 3 4 5

ISBN-13: 978-0-226-11094-3 (cloth)
ISBN-13: 978-0-226-82437-6 (e-book)
DOI: https://doi.org/10.7208/chicago/9780226824376.001.0001

Library of Congress Cataloging-in-Publication Data

Names: Guarino, Mark, author. | Fulks, Robbie, writer of foreword.
Title: Country and midwestern : Chicago in the history of country music
    and the folk revival / Mark Guarino; foreword by Robbie Fulks.
Description: Chicago : The University of Chicago Press, 2023. | Includes
    bibliographical references and index.
Identifiers: LCCN 2022042607 | ISBN 9780226110943 (cloth)
    | ISBN 9780226824376 (ebook)
Subjects: LCSH: Country music—Illinois—Chicago—History and
    criticism. | Folk music—United States—History and criticism.
Classification: LCC ML3524 .G83 2023 | DDC 782.42164209—dc23/
    eng/20220906
LC record available at https://lccn.loc.gov/2022042607

⊗ This paper meets the requirements of ANSI/NISO Z39.48-1992
(Permanence of Paper).

DEDICATED TO THE
MUSICIANS OF CHICAGO

Contents

IMAGE GALLERIES FOLLOW PAGES 180 AND 324

FOREWORD

Robbie Fulks

One day in August 1983, I told my boss, a hard-drinking, hot-tempered book publisher named Don Fine, that I was leaving my job and New York. He asked where I was headed. "Chicago?" he spat, incredulously. "You won't have any trouble making a living there. It's a hick town!"

Upon my arrival, a tiny slab of urban real estate that pops up in this book—three adjacent businesses on the north side of Randolph Street between Dearborn and Clark—became a landmark for me. In the Greyhound station men's room I sat most mornings, hick-like, thumbing the classifieds. Once I had secured a mindless, decent-paying job (Don had been right: within six weeks I got three offers), I started slipping off to the Woods Theater on slow afternoons to catch the latest slasher flicks with a few dozen of my fellow truants and a handful of popcorn-seeking rats.

Between the Woods and the bus station—below both street level and the attention, evidently, of the city sanitation department—sat the Bar R-R Ranch. It was a bar out of both time and place. Its time was 1960 and its place was, I'd say, small-town eastern Kentucky. My day-job friends had heard about the house band there, a grizzled trio named the Sundowners who rocked the room five days a week, six hours a night. Besides country-and-western music, the joint offered a clientele that didn't invite close proximity and a chili that positively repelled it.

The R-R wasn't a thoroughgoing anomaly. Chicago in the early 1980s still had a foot in the 1950s: saloon cars on the commuter Metra train, burly men making deals in Russian bathhouses, dusty memorabilia shops and chophouses with brothel lighting, Runyonesque scribes in crumpled hats with names like Kupcinet and Royko. Everyone smoked. We up-and-comers back then had our culture of punk clubs and mimeographed zines, of smart-ass irony and knowingness. What our working-class elders had—honky-tonks, hardboiled literature, a wearier irony, actual knowledge—we envied. Those more traditional assets and attitudes, we all sensed, weren't as everlasting as they appeared.

Yet, being in our twenties, my friends and I did feel somewhat immortal. We knocked back cans of cheap beer our first night at the R-R, we danced, we yelled. We dropped napkin requests on the bandstand for songs like Kenny Rogers's "The Gambler" (which the band knew all five verses of). As I returned, over the years, I started sitting in with the Sundowners and getting to know them a little. Don, Curt, and Bob offered me an early ticket into the tribe of Appalachian musicianship, with its fast, clean playing, its sentimental lyricism, and its correspondingly unsentimental approach to working and living. A number of Chicago singers and pickers followed them in forming me. In a short time, I went from gazing curiously at the thing, to admiring it, to imagining I could be it.

A dramatic comment made by my friend Jeff Perkins has stayed with me. In 1990, he left a line-dance country band I had briefly led to move to Nashville and play drums for Hank Williams Jr. Soon after, I called him and asked him what the music scene was like down there. "I'll tell you one thing," he said. "Nobody here gives a shit about what's happening in Chicago."

The idea that "what happens in Chicago stays in Chicago," along with the city's sometimes ambivalent relationship with its local creatives, has generated enough commentary to make a long and tiresomely repetitive book, in which Saul Bellow's chapter would be longest and most epigrammatically dazzling. Bellow noted the artistic cost-benefit ratio built into the Chicago identity: "Provinciality is not altogether a curse, we gain also from our backwardness." The main gain—speaking now as a country artist—is the freedom experienced in working out of view of the industry, with all its chatter and dull consensus. The gains are material, and social, too: a thousand great musicians, mostly unknown beyond a two-hundred-mile radius of Chicago, own pleasant houses in safe-ish neighborhoods, where they raise families, park free on the street, and enjoy collegial respect, middle-class incomes, and long lifespans. But Chicago's second-city self-awareness reliably produces insecure bombast. "Why do so many of your shows start with a speaker talking for ten minutes about how great Chicago is?" asked an out-of-town friend after a concert of mine.

This boast-free book, on the other hand, puts the record straight on Chicago country with balanced perspective, a wealth of insane research, and a writing style so smooth the book practically reads itself. The many chapters bringing long-dead people and scenes back to life gave me the most pleasure. Karl and Harty, Jenny Lou Carson and Tiny Hill, Billy Chips, Bob Atcher and his girls, the Southern Inn, Carol's Pub, twelve-hour jams at Andy's. Holy cow, what a riot. And it all provably happened, right in America's biggest hick town. Thanks, Mark.

INTRODUCTION

Chicago has no entrenched cultural tradition like New York, Boston, Philadelphia and Los Angeles. An idea can grow here without being required to conform. . . . Oh, I'm not suggesting that we don't have entrenched cultural organizations here, but by and large great sections of Chicagoans are able to view a new cultural movement without prejudice and with a healthy curiosity.

WIN STRACKE, CO-FOUNDER OF
THE OLD TOWN SCHOOL OF FOLK MUSIC, 1962[1]

In 1947, country music was a genre without a proper name. In the twenties and thirties, you could hear it on barn dance radio shows on stations from coast to coast. Early record labels tended to categorize the music in the simplest terms: "singing with guitar and autoharp" for the Carter Family; "singing with yodeling and guitar" for Jimmie Rodgers. By the late thirties, anything that wasn't a jazz orchestra or a race record—blues, jazz, or gospel music marketed to Black record buyers—earned a derogatory term that reflected what New Yorkers in the recording industry thought of its rural White market: hillbilly music.

The recording industry marginalized hillbilly music to protect the thing it was built to promote: the pop music of New York's Tin Pan Alley. Even though country music was quickly evolving from solo fiddlers to the blues yodeling of Jimmie Rodgers to the loud and fast rhythms of honky-tonk, the genre lacked the prestige of Irving Berlin, George Gershwin, Cole Porter, or George M. Cohan.

That bothered Ernest Tubb, a Texas singer and bandleader who by 1947 was already as big as you could get as a hillbilly. He had played starring roles in Hollywood features, and his jukebox hit "There's a Little Bit of Everything in Texas" had sold over two hundred thousand copies. That gave him the clout to approach Dave Kapp, president of the hillbilly division of Decca Records, and tell him the catalog needed a refresh, starting with the name "hillbilly."

"What would you call it?" Kapp asked. Tubb had the most practical of answers: "Well, I don't know, but most of us are from the country originally—call it country music." Kapp thought it over. Tubb was right, in a general sense. But another of Decca's hillbilly star acts was the Sons of the Pioneers, a group it placed in the subgenre "cowboy music." The Sons of the Pioneers sang of sleeping beneath open skies in ranch country far beyond the Mississippi River. "We couldn't call *them* 'country music,'" Kapp told his star.

Tubb had an answer for that too. "Well, what about 'Western'? 'Country and Western'?" Kapp agreed, and Decca's Summer 1948 catalog announced a complete listing of country and western records, with pages of subgenres aimed at rural customers, both White and Black: "Ballads, Blues, Folk Songs, Spirituals, Country Tunes, Gospel Songs." Tubb, Red Foley, and Jimmie Davis—the label's biggest stars—were now prominently pictured under a new title that affirmed their dignity and artistry: "Country Artists."[2]

Kapp was a record man from Chicago. He knew enough to watch which way the wind was blowing. Before he and his brother Jack co-founded Decca Records in 1934, they worked for their father, Meyer Kapp, who ran a franchised Columbia Records dealership in downtown Chicago called the Imperial Talking Machine Store. Meyer was known in Columbia circles as a "hit forecaster" because, as he delivered to and took orders from customers in his horse-drawn buggy, he came to understand and respect public taste. Jack was fourteen when he started working for Meyer; Dave followed. By 1921, the brothers had opened Kapp Music & Radio at 2308 West

Madison, a phonograph dealership where they also sold race and hillbilly records for eleven years. But they wanted to go beyond the sales counter. Dave knew the value of song publishing, so he used the store's address to solicit songs in the *Chicago Tribune* classifieds. Meanwhile, Jack worked his way up the ladder at Columbia, Vocalion, and Brunswick.[3] By scouring Chicago dance halls and clubs and taking road trips through the South to find new artists, the brothers, like their father, became experts at predicting what the public wanted to hear. They were melody men who believed good songcraft was the ticket to winning over anyone. The theory came from the store, where customers would routinely come through the door and admit they didn't know what they wanted, "leaving the rest to the dealer's judgment," said Jack.[4]

Decca was one of three major labels dominating the country music business, along with Columbia and RCA Victor. Under Dave Kapp, Decca's country roster flourished. He discovered and groomed Ernest Tubb, Milton Brown, Rex Griffin, Jimmie Davis, the Sons of the Pioneers, Red Foley, and the Carter Family. Kapp also brought country music to a national audience by borrowing songs that had momentum in the rural market and handing them to pop artists to record as national hits. It's why Bing Crosby, the most popular singer of his era and a Decca artist, had bigger hits with his versions of "You Are My Sunshine" and "It Makes No Difference Now" than Jimmie Davis, who recorded them first. That spirit of reinvention also played out over time. One of the sixty Carter Family sides that Kapp recorded between 1936 and 1938 was "No Depression in Heaven," a song that a central Illinois band called Uncle Tupelo recast fifty-four years later as loud and fast punk, unintentionally making it a touchstone for like-minded bands who sought new inspiration in the lyrics, themes, and melodies of recordings made before the rock and roll era.

This book is about Chicago's defining role in these kinds of improbable exchanges among artists who freely reinvented country and folk traditions, and their empowerment by a series of gatekeepers, some of them radical idealists and others hard-knuckled hustlers. Together, they kept the dance churning in Chicago, seemingly the least likely place for the music to flourish.

With its promise of opportunity, whether factory work, higher education, or simply a middle-class lifestyle, Chicago became an unusual hothouse for creativity. It offered economic stability, something other cities could not always promise. As the larger recording industry drifted to both coasts in the middle of the twentieth century, people followed, lured by the promise of fortunes. In Chicago, however, there emerged the figure of the working auteur who could freely experiment, perform, and collaborate because they existed far from the star-making structures of Hollywood, Broadway, and Nashville's Music Row. Chicago's artists were not roped off from their audiences; instead, they lived and worked alongside them. The immediacy of making music within such an incubator community naturally gave artists who were uninterested in chasing popular trends the support to pivot left. They could pursue other sounds or strike up creative partnerships or cull musical ideas from the past and forge them into something that felt modern but still wholly their own creation. No one was looking, until they were.

Reinvention became practice in Chicago. As early as 1924, the stars of WLS radio's *Barn Dance* modernized the sounds of country fiddlers and polished mountain tunes from Appalachia for contemporary ears. Kentuckians like Bradley Kincaid became commercial ambassadors of Appalachian regionalism. The same could be said of many others in his wake: John Prine, whose grandparents hailed from Kentucky, posed with bales of hay for the cover of his 1971 debut album, even though he later admitted it was the first time he had gotten that close to the stuff, having grown up in industrial Maywood, Illinois. Prine had twang, but his early songs were unmistakably Midwestern in their minimalism and comic despair. The same is true of the Handsome Family, a married duo who filtered an Edward Goreyesque humor through the Appalachian folk music of Dock Boggs. Califone, a band of indie-rock refugees inspired by the early twentieth-century country, gospel, and blues recordings in Harry Smith's *Anthology of American Folk Music* from 1952, built on their themes of loneliness and death using trip-hop grooves, electronics, and noise. Then there is Jon Langford, a Welshman who arrived in Chicago to use the city as the backdrop for his lyrical country songs, energized by punk rock but crafted in the shadow of Johnny Cash.

Why Chicago? Years before Nashville emerged as the commercial and spiritual heart of country music, Chicago was the most active center for country musicians. The presence of major record labels in the city meant that seminal figures like Bill Monroe, the Carter Family, and Gene Autry recorded some of their most legendary recordings there. WLS's *Barn Dance*, broadcast Saturday nights from the South Loop starting in 1924, flourished for two decades as the premier variety show of its kind before the *Grand Ole Opry* emerged as its more relevant equivalent just as honky-tonk was reinventing the genre. Then there were the hardscrabble scenes in Uptown and the near West Side, where Southerners who had relocated by the thousands looking for work created their own subculture in makeshift honky-tonks.

Chicago played an important role in the music's early development due partly to shrewd and ambitious entrepreneurs like the Kapp brothers who saw potential in making the themes, melodies, and even fashion of country artists accessible to pop audiences. John Lair, the impresario of the *Barn Dance*, took the same approach. Lair scouted performers from Appalachia and transformed them into entertainers who captivated audiences, packed theaters, and sold records by the millions. Decades later, similar reinventions were still at work in Chicago. In the 1950s, a nomadic showcase for radical politics called the College of Complexes gave folk singers a stage. Its antithesis was the Gate of Horn, the nation's first nightclub for folk music, opened in 1956 by a West Side hustler named Albert Grossman. Much of the music on his stage was older than the people performing it. Grossman cannily rejected the overalls and denim of the coffeehouse scene and presented his musicians in tailored suits and cocktail dresses for the businesspeople and suburbanites taking it all in for their first time. Jump ahead another decade, and there is Earl Pionke, a former boxer who in 1966 refused to believe folk music was dead and opened a club, the Earl of Old Town, that would extend its life in Chicago for at least another ten years. After that, country and folk music found homes in stranger quarters: Club Lower Links, a bar for performance art and free jazz, and later, Lounge Ax, an indie-rock club. When that scene died, the music moved to a former Irish factory workers' shanty named the Hideout, which carried it into the next century.

The reinventing rolled forward as the music was moved under new roofs, adopted by new performers, and discovered by new audiences. Chicago's openness to reinvention allowed fans of country and folk to become engineers of the scene themselves.

A Korean War vet named Mike Fleischer returned home, enrolled at the University of Chicago, and organized a folk festival on the Hyde Park campus in 1961. His vision was a weekend festival that could bring disparate cultures within the United States together, which it did by presenting traditional artists like Roscoe Holcomb, Elizabeth Cotten, and Frank Proffitt for the first time in a formal, urban setting.

Bruce Kaplan, a former student president of that festival, was so inspired by it that, not long after graduation, he founded Flying Fish, an independent record label that helped launch the careers of John Hartford, New Grass Revival, Tim O'Brien, and dozens of others.

At the Gate of Horn one night in 1956, a suburban homemaker, a classical music vocalist, and an ambitious folk guitarist—brought together by an intense love of the music—decided to form a school in the homemaker's living room. Within a few weeks, they had founded the Old Town School of Folk Music, which would sustain roots music in Chicago for more than sixty years.

When a house painter and graduate student named Rob Miller walked into Crash Palace in 1993, vintage country blasted out of the punk-rock bar's sound system courtesy of Nan Warshaw, a local scenester who presided on Wednesdays in the DJ booth, introducing the pierced and tattooed set to musicians like Bob Wills and

Lefty Frizzell. The next year, she, Miller, and Eric Babcock pooled their resources to document the local underground country scene with a compilation CD that was so successful it led to a record label, Bloodshot, that kept the momentum going. Like any entrepreneurs with an ear to the wind, Bloodshot's founders discovered an audience hungry for their flavor of country. Because this was Chicago, not Nashville, Bloodshot's founders dubbed the genre "insurgent," another reinvention. Like other good ideas before their time, insurgent country caught on, and eventually became widely referred to as "Americana."

Yet, despite this dense history, the wider public has little idea that Chicago played such an important role in the early development of country and folk music, or that it later served as a place where the music entered new sonic realms. By official scholarship, Chicago is recognized primarily for the birth of modern gospel, the development of electric blues, the advent of soul, and the creation of house music. But even within these acknowledged Chicago genres, country is present. Blues powerhouse Chess Records, home of Muddy Waters, Chuck Berry, and Willie Dixon, experimented with country and folk, as did Vee-Jay Records, its neighbor on Michigan Avenue's Record Row that specialized in R&B and jazz. When off the road, gospel singer Mahalia Jackson moved within the circles of the Old Town School of Folk Music. Seventies blues guitarists Lonnie Brooks and Eddy Clearwater both had country strains in their music, and the Roy Hightower Blues Band, a hardcore blues outfit from the South Side, toured overseas with Greg Cahill, founder of the pioneering bluegrass group Special Consensus. When Jon Langford put together a collective of alternative country musicians for a series of albums, among his guest vocalists was soul music great Otis Clay. But the partnership that represents the ultimate bridge between Chicago's South and North Sides is the one between Mavis Staples and Wilco's Jeff Tweedy. The three records Tweedy produced for the civil rights–era soul singer between 2010 and 2017 introduced her to new audiences worldwide.[5]

Chicago's role in country music and the folk revival has never earned a closer look. One reason is the City of Chicago's failure to promote cultural tourism that goes beyond large festivals and the fine arts. In New Orleans, Memphis, and St. Louis, museums and historical markers celebrate their place in the development of modern music, and their musical histories are central to their tourism messaging. In Chicago, by contrast, the longtime home of Muddy Waters, at 4339 South Lake Park Avenue, remained blighted for years, and in 2013 was put on the Ten Most Endangered Historic Places list by Landmark Illinois, a nonprofit advocacy organization. Nearby, the famed Forty-Seventh Street nightlife strip has been flattened, as have most of Chicago's other sites of important nightclubs and musicians' homes. If Chicago's response to the important strains of African American music it has produced is largely a shrug, what hope is there for country or folk music traditions?

But a more significant reason why Chicago's role in country music is overlooked is the neglect of music scholars and of institutions like the Country Music Hall of Fame and Museum in Nashville. The museum's telling of the music's development barely mentions the early twentieth-century fiddlers' contests, broadcasts, recording sessions, and rural listenership that spread across the Midwest with the advent of twin technologies: the radio and the automobile. With this omission, it confirms the Southern bias perpetuated by respected scholars like Bill C. Malone, whose landmark 1968 book *Country Music U.S.A.* and its many revised editions describe country music as a phenomenon inherently tied to the character of the rural Southerner, rather than that of rural working people not corralled by any specific geography. This limited focus on the South would be reasonable if one were to focus only on country music's emergence as a commercial art form in the post–World War II era. The catalyst for Nashville's prominence came only in 1939, when the WSM radio program *Grand Ole Opry*, just one of many barn dance shows in the prewar years, received network airtime on NBC. The program's focus then shifted from presenting sentimental portrayals of hillbilly music to focusing on newer stars who were modernizing the music. Overnight, the music sounded relevant, and people started buying. WSM's coast-to-coast broadcast brought music publishers, A&R representatives, and talent buyers to Nashville because there was money to be made there. The construction of studios followed, first at WSM itself and then elsewhere in town. Within a decade, Nashville had an established system in place to develop and grow country music as a legitimate art form and a profitable genre.

Still, as late as 1946, Chicago was the US city with the greatest concentration of country musicians. Chicago joined Dallas, Cincinnati, New York, and Los Angeles as a prime center for hillbilly recording sessions. Hank Williams made his first recording at WSM that year, but he was one of only a few recording in Nashville. Music City in 1946 was a one-note town.[6]

No specific region can claim to be the cradle of country music. Instead, its character emerged from rural communities that eventually connected to growing urban centers through radio, the automobile, and the railroad. For much of the country, Chicago was the closest city big enough to provide opportunities in commerce and education, so it naturally became a place where people could reinvent themselves, even if that meant smiling wide, deepening the twang, and downplaying the stories of the sorrow and hardship that people with little means endure.

For all the country and folk music played, performed, and recorded in Chicago, none of it came close to defining a unified sound. The blues that came from Chicago's South Side sounded distinct from that of the West Side: the first rooted in the Mississippi Delta, the second flashy and raw. The blues record labels—Chess, Motown, Stax—each released music with a particular sound characteristic of their respective cities. That is not necessarily true for country music, however. The contribution that Chicago made to that story was not always as much about artistry as it was about opportunity. The recording studios, powerhouse radio stations, and nightclub scene made Chicago a natural stepping stone to the next place the music would go. There was cross-pollination here: the Kapp brothers pushing hillbilly music into the pop charts, university students in Hyde Park presenting Appalachian musicians in a formal theater setting, the Gate of Horn bringing folk music out of the coffeehouses and into the nightclubs, and the underground rock crowd finding inspiration in lost and ignored artists of the past and creating something strange but vital that was neither rock nor country.

Win Stracke saw this restless reinvention as unique to a city that, in many ways, should never have emerged from the inhospitable wetland habitat it was built on and the 1871 fire that almost brought it down. Stracke, born in 1908, led the most American of lives: as an oil rig laborer, a sacred singer, a theater troupe actor, a children's television entertainer, a target of Senator Joseph McCarthy's blacklist, and then, near the end of his life, the visionary behind a folk music school that could, in his eyes, elevate the often unknown creators of America's songbook and give them as much dignity as any composer whose scores filled the music stands of the Chicago Symphony Orchestra. To Stracke, music was a pursuit that had dignity. Musicians were not entertainers. They were necessary to remind people where they came from and who they could become.

Ward committees, labor unions, organized crime—they thrust Chicago to prominence because they operated through alliances, powering everything from the South Side steel mills to the city's political machine. The alliances that could raise a city like Chicago from a swamp and then spread it in every direction into the prairies required an unforgiving drive. Stracke understood that musicians had the same kind of stuff. The idea of Chicago as an incubator for creative movements might sound preposterous, considering its tough character and harsh climate, but that's what it was, because the artists who took root there knew how to survive with what they had.

"Success on someone else's terms / don't mean a fucking thing," Jon Langford sings as he imagines his artist hero falling off a cliff, a sacrifice to the gods of music and mirth, who shriek and laugh and bang loud things until eventually what you hear is a symphony.

THE WLS BARN DANCE
AND THE CALL TO
CHICAGO

In 1973, the only way to hear Karl Davis pick his mandolin was to descend the man's basement stairs. There, Davis was no longer just a sixty-seven-year-old throwback at rock powerhouse station WLS, where he was kept on the payroll to "turn records"—a humdrum union job that involved handling turntables for disc jockeys like Larry Lujack and Dick Biondi. Beneath his Portage Park home, on the city's Northwest Side, Davis was once again the pioneering songwriter and mandolin player who was present at country music's beginnings.[1]

Hanging on his walls were framed photographs and posters from his early life as one half of Karl and Harty, a mandolin-and-guitar duo that recorded for Columbia and Capitol Records and filled theaters from the sticks to the big cities. Over sandwiches and soda, Davis told a visiting reporter how he and others from the upland South trekked to Chicago to appear on the *Barn Dance*, a Saturday night radio broadcast that played a critical role in the early development of country music.

From 1924 through World War II, the *Barn Dance* made Chicago the nation's commercial heart of country music. It surpassed the *Grand Ole Opry* in popularity, eventually drawing nearly three million people from all across the Midwest to participate in its live audiences.[2] The prolific recording output of *Barn Dance* stars alone accounts for more than 8 percent of all country music records made between 1921 and 1941.[3]

The *Barn Dance* survived Prohibition, the Great Depression, a world war, and the rise of television, but it ultimately could not withstand a genre considered more lucrative by parent station WLS: rock and roll. By 1960, the year the *Barn Dance* signed off forever, many of its artists, such as Gene Autry, Bradley Kincaid, Red Foley, Patsy Montana, Bill Monroe, and Lulu Belle and Scotty, had already moved on to greater prominence elsewhere. Others had quietly retreated to playing folk festivals.

Davis didn't protest the change. He told the reporter that some of what WLS was currently playing had grown on him. A year later, he would tell another interviewer that he recognized echoes of his generation's music in contemporary artists like Creedence Clearwater Revival, James Taylor, and John Denver: "They're similar. . . . Ain't no difference in what we did. . . . I think we were in it maybe a little too early, although we're thankful for whatever we did back there."[4]

WLS AND THE EXPLOSION OF EARLY COUNTRY RADIO

Radio in Chicago was still in its infancy in 1924, the year *Barn Dance* was launched on WLS. Batteries powered most radios, and listening required either a headset or a primitive horn-shaped loudspeaker. Three years earlier, on November 11, 1921, Westinghouse station KYW had broken open the Chicago airwaves with the sound of the Chicago Civic Opera, which the station broadcast afternoons and nights six days a week. There were only 1,300 wireless receivers in the Chicago area at the time, but excitement over the new technology emptied stores of their inventory and drove people to make their own sets at home. By the end of the winter opera season, 20,000 sets were powered up in Chicago homes. Seventy-five percent of those sets were homemade.[5] One writer scanned West Side neighborhoods and reported seeing "crude homemade aerials" fixed atop one in ten rooftops for miles. The changing landscape suggested better times ahead: "For thousands of families, life has acquired new savor through radio."[6]

The station's overnight success naturally sparked competition. By December 1921, nearly a dozen local stations were in the works.[7] With wireless receivers scarce or too expensive for many, if ordinary people wanted to participate in the new technology, they had to take it into their own hands. Young people led the charge. By fall 1922, up to 75,000 sets were in circulation in Chicago, thanks in part to the hard work of students at the city's four technical high schools—Crane, Lane, Harrison, and Washburn—who spent their summer vacations feverishly building sets. Speaking to the Chicago Rotary Club, the editor of *Radio Age* praised Chicago teenagers for mastering "the intricate science of transmitting telegraph code by wireless" that "brought the United States to the front as a radio country." "These boys, who saved their dimes and built their crude laboratories in city basements or country woodsheds, are the pioneers of radio," he proclaimed.[8]

As the technology craze took off, stations experimented with content. KYW expanded its daily programming to twelve hours and filled it with news bulletins, sports reports from boxing matches and major-league baseball games, children's stories at bedtime, jazz in the evening, chapel services on Sunday, and during the day, stock market reports from the pits of the Chicago Board of Trade.[9] The US Department of Agriculture delivered grain and livestock reports three times a day as well as weather updates.[10] By 1925, there were forty stations broadcasting out of the Chicago area, including WGN, WJJD, and WBBM, a jazz station started by two brothers in the basement of a Sheridan Road home.[11] Radio not only delivered entertainment into the homes of farmers, it empowered them.

"Thanks to his radiophone, the wheat grower in the remotest prairie is on an equal footing with the speculator in Chicago," one writer observed. "He would be in no better position were he at La Salle Street and Jackson Boulevard, watching the bidding and selling.... He is enabled by radio to sell at the most opportune moment, and his suspicion of grain dealers is abating as his confidence grows."[12]

The promise of radio was to narrow the gap between rural communities and urban centers. In 1925, the US Department of Agriculture reported that the number of sets on farms had doubled since the previous year, totaling 370,000 in all. As it broadcast agriculture news over more than eighty local stations throughout the nation, the government was an active partner in getting homesteads connected because it considered radio the best way to encourage modern marketing of farmers' products and to keep them current with news.[13] Yet there remained stark challenges: most farms did not have running water or electricity, farmers themselves were resistant to change, and, for a class of people struggling through an agricultural depression that brought low wages and falling crop prices, there was the cost: manufactured sets averaged $175 off the shelf and $83 for building one from scratch.[14]

Chicago-based retailer Sears, Roebuck and Company entered the radio market in 1924.[15] One year earlier, the company had created the Sears-Roebuck Agricultural Foundation, which conducted economic research intended to help farmers market their products and would serve as a public relations tool for the industry by publishing research data in local newspapers. The foundation's pledge: "Let the Sears-Roebuck Agricultural Foundation Help You Farm Better! Sell Better! Live Better!" With radio on the rise, it became apparent that the best way to follow through on those promises was to launch a station exclusively dedicated to farm programming. The decision was made March 1, 1924, and by March 21, Sears was broadcasting an hour-long noontime farm program from the downtown studio of WMAQ. Meanwhile, the company started constructing a small studio in the tower of its massive complex and headquarters west of downtown. The company also furnished a second studio on the mezzanine floor of the Sherman House Hotel in Chicago's downtown Loop district. Both connected to a transmitter in Crete, an Illinois town located about thirty miles south of downtown.[16]

During three consecutive evenings of test programming, listeners phoned in their approval. Sears's growing confidence must have factored into its hasty decision, made on the afternoon of the station's first official broadcast on April 12, 1924, to change its proposed call letters from WES (World's Economy Store) to WLS (World's Largest Store).[17] The bravado of the new name was prophetic. The opening night broadcast stretched over five hours, and the guests at the microphone included marquee comedians, film stars, and stage actors of the day like Ed Wynn, William S. Hart, Otis Skinner, and Ethel Barrymore. The evening was infused with drama when Barrymore, invited to approach the microphone to say a few words, fell silent with fright before shouting, "Turn the damned thing off!" They whisked her away before she could say more.[18] *Radio Digest* summed up the gala in one word: a "feast."[19]

Orchestrating the evening was station director Edgar L. Bill, formerly with the Illinois Agricultural Association. In his post for only a month, Bill had limited experience in any type of media, and his station already faced a landscape of competitors that were better established, better staffed, and better funded. While KYW, WMAQ, WGN, and WBBM all carved out separate niches, whether classical music or jazz, the stations generally followed a familiar pattern of live broadcasts of hotel orchestras, afternoon recitals, bedtime stories, and lectures.[20] No other station exclusively catered to rural audiences, and none would devote as much of its Saturday night to old-time music as WLS would.

The inaugural *Barn Dance* was broadcast from the WLS studio in the Sherman House Hotel on April 19, 1924, exactly a week after the station went on the air.[21] No audience demanded such a show, and it followed little planning. Bill would later admit that the show was an experiment. Like all stations of the day, he broadcast live dance orchestra music, bedtime stories for children, and Sunday services, but he also produced radio plays for children and Shakespeare. Radio was fresh soil and he was a pioneer. "We would try anything once," he said.[22]

To fill up the station's first Saturday night, Bill looked for "old-time fiddling, banjo and guitar music and cowboy songs," the kind of entertainment that he felt a farm audience would appreciate, just as they appreciated the agricultural news and market reports broadcast throughout the week.[23] The *Chicago Herald and Examiner* previewed the broadcast: "Young and old will have their fling from 8 p.m. till midnight, because Isham Jones' College Inn Orchestra will alternate with the fiddlers and other musicians of yesteryear."[24] The structure of the show suggested it was not meant just for armchair listeners: WLS wanted people to pull up their rugs and dance. But the orchestra's involvement also implied there were few old-time musicians to fill all four hours planned for the show. No recordings of that first night exist, and not all the names of the artists who performed are known. Years later, promotional director George Biggar recalled that one of the show's fiddlers that night was Tommy Dandurand, a streetcar operator from Kankakee, Illinois, who would be involved with the broadcast through the end of the decade.[25] (In the press, the lead fiddle was credited to "Timothy Cornrow" from "Ioway," clearly a pseudonym.) Over those years, Dandurand recorded fourteen sides for Gennett Records with a group credited as the WLS Barn Dance Gang.[26] Banjo player Jesse Doolittle accompanied him that night, as did Tom Owen, a local hospital employee who, upon tuning in, heard a request over the air for a square dance caller. Sleep could wait: he called the station and said he'd be right over.[27]

By the end of the evening, more than 250 telegrams had poured into the studio from happy listeners. "That was the answer to Saturday night on WLS from then on," Bill said.[28]

The first identifiable personality on the early *Barn Dance*, and on the station itself, was not a musician but the show's announcer, George Dewey Hay. Born November 9, 1895, in Attica, Indiana, Hay moved to Chicago while in the third grade.[29] As an adult, he found the city unfriendly and dirty, so he retreated to Memphis, where he took a job as a court reporter with the *Commercial Appeal*. Soon he was writing a humor column, titled "Howdy Judge," that depicted exchanges, in African American dialect, between a White magistrate and his Black defendants. This was the type of minstrel show humor that was in the midst of transitioning from the vaudeville circuit to radio, most notably popularized by the NBC sitcom *Amos 'n' Andy*, which debuted in 1928. Hay's column was so popular that in January 1923 the newspaper appointed him the announcer of WMC, a Memphis radio station it had purchased the previous year. Although still in his twenties, Hay adopted the nickname "The Solemn Old Judge." He would answer to it until his death.[30]

Radio captivated Hay, and he proved a natural showman with a command of sound. In his role of "Judge," he spoke in a deep baritone and had listeners imagine they were traveling aboard a Mississippi River steamboat. To open and close broadcasts, he blew a toy steamboat whistle he named "Hushpuckena" after an unincorporated Delta town. When he moved to WLS in May 1924, Hay adapted his act: the steamboat whistle became a train whistle, and he told listeners they were now aboard the WLS Unlimited. The gimmick reflected his own transition from a smaller and sleepier city to the excitement of the new industrial powerhouse that was Chicago.

Hay played an important role in branding WLS. His rhythmic station breaks—"WLS, Chi-CAW-go! The Sears-ROE-buck Station"—would become familiar to listeners. When the Columbia Phonograph Company from New York City staged a recording exhibition in Chicago to record WLS harmony duo Ford and Glenn, and Art Kahn and his Senate Theatre Orchestra, Hay appeared at the top of each cut to give an introduction "in the same inimitable manner" he was known for after just a few months on the job.[31] Hay injected folksy humor into the *Barn Dance* that would continue long after his exit.

In September 1924, after just five months at WLS, Hay was awarded the Gold Cup by *Radio Digest*. He won not only the 14-karat-gold trophy, but also $5,000 in cash and bragging rights as "the world's most popular radio announcer."[32] Another result was a job offer from Nashville station WSM, which launched in October and was eager to create a national profile. Happy to ditch the grime of Chicago again, Hay accepted and moved back to Tennessee in November.[33]

Hay's arrival at WSM in Nashville started the wheels turning for a new program to top the *Barn Dance*. He was now a station manager, and his first task was to create programming with more variety than the usual opera and light orchestral fare. He started getting acquainted with local old-time musicians who occasionally performed on WSM, including Uncle Dave Macon and Dr. Humphrey Bate, a country doctor with a band. He let it be known he "was going to start something like the *National Barn Dance* in Chicago and expected to do better because the people were real and genuine and the people really were playing what they were raised on."[34] The first show Hay organized, which aired November 28, 1925, featured seventy-eight-year-old fiddler Uncle Jimmy Thompson, who took requests via telegram for over an hour.[35] The success of that night led Hay to formally announce a weekly two-hour show called the *Barn Dance*, for which he booked local hoedown bands, fiddlers, and harmony groups. He eventually incorporated stage outfits such as overalls and straw hats as the broadcast transitioned to a full stage show. It took two years for the program to get a more ambitious title: the *Grand Ole Opry*.

Both WLS and WSM initially met some resistance for devoting valuable airtime to "old-time," or "hillbilly," music, which was considered primitive compared with the classical music and opera that dominated early radio programming. What helped smooth the transition was the brief but influential fiddlers' contest craze of the mid-1920s promoted by Ford Motor Company founder Henry Ford. As a child living outside Detroit, Ford developed an early interest in fiddle music and square dancing, and both played significant roles in his life. Square dancing, he believed, summoned "a time that was less hurried and more neighborly."[36] Ford became a patron of elderly musicians by recording them at the studios of his friend Thomas Edison, and he created a ballroom in a corner of a building of his Dearborn plant to host old-time dances. Ford dealerships that were especially ambitious arranged square dances among their new vehicles.[37]

Ford's campaign prompted a revival of fiddlers' contests, square dances, dance conventions, and talent shows that were sponsored by local radio stations, vaudeville theaters, and fraternal organizations; many of them became annual events in Illinois, Indiana, Texas, Kentucky, Oklahoma, Texas, Virginia, and elsewhere.[38] In summer 1924, the *Barn Dance* hosted its first fiddlers' contest, in which twenty teams representing five Midwestern states participated. At least twenty fiddlers appeared on the program's regular bill in those first few years, including Eugene Murdock and George Adamson, the winners of that inaugural contest, who were not from the South, but from Kenosha, Wisconsin.[39]

The popularity of fiddle music and the nostalgia for old dances it provoked established the *Barn Dance* as distinctly Midwestern and rural in flavor. For rural musicians who lived and performed throughout the Midwest, the explosion of radio broadcasting in the 1920s brought substantial opportunities to grow audiences and promote live appearances through the programs that relied on their talents. The *Barn Dance* stood tallest among these programs because, unlike smaller stations that paid very little or not at all, WLS offered substantial wages: union scale for musicians appearing for only a segment of the Saturday night broadcast earned them about $20; WLS staff musicians received about $60.[40]

BRADLEY KINCAID:
THE FIRST COUNTRY MUSIC RADIO STAR

By its second year, the *Barn Dance* was on the move. The broadcast relocated from the mezzanine floor of the Sherman House Hotel to a sixth-floor theater in the same building that was built to accommodate a live audience of a hundred people. In November 1925, the station also boosted its power signal from 500 to 5,000 watts.[41] That same year, a folk singer from Kentucky arrived in Chicago to attend college. He would become the *Barn Dance*'s first artist with sustainable star appeal, and his immense popularity would reflect the breadth and loyalty of its rural audience. With the *Barn Dance* still in its relative infancy, Bradley Kincaid's success served as a template for building a personal relationship between performers and fans.

Kincaid was not the first folk singer on WLS. That would be Chubby Parker, a five-string banjo player from Indiana who today is best remembered for the song "King Kong Kitchie Kitchie Ki-Me-O," first recorded in 1928 and later collected on the *Anthology of American Folk Music*, the influential 1952 compilation curated by Harry Smith.[42] Parker specialized in traditional, minstrel, and comic songs, and he recorded for several labels, including Gennett and the Sears labels Supertone and Conqueror. His songs, like "Oh Dem Golden Slippers" and "Nickety Nackety Now Now Now," were simply arranged—just voice, banjo picking, and fanciful whistling. Kincaid later described Parker as jealous of what he perceived as Kincaid's preferential treatment by both the station and its fans. Parker demanded that Bill, the station director, choose one man or the other. "Goodbye Chubby," Bill replied.[43] That was 1927.

Kincaid was an accidental star. Born in Garrard County, Kentucky, on July 13, 1895, he grew up in a multigenerational family that sang both popular songs from the turn of the century and old-time ballads and would accompany their singing on guitars and fiddles during social dances held on Saturday nights. Decades later, he would recall that those customs were already fading by the time he enrolled in nearby Berea College to complete his high school degree after serving in World War I. Opportunity was beckoning. "Country became more civilized, with the coming of roads [and] a way to get out," he said. Encouraged by his teachers, he started collecting the old songs.[44]

Kincaid came to Chicago to attend George Williams College in Hyde Park, where he planned to study to become a social worker. Already married, Kincaid paid the bills as a first tenor in the YMCA College Quartet, a group that toured throughout the Midwest, Pennsylvania, and West Virginia between 1925 and 1926. In the promotional booklet for that tour, Kincaid is shown bespectacled in a dark suit, his hair neatly parted.[45] Photos taken a few years later show him in a lumberjack shirt, rolled-up trousers, and boots, holding a Martin guitar given to him by his father, who, on a hunting trip, had traded a dog for it over a campfire. When WLS heard the story years later, it branded the instrument Kincaid's "Houn' Dog guitar."[46] In promotional materials, the bond between instrument and singer was described like that of the Lone Ranger and Silver, or Roy Rogers and Trigger. Through its catalog, Sears offered the Supertone "Bradley Kincaid 'Houn' Dog' Guitar," manufactured by the Harmony Company. It was the first "cowboy" guitar, a genre of mass-produced instruments sold in the 1930s through the 1950s, connected to popular cowboy singers like Gene Autry and Rogers.[47]

Kincaid's transformation from glee club singer to folk song custodian started in 1926, when the quartet performed on one of WLS's weekday programs. Word got to music director Don Malin that Kincaid was fresh from Kentucky and carried with him a repertoire of folk songs. Malin invited Kincaid to return that Saturday for the *Barn Dance*. Kincaid borrowed a guitar and performed "Barbara Allen," a song he remembered his mother singing to him as a child. Kincaid's switch from choral work to folk music was solely practical: Malin was offering real money at $15 a week, and it was steady. "For a college student that only has doughnuts and coffee for breakfast, that was pretty good," he recalled.[48]

Kincaid's repertoire of songs, handsome looks, and charming demeanor all played a role in making him the broadcast's first popular star. The station branded him "the Kentucky Mountain Boy," and fan letters poured in by the hundreds each week. WLS soon realized that not only were listeners focused on Kincaid, but people also wanted more information about his songs. That was a challenge, since none of the songs the Kincaid family sang were written down. "I was singing from word of mouth," he said.[49]

Sensing opportunity, the station suggested he transcribe from memory a selection of songs that could work together as a book. In producing this songbook, Kincaid established a standard for preserving folk music through the use of commentary and musical notation written by his wife, Irma Forman Kincaid, an Oberlin Conservatory of Music graduate. The process was grueling: Kincaid would hum songs to his wife, she would transcribe them as piano accompaniments and guitar chords, and he would later hammer out the lyrics on a typewriter. When he had twenty-two songs, he paper-clipped them together, slid them into a folder, and turned them over to Bill. Ten thousand copies of the songbook were ordered. Two days later, Bill called in an additional twenty thousand orders. The songbook, published in April 1928 as *My Favorite Mountain Ballads and Old-Time Songs*, sold more than a hundred thousand copies and went through six printings.[50] Its pages include gothic fare such as "Barbara Allen" and the murder ballad "Pretty Polly," and the first appearance of "Cuckoo is a Pretty Bird (A Forsaken Lover)," a song that Thomas Clarence Ashley would record in 1929 and that would then reappear on the *Anthology of American Folk Music*, leading to covers by Bob Dylan, among others.[51]

Radio was still in its first decade, and Kincaid's songbook stands out as one of the earliest ways a popular performer connected with a mass audience. He would publish thirteen different editions in all, more than any country star of the 1920s and 1930s, including the Carter Family or Jimmie Rodgers.[52] Total sales probably reached a half million copies.[53]

With mail pouring in, WLS realized it didn't want to lose its main star, so the station bumped Kincaid's salary from $15 to $100 a week.[54] Two years later, the station established the WLS Artist Bureau, a booking agency, to capitalize on Kincaid's popularity and to prime the audience for other performers. Soon, besides appearing on the *Barn Dance*, Kincaid was headlining at tent shows, fairgrounds, and theaters, where he sold songbooks from the stage and promoted his records. The circuit had already been established by vaudeville, so booking *Barn Dance* performers was easy; Kincaid remembers earning up to $400 for performing four to five shows a day. At first, he underestimated the power of his radio popularity. His first date was a matinee in Woodstock, Illinois. While approaching the theater, he saw a line of people trailing for several blocks. He stopped and asked what the commotion was all about. "Why that radio singer from WLS is going to be here!" he was told.

"That got me to thinking," Kincaid said, "that maybe there really was some money in the music business."[55]

The songbooks gave Kincaid material to record, which he did, under his own name and others, for nearly thirty labels, including Gennett, Brunswick, Decca, and Capitol. His sessions in Chicago and nearby Richmond, Indiana, for Gennett produced the majority of his prolific output, more than a hundred sides in all.[56] His songs were mostly Scottish, Irish, and English ballads, sentimental and novelty songs that he presented in simple arrangements, accompanying his tenor voice with his guitar. As in his songbooks, the central focus of the recordings was on the songs; by releasing them into the world, Kincaid not only contributed to preserving them, but also helped create a vocabulary for country artists in generations to come.

When Kincaid ran out of songs pulled from his childhood memories, he returned to Kentucky during vacation breaks to find more. Photos in his songbooks pictured him in the field, on front porches or in homes, among local musicians, giving readers a deeper understanding of where the songs developed. Inside the ninth songbook is a photo of Kincaid standing on the bridge in Clay County, Kentucky, near the home of "Old Joe Clark," the title character, a notorious moonshiner whose death remains a mystery. In all, Kincaid collected nearly three hundred songs between 1928 and 1948.[57] That work became his main calling; when he left WLS in 1930 to accept a job at WLW in Cincinnati, he didn't draw a salary, but told the station that all he required was its help in securing consistent theater bookings, which were far more profitable and where he could sell the songbooks.[58] He knew his worth: in his first month on the new job, Kincaid received fifty thousand letters from fans.[59]

PRAIRIE FARMER REFASHIONS
THE *BARN DANCE* FOR A MASS AUDIENCE

By the time Kincaid left Chicago, WLS had new owners. Under *Prairie Farmer*, the agricultural weekly that took ownership of the station in 1928, the *Barn Dance* reached thousands more listeners, expanded its cast of stars as well as its live audience, and increased its marketing capabilities, and broadcast two live shows every Saturday night totaling four hours. The show's aesthetic in sound, personality, humor, and even fashion emphasized a romantic view of rural life over its coarse realities, especially during the Great Depression and the difficult war years. Escapism was responsible for the program's enduring success.

Prairie Farmer had launched in 1841 and by 1928 was enduring a shakeup due to financial strain and increasing competition from a new crop of regional farm journals. Its paid circulation had passed 265,000 by 1928, but owner Burridge Davenal Butler had dreams of topping a million.[60] A radio station that could cross state lines would help. He had previously bought time on WLS for local farm programming, and he had hired stars from the station to provide live entertainment during circulation drives masquerading as variety shows. The magazine also ran a weekly column called "The Wireless Man," designed both to promote radio to farmsteads and to answer farmers' questions about a new medium they were just beginning to understand. When the magazine moved to its new offices at 1230 West Washington in January 1927, Butler installed a small studio so it could broadcast fifteen minutes of agricultural news every day at noon on WMAQ.

Butler had conducted research and discovered that WLS rated highest among farmers in Indiana, Illinois, and southern Wisconsin by 59 percent; except for WGN, at 10 percent, all other stations in the region earned low single digits.[61] Butler was convinced. On the day of the sale, he published a full-page advertisement in the *Chicago Daily News*, titled "Why I Bought WLS," that promised the station "will be a vibrating power working for better cooperation and understanding between Chicago and the cities and towns and rural communities of the great Mid-west."[62]

Butler had a deep personal investment in WLS, so much so that he wrote a provision into his will stating the station could not be sold until ten years after his death. Born February 5, 1868, in Louisville, Kentucky, he was raised by his mother and grandmother as his father relocated to New York City where he served as an editor and correspondent for Christian media outlets.[63] He later reunited with his wife, and the couple started a ministry in Michigan. Butler's parents were opposites in how they approached Christ's teachings: Thomas, his father, was a harsh disciplinarian who once spanked Butler when told his son questioned whether the Chinese went to heaven. Marie, his mother, wielded a far gentler touch. "My father was a preacher who pulled wings off of flies—He was a sadist. And my mother was a poet. I am a combination of both," he said.[64]

By all accounts, he was right. Butler belittled employees, held grudges, and was prone to violent acts. He was competitive and compulsive. Within his first year of moving to Chicago in 1909, he expanded the staff. Local news and information were priorities. He redesigned the front page of *Prairie Farmer* to emulate hard-hitting newspaper dailies. Photographs ran on thicker paper stock. The once sleepy journal became newsier, and editorials adopted a crusading tone. The facelift worked: by 1915, paid circulation more than doubled to exceed one hundred thousand.[65]

Butler was a high moralist. He shuddered at the popular image of the backward hillbilly, which he considered not just debased but corrosive to a national audience. His vision for the *Barn Dance* was to reflect the wholesome attitudes and values of *Prairie Farmer* readers. "I am proud to publish *Prairie Farmer* and to control a powerful radio station, both in the service of Agriculture," he wrote.[66] To him, show business was phony and facile. He rejected tawdry material and demanded that performers carry themselves in a respectable manner, both before the microphone and during public appearances. For the broadcast, he preferred that performers wear simple overalls and calico shirts, his imagined wardrobe of heartland folk. Anything that sparkled, or flowed, or, for women, was cut short, would be considered too "Hollywood." Because he cut an intimidating figure, he could demand a costume change on the spot and not be rebuffed. Singing cowboy Bob Atcher remembered Butler's talent for grabbing both sides of a collar and ripping a shirt straight off a performer's body. With Butler standing over six feet and weighing close to three hundred pounds, few protested the demeaning treatment. But some did. Once, disgusted by a lumberjack shirt worn by musician Hartford Taylor, Butler reached out and tore it off his body. Taylor whipped around and threw Butler against a piano, pressed his elbow against his throat, and gave his boss some news: "If you ever do that again, I'll kill you."[67]

The music of the *Barn Dance* also came under Butler's scrutiny. Davis remembered Butler refusing to allow him and Taylor to sing "I Didn't Hear Anyone Pray," their 1940 hit version of "The Wreck on the Highway," because it contained the lyric, "There was whiskey and blood mixed together / but I didn't hear anyone pray." One Saturday night, when Butler was out of town, the duo sang the song anyway. The live audience fell silent to listen. After they finished, the applause was so strong they returned to sing it two more times. Davis savored his brief victory: "Now that shows you how the audience responds!"[68]

In time, the *Barn Dance* established a full slate of commercially successful recording artists, some of whom would go on to Hollywood to star in a 1944 Paramount Pictures feature titled *The National Barn Dance*. But in those first years, the show fulfilled Butler's vision of wholesome entertainment with novelty performers like Pie Plant Pete, who played guitar and harmonica simultaneously; the Maple City Four, a comedic vocal quartet from LaPorte, Indiana; and Arkie the Arkansas Woodchopper, a rustic-minded fiddler and guitarist. Contrary to the Southern identity later embraced by the country music industry, the music in the broadcast's earliest stage was far from being exclusively Southern. In its promotional materials as early as 1930, WLS emphasized music that traveled beyond the Midwest but was presented as rural and nostalgic: "Old time music from the cabins of Dixie mountaineers, from cowboy bunkhouses, and from middle western farms is included on the barn dance. The variety of entertainers runs from a simple Jew's-harp up to a complete 'little German band.' Fiddlers, guitar and banjo teams, old-time soloists, yodelers, quartets, trios, duos, hymns, ballads, comical songs, a bit of jazz and harmonica music are all found on every dance. Champion old-time fiddlers and square dance callers of the middle west have frequently been decided as a result of contests on the *National Barn Dance*."[69]

The show's reach expanded in 1931 when WLS was granted access to a 50,000-watt transmitter owned by WENR in exchange for carrying ten hours of programming by WENR's parent, the National Broadcasting Company. The station's measure of success was mail: the following year, station mail spiked 39 percent, passing the one-million mark for the first time, and sustaining that rate for more than a decade.[70] WLS extended its reach still farther when it constructed its own 586-foot transmitter in 1938 in suburban Tinley Park, about twenty-five miles south of Chicago, which gave it a stronger signal downstate.

While radio stations in different parts of the country broadcast their own programs in the barn dance format, the WLS *Barn Dance*—carried nationally starting in 1933—was by far the most popular. Access had a lot to do with it. In 1930, 40 percent of homes in the United States owned at least one radio, and the majority of home radio ownership was in the North Central and Northeastern United States, which collectively represented 76 percent of the sets in the country. Comparatively, the South represented only 12 percent of home radio ownership. The story is the same with farm families: 45 percent of rural households in the North Central and Northeastern states owned radios, compared with only 5 percent in the South. Those numbers changed once rural electrification spread late that decade, but in the early days of radio, WLS reigned.[71]

As its radio audience expanded, the *Barn Dance* struggled to keep up with demand for tickets to attend the live broadcast. The problem was space: the *Prairie Farmer* studio could accommodate only a little over a hundred people, much like the show's previous home at the Sherman House Hotel. When the *Barn Dance* traveled to the International Amphitheater for a broadcast on October 25, 1930, nearly 20,000 fans from around the Midwest filled the seats, and another 10,000 people were turned away.[72] The next year, in August 1931, 16,000 people filled the seats when the *Barn Dance* cast played the Illinois State Fair in Springfield.[73] Clearly, the show was now a phenomenon, and careful planning was required to grow its profits.

The solution was the Eighth Street Theater, located at the northeast corner of East Eighth Street and South Wabash Avenue in the South Loop. Built in 1905, the former vaudeville house had 1,200 seats, which station management knew it could easily fill. So WLS decided to have two shows every Saturday night and, for the first time, to charge its live audience admission. After the first broadcast from the theater on March 19, 1932, proved that nearly 2,500 people were willing to pay for seats each week, the station immediately entered a contract with the theater to continue the shows indefinitely.[74] From that opening night broadcast through August 31, 1957, when the live broadcasts ended, the *Barn Dance* reaped 2,617,000 paid admissions at the Eighth Street Theater. On Saturday nights, the theater was dubbed the "Hayloft." A common sight on Saturday afternoons during those years was a line stretching down Wabash. More than half of those angling for a seat were from outside Chicago.[75]

JOHN LAIR CRAFTS
A COUNTRY MUSIC CAMELOT

Speaking to an interviewer in 1971, John Lair struggled to recognize modern country music from the traditional sounds and images he refined at the *Barn Dance* as a young man. He recognized there were fewer musical borders in his day, fewer characteristics to define the music that ordinary folks performed and enjoyed: "It's not a location that makes music, you can't call it country, you can't call it city or anything of the sort. Now you speak of opera, you know exactly what you're talking about. If you speak of religious music, you recognize it at once. But everyone has a different idea of what country music really is, and until we find a better name, I guess we'll have to use that."[76] Lair had coaxed the music of the upper South to Chicago, but he also recognized the power that same music held when it was unshackled from geography and free to go everywhere. His vision was to make the regional recognizable to the masses. If that meant diluting what made those homegrown sounds so special, well, that was a small price for progress.

Born July 1, 1894, in Mount Vernon, Kentucky, close to the foothills of the Cumberland Mountains, Lair arrived in Chicago in the late 1920s as medical director for the Liberty Mutual Insurance Company.[77] The job was strictly a cover for his true ambition: show business. He was an unabashed showman with a dream of packaging the music and humor from his upbringing in Appalachia into a stage show that would serve as a nostalgic restaging of his childhood experience. The *Barn Dance* was his Camelot, a mythologized environment where everything wonderful about his rural home could be brought to life, with all the rough edges, like poverty and violence, smoothed away.

Exposed to vaudeville during a stint in the military during World War I, Lair saw how old songs came alive in new settings. He did not see action during the war, but was stationed in Washington, DC, where he participated in theater productions and wrote sentimental prose. With the war over, he returned to Renfro Valley, Kentucky, and drifted through a series of professions—teaching, newspapers, and then insurance when Liberty Mutual hired him in 1922, which allowed him to travel to Boston, New York, and eventually Chicago. He had theater in his bones. When Virginia Crawford, his future wife, first met him, Lair was teaching math. "I could tell the first day he didn't know what he was talking about. Because he was making a game out of mathematics," she said. His daughter added of her father, "Everything was kind of a show or a production."[78]

Settled in Chicago, he heard Bradley Kincaid, also from Renfro Valley, on WLS and started pitching him songs. Lair talked his way into the station as a part-time employee, and his ideas soon broadened the show's sound. The *Barn Dance*'s transition from an in-studio broadcast to a live theatrical show before a paying audience was inspired by his experiments. Before the relocation, he convinced the station to remove the glass wall separating the audience from the performers. Then he set down loose wooden boards and brought in a fiddler for square dancing. A novelty for radio, the dancing transported listeners beyond their living rooms and into the action. "We put our play party people out on that floor and played for them, you could hear the feet romping across the floor!"[79]

As the station's librarian, Lair wrote a weekly column for its promotional magazine *Stand By!* that explained the origins of songs,
responded to inquiries from listeners, and often solicited their help
in finding more information. He claimed to have collected up to
twenty thousand songs.[80] Lair's interest in the old songs was less
musical than Kincaid's. He was most enthusiastic about establishing the real-life events that inspired their creation.

His sleuthing created opportunities for great drama. At a live
broadcast from the 1937 National Folk Festival in Chicago, he
appeared with Janie Jones, the wife of Casey Jones, the railroad
engineer immortalized in a controversial early twentieth-century
ballad that bears his name. After interviewing her about her husband and his efforts to stop a speeding train that resulted in the
1900 rail crash that claimed his life, Lair dropped a bombshell: he
revealed an older version of the song that "plays up the tragedy of
the song and sounds as if it might have been written by a sincere
friend of Casey Jones who mourned his heroic death." The published version known to most people, Lair sniffed, was "boisterous,
comic" and meant "to make the song sell better." Even the melody,
he told the widow, was stolen from versions dated to the previous
century. "I have traced it back to the eighties," he said, "to a song
called 'J. Gould's Daughter,' and also to a song about 'Jimmy Jones,'
a colored porter." To further shame the popular version, he asked
rhetorically if the widow believed the song tells the story "about the
way it actually happened" and, as a final blow, if she ever received
compensation. After she answered no to both questions, he replied,
"Well, that's the way it goes."[81]

Lair created a pipeline from Kentucky to bring musicians to
Chicago, promising them a weekly salary on WLS and residual
income from other radio and stage work during the week. Early in
his tenure, he solicited musicians by letter. In a 1930 exchange with
Ernest Hodge, a Kentucky fiddler later known as the "Stradivari of
the Appalachians" because of his nine years of classical training
in Atlanta, Lair announced he was assembling "an old-fashioned
barn dance orchestra" made up of three musicians who must "have

fairly good voices and play fiddle and guitar." Should Hodge and his brother Robert, a guitarist, accept, Lair told him, they would have to join the musician's union, whereupon they would earn thirteen dollars for each *Barn Dance* broadcast. As with most musicians Lair solicited, he wrote to Hodge with urgency, pressing for an immediate reply. The only requirement, he wrote in closing, was that they sign a contract making him their manager.[82]

Hodge and his brother, who were already on the radio in Cincinnati as the Hodge Brothers, responded favorably but wanted details: exact salary and Lair's split.[83] In his response, Lair announced a change of plans, blaming the station's program director, who wanted only musicians already on staff. However, Lair said both men were welcome "to take a run up here for a try-out." As for compensation, his answer was seductive: no salary, but a guaranteed twelve dollars per musician for each *Barn Dance* broadcast. "The real money comes from theatre and party work through the week when we could get as much as thirty dollars per man per night," he wrote. "I would manage the act, look out for bookings etc. and handle you as I do the other boys—that is, retain half of all you make above fifty dollars per week—or, if you prefer, take twenty percent of all your earnings." The clincher was the promise that WLS would soon boost its signal range, which "would allow them to reach over practically the entire country"—a suggestion of ample opportunities to come. "There is plenty of money in this thing if we can click."[84]

Signed contracts with other artists contain similar terms, with Lair collecting half of all earnings even from published music and recordings. Besides these profits, Lair insisted on the right to create or procure "all songs, music, routines, spoken lines or sketches," essentially brokering deals that allowed him to shape the artists according to his own vision.[85]

With the lure of the big city and big money, word spread. Musicians from smaller rural radio markets actively sought out Lair to lobby for a chance to get to WLS. Lair was relentless in finding out what they could deliver beyond their resumés. "You say in your letter that you play lead violin and guitar. Can you play the bass, fiddle,

harmonica or five-string banjo? What is your voice? Tenor? Baritone? And what type of songs do you do best?" he asked one fiddler
from West Virginia, after telling him to submit a list of "fifty favorite songs." Even though he was judging candidates for a radio job,
Lair also demanded a photograph and physical description. The fiddler took Lair so seriously he answered giving the color of his eyes.[86]

The first musicians Lair worked with were the mandolin-and-
guitar duo Karl Davis and Hartford Connecticut Taylor, whom listeners would know first as the Renfro Valley Boys and later as Karl
and Harty. Bradley Kincaid, impressed after hearing both men
picking during a visit to Berea College, sent them to Chicago to audition for Lair. It turned out that Davis and Taylor had been students
when Lair taught fourth grade in Mount Vernon, Kentucky.[87] Davis,
born December 17, 1905, and Taylor, born April 11, 1905, formed
an early string band called the Krazy Kats. By 1930, the group had
regular airtime on WHAS in Louisville.[88] They were harmony singers influenced by Lester McFarland and Robert Gardner, a blind
minstrel mandolin-guitar duo known as Mac and Bob who had several popular hits on Brunswick. Neither Davis nor Taylor sang lead,
but they switched back and forth depending on the melody range.
Their earliest ambition was to internalize the songs they learned
from older people in town or musicians who came down from the
mountain on Saturdays to play music on the courthouse lawn. Davis
later recalled watching with awe as one man spun his bow around
his fiddle with finesse, despite having hands that were deeply rough-
ened by weekly labor.[89]

Both men realized a golden opportunity in the *Barn Dance*:
in Chicago, they had been grinding away at factory jobs, and Lair
offered a salary of $60 per week. "We needed songs desperately. We
wanted to stay here," Davis recalled.[90] Davis wrote his mother to
ask her to head to the mountain and collect songs. Another source
of material was gospel songbooks, which he and Taylor used to
transform quartet notation into duets. They also made a beeline to
Montgomery Ward and ordered Carter Family records, then just
three years young. Soon, a total of fifty Carter songs were in the

duo's repertoire. Their records were the greatest source, Davis said, of "authentic, soulful, colorful songs, with a punch and with beautiful melodies." Just as important as the material was the sense that the Carters, whom Davis would soon get to know when the group recorded in Chicago in 1940, showed audiences their sound was true to back home: "The real thing is what counts, isn't it?"[91]

Karl and Harty were among the first to introduce Carter Family songs to a wider audience. Eventually the duo started writing their own songs, and they were prolific. Between 1931 and 1942, Karl and Harty released sixty-six songs under their own names and others, and recorded seventy masters.[92] The recordings had lasting influence long after the duo first quit the *Barn Dance* in 1937. Their biggest songs, "I'm Just Here to Get My Baby Out of Jail," "The Prisoner's Dream," and "Kentucky," earned them recognition decades later through cover versions by Hank Snow, Porter Wagoner, Marty Robbins, Chet Atkins, the Everly Brothers, and the Jerry Garcia Band, among others. Johnny Cash considered "I'm Just Here to Get My Baby Out of Jail" one of "the classic tragedy songs of country music." He chose it, among similar jail songs by Hank Williams and Jimmie Rodgers, to perform during his first prison concert in 1957, in Huntsville State Prison in Texas,[93] and again in 1968 when playing Folsom State Prison in California, where he recorded his famed live album.

Karl and Harty's "Kentucky," recorded in January 1941 and released on Columbia, was a sentimental hit, especially for soldiers stationed overseas who responded to songs that rhapsodized about the pleasures of home. "You are the dearest land outside of heaven to me," the duo sing with blended voices. The song resurfaced the next decade with a cover by the Everly Brothers and then again in 2013 with a version by Norah Jones and Billie Joe Armstrong of the rock band Green Day—a version NBC would choose to promote the 2014 Kentucky Derby.[94]

Although they augmented some of their recordings with fiddle and banjo, it was Davis's mandolin that drove Karl and Harty's sound. Bluegrass was not yet an identifiable genre, and the mandolin was associated more with Italian popular idiom and the vaudeville circuit. The mandolin's large curved back and strips of light and dark wood earned it the derisive name "tater-bug" from rural musicians because it looked like the insect that infested their tubers. When the Gibson Mandolin-Guitar Manufacturing Company in Kalamazoo, Michigan, transformed the instrument in 1922, flattening its back and later improving its design to give it fuller tone and greater volume, the mandolin seeped into recordings, the earliest by Doc Hopkins and Mac and Bob, both of whom migrated to WLS in the 1930s.[95] The instrument's adoption by harmony groups created a precursor for bluegrass.[96] At the same time, improved carbon microphone technology allowed singers to find more intimacy in their voices by no longer having to shout to the top of the rafters.[97] All of these changes created a new style of country music, but it took Bill Monroe, the "Father of Bluegrass," to step in and send that music to the world.

In fact, the first person Monroe remembered seeing play the modern mandolin was Karl Davis.[98] Monroe had arrived in nearby East Chicago, Indiana, in 1929 to join his older brothers Birch and Charlie at work at the Sinclair Oil refinery in nearby Whiting. The Monroe brothers were also displaced Kentuckians; Bill was born September 13, 1911, in Rosine.[99] When he was eight, Birch and Charlie, who played fiddle and guitar, respectively, gave him the family's antiquated "tater-bug" mandolin, and the three brothers played parlor parties and dances around town. Their father's death in 1928 disrupted the family's large farming operation and forced them to move north for more lucrative and steady work. At Sinclair, eighteen-year-old Bill Monroe unloaded empty fifty-six-gallon oil drums from freight trains and cleaned them with gasoline. As grueling and as dangerous as the work was, Monroe referenced the experience with pride throughout his life, saying five years on the job taught him the importance of a daily regimen.[100]

Monroe was already familiar with the *Barn Dance* and was fond of Bradley Kincaid.[101] Now with money in their pockets, the brothers became regulars on the local square dance circuit in Northwest Indiana. Tom Owens, the resident square dance caller on the *Barn*

Dance, observed all three men tearing up the floor with their girl-friends in Hammond, Indiana, one night in 1932. "How would you boys like to dance on the stage for a living?" he asked.[102] No convincing was required.

The Monroe brothers joined a WLS square dance team that toured small theaters throughout Indiana, Illinois, and Wisconsin for three months. The bill included *Barn Dance* stars Red Foley, the Maple City Four, and the Hoosier Hot Shots. The tour stopped at the 1933–1934 World's Fair in Chicago. The brothers' short-lived dancing career led to a new opportunity: playing music on WWAE in Hammond and then at WJKS in Gary, Indiana, where they hosted a fifteen-minute show, five days a week.[103] Around that time, Monroe ditched his "tater-bug" and purchased a Gibson F-7 flattop mandolin.[104] The Monroe Brothers, as they were billed, then started playing local live shows. Their earliest exposure to show business was playing a four-show-per-day bill at the New Palace Theater in Chicago's Loop district. Each time their fifteen-minute set wound to an end, twenty-six burlesque dancers suddenly appeared to whisk them off the stage. "Country boys out there and naked girls behind them!" Charlie remembered fondly.[105]

The Monroe Brothers' repertoire was limited to Carter Family songs and others heard on the *Barn Dance*. "We just had a lot of the old stuff. Neither one of us had ever written a song. Didn't know how to start one," Charlie said.[106] Karl Davis later recalled that when Bill visited backstage, he would ask to play Davis's mandolin, a Gibson F-2 model: "I've never heard anybody play as fast in my life. I went over across the stage, and I got Red Foley and Linda Parker and Harty. I said, 'Come over here and listen to this man play this mandolin.' Lightning, you know. Nobody had ever heard a mandolin like that."[107]

By 1934, Bill and Charlie had accepted an offer to perform at a sponsored show on KFNF in Shenandoah, Iowa. Birch chose to stay behind to support his family. The risk bore fruit: the two brothers signed to RCA Victor in 1936, and in 1939, Bill was invited to play on the *Grand Ole Opry*. But Bill was far from done with Chicago.

Bill Monroe made the seminal recordings of his career in Columbia Records' Chicago studio on the second floor of the Wrigley Building, a skyscraper tucked beside the Chicago River.[108] He first returned to Chicago to record eight sides for Columbia in February 1945. However, it wasn't until the following year that Monroe would begin recording the songs that would become bluegrass standards for generations. Monroe and his Blue Grass Boys recorded a total of twenty-eight songs over four days, including "Wicked Path of Sin," "Blue Grass Breakdown," "The Old Cross Road," "Toy Heart," "Summertime is Past and Gone," "Little Cabin Home on the Hill," "Blue Moon of Kentucky," and others. Taking place September 16–17, 1946, and October 27–28, 1947, these sessions were broken down into a few hours each in the afternoon and in the late evening. Unlike Monroe, most of his new band—Earl Scruggs on banjo, Lester Flatt on guitar, Chubby Wise on fiddle, and Howard Watts on bass—had no experience in a recording studio, which became an asset. They performed few takes and instead drew from the energy of performing onstage. These sessions introduced Monroe's raw and bending vocals, which he later described as "high lonesome," and Scruggs debuted his innovative three-finger picking style during the instrumental breaks. One Monroe original recorded on the evening session on September 16 became his most famous song. "Blue Moon of Kentucky" would live on nine years later in 1954 when Elvis Presley recorded it as the B side of his first single on Sun Records.[109]

Another famed instrumentalist whose first exposure to show business was on the *Barn Dance* was Les Paul, the electric guitar innovator who later recorded dozens of country standards with his wife, Mary Ford. Growing up in Waukesha, Wisconsin, Paul was an avid *Barn Dance* listener years before picking up a guitar. A chance meeting following a WLS road show with Pie Plant Pete, one of the station's earliest performers, led him to his instrument. Pete was influential in ways that weren't just musical. As "pie plant" was a common nickname for rhubarb, Paul would soon invert his idol's name and christen himself Rhubarb Red.[110]

Paul was eighteen when he moved to Chicago in 1933 to play

on WBBM for the World's Fair. By then he had formed a duo playing hillbilly fare with Sunny Joe Wolverton, a high school friend. Paul found steady work as an instrumentalist on the *Barn Dance*, but his real ambition was to gig at South Side jazz clubs under his own name. With fellow *Barn Dance* players Ernie Newton, a swing bassist, and Jimmy Atkins, a rhythm guitarist who was half brother to Chet Atkins, he formed the Les Paul Trio. Four years later, they moved to New York to further their careers. Paul would always credit his years with the *Barn Dance*, both as a listener and later on staff, as formative: "They were my teachers. That's where I learned to do everything."[111]

THE CUMBERLAND RIDGE RUNNERS AND THE PROMOTION OF MOUNTAINTOP NOSTALGIA

In 1930, John Lair convinced WLS to create a group consisting of musicians from his home in Renfro Valley. Lair hired Davis and Taylor; banjoist Howard "Doc" Hopkins, a barber in Mount Vernon who had played in the Krazy Kats; and Gene Ruppe, who played fiddle, banjo, and harmonica. The group's look and sound sprang from Lair's imagination. He called them the Cumberland Ridge Runners and dressed them in plaid shirts, suspenders, boots, neck scarves, and felt hats. He had them pose for photos in front of animated rural settings and wrote them scripts thick with mountain dialect. Two years later, he would rotate in other musicians, among them Homer Edgar "Slim" Miller, a lanky comedian and fiddler from Indiana with crooked teeth, who was often pictured barefoot, and Linda Parker, a young singer whom Lair topped with a sunbonnet. "Folks sometimes say that the Ridge Runners are like a chapter out of the past, suggesting the days of the long rifles and coonskin caps of pioneer Kentucky," the station's publicity copy read in 1935.[112]

The group's recording output was scant, amounting to two sessions in 1933. But they served as a flagship for WLS, used weekly on different shows and also in live appearances, where they performed instrumentals, old-time sentimental songs, or novelty numbers. One of their most popular was "Goofus," constructed with fiddle breaks that allowed the musicians to switch instruments with one another and continue.

Lair picked up a jug and inserted himself into the group. Early WLS promotional material shows him blending in with the others, in one picture with his head back, comically peering into the jug. Not long after, Lair composed photos with himself as the central figure and the others turned toward him as if for guidance. In copy, he is often described as their manager, as in this piece from 1933: "The only difference between John Lair in the office and John Lair before the microphone is that with his happy crew of Cumberland Ridge Runners, he relaxes and drops back into the native dialect of the mountains to which he was born, says 'you-all,' and 'hain't got no more time this mawnin', but mebbe we'll play it fer you tomorrer.' That's not 'put on,' either."[113]

Despite the caricatures that Lair perpetuated on WLS, he refused to use the word "hillbilly" and made it clear he considered it derogatory. He thought of himself as honoring a rural subculture by smoothing it out for city folks. "The fact is that if a radio microphone actually could pick up a real hill billy singing back in the hill country of the south, most listeners probably would tune out," he said. "The typical mountaineer who has never been out of the hills sings because he likes to. He's not too much concerned with how it sounds."[114]

The Ridge Runners lasted only five years. But in that short time, their act reflected both the commercial appeal of an Appalachian fantasy and an unease with the speed of change in America—its industrialization and dramatic shifts in family and cultural life. Their appearance at the World's Fair in 1933 was strategic: they performed in an 1863 barn that once held grain and livestock on the family homestead of Henry Ford's father. The automaker shipped the barn across Lake Michigan from Springwells Township to Chicago so it could be part of an exhibit on industrializing soybean production. Lair's script for the show, cast in exaggerated dialect, applauds Ford as a modern industrialist who, despite making great strides toward the future, has not done so at the expense of homespun American values: "This little old grey barn, tho, really stands fer something, folks. It brings home to us the fact that we're livin in a mighty wonderful country where in the brief span of a lifetime a barefoot boy kin go frum the hayloft of this old barn to the very top of the industrial world—an it speaks a lot fer a man who kin do all that an still find room in his heart fer the everday things of the simpler life he once led."[115]

Two years later, the Cumberland Ridge Runners broke up. No one in Elkhart, Indiana, knew on August 1, 1935, that they were watching the group's final appearance. But there was one sign.[116] Linda Parker, the twenty-three-year-old singer Lair had branded as "The Little Sunbonnet Girl," performed in pain, probably while holding her stomach. Eleven days later, she died of peritonitis, the result of a burst appendix. Thousands mourned her death, an outpouring stoked by WLS's publicity. The legion of martyred rock stars that die early is well documented, but back then, the sudden death of a performer, especially one perceived as the angelic embodiment of youth, was unprecedented. The grief spread far and wide because it was real.

But Parker transcended the circumstances of her death. She was the first female country singer to launch a successful solo career outside a group. Until then, the identity of a woman in the so-called hillbilly market was hitched to a male partner or existed within a vocal group. Women were side players. Parker may have started as the centerpiece of a group of men, but her singing voice, a sweet, crooning alto, gave her prominence. As soon as she joined, the Ridge Runners turned into accompanists.

Parker was a high school delinquent from Hammond, Indiana, who even as a teenager knew who she was and what she wanted to become. She was born January 18, 1912, as Genevieve Elizabeth Muenich, the daughter of local laborers who had a shotgun marriage after her mother got pregnant at age seventeen.[117] When Muenich herself was the same age, she was already out of school and singing pop tunes on WWAE, the station where the Monroe Brothers got their start. She also performed around town, playing

roadhouses and outdoor fairs. Even then, she had a rough edge. She
was kicked out of Hammond High for truancy and didn't last long
at Hammond Tech, the neighboring vocational school that took in
problem students. Her sights were set not on school, but on radio.
By September 8, 1929, the date of her WWAE debut, she had already
been branded with a stage name to remember: "Jeanne Munich,
Radio's Red-Headed Rascal."[118]

Muenich soon moved from WWAE to WAAF, a station broadcasting from the Chicago stockyards, and her following started to
grow. Lair took notice and, in an effort to widen the Ridge Runners'
appeal, signed her to a contract in April 1932. He became her business manager and booking agent, pocketing 20 percent.[119]

That contract changed everything. To distance Muenich from
WAAF, Lair gave her the stage name Linda Parker. As her contract
stipulated that Lair would furnish her with "all songs, music, routines, spoken lines or sketches," Muenich had no choice but to portray a fictional character who was not from industrial Indiana, but
from Lair's idealized version of his Kentucky mountain home. In
public and in pictures, she wore gingham dresses and a sunbonnet
with pearls and high heels. The meshing of rural and contemporary
styles added to the fantasy of "The Little Sunbonnet Girl," her new
moniker. In photos she clutched a banjo and dulcimer, but there is
no evidence she knew how to play them. When she married Arthur
Janes, a baritone singer in the Maple City Four, the station initially
kept it secret. WLS wanted Muenich's audience to know her only
as a dreamy, virginal sweetheart who served as a calming presence
amid the turmoil and insecurity of the Great Depression. "Lindy,"
the station told listeners, "is a slender, quiet girl of nineteen, serious faced, often getting a sort of far-away look in her eyes as if she
were day-dreaming of that beloved mountain country which she
sings about."[120]

Muenich's recorded output as Parker was slim: just four sides
released by the Sears label Conqueror in 1933 and 1934. Lair found
old Southern ballads for her to sing, mostly sentimental fare like
"I'll Be All Smiles Tonight," a waltz that pre-dates the Carter Fam-

ily's version by a year, and "My Ozark Mountain Home," a mournful-sounding ballad that sets her voice against Davis's trembling mandolin. As her popularity grew, Lair supplied her with original songs like "Mother's Old Sunbonnet," with lyrics that reinforced her nurturing image. Lair also reworked "Single Girl, Married Girl," an old folk song made famous by the Carter Family and sung from the perspective of a mother yearning for a different life. The new version, just titled "Single Girl," is less gloomy and instead idealizes the carefree life of youth: "Single girl, single girl, lives a life of ease / Married girl, married girl, has a boss to please."[121]

Muenich's popularity was boosted by Ridge Runner tours across the Midwest as well as the Saturday night broadcasts. But she also appeared solo throughout the week on WLS, playing Parker on *Mountain Memories*, *Play Party Frolic*, the *Hamlin Wizard Hour*, and the *Coon Creek Social*. Muenich became a reliable presence in listener households, which made her unexpected death a shock. More than three thousand people showed up for her funeral in La Porte, Indiana, where the Cumberland Ridge Runners served as pallbearers.[122]

Her death, in a way, fit her otherworldly image, and allowed WLS a final marketing opportunity. "Linda sleeps beneath the largest weeping willow in the cemetery," the station reported in its obituary, a fictitious detail meant to recall "Bury Me Beneath the Willows," the Carter Family song she reportedly sang in Elkhart just before being rushed to the hospital.[123] Lair later peddled the story in his column, recounting to readers "that dreary pain-racked afternoon."[124] By December, Muenich's smiling image floated above a transcription of the song in *100 WLS Barn Dance Favorites*, a songbook Lair rushed out in her memory. "Her sweet voice first brought you many of the songs which you will find in this book," he wrote in its dedication to her.[125] By January, Karl and Harty had penned and recorded "We Buried Her Beneath the Willow," a song that contributed to the official legend. The song is a simple but maudlin waltz that imagines why God chose Parker at such an early age: "A soft song fell within his hearing / he picked our girl / her soul, her voice," they sang. "Today our partner sings in heaven / God praised the angel for his choice." In 1959, Kitty Wells added a church organ to her version of the song, giving it a permanent place in the country gospel canon.

The Cumberland Ridge Runners also launched the career of Red Foley, who would become one of the most successful country stars of the postwar era, laying claim to the first million-selling country record made in Nashville. He too was a Kentucky boy, born Clyde Julian Foley in Berea on June 17, 1910.[126] When Doc Hopkins, the Ridge Runners' banjoist, left for a job at NBC in February 1931, Lair tracked Foley down and sent a panicked letter asking him to make the trip north by the week's end, even inviting Foley to crash at his apartment to defray expenses. As with all his recruits, Lair promised him steady work on *Barn Dance* broadcasts augmented by live dates on the side, which paid nearly double the weekly radio stipend.[127]

Foley had vocal training as a young boy and eventually studied music at Georgetown College, so when he arrived in Chicago there was polish in his voice. His Southern roots and vocal croon would both serve him well in crossing over to the pop charts. A writer christened him a "barnyard Bing Crosby."[128] Foley recorded with the Ridge Runners, but it wasn't until he signed to Decca Records in 1941 that his recording career took off. When he went to Nashville in 1946 to replace Roy Acuff as the emcee of the *Grand Ole Opry*, he was already a national pop star, even appearing on recordings with Lawrence Welk and his orchestra. He was well aware that his Midwestern credentials would make him suspect in Nashville: the audience, he recalled, "thought I was a Chicago slicker who had come down to pass himself as a country boy and bump Roy out of his job. It took me about a year to get adjusted." He did, and through his WSM tenure, which ended in 1953, Foley recorded forty-nine Top 10 hits.[129] His smooth vocal style helped establish the new cosmopolitan country sound.

During Foley's *Barn Dance* days, Lair paired him with Myrtle Eleanor Cooper, a singer from North Carolina he recast as Lulu

Belle, a comic tomboy character who wore checkered dresses and high-topped boots, pinned back her hair, and snapped her gum. This was 1932, and Lulu Belle's mountain girl character directly clashed with Linda Parker, the earthbound angel. She and Foley were billed as "sweethearts" in routines where she chased him for attention, dragged him into mischief, and sassed announcer Hal O'Halloran. Foley accompanied her on guitar for just two recorded sides, the best known being "Daffy Over Taffy": "Chewin', chawin', pullin', pawin' is the best of fun / in the kitchen, round the oven, lovin' till it's done," she sings over his playful fingerpicking. Her yodeling sews the song to a close.

When Foley married in 1933, his wife demanded that Lair put an end to the act, so he matched Cooper with Scott Wiseman, another North Carolina native who, under the tutelage of Bradley Kincaid, was a song collector and budding songwriter. Cooper and Wiseman married in 1935.[130] As one of the first husband-and-wife harmony duos in country music, Lulu Belle and Scotty sparked with listeners, and between 1933 and 1958 the couple served as the longest-running and best-loved act in *Barn Dance* history.

WLS promoted the union heavily, playing up the couple's hill country roots. A 1935 article in the station's magazine covered a visit to their childhood homes as an opportunity to reinforce the couple's rural biography. Photos show them picking berries, inspecting a "typical mountain home," and picnicking with locals. These home-spun details obscured the harsher reality of their backgrounds. Born December 24, 1913, in Boone, North Carolina, Cooper was the daughter of a convicted moonshiner and toiled in a hosiery mill as a teenager.[131] To escape the authorities after breaking out of jail, her father relocated his family to Evanston, Illinois, just north of Chicago. There, she continued to work menial jobs while performing around town with her guitar before auditioning at WLS.[132]

Wiseman, born November 8, 1909, was one of ten children raised on a farm in Ingalls, North Carolina. Because there were no paved roads to his high school, located seven miles from his home, he lived in a dormitory all week. There, he picked up a banjo or guitar at night to accompany school square dances.[133] He soon earned a reputation for knowing old mountain songs of the area, and caught the attention of Bradley Kincaid, who sought him out one summer during a scouting trip for one of his songbooks. Wiseman was not yet a teenager, but taught Kincaid what he knew. His generosity paid off: Kincaid recommended that WLS hire Wiseman. He gave up his plans to be a teacher and moved to Chicago.

Parenthood in 1935 boosted the couple's popularity. The uncertainty created by the Great Depression led to a demand for entertainment that emphasized stability, and the Wiseman family offered just that. WLS created a narrative of kindred souls lost in the big city—"aliens in an alien land" according to one writer. "Here they were, two youngsters fresh from the sticks, suddenly brought together at a radio barn dance in the heart of the city. It's the sort of thing you wouldn't credit if you read it in a book."[134] With their children—gossip magazines said their firstborn daughter Linda Lou was named to honor Linda Parker—the couple represented a family unit building a home without financial hardship, a fantasy most radio listeners were happy to indulge.

A sign of country music's ascendency in the American home came in 1936, when fans voted Lula Belle the "Queen" of national radio in *Radio Guide*, elevating her over popular stars like NBC soprano Jessica Dragonette, comedian Gracie Allen, and radio and recording powerhouse Kate Smith. Her victory appeared to surprise even the magazine's editors, who contrasted the "glamorous" Dragonette from "fashionable New York" with Cooper "from a mountain cabin," whose popularity had come "from nowhere."[135]

The couple became one of the highest-paying acts in the country. A prolific recording career followed, as well as personal appearances and starring roles in seven Hollywood features between 1938 and 1950. Beyond the charm of the couple's personality and rapport, they also wrote most of their own material. The primary songwriter was Wiseman, who contributed many early country music standards, including "Mountain Dew," "Brown Mountain Light," "In the Doghouse Now," "Remember Me," and with his wife, "Have

I Told You Lately That I Love You?" a song performed and recorded by dozens of artists, including Hank Williams, Elvis Presley, Eddie Cochran, Jerry Lee Lewis, and Ringo Starr.

Lulu Belle and Scotty directly benefited when in 1933, NBC created a coast-to-coast broadcast of *Barn Dance*'s second hour, making it the first national country music radio program.[136] The show changed its name to the *National Barn Dance*, and soon more than thirty stations were carrying the broadcast. Alka-Seltzer signed on as sponsor. The performers of the Great Depression years were dubbed "The Hayloft Gang," and they would all gain recognition far outside the Midwest. The exposure opened doors for them in Hollywood, in theaters across the United States, and in 1939, even in the White House.

SINGING COWBOYS AND COWGIRLS ON THE *BARN DANCE*

The characters that John Lair introduced to the *Barn Dance* may have been drawn to idealize Southern mountain culture, but they were stereotypes that to some appeared unsophisticated and even crass. Musicians wishing to break into show business but who wanted to project an image that was more romantic, with a dash of movie star glamour, could choose another character: the singing cowboy. By the late 1930s, the *Barn Dance* cast featured performers, dressed in classic western wear and topped with ten-gallon hats, who represented the frontier days of open skies and limitless possibilities—a potent image for Americans who were suffering under the hardships of the Great Depression and the brutalities of urban life.

Cowboys were already fixtures in Chicago by then. They can be traced back to 1893, when "Buffalo Bill" Cody's Wild West show made a stop in Chicago for the World's Columbian Exposition. Over the next few decades, the nation became fixated on the cowboy hero through Theodore Roosevelt's fascination with "taming" the West, the dime novels of Zane Grey, and the early screen cowboys of silent films. Chicago was no exception. Its society class took to cowboy country as an exotic playground. In 1933, the *Chicagoan* described Chicago's Loop district as containing many stores "filled with high Western saddles, cowboy's chaps, huge Stetsons, high-heeled boots, and sketches of rearing broncos" that served vacationers planning trips to dude ranches in Wyoming and Montana, some run by former Chicagoans.[137]

The singing cowboy represented clean living, positive values, and law and order. That this image would emerge in Chicago during an era of street violence represented by Al Capone was a matter of circumstance. Nashville was not yet the recording center it would become after World War II, Los Angeles was strictly about movies, and New York City was too remote. The *Barn Dance* entered more homes than any other country music program nationwide, and drew the biggest live audience, largely made up of rural transplants. In 1929, it wasn't uncommon to step onto a city bus at Howard Street and hear the driver singing cowboy songs, from "Goodbye, Old Paint" to "Whoopee Ti Yi Yo, Git Along Little Dogies," all the way downtown: the bus driver "sings, he says, because he once rode range and range songs are all the songs he knows," a writer explained.[138]

Soldier Field hosted rodeos starting in August 1925. The rodeo circuit's first promoter was John Van "Tex" Austin, who had already staged rodeos at Madison Square Garden and Yankee Stadium in New York and at Wembley Stadium in London. On the first day of a nine-day "Chicago Roundup," seventy-five cowboys and fifty cowgirls paraded through downtown Chicago on a double-decker bus before arriving at the stadium. Five hundred animals were required for the duration. With daily attendance averaging between fifty thousand and seventy thousand people, the city was pleased with the turnout, and Austin continued offering "prancing pintos, bucking bronc's and careening cowboys" for three more years.[139] Audiences grew, and movie cowboys like Tom Mix were added to the bill for star power.[140]

Chicago even had a self-professed cowboy for mayor: William Hale "Big Bill" Thompson. Newspapers around the country called him "the Cowboy Mayor," and Thompson became a character as big as the Stetson he wore around town. Western-style adventure had enticed him at a young age: at twelve he was among a gang of kids arrested for riding horses across the State Street bridge on a quest to capture imaginary Indians in Lincoln Park. Eventually his father fulfilled his son's fantasy by buying a 3,800-acre ranch in western Nebraska for him to manage.[141] He learned roping, riding, drinking, and telling tall tales, all traits he put to use when first elected mayor in 1915. That inaugural year, he ordered 165 motorcycles to transform police officers into "cowboy motor cops." "They will sweep around the outskirts of the city the same as a bird dog does in trying to pick up scent of game," he announced. The method was based on those "used in western round-ups of cattle."[142]

Thompson appeared at rodeos, trotted through Grant Park on horseback, and once rode a horse into City Council chambers.[143] Serving as Chicago's top official during Prohibition and the gang wars, Thompson developed an international reputation for largess. He hired well-known songwriter and sheet music publisher Milton Weil to write a theme song for him, "Big Bill the Builder." The song was such a hit he awarded Weil a job as assistant commerce commissioner for the state. Thompson "drank hard, ate heavily, and loved to talk about the days on the wide open plains, when he was a rootin' tootin' cowboy," remembered a *Chicago Tribune* reporter who covered the mayor until he left office in 1931.[144] To celebrate an election victory in 1927, he hired two steamboats for a river trip to New Orleans. He invited five hundred of his closest friends, topped them all in cowboy hats and, upon arrival, greeted New Orleans Mayor A. J. O'Keefe dockside with "the cow puncher's symbol of victory, a coonskin nailed to the cabin door."[145]

So when Gene Autry arrived in Chicago in 1931, the town was primed. Although Autry wasn't the first singing cowboy, his success helped move early country music off the Southern mountain and point it toward the west. Born September 29, 1907, as Orvon Gene Autry, he grew up in Oklahoma, where he worked as a teenage telegraph operator for the St. Louis–San Francisco Railway.[146] It was the era of desperadoes and train heists; Autry himself spent a night in a meat car after a holdup by the Matt Kimes gang in Weleetka. "I never carried a gun, even though we were in the middle of the Oklahoma oil fields, mean country," he wrote later. "Robberies were part of the job."[147]

A chance meeting with his hero Will Rogers in 1927 changed his life. Autry, nineteen at the time, was working at the depot in Chelsea, Oklahoma, that summer. As he sat there around midnight, strumming his Sears, Roebuck guitar, Rogers, in town visiting a sister, walked up to wire his newspaper column back East. According to the legend Autry recounted until his death, Rogers liked what he heard and told Autry to "get yourself a job on radio."[148] The next year, the young telegraph operator hopped a train to New York City to give it a try.

Autry auditioned for record companies but was told he needed to do something about his nervous energy, so he returned home and billed himself as "Oklahoma's Yodeling Cowboy" on KVOO in Tulsa. He was back in New York, recording for Columbia Records, in less than a year. Autry fashioned himself after Jimmie Rodgers, who was at the forefront of the yodeling craze and was singing songs with western themes. Autry recorded under both his own name and several pseudonyms, but even with modest success, he wasn't making enough to live on. The 1929 stock market crash limited steady work opportunities, so he relocated to the Midwest, settling in Aurora, Illinois, about an hour west of Chicago. There, he became a regular on WJJD by joining a hillbilly group called the Buckle Busters. From Aurora, he commuted to recording sessions at Gennett Records, which was just getting into the emerging hillbilly market.

By the time he made it to WLS, Autry was partnered with Art Satherley, an A&R man for the American Record Corporation and future vice president of Columbia Records, who is considered among the most influential executives in the development of early country music. Besides Autry, he is directly responsible for recording Bob Wills, Lefty Frizzell, and Roy Acuff, among many others. He also played a hand in developing blues artists Ma Rainey, Blind

Lemon Jefferson, Big Bill Broonzy, Leroy Carr, and Memphis Minnie. Satherley was tall, an Englishman, and much older than most of his artists—nearly twenty years Autry's senior. He answered to one nickname: "Uncle Art."

Indeed, Satherley was nearly twenty years Autry's senior when he stepped into the role of shaping Autry's cowboy image, moving him away from being just another clone of Jimmie Rodgers. Autry's first hit, "That Silver-Haired Daddy of Mine," released on ARC in 1932, sold thirty thousand copies in its first three months, on its way to an easy million. It was Satherley who suggested that same year that Autry move to Chicago and make WLS his home base. There, the singer would host his own morning show, appear frequently on the *Barn Dance*, and use his brief time in Chicago to build a following around the Midwest that would open the door to Hollywood.

Autry settled on the far North Side near the Edgewater Beach Hotel.[149] His first recording session in Chicago took place January 27, 1933, on a cold Friday morning in the depth of winter, at the Victor label's studio at 300 West Madison.[150] He hadn't been in a recording studio in six months, and the five songs he recorded that day—"Cowboy's Heaven," "The Little Ranch House on the Old Circle," "The Yellow Rose of Texas," "Your Voice is Ringing," and "Louisiana Moon"—were in direct contrast to the mountain ballads and Jimmie Rodgers songs of his previous few years.[151] These were songs that evoked his childhood, inhabited by frontier characters he had observed firsthand, but reimagined as romantic figures. By then he had developed an easygoing croon that contrasted with the belting-to-the-rafters style of most vocalists who had come up through vaudeville. His laid-back approach helped reshape the cowboy from a working-class roughneck into a figure relatable to people who would never travel west of the Mississippi River. "You like Gene's singing because he sounds so friendly and sincere, and that's just the way he is," WLS promotional copy assured listeners in 1932.[152] On "Louisiana Moon," the only song on which he received a songwriting credit, Autry, backed by harmony partner Jimmy Long, confesses his loneliness to the stars. The song is a slow waltz,

emulating the steady rhythm of a nighttime horseback ride following the "Southern moon." Backed by harmony partner Jimmy Long,
Autry's cowboy is a profoundly sentimental one, searching for home
while knowing it is far out of reach.

Just as Autry was turning a corner artistically, the sudden death
of Jimmie Rodgers in May 1933 suggested a turning point as well.
Sensing the moment, Satherley rushed Autry into the studio in June
to record "The Death of Jimmie Rodgers" and "The Life of Jimmie
Rodgers." In November, Autry added two more songs to the shellac
eulogies: "When Jimmie Rodgers Said Goodbye" and "Good Luck
Old Pal ('Till We Meet Bye and Bye)."[153] The send-off took place in a
transformational year for Autry. He had taken to wearing a full western outfit, including a white Stetson hat and fancy Nocona boots,
and had his 1927 Martin 00-42 guitar customized with pearl tuner
buttons, a peghead decal and binding, and his signature along the
neck in mother-of-pearl.[154] The visual package radiated star power
before he sang a word. All over the nation, country music performers followed his lead and started wearing western gear.

At WLS, Autry only made between thirty-five and fifty dollars a
week, but the exposure was priceless. A year earlier, Sears, Roebuck
had introduced a Harmony guitar with his picture and autograph on
the headstock, and Chicago publisher M. M. Cole had launched the
first in a successful series of Autry songbooks. Autry followed up by
self-publishing *Rhymes of the Range*, a digest of cowboy folk songs
in the public domain, and *The Art of Writing Songs and How to Play
Guitar*, a booklet that offered personal tips on his craft. He was busy
with live bookings all over the Midwest, including an appearance at
the 1933 World's Fair and the WLS Roundup, a road show of *Barn
Dance* stars that traveled throughout the Midwest that December.
Four shows a day were typical, many in local movie houses, where
he performed before the main feature. At the Joliet Penitentiary
in March, Autry played to four thousand prisoners, one of whom
was Nathan Leopold, the former University of Chicago student and
convicted murderer who had committed "the crime of the century"
alongside Richard Loeb. Leopold happened to be in charge of enter-

tainment that day. "I want you to know that while you're here you have nothing to fear. You are probably safer inside these walls than on the streets of Chicago," he told the star.[155]

By 1934, Autry was making enough money to pay his trio and his booking agent, Satherley, as well as all road expenses. In addition to appearing on the *Barn Dance*, he hosted a morning radio program several days a week. The public's growing appetite for western-themed music drove up sales of records, tickets, songbooks, and any other merchandise Autry could arrange. The opportunity to perform on horseback at the annual rodeos held in Soldier Field made his image even more potent. "I had no way of knowing then that my career was perfectly aimed. I was just right for those times, those deepening Depression years," he later recalled.[156] Years later, Autry hired Betty Johnson, a nightclub singer from North Carolina who appeared on morning radio in Chicago, to join him for rodeo dates. By then, Autry had perfected a stage show, featuring sequins, bright lights, parade horses, and cowboy songs, that dazzled audiences on a grand scale. "My god, I looked like a movie star," Johnson later recalled. "We would have these huge crowds. All I had to do was ride around the track and come back to him and stand beside him and then we would sing together."[157]

That summer, Autry connected with Nat Levine, an independent film producer from New York who made serials fast and on the cheap. Two of his key discoveries were John Wayne and the performing German Shepherd Rin Tin Tin. Levine had decided he wanted to create a series of singing cowboy movies. Herbert Yates, ARC's owner, steered Levine to Autry. Yates knew a movie career would drive up Autry's record sales, even though his opinion of the western film genre could be summed up in one word: "lousy."[158] Levine traveled to Chicago to look Autry over. Autry met him at the Blackstone Hotel in full cowboy regalia. Skeptical, Levine offered the singer a cameo in an upcoming Hollywood film as a kind of screen test. The pay: $500 plus expenses. "Sounds okay to me," Autry replied.[159] On the Fourth of July, he and his wife, along with sideman Smiley Burnette, jumped in their car and headed west on Route 66. Autry would return to Chicago for periodic recording sessions, but he remained in Hollywood to make his fortune.

WLS soon had a crowded stable of cowboys in addition to Autry. George Goebel, a teenage singer billed as "the Little Cowboy," sang popular western hits of the day. Stanley Leland Weed, known simply as "Tumble Weed," was a rugged rodeo champion from Arizona whose "high-heel boots didn't fit very well on city sidewalks."[160] In 1937, he too fled to Hollywood to become Bob Baker, a singing cowboy for Universal Studios. During his *Barn Dance* years he appeared as a sidekick to singer Romaine Lowdermilk, a cowboy singer-poet and Arizona ranch owner where Weed originally worked. "Cowboy Bill" Newcomb, another singing cowboy, dressed in all-black western wear. Like Weed, he was an expert ranch hand and roper due to his childhood on a farm in the Missouri Ozarks. He picked up the fiddle to accompany his father on a Joplin radio station. A series of amateur talent contests got him to Chicago in 1937.[161] There was also a cowhand humorist named Pokey Martin, who "arrived in Chicago driving a cattle truck because he didn't have bus fare," according to WLS.[162] Pokey was actually a radio actor and writer named Hoyt Allen, a journalism school graduate from Oklahoma who was in such demand that he rotated through seventeen different programs each week.[163]

The Swift Rangers first broadcast from studios located on the grounds of the Union Stock Yards at Chicago meat-packing giant Swift and Company. The group, dressed in a uniform of neck scarves and ten-gallon hats, shrunk from a sextet to a trio over the years. Leader Ozzie Westley, a North Dakota native whose recording career started when his glee club at St. Olaf College recorded for Victor in 1927, renamed the group the Rangers after their Swift days; he hustled to get them on several WLS programs, including the *Barn Dance*, but throughout the 1930s, the Rangers also played to the high-society set through long-standing engagements at the Blackstone Hotel, the Glass Hat Room in the Congress Hotel, and the equally swank Hotel New Yorker in Manhattan.[164]

Contrasting with all these cowboys was a single putatively Native

American figure: Hotan Tonka, a White man supposedly adopted by the Chippewa tribe after performing a "good turn" for its chief. In reality, he was Jack Rohr, from Naperville, Illinois, who after his service in World War I became an executive with the Boy Scouts of America, stationed in Chicago. His hobby was Indian folklore, and in 1927 he quit his job to pursue it full-time on the lecture circuit, appearing at more than twenty-five hundred schools, colleges, clubs, and churches across the United States while wearing a full headdress, beaded outfit, fringed leather jacket, and moccasins. Rohr joined WLS in October 1935, where he broadcast three mornings a week. The station played with the contradictions that Rohr represented: "In his ceremonial headdress of gaudy feathers, he might be either Indian or paleface, his complexion is of such a ruddy tan."[165]

The Hayloft lacked people of color, their absence partly a reflection of the highly segregated times. The *Barn Dance* aimed to soothe and entertain White audiences, not to challenge or provoke them. The station understood that listeners' embrace of the program's sentimental reimagining of rural life was a direct reaction against the growing popularity of jazz, which rural audiences tended to associate with immorality. "We think jazz is characteristic of the reckless-heedless-delirious attitude of some of our population," wrote Mr. and Mrs. C. W. Sherwin of Cannon Falls, Minnesota, to WLS.[166] Radio also provided the last refuge for vaudeville minstrels operating the "burnt cork" circuit since its heyday in the late nineteenth century. In 1935, WLS launched a road show called the WLS Minstrels that traveled throughout the Midwest offering "the flavor of an old-time Dixieland minstrel show." The group consisted of at least eight different performers or duos as well as the "WLS Minstrel Band," playing "music and song of yesterday's minstrel days." A truncated version appeared on the *Barn Dance*.[167] WLS was not alone in reviving blackface: WSM in Nashville had a similar road show as well as its own blackface comedians: "Jamup and Honey," who were hired in 1938, appeared several times a week, including every Saturday on the *Grand Ole Opry* from 1938 through 1953. The style of these minstrel humor acts, and many of their songs ("Turkey in the Straw," for example), directly influenced early country music. Radio forced minstrels to adopt new functions. On the *Barn Dance*, a minstrel named Malcolm Clair developed his character "Spareribs" into a popular children's storyteller.

As John Lair had done with his country artists, the WLS publicity machine was quick to make dubious claims about its western-style artists' backgrounds for appearances of authenticity. The Girls of the Golden West, a female duo who sang western songs in tight harmony, were presented as Millie and Dollie Good from Mule Shoe, Texas.[168] In truth they were Mildred Fern Goad and Dorothy Lavern Goad of Mount Carmel, Illinois, who had grown up in East St. Louis, where their mother taught them the old songs and created elaborately ornate matching western show outfits for them. They were unlike anything on WLS at the time: not only were they women who performed without male accompaniment, but their voices climbed into high soprano range. They often yodeled in harmony too. By 1933, they were recording songs for the Bluebird label that reflected a woman's perspective—also unusual at the time.[169]

The one group WLS had no need to invent a backstory for was Louise Massey & the Westerners. They were three siblings—Allen, Curt, and Louise Massey on guitar, fiddle, and piano, respectively—along with accordionist Larry Wellington and Milt Mabie, Louise's husband, on bass. The Masseys grew up in cattle country in New Mexico. Their father, Henry Massey, was an old-time fiddler and rancher who developed them into a professional band. The group eventually made it to Kansas City, where they played on local radio for five years. That experience set them up for Chicago in 1933.[170]

Popularity came quickly. The Westerners stood out because they knew the territory of their songs firsthand. They dressed in full western wear for their appearances, and they were often photographed on horseback at their home ranch, which WLS noted was near the "old stamping ground of Billy the Kid."[171] Louise Massey was a teenage rodeo champion and rider "at an age when many girls are just learning to stand up on roller skates."[172] WLS drove them hard. Besides the *Barn Dance*, the group appeared six mornings a week and on Thursday nights on various programs, and in between their radio schedule and live appearances they recorded more than a hundred sides for the American Recording Company and, later, Columbia between 1933 and 1942.[173]

The Westerners paid off for WLS—listener mail totaled two hundred thousand letters in just one month, a station record.[174] But their influence had wider reach: with all five members fluent in Spanish, they were one of the earliest groups to popularize Latin American material for English-speaking listeners, and their original songs referenced Mexico or had a Latin flavor. "My Adobe Hacienda," co-written by Louise, was one of country music's earliest crossover successes. The song lets the listener escape south of the border, where life's demands are few. "The soft desert stars / and the strum of guitars / make every evening seem so sweet," Louise promises as the band lightly swings behind her. Recorded in 1941, the song percolated until Columbia released it in 1947, then became the group's biggest hit, one that others, like Eddy Arnold, would revive. Hank Snow and Anita Carter even turned it into a duet. But by that time, the Westerners had disappeared. Louise and Milt retreated to the ranch life in Roswell. Brother Curt made it to Hollywood, where his western background was in demand: the theme to *Petticoat Junction* is his original, and his music is heard throughout *The Beverly Hillbillies*, for which he served as musical director.[175]

The final phase of singing cowboys on the *Barn Dance* followed World War II. The program's biggest star of that time was Rex Allen, one of Hollywood's last singing cowboys, who gained national prominence when he joined WLS in 1945. Born December 31, 1920, Allen grew up on a family ranch located about eighty-five miles east of Tucson, Arizona.[176] His father was a fiddler who encouraged his son to enter local contests, which led to Allen getting on the radio. After stints in different cities, Allen joined WLS in 1945, where he replaced Red Foley, who had just departed for Nashville. Showing up years after Autry and others, Allen could yodel, and, like Autry, had an easygoing vocal style and extensive range that opened the doors to Hollywood. WLS played on his good looks, reminding listeners he was single and giving away his photo for free. Mercury

Records signed him the next year, and he started recording cowboy ballads and, a few years later, modern country fare. Suddenly, Allen had a growing base of fans, making the next logical step Hollywood, where he moved in 1949.[177] Allen starred in nineteen singing cowboy movies for Republic Pictures, the last of which, *Phantom Stallion*, is considered the final installment for the genre itself. By then, he was so popular that he only had to play himself.[178]

Bob Atcher was the *Barn Dance*'s final singing cowboy, but unlike the others, he was already a recording star for Columbia Records and had been a presence on network radio for years when he joined the Hayloft. But he had not always been a cowboy. Born May 11, 1914, Atcher grew up on a tobacco farm in Hardin County, Kentucky, in a large family of fiddlers and singers who taught him the old songs. Because his father wanted someone to accompany his fiddle, he traded a championship coon dog for cash, which he used to order a guitar for his four-year-old son.[179] Years later, at the University of Kentucky, Atcher learned there was currency in his repertoire of nearly six hundred songs. Still a student, he found work at a radio station in Louisville, and then bounced between Lexington, Atlanta, Gary, and Chicago. He named himself "the Kentucky Mountain Minstrel," after "Kentucky Mountain Boy" Bradley Kincaid. In Chicago, where Atcher first landed in 1932, he appeared on three stations simultaneously—WBBM, WIND, and WJJD—and, in a foreshadowing of Chicago's Second City improv theater, was known for "singing news," in which he read newspaper stories and then retold them in song.[180]

In 1939, Art Satherley signed Atcher to Columbia, where he immediately cut the hits "You Are My Sunshine," "Why Don't You Haul Off and Love Me," "I Must Have Been Wrong," and "Pins and Needles (In My Heart)," among many others. He sang folk ballads and cowboy songs, often accompanied by just a guitar or an accordion. On his hit version of "I'm Thinking Tonight of My Blue Eyes," a Carter Family song, Atcher slows the tempo to a crawl and then belts the lyric through sobbing and high-pitched screaming, as a harmonica solemnly answers his blues. He called these vocal contortions his "panther yell."[181]

WLS was well aware of Atcher, as the station occasionally hired him for tours with their regular artists even though he was heard on national CBS Network programs. The station was willing to make him the highest-paid artist on the *Barn Dance* roster because, with Rex Allen gone, they were desperate for proven talent. The investment was worth it: by the time he joined in 1949, Atcher had made over three hundred recordings, and his record sales were in the millions.[182]

On WLS, Atcher became a full cowboy. He rode a stallion named Golden Storm around town and appeared in rhinestone western wear, often with his wife, Marguerite. In fact, Atcher was one of the first country stars to hire California tailor Nudie Cohn, who created elaborately sequined stage wear made famous by Elvis Presley, Porter Wagoner, and Gram Parsons, among others.[183] WLS got the most out of its investment: between 1950 and 1958, the station programmed Atcher seven days a week. Besides the *Barn Dance*, Atcher appeared on early morning and late afternoon programs and also did local television and live appearances. "I couldn't get too far away," he said.[184]

Yet he discovered western skies nearby. In 1954, upset about the density of Chicago, Atcher settled in an unincorporated area northwest of the city, populated by only a few German farmers. He found the area primitive—no post office or fire station, and only one store and one school. After living there for two years Atcher decided to help incorporate a town, which became the village of Schaumburg in 1956. Music became a part-time activity for Atcher between 1959 and 1975, when he served as village president and played a significant role in transforming the area into a major suburban metropolis.[185]

PATSY MONTANA: COUNTRY MUSIC'S FIRST MILLION-SELLING WOMAN

Cowboys, not cowgirls, dominated the *Barn Dance*. When women appeared, they usually existed within a group or as a comic foil. Patsy Montana changed that. She showed up in 1933 and two years later would record what would become the first song in country music by a woman that would sell more than a million copies. Her upbeat demeanor, yodeling style, and feisty spirit combined to create no less of a stereotype than any other character in the Hayloft, but during the Great Depression it represented a turning away from the sexualized images of damsels or vamps that pervaded films in the guise of Jean Harlow or Mae West. In Montana, audiences found a young woman who was accessible, strong, and independent. Most women could see something of themselves in her, or even if not, she presented an aspirational model of what they could be.

She was born Ruby Blevins, on October 30, 1908, on a farm in Hope, Arkansas.[186] The only girl in a family with ten brothers, she studied classical violin for years. When two brothers moved to California to look for work, Montana, only seventeen at the time, followed. She wanted to go to music school at the University of the West (now UCLA). Her father, a postal worker, went to the local bank to take out a loan to cover his only daughter's tuition. It was 1929, and the stock market would crush those hopes just a few months later.[187]

In California, Montana discovered the guitar and Jimmie Rodgers. The bank failure had evaporated her life savings—forty dollars—so she sought work and discovered that the yodeling she had practiced back home was a novelty in Hollywood. Soon she ended up on local radio as Rubye Blevins, the Yodeling Cowgirl from San Antone. Another station christened her Patsy Montana.[188] Her vocal trio was named the Montana Girls, and they told everyone they were sisters. They wore matching suede skirts, boots, blouses, and hats and played state fairs and rodeos up and down the coast with movie cowboys Hoot Gibson and Tom Mix.[189] In Pendleton, Oregon, a local radio station hooked up special microphones so all three girls could sing while clopping through the crowd on horseback.[190] Naturally, the movies called, and they starred in shorts. In 1932, the Hollywood press noted that the trio received five thousand fan letters in four short months, an endorsement that set them up for full-length feature work. Montana finally learned the thrill of having sisters, and she reveled in their new freedoms. Their days were spent riding motorcycles, playing in the ocean, and starring in shows alongside larger-than-life figures she had known only on the big screen a year ago. "I didn't know there was a Depression on!" she said later.[191]

But then the other two Montana Girls got married, and the fun ended as quickly as it had begun.[192]

The story should have ended there. Montana returned to Arkansas. Country star Jimmie Davis hired her for backup fiddle and vocal work for sessions in Camden, New Jersey, for Victor Records. Otherwise, she resumed farm work. But a healthy watermelon harvest the following year sent her life into a new direction. The 1933 World's Fair opened in May in Chicago, and the mayor of Hope decided his town needed recognition on the national stage. A monster melon would do it. He appointed two Blevins brothers to drive Hempstead County's biggest melon to Chicago to show it off. They did, bringing along their sister. Before they left, their mother took Montana aside to tell her that she had struck up a correspondence with the Girls of the Golden West because of their similarities to the Montana Girls. She pulled a letter out of her purse and gave it to her daughter to read. Apparently, her mother had talked up Montana to the Good sisters, and her persistence had resulted in an offhand comment that her daughter should stop by WLS to say "hi" if she was ever in town. Things suddenly looked up.

"Mama and I decided the letter was definitely an invitation," she said.[193]

With a nephew who played guitar, the three siblings formed a band to raise gas money for the trip. Fifty dollars later, in scorching August heat, their Pontiac, stuffed with clothes, instruments, and costumes, and towing a trailer containing the freakish melon nestled in hay, was on its way to Chicago. Their first stop was the fairgrounds. While the brothers set up the melon for display, Montana headed for the Eighth Street Theater. Miraculously, the Good sisters were in that afternoon and right down the hall. After introductions, Dollie Good remembered the letters. Montana was seven years her senior, but that didn't prevent Good from assuming a mentor role. As luck would have it, the Prairie Ramblers were holding auditions that afternoon for a girl singer. "Honey," Dollie told her, "go sign up."[194]

Montana retrieved her guitar and western costume from the car and changed in the bathroom. At the audition she sang "Texas Plains," a familiar western ballad. But for her second song she tried an original. Silence fell once she ended. "I don't believe I've heard that one," one of the Ramblers said. "It's one I wrote," Montana replied.[195] She got the job and sent her brothers home to Arkansas in the Pontiac without her.

The Prairie Ramblers were also newcomers to Chicago. When they arrived that January, they called themselves the Kentucky Ramblers to recognize their home state. Their name change suited *Prairie Farmer*, their new employer. They were string instrumentalists—Charles Gilbert "Chick" Hurt on mandola and four-string tenor banjo, Floyd "Salty" Holmes on guitar, Shelby David "Tex" Atchinson on fiddle, and Jack Taylor on bass—who played hot and clean, combining a rural sensibility with western swing. Bill Monroe was an early admirer, and for good reason: locked together, the band sounded like the future. "In spite of the instrumentation being right down the old bluegrass alley, except for the five-string banjo, their singing sounded the same. They used the same voicing, the same high pitch and everything as today's bluegrass," said Bob Atcher.[196]

The group expanded their sound with Montana, performing whatever was popular in any genre, but in their own style. Through yodeling, she added a fifth instrument. They played mornings and Saturday evenings on WLS and then throughout the Midwest. Touring was vigorous—sometimes two matinees and three evening shows in one day. Montana later remembered training herself to catch some sleep sitting on two chairs behind the movie screen while a western played: "In your ear, you'd be hearing a shooting . . . and you'd soon learn just when to get up and go brush your hair and get ready and put on a little lipstick for the next show. But I was getting my training."[197] Two years later, Art Satherley took the group to New York City for a full year to record for his American Record

Corporation. When they returned, they were a professional unit not just with big hits, but also with a star in Montana, who would dominate the group.

By then Montana was married to Paul Rose, a transplant from Tennessee who worked in the WLS booking office. One night after a show, Rose received a telegram asking him to return home to care for his dying grandmother. Alone, Montana remembered a piece of paper that Gene Autry's manager, Joe Frank, had given her and that she had stuffed in her purse. He had scribbled "Cowboy's Sweetheart" and figured she might find it useful for a song idea.

She did now. Montana wrote out of loneliness and yearning, not only for Paul but also for her Ozark home. The song spilled out in one sitting. Montana later said she wrote for herself because songwriters "certainly did not have anything for girl singers," primarily because there weren't any. "I needed a signature song of my own," she decided.[198]

Despite the title, "I Want to Be a Cowboy's Sweetheart" is not a love letter to a man, but to a lifestyle of roping steers, sleeping under the stars, and feeling the wind in your face while saddleback, "a thousand miles from all the city lights." The singer imagines she alone is the one heading west "to learn how to rope and ride." At night, only cattle, her guitar, and her yodeling keep her company.

"She says she wants to be a cowboy's sweetheart and she never mentions the guy again. In fact she'd rather sleep with the herd," said pop singer Cyndi Lauper, who recorded the song in 2016. "It kind of made me laugh, but it also made me think this was an important song to sing because it's very much a part of the history of women."[199]

The song, recorded during those New York sessions, established Montana as a personality, and throughout the decade, she recorded sequels to "Sweetheart," including "Cowboy's Sweetheart No. 2," "I'm a Wild and Reckless Cowboy (From the West Side of Town)," "Rodeo Sweetheart," and "Little Sweetheart of the Ozarks." "I just about milked that title dry," she recalled.[200] She also used her exuberant yodeling style on songs that ridiculed expectations of complacency for women and endorsed her own cowgirl image. The original "Sweetheart" did not die, but instead became a touchstone cover for female country artists over the decades, including Patti Page, Suzy Bogguss, LeAnn Rimes, and the Dixie Chicks.

In 1940, Montana went solo.[201] WLS was still grooming women artists mainly within vocal groups like Winnie, Lou and Sally, the Kentucky Girls, the Three Maids, and the DeZurik Sisters, but Montana took a leadership role in helping those women adapt to Chicago and the rigors of the road, since most had never traveled and didn't even know how to check into a motel.[202]

The DeZurik Sisters were particularly green. One of the rare *Barn Dance* acts to originate from the upper Midwest, they were born on a Dutch dairy farm in Royalton, Minnesota. Mary Jane and Caroline DeZurik were self-taught singers who had the unusual ability to imitate barnyard animals, all kinds of game, and the cackle of roosters and hens. Their talent emerged out of fancy and boredom. "To relax between chores on the farm they would sing together," explained Jim Klein, Mary Jane's son.[203] They also yodeled and eventually merged the animal sounds with musical instruments and sound effects like the Hawaiian guitar, musical saw, trumpet, hiccups, and bells. In 1934, both girls were cutting rye in the field when an uncle pulled up and announced he had booked them that night at the weekly band shell concert in town. The sisters sang three songs without microphones before the main event. But after the first song ended, they knew life would never be the same. "They screamed, they howled," Caroline recalled of the audience.[204] Two years later, the sisters were in Chicago, salaried on WLS. They were still teenagers.

WLS called the sisters' talent "trick yodeling" or, in some mentions, "double yodeling." They vocalized in harmony, even the tweeting, trilling, warbling, and cackling. Montana had already helped popularize yodeling on air, and the sisters heightened its potential with speed and wit. They were an instant hit. In 1938, they recorded six sides for Vocalion. Two years later, they moved to Hollywood to star in *Barnyard Follies*, a full-length musical comedy for Republic Pictures. They were a charming oddity. During the song "Poppin' the Corn," the sisters stroll onstage and sing in locked harmony until switching to a breakneck sequence of bird calls, not just in perfect rhythm, with the entire cast clapping along, but also in tune. The song is splashy big band gloss, but they inject mountain humor: while casually working toward their exit, Mary Jane pulls a whiskey jug from behind her back and the two girls switch to a staccato of hiccups until the cork flies high. The appearance clocks at thirty seconds, but economy is their secret weapon: not one breath is spared.[205]

THE APPALACHIAN JOURNEY
OF LILY MAY LEDFORD

One female performer who didn't need a WLS backstory because she actually came from the mountains was Lily May Ledford. The station promoted her as "Lily May, the Mountain Gal" and even featured her in a comic strip in its weekly magazine that played up common hillbilly stereotypes. But Ledford knew the harshness of poverty. She spent the first nineteen years of her life on a tenant farm in Powell County, Kentucky. Born March 17, 1917, she was one of fourteen children, four of whom died in infancy. The family also took in an orphaned cousin. They were one of a few families living deep inside the Red River Gorge who farmed corn and sorghum cane along the hillsides and riverbank.[206] Considering the isolation of her youth, forging a lifelong career in music must have been an unimaginable act; playing the White House must have seemed impossible. But Ledford accomplished both.

It was the fiddle that led her off the mountain. She and her younger brother Coyen started playing square dances and winning fiddle contests in Stanton, the county seat. As they walked back home, strangers who had seen them play would stop their cars and offer them change. Soon they formed a family band, the Red River Ramblers, with their sister Rosie and a neighbor boy, Morgan Skidmore, both on guitar. By listening to a neighbor's phonograph, they learned more songs, mostly from the Carter Family, Riley Puckett with the Skillet Lickers, and Jimmie Rodgers. Their popularity grew. Invitations to play outside Powell County rolled in.[207]

One of those invitations came from Albert Skidmore, Morgan's uncle, who lived in Rochester, Indiana, about 120 miles southeast of Chicago. Skidmore offered to take the band home with him so they could get an audition on WLS as well as dates around Indiana. In 1935, they left for Indiana and soon played Rochester's Char-Bell Theatre. H. Lisle Krieghbaum, the theater's co-owner, wrote WLS directly to tell them the teenage group was "a real find" and counted eighty songs in their repertoire. He was savvy enough to slip in a photograph to show they "were not bad-looking kids," either.[208]

John Lair presided over the audition and was impressed with only Lily May. Yet he couldn't convince WLS program director Harold Stafford, who wasn't at the audition, to agree that the station needed another young Kentuckian. The news was devastating. Albert Skidmore's letter to Lair reflects the desperation of the Great Depression:

These girls are nothing to us only our desire to help better their chances for a decent living. . . . These two girls and the small boy were working on the road at 75cts a day 2 days per week. They haven't any instruments of their own and never owned any. Neighbors have been good enough to lend to them. We have bought their clothes and kept them since the first part of Oct. and don't begruge [*sic*] it any, but would like for it to have done some good. It will be the hardest thing I've ever done to take them back to same conditions we found them. I can't resist making this last appeal to you in their behalf.[209]

Skidmore's worry was in vain because Lair had plans for Lily. He wrote the girl and told her to practice hard because he wanted her to play a July fiddlers' contest in Mount Vernon, Illinois. Stafford would be there, and Lair wanted him to see the girl alone. By September, Ledford was in Chicago. To afford the train fare, her father sold a pig.[210]

Ledford lived with Lair and his wife at their home on the far North Side, 6921 North Ridge Avenue, and drove with him to work every

morning, before she found her own room nearby.[211] Even though
the fiddle was her main instrument, Ledford switched to five-string
banjo at Lair's urging. He also dictated an appropriate outfit: long
old-fashioned dresses, lace-up shoes, no makeup, no hair curls. He
even discouraged her from improving her grammar. "Be genuine
and plain at all times," he instructed. The teenager complied, but
grudgingly: "I felt like an old lady and not at all pretty."[212]

Ledford's experience exemplified the hardships many Southerners dealt with when forced to relocate to Chicago to make a better
life. The rewards of more income and opportunity were balanced
with crime, noise, filth, and density. But the harshest challenge
may have been homesickness. Ledford missed her large family,
with whom she had lived in tight quarters, worked in the fields,
commiserated after tragedies, and made music at night. She had
survivor's guilt, she confessed many years later. One night on the
Barn Dance, she was invited to the microphone to talk with a child
fiddler who had hitchhiked from southern Indiana to appear on the
program. Moments earlier, the waifish boy had torn through fiddle
breakdowns with the speed and confidence of a professional twice
his age. She put her arm around his small shoulder to tell him how
proud she was of his talent. But words didn't flow, tears did. The
boy, his clothes shabby and torn but who played with regal poise,
reminded her of her fiddler brother Coyen, who had been sent back
home. Ledford ran off the stage and cried it out in the dressing
room.[213]

The incident endeared her to the WLS audience even more, likely
because they shared her story. "They saw that it was a genuine thing
with me. They knew it was genuine tears," she said decades later.[214]
For months, Ledford received gifts to remind her of home: homemade cookies, candies, roses, clothes. Her mother sent a dressed
chicken and jars of blackberry jam, molasses, and pickles. But one
gift from an anonymous listener topped them all: a crate containing
a live baby opossum. After the animal escaped into the station coal
bin, Ledford donated it to the Lincoln Park Zoo.[215]

THE *BARN DANCE* BECOMES
A MAINSTAY OF AMERICAN LIFE

Lily May Ledford lasted on WLS for only thirteen months, but her impact was substantial. With four other women, she co-founded the Coon Creek Girls, country music's first all-woman string band, which recorded traditional folk songs for Vocalion.[216] They became the first *Barn Dance* act to make it to the East Room of the White House, where, on June 8, 1939, they performed on a bill titled "A Program of American Music," organized especially for visiting British monarchs King George VI and Queen Elizabeth. With President Franklin and First Lady Eleanor Roosevelt presiding, the program featured Alan Lomax singing cowboy ballads, pop star Kate Smith singing traditional folk songs, contralto Marian Anderson singing spirituals, and opera singer Lawrence Tibbett singing works by American composer Oley Speaks. The evening was a showcase of music considered "rich and strange but vital and undeniably American."[217]

The Coon Creek Girls were there to present folk songs with roots in Black America. The program notes stated that while American folk music was derived from the British Isles, it had since "undergone sea change in its migrations across the Atlantic" and that "above all, the Negro has made the most distinctive contribution." The group had four songs to sing—"Cindy," "The Soldier and the Lady," "Buffalo Gals," and "How Many Biscuits Can You Eat?"—that exemplified the uniquely American pastiche. With John Lair directing and Ledford leading on fiddle, the group gave speed and pluck to the African American folk tunes, two of them common on the minstrel circuit. The king "looked pretty sour" at the beginning of the performance, Ledford remembered, but by the end he was tapping his foot. "I knew I had him."[218]

In case that music proved inexplicable to the visiting royalty, when the group finished, they stayed to play music that appeared more in their element: square dance music for a North Carolina troupe directed by folklorist Bascom Lamar Lunsford.[219]

The White House appearance signaled how far the *Barn Dance* had traveled in its fifteen years. As the station's talent bureau successfully delivered its stars to theaters, auditoriums, and local fairs in towns across the United States, its roster was soon in demand for bigger stages. State fairs, livestock shows, rodeos, and agricultural anchors like the National Corn Husking Contest drew tens of thousands of people to *Barn Dance* broadcasts. Road shows traveled by automobile, by train, and in 1933, by steamer across Lake Michigan when WLS hosted one-day "picnic trips" that carried a thousand listeners from Chicago to shoreline cities like Michigan City, Indiana, and Benton Harbor, Michigan. These events were built for drama, with thousands more fans watching the ship slowly approach and dock, and the Hayloft performers then disembarking like royalty.[220] In 1935, WLS even put together an eleven-day train tour that took 160 listeners to "historic spots" of Mexico, Texas, and Louisiana, with *Barn Dance* musicians providing the appropriate accompaniment.[221]

The benchmark event was the broadcast from the 1933 World's Fair. *Prairie Farmer* hired a plane so its announcer could see and describe the throng of people descending upon the lakefront on the opening day. In addition to performing live on-site, *Barn Dance* entertainers were shuttled to a special lounge at the Foods Building on Northerly Island where they could interact with the crowd.[222] Having the Hayloft regulars serve as informal hometown hosts set a precedent for future events. At the Illinois State Fair in 1936, eighteen thousand people showed up to listen to a live broadcast of the *Barn Dance*, a five-hour affair that made news when Lulu Belle broke ranks to plant a kiss on the cheek of Illinois Governor Henry Horner after his speech.[223] That October, twenty-four thousand people crammed inside Chicago's International Amphitheatre for another live broadcast, followed by an arena-sized square dance. The next year, when Chicago celebrated its centennial, the city hired the entire *Barn Dance* cast to perform at Soldier Field, complete with square dancers—"the largest barn dance ever held," the station exclaimed.[224]

Serious folklorists and the Smithsonian Institution took notice when the National Folk Festival, an international event presenting indigenous folk cultures from the United States and abroad,

announced it would host its fourth annual festival at Orchestra Hall
in Chicago May 22–28, 1937, the first time it had been held north
of the Mason-Dixon line after traveling through St. Louis, Chattanooga, and Dallas. Sarah Gertrude Knott, a New Deal–minded
organizer, had founded the festival. A nonacademic herself, she
worked with several prominent folklorists, including writers Paul
Green and Zora Neale Hurston, to create a festival that included
performers who went far beyond Anglo-American folk culture. She
had had success with the first three festivals and saw Chicago as
presenting an opportunity to include performers from the upper
Midwest, such as Scandinavian folk dancers from Minnesota, Win-
nebago Indians from Illinois, German singers from Chicago, and
singing lumberjacks from Michigan and Wisconsin. Knott was
fiercely anti-segregation, so each night of the four-day festival featured spirituals from African American choirs pulled from local
glee clubs, churches, and the Wabash YMCA. The final night featured the Chicago Negro Group, a special choir of 750 voices featuring song leader Thomas A. Dorsey, the gospel music pioneer.[225]
One of the choirs involved came from the Metropolitan Community
Church in Bronzeville, on the near South Side, and was the first
Black choir to make a commercial record and to perform frequently
before racially mixed audiences. The choir also became the first to
appear over the commercial airwaves when, in 1927, WLS gave it a
program to broadcast every other Friday night.[226]

Knott was impressed with what she found in Chicago. "Right
here in this city it has been a pleasant surprise to find that there
are many nonprofessional Negro singers who have learned from
their parents or grandparents the real songs of the cotton fields and
southern camp meetings," she told the local press.[227]

Chicago embraced the festival. Mayor Edward J. Kelly declared
the week National Folk Festival Week, and the event was immediately
included as part of the city's centennial anniversary programming.
John Lair and WLS served as important intermediaries. Promotional
director George Biggar wrote Knott to direct her to old-time fiddlers
and harmonica players, including Tommy Dandurand, the *Barn*

Dance's first musician, who, Biggar promised, "plays with the real swing as used in rural communities for dancing many years ago."[228]

The station also promoted the festival, bringing some of its artists on the air, including organizer Bascom Lamar Lunsford, Appalachian ethnomusicologist and founder of the Asheville Folk Festival. Upon arriving in Chicago, Lunsford met up with Scotty Wiseman, another North Carolinian, and played him "Good Old Mountain Dew," a song he had recorded for Brunswick in 1928 about a moonshiner who escapes a court conviction after the town partakes in his product. He offered it to Wiseman for $25, the cost of a train ride back home. Two years later, Lulu Belle and Scotty had the first hit with the song, retitled "Mountain Dew," which became a country standard covered by hundreds of others, including the Stanley Brothers, Glen Campbell, Roy Acuff, and Willie Nelson. Wiseman had rewritten the lyrics to make them simpler and to include a verse about President Franklin D. Roosevelt's approval of the drink. Despite the song's popularity, WLS still wouldn't let the couple sing it on air.[229]

By the 1940s, most of the biggest *Barn Dance* stars had Hollywood careers. Following in the steps of Gene Autry, Lulu Belle and Scotty played themselves in four films, starting in 1938 in *Shine On Harvest Moon*, where they shared the bill with Roy Rogers. Patsy Montana starred with Autry in *Colorado Sunset* in 1939. In *The National Barn Dance*, a 1944 feature for Paramount, the entire cast played themselves in a kind of fantasy retelling of their journeys from the rural outback to Chicago.

Another *Barn Dance* act that had a prolific movie career was the Hoosier Hot Shots. They were a jazz novelty group that preceded Spike Jones and His City Slickers in their use of unusual instruments like the slide whistle, bicycle horn, and washboard, and anticipated "Weird Al" Yankovic with their satire and dunce humor. Three of the four original members were true Hoosiers from central Indiana who were already established on the vaudeville circuit before WLS hired them in 1934, giving them a national audience. Quickly, songs like "I Like Bananas, Because They Have No Bones,"

"From the Indies to the Andes in His Undies," and "Sioux City Sue" became pop hits, and "Are you ready, Hezzie?"—shouted by Ken Trietsch to his brother at the beginning of each song—became a national catchphrase for many years. The Hot Shots ended up starring in twenty-one films.

Listener mail during the thirties soared to more than a million letters a year, and accolades and rebuttals filled the station's weekly magazine. The Hayloft Gang, often posed in WLS marketing material with their children and spouses, were received as important fixtures in the personal lives of their listeners. Mrs. Lawrence Wright of Whitewater, Wisconsin, wrote that her family listened to the *Barn Dance* in the most important place in their lives: their barn. "With the radio tuned to the old Eighth Street Theatre we are always milking by six on Saturday nights," she wrote.[230] Readers who attended the live broadcasts were prone to describe the experience as a reunion: "I didn't realize that the entertainers could make you feel so much at home as was the case last night. The hall was filled with one big happy family and everyone seemed to feel they had lived neighbors to the entertainers for years," wrote Marline Kent of Apple River, Illinois.[231] Mrs. Earl Spaulding of Marion, Indiana, was more to the point: "I feel that WLS is our station; the staff is so friendly that they seem like real friends. And as someone put it the other day, the programs are so clean."[232] For others, WLS was simply a portal to the home they left behind: "Attica, Indiana, is my birthplace.... I came to Chicago to live two years ago and I miss that friendliness we have in a small town, but I have WLS still to listen to," wrote Ida Haines of Oak Park.[233]

But the ties that bound listeners to the *Barn Dance* singers, comedians, and musicians couldn't last. WLS didn't pay enough, and the lure of better money and opportunities called. The catalyst was John Lair. In 1937, just months after the National Folk Festival, he moved to Cincinnati to be his own boss.[234] His absence started a slow exodus of talent from WLS that the station did nothing to stop until it was too late.

THE *BARN DANCE* DOORS
SLOWLY SHUT

The success of the National Folk Festival in Chicago gave Lair stature in the eyes of the folk music establishment. The next year, Sarah Gertrude Knott appointed him to the festival's board, and he soon became involved in programming subsequent festivals of national stature. In Cincinnati, he produced the *Renfro Valley Barn Dance*, which debuted October 9, 1937.[235] The show was broadcast live each week on WLW and toured the upper South and Midwest, playing to more than a half million people in under two years. But it wasn't until Lair moved the show into a tourist complex he built alongside Highway 12 in Renfro Valley, about fifty miles south of Lexington, that he would come into his own. On November 4, 1939, Lair opened his broadcast in its new home: a pioneer-style barn with a capacity of a thousand people, all of whom he could feed at his restaurant, house in his cabins, fit comfortably in his lodge, and sell goods to at his trading post.[236]

The impact Lair's move had on the Chicago *Barn Dance* was substantial. He successfully lured many key players from the Hayloft Gang to Kentucky, including Red Foley, the Duke of Paducah, the Girls of the Golden West, and members of the Cumberland Ridge Runners and the Coon Creek Girls. By then Gene Autry was gone, and Patsy Montana would soon move west. For them, and for others who would leave in the coming years, the choice was made simpler by union politics.

The catalyst was James C. Petrillo, the powerful president of the American Federation of Musicians. After stepping into the role in 1940, he created a wage scale of $40 per show for musicians and deemed that every thirty minutes of radio airtime constituted a single show. That proved disastrous for WLS, as the *Barn Dance* was a variety show cut into half-hour segments that stretched four and a half hours in all, meaning the station had to pay musicians up to nine times the rate per show, a difficulty since the Hayloft Gang numbered up to seventy-five players on any given Saturday night.

Sponsors refused to shoulder the increase, and ticket sales weren't enough to cover it. "The cost of the show soon went right out the ceiling," said Bob Atcher. "The station was not able to get enough for the airtime to meet that kind of a nut."[237]

Petrillo also refused to consider the stars a separate class of musicians, which meant WLS now had to pay, on top of their salaries, extra compensation for its entire cast, which the stars saw as threatening their jobs. "We had no qualms at all about paying a tax to the union on what we could make out on the road if they would let us do the jobs back here in the broadcast field . . . so the station could afford then to keep us on the air. Well, they never did see it our way, and that's what killed the *National Barn Dance*," Atcher said.[238] Petrillo's two-year ban on recordings in 1942, even though it was intended to fight for artist royalties, also caused resentment because it stifled the earning potential of musicians and drove some to Hollywood to further their careers. Petrillo also pressured union members to not join the American Federation of Radio Artists, which he considered competition. For the *Barn Dance* cast, already toiling under the thumb of Burridge Butler, the Petrillo dictates became too much. "We called him Mussolini," said Patsy Montana.[239]

The migration of talent eroded the *Barn Dance*'s identity. The union insisted that the show use professional musicians, which meant that musicians who left were replaced by moonlighting Chicago Symphony Orchestra members. "The Chicago Musicians Union's band members were about as far removed from agriculture as you could get," said *Prairie Farmer* editor James Thomson.[240] "They were excellent musicians. But they weren't country," Atcher added.[241] To cut costs, WLS installed a fifteen-piece orchestra of its own that would provide accompaniment, introducing horns and strings. Under Lair, the *Barn Dance* intentionally presented "old-time" music with regional quirks and inflections, but the newer groups were polished, and they chased pop trends.

"It would still be going if they didn't try to take it high class. Country music was big in Chicago. Then they ruined it," said Roy Acuff.[242]

More slots were being taken up with groups like the Dinning Sisters, a trio fashioned after the Andrew Sisters; the Williams Brothers, a pop quartet featuring a young Andy Williams; and Captain Stubby and the Buccaneers, a novelty act. Even the Prairie Ramblers, years after splitting with Patsy Montana, sped up the beat, added an accordion, and in the 1950s renamed themselves Stan Wolowic and the Polka Chips. "Country is in my blood, but times changed," explained guitarist Ralph Gill.[243]

The *Barn Dance* clung to a variety show format, dominated more by corny humor and personality than by music. Promotion director John C. Drake defended the format in 1949: "The success of folk-music programs is not so much the kind of music, as it is the way these programs have combined a sense of reality, spontaneity, informality, and the power of personalities."[244]

However, new singers like Hank Williams, Hank Snow, Kitty Wells, Ernest Tubb, and Webb Pierce were modernizing country music by moving it away from the hillbilly stereotypes that were so pervasive on the *Barn Dance*. Fred Rose, the songwriter-turned-publishing-giant who played a major role in transforming country music in Nashville, expressed this shift in an open letter to *Billboard* in 1946. Addressed to advertisers and radio program directors, it blasted the industry for patronizing the music, something that would be unheard of when appreciating European "folklore"—opera.

> We read all kinds of books that will give us an understanding of foreign "folklore," but what do we say and do about our own good ol' American "folklore?" We call it "hillbilly" music, and sometimes we're ashamed to call it music.[245]

In fact, just as the *Barn Dance* was doubling down on novelty acts, the *Grand Ole Opry* was entering its golden era. Program director Harry Stone worked for years to steer the show away from the variety format and toward one that focused squarely on cultivating stars. While the *Barn Dance* clung to the concept of the Hayloft Gang as a democratized family of performers, the *Grand Ole*

Opry evolved into a modern showcase for relevant recording stars, including Eddy Arnold, Bill Monroe, and Minnie Pearl as well as Tubb, Snow, and Williams. Bob Atcher said WSM's star system succeeded because it harnessed the power of the live performance, in contrast to the *Barn Dance* format, "where the lowest picker on the list was considered to be just as important as the biggest star."

> But nevertheless, when you were scheduled to do a song or, on rare occasions, two songs, one following the other, you could go out there and stop the show colder than kraut and were not allowed to do an encore. On the other hand, a fiddler or a mandolin player or whatever could get up and do something and get next to no applause, and he would get his second number. . . . So many times I've seen those people standing up yelling for more for a performer, and the performer was not allowed to do it.[246]

By the time the *Grand Ole Opry* moved into Nashville's Ryman Auditorium in 1943, NBC carried the program nationally. Three years later, on September 8, 1946, the same network dropped *Barn Dance*. Miles Laboratories, maker of longtime sponsor Alka-Seltzer, ended its affiliation with the *Barn Dance* a month later. After broadcasting coast to coast on 133 stations, the Hayloft Gang's wide reach contracted, and it became nothing more than a local show.[247]

WSM spent more for talent and allowed performers to hawk mail-order merchandise, live appearances, and records on the air, a complete reversal of the policies at WLS that had earned the station a reputation for "World's Lowest Salaries," according to mandolin player Jethro Burns.[248] Much of this change followed the 1948 death of owner Burridge Butler. His successful strategy of presenting station personalities as a family had provided continuity for listeners and support for the cast. His absence gave station executives permission to abandon Butler's mission. With rock and roll on the horizon, and the country music recording industry already established in Nashville, the *Barn Dance* looked less and less like a profit center that would serve the station well in the future, so they did the minimum to keep it afloat. Making things worse, the *Prairie Farmer* editors resented playing "second fiddle" to the WLS stars, and a cultural divide yawned between the magazine and the station. "It was discouraging. . . . Farmers never asked about *Prairie Farmer* writers. It was always, 'Do you know the Arkansas Woodchopper? Lulubelle and Scotty? Red Blanchard? What are they really like?'" said Thomson.[249]

The program died a slow death. The station sold the Eighth Street Theater to the Hilton hotel chain in 1957 and announced the program would retreat into the WLS studio. Without a live audience, the *Barn Dance* fundamentally changed. After decades of booking the *Barn Dance* cast to broadcast live to thousands of people, in 1959 the Illinois State Fair booked the *Grand Ole Opry* cast instead. Then, in March 1960, *Prairie Farmer*, including WLS, was sold to American Broadcasting–Paramount Theatres, Inc., which ended the program on April 30. The cast was not told until just before they went on the air on what became their final Saturday night broadcast.[250] The next Monday, the station switched to rock and roll. Its thirty-six-year run as a farm station began with Tommy Dandurand fiddling live before a microphone and ended with the spinning of "Alley Oop," the novelty pop single by the Hollywood Argyles that the station had chosen to announce its new sound.[251]

The sudden change and lack of warning shocked and angered the station's audience. "Like the outbreak of World War III," said Thomson, the *Prairie Farmer* editor. Management instructed the magazine's editorial staff to tell farmers that WLS had been losing money catering to rural audiences, although that wasn't true. "The truth was that money was the principal consideration. . . . They were offered what they thought was a good price and [*Prairie Farmer* President James E.] Edwards was about to retire and so Edwards decided that this was a good time to take the money and run," Thomson said.[252]

Doubts about the program's modern viability proved wrong. After WLS dropped it, the *Barn Dance* hung on throughout the sixties. WGN eventually picked it up and ran it Saturday nights for ninety minutes, with a thirty-minute version for television. Both ended by 1969.[253]

By that time, Nashville claimed country music as its focal industry. Chicago lacked the urgency to contest that claim. Even though the *Barn Dance* had served as the prewar incubator for what would become the country music industry, by its end Chicago was establishing itself as a global headquarters for professional services, as demonstrated by new high-rise office towers and hotels, multi-story parking garages, the sprawling McCormick Place convention center, and even the demolition of the Eighth Street Theater in 1960 to make way for a 75,000-square-foot convention facility for Hilton. Regionalism took over, and the sound, themes, and down-home culture of country music started to sound more comfortable nestled in the South than in the sleek skyscraper canyons of Chicago.

Aside from the *Barn Dance* performers who extended their careers elsewhere, there were many who stayed behind and found life outside the music industry. Patsy Montana, Bob Atcher, Lily May Ledford, and Doc Hopkins were among those who were rediscovered by folk music audiences in the 1960s and 1970s, which opened a second chapter for their careers. Others stepped away from the microphone and never returned. Hartford Taylor, once one of the most recognizable stars of WLS, put his mandolin down and bounced between jobs, including a stint at the Regal Musical Instrument Company as a salesman, before he ended up inside an Illinois State Tollway Authority booth, collecting change from commuters until his death in 1963. "He never had any desire to perform again," his son Bill Taylor recalled.[254] Unlike her sister Caroline, who continued to perform, Mary Jane DeZurik became a switchboard operator at a local college. She rarely talked about her *Barn Dance* days, remembers Jim Klein, her son. One day he unearthed memorabilia from the radio show in the family basement and carried it upstairs to show his mother. "She burst out crying and didn't want to look at it," he said. "There was real sadness."[255]

The world had changed, the city had changed, and so had the music they played that made so many people happy. "He loved music but he never thought of it as special. When he first started to be in the music business, if somebody wanted to pay to listen, he figured he would play," said Taylor of his father.[256] But then people stopped paying.

On March 29, 1967, Patsy Montana wrote a letter to John Lair, her first boss. "I am still in the recording racket, it's not fun like it use [*sic*] to be, too commercial. . . . Personally, I am growing tired of the 'Nashville Sound' and am trying in my own small way to help bring back some of the good old tunes." Montana told Lair of getting on a stage to play to soldiers on their way to Vietnam. She had intended to play only the hits of the day—"all the current Nashville songs"—but the band got to them before she appeared onstage.

So the fifty-nine-year-old singer walked out and belted what she knew best—"Reckless Cowboy," "I'll Remember You Love in My Prayers," and the song that made her famous three decades prior, "I Want to Be a Cowboy's Sweetheart."

Time froze. On her last note, the young men jumped to their feet. "I was the only one that stopped the show," she told her former mentor, "And this was from the younger generation!!!!!"[257] The Cowboy Sweetheart, one more time, was a star.

"HILLBILLY HEAVEN"
IN CHICAGO

UPTOWN AND SKID ROW

The beer wars of the Prohibition era gave Chicago an international reputation for violence and vice, an image that, by the 1950s, the city was eager to shed. The extension of the central business district from the Loop to North Michigan Avenue created a luxury shopping district amid an urban renewal boom that fortified downtown with corporate headquarters, high-rise hotels, and apartment buildings for downtown professionals. Nearby, investments were made in cultural and educational institutions such as a satellite campus for the University of Illinois, the expansion of the Illinois Institute of Technology, and new administration facilities for county, state, and federal governments.

When the Prudential Insurance headquarters opened its doors in 1955, it was the first new skyscraper built downtown in twenty-one years.[1] In the building boom that followed over the next two decades, downtown office space nearly doubled in capacity.[2]

For the working poor, however, the boom meant not dollars, but displacement.

Single-room occupancy residents, the majority White unmarried men, were largely clustered in a district anchored by West

Madison between Jefferson and Des Plaines, which at one time had even encircled the Loop. Called the "Main Stem" in the early twentieth century, the district housed saloons, cheap hotels, gambling dens, fortune-tellers, and employment agencies catering to seasonal laborers and hoboes brought to Chicago by the thirty-nine different railroads that serviced the city. By the 1950s, the area had shrunk to just the Madison stretch, and was known by a new name: Skid Row.[3] By 1965, more than four thousand transients lived along the West Side strip, and the city was determined to get them out for good.[4]

Country bars, most of which featured live music, lined West Madison. They, along with the honky-tonks on the near North Side, had names above the door that told recent arrivals from the South they were welcome: the Southern Inn, the Hillbilly Nitery, the Hillbilly Inn, the Memory Ranch, Tex Carter's, the Ringside Ranch, the Dude Ranch, the Wagon Wheel, and Dome Stables, which presented strippers backed by a country band. By 1959, it was clear the days of all these bars were numbered. In January, to kick off his campaign for a second term, Mayor Richard J. Daley announced a $1.5 billion plan to create "wholesome suburban living conditions at the fringe of Chicago's busy Loop," intended to attract middle-class families downtown and to redefine Chicago as a world-class city comparable to Paris or New York. The plan targeted the area from North Avenue south to Twenty-Sixth Street and from Ashland Avenue east to Lake Michigan. The window of time slated to complete this massive overhaul was twenty-two years.[5] The estimate was almost exact: the final Skid Row flophouses would fall in 1982 to make way for Presidential Towers, a series of high-rise residential units at 555 West Madison.[6]

Yet even with bulldozers approaching, the country bars did not fade easily. There were too many of them for the city to control. According to city records, the number of liquor licenses in Chicago more than doubled between the time before Prohibition and the late 1940s and early 1950s. In 1916, Chicago had 3,496 liquor licenses on record, but by 1948, that number had catapulted to 10,034.[7] Clearly, tavern owners were catching up with both the pent-up demand for

alcohol and a population spurt of more than a million additional
people since Prohibition. In its final incarnation, West Madison
was derided as a strip of sin, offering illicit sex shows and gambling,
which brought about violence, drunkenness, homelessness, disease, and even voter fraud. "It was a sleazy scene. They were rough,
they were violent, they weren't pleasant," said Joan Delaney, wife
of Curt Delaney of the Sundowners, a country trio that performed
in the Loop.[8]

Harmonica player Charlie Musselwhite, a White Memphian,
drove to Chicago in November 1962 seeking factory work. He was
eighteen. He settled with a friend in a furnished apartment in
Uptown at 4040 North Broadway Avenue. Rent cost $25 a month,
and dinner was peanut butter and canned tuna. "I was too broke to
do much of anything," he said. Entertainment consisted of buying
a pint of whiskey and standing in the doorways of the honky-tonks
to listen to local country bands from the sidewalk. On days he had
money in his pocket, he'd go inside just to watch the fights. Stepping
over fresh blood on the sidewalk from knifings earlier that day was
common. The bars that were the most unpredictable were the ones
on Skid Row.

"People talk about how rough the blues clubs were, but actually,
these places were worse. Because a fight in a blues club was usually
about something. A fight in these places might not be about anything. Everybody was just angry. Life had really fucked them over,"
Musselwhite said. "I'd see people just sitting nursing a drink and
looking at everybody. And if he caught anybody's eye, he would give
them the finger. Just to start something. Just to put some excitement in their life."[9]

Songwriter John Prine has memories of his father, Bill Prine, a
tool and die maker who grew up in the coal country of Kentucky, taking him to Chicago Cubs games. They'd arrive in the neighborhood
early to stop by the honky-tonks—"real doozies"—that lined Clark
Street near Wrigley Field. Bands played music on stages encased in
chicken wire while punches flew to the music. Prine's father would
sit his son down with an orange soda and listen to the songs from

back home while nursing a beer. His words of advice about drinking alone: "You walk in and you find yourself a place at the end of the bar. And you order two beers—one to drink and the other to hit the guy over the head with if he attacks you."[10]

As urban renewal crept forward, police raids on bars were frequent, followed by charges of prostitution, gambling, and underage drinking. Often the situations that drew attention from police involved tourists or other run-of-the-mill naïfs getting fleeced. A New Jersey man complained to a federal judge in a 1960 court case that he woke up in his hotel room in the Loop "violently ill" after passing out at the Show Lounge, 3040 West Madison, with the $800 in his pocket gone.[11] At the Liberty Inn, 661 North Clark, police arrested four men and five women for solicitation in 1953; two ministers from nearby Gary, Indiana, told police they were only there "observing night life conditions in Chicago."[12] At Papa Joe's Tavern, 1303 Jackson, the bartender beat a man bloody with a baseball bat in 1961 after he objected to the solicitations of a showgirl who slid onto the stool next to him. Mayor Daley revoked the bar's license for that.[13] Maybe the most notorious showdown was at Tex Carter's, 3777 North Broadway, where a predawn brawl in 1958 involving pocketknives and broken beer bottles took place after four men were turned away for not having IDs. They returned forty minutes later, in three cars carrying an additional eight men, all recent Kentucky transplants. A struggle broke out inside the club, but trailed outside when owner Everett "Tex" Carter himself chased one marauder down the street and shot him in the right foot.[14]

The music was just as wild. Dale Watson, the Texas honky-tonk singer, remembers spending his early childhood watching his father lead the house band at the Wagon Wheel, 1001 North Clark. Don Watson, who had grown up in Hazard, Kentucky, moved his family to Chicago in 1965 because he heard the music scene was so active. He pumped gas at a North Side Amoco station during the week, but every weekend he headed Don Watson and the Make-Ups, a group that also recorded for local country label Chaparral. His son would often pass through the swinging front doors of the Wagon Wheel to watch his father rehearse. The music ran fast and hot. "Chicago definitely had its own sound," Watson said.[15]

One of the most notorious clubs was the Southern Inn, 3409 West Madison. Three brothers, Johnnie, Walter, and Earl Glisson, decked the bar and dance floor, which held about three hundred people, with western kitsch. They were ruthless in their business dealings—"sons of bitches," according to Johnny Pitts, an Alabama-born guitarist whose first job in Chicago was playing the club in 1956. He was twenty when he backed Buck Owens, long before his Buckaroos days, during a three-week stand before the Chicago weather convinced Owens to return to Bakersfield, California. Pitts then became the house guitarist.[16]

The Southern Inn had one of the biggest dance floors in town and booked the hottest bands, but it was violence from rival gangs, and even rival club owners, that kept it in the headlines. In 1950, two men tossed a "stench bomb" on the dance floor and then sped off in a car after spraying the tavern walls and windows with bullets.[17] That was topped in November 1956 with what the *Chicago Tribune* called "one of Chicago's wildest bar fights."[18]

That night, Pitts was on the bandstand playing a new Fender Stratocaster guitar to back up Bobby Soots, a fellow Alabama native who had come to Chicago the previous decade to play the clubs. Bandleader Gene Krupa had hired "the novelty hillbilly singer" in 1950 as his lead vocalist to help him break into the Dixieland market, and with him recorded a version of "Bonaparte's Retreat," a Top 20 single that year.[19] But by 1956, Soots had long since left Krupa and had recorded a few singles of his own for Mercury Records. The Southern Inn was his final rodeo.

Around two o'clock in the morning, a gang of men crashed through the doors firing guns, sending glass flying and furniture crashing. Heading the pack were Christ and Thomas Boulahanis, a rival set of brothers who owned the Memory Ranch, a country music tavern across the street at 3330 West Madison. Fifty people brawled with chairs, bottles, and barstools. Nearly sixty years later, Pitts still remembered a bullet ricocheting off the floor and hitting the truss rod on his guitar neck, destroying his new instrument at the exact moment he was striking a G chord. "Scared the living hell out of me," he said.[20] By the time police arrived, bodies were crawling on the floor, but miraculously not a single person had been shot. Earl Glisson, bleeding from the head, greeted them on the dance floor, in each of his hands a smoking pistol.[21]

This was why most bands played inside cages of chicken wire. Jukebox hits of the day filled their sets during a period when country music was discovering speed and the pedal steel guitar, and honky-tonk audiences were drawn to darker themes like drinking, desolation, and hard times. But the national dominance of the WLS *Barn Dance* also meant that Chicago was home to songwriters with their own material. One consistent bandleader from the mid-1940s through the late 1950s was Arbie Gibson, a Wisconsinite with Kentucky blood. He produced a consistent output of hits that were recorded by a long list of people, including Jerry Lee Lewis, Elvis Presley, Roy Acuff, Rex Allen, and Ernest Tubb.

Born September 1, 1914, Gibson spent his teenage years in Crandon, Wisconsin, a town nicknamed "Little Kentucky" because of the mass migration of loggers who had moved there earlier that century to work the timber mills. He entered show business in 1933 when he walked through the stage door of the local opera house in nearby Antigo, where Gene Autry was headlining.[22] A friend snuck him behind the curtain, and Gibson cornered the cowboy star long enough to play him eleven songs, his total output to date. The next two nights, Gibson showed up again, and on the third, Autry offered him ten dollars for the lot. For a boy whose lack of education was a handicap, the only logical answer was yes.

Two of those songs, "You're the Only Star in My Blue Heaven" and "Dear Old Western Skies," became hits the following year, earning Autry a substantial payday. Gibson, unaware of the concept of publishing royalties during their first meeting, showed up backstage at Autry's next date in town. "White as a sheet" is how Autry looked when he saw the boy walk in and ask about royalties. Autry told him nothing could be done, but he offered to set Gibson up with song publishers and radio stations if he followed him to Chicago. Gibson did, and soon he was playing guitar on WLS road shows while circulating his songs. His band, the Drifting Cowboys, backed him at the New Buckingham Inn, 2142 West Madison, where he played for ten years starting in 1943.[23] Outside of town, he was bandleader for Jenny Lou Carson, a *Barn Dance* veteran and a prolific songwriter herself. As luck would have it, her husband was Tiny Hill. Weighing over three hundred pounds, Tiny was a local big band leader who accepted a job as folk music director for Mercury Records in 1945, the founding year for the Chicago label. The first meeting between Hill and Gibson was brief: "We need some songs," Hill told Gibson. "I need some money," the songwriter replied. Five hundred dollars later, the audience for Gibson's songs grew overnight.[24]

"Letters Have No Arms," Gibson's most enduring hit and a postwar classic, traveled far for many years, with versions recorded by Ernest Tubb, Faron Young, Kris Kristofferson, Ray Price, Brook Benton, and Cajun fiddler D. L. Menard, among many others. In Tubb's 1950 version, the sexual frustration of the letter holder flickers just within reach: "Kisses on paper are so cold," he sings. "Letters never bring me the touch of your hand / Or none of your sweet lovin' charms."

Gibson corrected his earlier mistake with Autry and established a publishing company to handle dozens of his songs, many of which, like "Honey, I'm in Love with You" and "Soap and Water," became standards of their day. During a prolific ten years as a working musician, Gibson was forced to turn down offers to relocate to Los Angeles and Nashville for one simple reason: his wife refused to move. In 1952, he took a job at a steel mill and put down his guitar for good.

The Mercury connection also proved fruitful for Arbie's younger brother Art. Art Gibson spent time in North Dakota before moving to Chicago, where he quickly signed to Mercury and recorded for the label through 1949. Backed by a band that included steel guitar and piano, Gibson sang mostly raucous honky-tonk fare like "I'm A Truck Drivin' Man" and "Honky Tonk Mama." Most were originals. "No More Records" in 1947 playfully lamented the pending strike by the American Federation of Musicians that banned new recording sessions throughout 1948. "What would we do without our records? / When we can't play our phonograph no more? / What will we do for entertainment? / When there's no more records in the stores?" he sang as a steel guitar bounced behind him.

Art Gibson's life ran as wild as his music. Different women and copious amounts of liquor were frequent companions. After a fight on the road, a girlfriend pulled out a gun Art carried in the car's glovebox and put it on the seat, then called the county sheriff. Lack of a gun permit put him in jail for a year. He died of liver failure in 1971, twenty-six years before his older brother.

LIVING HARD AND
HARD LIVING IN UPTOWN

On a Sunday afternoon in 1965, William Chipman stood, guitar in hand, in the foyer of St. Mary of the Lake School, 4201 North Kenmore. Billy Chips, as he was known, lived just down the block. He played music in the two places his neighbors frequented most: taverns and church. Yet church was over for the day. Chips was heading a hootenanny intended for neighborhood children and their parents. Neither came.

So he and others spread out to round up people huddled against bar rails. "I'm not going to play anymore in them taverns," Chips said, disgusted. "People are there just to hear noise. They don't appreciate it."[25]

The noise of so-called hillbilly bars indeed ran up and down Chicago in the postwar era, from the South Side to the North. The farthest north were in Highwood, a suburb on the far North Shore that primarily served Fort Sheridan, a mobilization and training center for the US Army that opened in 1887. The leafier and sleepier communities of its southern border also supported Highwood because it was their local vice district, a convenient escape known as Whiskey Junction. The row of taverns filled with suburbanites fleeing local temperance laws and soldiers on weekend leave. Speakeasies flourished during Prohibition, and when it was over, they went legitimate. By the 1930s, recreational drinkers had the choice of getting their fix at Marge's, Midge's, Pearl's, Santi's, Bob Saielli's, the Bear Hut, the Village Inn, My Favorite Inn, Del Rio, Pagoda, Sunnyside Inn, the Rainbow, Lorraine Gardens, the local American Legion Hall, or the Labor Temple—all watering holes that featured live bands.

Like that on Skid Row, the Highwood scene was rough, especially since most of the audience were servicemen looking to blow off steam. Hayden Thompson, a Mississippian who moved to Highwood in May 1958, recalls business as thriving—he fronted a band five nights a week at the Tally Ho Club. But it took a toll. "Guys liked to come and throw things at me," he said. It wasn't how Thompson sang, but how he dressed—black-and-white shoes with lightning bolts on the side, pink striped jacket, and checkered shirt. Apparently, the rockabilly look had not yet reached the upper Midwest. "People came to see the monkey," he said. "But the point is, they came."[26]

Born March 5, 1938, in Booneville, Mississippi, Thompson was an only child raised on country crooners like Hank Snow and Eddy Arnold, even though at night he turned the dial to the up-tempo blues and gospel emanating out of WLAC in Nashville. The release of Elvis Presley's debut single "That's All Right" in 1954 gave him direction: at age sixteen, he walked into a local radio station and cut two singles himself. Soon enough, he and his band toured the South's movie theater circuit, playing before and after the film *Rock around the Clock*. Presley's success put teenagers like Thompson in high demand. "Everybody wanted to get a record out, everyone wanted to make money and drive a Cadillac. We all figured if Elvis had four, we should have at least one," he said. In 1956, Sam Phillips, the man credited with discovering Presley and recording him at the Sun Records studio in Memphis, invited Thompson to record a cover of Junior Parker's "Love My Baby," which featured piano by a then-unknown Jerry Lee Lewis. Thompson ended up recording nine sides at Sun.[27] But times were too good for Sun to give Thompson a shot: still reeling from Presley's popularity, the label had few resources to promote him. Years later, Phillips said he had "no explanation" why Thompson didn't become a star: "His 'Love My Baby' is one of my favorite records. It was a classic. . . . I would like to have had more time with him. Maybe there was too much of an Elvis influence in him; that's all I can think of."[28]

When a childhood friend phoned to say he had just purchased a club a few miles north of Chicago, Thompson, disillusioned with the Memphis scene, packed his bag and drove north. Over four years, he pounded the piano, played guitar, and belted rockabilly songs with the house band at the Tally Ho, a venue just as unpredictable and wild as any twenty-year-old man could imagine. Soon, the 250-seat club was attracting audiences from as far away as Wisconsin and Michigan. One asset under Thompson's belt was his rhythm guitarist: a fifteen-year-old Michael Bloomfield, who later played lead guitar for Paul Butterfield and Bob Dylan.[29] "It was just a happening place because nobody was doing what I was doing," Thompson said. "I came up and brought that rockabilly scene to Chicago."[30]

Highwood aside, the densest concentration of country music was in Uptown, a Chicago neighborhood loosely bound by Foster Avenue, Irving Park Road, Ravenswood Avenue, and the Lake Michigan waterfront. Chicago annexed Uptown in 1889, but before 1900 there were relatively few homes there.[31] It took rapid transit—four electric streetcar lines and elevated train service—to make the area appealing to downtown commuters. Soon enough, high-rise hotels, marketed to middle-class sophisticates, sprang up on its major arteries. Accommodating the growth was an upscale entertainment and shopping district designed to compete with downtown. The very name "Uptown" was formally chosen in 1921 by a local retailer who felt "Wilson Avenue District" failed to adequately describe the excitement of what was happening there. The concept of modern living took root at these intersections. The 46,000-square-foot Uptown Theater, opened in 1925, was the first in the nation to rival Radio City Music Hall in size and grandeur. The Aragon and the Arcadia, ballrooms at 1106 West Lawrence and 4432–4456 North Broadway, respectively, hosted Black jazz bands from the South Side and held dance competitions that had strict dress codes. Smaller nightclubs showcased Black jazz groups and vaudevillians. Hollywood lights came to the neighborhood through the De Luxe Theater, 1141 West Wilson, and the Riviera Theater, 4746 North Racine, two movie houses that opened in 1912 and 1918, respectively.[32]

But the Great Depression ended all that. Overnight, Uptown turned to the economy of vice, a natural outgrowth of its entertainment halls and booze lounges. Gangsters took control of the district, most notably Al Capone, who owned several local speakeasies and clubs, most famously the Green Mill at 4802 North Broadway, where tunnels were installed under the bar to smuggle in alcohol. A housing shortage after World War II turned single-family homes into rooming houses, and the high-rise hotels became overcrowded rentals with substandard upkeep. Between 1950 and 1960, Uptown's property values fell as much as 26 percent in some years as people fled to burgeoning suburbs that promised more space and less crime.[33] The old neighborhood was handed over to the poor and indigent. Slumlords scooped up buildings for little to nothing and refused to make repairs. Then came the blight.

The abrupt transformation happened to coincide with the migration of Whites from the upland South to urban areas across the Midwest. About 3.3 million people left Appalachia between 1950 and 1969.[34] Although Southern Whites came to Chicago from ten states, the majority originated from Kentucky and West Virginia. Sixty-five thousand Appalachians were living in Uptown by 1968.[35] The neighborhood became a port of entry for these migrants.

There were many reasons for the mass exodus from Appalachia, but the greatest was the automation of coal mining and cotton picking. Between 1950 and 1959 alone, the number of farmworkers in the South dropped by half. Coal mining jobs in eastern Kentucky were also halved, but their demise took less time, only five years.[36] Unlike Black Southerners, who dominated jobs at the stockyards and steel mills of the city's South Side—along with the Poles and Lithuanians—White Southern migrants were geographically restricted to the opposite end of town. Unskilled laborers readily found work at places like Bell & Howell, Crane Packing, General Valve, Stewart-Warner, and Bell & Gossett, all operations located north of Fullerton.[37] The city needed to expand its labor force, but with workers packed into such a small geographical footprint, it didn't know what to do with them once they arrived.

Uptown had already become home to upland Southerners by way of the WLS *Barn Dance*. In 1932, Gene Autry and his new wife, Ida Mae, moved into their first home together, a two-bedroom apartment on the top floor at 4501 North Malden Street.[38] The yellow brick building was relatively new, and the landlady, a Mrs. Smith, "loved show people" and didn't mind the unconventional hours they kept. So she rented primarily to WLS performers. Les Paul, Patsy Montana, Louise Massey & the Westerners, and the Hoosier Hot Shots, among others, rented units there.[39] Many were starting families, so the building became a gathering place where potluck dinners were exchanged and bonds formed.

Moving forward two decades, it's not certain that any landlord would be so accommodating. Uptown is where poverty festered, where newcomers to the city were forced to survive in crowded, filthy, and unsafe living conditions that they did not create, but for which they were often blamed. The real culprit was density: families were forced to live in one- or two-room units, which represented over half the total housing units in 1960. More than a quarter of units lacked proper plumbing.[40] Relocation to the city meant accepting confinement. People who once lived proudly on land that belonged to their families over generations now squeezed into close quarters that weren't their own. Sidewalks became an extension of the home. Children played amid broken glass and trash under the elevated train tracks. Men could neither hunt nor own a gun. White Southerners now shared the factory floor with the same minorities they were segregated from back home. Women as well as men found jobs waiting for them—waitress, sales clerk, hospital attendant, factory worker—which meant they left the home and were not confined to domestic duties. Children were left on their own during the day, and truancy rates spiked. With the Uptown commercial area losing jobs, the neighborhood itself offered little upward mobility. By 1961, 11 percent of storefronts were vacant, 21 percent were marginally used as itinerant churches or pawn shops, and 17 percent were taverns.[41] Alcoholism and disease spread.

Robert Rehak was a junior copywriter at Leo Burnett when he developed a routine of gazing through train windows during his daily commutes to and from his home in Rogers Park. Uptown held his eyes the longest. One evening in 1973, he decided to make an early exit at Wilson and shoot photographs, a decision that turned into a four-year project and five thousand images. Walking Uptown's streets led him into homes and businesses and lives, and even though he lived about four miles up the road, Rehak discovered a neighborhood that resembled a forgotten island.

"Lots of rats, lots of roaches, lots of graffiti, buildings were crumbling," he said. "The living conditions were abysmal."

His photographs show the diversity of Uptown—besides Southerners, the people in the doorways, streets, and alleys and beneath the elevated tracks are Puerto Ricans, Native Americans, East Asians, Japanese, all connected by poverty and marginalization by Chicago's gilded class. One photograph from 1976 shows a Latin Kings leader wearing a T-shirt for the Unknowns, their softball team. "These were people who were ignored by society. They were the forgotten ones. Why would a softball team call themselves the Unknowns? Because they were invisible," he said.[42]

By the early 1960s, many different public and private social service organizations took root in Uptown, and by 1968, their number boomed to at least twenty-six. There were also twenty-four churches in the 120-block area, all in the business of providing basic needs like food, medicine, childcare, and job placement. The Old Town School of Folk Music established a strong presence in Uptown by providing free music lessons, instruments, and performances. As early as 1965, the school ran guitar lessons for children out of an apartment at 4240 North Kenmore. School co-founder Dawn Greening found nineteen free guitars for the children, ages ten to sixteen. The school's purpose was to generate pride. Said Greening,

"We should let people know that the culture they bring to the city is truly worthwhile, and encourage them to recognize their own traditions."[43] Through music, the school created a litany of community events. The most ambitious was the Chicago Poor Arts Festival, a twenty-two-day event in 1972 held at the Uptown Center–Hull House on North Beacon. The festival, drolly subtitled the "un-Ravinia" in reference to the tony summer festival on the far North Shore, featured the full slate of Old Town School teachers, who performed with blues sets by Carey Bell, Mighty Joe Young, and the Siegel-Schwall Band.[44]

The most prominent social service organization was the Chicago Southern Center, at 1028 West Wilson, a community center dedicated to aiding the poor through health care, job assistance, food, education workshops, and cash. What made it different from other similar groups was its affiliation with the Center of the Southern Mountains, a missionary organization involved in both advocating for Appalachian heritage and fighting for worker rights for fifty years from its headquarters at Berea College, Kentucky. The Chicago center was one of five the organization had opened up in the Midwest. In a previous incarnation, the Southern Center had focused on the problems posed by industrialization, but by the time the Chicago center opened in 1963, its mission had changed to preserving Appalachian identity and helping White migrants in the city adjust to the challenges of their new setting.[45] Among its programs were a group orientation to Chicago amenities like museums, public transit, and schools; a clothing exchange; job training; an Alcoholics Anonymous chapter; youth tutoring; and social clubs. Another way it created a home away from home was through informal jam sessions where musicians were invited to "air their thoughts in addition to playing" their instruments.[46]

Music was central to the Southern Center's programming. Roger Bellow, a fiddler and banjoist who grew up nearby, moved to Uptown in 1966. He was a teenager when he sought out weekend shows at the Southern Center. Soon he joined up with Jimmy Rippy, a Savannah, Tennessee, native who headed a country band with his wife.

Rippy played electric guitar, his wife sang, and the band's repertoire covered the songbook of Hank Williams and more. Their Saturday night variety show was raucous; Rippy emulated the *Barn Dance* formula and even included a comedian who, dressed like David "Stringbean" Akeman from the *Grand Ole Opry*, called himself Uncle Hayseed. Bellow joined on banjo. He was already immersed in folk music through the Old Town School of Folk Music, where he had started lessons at age nine. Learning country music directly from Appalachians felt like bringing his education full circle. "I was just overjoyed to be playing. It was fun as can be," he said.

Bellow witnessed both the passion displaced Southerners had for playing music from home and the desperate lives they lived once they put their instruments down for the night. Most returned to apartments without heat, and moving from building to building was constant. "The housing was rotten. They seemed to be getting by, but they were living pretty close to the edge," he said.[47]

NORMA LEE BROWNING: MUCKRAKER OF THE *CHICAGO TRIBUNE*

While the social service agencies operating in Uptown needed to court the media to keep donations flowing in, the Chicago media was, by most accounts, their worst enemy. Newspapers played a significant role in stoking public fear over the Southern "invasion" of low-income Whites who threatened to upset the social order, and often portrayed them as so-called disgraces to their race. No reporter was more dedicated to promoting this narrative than Norma Lee Browning. After getting her master's degree at Radcliffe College, Browning joined the *Chicago Tribune* in 1944 as a feature writer. Her writing voice sneered at fads and ridiculed any group she suspected of frivolity, be it beatniks or bobbysoxers. The *Tribune* crowned her its "girl reporter." Browning's relative youth was an asset because her derision came from the same generation the paper sought to put in its place.

In March 1957, the *Tribune* ran a nine-part series that promised an in-depth look into the "jungles of hillbillies" taking root in neighborhoods that "are considered the wildest in the city." Writing in the guise of a safari guide, Browning told readers that their city was being "taken over by clans of fightin', feudin' southern hillbillies and their shootin' cousins, who today constitute one of the most dangerous and lawless elements of Chicago's fast growing migrant population."

"Their hangouts advertise: 'Hillbilly Music,'" she warned readers. "Best you stick to calypso."[48]

Using no data and quoting only the Chicago Police Department, Browning reported over weeks that the North Side was under siege by people who brought with them child brides, common-law marriages, rampant crime, delinquency, primitive sanitation practices, illiteracy, and even a resistance to immunization and education. The police told Browning that, granted, the Southerners have the right to settle wherever they wish, but suggested it would be better for the city if it weren't near the lakefront. "They have turned the streets of Chicago into a lawless free-for-all with their primitive jungle tactics," said one Chicago crime commissioner. "[Authorities] agree that the Southern hillbilly migrants, who have descended on Chicago like a plague of locusts in the last few years, have the lowest standard of living and moral code [if any] of all, the biggest capacity for liquor, and the most savage and vicious tactics when drunk, which is most of the time," Browning explained.[49]

Her reports started with the bars. "Ten years ago 'hillbilly music' dives were unknown in Chicago. Today they're splashed all over the city," she wrote, singling out the stretch of Madison from Kedzie to Homan, as "wilder than any television western." Most bars Browning attended had dance floors with live bands playing "the Tennessee stomp." The dancers Browning encountered there were under the age of thirty, all driven, she concluded, by "liquor, sex, and cars." Her reporting shows how alien everything about Southern culture was to the society class, even down to the fundamentals:

It's easy enough to tell a hillbilly dive from the ordinary saloon—even without that awful racket from the bandstand. It is distinguished by its odor (not Chanel), acrobatics, and fascinating attire. The women wear blue jeans, sacks (preferably red plaid), or cheesey brocade and spangles. Men are in work pants, coveralls, leather motorcycle jackets, and Presley sideburns. In some 30 joints we only saw one "square" in a suit.[50]

After the first installments, letter writers pounced on Browning and the *Tribune*, calling her vindictive and charging her employer with scandalmongering. Some demanded an apology. Only one defended the reporting. Most writers were displaced Southerners themselves who were unapologetic about their birth homes. "I am a hillbilly and thank God I am. I know one thing—where I come from down South we don't have to worry about gangs beating up our children when they go to school," wrote Anna Wright. C.B. of Chicago told Browning she needed to "cheer up." "The youths in blue jeans and leather jackets she saw . . . were probably not the remains of the Confederate army, come to drag her off to Andersonville, as she seems to think. That is almost the universal garb of teen-agers."[51] Mrs. Michael Tito added that during World War II, "we were not called hillbillies but Americans. I had six boys in service; one was killed."[52]

Many letter writers contradicted the depictions of Southerners as lowlifes, and one, Richard D. Miller, reminded the *Tribune* that what Browning was witnessing had less to do with character flaws than with the economics of class.

If Miss Browning can get out of the taverns, brothels, and opium parlors . . . long enough to look in the right places, she will find southern hillbillies writing novels and plays of lasting worth, issuing court decisions and opinions of historic significance, serving the nation and its communities well in public office, acting and singing competently, teaching and learning in university classrooms, designing, building, and operating the equipment essential to our technological progress, and even publishing newspapers.

As a hillbilly descendant of many generations of hillbillies, I resent being regarded as an undesirable alien in my own country.[53]

The letters ran for three days. They forced Browning to soften her tone, but only slightly. "The word 'hillbilly' set off a powder keg that exploded with all the ferocity of the long-feudin' Hatfields and McCoys," she wrote at the start of one piece.[54] She then chided Chicagoans who wrote to the newspaper, explaining that, to Southerners, the term "hillbilly" was a matter of pride.

Thousands of letters poured in after that.[55] Browning eventually backpedaled with a sympathetic profile of a family from Roanoke, Virginia, who she found toiling in Chicago, not because of any natural deficiency but because of proven socioeconomic ones. "There they had a five room house, a big yard, a nice gas stove for cooking. Here, tho they have no complaints, they are paying $21 a week for what anyone but the landlord would consider a substandard firetrap," she reported.[56] That May, Browning wrote that her series "had a nationwide response—and repercussions" because newspapers in Nashville and other Southern cities were now starting to publish exposés and editorials that explored joblessness in their regions and the exploitation that awaited Southerners moving north. She accepted the invitation of some readers to visit Appalachia and announced the *Tribune* would soon launch a new series that promised to reveal "what is creating the huge exodus into northern industrial cities."[57]

But the damage was done. Other media had picked up Browning's series and splashed it across their pages, either as a full reprint or as a springboard for further commentary. "The Hillbillies Invade Chicago" screams the headline of a *Harper's Magazine* story that plucked Browning quotes for use throughout. "They are worse than the colored. They are vicious and knife-happy," a police captain says. The writer eventually concludes that lack of fair housing, not delinquency, is at the root of the problem, and he reminds readers that, as White Protestants, the Southerners are descendants "of the yeoman of Jeffersonian democracy" and therefore have "every attribute for success according to the American dream—even in its narrowest form." In other words, White-against-White prejudice should be denounced because it's not the same as prejudice involving skin color.[58]

An editorial in the *Pittsburgh Courier* was less introspective. In one short column, the editorial board blamed all the industrial North's problems on Whites from the upland South. "If they would go back where they came from," the column concluded, "we would all be better off."[59] Locally, other newspapers, like the *Edgewater Uptown News*, also fanned hysteria against low-income Whites, commonly noting in crime stories when the assailant had a Southern accent. Reporting during this period leaned heavily on generalizations and was always light on data. "Hillbilly" came to represent an undesirable, regardless of origin or background. Vice had existed long before Uptown's decline, but memories were short. To the people living in wealthier enclaves bordering Uptown, the Southerners became the face of modern blight. For North Side property values to hold, something had to be done to remove the threat.

THE MUSIC OF RESISTANCE IN UPTOWN

The jeering in the media reflected what most Southerners experienced on the streets. The everyday harassment had many flavors: from a waitress rolling her eyes because she can't make out words through a Southern accent, to the police waiting outside bars to pick up unsuspecting locals meandering home, to the worst kind of intimidation: arsonists hired to smoke out the newcomers for good.[60] "Every place has a group to pick on. And I guess it was our turn," said Hy Thurman, who arrived in Uptown from his hometown of Dayton, Tennessee, in 1967, looking for work.[61] He was seventeen.

Before he became known around the world as a master of the blues harmonica, Charlie Musselwhite sounded funny to people he came up against in Chicago, his tongue the product of being raised in Memphis by a single mother born further South along the Mississippi Delta. "My accent back then was so thick that even in Memphis other Memphians would comment at how heavy it was," he said. Exhausted from the physical strain of laying concrete for cotton warehouses in Arkansas, he moved to Chicago and ended up as a driver for an Uptown exterminator named Harry Zimmer. The new job forced him to learn all corners of the city, particularly the South Side, where he would return at night to frequent blues clubs he'd seen during the day. He was more comfortable there because, among Black Southerners, "nobody laughed or couldn't understand me when I talked. They knew exactly what I was saying."

In the five years Musselwhite lived in Chicago, he traveled between the North and South Sides, and discovered that the more he was welcomed inside the basement taverns and corner taps in Woodlawn, or on Maxwell Street, where he played blues with Johnny Young and Robert Nighthawk and Carey Bell, the more he stood out as troublesome to the police. They harassed him routinely, and his predicament got worse when he opened his mouth and revealed a twang.

Late one summer night in 1964, at a bus stop on Cottage Grove, Musselwhite sat atop a plastic bench waiting for a bus to take him north. Drummer Frank Kirkland, who was Black, stayed with him to keep him company. Soon enough, a police cruiser passed by, and within seconds did a U-turn and parked across the street. "And they were looking at us, probably wondering who I am and what I'm doing there. I had my little case of harmonicas. I said to Frank, 'they're probably wondering what I had in the case.'"

Finally they pulled up in front and got out. There was a white cop and a black cop and they both said to us, "What do you mean sitting there with feet on city property?" It was funny, they never asked anything about the case. I said, "I'm just waiting on the bus." They asked me if I was trying to be smart. I said, "No, you asked me what I was doing." They told me get into the car and they told Frank to go home and they took me to jail. I remember the white cop telling me I ought to go back wherever I came from.

The next morning in court the black cop was there. He told the judge I appeared to be under the influence of something other than alcohol and I was cussing everyone out and I wouldn't let anybody sit on the bench. They had these signs up on the wall and number one was you are supposed to have a phone call. When I would ask to make my phone call, they'd just laugh. Nobody got a phone call. So there I am in court. Still no phone call, nobody knows that I'm in there except probably Frank and I don't know where he went to, but he couldn't help me. When I tried to tell the judge I wasn't allowed a phone call, some guy behind me, the bailiff I think, held my right hand up to swear me in. I told them that the cop was lying that none of that was true that I was just trying to go home. And the judge gave me thirty days for disturbing the peace. In Cook County.[62]

In Uptown, White Southerners fared even worse. Hy Thurman had been in Chicago only a few weeks when two police officers interrupted his walk down Sunnyside by throwing him in handcuffs and pushing him into the back of their car.

They said there'd been some burglaries in the area and they wanted to know where my burglary tools were. I obviously didn't know anything about it. . . . And this one cop said after he heard my Southern accent—it was very strong then because I was just seventeen—he said, "Oh my god, not another fucking hillbilly. You guys are just taking over. Why don't you go home and fuck your mother and your dog and your pig and your sister and your brother, or whatever you fuck down there?" That was their attitude toward us. That's the way we were looked at.[63]

Fear of blight mobilized the neighborhood's wealthiest inhabitants to organize against the urban newcomers. Central to the fight was the Uptown Chicago Commission. Formed in 1955, it was made up of local bank presidents, real estate developers, and executives, most of whom had direct ties to Mayor Richard J. Daley, the lead advocate for urban renewal during this period. The UCC's mission was to promote neighborhood safety, but its initiatives were clearly intended to keep property values from collapsing, a scenario that threatened to erode the tax base and, for banks, cause borrowers to default. Through its political connections, the commission got the city to dispatch building inspectors into the neighborhood to enforce code violations and to clamp down on apartment buildings converted into overcrowded rooming houses. In one case, eighty-two people were discovered living in a building with just thirty-one single rooms.[64] The commission secured city money to beautify the neighborhood by creating cul-de-sacs and improving Wilson Avenue. But eventually, the UCC became focused on pushing low-income Whites out. Editorials at the time railed against the blight spilling over into districts dominated by single-family homes, and the UCC was on the front lines representing the interests of power brokers who wanted to speed up redevelopment at the expense of affordable housing.

COUNTRY MUSIC AS WITNESS

The bleak living conditions, racial tensions, and the everyday threat of police brutality left the working poor of Uptown to fend for themselves. As a result, an activist movement emerged in the late 1960s that created unlikely alliances among young Whites, Blacks, and Puerto Ricans in an attempt to push back against the threats facing all three. As in any radical movement, music played an important role in articulating their struggles, but in this case it also served to shape their identity. For White migrants, country music became a cultural touchstone that was integral to their perseverance amid their struggles in their adopted city. If they were treated as strangers in a strange land, the music spoke of home.

The Young Patriots emerged around this time as the leading community organization advocating for neighborhood rights and better living conditions. The members were mostly young White men from the upper South whose families were directly impacted by the city's push for urban renewal. One of their major accomplishments was a storefront health clinic, run by a volunteer medical staff, that operated seven days a week.

The progressive student activism surrounding the Vietnam conflict helped set the stage. Many members from the Students for a Democratic Society (SDS) descended on the North Side during this time, escalating in the protests staged during the 1968 Democratic National Convention. One of SDS's initiatives was Jobs Or Income Now (JOIN), which in 1964 opened its flagship office in Uptown and over the years practiced immersive organizing among poor Whites. JOIN's presence attracted student radicals from outside the neighborhood and even high-profile figures in the movement, such as actor Harry Belafonte, who visited in spring 1965. The Young Patriots initially spun off from JOIN to confront police oppression. They dressed like any other gang of urban greasers: white T-shirts and black pants, but with sleeveless denim vests or leather jackets adorned with the Confederate flag or buttons that read "Free Huey" or "Resurrect John Brown."[65] While they formed with the intent to serve "hillbilly nationalists," as they called themselves, they soon made it clear they were fighting not just for oppressed Southerners, but for all minorities in Chicago who were under the thumb of the Daley regime. Borrowed from the Chicago Police, "We Serve and Protect" became their official motto, reflecting the belief that they had no one to help them but themselves.[66]

In 1969, the Young Patriots were invited to join an alliance with the Illinois Black Panther Party and the Young Lords, a former Puerto Rican street gang that now stood for racial equality across Chicago. This three-way partnership, called the Rainbow Coalition, chose a symbolic date for its first press conference: April 4, 1969, the first anniversary of the assassination of Dr. Martin Luther King Jr.[67] The alliance was a strange one only on the surface, as the police antagonized all three groups. As a result, each one fell under FBI surveillance, and tension on the street mounted.

Soon after the Rainbow Coalition took hold, the Young Patriots invited non-Whites into their ranks, including Cubans, Native Americans, and Blacks.[68] Adopting the Black Panther ideology forced the Patriots to reshape the Confederate flag as a symbol not of racial hatred, but of tolerance for the oppressed. The Patriots who wore the flag made sure to decorate it with Black Panther or Rainbow Coalition buttons to reverse its meaning so the few Blacks living in Uptown would understand they were allies. But the symbolism was also meant to tell Mayor Daley that segregation would not work so easily to divide people on the North Side and "that his plan of racism and repression had failed," said Hy Thurman.[69]

As with any community organizing, there was music. The student activists who arrived in Uptown during the 1970s were educated in the songbook of the civil rights movement from the previous decade, and those songs rang out during meetings and on the streets. But the music that originated from the Southerners themselves was different, because it was original and came directly from their experience.

The Chicago Area Black Lung Association (CABLA) formed in 1976 to help displaced Southern coal miners receive the federal benefits they deserved. Nine hundred ex-miners signed up. About ten thousand more were living in the metropolitan area. "In Chicago they were an invisible population, they couldn't get anywhere," said Paul Siegel, a young activist from the University of Wisconsin who helped organize the group after he moved to Chicago in 1972. CABLA fought to make the claim process fairer and less cumbersome, trained paralegals and attorneys to get claims through the system successfully, and opened the Uptown People's Health Center, a clinic dedicated to the aging miner population. Three former miners, Bob Cline, Donald "Fuzzy" Ratliff, and Bill Mullins, formed the Blue Ridge Mountain Boys, a bluegrass group that played throughout the neighborhood, at various evening functions and often during the day in the alley next to CABLA's headquarters at 1222 West Wilson. "For the down and out guys in Uptown, the music gave them something," Siegel said.[70]

The hardships of those years filtered into poetry and songs written by the people who experienced them. The Columbia College Press joined with the Young Patriots to collect their work, which it published across four separate chapbooks titled *A Time of the Phoenix*. Doug Youngblood, a Young Patriot, spearheaded the project. Born September 16, 1941, Youngblood grew up in Alabama and Kentucky before moving to Chicago in the 1960s with his mother, Peggy Terry, who would become one of Uptown's most prominent activists.

Terry co-founded JOIN and worked to take Uptown's problems to the national stage.[71] By the time the chapbooks were published, she had run on a national presidential ticket in 1968 with Black Panther leader Eldridge Cleaver. Terry, born October 28, 1921, grew up between Oklahoma and Kentucky; as a teenage bride during the Great Depression, she hitchhiked through Texas looking for farm work. "When I read *The Grapes of Wrath* . . . that was like reliving my life," she told Studs Terkel.[72]

Youngblood, who adopted a family name on his father's side, was self-educated and shaped his identity through Uptown's struggles. "Before I started doing this I was nothing. I would have kept on being nothing. Now, for the first time, I'm really doing something worthwhile," he said in 1968.[73] Despite only having completed grammar school, Youngblood read every book within reach and wrote prodigiously. "You're talking about a kid with no education who became a master of words. He was the smartest man I knew," said Carol Coronado, his wife.[74]

Youngblood played guitar and composed songs that reflected the harshness of poverty, but went deeper in expressing the hurricane of emotions that came with it: paranoia, bitterness, anger. On "Uptown Chicago Kind of Blues," from 1975, Youngblood describes watching children playing in rain puddles underneath the L tracks while thinking of the wealthy's children ensconced from all want. "Fingers of fire / keep a-reaching for my brain," he writes. The harrowing image answers each verse, including the last, in which he directly addresses those "who rule us with pistols and moneyed chains." "There's gonna be a difference 'cause we're gonna rearrange / All that you've erected made of hunger, hate and pain," he sings.[75] "Day Labor Blues," from 1977, describes waiting all day in line for the promise of work. There is the absurdity of the situation—"wasting my time day labor blues," the chorus goes—but also the terror: "I really don't know what I'm gonna do / My kids are in the car and they're hungry."[76]

The bitterness was real. Police harassment was routine. One Thanksgiving, the police tailed Youngblood and Coronado home.

When the couple stepped out of their car, officers ordered them inside the building and proceeded to tear the car apart. Another time, police pulled Youngblood from his car and smashed his ribcage. Cradling their baby in one arm, his wife called their attorney as she watched from their apartment window. "They targeted him because of our politics," said Coronado. "They were terrible."[77]

Many songs from this period read as if torn from a reporter's notebook—"Wilson Avenue" by Buddy Thompson, from 1965, asks the listener to "think of a street seven blocks long / and countless people who just drink and roam."[78] But mostly the desperation turns inward. "My Mind" by Susan Jah Jah, from 1973, is an account of teenage junkies, shoeless children, and prostitutes, everyday images that send the narrator to the nearest bar. "The last bottle I bought / brought thoughts of Wilson Avenue," she writes, adding what could be a jail sentence: "Where I live or exist."[79]

The lurid, unvarnished tales of drunkenness reflect the raw desperation on the street. "White Port Wine" by Roger D. Phillips, from 1976, is told from the viewpoint of a child whose mother and brother have both died from the cheap liquor. Now his father is on the same stuff, and the boy realizes, "I don't got too much time / to see my dad a'living."[80] "Uptown" by Carl Lorig, also from 1976, takes place on the sidewalk, where the narrator has ended up after being thrown through a tavern door. A priest—"his collar on backwards"—walks by, takes notice, but is only interested in learning what the sad sack had to drink. "First they fill you with lickor [*sic*] then they cut off your head," Lorig concludes wearily.[81]

Uptown emerges as a dream turned nightmare. In "Hillbilly Harlem," from 1973, William "Preacherman" Fesperman, a Young Patriot leader, writes of the dream undone:

If you travel route 41
From Nashville to Chicago
You better know what you've done
'Cause there on the north side's a sight
To behold

Forty thousand hillbillies shivering
In the cold.

Just behind the Gold Coast
Right next to Lake Shore Drive
Is where the people from the country arrive.
They find it hard goin' on
Day labor pay
But the poor old Hillbilly can't
Have his say

But the mines of Kentucky
And the farms of Tennessee
He comes to the city to save his family.
But plowing ain't so easy on concrete
And stone
And the jails of Chicago
Become the Hillbilly's home.[82]

Music was also the expression of choice for the Young Lords, the
North Side gang that comprised the sons and daughters of Chicago's
first wave of Puerto Rican immigrants. The music heard on their
streets was jibaro music, often referred to as "Puerto Rican hillbilly
music" because it developed in the island's countryside and involves
primarily stringed instruments, not percussion or horns. José "Cha
Cha" Jiménez, a Young Lords co-founder, remembered hearing it
played on sidewalks and during church services in "La Clark," the
Puerto Rican stronghold bordered by Ohio Street, North Avenue,
Dearborn Avenue, and Halsted Street. When he finally made it to
Uptown, he witnessed Appalachian Whites picking away at a similar frenzied brand of mountain music out of place in an unwelcom-
ing and cold city. "That was the bond," he said.[83]

In 1973, after the Young Lords evolved from a street gang into an
active political organization, Jiménez announced he would run for
alderman of the Forty-Sixth Ward, in response to the urban renewal

policies that were pushing Latinos out of La Clark into Lincoln Park and beyond. The Young Lords had already made the United Methodist Church on Armitage their headquarters, providing free dental and health clinics and food programs for children. They, like the Young Patriots, were under siege from police violence and under pressure to stay afloat amid blighted living conditions and substandard wages. To launch his campaign, Jiménez found an unlikely partner: folk singer Bob Gibson.

Gibson, who was living down the street, was by then a national figure on the folk music scene. In 1970, he showed up uninvited at a Young Lords rally and stepped up to the microphone to play a song from a recent album of his that would have special significance for the audience: "The Ballad of Mark Clark and Fred Hampton." The song details the brutal killing of both Black Panther leaders by fourteen Chicago police officers in 1969. The first verses detail the police climbing the apartment stairs "like jackals used the darkness" and wearing "smiling faces" after dragging both bodies away. The final verse is tailored for revolution:

> Well we're taking off our masks, we're crying "Power to the
>   People!"
> We're holding up our guns, we will charge the barricades
> Sing a battle cry for freedom, keep the mighty legion marching
> The tide is swiftly turning, and new history's being made[84]

Jiménez broke bread with Gibson over a shared heroin bag, and the two would remain friends during their different stages of addiction and recovery. Jiménez, who had cleaned up by the time of his alderman run, asked poet David Hernandez to write a song with Gibson they could use for campaign rallies. The collaboration was perfectly tailored to reach all the groups who would be sympathetic to Jiménez's message of affordable housing and human rights: "It had country music, it had jibaro music, it had the folk music of the lakefront liberals. I thought 'wow, this will relate to everybody,'" Jiménez said.[85]

The song, "Dawning of a Brand New Day," was performed for
two years throughout the North Side. It served as a rallying cry to
motivate constituents to get on their feet and vote, but it also aimed
directly at the city government itself:

There will be a Nuevo dia
No more roaches in casa fria
Politicians don't you know
Estamos aqui means you got to go

We won't move and we won't go
City hall we tell you so
If you don't or won't believe us
We will show you we mean business[86]

The campaign reached far beyond Chicago's Puerto Rican population. Jiménez ended up receiving 27 percent of the total vote in
the February 1975 election.[87] The coalition building would pay off
seven years later when, in 1982, Jiménez served as North Side pre-
cinct coordinator for Harold Washington, helping drive the Puerto
Rican vote his way during that historic campaign for Chicago's first
Black mayor.

TAVERNS, JUKEBOXES, AND RECORD STORES

By 1966, 17 percent of all storefronts in Uptown were taverns.[88] They
all relied on regulars, but it was their music that set most of them
apart, be it on a stage or booming from a jukebox speaker.

The taverns gave Southerners a chance to shut out the hostility
of their new city, and music served as the most recognizable portal to what they had left behind. "When you get off from work, you
head right for one of the hillbilly bars, where you're among your own
people and you feel free and you don't have to worry about how your
voice sounds, how you're dressing," said Doug Youngblood.[89] And
for people from areas of the South where moral codes and local laws

prohibited liquor sales and consumption, the taverns of Chicago represented a new kind of freedom that wasn't easily enjoyed back home. "Music was a very big part of the culture," said Hy Thurman. "You could hear it blasting out any of the bars. Every bar was a country bar. There was one on every street."[90]

The majority of jukeboxes in Uptown were controlled by ABC Music Service Corporation, Chicago's largest jukebox operator from the 1950s onward. The company started in December 1945 by purchasing smaller operations, and by the time it set up its new headquarters at 725 North Western, it held a tight grip on its routes, which had increased to twelve.[91] Hillbilly music dominated the machines on two of those routes—one that covered the whole of Uptown and a second located between California and Kedzie on the city's North Side. ABC developed a reputation for anticipating customer demand, but also catered to the competing musical tastes of different neighborhoods. By 1952, the company's record library had grown to twenty-five thousand discs, with a thousand new titles coming in each week.[92]

Besides frequenting taverns, people attended jams at neighborhood community centers or gathered in one another's homes to play. Music also made its way to the sidewalk. "You'd see people playing on the street. The music was everywhere," said Roger Bellow.[93] In summer, this was the practical choice, as barely any of the apartment hotels had air conditioning, but when musicians gathered outside a bar in the afternoon, it was usually to market the sounds booked for that night. A photo from 1974 by Robert Rehak, part of a four-year project that produced thousands of images of Uptown life, shows two men performing across the street from the Wooden Nickel, 1140 West Wilson, where they would probably be performing that night. One with a banjo and the other a guitar, they are turned toward each other, eyes shut in concentration as they played "Dueling Banjos," the theme from the hit film *Deliverance*, released just two years prior. The image shows a moment of spontaneity—the trunk of a parked car is still hanging open with a fresh beer abandoned atop a tailfin. The passenger door of the car parked behind

it, probably the guitarist's, cuts across the sidewalk between the
two men, revealing a glimpse of a woman and all the possessions
the couple own. "They were very good, almost as good as the pickers in the movie," Rehak recalled decades later. "They had come to
Chicago in those cars. . . . Musicians were itinerant during those
days. They'd play for supper money and a couple of beers and move
onto the next place. These people brought their music with them."[94]

The informality of the scene made it easy for younger musicians
to hunt down older ones to learn directly from the source. Around
1973, aspiring bluegrass banjoist Greg Cahill found Leon Jackson
in a condemned building in Uptown. Years earlier, Jackson had
played with and written songs for Bill Monroe, including the standard "Love Please Come Home," and had briefly recorded for King
Records. When Cahill found him, he was homeless.

Jackson played banjo Sunday afternoons in local bars, where he
also stored his instrument at night because he feared it would be
stolen from wherever he crashed. An acquaintance, named Lloyd,
was tasked with holding onto Jackson's songbook, into which he was
"still cranking out killer songs," Cahill said. Over a few years, Cahill
would sit with him and play, and Jackson would pitch his young
student songs, his voice sometimes indecipherable because of the
treatments for jaw cancer he was receiving at the nearby VA hospital. "Here's one I think you'll like! I wrote it last year. Lloyd where'd
you got that book?" Jackson would shout out in the middle of a session. Two of those songs—"Late Last Night" and "Long Winter"—
ended up on the 1979 debut album by Special Consensus, Cahill's
groundbreaking bluegrass band. "It was an honor," Cahill said.[95]

Record stores, too, were part of Uptown. For a time, the highest volume of country record sales in Chicago took place at one
store: Wil-Ken Recordtown at 1038 West Wilson. Thirty percent
of the records that moved out of that store were country, compared
with 2 percent citywide. "Wherever you find furnished rooms and
low-priced hotels, you find country and western music," explained
owner George Topper.[96] One of the store's earliest customers was
Greg Gibson, who later ran a family-run chain of record stores that

expanded from its original location near the Union Stock Yards. Gibson Music, 1956 West 51st Street, anchored the country music scene on Chicago's Southwest Side, an area where clubs like Swing Town, the Sabre Room, and even the Baby Doll Polka Club featured country bands on different nights. Gibson's father, Arbie Gibson, opened the business in 1962 after leaving steel mill work and long after his own musical career had subsided. The store developed a reputation far outside Chicago not only for having the deepest stock of current hits, but also for its extensive catalogs of individual artists. Stars like Charley Pride, Billy Grammer, and Merle Haggard were frequent customers, often buying up all their own singles because they hadn't kept track of their own music through the years. Greg Gibson remembered fielding phone calls from Pride, who wanted to know how fast his current single was moving. Once, in 1966, he told Gibson he was sending his brother in to pick up twenty-five copies of "The Snakes Crawl at Night," his debut single on RCA Victor out that year.

> Around two o'clock here comes this mean-looking Black dude about six-foot-four, all muscles. He comes up to the counter and says, "I'm here to get these records for Charley Pride." I said, "I thought Charley said he was going to send his brother." And he said, "I *am* his brother!" and then he cracked up. It was funny. Because Charley had told him we didn't know he was Black.[97]

Color mattered little at the shop because many of Gibson's customers were Black. "They grew up on country music in Mississippi and Alabama and Georgia and listened to the Opry as kids," Gibson said. "They would come in the store and buy nothing but country music."

Gibson's father sold him the business in 1978. Soon Gibson Music migrated north, with locations at 4549 North Western in Lincoln Square and later at 6003 West Belmont on the Northwest Side. Gibson captured the Uptown market when he bought Uptown Records and Tapes, at 4707 North Broadway, owned by a couple who had fallen into debt.[98]

While all these stores sold primarily music, one store in Uptown catered to Southerners who wanted to fully disappear into the country lifestyle. The Johnny Pitts Musical Showcase was open for only two years, but its comprehensive inventory and full-service sales approach was as colorful and multifaceted as its owner.

Pitts was born April 26, 1935, in Columbiana, Alabama, but left the South when he was three after his mother answered a want ad for a housekeeper in Six Lakes, Michigan. She worked on a 50-acre farm owned by Hans Hansen, an elderly farmer who lived to age 105, then left her everything he owned. Once a concert pianist and accordionist, she took on the role of head of the household, which often left her son to spend time on his own, picking potatoes or doing other chores. They spent Saturday nights listening to the *Grand Ole Opry* on the family Grundig. It wasn't long until Pitts imagined himself onstage with Hank Williams, Roy Acuff, Hank Snow, and others he listened to week after week. "Damn, I want a guitar," he told himself. So he started to save money every way he could. After one lucrative potato harvest in 1949, he had his chance. That morning, Pitts said goodbye to his mother and hitchhiked to Grand Rapids, where he hopped a train to downtown Chicago. After a night spent at an aunt's house, he woke up and walked to Chicago Avenue and through the doors of a Montgomery Ward, where he plopped down $29.95 for a Roy Smeck Harmony guitar. After a quick bite at the store's lunch counter, he was back on the train, back thumbing on the road, and back home in bed. It was forty-eight hours well spent. He was barely fourteen.[99]

The determination it took to get that guitar was matched by the dedication Pitts put into mastering it. In just a few years, he was playing for local radio stations and dance halls. Soon it was time to take the next step. "I had heard that if you wanted to learn guitar to come to Chicago, don't go to Detroit, don't go to Los Angeles, don't go to New York, come to Chicago because some of the best guitarists in the country are in Chicago," he said. "And that was the damn truth."[100] In July 1956, he arrived in a city he soon realized was populated by musicians all born in the South. By the second week, he met Wally Doss, a country singer who had a standing gig at the Dude Ranch on Rush Street. Wally recruited him to replace Top Porter, a guitarist who was returning home to Alabama. The decision was easy. Chicago was full of hot players, but not many had the chance to step out of the accompanist role to serve as the main attraction. Having memorized every song by Merle Travis and Chet Atkins, Pitts established a following by composing full sets of instrumentals, including his transcription of "Orange Blossom Special," a cherished fiddle tune from the 1930s that two decades later was revived by bluegrass groups.

Before rock and roll struck a blow to the nightlife scene, Chicago's downtown was "a mecca for country music." The tips were generous, sex was everywhere, and musicians could play seven nights a week at dozens of clubs that stretched from the Loop down Madison. On Sundays at Andy's, 1509 West Madison, Pitts played twelve-hour jam sessions that started at three o'clock in the afternoon.[101] For a time, the pace was unrelenting; nothing, it appeared, could slow the scene down.

But when it did, Pitts walked into the offices of David Wexler and Company, a wholesale instrument distributer at 823 South Wabash. He became the company's primary guitar demonstrator and troubleshooter, flying to conventions and factories all around the world to showcase the latest guitars, five-string banjos, and mandolins.

The industry connections were helpful when Pitts took over Bocian Music House, an instrument shop in Uptown at 4453 North Broadway, and expanded it into a magnet for country musicians. When it reopened in 1967 as the Johnny Pitts Musical Showcase, it promised a "complete musical merchandise and accessory line, showcase recording studios," and "western show apparel." "Where the stars buy their instruments and accessories," a sign announced in its front window.[102] The shop became a gathering place for musicians, both locals and those passing through town. Pitts moved his family to the second floor. Downstairs housed a paradise of instruments—Gretsch, Gibson, Fender, Franklin, Martin, and Ovation guitars, and even Steinway pianos; tape recording equipment and amplifiers; and racks of western show clothes, including those from famed West Coast clothing designer Nudie Cohn, who was known for elaborately stitched suits designed for Hank Williams, Gene Autry, and Porter Wagoner. A recording studio was in full operation in the basement, and a label, Showcase Records, was in the works. Songbooks were available for students, and guitar, voice, drum, and organ lessons ran all week.[103] On weekends, Pitts set up fifty folding chairs and a stage for afternoon jam sessions that ran both days. Saturday was reserved for a two-hour radio show broadcast on WEAW in Evanston that featured local talent plus traveling acts like Hank Snow and Flatt & Scruggs. The crown jewel of the shop was in a glass case mounted on the wall: a fringed buckskin leather jacket once worn by Hank Williams. Irene Williams, Hank's sister, was a family friend and stayed upstairs for several weeks a year.[104] Years ago Pitts only had the dial of his kitchen Grundig to transport him into this world. Now, the storefront served as an open portal to his dreams. "Everything I ever wanted in my life I had in that store," Pitts said.[105]

But this was Uptown in the late 1960s, a place where precious things did not last.

Almost as soon as Pitts opened his doors for business, city inspectors were dispatched to make sure he closed. The first inspectors told him the building needed new electric wiring on all three floors. Three months later, they returned to tell him his roof was a firetrap. Nine months later, he was told he needed a rear egress. Each time, Pitts spent thousands of dollars to comply. Six months later, his building was torched.

"An Uptown thing" is what it was. "It could be because I was from Alabama and my wife was from Tennessee. But they had it in for us," he said.[106]

According to Pitts, at ten minutes past three o'clock in the morning of April 8, 1969, a fireball blew through the store, originating from nearly fifteen gallons of gasoline splashed across the carpeting of the basement recording studio through the back door, pried open by a piece of sheet metal. A fuse six feet long ran to the alley. Marie,

Pitts's wife, managed to get through the front door and call the fire department from across the street. The fire trucks retrieved Pitts and his children from the roof. Instruments boiled, recording tape melted, the Hank Williams jacket was left in shards. Nothing was saved. The gas even burned the eyes of the family German shepherd. Pitts put his family in his car and drove west. He didn't return to Chicago for years.[107]

The brutality of the act reflected the ugly truth of Uptown in those years. Because Southerners were perceived as the cause of blight, they, and anything related to their culture, were expelled with harassment, and then violence. Arson was so frequent in Uptown and the surrounding area that in 1976 the Illinois State Senate directed a special commission to investigate. Two years later, its report cited several reasons for the prevalence of arson: slumlords, poor enforcement of housing codes, building abandonment, inadequate penalties for arsonists, vandalism, and even terrorism from the Puerto Rican liberation movement. The city's rate of clearing arson cases was unusually low, the report noted, because the Chicago Police Department's Bomb and Arson unit had "a very informal system of record keeping," consisting of "a rather crude log book" listing rudimentary information, such as addresses and victim names, and little else.

Uptown was one of the nine neighborhoods where half the city's arsons took place, all of them with large minority populations. The 1978 report concluded, first, that arson would be better understood only if the police department raised the quality of its recordkeeping above its current level of "very poor." Second, it blamed the Chicago Building Department, which stalled the commission by refusing to cooperate with the investigation.[108]

If the trials of Uptown residents like Pitts were barely recorded by authorities who had little to no incentive to solve the arsons, local media coverage was also scant. Arson was so under-policed that, between 1975 and 1979, fifteen buildings operated by the same slumlord were destroyed by fire with no repercussions.[109] The message was clear: the lives of Uptown held little value compared with those of the people in power. The arsons continued. "The smell permeated the air," said Paul Siegel, who moved to the neighborhood in 1972. "There was a fire every night."[110]

In 1976, the same year state authorities commissioned their arson report, Harry S. Truman College opened its doors. The symbolism could not have been greater: Building Truman meant demolishing more than a thousand low-income housing units, which pushed thousands of people out. Real estate speculation rose with the news of the city's plan, which meant a dramatic rise in arson for profit.

John Harding, a firefighter with Engine Company 83 in Uptown during that time, described the entire neighborhood as "burning down." "That was the way you renovated," he explained. "You start out with as big a fire as you could and then you bring the bulldozers in. That's what they did with Truman College. They would blatantly burn down buildings full of people. It was terrible. That was just the way of doing business."[111]

THE LOST HOPE OF
HANK WILLIAMS VILLAGE

What briefly stood in the way of what the city planned for Uptown was Hank Williams Village, a proposed multi-use housing and retail development designed by and intended for Southerners. The project imagined lifting people out of poverty and giving them more autonomy within their community by freeing them from the control of slumlords. More importantly, the plan originated from the people in the neighborhood, as an act of insurgency against the city's political and business establishment that wanted them displaced.

By 1968, Hank Williams had been dead for fifteen years, but he remained a figure of pride, not just for the stars who performed his songs, but for ordinary people who recognized the hardships he sang about. He channeled the sound of home, which is why, with his songs blaring from their jukeboxes, the taverns on Wilson Avenue felt as familiar to them as any bars on the back roads of Alabama. A year before the plans for Hank Williams Village were under way, the

Young Patriots and other community organizations had success-fully petitioned the Chicago Park District to create a playground on Sunnyside and name it in the singer's honor.[112]

Hank Williams almost made it to Chicago, but was derailed by Fred Rose, his song publisher. By 1946, when Williams signed with Acuff-Rose Publications, the powerful music publishing firm that created the blueprint for the modern music industry in Nashville, he was known only regionally on the honky-tonk circuit of his native Alabama and through regular appearances on WSFA in Montgom-ery. Taking his career to the next level would require establishing Williams on one of three powerhouse radio programs: the *Grand Ole Opry* in Nashville, the *National Barn Dance* in Chicago, or the *Louisiana Hayride* in Shreveport. In 1948, Rose knew Williams was not yet big enough for the *Opry*. The *Barn Dance* was elimi-nated because by that late phase in its history, the program, with its pop vocalists, novelty acts, and even polka bands, had veered from where country music was heading. It wasn't the future, and Rose knew it. So Williams went South to make his name in Shreve-port. Ten months later he was a star. He made his *Opry* debut the following year.

"The *Barn Dance* . . . had some pop singers on it. A kid like Hank might have listeners in Chicago saying, 'Boy, he's awful.' We didn't really care what they thought because we were trying to make Hank the number-one country artist," said Wesley Rose, Fred's son. "My father knew he'd get a straight reaction on Hank in Shreveport. The people there are real country fans."[113]

Fred Rose was vocal late in his life about his distaste for what the *Barn Dance* had become. He was a purist, drawn to artists who left audiences on their feet with songs that were open with raw emotion. He loved the early *Barn Dance* because he started his career in Chi-cago and knew it well. Born August 14, 1898, in Evansville, Indiana, Rose was a piano prodigy; he made his way to Chicago as a teen-ager in 1917, where he played South Side speakeasies and eventually found work with bandleader Paul Whiteman.[114] Early *Barn Dance* star Bradley Kincaid recalls Rose singing on the program, but apart from the jobbing, Rose made a name for himself as a songwriter of the Jazz Age, writing novelty songs and popular hits including "Red Hot Momma" for Sophie Tucker, "Deep Henderson" for King Oliver, and "Honest and Truly" for bandleader Isham Jones.[115] Numerous jazz orchestras of the day recorded his songs, which he popularized on "Fred Rose's Song Shop," a daily radio program on WBBM that relied on his talent for writing songs on the spot, inspired by titles made up by listeners. After his drinking cost him his last radio job, he moved to Nashville in 1933.[116] Gene Autry, Bob Atcher, and other former *Barn Dance* stars would later record his songs.

Chicago also played an early role for Rose's business partner Roy Acuff. After a season of singing and fiddling in a medicine show traveling across the Tennessee-Virginia mountains, Acuff moved to Knoxville and formed Roy Acuff and His Crazy Tennesseans, an acoustic string band that made its first recordings in Chicago for the American Record Corporation over a four-day period in October 1936. Besides recording "You're the Only Star in My Blue Heaven," written by Arbie Gibson, the sessions included "The Wabash Cannonball" and "Great Speckled Bird," two hit songs that reached a national audience that decade.[117] His brief time in Chicago inspired Acuff to write two more songs—"When Lulu's Gone" and "Doin' It the Old-Fashioned Way"—when pining away one night at the Knickerbocker Hotel. The latter is a sly tribute to the simple pleasures of country life, while the former is more direct: "Bang away, my Lulu, bang away good and strong / What are you going to do for banging when Lulu's gone?" goes the chorus. Later known as the "King of Country Music" as a key member of the *Grand Ole Opry*, Acuff wisely decided to release the pair under the pseudonym the Bang Boys.[118]

Hank Williams made it to Chicago at least once—in March 1950, he attended the Music Operators of America convention at the Palmer House, a three-day event for five hundred jukebox and phonograph companies all over the United States.[119] Williams, accompanied by Rose, was there to promote his latest single, "Long-Gone Lonesome Blues," on MGM Records.[120] The next week's *Billboard* shows Williams squeezed in the middle of nine record industry executives, both his hands stuffed into their own. He is dressed just like they are—dark suit, tie, name tag with ribbons dangling off his lapel—distinguished only by an awkward smile and a white cowboy hat cocked on his head. "Leading juke ops at the Chicago convention glad-hand Hank Williams," reads the caption. Williams would be dead in less than three years.

Hank Williams Village was meant to honor his legacy. Advocates conjured up the plan after learning that four thousand units of low-income housing would be flattened to make way for Harry S. Truman College. This was the era when higher learning was often an anchor for large-scale urban renewal projects. A decade earlier, the University of Chicago had cleared out thousands of housing units in Hyde Park and Kenwood using $50 million in state and federal funds, and in the 1960s, the University of Illinois at Chicago had decimated housing in the Italian, Black, and Mexican neighborhoods intersecting Maxwell Street.[121] By 1965, the Daley administration approved the redevelopment of a 150-acre tract of land in Uptown occupied not just by housing units, but also by the transient hotels and taverns that local business leaders had long identified as hindering their long-range plans for gentrification. In 1968, the board of the Chicago City College system approved plans for building Truman, creating a flashpoint for activists who saw the land as representing the heart and soul of their community.[122]

Residents had reason to believe the $25 million project was specifically designed to root them out for good. The Chicago media framed the development as progress, while city leaders derided what would soon be swept away. "The college might also work for the upgrading of the community by causing the demolition of many of the taverns on Wilson avenue," Illinois Senator Robert Cherry told the *Chicago Tribune*. Local alderman Robert O'Rourke agreed, saying that the junior college would attract "stable income families" and, according to the *Tribune*, "would eliminate many of the problems caused by bars in Wilson avenue."[123]

But residents pushed back. "If a guy doesn't live in the neighborhood he forgets there are human beings there," said Chuck Geary in

1968. As founder of the Uptown Area People's Planning Coalition (UAPPC), the organization that proposed Hank Williams Village, Geary was a leading figure in opposing the urban renewal projects proposed by the Uptown Chicago Commission. "The only hope for lower income people is cooperative housing. Only those that have been poor know what it is like for us. We don't want welfare based on the profit system," he said.[124]

Geary immediately asked architect Rodney Wright and his wife, planner Sydney Wright, to begin work on an alternative development plan with feedback from neighborhood residents. They envisioned Hank Williams Village as a small Southern town within the city that would encourage residents to put down roots. The design showed cul-de-sac streets, generous green space, a town hall for community meetings, childcare and recreational facilities, a medical clinic, a grocery co-op, a pharmacy, and an employment center, all within walking distance. Instead of razing the standing housing stock, units would be refurbished with minimal displacement of their residents.[125] Alleys would be converted into parking areas, walkways, and playgrounds. A new structure at Racine and Sunnyside would serve as an entrance and a community house for new immigrants. In all, Hank Williams Village, bordered by Wilson, Broadway, Montrose, and Clark, would be home for eight thousand people.[126]

While the plan was a source of pride for the community, it also sent a clear message to Daley's Chicago. "It was self-determination. We really wanted to show we weren't just a bunch of ignorant and stupid hillbillies but that we were a very intelligent group of people," said Thurman.[127]

Rodney Wright was able to get the Uptown Conservation Community Council (UCCC) to recommend his plan to the city's Department of Urban Renewal, but he was up against pressure to show that financing would be a lock. At the following meeting, he announced he had nearly $500,000 in preconstruction commitments and a $10 million agreement from a developer to build a twenty-two-story high-rise. However, political pressure set the approval process at a glacial pace, and in June 1970, the UCCC reversed its recommendation, saying the financial commitment was not enough to secure Federal Housing Authority loans. The wrecking balls were finally allowed to clear space. By the end of that year, 273 apartments were demolished, and the city made no plans for replacement housing for those who were displaced.[128] Families scattered to other parts of the city, to the suburbs, or back home. Geary hung on for a few years, but eventually returned to his birthplace of Horsebranch, Kentucky.[129]

It took years for Uptown to shed its association with Appalachia. Twelve hundred units of low-income housing were sacrificed for Truman College between 1970 and 1976, pushing out between 1,800 and 4,000 low-income people.[130] In 1960, 80 percent of Uptown's population had been born in the South; by 2000, that number had fallen to less than 4 percent.[131] The exodus silenced the music. The neighborhood taverns that once featured live country music or jukeboxes generously stocked with country hits closed, one after another.

The final holdout was Carol's Pub, a corner honky-tonk featuring live country music at 4659 North Clark, once called "one of the toughest bars in Uptown" by a *Los Angeles Times* writer.[132] As late as the 1990s, the bar still earned the reputation. Rob Miller and Nan Warshaw, co-founders of Bloodshot Records, once escorted Ryan Adams and Caitlin Cary to the bar after their band Whiskeytown played Metro in 1998. Upon arriving, they discovered police tape surrounding the front door, police circulating, and a fresh pool of blood on the sidewalk from a knifing. Carol Harris, the bar's owner, was outside, and she wasn't about to let the incident deter paying customers. "Don't worry about it, they were friends," she said, lifting the tape so the group could duck inside for a drink.[133]

But Carol's, too, could not last. In September 2016, forty-three years after opening in 1973—back then, it was called Pam's Playhouse—the bar closed its doors. This time, the Illinois Liquor Control Commission had the final say: the liquor license was pulled after the bar accrued nearly $55,000 in unpaid state taxes.[134]

Unlike the other lost country bars of Chicago, Carol's found a benefactor: Ed Warm, a co-owner of Joe's Bar, the longest-running venue for live country music in Chicago, and president of the Academy of Country Music in California. Warm purchased Carol's and reopened it in December 2018. The new incarnation paid homage to its past—outside, the red arrow of the original sign still shoots toward the front door, and inside hangs a framed photo of former owner Harris—but Warm let light in by replacing the brick walls with windows, and he put in a superior sound system. He also cleaned up the bathroom funk. In a way, the modern Carol's represented how far country music had traveled since mainly blue-collar households occupied Uptown and the city's North Side. On opening night, decades-old regulars and young professionals wove through the dance floor as Diamondback, the house band since the 1970s, played standards by Merle Haggard and Alabama.

"They kept the old charm but cleaned it up," said Hope Brown, age seventy-two, who returned to the bar that night after having been a regular for nearly thirty years. "It's nice to see this many people coming out to hear the old country."[135]

THE FIRST ALL-COUNTRY
STATION OUTSIDE NASHVILLE

The weather forecast on February 15, 1965, was typical for Chicago: cloudy with snow flurries and highs in the 40s. But as soon as the announcer finished delivering the dreary news, Buck Owens took WJJD listeners to another world. His voice suspended the first two notes before the music kicked in. With guitars snapping alongside him, Owens sang "I've Got a Tiger by the Tail," its bright and cheery harmonies making it a perfect country pop hit at under three minutes long.

Over the next hour, Chet Atkins, George Jones, Hank Locklin, Jim & Jesse, and other names from WJJD's "million dollar library" followed.[136] Compared to the *Barn Dance*, there was no cornpone humor, no twang in the announcer's voice. "We don't do it hokey," explained program director Chris Lane. "None of this 'we'll be back tomorrow be the good Lord willin' an' the cricks don't rise.'"[137] Instead, in its quest to succeed as the first all-country station in the biggest US radio market outside Nashville, WJJD went for the hits, hired disc jockeys with hip deliveries, and invested heavily in research to understand what listeners wanted. General manager George Dubinetz warned other stations considering the switch that country music's broad appeal—for "the sophisticate as well as the plebian"—meant there was no room for "a second-rate programming environment." In other words, just because the music had twang was not an excuse for sloppy broadcasting. "All the programming ingredients that make a successful pop, middle-of-the-road, talk, classical or any format station are just as important for a country station, maybe even more so," he said.[138]

He was right. Eight months later, WJJD was pulling in 25 percent of Chicago's radio audience, or about a half million households, and it moved from barely ranking in the *Pulse* ratings book to number four.[139] The station's success would be confirmed by a *Billboard* poll, which showed that 89 percent of all country music record sales in the Chicago market were a direct result of the station's format switch from Top 40 to country. "Not only has the station received unqualified acceptance by the market and proved a tremendous impact to country music sales, WJJD has been a springboard and guiding light for the launching of other country music formatted radio stations around the nation," the magazine wrote. By making Chicago the biggest market to date to have a full-time country radio station outside of the South,[140] WJJD proved there was an audience for country music in the big city. In just under a year, similar switches were made by stations in Charlotte, Miami, Newark, Rochester, and Buffalo.[141] In 1963, there were 115 radio stations across the country with a full-time country music format; by 1966, a year after WJJD made the switch, there were 285 stations.[142]

Making the format change was not easy. National advertisers were snobbish about country and didn't believe that it held any appeal for the affluent middle-class consumers they were chasing. This view was pure class prejudice: all the images that early country radio endorsed and that the media exploited—namely, that the musicians and their fans were ignorant hillbillies—were cultural roadblocks to country music's acceptance. In 1958, the Country Music Association was established in Nashville with the specific goal of persuading sponsors that country music could sell their products. Today, the CMA is best known for its annual awards show, which launched in 1967. However, it spent its first decade actively targeting radio programmers to convince them to play country music and conducting research to demonstrate to advertisers that modern country broadcasting was good for profits.

What convinced WJJD to make the format switch was the success of *Suppertime Frolic*, a long-running country music show that it broadcast two hours a night, six nights a week, for three decades. Along with the *Barn Dance*, it was one of the earliest radio shows that popularized country music across the Midwest.

Hosting the program was Randy Blake, a trained opera singer. Born in Chicago on June 3, 1906, he played vaudeville's Orpheum circuit for three years as a teenager, and then ended up with an advertising job back home, where he scouted talent to package for sponsored radio shows. In 1937, tired of seeing others get airtime, he talked his way into a job on *Suppertime Frolic* as a sacred singer, eventually working his way up to announcer.[143] While Blake worked intermittently on the show, station music director Ken Nelson created its format. Nelson, born January 19, 1911, in Minnesota, also arrived at WJJD with a strong interest in classical music, which led him to becoming the city's top announcer for broadcasts by the Chicago Symphony Orchestra. Eventually, Nelson was assigned to *Suppertime Frolic*, where he scouted talent and built a live roster that included the Cumberland Ridge Runners, Karl and Harty, Bob and Bonnie Atcher, and Uncle Henry's Original Kentucky Mountaineers. By 1948, *Suppertime Frolic* had built enough of a national reputation that Nelson was hired by Capitol Records in Hollywood to head its country division. At Capitol, he became one of the key figures in shaping the postwar growth of country music by bringing artists like Buck Owens, Merle Haggard, Hank Thompson, and the Louvin Brothers to the fore and producing their landmark sound over thousands of recordings.[144]

As influential as Nelson was in shaping the "Nashville Sound," it was Blake who established the role of the country music deejay by elevating the music in his delivery and not bowing to stereotypes. "He played it straight, without regional accent, and his presentation of hillbilly music had a dignity and authority not before identified with the music," said veteran Nashville deejay Hugh Cherry.[145] Indeed, Blake's daughter Penny Winston Blake Stein said her father "didn't pretend to have a thick accent." "He was such a city slicker. He spoke like a Chicago announcer." Blake also turned his back on the Nashville Sound and wouldn't play records that had orchestration. "He didn't think that was authentic country music," his daughter said.[146]

Writing in the influential jazz magazine *DownBeat* in 1955, Blake even advocated for keeping country music separate from other genres like pop and R&B, suggesting that one shouldn't threaten the other. That same year, *DownBeat* publisher Maher Publications, headquartered in Chicago, segregated its country music coverage with the launch of *Country & Western Jamboree*, a new magazine it claimed was "the first major monthly publication designed exclusively for all country and western fans."[147]

Blake was enormously popular across the Midwest, and his name would regularly end up in top slots of *Billboard* reader popularity polls. He was also a hustler who, besides his nightly radio job, wrote songs for other artists, co-founded a song publishing company affiliated with BMI, recorded sacred music for Capitol Records, and even ran a company that supplied promotional giveaways. By the late 1940s, *Suppertime Frolic* had switched from live talent to records, which immediately made Blake an influential tastemaker for record labels in Nashville. Up until his death he claimed that he was solely responsible for breaking Hank Williams nationally after MGM Records asked him to play "Move It On Over," Williams's first record to make the *Billboard* charts. Blake later admitted he felt the song "sounded pretty horrible" but promised MGM's president he would deliver: "Obviously he has a lot of talent because he writes and writes and writes. I'll tell you what I think of this record: I think you should put it out. I'm giving you an order right now for 10,000 of them."[148]

Blake had moved on by 1957, the year WJJD switched to a full-time Top 40 format. The station was owned by Plough Broadcasting, which had little success programming the station from its Memphis headquarters. Soon enough, Plough president Harold Krelstein ordered research to see if there was a void in country music programming in Chicago.[149] Plough discovered that 23 percent of country albums sold nationally were sold in Illinois, Wisconsin, Indiana, Ohio, and Kentucky—all within range of WJJD's 50,000-watt signal. Assuming its first wave of listeners would be blue collar, the station was pleased to learn that not only were 63 percent of Chicago's workers working class, but that half of them earned more than the national average. Once Krelstein gave the green light, the station started hiring outside talent and allocated a budget of $50,000 for advertising. The country format was such an overnight success that the full sum was never spent.[150]

The CMA persuaded advertisers to stick with the station. It helped that two years earlier, it had created a sales presentation titled "The Selling Sound of Country Music," which, between 1963 and 1967, it unveiled before advertising executives in New York, Chicago, and Detroit as well as smaller markets like San Diego and Norfolk, Virginia. The presentation's mission was to sell country music's newfound respectability and to emphasize that its consumers were professionals, not hayseeds, and its artists serious craftsmen like any others on the pop chart.[151] "We're aware that country music often has a stigma attached to it. However, we feel it's due to a lack of knowledge and prejudice—not fact," Jo Walker, the CMA's executive secretary, explained. WJJD asked for the CMA's help in 1964, and by July 1965, the organization was in Chicago presenting "Selling Sound" at a convention sponsored by *Advertising Age* and attended by six hundred executives from every state.[152]

To impress the money men, the hour-long presentation was "fact-packed" with revenue numbers, starting with a big one: $100 million, the annual value of country radio broadcasting. Presenter

LeRoy Van Dyke then gave them a short course in music theory, going so far as explaining country music's roots and drawing the line from there to the folk revival earlier in that decade. He suggested that young consumers, recently taken with the banjos and twelve-string guitars of the folk revival, were now hungry for the real thing. The "popularity and appeal of a country song was in the simple, easy-to-sing melody and the lyrics that depicts the everyday life of the average person, and the average person is the one that you, the creative advertising specialist, likes most to reach," he said. Van Dyke's "average person," of course, did not mean the day laborers of Uptown or other displaced Southerners scratching out a living in Chicago's slums. He told the executives that the long roads country musicians traveled now led to upscale hotels and downtown nightclubs. "You see, country music does get around," he said.[153]

COUNTRY MUSIC EXPANDS
FROM BARROOMS TO BALLROOMS

Key to WJJD's rollout were live concerts at the Arie Crown Theater, the lakeside venue that opened in 1960 as part of the McCormick Place convention center. The venue held more than five thousand people, a far cry from the North Side honky-tonks, and was far more respectable, too. WJJD made sure to snap photos of the neatly dressed professional men and women who flowed through the turnstiles. The concerts were opportunities to conduct early market research to support the format switch. The station handed out surveys to tally data on income and home ownership to show that the new country audiences were from the consumer class. "We took this material to the advertising agencies and said, 'Look, there's nothing wrong with these people. They work for IBM, Illinois Bell and there's nothing strange about them,'" George Dubinetz said.[154]

One day before the format switch, on February 14, 1965, the station hosted "A Country and Western Jamboree," an all-day event featuring Lester Flatt and Earl Scruggs, Ernest Tubb and His Texas Troubadours, and others.[155] A month later, WJJD kicked off its first "Shower of Stars," an all-day blowout featuring Buck Owens and the

Buckaroos, Tex Ritter, Del Reeves, Lamarr Morris, Jan Howard, and Hank Williams Jr. alongside Audrey Williams, his mother. (Johnny Cash appeared on the bill but never showed up.)[156] The station sold out both events, for a total of eleven thousand tickets.[157] "Shower of Stars" became a tradition the station would repeat several times a year through 1972.

There was no shortage of country shows in downtown Chicago in the 1960s. Each year averaged three to four shows spread across the seasons. When the Arie Crown suffered a massive fire in 1967, the shows alternated between the Civic Opera House and the Medinah Temple and featured a constant flow of Nashville stars.[158] But these marquee acts were not just booked downtown. Touring artists also appeared at the Genesee Theater in Waukegan, the Paramount Arts Centre in Aurora, and the Hammond Civic Center in nearby Indiana.

One venue that reopened the same year WJJD went country was the Rivoli Continental Show Lounge, a terraced ballroom at 4380 North Elston on the city's Northwest Side. The thirteen-hundred-seat theater opened in 1923 for vaudeville and then ran for decades as a movie palace until the lights went out in 1951, after which it was used as a warehouse. The 1965 incarnation was built for lavish entertainment; Albert Donner, who had designed the newly reopened Playboy Theater downtown, was hired to bring it back to life. Although it was comedian Henny Youngman who performed on its opening weekend, it would soon be known as Chicago's country music hotspot.[159] Right away, its owner, a native New Orleanian named Sam Conzeneri—known around town as "Sammy C"—imagined a yearly country music festival the size of the Newport Folk Festival in his adopted home city. "We have as much interest in country music right here in the Middle West as in any other part of the country," he said. He soon made enough noise to win the endorsement of Mayor Daley, who, through a spokesperson, said the idea played into Daley's interest in advancing the city as "the nation's music center."[160] By December, Conzeneri had formed the Midwest Country Music Committee and appointed all the right people: WJJD and WGN staffers; Chicago aldermen; advertising executives from United Airlines, Gibson Guitar, and Nashville Guitars; artists Homer & Jethro, Ray Price, and Roy Clark; and record executives from all the right labels: Columbia, Decca, and Mercury. A date and venue were set: four shows at the International Amphitheater on August 20–21, 1966.[161] Conzeneri anticipated a crowd of forty thousand people.[162] He called the festival his "dream." "As Newport has been for jazz, Chicago could be for the whole C&W field," he said.[163]

There is no record that Conzeneri's dream came true. One reason could be that it didn't receive the support it needed from the CMA. Conzeneri wrote the organization's board of directors to ask that they add it to their next meeting agenda, and he visited Nashville to start networking. But it was obvious that the CMA had little interest in promoting a country music festival of such wide scope outside its home base. Jo Walker, CMA's executive director, told *Billboard* that the organization was indeed planning to sponsor "a world country and western music festival," but added, "We would probably hold it in Nashville."[164] In 1967, the following year, the first CMA Awards were held in Music City, not Chicago.

Nevertheless, the Rivoli emerged as Chicago's headquarters for country music between 1965 and 1968. Weekends were booked with acts that could fill the dance floor to capacity: Buck Owens and the Buckaroos, Jerry Lee Lewis, Roy Clark, Bill Anderson, Hank Snow, Connie Smith, Ferlin Husky, and Jimmy Dean and the Western Gentlemen. Couples decked in dark suits and cocktail dresses danced to Ernest Tubb and his band amid the hundreds of balloons that fell to ring in 1967.[165]

By then, Hayden Thompson, who had jump-started the rockabilly scene in Highwood, was retired. His new steady paycheck came from driving a truck. Suddenly he noticed WJJD was creating new work for musicians like him. So in 1965 he signed on to play guitar in the Rivoli's house band, backing up Nashville up-and-comers like Waylon Jennings, Bobby Bare, and Merle Haggard. Stage work was now plentiful: "Country music was coming back and I was Chicago's local boy," he said. But Thompson's network extended beyond Chicago: he played the *Grand Ole Opry* three separate times in 1966 at the invitation of Roy Acuff, who collared him one night at the Rivoli; that same year, he was in Nashville cutting his own album. Those opportunities paid dividends in keeping him working into the mid-1970s. The resurgence of country, he recalled, "was unreal."[166]

At that time, the infrastructure for booking country artists in Chicago ballrooms and theaters did not exist in a way we would recognize today. Blockbuster acts, sports arenas, and the lucrative sideline of merchandising had not yet been set in place, which meant that booking agents dealt primarily with local hustlers who knew the market, could spread the word, and could get tickets out the door. In Chicago, that meant Cal Starr.

Starr knew his way around a stage. With his hair slicked back, and decked in a dark evening suit, he was a crooner who connected with the stars he ushered to the big city because he was one of them. Born Calvin Martin Stallard in 1930, he relocated with his family from Chicago to his grandparents' farm in Wesleyville, Kentucky, after his father was diagnosed with crippling rheumatism. The family knew poverty. Without electricity, all five children and both parents huddled in one bed during cold nights. To listen to the *Grand Ole Opry* meant crossing a creek every Saturday night to home in on a neighbor's radio.[167]

Starr learned guitar in church, where he played alongside his father, a fiddler. Soon he was winning talent contests, which set him on the road performing radio stints in West Virginia, Texas, and Ohio. The work got him to Shreveport, Louisiana, where he hosted a fifteen-minute television show in 1955. After signing with a Chicago booking agency a year later, he moved to Chicago and played clubs, including the Original Key Club, 150 East Ontario, a location popular with media and sports celebrities. With only his guitar, he was making $500 a week.[168] Naturally, the work led to record contracts. *New Voice in Town*, released on the Chicago Capaco label in 1962, contained mostly covers of current hits. In 1966, Starr went to Nashville to record *Starr and Guitar in Nashville* for Fraternity

Records, based in Cincinnati. The album was produced by Ray Pennington, a fellow Kentuckian who would later write the enduring Waylon Jennings hit "I'm a Ramblin' Man."

Yet Starr sensed more ground to till. "There were no promoters here," he said. Starr knew he could talk, so he walked into the headquarters of Sears, Roebuck and Company and coaxed help from strangers. The next week he reached a deal to ship handbills for a country show to the company's mailing list and get show posters plastered throughout its stores. Some stores doubled as ticket outlets. He promptly turned his garage in Evergreen Park into an office and worked two phones on his desk. "Sometimes those phones were so hot you couldn't keep up with it," he said.

For twelve years, "Cal Starr Presents" topped the marquee above every top country name that came through Chicago. By the late 1960s, Starr was able to pocket thousands of dollars from the biggest artists of the day—$60,000 net from four shows by Loretta Lynn, $55,000 from Marty Robbins. At the time, getting country fans to the Auditorium Theatre or the Arie Crown or the Genesee in Waukegan meant first dialing Starr, and he knew it. "I did more for Chicago as far as country music is concerned than any other person," he boasted. To save money, he opened some shows with a family band consisting of his wife and three daughters. But audiences didn't mind, since his operation had class: alongside each set of tickets Starr mailed from his garage, he included a personalized note of thanks.[169]

THE GATE OF HORN
AND THE CHICAGO
FOLK REVIVAL

On August 3, 1955, Pat Philips, a young woman just a year out of Northwestern University, made the decision to become a concert promoter for one night. Not because she aspired to, but because the music she was drawn to did not have a respectable home.

By the mid-1950s, folk music was on the move, shifting away from neighborhood taverns and university halls, where it had percolated, to swank downtown eateries and stately orchestral halls, where it would reach the masses. The benchmark for this transformation, in 1956, was the opening of the Gate of Horn, the nation's first nightclub exclusively dedicated to folk music, where many of folk's biggest names got their start.

But that benchmark was a year away. To hear folk music in 1955, Philips and her friends had to seek out coffeehouses or travel to oddball venues like the College of Complexes, a nomadic showcase for radical politics, theater, and debate.

There, Big Bill Broonzy inaugurated a Wednesday night folk music series, an event significant enough to earn notice in the *Chicago Tribune*.[1] By that time, Broonzy was an established star in the folk world, having already expanded his popularity from South Side clubs to North Side halls and hootenannies, and reaching an even wider audience in Europe. His song "Black, Brown, and White Blues" helped endear him to White audiences because of its direct criticism of racial discrimination. The song had emerged as an "internationally recognized call for racial justice" a decade before the civil rights anthem "We Shall Overcome."[2]

But the times had not fully changed in Chicago. Philips recalls that Broonzy's debut at the College "wasn't just inhabited by college students, there were also street kids and guys in gangs."[3] In the silence before Broonzy sang his first note, a racial epithet cut through the air.

Philips flashed with anger. She stood, walked up to the audience member who had said it, and slapped him hard across the face. The room fell silent. The man pulled a knife. Seeing that, Broonzy started to pack up his guitar. He was the only one in motion. Philips calmly walked back to her seat, sat down, and did not move. "That ended it," she said. "And Big Bill left, of course."

Philips wanted to make up the night for Broonzy, so she became a grassroots concert promoter. She solicited her friends to volunteer, secured Fullerton Hall at the Art Institute of Chicago as a venue, and even persuaded the printer who published the *Daily Northwestern*, her former student newspaper, to print posters for distribution in Evanston and Hyde Park. She titled the September concert, which paired Broonzy with banjoist-singer Bob Gibson on a double bill, "Tempo Times Two." "Bill will sing the blues that made him famous in the '30s and Bob will do West Indies songs in calypso tempo," the *Chicago Tribune* promised. Broonzy appeared on Studs Terkel's radio program on WFMT to promote the concert. The tickets sold out, and everyone got paid. The concert would be Broonzy's last local appearance before he departed in October for a six-month concert tour of Europe, where his autobiography, just published, was gaining popularity among British jazz and blues critics.[4]

Philips was of a generation drawn to folk music as an alternative to the pop mainstream. "We were smart, talented, self-motivated, and with a high sense of adventure. Comfort and conformity were not on our radar," she recalled.[5] For her, folk music possessed qualities that ten years later would be associated with rock and roll: it served as a vehicle to challenge established views on politics, social norms, and most importantly, race. "I never saw a television show in the fifties that had anything substantive to say. Everything was bland," she said.[6]

She joined an underground circle of radical thinkers, left-leaning college students, and, in College of Complexes founder Myron R. "Slim" Brundage's words, "drifters, junkies, nymphos, homos, and rejectees from Kankakee."[7] Their gathering place was the College, a tavern and then coffeehouse that promoted itself as a place "where the literati linger and the cognoscenti congregate."[8] The College, which drifted among six different locations over nearly forty years, was Brundage's life mission. The local media latched onto his hard-scrabble backstory and grizzled persona, which grew more anachronistic as nightlife in downtown Chicago became more affluent.

THE COLLEGE OF COMPLEXES: A REFUGE FOR RADICALS

Folk music found a home at the College before a club scene for it existed. While national touring artists like Burl Ives and the Weavers could fill Orchestra Hall or find ready-made audiences at the University of Chicago and Northwestern, Chicago did not yet have an informal listening room dedicated to folk music. At the College, "music was the dominant element. It was a fertile place," remembered Pat Philips.[9]

Ella Jenkins, who had a long career on Folkways Records starting in 1957, said the College was where the folk crowd went "to find out what was happening musically."[10] In the days when song swapping was critical to building up a repertoire, the College represented the first organized place for young people to learn. "People weren't trying to show off, they were just up there trying to do what they could do and share," Jenkins said. "People were always there writing or had their tape recorders. Because it was informal. People who had been very shy about singing could get into it quite easily."[11]

Slim Brundage was born November 29, 1903, in a mental hospital in Blackfoot, Idaho, where his parents both worked.[12] He arrived in Chicago in 1922 and found work as a house painter, as a handyman, and eventually as a bartender at the Dil Pickle Club, a gathering spot for Chicago writers, academics, artists, musicians, anarchists, and radical freethinkers, including Carl Sandburg, Ben Hecht, Clarence Darrow, Emma Goldman, Theodore Dreiser, Ring Lardner, Edgar Lee Masters, Charles McArthur, Jack Johnson, and Sherwood Anderson.[13] "Where wits and orators and literati and vagrants were wont to gather," the *Chicago Daily Tribune* said of the club.[14]

It was located at 18 Tooker Place, but accessed through an alley entrance at 867½ North Dearborn.[15] A sign over the door hinted at the activity inside: "Step High, Stoop Low, Leave Your Dignity Outside."[16] Starting around 1916 and continuing through 1932, the Dil Pickle was the heart of Chicago's bohemian culture. Founder Jack Jones, a former organizer for the Industrial Workers of the World (IWW), aimed to "outdo Paris and N'Yawk Bohemians," announced the *Tribune* in 1920. "The Dill Pickle club has it all over Greenwich Village. We're Art for Art's sake and we're going to make Chicago the center of intellectual expression, the Mecca of the free minded," Jones told the reporter.[17]

Many years later, in 1964, Brundage would return to that theme, asking in print what had made the Dil Pickle Club different. He concluded it stood in "the intellectual center of America." While Greenwich Village could rightfully claim its title as the nation's artistic home, to which aspiring artists flocked to develop their craft, Chicago's near North Side represented a place where you could find "bums who talked like professors."[18]

Pressure from both the city and the mafia led directly to the Dil Pickle's demise in 1933. To Ben Reitman, a Chicago physician who programmed the club, the Dil had proved too successful. "There's one thing about a gangster and a crook—he always has an eye for business, and business was good at the Dil," he wrote.[19]

Building inspections and police raids increased during the club's final years. Brundage himself was jailed for thirty days after selling liquor to two federal agents.[20] "Late one night I arrived to find a group of young, well-dressed, close-coupled, and armed men in control. Jack got them out, but others came. Rather than sell out to Capone, Jack closed down," one regular reminisced.[21]

The College of Complexes, first opened by Brundage on January 6, 1951, at 1651 North Wells, operated as the post-Prohibition successor of the Dil Pickle, with an emphasis on free-speech forums that encouraged loud, boisterous debate.[22]

Brundage struggled to support the club's operation through a lifelong career as a house painter and a $6,000 insurance settlement he received in the late 1940s. He had broken his back in 1945 in a fall from a New York elevated train platform when he was in that city making the rounds of major publishing houses with his first novel.[23] (His inability over his lifetime to sell any of his five books earned him the title "King of Failures" from the *Chicago Tribune*.)[24]

The "college" component of Brundage's programming consisted of open forums with topics such as "The Farce of the So-Called Paris Peace Conference," "Can Hippies Make a Happier World Despite the Status Quo of the Squares?" "Are Beatniks Immoral?" "The Chicago Police Department and Its Terrible Record of Civil Liberty Violations," "Will the U.S. Have Second-Raters in the Next Olympics?" "Do Europeans Have a Healthier Attitude toward Sex Than Americans?" and "Jazz Is Beautiful When It Pays."[25]

A typical weekend at the College merged music, game playing, oratory, and debates pitting authors, clergy, veterans, professors, and others with starkly opposite views, goaded by the audience to pull emotional and intellectual triggers meant to maximize the evening's liveliness. Because Brundage was committed to free speech and doled out time to both the radical left and the far right, controversy was common, and so were visits by the police. "I have always had the conviction that anyone running a free-speech emporium couldn't deny the platform to anyone with something valid to say," he explained.[26] A program titled "Chicago's Criminal Cops" in March 1954 further degraded his relationship with the city, and the next year, when he moved the club to 862 North State, Captain

James Hackett of the Chicago Police Department recommended that Mayor Martin Kennelly refuse Brundage a liquor license, as he "contended it had been a gathering place for undesirable persons."[27]

But Brundage had always booked talent that ran the gamut. The College became a place where Chicago writers like Nelson Algren and Herman Kogan held fetes to celebrate new books, and where, early in the civil rights movement, the public could meet Olympian runner Jesse Owens, prominent officials with the Urban League and the NAACP, and traveling political figures from Africa.[28]

Like Jones in the waning years of the Dil Pickle Club, Brundage grew weary of continually battling the city over alleged building code violations, failing to obtain a liquor license, and dodging the local mafia. The Internal Revenue Service was also on his back. He shut the club down in May 1961.[29] In a 1967 letter to the *Chicago Tribune*, Brundage lamented Chicago's corruptive elements and compared his city to fallen empires across Europe. "Certainly there have been enough social scientists around this town warning that this would happen here," he wrote.[30]

After trying to reopen it in fits and starts, he eventually gave up on the College in 1972 and moved to Guadalajara, Mexico, and then El Centro, California, where he died of a brain hemorrhage at a senior citizens' bingo party on October 18, 1990.[31]

THE GATE OF HORN MOVES FOLK MUSIC TO THE NIGHTCLUB SCENE

A catalyst for folk music's development in Chicago was "I Come for to Sing," a successful and long-running folk revue featuring Big Bill Broonzy, actor and radio host Studs Terkel, folk singer Win Stracke, and tenor Larry Lane. The revue presented traditional folk and blues songs and Elizabethan ballads, grouped under different themes that Terkel would highlight with narration. Making its debut in 1947 at the University of Chicago's Mandel Hall, it marked the first significant event in the postwar era of Chicago folk music.[32]

In 1952, the revue moved north to 56 West Madison, playing a three-show-a-night Monday residency at the Blue Note. There, jazz

titans Stan Kenton, Buddy Rich, Benny Goodman, and Duke Elling-
ton took in the show and sang its praises. Its commercial viability
signified folk music's successful transition from coffeehouses and
theaters to the nightclub scene.

The revue's success set the stage for what would become the
nation's first nightclub dedicated exclusively to folk music: the
Gate of Horn. The Gate represented a new face for folk music in
Chicago: neither a coffeehouse nor a campus auditorium, it was
meant to appeal to the same well-heeled crowd of professionals who
were packing the downtown supper clubs and jazz lounges that had
sprung up in the 1950s—the Sherman House Hotel's College Inn,
the Hilton's Boulevard Room, the Blue Angel, the Empire Room at
the Palmer House, the London House, the Black Orchid, and Mr.
Kelly's, as well as the Blue Note—during what is considered Chicago's second jazz age.[33]

Les Brown, an editor at *DownBeat*, and his college friend Albert
Grossman, who worked at the Chicago Housing Authority, both saw
folk music trending. "A certain kind of person went to those concerts that we didn't see at nightclubs and jazz clubs and other places
like that. We thought that was a niche," Brown said.

Neither Grossman nor Brown knew much about the music other
than that it was popular. But both were impressed by a twelve-hour
show performed by Bob Gibson at the Off Beat Room, a short-lived
spoken-word and music cabaret at 1037 West Granville on the city's
far North Side.[34] Owner Ken Nordine, a radio announcer and future
creator of *Word Jazz*, enforced a strict no-talking rule during the
music, which was unusual at a time when music largely served as a
background.[35] Grossman took note. According to Gibson,

> Albert saw that Ken's approach, this respect for the performers,
> would work and planned to use the same idea. He said, "This is
> interesting; a place like this could work downtown." It wasn't the
> folk music, because Albert knew nothing about folk music and could
> have cared less when he opened the Gate of Horn; he knew that a
> listening room would work. He told me about his idea, and he asked

me if I'd like to work there sometime and I said, "Sure." It sounded great. That idea became the Gate of Horn.[36]

Grossman pressed to call their club the Shingled Banjo, but Brown chose the Gate of Horn, a classical literary image that dates to Homer's *Odyssey*.[37]

The Gate's opening night on February 29, 1956, promised "folk singers, kicking off with Parisian Luc Poret and Hoosier Katie Lee."[38] Lee was not, in fact, from Indiana, but was born in Tucson, Arizona, and had already had a career as a radio actress in Los Angeles while moonlighting as a folk singer. During that time she had learned songs from Burl Ives, calypso from Harry Belafonte, and blues guitar from Josh White, and in 1956 recorded her debut album, *Katie Lee Sings Spicy Songs for Cool Knights*, on the Los Angeles label Specialty.[39]

Ives had taken Lee under his wing in California, helping her pick songs for her repertoire and explaining how to sell them to an audience. Lee remembered that Ives called Hollywood too self-conscious for folk music, saying "You need to take these folk songs and you need to get out of here."[40] He persuaded her to move to Chicago, where he set her up with his agent and publicist. Chicago had a circuit of folk venues, coffeehouses, and cabarets, more than the West Coast had at the time, and a media presence that would quickly cotton to a young, fresh up-and-comer. One tip Ives passed on to Lee: if a newspaper columnist says something nice about you, call them up the next day or send a card to say thank you. In Chicago, that worked.

Lee was talented—she played guitar and sang—but she was also naturally gorgeous. At the time, beauty worked against other folk singers like Jean Ritchie, who downplayed their appearance. Not Lee: the cover of *Spicy Songs* pictures her in a flirty embrace with a suit of armor; the back cover promises "lusty songs with her own unique blend of salty nuances, good strong spirits, ladylike leers and dramatic spice."[41] On *Songs of Couch and Consultation*, her second album from 1957 on Commentary Records, she reclines on a therapist's couch in a cocktail dress and heels, beaming into the photographer's lens while a goateed and horn-rimmed therapist peers into her bosom. The music, all co-written by Lee and swing-era saxophonist Bud Freeman, was equally audacious, lampooning psychoanalysis in a series of musical styles, from big band jazz to cowboy songs.[42]

"I didn't dress like the dirty sandal group at all," Lee said. "I dressed totally different—flashy big skirts and fancy tops. I didn't fit into the folk clubs, so they didn't know what to do with me. They didn't know if I was a pop singer or a folk singer but I know who I was, dammit, I was a folk singer!"[43]

Poret and his wife, the single-named French singer Genevieve, were also regulars on the Chicago lounge circuit. That same week, "the cherie from Paree" was "chansoning at the Empire Room" while her husband helped open the Gate.[44] Less than a year earlier, a *Billboard* review of their performance opening the Saxony Hotel in Miami compared her to Edith Piaf and Jacqueline François. "She has big, dark, appealing eyes, and sings the songs heard in the dark cellars of Montmartre," the reviewer wrote.[45]

Indeed, the Gate of Horn was located in a dark cellar, beneath the Rice Hotel at 755 North Dearborn on the southeast corner of Chicago and Dearborn, just one block south of where the Dil Pickle Club once bloomed. Pat Philips, who attended opening night with her boyfriend, remembers stepping down into the dimly lit room, where Grossman greeted her, as he did all his guests. "The College of Complexes sat more people; the Gate of Horn sat fewer than a hundred. But it was much more of a nightclub," she recalled.[46]

Lee's opening night booking extended fourteen weeks. The Gate would relocate to a bigger space, and above ground, in less than two years, but before that happened, she remembered the club as "a total mess." Prostitutes lived upstairs, the dressing room had a dirt floor, and performers were forced to hang their clothes on heating pipes. "I'd have to bring in my clothes and be damned careful to make sure they didn't fall on the floor," she said.[47]

In the beginning, the Gate rejected songwriters with leftist material, and instead brought in performers who played well to tourists and young professionals. A month after its opening, the *Chicago Tribune* praised the Gate for its intimacy, describing it as "one of the more comfortable cellars around town, attractively lit, tastefully furnished, and apparently bent on producing an atmosphere of quiet informality. You actually can hear, and the music is worth hearing."[48] The respectful ambiance at the Gate suited not just performers, but a clientele that wanted their folk music polished and upbeat, not raw and dark.

To John Cohen of the New Lost City Ramblers, a New York City trio that performed Southern roots music in traditional arrangements, the Gate "was uptown and sophisticated and had drinks and a crowd that was getting interested in this music." But by the time the Ramblers auditioned for the Gate, on May 22, 1960, commercial folk music and the kind embraced by college audiences was firmly divided.[49] "This was new music to [the Gate audience] and we had never played in such a sophisticated club before. In the middle of our second set, in the middle of our second song, half the audience got up and walked out," remembered Cohen. "They were on a Gray Line tour of hotspots in Chicago and the bus had just arrived. That will tell you what that place was."[50]

Grossman and Brown calculated right. In November 1958, less than two years after the Gate opened, the folk revival accelerated thanks to "Tom Dooley," the Kingston Trio's smash hit that reached number one on *Billboard*'s Hot 100 chart, subsequently sold more than three million copies, and even won a Grammy that year for Best Country and Western Record, because there was not yet a folk category.[51] The song, a traditional Southern mountain murder ballad, became folk music's biggest moment to date. National artists, like Josh White, Big Bill Broonzy, Bob Gibson, Odetta, Jo Mapes, Theodore Bikel, Brother John Sellers, the Gateway Singers, Peggy Seeger, Glenn Yarbrough, Gina Glaser, and Barbara Dane, soon got on the calendar.

Both coasts took notice. "The Gate of Horn was the place to go. That was the leading club," said Jac Holzman, founder of Elektra Records, the label that launched the careers of Josh White, Bob Gibson, Judy Collins, Phil Ochs, and in the later rock era, the Doors, the Stooges, and Queen. "The Gate of Horn had the folk thing pretty much locked up, it had a more lounge atmosphere than the Bitter End [in New York City], which was cider and maybe hot chocolate. You had to go to Chicago to keep your career going."[52]

By the mid-fifties, few nightclubs were as plugged into the folk circuit as the Gate. Its central location between the coasts was also key because artists could build a touring network and then expand. The West Coast folk scene was still nascent. The more developed network of clubs stretched between Chicago, Boston, and New York. "We all knew that Chicago was the second biggest city in the country at that time, and it was a force field," Holzman said.[53]

In those early days, folk artists in New York targeted the Gate not only to gain traction in their careers, but also to develop valuable stage experience. Those artists included Peggy Seeger, the singer and banjoist who was also half sister to Pete Seeger and sister to Mike Seeger of the New Lost City Ramblers. In 1957, at age twenty-two, she hopped on her Lambretta scooter with only a suitcase, knapsack, and banjo and rode to Chicago, where she played her first paid job: a three-month residency at the Gate. She performed on a nightly bill with Bob Gibson and Big Bill Broonzy. Music started at 10:00 p.m., and she played three or four forty-five-minute sets each night, getting back to her Wells Street apartment close to 4:00 a.m. The Gate audience was devoted but demanding.[54] "There would be people who came every night and they would expect a new song every night," she said. "Not a new made-up song, but one they had not heard before. So I had to comb through my repertoire. I had sung very, very little at that point."[55]

Backstage, she got to know Gibson and Broonzy, but soon found that the Chicago scene represented by those two local icons was quite different from what she had been used to back home, or in England earlier that year, where she sang union songs in labor marches. "We didn't hit it off chiefly because our approach to folk music was so different, [Gibson] was more popular-minded than I was. I was still trying to sing [songs by early twentieth-century union activist] Aunt Molly Jackson." Broonzy was more congenial. But as Seeger sipped coffee before her late-night set, she watched Broonzy swallow brandy. "It was just a recognition that there's not much in common here," she said.[56]

Indeed, the Gate embodied the hearty appetites of the steak-houses, supper clubs, and nightclubs that dominated Chicago nightlife, in contrast to the subdued and bohemian nature of the New York coffeehouse circuit. Joan Baez was eighteen in 1959 when Grossman coaxed her to Chicago to perform. After two weeks of shows, she left "baffled, flattered and terrified" by the experience."[57] Baez recalled struggling with "the maleness around me, the overt sexuality that erupted as inhibitions were anesthetized by alcohol. I knew only that at age eighteen, I was not cut out for the cocktail crowd. I needed my academic, rebellious coffee-drinking admir-ers who listened single-mindedly to their madonna, and dared not touch her."[58]

The club had two rooms: a front bar and a back room with a stage. Frank Hamilton, the house guitarist, played to celebrities, tourists, college students, writers like Saul Bellow, Nelson Algren, Lionel Trilling and William Styron, actors from the Second City, Playboy Club bunnies off their shifts, gangsters and their molls.[59] "Lots of drugs floating around the place. They plied the crowd with liquor and there was too much smoking," he said. "It was a hole in the wall to start with, but not a bad hole in the wall."[60]

As they had at the Dil Pickle and the College of Complexes, the Chicago Outfit inevitably surfaced. "Al knew a lot of shady people," Hamilton said. "There was an underworld community that hung out on the fringes."[61] According to Les Brown, it appeared in the guise of a man named Wally who showed up one day to demand $100 a week as a "consultant." His outfit sent a jukebox, but the Gate didn't have it installed. Wally's bosses paid the club a visit and watched a show; impressed, they asked Grossman and Brown to help them manage a few jazz clubs they owned on Clark Street. That spooked Brown enough that he left the club business. "You don't want to get mixed up with these guys," he told Grossman.[62]

Grossman held court in the front bar. Bob Dylan biographer Bob Spitz recalled that while folk singers performed in the back room, "Al chatted with the 'dignitaries' out front at the long, crowded bar, working very hard to create an atmosphere of cultural sophistication. Taste, refinement, provocative conversation, political and intellectual savvy—These are the qualities Al Grossman sought to cultivate as part of the Gate's highbrow mystique."[63]

Aspiring folk singers eager to play the Gate soon realized they were at cross-purposes with the club: Grossman was less interested in where folk music had come from than where it was headed. Dave Van Ronk, who later became the dean of the Greenwich Village folk scene, hitchhiked to Chicago in late 1957 to audition for Grossman at the suggestion of Odetta, whom Grossman managed. "The Gate of Horn was an important club they were all aware of. That was a goal for all of them who wanted to be in this business. There was a lot of prestige to be accepted there," said his widow, Andrea Vuocolo Van Ronk.[64]

In his memoir, Van Ronk recalls showing up in Chicago high on the Dexedrine he took to stay awake during the twenty-two-hour trip. Dropped off in the suburbs, he hopped a bus to the Loop and then took a taxi straight to the club. Entering the room as staff were removing chairs from tables to set up for the night, he saw a "heavy-set man with graying hair in a too-tight suit" at the bar. Van Ronk introduced himself to Grossman and said he should have received his demo tape from Odetta. Grossman said he hadn't.

So I told him my sad tale, how I had hitched all the way from New York, blah, blah, blah. He heard me out noncommittally. "Well," he said, "you've come all this way. . . . Why not audition right now? There's the stage."

This wasn't going according to my script at all, but maybe I could still pull it out. I got onstage and launched into a set of my biggest flag-wavers: "Tell Old Bill," "Willie the Weeper," "Dink's Song," and suchlike. I could see Albert plainly—the house lights were still on. His face had the studied impassiveness of a very bad poker player with a very good hand. All around me chairs and tables scraped and thumped, glasses and silverware clinked and rattled, but I forged on. This was D-Day goddamnit, and I was showing this hypercool Chicago hick how we did it in Washington Square.

I'm afraid that's just what I did.

When I got off, Albert still had not batted an eyelash. "Do you know who works here?" he asked. "Big Bill Broonzy works here. Josh White works here. Brownie McGhee and Sonny Terry play here a lot. Now tell me," he went on, "why should I hire you?"[65]

Van Ronk returned east. The incident, which filmmakers Joel and Ethan Coen fictionalized in their 2013 film *Inside Llewyn Davis*, confirmed his suspicion that clubs like the Gate of Horn were not interested in performers who lacked the backing of influential managers and record promoters. The trip was "a real turning point in his life," said Vuocolo Van Ronk. "That's when he decided to just do the music."[66]

ALBERT GROSSMAN:
FOLK MUSIC'S MOST NOTORIOUS IMPRESARIO

On the day the Gate opened, a columnist for the *Chicago Daily News* ended his dispatch with a brief observation: "Al Grossman used to be in the construction business, so you ask him about the new night spot, Gate of the Horn [*sic*]. . . . And the first thing he mentions isn't the talent, but the dandy new sound-deadening cork floor he put in."[67]

Grossman knew talent, but it was his focus on presentation that would make him one of the most powerful artist managers in the 1960s. Selling the Gate of Horn to his manager in 1959, and leaving Chicago the next year, allowed him to forge a new role that had never existed in rock and roll, let alone in folk music. Grossman created folk supergroup Peter, Paul and Mary and represented Odetta and Bob Gibson, and he later took control of the careers of Janis Joplin, Paul Butterfield, the Electric Flag, The Band, Gordon Lightfoot, and Richie Havens. But it was his early control over Bob Dylan's career between 1962 and 1971 that made him wealthy and notorious.

Grossman famously rewrote the rules on personal management,

gaining control of publishing rights for his clients and earning them a higher stake in royalties. He also understood the long-term potential in the sources of residual income that were emerging in that decade, such as festivals, overseas licensing, film soundtracks, and large-scale touring. As the music industry grew, Grossman was one of the first managers to see that the real money was no longer in the nightclub and promotion business, but in developing commercial brands that would have staying power.

"He was all business. I could see the gears moving in his head," remembered Elektra Records founder Jac Holzman. "He realized that there was no way he could leverage a club unless he opened Gate of Horns all around the country without management and mess. He understood that leverage was critical to being financially successful, and controlling an artist's career would give him a lot of leverage."[68]

Former Elektra Records chairman Bob Krasnow said Grossman leveled the playing field between his artists and the record labels and publishing companies that were gaining prominence, especially in the emerging singer-songwriter era when artists like Bob Dylan not only could earn money by recording their own songs, but could generate double that or more from cover versions by other artists. "What you see today in the music business is the result of Albert. He changed the whole idea of what a negotiation was all about. Albert understood that music was becoming an industry."[69]

Grossman was born May 21, 1926, on Chicago's West Side to parents who were recent Russian immigrants. He rotated through different jobs, including shoe salesman and later management aide at Dearborn Homes, a public housing development run by the Chicago Housing Authority in Bronzeville, on the near South Side. He was fired from that job for "gross irregularities."[70] Faced with few job prospects, he put his economics degree from Roosevelt University to use by opening the Gate.[71] Even though he was three months shy of age thirty by opening night, he had prematurely gray hair and carried the natural heft of a much older man who had earned his chops as a street hustler. Dylan remembered eyeing Grossman in the early days of the Gaslight Café in Greenwich Village:

He looked like Sidney Greenstreet from *The Maltese Falcon*, had an enormous presence, dressed always in a conventional suit and tie, and he sat at a corner table. Usually when he talked, his voice was loud, like the booming of war drums. He didn't talk so much as growl. Grossman was from Chicago, had a non-show business background but didn't let that stand in his way. Not your usual shop-keeper, he had owned a nightclub in the Windy City and had to deal with district bosses and various fixes and ordinances and carried a .45. Grossman was no hayseed.[72]

Indeed, Grossman operated like a Chicago ward boss: on the folk scene, he ruled by dividing and conquering, as if presiding over a chessboard. Dylan told biographer Robert Shelton that when he first met Grossman he "thought he was just a street bear." Shelton countered that Grossman "was a teddy or a grizzly, depending on your point of view."[73]

In true Chicago fashion, Grossman rewarded loyalty and slammed doors on those he either didn't need or couldn't win over. "He preferred to work in the shadows, seeking neither credit nor limelight, but he appreciated his growing reputation as a king-maker. Enduring his charges' idiosyncrasies, he was confessor and psychiatrist to them all," wrote Shelton. "His chief reward was money—tons of it, bags of it. His subsidiary reward was power, which he used judiciously at first, until he gradually became pos-sessed by it."[74]

He was deeply committed to his artists, but fiercely insistent on what he wanted. Baez remembered Grossman intimidating her and her parents in his effort to get her to Chicago, but not in the obvious ways. He was, after all, a genial-looking gangster who had "a round form, round face, round eyes, and round glasses."[75]

He terrified me by saying things like, "You can have anything you want. You can have any*body* you want. Who do you want? I'll get him for you." I wanted Marlon Brando, but wanted more for Albert to quit talking that way.

My father was impressed by the kind of money Albert was talking, but I didn't trust him. Neither did my mother.[76]

The Gate served as headquarters for his looming management
career. He would cajole artists he had scouted to come to Chicago
to polish their acts, promising them weeks of well-paid work and
national exposure, and would eventually get them to sign personal
management contracts. He lured Peter Yarrow from New York so
he could improve as a club performer, and later tried to slot him
into a trio with Bob Gibson and Carolyn Hester in an effort to create a folk supergroup he envisioned as an alternative to the Kingston Trio. When that didn't click, Yarrow suggested Mary Travers,
a Greenwich Village native with little singing experience. Finding
their voices meshed well, Travers suggested adding Noel Stookey, a
friend and stand-up comedian who regularly worked at the Gaslight
Café in the Village. All three singers were untrained and had limited experience onstage, but Grossman smelled potential. He hired
Milt Okun, a producer and arranger who had worked with the Chad
Mitchell Trio and Harry Belafonte, and forced them all together
into rehearsals for seven months. When they emerged, Grossman
made some finishing touches: Noel had to become Paul, the men
needed to maintain mustaches and goatees to signal Beat culture,
and Travers must remain mute between songs in order to preserve
an air of mystery.[77]

Musician Eric Weisberg recalled standing next to Grossman
during an early Peter, Paul and Mary show at Gerde's Folk City in
New York and being less than impressed. "I didn't really like what
they were doing. . . . He may have asked what I thought, but he didn't
really care, because he said to me, 'Well, they're going to be huge.'
And he was right."[78]

Weeks later, Grossman secured the group an unprecedented (for
an unknown folk group) $30,000 advance from Warner Bros. as well
as two perks: recording sessions in New York, not Los Angeles, and
the freedom to handle the art design of their own album. *Peter, Paul
and Mary* ended up selling over two million copies and won two

Grammys in 1962.[79] Their breakthrough would solidify Grossman as an industry power broker.

"He fights for his singers better than anybody," Izzy Young, proprietor of the Folklore Center in New York, told an interviewer in 1969. "Some people hate him for it, but I've never seen anyone not want to be managed by him. It's the other way around." Grossman, Young said, knew of his reputation and once jokingly referred to himself as "the source of darkness."[80]

Grossman could indeed land major-label deals for his clients, but that service came with a price. Less than a decade after the Gate of Horn opened, when his success with Bob Dylan had made him a formidable tastemaker, artists had little choice but to agree to his terms.

When Michael Bloomfield, the guitar prodigy who grew up in Glencoe, a suburb north of Chicago, departed the Paul Butterfield Blues Band to form the Electric Flag, he retained Grossman, who had managed his former band. After relocating to San Francisco from Chicago, the band awaited Grossman's arrival with their contracts. According to vocalist Nick Gravenites:

> When Albert came out, he came out with contracts—contract after contract. He had a recording contract. He had a personal management contract. He had publishing contracts. I was perfectly willing to sign a recording contract and my personal management contract, but then he told me I had to sign over my publishing to him, too.
>
> I got a little quirky. I thought, Man, this guy wants everything. Why? Why? For the money, of course. I said, "Man, you know, Albert, I don't know about this. I just went through years of having a publishing deal with Elektra, off of Butterfield's first album. I've been waiting for years to get out of that thing, and it's up in about three or four months. I'm not ready to sign another deal. Anyway, even if I was ready to sign another deal, I can't. I'm signed to another company."
>
> Albert says, "No, you either sign or you're out." So I signed, which was a major mistake.[81]

Wherever Grossman looked, he saw potential. But some artists didn't cooperate. When Ella Jenkins was performing at the Gate, Grossman approached her with the idea of making her the next Odetta, his first star client and another Black woman embarking on a career singing folk songs to mostly White audiences. But Jenkins, born two years earlier than Grossman, envisioned a career performing music for children. At the time, children's music may not have been taken seriously by her peers, but as someone who started out teaching music to teenagers at the YWCA, and who spent a summer leading sing-alongs with Big Bill Broonzy at a folk school in Michigan, Jenkins wanted the informal camaraderie of group singing, not a career in show business.

At the Gate, "they all played guitars and banjos and used to laugh at me because I came with a baritone ukulele and harmonica," she said. Besides her resistance to giving up children's music, she was reluctant to sign up for professional management: "I saw how a lot of other people who had gotten under managership and I didn't like it. You had to be responsible then, you had to be in a certain place. Then they told you how you had to sing, what you had to sing. That didn't seem free."[82]

In 1962, the same year he struck gold with Peter, Paul and Mary, Grossman approached Judy Collins, who had been performing at the Gate for about a year, and proposed she form a trio with singers Jo Mapes and Judy Henske, to be called the "Brown-Eyed Girls." "I think it would work," he told her. "You can get brown contact lenses!"[83]

For musicians passing through the Gate whose spirits were rooted in the music's radical past, Grossman personified a troubling contradiction: he was an efficient taskmaster with questionable principles, but one who created a forum for the music. Grossman hired Frank Hamilton, a young guitarist from California who had studied with Woody Guthrie, to serve as a house musician accompanying touring acts. "I felt like a product around him more than anything else," Hamilton said. "He was more interested in people he could go someplace with and make money off of."[84]

The Gate was not without its radicals, although Grossman shrugged and looked the other way. Martha Schlamme, a Vienna-born cabaret singer known in the next decade for her interpretations of Kurt Weill songs, was performing at the Gate in 1956 when she was solicited by local activists involved in the American Socialist Party to take part in a benefit performance.

Frank Fried, a former steelworker, remembered going to the Gate to pitch the idea of the benefit to Schlamme because he had heard she was sympathetic to the party due to the rampant McCarthyism of the time. After an introduction, she called Grossman over.

> I explained to the two of them how badly the Eugene Debs Forum needed to raise some money, and how a small benefit concert could help. We were trying to get the word out, I told her, and that was expensive. . . . Martha thought that sounded good and she'd like to help out. Grossman said it was fine with him. He was not unsympathetic, he was just bemused at how hard some people would work for no money, and for a lost cause, as far as he was concerned.[85]

Grossman ended up giving Fried work selling tickets for concerts he was promoting at larger halls around town. Eventually, Fried opened Triangle Productions, a company that produced folk concerts in Chicago by performers who held political values and an artistic aesthetic closer to his own.[86] Fried later suggested that his approach to presenting folk music was contrary to that of Grossman, who "had no moral code or a political outlook that gave him a sense of morality so he was essentially an amoral person. He led a very consistent life, which is more than most people can say, and he stayed the course."[87]

What got Grossman to New York permanently was the inaugural Newport Folk Festival, held July 11–12, 1959, in Newport, Rhode Island. The festival established folk music as the dominant commercial music of that period and would serve as a beacon to draw young audiences to older traditional artists like Jimmie Drift-wood, Frank Warner, Reverend Gary Davis, and the Stanley Brothers. The Kingston Trio, a pop group derided by purists but whose popularity ensured crowds, headlined. Twelve thousand people bought tickets.[88]

Grossman produced the festival at the invitation of George Wein, a Boston jazz club owner who had organized the first Newport Jazz Festival in July 1954. Wein knew little about folk music before Odetta performed at Storyville, one of his two Boston clubs, in 1958. "While business was less than sensational during the nighttime performances, on Sunday afternoon I found the place completely packed. The crowd consisted entirely of young people. What was happening here? Though Boston was the base of my life in jazz, I was not aware of the folk movement evolving on the Cambridge side of the Charles River," he said.[89]

Wein immediately made plans to dedicate an afternoon of his jazz festival to the new folk movement and booked the obvious choices: Odetta, Pete Seeger, the Weavers, and the Kingston Trio. But after more research he realized the folk movement was much bigger than he anticipated and that it deserved its own festival. But he needed a producer. He turned to Odetta's manager, who struck him as the consummate insider to the folk scene. Grossman, eager to expand his reach to the East Coast, readily signed on.

Grossman succeeded in the new role because, as at the Gate, his programming made no attempt to dictate folk music's new direction, but instead offered many strains of folk music to appeal to its different factions. The format mimicked the Newport Jazz Festival: each day featured afternoon and evening performances, with reserved seating at both. Grossman solicited familiar names from Chicago: Frank Hamilton, Bob Gibson, and emcee Studs Terkel. Rounding out the festival were artists who appealed to those wanting traditional music (the New Lost City Ramblers, Jean Ritchie, John Jacob Niles, Frank Warner), blues and spirituals (Leon Bibb, Odetta, Brownie McGhee and Sonny Terry, Barbara Dane), Appalachian music (Earl Scruggs, Billy Faier), and names familiar to the New York folk scene (Cynthia Gooding, Eric Weisberg, Oscar Brand). Pete Seeger and the Kingston Trio co-headlined the bill.

To Wein, the music Grossman brought to Newport that first year "constituted more than a revival; it was a transformation. A synthesis of traditional sounds with new ideas and perspectives were put into motion."[90] Reviewers unanimously approved, ensuring that the festival would continue. Robert Shelton praised it in the *New York Times* as "perhaps the most ambitious attempt ever made at delineating a cross-section of the nation's folk music."[91] Izzy Young, in his *Caravan* review, agreed: "Every aspect of human emotion was displayed there. Folk music was proven to be a great art form, and not something to be listened to necessarily because it is cultural or traditional," he wrote. "Albert Grossman succeeded at Newport without making cerebrations of what the singers should sing. Grossman did not demand that the show revolve around his idea of what folk music should be. The singers sang what they wanted."[92]

Grossman had traveled back and forth from Chicago in planning for the festival, but in 1960 he moved to New York permanently, having already formed a company, Production and Management Associates, with Wein and Eddie Sarkesian, a jazz promoter from Detroit.[93] The partners had grand plans to produce jazz and folk festivals in all three cities, but the partnership would not last. Grossman had moved in with Wein and his wife, and it soon became evident that the Chicago folk hustler and the East Coast jazz aficionado occupied different worlds. Said Wein:

[Grossman] brought with him a lifestyle not entirely compatible with ours. On numerous occasions Joyce and I would come home to discover Albert sitting on the floor with a friend, passing a pipe or makeshift hookah between them. This provoked some consternation from my wife. I wasn't exactly thrilled with it, either. Another problem was Albert's callous concern for the people to whom he owed money. These unwilling lenders figured that 2 or 3 a.m. was the only time they could catch Grossman at home. So the phone would ring at all hours of the night. Grossman never picked up the receiver. It didn't take long for Joyce and me to grow tired of answering these calls.[94]

Wein dissolved the company in 1961, the year before Grossman would be catapulted to success with Peter, Paul and Mary. The
breakup left Wein carrying $15,000 in office expense debt, half of
which was Grossman's share. In later years, when Wein would ask
for the money, Grossman's answer was always the same: "You've
been telling everybody that I owe you money. That's why I haven't
paid you."[95]

The year before he moved to New York, Grossman sold the Gate
of Horn to the club's manager, Alan Ribback, who had experience
promoting concerts in Bloomington, Indiana, while a graduate student at Indiana University.[96] Grossman continued to send artists
to Chicago, but in 1963 he returned to his hometown to open one
more club, the Bear, with partner Howard Alk, a co-founder of the
Second City who also ran the lights at the Gate of Horn.[97] The new
club was located on the Gold Coast, at 22 East Ontario at the corner
of Wabash, the former site of L'Aiglon, a longtime French Creole
restaurant that opened in 1926 and in its former life was known
for dance orchestras and female gypsy "strollers" who sang among
diners, playing mandolin and accordion.[98]

Alk's management of the Bear was a problem because he was
involved with drugs. He would eventually get clean, but his criminal
associations filtered into his new responsibilities. "[Alk] had hired
a friend of his to work valet parking for the nightclub and [the valets
operated out of] the basement. One day he goes down there and
there's a key cutting machine. And Howard realized, 'I guess hiring
my friend whose real career was as a professional burglar wasn't a
good idea,'" said friend Gordon Quinn.[99]

The Bear wouldn't last a year, but it is still remembered as
the place where Grossman promoted Bob Dylan in Chicago eight
months after signing him.[100] It's also where Dylan met guitarist
Michael Bloomfield.

On April 25, 1963, Dylan already had released his debut album,
but it didn't sell well as he wasn't very well known outside Greenwich
Village. His second album, *The Freewheelin' Bob Dylan*, would be in
stores in May.

At the Bear, Dylan was hot from his eighth and final *Freewheelin'* recording session, which had taken place a day earlier at Columbia Recording Studios in New York. In Chicago he debuted many of the album's new songs—"Blowin' in the Wind," "Honey Just Allow Me One More Chance," "A Hard Rain's A-Gonna Fall," "Talkin' World War III Blues," "Bob Dylan's Dream," "Girl From the North Country," and "Masters of War"—both at the Bear and on an hour-long radio broadcast the following morning on WFMT. In the studio with host Studs Terkel, Dylan performed songs that never made it onto that second album, or any other, such as "Talkin' John Birch Paranoid Blues" and "Farewell."[101]

The audience at the Bear for Dylan's Chicago debut was made up mostly of guitar students from the Old Town School of Folk Music, corralled by school co-founder Dawn Greening. The Bear didn't have a liquor license for the opening and served only coffee.[102] The students filled two long tables set with white tablecloths and coffee mugs. There was no stage, no microphone. Dylan stood in front of the tables on the wooden floor with just a guitar and harmonica.[103]

That Thursday night, Dylan played some of his starkest material—"Talkin' World War III Blues," "A Hard Rain's A-Gonna Fall," "With God On Our Side," and "The Ballad of Hollis Brown"—in a room barely lit by candles. Dylan's audience of peers, many his age or barely older, were hardly prepared for the bleak evening.

"Lots of hair, skinny Jewish guy, strings hanging out of the head of his guitar," is the picture that remained with Marcia Johnson of that night. "We said to each other, 'this guy is going nowhere, he's so depressing.'"[104]

Jo Razowki, another Old Town student, said Dylan's baby face and lithe body contradicted the gravity of his songs and the weariness of his voice. "How come he's so young and so upset at the war like he'd been in it?" she remembered asking friends.[105]

That evening was fortuitous for Dylan because he would meet two core members of his entourage: Victor Maymudes, who would later serve as his tour manager for decades, and Alk, who would leave improvisational comedy behind for a career as a cinematographer and film editor, working primarily on Dylan projects between 1967 and 1978.[106] However, the most profound connection Dylan made was with guitarist Michael Bloomfield, who would later aid Dylan's transition to rock and roll by playing on the 1965 album *Highway 61 Revisited*, dominating each track with his lead guitar. Bloomfield, along with the Paul Butterfield Blues Band, would also join Dylan on the road that summer.[107] In 1968, Bloomfield told *Rolling Stone*'s Jann Wenner:

> I met Dylan at this funny little club called the Bear in Chicago just after his first album came out. The liner notes described him as a real hot shot, you know, a real great guitar player. And I heard the album and it sounded just shitty. He came to Chicago and I welcomed the opportunity to go down there and cut him. So I went to see him in the afternoon to talk to him and he was really nice. He was just so nice. I saw him at a few parties and then out of the clear blue sky, he called me on the phone to cut a record which was "Like a Rolling Stone." So I bought a Fender, a really good guitar for the first time in my life, without a case, a Telecaster. And that's how. He called me up.[108]

By the time Dylan appeared in Chicago to headline at Orchestra Hall in December 1963, the Bear had vanished.[109] The name, however, would loom large in Grossman mythology. After becoming a multimillionaire through Dylan, he started purchasing land on the eastern edge of the Catskill Mountains and settled there in 1964. Over two decades, he assembled a sprawling 15-acre creek-side campus of converted farmhouses and barns, located in a hamlet on the edge of Woodstock, New York, called Bearsville. He established a recording studio, a record label, a music video center, a restaurant called the Bear Café, and the Little Bear, an adjoining Chinese restaurant. By the early 1970s, he had largely extracted himself from personal management. He had little choice: Peter, Paul and Mary had broken up, and Janis Joplin had died of a heroin overdose in 1970. Dylan refused to re-sign with Grossman in 1971 and claimed, in a long-running series of lawsuits, that Grossman had exploited him. Dylan had signed a contract that gave Grossman 20 percent of his earnings and 25 percent of his recording royalties, which was more than double the rate other theatrical agents charged at the time. Dylan's attorneys showed that Grossman wasn't even licensed as a theatrical agent in New York. "Arguably, the whole thing was illegal," wrote Dylan biographer Howard Sounes.[110] In a 1981 deposition, when asked how long he had known Grossman, Dylan coolly replied, "Well, I don't think I've ever known the man."[111]

At Bearsville, Grossman quietly presided over an artists' utopia. With a long mane of white hair knotted behind his neck and a wardrobe of Indian peasant shirts, he embraced the role of the creative guru. "We've tried to allow people to present themselves in a positive way as possible to provide those facilities to them. And I think it's what it's all about, just sort of trying to make Bearsville a nice place to live in," he told a British television interviewer in 1977.[112]

Muddy Waters, Todd Rundgren, NRBQ, Jesse Winchester, The Band, Paul Butterfield, and Foghat recorded at Bearsville under Grossman's watch, while others, including the Rolling Stones, used it as a personal refuge. "He made this place attractive for musicians. He amplified a lot of what was already implicit in the town of Woodstock, and out of him sprung the Woodstock festival and that whole legacy, as well," said Michael Lang, producer of the 1969 Woodstock festival. "He was a very bright and talented man. But he was also not entirely a happy man."[113]

Grossman died of a heart attack on January 25, 1986, on a plane headed to London to scout a potential new client.[114] He remains at Bearsville, buried in a pine grove not far behind the buildings, under a headstone encircled in ivy.

THE RISE, FALL, AND TWELVE-STRING LEGACY OF BOB GIBSON

Six years before Dylan, Bob Gibson was the first client Grossman managed. The two were roommates, but besides that, it was easy to see what the aspiring mogul saw in the musician: Gibson was talented, easygoing, clean-cut, wore a flattop, and had no qualms about presenting folk music as upbeat entertainment. He went national in 1957 after winning the *American Idol* of the Eisenhower years: *Arthur Godfrey's Talent Scouts*. Impressed with his banjo playing, Godfrey signed Gibson to appear on his variety show, *Arthur Godfrey and His Friends*, for seventeen consecutive weeks, and with Godfrey on the baritone ukulele, the pair often appeared playing duets.[115] Through their screens, viewers saw a man John Cohen described as "Mr. Good, Wholesome, Healthy and Uplifting." What they didn't see was that Gibson was secretly addicted to heroin, a habit that would later derail his career at the same time the tidal wave of rock and roll washed away most folk acts.

"In terms of the guys who really got commercial after him, he was small peanuts. But he set the stage for the club scene," said Cohen. "He was trying to make the music alive on the terms he was able to do it."[116]

Gibson started on banjo but switched to the twelve-string guitar, an instrument that was not the norm in the folk world but would later be taken up by a younger generation that admired his deep knowledge of the folk tradition and his winsome personality needed to win over nightclub crowds, as well as his virtuoso playing. David Crosby, of the Byrds and Crosby, Stills, and Nash, considered Gibson a "hero" to young musicians. "He was a mentor of mine. I bought a twelve-string trying to be like him because he played twelve-string fantastically well," Crosby said. "He made me love the idea that the song had to have content, not just be this kind of highly polished nothing, which is what pop music is now. It had to have meaning, it had to take you on a little voyage, it had to express something to you. People like Bob were good teachers for that."[117]

"We learned a lot from Bob," said Peter Yarrow of Peter, Paul and Mary. "He started out as a scholar of folk songs, but he bridged the gap between the purist point of view, playing [folk music] in the strictly traditional fashion, and the idea that if you were tasteful, you could express yourself in a contemporary way that carried on the tradition. That was not an easy thing to achieve."[118]

Gibson was born November 16, 1931, in Brooklyn and grew up in Putnam County in the lower Hudson Valley.[119] He would later tell people of the anger he carried throughout his childhood. At age ten, rheumatic fever forced him to be hospitalized for months and then housebound for nearly a year. He was an outcast. A distracted father who commuted four hours a day to and from the city and an alcoholic mother who showed little interest in him meant more or less being on his own. Freedom came when forced to attend Catholic school in the Bronx; Gibson often rode the train into Times Square instead and watched movies all day, his real education. Hitchhiking became his hobby before graduation. From odd jobs across the country to a stint in the Merchant Marine, Gibson adopted a freewheeling path of self-discovery that many of his generation followed.

> The idea of being destructive, being vandalistic, of being wantonly destructive was appealing to me. I did enough kid vandalism. I remember there was a time after I'd left home, I was trucking around New York a lot, and I was running in some seamy circles. I was fascinated by people who were street hip; fascinated by street cunning. I always had been. There was a time when I was 17, I was running around carrying a gun regularly, which shows you a certain amount of hostility and paranoia. . . . No one messed with me, though. I think they probably thought I was a crazy little bastard.[120]

By the time he returned to Washington Square Park as a folk singer, the music had taken hold. On a lark one Saturday in 1953, Gibson and a friend hitchhiked up the Hudson River to meet Pete Seeger. When they arrived in his yard, Seeger was in the process of building a chimney and, spotting two extra sets of hands, enlisted them to help. Their reward that evening was a home-cooked dinner prepared by Toshi, Seeger's wife. The group ate outside, overlooking the Hudson as the sun set. Gibson recalled that the conversation quieted and things felt "kind of holy." Seeger stepped inside for his banjo and returned to play them songs, one of which Gibson remembered as the English ballad "Leather-Winged Bat." His young ears had never heard anything so sophisticated or mature. He knew it was a traditional song, yet Gibson was overcome with how "hip" Seeger made it sound, like it could have been written that year.[121]

"It changed my life . . . here was a committed man. I knew that he lived the life he talked and sang about. He didn't just talk the talk," Gibson later said. "His songs are more than just the way he makes his living."[122]

Gibson spent the next two years honing his craft in New York, Cleveland, and far-flung places like the Caribbean and Miami, where an agent booked him in bars and lounges seven nights a week. He arrived in Chicago in 1955 and played his first gig at the Raths-keller of the Old Heidelberg, a German beer hall in the Loop.[123] "The act I followed was a guy who had been working there for 14 years. He sang German songs for the furniture makers from Wisconsin and Michigan who were in town on buying trips. I was a guy with a banjo and a crew cut, singing calypso and Appalachian mountain ballads, and they didn't care for me at all. I was fired after the second set," he said.[124]

By the time Gibson got to the Gate of Horn, he had already spent a few years on the nightclub circuit learning how to win over tough crowds. One Miami club, for example, was located above a strip joint that catered to mobsters, who would take clients to the upstairs club "for the class acts," Gibson said. Customers pounded the tables with little wooden mallets instead of applauding. He shared a dressing room with twenty naked women.[125]

Unlike other young folk singers on the circuit, Gibson did not imitate Woody Guthrie or Seeger, nor did he have any interest in presenting songs as museum pieces. He may have devoured holy texts like Carl Sandburg's *The American Songbag*, but note-perfect covers bored him. Instead, he used traditional songs as source mate-rial to create something new and pleasing for audiences:

> The songs had a lot of obscure references and archaic language in them, some of which was wonderful, because it was beautiful use of language. But when it confused or confounded the audience, then I

thought it was time to change the language a little. . . . I also found that singers in the traditional setting—sitting around the back porch, swapping songs—seemed to have a lot more time to spend on music. So there would be lots of verses, a lot of repetitive and redundant material. I did not have that kind of time when I was on stage; I was dealing with urban audiences who were used to songs on the radio that lasted two and a half or three minutes, tops. If you couldn't tell the story in that amount of time, you'd lose them.[126]

Gibson was upbeat, told jokes, looked like he worked the tie counter at Burberry, and knew what it took to quiet those pounding mallets—a talent that came from making music in spaces where liquor poured freely. Impressing his audience with the social history behind the music wouldn't work on the nightclub circuit. Gibson was more practical:

I have to remember that although the spotlight is on me, and I have the microphone, and my name is out in front in two-foot letters, and I'm being grossly overpaid to be on that stage, I'm still not the center of attention. The guy who pays five bucks to sit out there thinks that he is. He has come to me for a service; I'm in a service business . . .

It isn't art. I'd like to have art overtones, and I would love it if people would sit around and discuss old Gibson's 'art,' but, you know, basically, I'm a saloon singer.[127]

Gibson played the Gate eleven months in its first year, which established him as the club's house act. Then things happened fast: he signed a contract with Riverside Records, which released *Offbeat Folksongs*, his debut album. In February 1957, Gibson headlined Carnegie Hall, and a live album followed, his second of two for Riverside in that year alone. Then Godfrey called, and by the end of the decade Gibson was a headlining act at every major folk club in the country and had earned his place on the roster of Elektra, the dominant folk label at the time. "His incredible guitar playing and very winning stage presence" is what convinced Jac Holzman to sign him. "He was doing a lot of traditional material and he was pretty much the best of the lot. He did it well and he did it with great authority. That made him highly desirable."[128]

Gibson didn't carry lefty baggage. His approach to folk music tradition was to strip it of politics and social change and make it relevant but not divisive. Bob Dylan looked up to him in the early days. Comedian George Carlin recalled that Dylan "copied down Bob Gibson's chord changes" at the Gate. Later, Dylan name-checked Gibson on his *Self-Portrait* album.[129] But as Dylan honed his craft in Village folk clubs, he grew to perceive Gibson as one of the "commercial folk snobs":

> These kind looked down on the traditional singers as being old-fashioned and wrapped in cobwebs. Bob Gibson, a clean-cut commercial folksinger from Chicago, had a big following and some records out. If he dropped in to see you perform he'd be in the front row. After the first or second song, if you weren't commercial enough, too raw or ragged around the edges, he might conspicuously stand up, make a fuss and walk out on you. There wasn't any middle ground and it seemed like everybody was a snob of one kind or another.[130]

To others, Gibson became a mentor. Judy Collins, eight years his junior, said Gibson was responsible for getting her to the Gate in 1959, which launched her career. She later paid him back by recording his songs on her third Elektra album. "I had listened to his albums in high school and knew his rich, clear tenor and engaging playing well. I fell in love with Bob's finger-picking wizardry, so crisp and free."[131] At the Exodus in Denver, where they first met, Gibson "would haul out his banjo, open his mouth, and charm the birds out of the trees." Every night he would pull her aside for tips: "You gotta smile! You're killing 'em with all those serious songs. Make 'em listen, give 'em contrast!" she remembered. "He had a point; I was grim, tightlipped, all business."[132]

"Bob's role in establishing the singer-songwriter tradition is never properly acknowledged. His eye for talent, his unquestionable taste in songs, his enthusiasm, even his friendship—with Albert Grossman, with Odetta, with Joan Baez, with me—have slid somehow under the radar," Collins later wrote.[133]

Joan Baez's career broke open in one night when Gibson called on her to join him onstage at the first Newport Folk Festival in 1959. She was eighteen, unknown, and had just played her two-week stint at the Gate. "I got a crush on Bob, of course, and was terrified of him because he was at home in a den of sin called a nightclub, was marvelously sarcastic and funny, drank too much, sang both serious and silly songs, and cracked jokes," she wrote later.[134] Gibson performed his set before an audience of thirteen thousand people and then asked Baez to join him on two spirituals, "Virgin Mary Had One Son" and "Jordan River." The religiosity fit her outfit: a bright orange Mexican rebozo and gladiator sandals. The performance not only introduced her to a mass audience, but captured the attention of the national and international media, which gave her a lasting nickname: "The Barefoot Madonna." When she returned to Harvard Square the next week to play her weekly residency at Club 47, a line of people trailed around two corners of the block.[135] Her debut album on Vanguard appeared the following year.

Gibson's incorporation of the electric twelve-string guitar, which gave his music a richer and fuller sound, was an innovation in a movement dominated by the six-string guitar and banjo. The instrument's notoriety influenced the coming folk-rock generation, particularly Roger McGuinn, who was a teenager named Jim McGuinn when Gibson performed in his classroom at the Latin School of Chicago. "It was so inspiring that I immediately enrolled at the Old Town School of Folk Music. I bought a banjo and a guitar and became a folk singer, just based on Bob's performance," he said.[136] McGuinn would later revolutionize rock music with the full power of his twelve-string Rickenbacker and would credit Gibson as the link.

"Gibson was the first guy to take a 12-string knowing what Leadbelly had done with it, knowing how to jazz up a folk strum a little.

Gibson was a masterful strummer with a very, very light and agile touch. When he played, he sang very light and easy, but the 12-string was really slammin'. He wasn't using drums, but he was getting the effect by just the use of accents and things in his guitar style," said John Sebastian, founder of the Lovin' Spoonful.[137]

To folk singer Art Thieme, also a Gibson acolyte as a teenager, the guitarist's performances "got so infectious" when he transitioned from the banjo to the twelve-string. "He put chords together in ways that made emotions from the sounds of the changes like nobody else," he said.[138]

Albert Grossman introduced Gibson to Bob Camp, an actor and singer who was playing folk clubs in the Village. He had initially eyed them for the trio that became Peter, Paul and Mary, but it soon became obvious that the two men were better suited as a duo. In April 1961, after playing a string of dates at the Playboy Club in Chicago, they recorded the touchstone album of their career, *Gibson and Camp at the Gate of Horn*, on Elektra. The album, which featured Gibson playing banjo and his twelve-string guitar, and Herb Brown on bass, became a definitive document of the folk revival. Both Gibson and Camp were humorists who freely retooled traditional songs with contemporary lyrics and arrangements that cleverly played their voices against each other, but also pressed them together in harmonies that just a few years later were recognized in Simon & Garfunkel and the Smothers Brothers.[139] "Betty and Dupree," a speedy number about lovers who get involved in a jewel heist, is based on "Frankie and Johnny," while "The Thinking Man," a talking blues song based on "The Wayfaring Stranger," lampoons the anxieties and absurdities of the atomic era (to prove they can play it straight, they follow the update with the traditional version).

While the cover art pictures both singers dressed in the uniform of the day—sports jackets, ties, and white collared shirts—their music is tinged with subversion. Producer Jac Holzman's decision to include audience noise and stage interaction captures the loose mood of a late-night set at Chicago's Second City theater.[140] The song "Chicago Cops," co-written with Frank Hamilton, skewers police corruption: "The title of this song is 'I Think It's a Terrible Shame That It Only Takes 10,000 Crooks to Ruin the Reputation of One Honest Cop,'" Gibson quips. "The Thinking Man" follows John Henry, a village idiot who discovers a perfect job in the corporate world "at the *Chicago Tribune* thinking up thoughts of the day," Gibson explains. "For a while, he had a job at the Atomic Energy Commission thinking up bombs," answers Camp. One song, "Butternut Hill," a rewrite of the Irish ballad "Johnny Has Gone for a Soldier," mentions Frances Faye, a lesbian cabaret performer who often referenced her sexuality in code but was not yet fully out of the closet: "Me oh my, ah well a-day / Johnny's gone the other way / Now he's just like Frances Faye," they sing, followed by audience gasps.[141] Fay filed a $500,000 lawsuit against both men in January 1962, saying the song caused her "irreparable injury."[142] All copies were yanked from the shelves, and the song was replaced in future pressings.

In his stream-of-consciousness liner notes, *Playboy* cartoonist and songwriter Shel Silverstein described the Gibson and Camp scene at the Gate as a bacchanal:

Gibson would be up there cool and cocky, playing that 12-string and singing and Camp would be like a little rooster with his head back screaming and bouncing up and down and it was really something. After the show we would be out front, Gibson, Camp and Joel something, and the bartender with the mustache and Ira and Inman and Camp's chick. . . . Ginger or Camp's chick Margaret or Gibson's chick Gloria or Gibson's chick Patty or Gibson's chick whatever the hell their names were I don't even remember their names and there was a lot of booze being sopped up between sets and a hell of a lot of musical chairs being played with the girls around there . . .

And that is where we would sit and booze and talk about the new songs we were going to collaborate on and plan the party that would start around 3 o'clock in the morning—maybe at Gibson's room, at that whore hotel he was staying in or in Camp's apartment which was some girl's apartment or at somebody elses [*sic*] house, sometimes the waitresses. That bar was really the social center for the hip crowd. Gibson and Camp were the social directors. And they would sit there and whisper and work up wild scenes that couldn't possibly turn out as great as they sounded.[143]

Judy Collins opened many of the duo's shows. On a night she was too drunk to walk back to her room at the Cass Hotel, Gibson offered her his handgun for protection. Inside her room, Collins held the gun straight, and it discharged. Frightened, she ran to the window and expected to hear police sirens. But this was Chicago in winter: "No one in the street looked up," she said. The next night she returned the gun to Gibson and told him what had happened. "He laughed and told me I didn't know how to handle a gun," she said. Then, incredibly, the gun fired again in her hand and put a bullet in one of the club's back doors.[144]

The party didn't last. Despite the success of the album, Gibson and Camp remained a duo for only two years before drinking and drugs took hold. Camp moved to Los Angeles, changed his first name to Hamilton, and became a successful character actor in film and television. Gibson turned in one more album for Elektra, but struggled with a heroin addiction throughout the 1960s and into the 1970s. Despite appearances on network television, publishing deals, and constant touring, he reverted to the street hustling of his earlier life. Drugs were never recreational to him, he later wrote; he needed them just so he could persevere. Quitting never took. "I remember looking at my arm and saying, 'Why'd I do that? Why?'"[145]

Gibson had used amphetamines to get him through years of touring, but with heroin, he found the perfect treatment for his anxiety. "I took to it like a duck to water. I thought it was wonderful," he said.[146] At the same time, Grossman was shifting his priorities from Gibson and Odetta to Peter, Paul and Mary and Bob Dylan, who represented greater potential. Gibson, "immature and crazy," felt threatened. "I was incapable of dealing with it," he said.[147]

His addiction often forced him to sell instruments for cash and borrow guitars when he had none. In 1965, Gibson hired Skip

Haynes, later of the rock group Aliotta Haynes Jeremiah, to accompany him on bass for a week of shows at the Plugged Nickel in Old Town. On the last night, Gibson told the young musician he didn't have the $300 he owed him, but could give him something better: $80 in cash and his Vega twelve-string guitar, the very one he is pictured holding on the *Gibson and Camp at the Gate of Horn* album cover. Haynes, who had grown up idolizing both Gibson and that album, didn't think twice. "I would have sold my car for that instrument," he said.[148]

Gibson's habit shifted his priorities away from music, and what followed that decade was the fallout: missed shows, stints in jail, police busts. "He was unreliable, and he wanted to be reliable. He tried really hard, but he had a great deal of trouble kicking," said Holzman, who dropped him in 1964 after his fourth and final Elektra album.[149] McGuinn recalled living in Los Angeles and receiving a late-night phone call from Gibson asking him to help him score. "It was really upsetting," McGuinn recalled. "Here he was, my idol, calling me to get him some heroin."[150] Gibson was living in New York City when he quit the music business in 1966 and moved his family upstate to get clean. That didn't last, and he went back on the road. In August 1969, he made headlines in Chicago when he was arrested in a Marina City apartment for possession of hypodermic needles and drugs. It was three months before his fortieth birthday.[151]

Gibson had a final opportunity for a comeback in 1970 when Capitol tried to relaunch him into the looming singer-songwriter era with a new album. The cover art of *Bob Gibson* pictured the singer in denim and cowboy boots and reclining in a Prairie-style chair with a shaggy dog at his feet. The album was primed to fit Gibson into the country-rock scene by accompanying him with the young guns of that era: McGuinn, Crosby, Chris Hillman, "Sneaky Pete" Kleinow, and Bernie Leadon, who collectively represented the Byrds, the Flying Burrito Brothers, and the Eagles.[152] Despite that star power, the comeback would never get off the ground. Gibson had lifted the song "Sam Stone" off a demo tape by a Chicago up-and-comer named John Prine, who had reportedly not given Gibson his permission because he had already recorded his own version for his debut on Atlantic Records, due out the following year. Even though Prine was credited on the album, Gibson had not registered the song with his publishing company. Capitol pulled the album after only 17,500 copies were pressed.[153]

Gibson finally entered recovery in 1978 and spent his last two decades playing folk shows and festivals, collaborating with Shel Silverstein, and releasing new music without the pretense of becoming a star. He started producing folk shows for children, created a stage show about Carl Sandburg, and in 1986, reunited with Camp. They would perform intermittently into the next decade.

"When he came back, his audience was gone," remembers his longtime friend Tom Paxton. "The harsh truth is that he lost the edge that he had when he was killing himself. There was that outlaw edge when he and Camp were doing drugs, which was gone. He was content, but it was gone. He never got that audience back."[154]

On September 27, 1994, after Gibson was diagnosed with progressive supranuclear palsy, a rare neurological disorder that affects the brain, a long list of friends, including Camp, McGuinn, and Peter, Paul and Mary, played a benefit at the Vic Theatre, raising $50,000 to pay his medical expenses.[155] By then, Gibson's condition prevented him from playing the guitar, but he harmonized with Camp on a few songs before a standing-room-only crowd.[156]

One week before his death, on September 28, 1996, Gibson hosted a farewell party in a conference room at the Sheraton North Shore in Northbrook.[157] "This may be the last chance I have to see many of you," he wrote in an email invitation. "I won't be able to play and sing with you, but I'm really looking forward to being an audience of one!"[158] Shel Silverstein, Roger Ebert, Studs Terkel, and others shared remembrances in what Ebert later described as a wake for a living person. In front of his friend, immobilized in a wheelchair, Silverstein told the room how profound Gibson's influence had been, not just on him, but on everyone who heard him play during those golden Gate years.

"He set the time for us," Silverstein said. "To be there was to be at the best place in the world. . . . I've never known anything better."[159]

As with prominent Chicago jazz clubs like the Pershing Lounge, Mr. Kelly's, the London House, and the Blue Note, the Gate of Horn became a national brand and a popular spot for live recordings. Odetta, Gibson and Camp, Memphis Slim, Martha Schlamme, and David Troy all recorded live albums there. Although the club would continue to be associated with Grossman even after his departure to New York, the programming would broaden to include sketch comedy from the Second City, stand-up comedians, cabaret revues, a Leonard Bernstein one-act opera, and the "Monday Omnibus" hosted by Studs Terkel, which featured "singers, guitarists, comics, satirists, storytellers—anything that qualifies as entertainment."[160]

Owner Alan Ribback pressed for more stage plays and presented short works headed for Broadway. He also integrated the Gate, both on and off stage. In 1959, the Gate featured Barbara Dane, a White vocalist from Detroit who had already established her name on the West Coast circuit, performing with Louis Armstrong, who told *Time* she was a "gasser."[161] Her band featured bassist Willie Dixon, the staff songwriter at Chess Records, and Memphis Slim on piano. Her Gate performance landed Dane a five-page spread in *Ebony*, a first for a White performer in the Black culture magazine. Subtitled "Blonde Keeps Blues Alive," the spread described her as "making a name for herself in a realm of the entertainment world once thought to be the exclusive property of the Negro Race" and through which "a lot of dark-skinned people hope to keep the blues alive and the royalties flowing."[162]

The *Ebony* writer remarked that Dane had already lost gigs in Dallas and Las Vegas for playing with Black musicians. Her outspoken thoughts on race probably didn't help. "This was sung at a time when, believe it or not, it was legal for one person to actually own another human being. Boy, you think people are sick now!" was her introduction to one song at the Gate. "Such comments do not always endear her to club management," *Ebony* noted.[163]

As early as 1960, the Gate held benefits for college scholarships for Black youth in the South,[164] and it is listed alongside the Sutherland in Bronzeville as participating in a fundraising night for the Congress of Racial Equality.[165] The club also gave the first out-of-town break to Bill Cosby, who was then honing his routines between folk acts at the Gaslight Café in New York. Cosby remembered Ribback showing up at the Village club in 1963. He took one look at Cosby and made his decision: "I want this guy."[166]

> The guy sent me a round-trip ticket and paid me one hundred fifty dollars a week (I was making sixty dollars at week at the Gaslight Café). I thought, "This is show biz! I'm already head of the game. I've made more money than my father made last year!" . . . I open for Oscar Brown Jr. Oscar and I sold the place out. The announcer says, "And now, one of the leading Negro comedians in the world, Mr. Bill Cosby!"
>
> I come out, I've got thirty-five minutes of material planned; I don't get into any of it. I ad-lib and the people fall out of their chairs. They're loving me; I'm loving them. And I do two weeks there. Alan Ribback brings me back in August and I open for a group called the Terriers. I do the same thing; I just have a ball.[167]

Neither Grossman nor Ribback may have explicitly intended for the Gate to integrate Chicago nightlife, but their programming choices were often pioneering. The best example was when Grossman invited Maya Angelou from New York to Chicago to open for the Irish folk group the Clancy Brothers and Tommy Makem for a two-week engagement. The future poet, activist, and author of *I Know Why the Caged Bird Sings* was a struggling calypso singer at the time, and the money, she later said, paid for two months' rent.[168]

She arrived at the Gate during the headliners' afternoon rehearsal. They were singing the Irish street ballad "The Wearing of the Green," which laments the 1798 Irish Rebellion against the

British. One line caught her ear: "The shamrock is forbid by law / to grow on Irish ground."

"If the words Negro and America were exchanged for shamrock and Irish, the song could be used to describe the situation in the United States. The Clancy Brothers already had my admiration when we met backstage," she later wrote. On opening night she watched the Irish group with Odetta, jazz pianist Oscar Brown Jr., and jazz vocalist Amanda Ambrose. Together they "made joyful noises as the Irish singers told their stories."[169] Over those two weeks, the engagement briefly linked two otherwise disparate worlds, which in 1960 was not common in deeply segregated Chicago, let alone the nation as a whole. Angelou remembered:

> Closing night had been a hilarious celebration. The Clancy Brothers' fans had found room to accept my songs, and the black people who had come to hear me had been surprised to find that not only did they enjoy the Irish singers' anger, they understood it. We had drunk to each other's resistance.[170]

Angelou later discovered she was booked on the same return flight to New York as her new Irish friends. The trip, she remembered, "was riotous." "Many passengers were incensed that four white men and a black woman were laughing and drinking together, and their displeasure pushed us toward silliness."[171]

The Gate also booked local Black folk artists like Willie Wright. Wright had been a teenager in the city's thriving doo-wop scene—he was in a group called the Quails alongside future soul-music great Jerry Butler.[172] Upset that none of his groups had achieved success, he picked up a guitar and transformed himself into a folk singer. *I Sing Folk Songs*, declared the title of his 1958 debut album. At only twenty-three, Wright sang in an ethereal tenor, often rising into the high registers and using vocal accents like grunts, hiccups, and moans, and the reverb on the recording bathed the minimalist setting in a holy glow. Wright recorded a follow-up, *I'm On My Way*, for Argo, the pop/jazz division of the seminal blues label Chess Records.

It featured some Gate regulars, like Old Town School of Folk Music teacher Ray Tate on guitar, and a song by Bob Gibson. Both records served as an important bridge between folk music and soul, setting the stage for future singer-songwriters like Terry Callier.

CITY HALL CRACKS DOWN

But as the Gate gained national prominence, it would be confronted by inevitable bad luck, and by City Hall.

An early morning fire destroyed the roof, fifth, and fourth floors of the Rice Hotel on April 8, 1959, forcing a hundred guests to take refuge at the YMCA across the street.[173] The Gate took on several feet of water and closed for two months. During that time, Grossman sold the club to Ribback, who reopened on June 16 with Bob Gibson on the bill, along with Bill Daily, a comic, and Joan Baez.[174] Two years later, on April 23, 1961, Ribback reopened again at 1036 North State. The new space was larger, above ground, and had already served as home to several clubs: the Miami, the Club St. Elmo, and Lou Forrest's. "Terraced and streamlined, beautifully lit and intelligently focused on the second floor stage, it promises to be one of the town's most interesting evening retreats," the *Chicago Tribune* predicted.[175]

But not for long. In two years, Ribback would be out, and one year after that, the city would padlock the door. The club's demise can be traced to a December 5, 1962, performance by comedian Lenny Bruce, who had been through Chicago many times before, but at that time was getting arrested for using profanities onstage and pushing the envelope with his material. Ribback had booked Bruce for five weeks starting in late November and had prepared Chicagoans for what to expect. A sign over a door warned, "Let the buyer beware."[176]

The warning wasn't enough. More than a third of the way into Bruce's set that night, Chicago police detective Arthur Tyrrell stood up in the audience of thirty people.[177] "Show's over, ladies and gentlemen," he can be heard saying on a recording made that night.[178]

He and two other detectives planted in the room tell everyone to have a seat so they can check IDs to catch minors. They do catch one: a sixteen-year-old girl.[179] The house music comes on, a mournful jazz saxophone plays. Bruce, in a mock Russian accent, says, "Ladies and gentlemen, we now have new star of our show."[180]

Bruce was charged with obscenity and contributing to the delinquency of a minor.[181] Ribback and bartender Herbert O'Brien were charged with keeping or being inmates in a disorderly house.[182] Also arrested and charged with disorderly conduct were two audience members: Roger Pittman of Elmwood Park and George Carlin, the future comedy star who would later say the event "had a radicalizing effect" on him.[183]

"Purposely I arranged to be almost the last going out. The policeman said, 'I wanna see your ID.' I said, 'I don't believe in identification. Sorry.' And I tried to give some kind of fucking stupid drunk speech. The cop grabbed me by the collar and pants in the old buncheroo fashion and hustled me down the stairs and through the lobby to the front door," Carlin remembered.[184]

Soon it became clear to Ribback that the Gate was now a target of the Irish Catholic hierarchy that ruled the city at the time and had taken offense at Bruce's material mocking the Vatican. "I'm not doing this as a cop, I'm doing it as a Catholic," one of the arresting officers told Ribback that night.[185] Later, when Bruce was released on bail and continued his Gate residency, a police official showed up to convince Ribback to fire the comedian or lose his liquor license. "He mocks the Pope," the cop said. "I'm here to tell you your license is in danger. We're going to have someone here watching every show."[186]

Ribback didn't budge, so the Gate's fate was sealed. "Gate of Horn's Liquor License Up to Mayor," the *Chicago Tribune* announced on January 31, 1963.[187] Chicago Mayor Richard J. Daley, a devout Irish Catholic from Bridgeport, had ten days to rule. Novelist Nelson Algren was one of the witnesses who defended both Bruce and the Gate on First Amendment grounds before the city liquor commission.[188] But nothing worked: Daley revoked the license on February 9, 1963, for fifteen days.[189] Ribback sold the club the next month and left Chicago for good.

New Gate owners Hal Stein and Rudy Orisek were already business partners in local broadcasting. *International Café*, their hour-long weekly television show, aired on WGN and featured popular folk stars such as Peter, Paul and Mary, Tommy Makem, Theodore Bikel, Odetta, and the Clancy Brothers, as well as singers from Europe, Mexico, Russia, and elsewhere, performing in a setting that emulated a European café. "Starring foreign folk singers is serving a kind of moral purpose. When one group understands the talent and artistry of an unfamiliar tradition, then peoples and cultures begin to understand each other," Orisek explained.[190]

Their new proprietorship of the Gate gave Orisek and Stein access to emerging talent they could book for both their club and their television program. It's no coincidence that in July 1963, just four months after they took control of the Gate, they launched *Folk-fest*, a live half-hour show, also on WGN, that emulated *Hootenanny*, the popular national hit.[191] On the set, well-heeled young couples in suits and cocktail dresses sat with drinks at bar tables. Orisek's live narration at the top of each episode was a gauzy attempt to summarize the folk trend:

> America is a song. From the wide Pacific Ocean to the rock bound shore of the Atlantic. From the Alleghenies and the Appalachians to the Great Lakes to the Great Plains and beyond. Sometimes it's played on an old guitar and sometimes on a guitar that's held together with determination and a few strings. But wherever you go, you can hear a song that is America.[192]

When Stein and Orisek reopened the club in March 1963, they promised musical unknowns who were unlikely to stir up any trouble. Their reputation for presenting "clean" entertainment across established local radio and television stations helped. "The club was put up for sale, but the only person who could obtain it and the licenses you needed to run it had to have a squeaky-clean reputation . . . well, guess who that was?" Orisek later said.[193]

But a heavy police presence remained. Performers at the new Gate knew they had to watch what they said. David Somerville, co-founder of the Canadian doo-wop group the Diamonds in the previous decade, was booked to open the Gate as David Troy, a stage name he adopted to launch a folk career. He remembered:

> Someone at the club said to me that "the cops around here can be bought." That if you're out driving, get stopped and you offered a bribe, you could get out of a ticket. As a matter of fact, about a few days after that, I got stopped. And I said, "Is there any reason that I could give to work things out?" And he said, "You'll have to have at least twenty good reasons." I reached into my pocket and gave him a twenty-dollar bill and I drove away. I wanted to tell that story onstage, which would have been very, very dangerous. So I didn't.[194]

The *Chicago Tribune* tried to help boost the new Gate's chances of survival, suggesting it was a throwback to the club's heyday when it was possible to catch rising stars like Troy on the way up: "If the Gate of Horn can maintain a policy like this, of low budget shows that crackle with enthusiasm and talent, it can't lose."[195]

It lost. On February 13, 1964, the city's revenue department padlocked the club's doors and held an auction to satisfy a $5,235 debt in cabaret taxes. All that was left of the Gate after eight years was 189 bottles of whiskey and ninety tables.[196]

Incredibly, the Gate of Horn name would resurface in 1968 when Henry Norton opened a new Gate in Lake View, at 3144 North Broadway. An advertising executive who retired from the industry in 1959 to get into the club and eatery business—he owned many Rush Street clubs including Aide's, LePub, Alfie's, Shuckers, and later the Chicago Chop House—Norton announced a policy change for the Gate in November 1972: folk acts would no longer be welcome, and he would feature only soft rock or other "contemporary sounds rather than folk music."[197] He also added a dance floor. The reason: good business.

"Our present physical layout makes it difficult for a single per-former," Norton told a reporter. "Unless you feature in incredibly sensational, well-known groups, the people in Chicago do not sup-port them."[198]

SETTING THE STAGE
FOR THE NEXT GENERATION

The Gate of Horn name may still have filled seats, but for most people involved in the Grossman and Ribback years, its relevance had long expired. In 1974, Roger McGuinn, newly out of the Byrds, recorded a musical tribute to the club, which largely honored Bob Gibson, his early mentor: "How I wish that I was there / Standin' at the bar / Listenin' to Mr. Gibson play / On his fine guitar / It's a big old twelve-string / And it went like this," he sings before launching into an imitation of Gibson's technique.[199]

The more lasting legacy of the Gate may have come from its role in nurturing informal social networks for Chicago musicians to meet, learn from each other, and collaborate.

On May 26, 1957, Win Stracke played the first night of a nearly two-week stand at the Gate, filling in for Bob Gibson. To accompany him, he hired Richard Pick, a classical guitarist and composer more commonly found in recital halls around town, and who had been the first guitarist to perform with the Chicago Symphony Orchestra.[200]

Choosing a guitarist from the classical world suited Stracke: his own baritone voice was familiar to Chicago folk audiences, but he also performed solo classical work at the Fourth Presbyterian Church and sang with the Chicago City Opera Company. At age forty-nine, Stracke had already lived many lives: as an ensemble singer on the WLS *Barn Dance*, a World War II veteran, a local the-ater performer, a television actor and children's program host, a victim of the Communist blacklist, and a folk song collector and instructor. But at the Gate that spring, he would unknowingly start on the path toward his most enduring legacy through an unlikely encounter with two people he appeared to have little in common with: Frank Hamilton, the Gate's wiry and well-respected house guitarist, nearly thirty years his junior, and Dawn Greening, a suburban homemaker and folk music evangelist.

The three were of different backgrounds, generations, and temperaments, but their chance meeting would lead to Chicago's most towering contribution to American roots music from that decade onward: a not-for-profit school where the music no longer had to struggle under the uncertainty of tavern life, city politics, or the mob, but would give ordinary people of any background the opportunity to learn and make music among peers. Bars, coffeehouses, and nightclubs would continue to play important roles in Chicago, as they would in any city, but nothing existed on either coast that could match what the Old Town School of Folk Music had to offer: an institution of communal music learning that would continue developing folk music long after rock and roll had forced it off the national stage.

WIN STRACKE AND
THE OLD TOWN SCHOOL
OF FOLK MUSIC

On June 14, 1990, Win Stracke sat in his room at the North Shore Retirement Hotel in Evanston, Illinois, answering questions from Mark Dvorak, a young folk music teacher who had been dispatched to collect the eighty-two-year-old's life story in five hundred words for a newsletter. They had just returned from lunch at a hotel restaurant. "Everybody knew him," Dvorak remembered. "We walked down the hall and it was all 'Hi Win! Hi Win! Hi Win!'" Over soup, Stracke had struggled to get the spoon to his lips with his trembling hand. He knew it was awkward to watch and made Dvorak comfortable by joking at his own expense.[1]

Back in Stracke's room, Dvorak started a recorder and began the first in a series of interviews he would conduct with Stracke that summer. Stracke's memory was sometimes shaky. He told Dvorak that the Old Town School of Folk Music had opened on December 1, 1937. Dvorak corrected him: "1957." "1957," Stracke repeated.[2] Between interviews, they did what folkies always do when they feel a connection with each other and the old songs: they sang together. Eleven months later, Stracke would die in that same room of natural causes. But as he spoke with Dvorak, taking long pauses between thoughts, his baritone voice still carried the dignity that had made him a pillar of Chicago cultural life for decades.

The Old Town School of Folk Music—the first folk music school in the United States and now the oldest still in operation—established Chicago as a primary center for the music during the 1950s folk revival. Stracke co-founded the school with Frank Hamilton, a wiry and enthusiastic guitar teacher from the West Coast, and Dawn Greening, a homemaker and folk music matron from Chicago's western suburbs. Together, they created a nonprofit school imbued with social consciousness: learning guitar or singing or dancing was considered a gateway to community. Before the Old Town School, music lessons were largely confined to private conservatories, accredited schools, and for-profit businesses. What still connects the Old Town School to Stracke's original vision is not necessarily the style of music heard there, but the populist approach to teaching music that continues to thrive in its classrooms and concert halls.

"Here we teach guitar and we teach banjo certainly, but most importantly, we teach the simple and exalted joy of the music that comes from the hills and valleys, the meadows and the mills, the fields and the hearts of people everywhere," Stracke told an interviewer in 1969. "Folk music doesn't belong to black folks or white folks or blue folks, it belongs to people."[3]

Today, the notion of a "people's music" seems quaint. But in 1957, the ideal of music shared among races and across history was liberating, not just for the singer but also for those emboldened by the song. Once sharing and cultivating folk songs became linked to New Deal politics and the labor and civil rights movements, however, the "people's music" felt to many Americans like a tool of radicals intent on subverting the social order. Chicago was hardly isolated from the Communist scare that arose after World War II. All three founders of the Old Town School were under steady surveillance for many years by the Federal Bureau of Investigation. Stracke was ultimately blacklisted because of his associations with the radical left, which ended his lucrative television career and left him with a deep sense of sorrow he could never shake.

STRACKE'S EARLY LIFE
OF MULTITUDES

Win Stracke was a multifaceted figure in Chicago's cultural history: he sang bass harmony in a vocal quartet on the WLS *Barn Dance*, hymns as a soloist at the Fourth Presbyterian Church, labor songs at union rallies, commercial jingles for local businesses, and children's songs on local television while surrounded by live animals. He knew too well the inside of Old Town saloons, but he was also comfortable among the Gold Coast elite at Orchestra Hall and at any number of synagogues, schools, and churches when a singer of his caliber was needed for hire. His musical passion was regional: he wrote songs about Chicago winters, political cronyism, early Illinois history, and the state's rivers and prairies. When Illinois celebrated its sesquicentennial in 1968, the person chosen to write a new version of the state song was Stracke, the same man blacklisted a decade earlier during the McCarthy era.

On that June day in 1990, Stracke told Dvorak about the first song he had written, one he would sing with fellow troops while serving as a corporal in an anti-aircraft unit in Europe and North Africa during World War II.[4] Stracke searched for the words. After a first verse came another long pause. Then, in a faint voice, Stracke continued:

> Now someday soon, we'll start a second front
> and we'll cross right over the Rhine
> and we'll take Schicklgruber, Hirohito, Mussolini
> and string 'em to a damn good line

The last time he sang that song, Stracke told Dvorak, was with Pete Seeger at Orchestra Hall.

Chicago's Old Town neighborhood defined Stracke. Not only was it the place of his early childhood, but as an adult he returned to live there at different times in his life. He was born February 10, 1908, in Lorraine, Kansas, to German immigrant parents, the youngest of seven children. His father, Robert Stracke, was a conservative

Baptist minister who moved his family to Chicago and settled in Old Town, where he operated the Second German Baptist Church at the corner of Willow and Burling.

Those early years in the bustling immigrant neighborhood gave Stracke a sense of community. Nearly forty years after the Great Chicago Fire, Old Town still had the rebounding energy of a city bridging the Old World and the New. All day the streetcars on Halsted rattled by, as did the trains on the elevated line that took the triple curve at North Avenue and Halsted. But horse-drawn wagons also passed down Burling, newly paved with granite blocks, as did two-handled carts pushed by shouting peddlers. Stracke's earliest memory of a musical group was one he called the Hungry Five, who showed up at the family home to play cornet, alto saxophone, clarinet, trombone, and bass. His mother, in a gesture to their dignity, folded a quarter into a piece of paper and gave it to one of her children to present to their leader.

Stracke remembered New Year's Eve, 1913, when as a five-year-old he attended a basement service at his father's church. The congregation sang hymns common at the time—"When the Roll Is Called Up Yonder," "We're Marching to Zion," "Safe in the Arms of Jesus." A man confessed his sins of attending movies and taking drink, followed by an older woman who thanked God for the wine she drank to ease her aching bones. Then, minutes before midnight, silent prayer. At the stroke of twelve, night watchmen from surrounding factories pulled their steam whistles and the night was filled with magnificent noise. The adults hugged, kissed, shook hands, and gathered around the piano to sing in fellowship. "It was wild and glorious," Stracke said.[5]

As a young man, he was set for adventure. After graduating from high school in 1926, he drove a Model T Ford to Thermopolis, Wyoming, to work on an oil rig at $25 per week. The work was rough and the environment harsh. He met a coal miner named Flat Wheel Harry who dragged a lame leg, the result of a bar fight or a mining accident. Flat Wheel Harry was a member of the Industrial Workers of the World, a "Wobbly," who spun long yarns about Babe the

Blue Ox and taught Stracke songs like "The Big Rock Candy Mountain." Characters like Harry didn't exist in the Chicago Stracke had known, and he later said his new friend was the first person who gave him the sense of oral tradition in American folklore.[6]

Stracke soon felt comfortable enough to perform popular songs at the Ritz, a public tavern and brothel, where he enjoyed watching the reactions of men who were twice his age or older. But he didn't stay long in Wyoming. Soon he was in California, where he joined the engine room crew on an intercoastal freighter. In his late twenties, he jumped among similar jobs—fruit picker, gas station attendant, suit salesman—all the while learning new songs and forming a sense of class structure that would broaden his horizons past his respectable middle-class roots.

In 1931, Stracke was back in Chicago and had found a job on the WLS *Barn Dance* as bass singer for a quartet called the Melody Men. The work earned him $40 a week.[7] As Flat Wheel Harry had taught him the tall tales of American folklore, the *Barn Dance* introduced him to the corresponding worlds of country and folk music. "I liked it. Of course, my peers, who were serious singers, would say, 'Hmmph, hillbilly music!' and dismiss it. But to me there was magic in it."[8] Each Saturday night at the Eighth Street Theater he watched *Barn Dance* star Bradley Kincaid sing "Barbara Allen" in response to an outpouring of weekly requests. It was then that Stracke understood how an unadorned presentation, a simple melody, and a poignant story in verse could hold people captive. Fifty years later, he told Mark Dvorak that "Barbara Allen" was an example of how certain songs "seemed to have entered the subconscious of American life."[9]

While appearing on the *Barn Dance* periodically, Stracke grew dissatisfied with the way the show's producers allowed advertisers to exploit the music in their on-air plugs. Alka-Seltzer especially rankled him when it used a country fiddler to play background music during sponsored messages, which he felt cheapened the music. The ads "injected showmanship and comedy," he complained, "and the folk content was corrupted."[10] For Stracke, this would become a lifelong refrain.

FIG. 1 John Lair's talent as a showman and business manager helped make WLS radio's *Barn Dance* a major catalyst in the early commercialization of country music. The Kentucky native built the show around an imagined rural America and scouted native Appalachian performers to bring it to life. JOHN LAIR PAPERS, SOUTHERN APPALACHIAN ARCHIVES, SPECIAL COLLECTIONS AND ARCHIVES, HUTCHINS LIBRARY, BEREA COLLEGE.

FIG. 2 The first mass-marketed country music star was Bradley Kincaid, a Kentucky native who joined the *Barn Dance* in 1926. Promoted as "the Kentucky Mountain Boy," Kincaid is responsible for preserving nearly three hundred folk songs between 1928 and 1948. BRADLEY KINCAID PAPERS, SOUTHERN APPALACHIAN ARCHIVES, SPECIAL COLLECTIONS AND ARCHIVES, HUTCHINS LIBRARY, BEREA COLLEGE.

FIG. 3 One of John Lair's greatest successes was recasting Myrtle Eleanor Cooper and Scott Wiseman, both North Carolina natives, as Lulu Belle and Scotty, one of the first harmony duos in country music. The couple became one of the highest-paid country acts in the United States, starred in numerous Hollywood films, and enjoyed a prolific recording career. KEVIN PARKS EARLY COUNTRY MUSIC RESEARCH, SOUTHERN APPALACHIAN ARCHIVES, SPECIAL COLLECTIONS AND ARCHIVES, HUTCHINS LIBRARY, BEREA COLLEGE.

FIG. 4 A wrangler rides a bucking bronco during a rodeo at Soldier Field in 1926. Promoter John Van "Tex" Austin, who also staged rodeos at Madison Square Garden and Wembley Stadium, first brought rodeos to Soldier Field a year earlier. © SUN-TIMES MEDIA, LLC. ALL RIGHTS RESERVED. CHICAGO SUN-TIMES/CHICAGO DAILY NEWS COLLECTION, CHICAGO HISTORY MUSEUM.

FIG. 5 Chicago Mayor William Hale "Big Bill" Thompson (*second from right*) spread his childhood love of cowboy culture across the city. Called "the Cowboy Mayor" by the press during Prohibition, Thompson promoted cowboy regalia and music, regularly appeared on horseback, and once rode a horse into City Council chambers. CHICAGO DAILY NEWS NEGATIVES COLLECTION, CHICAGO HISTORY MUSEUM.

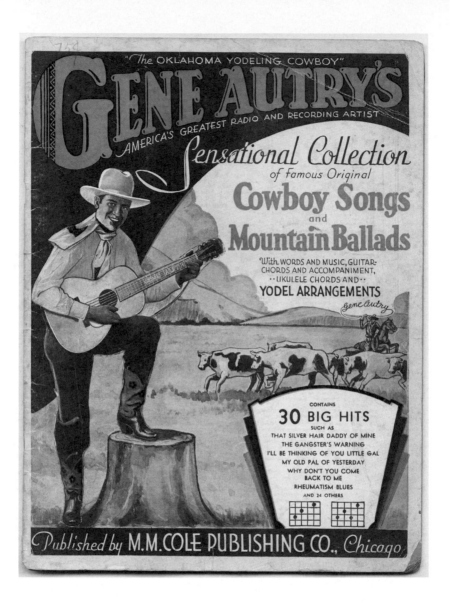

FIG. 6 In 1932, Chicago publisher M. M. Cole launched the first of many country music songbooks featuring Gene Autry, who had moved to Chicago a year earlier on the advice of Art Satherley, an A&R man for the American Record Corporation. In Chicago, Autry developed his cowboy image, recorded his first million-selling hit, and hosted a morning show on WLS. PRIVATE COLLECTION.

FIG. 7 The Windy City Ramblers play for square dancers in Grant Park in 1974. The Chicago Park District started hosting citywide square dances in the 1940s.

FIG. 8 Bob Gibson performing at the Crystal Palace in 1963. The folk revival made him a national star, and his banjo and twelve-string guitar playing directly influenced David Crosby and Roger McGuinn, among others.

FIG. 9 Dawn Greening, a folk music fan from Oak Park, and Frank Hamilton, the house guitarist at the Gate of Horn, helped co-found the Old Town School of Folk Music in 1957. Here, they exchange words at Hamilton's farewell concert in 1962 when he left to join the Weavers.

FIG. 10 *Facing* By the time Win Stracke helped launch the Old Town School of Folk Music in 1957, he had lived multiple lives as a classical singer, children's performer, actor, and broadcaster—all of which ended when the FBI classified him as a Communist. The school became his second chapter in life and in music. Here he performs at the inaugural University of Chicago Folk Festival on February 4, 1961.

FIG. 11 *Above* Old Town School banjo instructor Fleming Brown (*right*) was among the first in Chicago to expose a new generation to the Appalachian banjo style he revered. In 1962, he invited Frank Proffitt (*left*), the Appalachian banjoist known for preserving the song "Tom Dooley," to the school for a conversation and concert.

FIG. 12 When Albert Grossman approached Ella Jenkins to manage her, Jenkins turned him down. "That didn't seem free," she said. Jenkins, here performing for children in her Hyde Park home in 1961, carved her own path by becoming the first folk artist who recorded exclusively for children. Starting in 1957, she recorded more than sixty albums, and in 2004, she received a Grammy Lifetime Achievement Award. © CHICAGO HISTORICAL SOCIETY, PUBLISHED ON OR BEFORE 2017, ALL RIGHTS RESERVED. CHICAGO HISTORY MUSEUM, RAEBURN FLERLAGE, PHOTOGRAPHER.

FIG. 13 The New Lost City Ramblers—a folk revival trio from New York City—is directly responsible for building bridges in the early years of the University of Chicago Folk Festival. Maybelle Carter was fifty-four when Mike Seeger (*left*) of the Ramblers convinced her to play at the festival in 1964. With Seeger and John Cohen (*right*), she performed songs from the Carter Family's historic 1927 recording sessions. © CHICAGO HISTORICAL SOCIETY, PUBLISHED ON OR BEFORE 2017, ALL RIGHTS RESERVED. CHICAGO HISTORY MUSEUM, RAEBURN FLERLAGE, PHOTOGRAPHER.

FIG. 14 Before the urban renewal of the 1960s, Madison Street, just west of the Chicago Loop, was populated with honky-tonks like the New Buckingham Inn. Here, Arbie Gibson (*second from right*) poses with the club's house band, which includes (*from left*) Eddie Evans, Gene Bera, and Bill Balasty, in 1947. Two songs that a teenage Gibson sold to Gene Autry in 1933 became the cowboy singer's earliest hits. Jerry Lee Lewis, Elvis Presley, Roy Acuff, Ernest Tubb, and others later recorded Gibson's songs. PHOTOGRAPH COURTESY OF GREG GIBSON.

FIG. 15 *From left*, Curt Delaney, Bob Boyd, and Don Walls in the early 1960s. As the Sundowners, the trio performed five times a week between 1959 and 1989, entertaining tourists, celebrities, and conventioneers until eventually their marathon sets became requisite master classes for up-and-coming musicians eager to learn the music. "Watching those guys perform was like watching someone fill a glass of water—effortless, smooth, and perfect," remembered one. PHOTOGRAPH COURTESY OF JOHN RICE.

FIG. 16 Standing on Wilson Avenue in 1974, two men perform "Dueling Banjos" from the hit film *Deliverance*. "Almost as good as the pickers in the movie," remembers photographer Bob Rehak. By then, Uptown was crowded with Southern Whites seeking work. Sixty-five thousand Appalachians were living in Uptown alone by 1968. The Wooden Nickel, visible across the street, was a popular spot for live music. PHOTOGRAPH BY BOB REHAK.

FIG. 17 In 1967, musician Johnny Pitts opened a store in Uptown that sold instruments, songbooks, show wear, and even full suits designed by Nudie Cohn, known for outfitting Hank Williams and Porter Wagoner. Pitts, a guitarist who performed in the Madison Street honky-tonks, also broadcast a live country radio show from the store each Saturday that featured traveling acts like Hank Snow and Flatt & Scruggs. "Everything I ever wanted in my life I had in that store," Pitts said PHOTOGRAPH COURTESY OF JOHNNY PITTS AND LYNN STRAUCH.

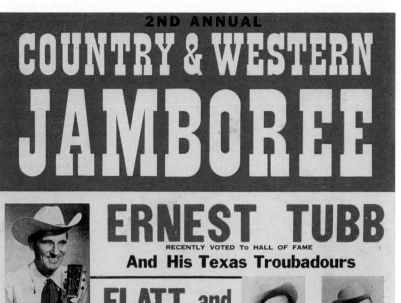

2ND ANNUAL
COUNTRY & WESTERN
JAMBOREE

ERNEST TUBB
RECENTLY VOTED To HALL OF FAME
And His Texas Troubadours

FLATT and SCRUGGS
and the Foggy Mountain Boys

Porter Wagoner & Norma Jean
& the Wagon Masters

Cal Starr

CAPT. STUBBY - M.C.
ROY STINGLEY - M.C.
JACK GREEN

Special Added Attraction "LITTLE BILLS"

Jimmy Martin

McCORMICK PLACE
ARIE CROWN THEATRE 23RD AND THE LAKE

TICKETS: $4.50 - 3.50 - 2.50 TAX INCL.
MAIL ORDERS enclosed self-addressed stamped envelope. Make Check or Money Order
payable to "Country and Western Jamboree", McCormick Place, Chicago, Illinois 60616
TICKETS ALSO AVAILABLE AT ALL: SEARS CUSTOMER CONVENIENCE
CENTERS OR BOX OFFICE AT McCORMICK PLACE
Additional Information Call: 327-6286 or Box Office at McCormick Place 225-6350

SUN., FEB. 6th
2:30 P.M. AND 7:30 P.M.

FIG. 18 Cal Starr, a Kentucky native, started out as a singer but later saw that the real money was in producing all-day country music concerts like the one advertised here. In the 1960s, he became the first promoter in Chicago to usher the music into large ballrooms and theaters. PHOTOGRAPH COURTESY OF CAL STARR.

FIG. 19 Bruce Kaplan stands on the balcony of "the Fish House," 1304 North Schubert Avenue, the home of his record label, Flying Fish, in 1980. Between 1974 and 1995, Flying Fish helped launch the careers of John Hartford, New Grass Revival, Tim O'Brien, and dozens of other folk and country artists. By 1979, the roster had twenty-five artists, had annual sales of $1 million, and helped earn a Grammy for Hartford. PHOTOGRAPH © MARC POKEMPNER.

The *Barn Dance* avoided direct political or social commentary, as did other network radio shows on which he worked: *The Chicago Theater of the Air*, *Alec Templeton Time*, *Hymns of All Churches*, and *Saturday Evening Symphony Hour*. Stracke satisfied that itch in 1938 by joining the Chicago Repertory Group, a theater company and school that produced works celebrating the labor movement. The company performed wherever they could: union halls, picket lines, and soup kitchens. One of Stracke's fellow actors was Studs Terkel. "Its audience was made up of teachers and social workers and cabdrivers," Terkel remembered. "It was the Great Depression and this was the theater of then."[11] Stracke impressed the group with his musical training and experience, even though Terkel later said he "looked like a banker."[12] The two men would become lifelong friends, collaborators, and supporters. "Studs was the person who radicalized me," Stracke said.[13]

World War II dispersed the group. Afterward, Terkel and Stracke returned to Chicago and, with Big Bill Broonzy and tenor Larry Lane, formed "I Come for to Sing," a folk revue that debuted in 1947. Then came television. The medium was in its infancy when Stracke played the role of a singing handyman on *Studs' Place*, a half-hour Terkel vehicle that launched on network television in 1949. Set in a cellar-level Chicago restaurant with Terkel as the proprietor, the show was largely improvisational, with story lines only loosely sketched before the live taping at a Merchandise Mart studio. Terkel chose Stracke because he wanted music woven into his plots. It helped that Stracke was as comfortable improvising lines as he was pulling his guitar off the wall and singing. Stracke's co-stars on the show included Chet Roble, a popular jazz pianist on the downtown nightclub circuit, and actress Beverly Younger, who Nelson Algren said had "more class than Eve, Joan of Arc, and the Virgin Mary put together."[14]

The show had no ambition but to portray the ordinary day-to-day drama of working people. The comedy was sweet, the tragedy gentle. In one episode, Terkel and Roble marvel at their new bowling shirts until Younger, in her role as Grace the waitress, discovers that there isn't one for Stracke. Terkel tells her he isn't invited to join their

team because his bowling isn't up to snuff. Both men worry about
how they're going to break it to their friend until Stracke bounces
into the restaurant with news that he's upped his score. After learning his friends have abandoned him, he sits down, picks up his guitar, and sings "Go 'Way From My Window," a song of loneliness and
loss by John Jacob Niles. In between verses, Younger cheers him up
enough that he agrees to see a movie with her. Then Terkel enters,
swallowing big yawns and reaching for a chair. He has mistaken
Stracke's sleeping pills for aspirin and now can't play in the tourna-
ment, making Stracke an accidental hero: he apologizes to Younger
for skipping their date and heads to the bowling alley with refreshed
purpose.[15]

The show lasted until 1951, when ABC abruptly canceled it. Terkel was blacklisted for participating in so-called radical events at
union halls. According to Terkel's FBI file, he had been under surveillance since 1945.[16]

FBI SURVEILLANCE:
A PROMISING CAREER STUMBLES

Stracke, too, was an FBI target. He was under intermittent surveillance between 1940 and 1972. Even though the records show he was
never charged with a crime, and his FBI file contains nothing more
than innuendo and anecdotal charges, the FBI's harassment over
decades inflicted serious damage, derailing his career as a singer
and affecting his mental health.

That FBI file, finally declassified in 2015, reveals the full, ugly
story of the FBI's pursuit of Stracke. In 1941, an informant in the
Office of Naval Intelligence warned the agency that Stracke was
"a fanatical Bundist, a leader of a 'cell' who meet religiously every
Wednesday night." FBI director J. Edgar Hoover told the Chicago
office that April that he worried Stracke "could do considerable
damage to defense work" if drafted into the Army.[17] Three months
later, Hoover's description of Stracke was updated to say the singer
"often stated that he hates America and that Germany and Russia are his idea of heaven."[18] Agents then dispatched local police to

interview Hertha Sibbach, Stracke's sister, in the western suburb of Maywood. She informed them that her brother's first marriage had ended because he complained about the government, although she hypothesized that her brother "was a good American citizen" who was simply corrupted by books their father owned.[19]

From there, the FBI instructed the Chicago Police Department to send officers knocking on doors. First up for a visit was John Depner, the janitor in Stracke's apartment building at 321 Webster. Depner said he had never heard Stracke make "any anti-American remarks, nor had ever he heard from anyone else that Mr. Stracke's interests were in any way un-American."[20] A dead end. Next was Agatha Lewis Stracke, his first wife. She confirmed that they had divorced, but dismissed the suggestion it was because he was a Communist. In fact, she told her questioners that Stracke "only had two bad faults—namely, he talked too much, saying many things just to hear himself talk to aggravate someone, and the other fault was that he was over-anxious to help the less fortunate." To make her point, she recalled the time Stracke noticed a homeless waif in Lincoln Park and brought him home for a bath and meal. The interview ended, the officer noted, when she grew "hysterical" and said the rumors about her former husband were being spread by people jealous of his success and determined to "ruin his career."[21]

The interviews continued with many others—the music director at the Fourth Presbyterian Church, Stracke's vocal instructor at the Fine Arts Building on Michigan Avenue, his employer at WBBM in the Wrigley Building, and regulars at the two Italian restaurants he was known to frequent along Taylor Street. None led anywhere.

Later in 1941, the FBI closed the case—for the time being. The following year, Stracke entered the US Army and spent three years in Europe as a corporal, returning home from the war with several medals, including six bronze stars, along with a spotless record. Yet in 1953, the FBI classified him as a Communist on the basis of the affiliations he had formed years earlier as a performer.[22] Over twelve pages in his file, each encounter is parsed with specificity: a singing date at a Communist Party convention sometime between

1934 and 1938, an appearance at an American Youth for Democracy event in 1947, a May Day rally in 1948, singing classes he conducted for the Progressive Party in 1948, his performance of the national and Soviet anthems at a celebration of the American Soviet Friendship organization at Orchestra Hall in 1945. His early participation in the Chicago Repertory Group was also noted. An informant said Stracke was "closely associated" with the Communist Party unit of the American Federation of Radio Artists, the labor union that routinely hired him to perform at meetings, birthdays, and even funerals.[23]

The scrutiny cost Stracke his living. In 1940, he was fired from the Fourth Presbyterian Church because it became known that he sang labor songs at a strike meeting for farm equipment workers. After delivering the bad news, the minister prayed with Stracke and then suggested he leave town and change his name.[24] After *Studs' Place*, Stracke bounced around on television until 1953, when he landed on *Animal Playtime*, a children's show on NBC that featured live animals borrowed each morning from Animal Kingdom, a store on the city's Northwest Side. The show became a hit, but was abruptly canceled in March 1954. He was also yanked from his role as the guitar-strumming philosopher Laif Flagle on *Hawkins Falls*, a daily soap opera that ran weekday mornings. The reason for both: he was blacklisted for his appearances at union halls.[25] The process began in October 1953, when NBC personnel manager Robert Kendall fed Stracke's personal information, including his Social Security number, to the FBI.[26]

ABC hired Stracke in 1955 to host *Time For Uncle Win*, another children's show. He was paid one-third of his previous salary. The show lasted a year.[27] The final straw was likely his naming by television writer and producer Kenneth Pettus at an executive session of the House Un-American Activities Committee in Los Angeles on October 14, 1955. In his testimony, Pettus said that as early as April 1942, Stracke was a member of a "Communist Party group which was connected with the entertainment industry."[28]

Stracke struck a weary tone when looking back at the persecu-

tion that cost him his livelihood and, for a long while, his reputation. "I accepted it as a product of the times. I've always felt that
Studs . . . reacted in a much more healthy way; he wanted to get up
and fight. But I didn't have strong feelings of anger, which I think I
should have had," he said.[29]

To support his family, he returned to the live performing circuit. A brochure he created to market his services did not mention
his television work, but rather emphasized qualities that churches,
schools, and civic organizations would find acceptable: his army
service, past appearances with the Women's Symphony and Grant
Park Symphony, and a repertoire that included oratorios by Bach,
Handel, Haydn, Verdi, and Brahms.[30] "There weren't a lot of
options," said his daughter Jane Bradbury. "It must have been horrible because the last thing he wanted to do was sing. Because he
was depressed."[31]

Stracke endured until 1957, when opportunity presented itself
in the form of the Gate of Horn, a new nightclub located downtown
that exclusively booked folk singers. Stracke by then had stopped
playing guitar. Union rules had not allowed him to accompany himself on television, and a pianist was best suited for his local recitals
of classical works. "Necessity was the mother of invention" was the
Chicago Tribune's explanation of the partnership Stracke formed
with Richard Pick, a classical guitarist from whom Stracke had
begun taking lessons.[32] Quick on his feet, Stracke put together a
program of folk music that he would sing to the Gate of Horn's late-
night clientele, with Pick accompanying him on guitar.

The duo lasted less than two weeks because they were hired only
as a substitute act for Gate star Bob Gibson. But that was enough
time for Stracke to hang around every night and listen to Jo Mapes,
another singer on the bill. What impressed him most was Frank
Hamilton, her tall, wiry, and bespectacled guitarist, a twenty-two-
year-old who looked half his years. Yet Hamilton had already packed
years of experience into his short life: he had learned guitar from
Woody Guthrie in Los Angeles, had played the folk circuit in New
York City, and had roamed the back roads of Southern states col-

lecting songs and learning about rural America. He took traditional music seriously, was committed to playing it, and was energetic about spreading its gospel. Stracke would later tell people how joyful Hamilton appeared to be, both as a person and through the sound he summoned through his fingers.

"I visualized a school. Frank Hamilton was the person," Stracke said later. "It was a whole new feeling."[33]

FRANK HAMILTON: THE OLD TOWN SCHOOL'S FIRST INSTRUCTOR

Born August 3, 1934, Frank Hamilton was fifteen when he met Woody Guthrie in 1950.[34] The teenager was a loner who had discovered in folk music a refuge from a household he had little in common with: his mother taught classical piano, and his stepfather worked odd jobs. He played trombone and was already performing in the LA City College Dance Band and sitting in with local Dixieland and jazz groups.[35] Folk music came into his life when he heard Pete Seeger sing "Hold the Line" on a 78 rpm record his aunt played for him, hoping to get her nephew interested in music she felt was more socially relevant than the classical music he toiled over at home. The song led Hamilton to the banjo, and the banjo led him to gigs in restaurants around Los Angeles with an informal group called the Sierra Folksingers, made up of musicians nearly three times his age. Its leader was a man named Bart van der Schelling, a Dutch-born singer and Spanish Civil War veteran who was prominent in the city's left-leaning folk scene.

At one venue off Santa Monica Boulevard, after the group had performed the English folk ballad "Sam Hall," a burly, bearded man who looked like he had tumbled off a mountain approached the teenager. "I like the way you sing, kid," he said. "I want to invite you to a party." The man was Will Geer, an actor who decades later would become familiar to millions of television viewers as Grandpa Walton on the CBS drama *The Waltons*, but at the time was a New York stage actor and labor rights activist credited with introducing Woody Guthrie to radical politics. Geer not only had brokered an introduction between Guthrie and novelist John Steinbeck at a film shoot, but had later organized a benefit concert in 1940 for the John Steinbeck Committee to Aid Farm Workers, an event that would introduce Guthrie to Pete Seeger at a time when both were relatively unknown. "You can date the renaissance of American folk song from that night," Alan Lomax said later.[36]

Hamilton agreed to the invitation and traveled up Topanga Canyon to a hootenanny at Geer's house, known as "a halfway house of sorts for lost souls and refugees from the political storms of the period."[37] He walked through the door and in one night, he met the most prominent figures of the folk era: Guthrie, Cisco Houston, and the Weavers, featuring Pete Seeger in the flesh.

There was no turning back. The introduction made Hamilton a true believer, and he returned time and again to Geer's home to accompany Guthrie on banjo and get lessons in harmonica. Signs of the Huntington's disease that would take the folk poet's life in 1967 appeared to Hamilton and others as slight tremors. At first they thought Guthrie was an alcoholic, but they didn't smell anything, nor did they see him take a drink. "He wasn't singing as well as when he did as a young man, but he still had a lot to say," Hamilton recalled.[38]

During that period Hamilton also got to know folklorist and teacher Bess Lomax Hawes—daughter to song collector John A. Lomax and sister to ethnomusicologist Alan Lomax, both of whom she had collaborated with on *Our Singing Country*, their influential 1941 anthology of traditional songs. When Hamilton showed up in her Santa Monica living room, she was making a living teaching UCLA extension classes in singing, folklore, and traditional instruments, using a method that was new to the West Coast folk scene. That method relied on community instruction designed to tear down the traditional conservatory approach. Instead of focusing on the individual, Lomax Hawes taught multiple students in the same room at once to clear away all differences in status due to class or ethnicity or gender. She was not interested in grooming stars or virtuosos, but instead emphasized rudimentary skills. She valued learning music by ear over learning on paper, and she taught songs, not notes. Instruments were there only to accompany the songs. Folk music was not just a craft, she emphasized, but a social expression that would make life better by strengthening communities.

Talking to *Sing Out!* in 1961, Lomax Hawes called singing "a natural thing, like speech, for which we need special training only in special circumstances. In fact, the first thing to know about singing is that it is an extension of speech." To teachers, she suggested positive interaction with students, not rebukes for mistakes. Her advice: "Use every device you can think of to encourage listening, relaxation and confidence."[39] In a perfect world, under her instruction, people would no longer be embarrassed to sing, but would open their mouths naturally in song to connect with strangers, and in doing so, would strengthen the greater good.

Through Hamilton, her teaching philosophy became the fundamental idea behind the Old Town School. Hamilton monitored her singing classes and helped her by accompanying the novice vocalists on his guitar or banjo. He found her warm, intellectually exciting, and given her East Coast pedigree and the renown of her family, strangely accessible. By the time he left Los Angeles in 1953, Lomax Hawes had convinced him that music could be far more than entertainment. Through teaching, it could be a catalyst for change.

"I wanted to be a performer, but I began to see teaching was an important thing to do," he said.[40]

Hamilton hitchhiked to New York to find work. That summer, he took a six-week road trip through the South, for the same reason many young people did during that era: to discover the America they had heard about through the Library of Congress field recordings the Lomax family had collected and popularized. His companion for the trip was Guy Carawan, a fellow folk singer in Greenwich Village with whom Hamilton had performed in the Sierra Folk Singers back in Los Angeles. Carawan had a car and planned to pick Hamilton up at Pete Seeger's house in Beacon, where he was staying temporarily. Before the trip, they met in a Harlem club to hear blues singer Brownie McGhee. There they bumped into Jack Elliott, a folk busker who had already hitchhiked out west and had returned transformed, in western wear and topped with a Stetson hat. Upon hearing their plans, Elliott begged to join them. "Oh hell, why not," Hamilton said.

The trip eroded the romanticism with which they, and many of their contemporaries on the Greenwich Village folk scene, had viewed the South, and gave them a deeper sense of the despondent and sometimes violent environment of the songs they had chosen to seek out.

Threatened with arrest for busking in Norfolk, they were driven out of Merry's Point, Virginia, by the sheriff and members of a local Ku Klux Klan chapter, who suspected they were labor agitators. Elliott's long hair and drifter attire didn't suggest otherwise. In New Orleans, Hamilton and Carawan had to spring Elliott from jail after he was arrested for vagrancy in the French Quarter. Wherever they went, locals "looked askance at anybody who didn't look squeaky clean," Hamilton said. "We were naïve and didn't have a clue. It opened up my ears and my eyes to what the world was like."[41]

In Asheville, North Carolina, they sought out Bascom Lamar Lunsford, the founder of the Asheville Folk Festival, who had introduced the five-string banjo to Pete Seeger in 1936 when Seeger was a teenager. Lunsford suspected they were Communists and complained bitterly of their kind sweeping through his part of the world, armed with tape recorders to collect songs for causes people like him didn't support. They left amused but dejected. "He's a shit and how," Carawan later said.[42]

Despite the hardships of being broke, almost homeless, and threatened by authorities almost everywhere they stopped, the three Northerners did their best to seek out music. Like Stracke in Wyoming, they found that hearing music performed by people in their homes, or against the backdrop of where it originated, gave it context and deepened their understanding of what gave it such power. Hamilton felt the hand of his former teacher Lomax Hawes, who pushed her students to value the song as opposed to the performance: "I wanted to learn who sang them. I was really curious who they were as people, what inspired them to keep the folk tradition alive in those areas," he said.[43]

In Maces Spring, Virginia, they appeared on the doorstep of A. P. Carter, the patriarch of the Carter Family, country music's earliest recording artists. They ate and sang together, and then Carter, sixty-one at the time, invited them to stay the night to rest up for the next day's drive. The boys took in two nights of country music at the *Grand Ole Opry* in Nashville, where the bill featured Roy Acuff, Hank Snow, Chet Atkins, Grandpa Jones, and country comedian David "Stringbean" Akeman.[44]

They mingled with kindred spirits down the road at the Highlander Folk School in Monteagle, Tennessee, a tiny oasis of leftist values atop a mountain in the Cumberland Plateau. The visit would inspire Carawan to return six years later to remake the school, originally formed to organize the labor movement, into a galvanizing force for training civil rights workers the following decade. His work there helped make songs like "We Shall Overcome," "We Shall Not Be Moved," and "Keep Your Eyes on the Prize" into global anthems.

By the end of the six weeks, road sickness was taking its toll. Wary of Carawan's driving skills, Elliott jumped out of the car in North Carolina and announced he was hitchhiking back to New York.

Over the next two years, Hamilton shuttled between New York and Los Angeles in search of studio auditions and permanent work. In New York, he met Bob Gibson, then a rising star on the folk scene, who would move to Chicago in 1955. By late 1956, Gibson was packing in crowds at the Gate of Horn. Gibson invited Hamilton to Chicago to serve as his accompanist, a job that would allow him a nightly solo set.

The two became partners and roommates, but not friends. Hamilton didn't share Gibson's hard-partying ways. Instead, he quickly established himself in town as a private guitar instructor. David Gedalecia was one of many aspiring guitar players at the University of Chicago who traveled to the North Side each week to sit with Hamilton. Even though he was just a few years older, students viewed him as a skilled professional and were surprised that he would even give them his time. During his lessons, Hamilton let them play his Martin guitar and taught vocal harmony. More than fifty years later, Gedalecia is still struck by the experience. "You could tell he was listening to what you were doing and he was trying to bring out the best in you," he recalled. "You don't meet people like that."[45]

As with Stracke, the FBI was watching Hamilton. However, his records were lost to history when the agency destroyed them on February 1, 1997, for unspecified reasons.[46]

A CATALYST NAMED DAWN GREENING

Hamilton had been at the Gate of Horn less than six months when he met the person who would give him the opportunity to take what he had learned from Lomax Hawes and expand it even further. Dawn Greening was neither a musician nor a singer and she had no stake in the club business, or in any aspect of the music industry. She was a homemaker in Oak Park, a village bordering the city's West Side, where she tended to four children while stoking her life's greatest passion: proselytizing for folk music and musicians.

Dawn McCulloch was born May 4, 1922, and grew up in Oak Park, where she met Nate Greening while both were students at Oak Park and River Forest High School.[47] They married shortly after graduation, in December 1941, and settled in the area. The couple started a family, and after several moves, ended up at 327 South Lombard, near the village's eastern border.[48]

In the era of legal segregation, Oak Park was prosperous and predominantly White. Dr. Percy Julian, a renowned chemist, became the village's first Black resident in November 1950, but before he moved his family from nearby Maywood into their new fifteen-room mansion at 515 North East, arsonists splashed gasoline across the floors and walls and tried unsuccessfully to burn it down.[49] The next year, vandals threw dynamite at the house and blew a hole in the front lawn.[50] Both incidents made the pages of the *New York Times*.

The incidents rallied sympathy among some Oak Park resi-

dents, particularly younger ones like the Greenings who considered themselves more racially progressive. They had Black friends
and regularly hosted dinners for them. Neighbors took notice and,
according to son Lance Greening, the family earned a nickname
on their block: "N—— lovers." Nate Greening had little tolerance
for bigots, and a single slight in his presence was enough for him
to order guests out of his house while shouting "you damn Nazi,
you racist!" Dawn was the counterbalance, telling guests that it
wasn't that they weren't welcome in their home, it was simply that
her husband didn't agree with their particular point of view. "My
mother was always the soother," said Lance. "She was in everybody
and anybody's corner."[51]

Her nurturing demeanor extended beyond her children to a
class of people who needed someone to look after them, feed them,
and give them a touch of home: traveling musicians. Over many
years, the Greenings opened their home to musicians who found
themselves in Chicago playing engagements at the Gate of Horn
and elsewhere. While club owner Albert Grossman maintained an
apartment on Wells Street where his musicians could crash, many
chose the Greening home, primarily due to Dawn's hospitality.
"They treated me like a son. Dawn was like your mother," said Ramblin' Jack Elliott, who stayed at the Lombard house for a summer.[52]

Lance Greening's memories of his teenage years featured Big
Bill Broonzy telling stories of his exploits around the kitchen
table; Pete Seeger cooking baked apples; dinners with Odetta, with
whom his mother maintained her closest friendship; and visits by
Jo Mapes, José Feliciano, Joan Baez, Peter Lafarge, Jimmy Driftwood, Brother John Sellers, Carolyn Hester, and Mance Lipscomb,
among others.[53] Peggy Seeger remembered the Greening home as
"a kind of salon for folk singers," for which the young woman traveling through Chicago on her own for the first time was grateful.
"Somehow having a family I could go home to was wonderful. They
made me feel totally at home," recalled Seeger.[54]

The activity at the Greening home attracted attention from the
FBI as early as August 1950, the year an unnamed family friend noti-

fied the agency to report that he believed the family was "harboring a Communist cell." As with Stracke, the agency conducted surveillance based on innuendo, but that was enough for their family home to remain a target for many years.[55]

The initial informant told the agency that Nate and Dawn Greening had told him they were "'card carrying' members of the Communist party" one year earlier and that at dinner parties the couple often expressed "very strong pro-Communist" beliefs. There was something very troubling about their home—the informant could not understand how the Greenings could afford to entertain as often as they did, and they often had temporary guests staying with them—including "several unemployed students" and, at one time, "an elderly gentleman whom [the informant] could swear was a Russian but who claimed to be a Prussian." The couple introduced the man as their uncle, but even that was puzzling because his name "was a peculiar one" and it was evident he was "quite wealthy" and generally out of place.[56]

The Greenings, the informant said, also had questionable moral values. He charged that Dawn Greening was "an advocate of 'free love'" and "discussed the advantages" of such to him one time when Nate was not at home.[57]

From there, other informants stepped forward, all identified as neighbors and close family associates. A high school friend of Dawn's told the FBI her friend was always "out-spoken and radical in her thinking" and in 1948 persuaded her to attend a meeting of the Progressive Party in Oak Park. The friend admitted "there were no direct Communistic remarks made by [the speaker] but that there seemed to be a Communistic under current [sic]" to the evening. The report also mentions what was likely the most troubling to the neighborhood: they often hosted Blacks in their home and one time visited New York City where it was known they had Jewish friends.[58]

Two years later, on December 12, 1952, the FBI showed up on the Greenings' doorstep and began one of several living room interviews to determine what the couple was up to. According to agent reports, the couple always accepted their visitors cordially but denied they were members of the Communist Party, saying they were instead supporters of the Progressive Party. They also refused to hand over names of friends under similar scrutiny.

Dawn Greening explained they were likely thought to be radical because of who they entertained in their home: Blacks. "Many of her neighbors had said unkind things to her, and that one time a member of the township government had visited her to talk to her about 'town policy' concerning Negroes and Jews," the agents wrote. Greening informed them "she is a person who keeps an open mind on all questions" and that she and Nate "have read and discussed all kinds of philosophies, religions, and political views."[59]

The FBI still wasn't convinced. After each of their visits, which continued through late 1953, agents reported they believed the Greenings were active Communists and said they tried to give them quasi-history lessons on the "revolutionary character" of the movement. Agents left the couple of pamphlets published by the Anti-Defamation League for further reading.[60] The Greenings continued to insist they were not Communist Party members, but said they had at one time attended meetings in Austin on the city's West Side. The party's appeal, they said, was that it was the only organization talking about "social problems, such as discrimination of racial and minority groups, rent control, etc." Nate Greening later said they didn't go further with the party because it appeared to want only to "stir up a lot of trouble and accomplish little or nothing."[61]

The agency always ended its reports with the same conclusion—that the Greenings were indeed Communists—but withheld details because Nate's job was at stake. That ended on November 9, 1953, when Dawn Greening called the FBI to report that her husband had been fired from Hills McCanna, where he worked as a chemist, because the company had mysteriously learned of his family's "activities."[62]

The agency answered ominously. "Mrs. Greening stated that she really did not know why she was calling the writer, but did want to report the above fact. The writer sympathized with her, but reminded her that the FBI is a fact finding body, which is charged with the responsibility to furnish facts to other governmental agencies."[63] That ended that.

When Greening became the administrator of the Old Town School, her relationships with musicians deepened. She organized and promoted performances, connected artists with key players in the city like record stores, promoters, radio personnel, and journalists, and performed tasks as minor as holding redirected mail and lending money. Maybe most importantly, she served as a confidant and active correspondent through letters in which the musicians expressed personal hardships, anxiety over their careers, marriage difficulties, loneliness, and sometimes affection. Writing from Paris in 1968, Brother John Sellers told Greening of injuring his leg during the student riots; the death of his friend, bluesman J. B. Lenoir; and how another friend had stolen more than $4,000 from his bank account. Despite all that, he switched to complimenting the beauty of her legs and smile and admitting that his mother suggested to him he might be in love: "I said may be she said one would never no [sic] when you were in love with them cause you have a funny way of showing it," he wrote.[64]

As devoted as Greening was, the musicians were fiercely loyal in return. Cowboy singer Bill Chipman, also known as Billy Chips, sent her a three-page apology for being slow to repay the $24 she sent him as travel money, explaining he was broke, stranded, and trying to scrape together enough money to return to Chicago. His letter portrays the hardscrabble life of many of the musicians she took under her wing:

> You don't no [sic] how I worried about that money GOD ONLY KNOW'S and I hope and pray you ain't mad [at] me. The reason I haven't wrote you before is because I didn't know where I would be as I slept mostly in the car for 3 weeks after I got here, but GOD has been good to us as I arrived here safe & sound.[65]

Greening never tired of the role she played, and her family followed her lead, spending weeknights and weekends at the Old Town

School, where they served cookies and coffee to students, cleaned and organized, and doted on the musicians. Chicago folk singer Fred Holstein once asked Lance Greening if he ever resented all the love his mother heaped on the multitudes outside their family. "God no, I'm so glad she's dissipating it on someone else," Lance responded. "There's plenty of my mother to go around."[66]

Greening had no interest in playing an instrument, but it was a banjo that first drew her into the world of musicians. The instrument hung in the window of an antique store on Chicago Avenue, and she talked the price down from $25 to $17.75.[67] Lance would learn how to play it, she decided. After all, the Greening family had already discovered *The Midnight Special*, a Saturday evening program on classical station WFMT that surveyed the local and national folk scene. When she heard a Studs Terkel interview with Bob Gibson, she made a beeline to the Gate of Horn to see if Gibson gave lessons. He didn't. She then showed up at a concert Win Stracke gave at the First Presbyterian Church in Oak Park. He, too, brushed her off, telling her, "I don't teach people who don't know music. But I'm starting a music school and whenever I do, I'll let you know."[68]

LIVING ROOM SESSIONS
IN OAK PARK

Her opportunity to get her son a lesson came through Frank Hamilton. Odetta was visiting and she and Greening had plans for a Sunday night dinner in Oak Park. At the last minute, the singer asked to cancel because she wanted to see Hamilton, whom she knew from the early folk scene in Los Angeles. At first Greening was insulted because not only was she being stood up, it was for someone she didn't know. So she drove to the Gate to see what the excitement was about. After watching Hamilton perform, she engaged him in conversation. Within minutes, she had found her teacher. "We hit it off instantly," Hamilton said.[69]

Hamilton became another person for her to look after. Seeing that he wasn't rooted in Chicago and sensing he needed some grounding, she invited him to conduct lessons in her living room, which would provide him a stable income. He agreed, and in October 1957, Hamilton held weekly lessons for nearly fifteen students, who included the entire Greening family as well as Stracke, who showed up at Dawn's invitation. He hadn't held a guitar since before his blacklisting and he wanted to improve his fingerpicking. "I was told that Frank Hamilton would teach different levels at the same time. And by god, he could," he said.[70]

The arrangement was beneficial for everyone. The folk scene did not yet have anyone of Hamilton's instrumental proficiency who also had the energy and aptitude for teaching students no matter their age or background. And after many years of professional uncertainty, it was a chance for Hamilton to settle into a role that was a refuge from the nightclub scene and would give him his first real opportunity to implement the methods he had gleaned years earlier from Bess Lomax Hawes. There was also a practical benefit: the next month he would marry Sheila Lofton, sister of Nate Lofton, the school's future dance coordinator, so a steady income was welcome.[71]

Those early lessons created the blueprint for the way classes are conducted at the Old Town School today. Like Lomax Hawes, Hamilton taught not scales or notes, but songs. He arranged students in three different rooms of the house by their level of proficiency and rotated among them as they all practiced the same song. Then, he devised "The Second Half," a time for everyone to join together in the same space to sing and play the same song. In a single session, the instruction eroded the mystique of playing music. What made the folk revival different from earlier popular music trends is that it drove ordinary people to want to pick up banjos and guitars and play among themselves. The method of instruction Hamilton tried out in the Greenings' living room accommodated that homegrown movement, as it was designed to produce music for the sake of personal enjoyment as opposed to shaping future stars.

"People wanted to learn this music and we had to convince them they could do it. And once they had a guitar in their hand and started to do it, word of mouth spread," Hamilton said.[72]

Hamilton's teaching nudged students toward traditional songs that, for many amateurs, were not as familiar as what they were hearing on the radio from groups like the Limeliters and the Kingston Trio. He taught popular hits of the day, but with the idea of broadening his students' tastes by weaning them away from the familiar. The first song of the first session in the Greening home was "Wreck of the John B" by the Weavers. As the weeks wore on, Hamilton would show up with music he would hear at the Gate: African, Israeli, Yemenite, Appalachian.[73] After the dejection of the blacklist and the drifting he felt in recent years, Stracke watched this twenty-three-year-old teacher with delight. One night he leaned over to Ted Johnson, another student, and whispered, "You know, I'm going to start a school around this."[74]

This time he wouldn't let the idea pass. After classes ended and everyone went home, Stracke stayed behind and, over coffee and cake, sketched out plans with the Greenings. They offered Hamilton a yearly salary of nearly $13,000 to stay in Chicago and be their lead instructor of a new folk school.[75] Stracke already had a location in mind: 333 West North Avenue, home to the former Immigrant State Bank in Old Town, where he was renting a studio on the top floor. The building had a storied history. Built in 1878, it was a German social hall until 1907, when it turned into a "nickel" movie theater. The bank took over in 1922, but collapsed in the Depression. After that, a men's hat store on the first floor fronted a backroom bookie joint, and a dance hall operated upstairs.[76]

The location was familiar: just two blocks away from Stracke's house at 411 West Eugenie. He could walk to work. While he would continue to hustle for concerts and other jobs, the school afforded him something that had been stripped from him in recent years: a place where he belonged.

THE DOORS OPEN ON
NORTH AVENUE

Opening night took place December 1, 1957.[77] Stracke used his connections to fill the room with tastemakers who would spread the word. Among them were the poet Paul Engle, director of the Iowa Writers' Workshop at the University of Iowa, novelist Jack Conroy, local journalists and music critics, assorted art patrons, his friend Studs Terkel, and Mathias "Paddy" Bauler, the famously corrupt Forty-Third Ward alderman who once ran his political office out of De Luxe Gardens, a saloon he owned on the school building's first floor, using the former bank deposit vaults to store beer.[78]

Stracke's close relationship with Bauler was critical for the school's early survival in Chicago's rough world of tribal politics. The two men lived across the alley from each other, and when Bauler announced his retirement in 1967, Stracke said he would run for his seat as an independent.[79] Bauler kept close watch on his neighbor, and one day after an election asked him why he didn't vote a straight ticket. "How did you know?" Stracke asked. Bauler explained he hired a teenager to sit on a balcony to keep track of the voting below.[80]

Bauler appeared at many Old Town School functions in the early days, for which Stracke was grateful. For the alderman's seventy-fifth birthday on January 27, 1965, Stracke performed "Paddy's Song," which he composed to celebrate all the factors that had kept Bauler in office since 1933: his saloon, his taste in beer and sausage, and his iron might. "So up with Bauler and down with the blues / We'll rush the growler and holler the news / He runs a great ward and he runs it good / And he'll never run out on the neighborhood," Stracke sang at the Germania Club that night.[81]

Bauler returned the favor not long after when thieves audaciously shimmied down a manhole and tunneled under the sidewalk and into the wall of the school building, where they stole instruments and tape recorders weighing a hundred pounds from the Old Town Folklore Center, the school's retail outlet. When Stracke found out, he dialed Bauler, who contacted a street fence who had the entire haul. The school quietly paid the going rate for each item's return. "He was connected," Art Thieme, the center's assistant manager, said of Stracke. "Nobody said anything more about it."[82]

Stracke wrote personal invitations to opening night in which he set the school against the national trend: "The formation of the school is a natural result of the tremendous upsurge in the interest in folk music. Locating a school such as ours in Old Town also seems to be a natural step, in view of the contribution Old Town has already made in responding to the cultural needs of our time." He ended with a promise: "Studs Terkel will be there to add sparkle, and you will meet other well-known folk singers and musicians."[83]

Stracke later reported that several hundred people showed up, the majority of whom were prospective students.[84] The evening opened with a bagpipe introduction by George Armstrong, followed by a demonstration: Big Bill Broonzy performed a song and Hamilton notated his technique on a blackboard, then used it to teach the song to a group of student beginners, including Lance Greening and Ted Johnson, who were playing the riff minutes later. The notation method was a visual tool Hamilton had devised to make the fingerpicking understandable. Stracke told invitees the visual tablature was designed specifically to study "the techniques of famous folk artists of the country, including those of Huddie (Leadbelly) Ledbetter, Merle Travis, Earl Scruggs, and many others."[85]

Johnson remembers the audience held rapt as he and his fellow students were guided through Broonzy's "Glory of Love" on their guitars soon after Broonzy himself had performed it to dazzling effect. This was, after all, the era of the classical conservatory method, in which music learning took place in a one-on-one setting and required intense memorization skills and theory comprehension. In its simplicity, Hamilton's presentation that night was a genius marketing pitch and effective theater rolled into one. "Transmitting this supposedly arcane thing for these ordinary people who had never done that before—it was really dramatic," Johnson said.[86]

Broonzy's presence on opening night gave the school authority and relevance. He was a major star in the folk world, and a year earlier, on October 25, 1956, he had performed a concert with Pete Seeger at Northwestern University's Cahn Auditorium in north suburban Evanston. Recorded by WFMT, the concert was eventually released by Folkways through Verve Records, becoming Broonzy's first live album recorded before an American audience.[87] In Chicago, he was a familiar face at the Gate of Horn and was heard often on WFMT's *Midnight Special* and *Studs Terkel's Almanac*.

But Broonzy had lung cancer. Four days before the Old Town School opening, on November 27, his friends held a three-hour benefit concert at Temple KAM in Hyde Park to raise money to offset his medical expenses. Terkel emceed, and the bill reflected the diversity of the contemporary folk music community: topped by gospel star Mahalia Jackson, it included Pete Seeger, Odetta, Stracke, Hamilton, banjo player Fleming Brown, and blues performers Sunnyland Slim, J. B. Lenoir, and Little Brother Montgomery. Terkel read telegrams of support from Muddy Waters and Memphis Slim. Broonzy didn't sing, nor did he four days later at his Old Town School appearance. He would die the following August.[88] The fact that he helped the school while in such a weakened state reflects the strength of his friendship with Stracke and Terkel, his former partners in "I Come for to Sing," and with the folk music community in Chicago that supported him in kind.

THE SCHOOL'S EARLY YEARS

Opening night ended with a coffee break and then a sing-along. By nine o'clock, dozens of people had registered for classes. In doing so, they met Gertrude Soltker, the school's first administrator. Soltker's relationship with Stracke dated to 1934, when they had both helped found the Chicago Repertory Group.[89] It was Soltker who established the Old Town School as a nonprofit organization, and in her two years on the job she got the bookkeeping in order, just as she had with the Old Town Players, the long-running theater troupe where she served as a company member and bookkeeper.[90]

Born July 22, 1912, Soltker was well suited for a job requiring discipline and organizational skills, especially among artists. She was an American Red Cross worker who helped establish tent clubs for infantry regiments in Europe. Those who encountered her were immediately made aware she didn't suffer fools gladly. "She was the hammer. She made it come together," said Nate Lofton.[91]

Like Stracke and Greening, Soltker was an FBI target. Her background in leftist politics attracted the agency's attention. She and husband David Soltker, an architect, were reported as members of the Communist Party as early as 1934, and between 1958 and 1969 were active participants in the Chicago chapter of the Committee to Secure Justice for Morton Sobell. The group advocated for the release of Sobell, a US citizen who was imprisoned in 1951 for spying for the Russians. An informant scrutinized the couple in 1960 in relation to Sobell, but in 1973 they resurfaced when the agency tried to link them to an alleged assassination plot against President Richard Nixon.

They were friends of Mariana Yampolsky, a Chicago-born photographer who relocated to Mexico City to study painting and sculpture, and had taken up with an expatriate community of Communist sympathizers. Yampolsky's mother Hedwig, also in Mexico, had told FBI informants her "comrades" in New York and Chicago feared the president and, during a trip to Chicago, talked to a number of people about a plan to raise money to hire an assassin.[92] That brought agents to the Soltkers' door on February 2, 1973. The couple denied knowing Yampolsky. In the report is a note that Gertrude was "very antagonistic," especially upon hearing they were accused of possibly funding an assassination plot against a sitting US president. "That is so wild, I wouldn't even discuss it," she said. The case was dropped twelve days later.[93]

By 1960, Soltker had left the school to return to the stage, and the role officially shifted to Dawn Greening.[94] Their styles were different—Soltker's warmth was finely measured, while Greening's spilled into everything she touched. But by that time, the structure Soltker instituted had made the school operable. "She's the unsung hero of the whole thing. She did everything," Lance Greening said.[95]

In the early days, classes for guitar and five-string banjo ran from 8:00 p.m. to 10:30 p.m. Tuesdays and Thursdays, and a Saturday class for both children and adults ran from 1:30 p.m. to 4:00

p.m.[96] Ten-minute coffee breaks were mandatory for every class. Their purpose: "a time for socializing—comparing notes and meeting visiting folksingers." The social component was critical. Visiting curiosity seekers were welcome to any class, but if they brought an instrument or took notes, they would be charged. In its early literature, the school emphasized that it was not simply interested in teaching people chords and technique; instead, its mission was to draw them deeper into the bottomless well of American songs to emphasize their "historic and cultural background." A pecking order was made clear: "All classes are in the study of folk songs and their accompaniment," not the other way around.[97]

Hamilton not only headed the curriculum, but he taught every class for the first month. That didn't last. "It was crazy, I couldn't do it all," he said.[98] Soon, a first-generation faculty emerged to teach introductory, advanced, and intermediate levels.

Within months, enrollment reached nearly two hundred students. Local media accounts show that folk music was perceived as part of the world of beatniks and bebop, and that the desire to learn instruments like banjo, harmonica, or guitar, or to sing songs with themes like killing, infidelity, or liquor, was not seen as respectable. This view reflected the cultural divide influenced both by the rise of affluent urbanism, which embraced rapid new developments in consumerism, and by the shrinking of interest in the past, which summoned only images of poverty or struggle. Most early stories on the school used phrases like "hillbilly" or "mountain music" to scorn what it depicted as primitive or unsophisticated. As Chicago neighborhoods on the North Side swelled with White Southerners in 1957, media reports clearly illustrate the anxiety many Chicagoans had about efforts to make Southern culture respectable. "Hillbilly for cultured" is how the *Chicago Tribune* summed up the folk phenomenon in 1960. "Most of them do wear shoes. Some are quite brainy."[99]

At its opening, the Old Town School was considered a curiosity at best, and at worst, an example of a fleeting craze. In April 1958, only five months after opening night, the *Chicago Tribune* called it "probably the strangest educational establishment extant," but reported that "its students have all the outward manifestations of normal citizens." Even the occupations of its students were listed to reassure skeptical readers: "doctors, lawyers, stock brokers, bankers, teachers, research chemists, geographers, stenographers, housewives, and whole families who share a common addiction that drives them all the way in from Evanston, Oak Park, Deerfield, and Blue Island just to plunk and sing."[100]

Reporters often highlighted the Greenings as an example of such a family transformed. All four children took lessons, as did Nate Greening, the patriarch, who at the time worked as a research chemist. In photographs, they looked angelic singing together. Dawn assured one writer that "folk music is not for the beatnik and bop crowd. It has substance and esthetic value. The folk music of other countries all over the world is much more appreciated than in our own country. I think our present resurgence of interest in it is a wholesome thing—and certainly a fascinating family hobby."[101]

The school's early quarters were modest. Students tramped up three flights of creaky stairs to two large classrooms, one that was partitioned to include a small entertaining area where coffee and cookies were served before "The Second Half." The second floor housed the school's office. Oftentimes, for a concert or special event, the school rented "The Rainbow Room," a large room on the third floor that earned its name from a colorful mural on a back wall. It had a bar, and when the school wasn't using it, it would be occupied by other events, from Puerto Rican weddings to meetings of the Industrial Workers of the World.[102]

By 1960, the idea of a center exclusively devoted to the teaching of folk music was still unique. That year, *Sing Out!* reported that Greenwich Village folk performers Happy Traum and Dick Weissman had started the New York School of Folk Music, "patterned after Frank Hamilton's Old Town School of Folk Music in Chicago."[103] Despite its lofty name, the New York equivalent was actually just a room in the basement of a music shop and didn't last a year.[104] In March 1963, a guitarist from Philadelphia named Harry

Tuft launched the Denver Folklore Center in the back of a guitar shop he had opened a year earlier when he saw a demand for guitar instruction. His Saturday classes featured students in groups, a method he had observed at the Old Town School when he visited in 1959. "The whole idea of teaching a group of folks was just not done. That alone was something very different," Tuft said. "And then the idea you could teach them in such a way that they could then play together was another aspect that worked really well."[105]

Expanding its outreach past the North Avenue location was an early mission of the school. Stracke continued hustling for engagements throughout the city and suburbs, but the folk circuit now included many of the school's instructors, who were in demand for fundraisers and concerts. They were often packaged together to play dates around town. One advertisement for a hootenanny at the O'Hare Inn Auditorium advertised an "all star cast" consisting of Stracke and three other Old Town School instructors.[106] In 1959, Hamilton and instructors Fleming Brown and Valucha Buffington appeared on a bill at the Circle M Ranch, a private day camp in Wheeling, to raise money for the Henry Booth Settlement House, an after-school facility for children in the city.[107] They were invited back for repeat benefits, all of which suggested the respect the school had earned in society circles.

STU RAMSAY:
REFUGE FOR A BLUES PRODIGY

Students became teachers. In 1960, the Old Town School had a faculty of twelve instructors; by 1967, the staff had grown to forty-four.[108] The first teacher Hamilton hired was Ted Johnson, a twenty-nine-year-old folk music enthusiast from Evanston who had first appeared in the Greenings' living room and participated in the opening night demonstration. Teaching beginner guitar classes convinced Johnson that he loved the classroom, so he enrolled in a doctorate program in English at Northwestern University and, once he graduated, moved from Chicago to pursue a full-time career in academia. "Teaching and learning, it's hard to tell where one stops and the other [starts]. . . . It seemed natural that sooner or later you'd begin to pass things on. Especially in folk music," he said.[109]

Another student introduced South Side blues to the curriculum when he was only a teenager. Born February 26, 1944, Stu Ramsay grew up in Elmhurst, a western Chicago suburb, where his father entertained the family at night by playing the harmonica while he and his mother and sisters danced.[110] Ramsay heard blues on *The Shopping Bag Show*, a daily radio program hosted by Big Bill Hill, an R&B deejay who brokered time at WOPA, which broadcast from atop a hotel in nearby Oak Park. Soon Ramsay was playing guitar, and at age fourteen, bought his first banjo.

By that time, Ramsay's home life was deteriorating. He was the oldest of six children, and his father drank. The evening music sessions he had enjoyed as a child soon ended. He started hopping trains to get away from home. "I couldn't stand the fucking place," he said.[111] When a local judge threatened to ship him to the St. Charles School and Home for Boys, a state institution for delinquents, his parents encouraged Ramsay to commit to something to keep himself out of trouble. He chose music, and soon was commuting to the Loop, where he played on street corners and L platforms and hung out at the Jazz Record Mart. His mother read about the Old Town School and accompanied him there for an introduction. He met Hamilton and started taking classes. It was 1959, and he was fifteen. "It was better than any place I had ever been. The people there were the most kind, generous, wonderful people you could ever possibly meet," he said.[112]

Ramsay was considered a prodigy. One evening after class, Dawn Greening noticed him alone with his Stella guitar and asked what he was playing. Songs by Jimmy Reed, he told her. Days later, she told him she wanted to make an introduction and drove him to an Elks Lodge on the South Side, where guitarist-singer J. B. Lenoir was onstage. "He had gold teeth with 'JB' etched in them," Ramsay remembered.[113] That night, he sat in with the band. Greening took particular interest in Ramsay and introduced him to other bluesmen, including Muddy Waters. One afternoon, Big Joe Williams, the Delta bluesman known for playing a nine-string guitar, summoned Ramsay to the Gate of Horn to play alongside him. When Ramsay's father died of alcoholism in 1965, Williams became a father figure to him.

Ramsay started teaching at the Old Town School in 1961, when he was seventeen. He immediately took to the method Hamilton had designed, noticing that the instructors, unlike those in instrument shops or music studios, were not expected to prolong the learning process over weeks in order to upsell students on instruments, books, or equipment. Nothing was expected of him but to make music and grow. He felt free. "It was a place where I could play my shit and nobody is going to say 'fuck you.' They were going to make something out of me," he said.[114] He started joining other instructors, including Stracke, for dates outside the school. In Ramsay, the school had a fresh, young face it could pin its success on.

He became the first faculty member to sign a commercial record deal. Concert promoter Frank Fried got a whiff of his talent and, serving as his manager, helped lock down a contract with Mercury Records. Ramsay went into Universal Recording Studios for three days in January 1963, and *Stu Ramsay Loves Dobro, Banjo, Guitar and Harmonica* was in stores that May. The cover art exuded youthful mischief, with Ramsay, dressed in a crew-neck sweater and leaning against a brick wall, confidently tilting his head back to smile at the album title scrawled in white paint above his head. In his left hand, a paintbrush.[115]

The album was a stealth advertisement for the Old Town School. The liner notes championed Ramsay's versatility and noted that he had started playing the dobro only eight months earlier. "How he developed so much talent so early, so fast, and so well is difficult to say," Chad Mitchell wrote in the liner notes. He mentioned the Old Town School ("a unique organization devoted to instruction in folklore") and Frank Hamilton ("an outstanding folk musician"), as well as Ramsay's associations with Big Joe Williams and blues singer Estelle "Mama" Yancey. The notes emphasized the use of overdubbing, which was still in its infancy. The technique allowed

multi-instrumentalist Ramsay to be heard playing two lead instruments at one time. "And by the way, the horse trotting through *Good
Timin'* is really Stu tapping his feet. He was so naturally energetic
about this during the recording session that we couldn't resist putting a microphone on the tapping for this one number," the notes
read.[116]

The Old Town School held a release party to celebrate Ramsay's
achievement. ("They say he's a budding Segovia-Montoya," the
Chicago Tribune gushed that morning.)[117] The album's traditional
music fit with the school's mission, but it also had personality and
youth, two commodities that were valuable to keep the school growing in the public eye. The songs, all instrumentals, ran the gamut
from Chicago blues to old-time jazz to speedy banjo workouts, all
bathed in reverb to evoke the mood of something from the streets,
or lurking down an alleyway.

But Ramsay's fling with the record business didn't last. His
request to have Big Joe Williams on the album was refused. Mitchell, the leader of the commercial folk group the Chad Mitchell Trio,
was dispatched to serve as the label's A&R representative, and to
Ramsay, it was obvious that Mitchell's job was to shape him into
someone he was not. He wanted to play blues. Mitchell wanted
wholesome hootenanny fare and gave Ramsay's instrumentals
song titles ("Daybreak in Dixie," "Traveling Dobro," "Stu-in'") that
reflected that image.[118] The arrangements, the use of multi-track
recording, even the album's title, were all out of Ramsay's control.
He "wanted to drop that whole thing like a hot potato."[119]

He soon left Old Town to enroll in the music program at Elmhurst College, a small liberal arts school in his hometown associated
with the United Church of Christ. Because folk and blues guitar
were not on the curriculum, he studied voice. His banjo playing was
relegated to the student café. Soon enough, some students mocked
the instrument; one told him to take it back to Virginia where it
belonged. But the college was in the midst of being integrated, and
a group of Black students who heard him play learned of his association with Big Joe Williams and other bluesmen. They invited Ram-

say to perform blues at Hammerschmidt Memorial Chapel during a service presided over by Dr. Martin Luther King Jr., who was in Chicago for two months, leading marches in all-White neighborhoods to promote fair housing.

On July 8, 1966, a Friday evening, Dr. King, school leaders, and the entire student body listened to Ramsay perform music he had first learned in Chicago bars and lounges and had never before made its way into such a sanctified place. A local report said that among the crowd of twelve hundred people, only fifty were Black—it was "a virtually all-white crowd of suburbanites."[120] Ramsay's peers, steeped in sacred and classical music, listened to his performance "with their eyes wide open and their jaws hanging open." Many had never heard the blues, no less played by one of their own. In one night, everything the Old Town School stood for became a living thing.

"I guess you could call that the purpose of the Old Town School, to go out into the world and do good," Ramsay said. "The music had to speak. It wasn't about commerce. It was about having human value."[121]

FLEMING BROWN:
THE SONG CHOOSES YOU

The first generation of teachers the school hired were not professionals in the commercial sense of pursuing recording careers. For them, music was a vocation through which they could better their community and make themselves whole. "A complete man" is how banjo instructor Fleming Brown described himself after honing his craft free of the pressure of needing it to survive. Only "the best of the amateurs are the professionals," he said.[122]

William Fleming Brown joined the faculty in 1960 and stayed for thirteen years. By the time he left, he had taught more than three hundred people to play the banjo, and in doing so, was one of the first instructors in Chicago to expose others to the originators of the Appalachian banjo style he so fully mastered and revered.

Brown was born in Marshall, Missouri on March 1, 1926.[123] Four years later, his family relocated to Glen Ellyn, a western suburb of Chicago, where he later settled with his own family. As with so many others of his generation, the person who provided a guiding hand in his musical development was Pete Seeger. When Seeger passed through Chicago in 1948, campaigning for Henry Wallace's Progressive Party bid for the White House, Brown approached him at his hotel room, asking if he knew a banjo tutor in town. He had purchased a five-string banjo two years earlier but was confounded by how to tune it, let alone play it.[124] Nevertheless, he was determined, because the sound of the instrument was ingrained in his head. "There's something about the banjo, the cutting quality of it and the raw dynamics, for lack of anything else to describe it, and there was an earthy quality," he said.[125]

Seeger steered him to Doc Hopkins, by then a WLS *Barn Dance* veteran of eighteen years who also hosted a morning show on the station. Seeger credited Hopkins as an influence, and to Brown, he represented the real thing. Born January 26, 1900, in Harlan County, Kentucky, Howard "Doc" Hopkins performed in a medicine show as a teenager. After serving in World War I, he returned home to play steel guitar and banjo in a number of groups before relocating to Chicago to join the Cumberland Ridge Runners, a group that recorded for the Paramount and Decca labels. Hopkins received Brown warmly even though he had never given a proper lesson in his life. "I can't teach you, but I can show you," he said. "Come by around five." He meant five o'clock in the morning, a half hour before his radio program started. Brown showed up and didn't look back.[126] Those early morning lessons turned into an apprenticeship, taking place twice a week for several years.[127]

In 1950s suburbia, Brown was a man out of time. He named his Glen Ellyn house Stingy Ridge after the Kentucky edge of the Cumberland Mountains. Instead of filling his house with modern appliances, he owned household items from the frontier days, like the spinning wheel he and wife Jean used to make their own clothes. The couple collected bark, berry juice, flowers, and roots to make their own dyes. After visiting their home, a local reporter wondered "whether the 'progress' we have made in the art of living during the last 300 years is really progress at all."[128]

In 1957, when Stracke became too involved in the school to tour with "I Come for to Sing," Brown was chosen as his replacement.[129] By then Brown was a regular on the folk circuit.[130] Everywhere he showed up, he carried with him a repertoire of songs he had learned from Hopkins or culled from recordings issued by the American Folklife Center Archive of the Library of Congress. Eventually Brown traveled south himself to record the people he had heard on those records. He later created tablatures of their songs for his students, and then elaborated on them in class by discussing how the idiosyncratic performances of the older players completed their emotional power. For him, technique was important, but it was secondary to knowing how to enter the world of the song and, in an almost sanctified way, committing so fully you momentarily shed your identity and became what it contains. "That's the way to sing a song. I can't sing a song I don't believe," he said.[131]

He often told his students that imitation is pointless. Instead of starting lessons, he encouraged them to buy a dozen records, go away for a year, and absorb them like sponges. Then, he said, it will be time to pick up an instrument and "see what you've done with them."[132] He believed personal immersion was the only way to find purpose within the song.

"The song chooses you. There is a song that needs to be sung," he said. "There is a song that I want other people to hear, and I want them to hear it the same way I hear it."[133]

On his eponymous debut album on Folk-Legacy Records in 1962, he modified songs he learned from his travels to make them personal, such as "Reek and Rambling Blade," an Irish folk ballad whose lyrics he patched together from two separate versions. Another song, "Flag of Blue, White and Red," documents the paradox of a miner wanting to feed his family but forced to strike by the union: "I tell you boys, it is a crime / That has transpired in many a mine / You do the work the best you can / You get beat up by idle men." With folk music so aligned with organized labor, the song's dark side was shocking. The liner notes say that Brown learned the song from a Missouri woman who "insisted that her name be kept secret, as she was 'afraid of reprisals.'"[134]

That woman turned out to be Brown's mother. She co-wrote the song with him about a 1951 coal mine strike in Southern Illinois and the beatings she witnessed when miners crossed the picket line. More than ten years after the record's release, Brown confessed to the ruse. The actions of the union, he said, were just as bullying as McCarthyism. By then the song had taken on a life of its own—University of Illinois folklorist Archie Green, who specialized in labor songs, produced a paper on the song, and Pete Seeger included it in his 1972 book *The Incompleat Folksinger* and performed it regularly. Brown's reluctance to reveal its true authorship reflects not just his worry about the Left's reaction, but also his concern that many in the folk world were not ready to hear an original song written by one of their contemporaries. In a single stealth action, he proved that it's not the time period that gives folk songs their power, but whether or not they are rooted in something real: "I was angry about something. And that's where the song's validity lies."[135]

By the 1980s, Brown had been embraced by the new generation of folk singers, like Steve Goodman and Fred Holstein, and played with them in the new clubs that popped up along Lincoln Avenue. He connected them with Appalachian elders like Frank Proffitt and Hobart Smith, whom he hosted in Chicago. The road held little appeal. He chose to stay close to home because he had a job that funded who he really was, a pact that made him no different from the rural laborers whose living rooms he sat in as a younger man. "I wanted to be an independently wealthy folksinger. I didn't want to depend on it. I wasn't going to get into the 'business' of being a folksinger," he said.[136]

He remained in touch with Doc Hopkins and invited him to his home in 1982, where the two men, generations apart, were joined by Stephen Wade, then a twenty-nine-year-old banjo prodigy who considered Brown his mentor. The three men sat in a circle and played songs that preceded them all, but connected them through the precision of their playing and their shared intuition for the music. "We are family," Brown declared when the session was over. "Family is not necessarily flesh and blood."[137] Two years later, on December 6, 1984, he died of cancer at Northwestern Memorial Hospital.[138]

INCORPORATING INTERNATIONAL MUSIC AND DANCE

Frank Hamilton had established the Old Town School curriculum with international music in mind. His view corresponded to the global perspective of Pete Seeger and many other prominent folk musicians. To them, pluralism was integral to the music, and learning songs required understanding the culture they came from. Valucha Buffington, a Brazilian-born student who spoke Portuguese, French, Italian, Spanish, and English, brought this pluralism to life. By the time she showed up at the Old Town School to take classes, she had traversed both Americas. Born October 10, 1930, in the state of Minas Gerais, she spent her teenage years in Rio de Janeiro before moving to Des Moines, Iowa, to attend Drake University. She married and followed her husband to Chicago.[139]

The Old Town School recognized Buffington's value and soon offered her a job teaching Brazilian folk music. She frequently sang in solo performances at the school as well as at the Gate of Horn. Dawn Greening said Buffington was a "good example" of the cultural exposure the school strove to offer beginner students who were using the school to step out of their comfort zone:

> Many of the people who come to the school are from the suburbs. They've not been exposed to other cultures. They come into the neighborhood, which is a conglomeration of cultures. And through the school we have people singing Brazilian songs, teaching South American cultures. We have people from the French Navy coming up and singing for us. And Negro students attending the school who have brought many things from their own culture.[140]

Buffington eventually made a debut album with Hamilton that Phillips Records released in 1962. *The World of Frank and Valucha* featured fourteen songs from eight different countries: France, Israel, Brazil, Yugoslavia, Chile, Greece, Russia, and the United States. Their two voices, one alto and the other tenor, blend naturally in duet arrangements with accompaniments—primarily Hamilton on guitar—that are faithful to their region.[141]

A leading component of the school's expansion of its multi-ethnic curriculum was international dance. Within its first few years the school hosted a Wednesday night "Folk Dance Circle" that featured instruction on the dances of Greece, Japan, Scotland, Sweden, Norway, Israel, the Netherlands, Germany, Russia, and—quite naturally, given the city's booming population of Eastern European immigrants—Poland, Hungary, Croatia, and Slovakia. The lessons were intended to be just as accessible as the music classes, as there was no requirement to know the language or culture. Often the school would invite ethnic musicians, whether visiting or were based in Chicago, to provide accompaniment. Leading the sessions was Nate Lofton, a public high school science teacher invited to the school by Hamilton—by then his brother-in-law—to take guitar classes.

Lofton was born January 4, 1928, and grew up on Chicago's South Side, where his father, a jazz guitarist, played in professional swing bands. As the Second World War was winding down, he found himself based in Germany, from which his travels took him to places as far-flung as Yugoslavia and Romania. He was already interested in folk culture and wherever he landed he would network with the townspeople in the hope they would invite him home so he could watch them dancing.[142]

As a Black man teaching dance to predominantly White students, Lofton stood out. Paul Collins, who would eventually succeed Lofton as the Old Town School's dance instructor, first took notice of Lofton in 1963 at the yearly conference of the Illinois State Square Dance Association at McCormick Place, where Lofton was leading a forum on international folk dance. Collins, also Black, saw Lofton as a role model and signed up for his Wednesday night class that summer.[143]

SQUARE DANCING MANIA ARRIVES

Square dancing had taken hold in Chicago more than a decade before the Old Town School. Its origin can be traced back to the Chicagoland Music Festival, held in Soldier Field, one of the largest outdoor musical gatherings ever staged in Chicago.

The WLS *Barn Dance* supplied talent to a number of folk festivals and events that emerged in the 1930s and 1940s as interest in traditional music grew. Besides the 1933–1934 World's Fair, the most prominent musical gathering in downtown Chicago was the Chicagoland Music Festival. This annual event, which was launched in 1930 and ran through 1964, was a pageant of Midwestern pride. Chicago Tribune Charities, the festival's lead sponsor, intended it as a successor to the 1873 Chicago Jubilee, a musical spectacle that celebrated Chicago's rise from the ashes of the 1871 Great Fire.

The one hundred and fifty thousand people who were packed into Soldier Field on August 23, 1930, listened to music performed at that earlier festival: the "Anvil Chorus" from Verdi's opera *Il trovatore* and various John Philip Sousa marches.[144] A thousand-member Black choir also performed—the women dressed in white, the men in black. They sang spirituals, including "Swing Low, Sweet Chariot." In an unusual break from the deep segregation that halved the city, a choir of two thousand White singers joined them. Together they sang the "Hallelujah Chorus" from Handel's *Messiah*.[145]

Although the festival's early years were devoted to classical music and patriotic marches, its later years featured entertainment as diverse as Black church choirs from Bronzeville, yodelers, accordion bands, concert bands, baton twirlers, pianist Liberace with orchestral accompaniment, and in 1951, a seventy-eight-year-old dulcimer player from Catlettsburg, Kentucky, named Aunt Polly Triplett. However, as early as the late 1930s, the festival also held public square dances as a way to promote nostalgia for a simpler time. "What has been fun for 150 years and what brought smiles to our grandfathers when the United States was in its teens will be fun again this summer," exclaimed V. K. Brown, an administrator of the 1939 festival. The event's ambition was great: John Dolce, the square dance caller, used Soldier Field's public address system, and the music was provided not by a fiddler, but by a forty-piece concert orchestra playing songs like "Turkey in the Straw."[146] A thousand dancers participated.[147]

Driving the craze was the Chicago Park District, which coordinated barn dance groups at parks throughout the city, particularly on the Southwest Side. By 1947, the district reported it was conducting twenty-five dances a week around the city; by 1950, the number had grown to forty. Field house dances ran three and a half hours with few breaks; to break up the monotony, callers would routinely interject ballroom dances or polkas accompanied by a fiddle or guitar.[148] By that time, the dances were catering to seventy-five thousand people a year.[149] Many dancers dressed the part—plaid shirts and neck handkerchiefs for men, calico gowns for women or "old fashioned percales that their great-grandmothers probably wore for the same kind of dancing a century ago. Some complete their costumes with sunbonnets."[150]

Competitions fanned across the city, the suburbs, and then the greater Midwest. On October 28, 1950, WLS hosted the city's first International Square Dance Festival at the Chicago Stadium, which featured square dance groups from more than twenty states. The program was widely inclusive, with sets for children recovering from polio, the blind, and Canadians dancing to calls in French.[151] When the park district announced a square dance contest at the International Amphitheater in 1953—an event that promised fifteen continuous hours of square dancing—ten thousand people showed up from as far away as Massachusetts and South Dakota. Clearly, a mania was taking hold. "All square dancers are mad—mad—mad," said one district manager.[152]

The large-scale events came straight from the imagination of John Dolce, the WLS *Barn Dance*'s official square dance caller, whose day job happened to be head of recreation for the Chicago Park District.[153] Dolce consulted on and called all the festivals, but he also organized workshops and classes that encouraged people to learn, and which got them interested in the district square dance clubs organized throughout the city. Dolce had Southern roots, but in Sicily. Born in 1907 in Montemaggiore Belsito, southeast of Palermo, he settled on Chicago's West Side with his family in 1914. After graduation from DePaul University, he joined the Chicago Park District as a physical education instructor, where he organized boxing tournaments and eventually square dances at local parks. The dances drew crowds, which sent Dolce conjuring up bigger dances, which brought WLS calling. Throughout his thirty-eight years on the job, Dolce preached the physical and mental benefits of square dancing. There was no limit to his promotional skills: one year he organized a square dance that stretched ten blocks, from Lake Street to Congress Parkway. Eight thousand people danced in the streets as his voice boomed out of sound trucks parked at each intersection.[154] Dolce's efforts paid off in 1990, when Illinois Governor James Thompson declared square dance the official folk dance of Illinois—"endemic to Illinois as the prairie plants," he said at the signing.[155]

Square dancing was also popular among Chicago's Black population, but as was typical of the time, Black dances were segregated to the South and West Sides. Born June 5, 1947, Paul Collins grew up in Washington Park and remembers attending a live taping of the WLS *Barn Dance* at the Eighth Street Theater with his grandfather, who introduced him to country music. Both of Collins's parents, who were public schoolteachers, danced weekly. They took him at age eight to Saturday night square dances for Black adults at a neighborhood YMCA. Sam Roberts, a caller, splintered from that group and started hosting competing Saturday night dances in the basement of his two-flat building at 7312 South Saint Lawrence. He named it Robert's Barn. The walls were decorated with pictures of hay bales, and local boys, including Collins, helped cover the concrete with tile to make a dance floor. Roberts wore cowboy boots and western shirts he picked up at Morris Men's Shop near the Chicago stockyards. The group that showed up in his basement to dance sometimes totaled more than sixty people. Their name: the Chicago Hoedowners.[156]

The Hoedowners was one of several square dance clubs in the city's Black belt in the 1950s and 1960s. They had names like the Chicago Hashers and the Chi-Squares. As popular as they were, the clubs were still puzzling to the larger neighborhood population. When Collins tried to start up a club at Tilden Technical High School, he was jeered. "They thought it was the furthest thing from fun," he said. In the early civil rights era, he tried persuading local groups to host dances "to bridge the gap" between Blacks and Whites in the name of racial reconciliation, but his idea was never implemented.[157]

Whites did not tolerate Black square dancers either. When Blacks showed up at a Park District square dance in Gage Park, a solidly White enclave on the Southwest Side, their cars were vandalized. Black dancers were shunned at the first state square dance convention, as some Whites simply walked away when they entered to dance. Some Whites stayed, however, and others joined when they saw what was happening. For the most part, the Black square dancers danced in their own sets.

By the time Collins enrolled in the University of Chicago, he had the opportunity to dance every night of the week. Besides square dances, ethnic folk dances were held at the Hyde Park Neighborhood Club, the University of Chicago International House, and other venues where Collins danced and also taught. When Ray Tate, the director who succeeded Win Stracke at the Old Town School, asked Lofton in 1972 to come back to the school to lead its dance programming, he declined, but suggested Collins as an alternative. Collins would lead the dance programming there for ten years.

ELLA JENKINS AND HER QUIET REVOLUTION IN CHILDREN'S MUSIC

By the mid-1960s, the Old Town School started offering more specialized classes, which meant expanding the faculty. Students were

moving beyond guitars and on to more exotic instruments like mandolin (taught by Ray Tate), classical guitar (Jim Norris), bagpipes
(George Armstrong), and plectrum banjo (John Carbo). "I really
think if we had students interested in zither, we'd go out and find
somebody to teach the zither," Dawn Greening said.[158]

Children's music emerged as a priority through the presence of
Ella Jenkins, the first folk artist who recorded exclusively for children. Jenkins was born August 6, 1924, in St. Louis, but her family
relocated to Chicago a few years later and settled near Hyde Park.
Floyd Johnson, an uncle from Arkansas who lived with the family, played harmonica and set up his jukebox in the family dining
room. He played strictly acoustic blues and early jazz. "It was like
country music, it told stories. I loved the way the singers sounded so
relaxed when they sang," Jenkins said. She would memorize lyrics
and, if she fumbled for words, she would sing her own lines. What
mattered, she discovered, was capturing where the song came from,
not copying what it said. "Back then, people used to sing from the
heart."[159]

As a teenager, she absorbed the music that permeated her neighborhood: gospel from the storefront churches that lined State
Street, current hits blasting from loudspeakers outside record
shops, international music she tested in listening booths, and
sidewalk rhymes and chants children sang in playgrounds and in
front of stoops. "I used to travel around the world in my head, from
one place to another. I'd get records from the Middle East and from
Africa; I got interested in these exotic sounds. It was a very informal
musical education," she recalled.[160]

Jenkins ended up in San Francisco to earn a sociology degree
from the state college, but that port city also expanded her musical interests to include Cuban, Latin, and Mexican music. She
started performing at local folk clubs and coffeehouses, where she
accompanied herself on homemade percussion instruments, a Chinese tom-tom, and later, a baritone ukulele. Back in Chicago, she
attended the living room sessions at the Greening home in Oak Park
and was present at the Old Town School's opening night. By then,

she was frequenting the Gate of Horn, where she often performed as a duo with Bob Gibson. She liked his informality and his need to entertain. "I always felt that if you were in the folk world, you should be pretty down to earth," she said.[161]

Despite pressure from club owners to go commercial, Jenkins was committed to community singing. She taught workshops to children at the Old Town School, YMCA clubs, hospital wards, churches, and summer camps, as well as workshops for blind, deaf, and mentally disabled people. In her "Adventures in Rhythm" workshops, she crafted a method built upon meaningless phrases (like "Tah-Boo" or "Zeembah") that children are encouraged to repeat, accompanied by minimal rhythm on a piano, conga, tambourine, or bongo drum. The lessons evolved, incorporating African, West Indian, and Middle Eastern rhythms. News of her workshops spread, and she was eventually hired to appear on *The Totem Club*, a children's show on WTTW. When the show switched from weekly to daily, she was given "This is Rhythm," a segment that featured cameos by Odetta and Big Bill Broonzy, among others.[162]

Up until then, children's music was not taken seriously, and records intended for young listeners were largely nursery rhymes, novelty songs, light classical music, or music from Disney films. *American Folk Songs for Children*, the 1953 album by Pete Seeger on Folkways, broke new ground because, while it was intended to entertain, it also served an educational purpose in exposing listeners to the stories behind songs and the cultures where they originated. There was also a community aspect, as the recordings often featured groups of children singing along, encouraging their at-home counterparts to join in rather than just passively listen. The success of that album then prompted Folkways to release *Songs to Grow On for Mother and Child* by Woody Guthrie in 1956.

Jenkins sent Folkways founder Moses Asch a demo in 1956, which included some original songs and others she had adapted from North Africa, West Africa, the Middle East, and a Southern chain gang recording. He signed her, and the next year, released *Call-and-Response: Rhythmic Group Singing*, the title of which described the method she used in her workshops. She later said it wasn't just the exchange of singing found in churches and synagogues that inspired her call-and-response style, but also the music of bandleader Cab Calloway, whom she often saw perform when she was a child.

The ten songs are minimal—just handclaps and voices, supplied by children at the Howalton Day School, the first private K–8 school for Black students in Chicago. While some songs introduce instrumentation like bells and tambourines, the music is always accessible and spontaneous.[163]

The success of *Call-and-Response* gave Jenkins a career. She recorded more than thirty albums for Folkways and traveled internationally, becoming the label's only artist to tour all five continents.[164] Her 1966 album *You'll Sing a Song and I'll Sing a Song* became the best-selling title in Folkways' history and entered the National Recording Registry in 2007.[165] In 2004, Jenkins was awarded a Grammy Lifetime Achievement Award. She laid the groundwork for children's music as a distinct genre, although it would take until 1995 for *Billboard* to launch its first "kid album" sales chart.

An early protégé of Jenkins was Virginia "Ginni" Clemmens. She was born February 28, 1936, in Evergreen Park, a South Side suburb.[166] In her early twenties, she worked as an occupational therapist at a school for children with intellectual disabilities. At night and on weekends, she became a regular at hootenannies hosted by Bob Gibson at the Gate of Horn. When the Old Town School opened, she was first in line, learning guitar from Frank Hamilton and, later, banjo from Fleming Brown. Soon, as she became the first woman in Chicago playing banjo in folk clubs, Clemmens joined the faculty.

Clemmens incorporated singing into her therapy work, and her reason for taking lessons was to learn how to accompany herself in front of her kids. She even tried introducing the Old Town School's method of guitar instruction to her classes, and when her school wouldn't pay for instruments, she got Win Stracke to call the president of the Key Musical Instrument Company, who ended up donating six guitars.[167]

When a music career beckoned, she followed, first working the circuit in Greenwich Village and then on the West Coast before returning to Chicago. Jenkins invited her to perform on her 1963 Folkways album *Rhythms of Childhood*, not just as a harmony singer and accompanist, but also as a soloist with her banjo on some songs. Two years later, Folkways released *Sing a Rainbow*, Clemmens's first album for children, recorded at the Old Town School. Arranged much like her therapy sessions with students, the songs were preceded by invitations to clap, dance, and sing on the choruses. Clemmens would later become a regular on the 1970s nightclub scene on Wells and Lincoln, but she always said performing for children remained her truest work.[168]

"They don't respond to the show-biz stuff. You have to be real for them, or they'll just ignore you," she said in 1979. "When I need to level out, I always try to sing with and for kids. Then I can carry some of that energy into my other musical work."[169]

OLD TOWN SCHOOL EXPANDS ITS REACH

Meanwhile, the Old Town School had emerged as the leading producer of folk concerts in Chicago, both at the school and at other venues like Orchestra Hall. As the Gate of Horn wound down, many of the most respected artists of the folk revival were performing under the Old Town School banner, including Mahalia Jackson, Doc Watson, Frank Proffitt, Odetta, Reverend Gary Davis, Gus Cannon, Hobart Smith, Bill Monroe, José Feliciano, Terry Callier, Mama Yancey, Josh White, the Clancy Brothers and Tommy Makem, Sonny Terry and Brownie McGhee, John Jacob Niles, and Glenn Yarbrough and the Limeliters. Not only was the school reaching students in the suburbs and cities, it was also offering four-week summer courses for students throughout the United States and in Europe and worked with the State Department in hosting visitors from Austria, Germany, France, Brazil, Japan, India, Nigeria, the Netherlands, and Bolivia.[170]

For Peter Feldmann, who moved from Switzerland to Los Angeles as a child, the Old Town School was a refuge where he could discover an American culture otherwise hidden from him. He dropped out of the University of California at Santa Barbara in 1961 and moved to Chicago, where a neighbor referred him to the school. He enrolled in Hamilton's class, where he learned Maybelle Carter's rhythmic guitar style. He discovered that if he sat in the back of the class he could also observe Fleming Brown, in the classroom across the hall, who was teaching clawhammer style banjo. "I was overloaded on information," he recalled.[171]

The Old Town School stoked the hunger of students like Feldmann by publishing reference lists of Library of Congress field recordings and even by hosting special workshops with indigenous musicians who appeared on those recordings. Enamored with North Carolina banjo player and singer Frank Proffitt, Feldmann volunteered to usher him around Chicago during his three-day visit. More than fifty years later, his memory of taking Proffitt to the Field Museum of Natural History and watching him run his fingers through animal pelts from Siberia and South America is still a powerful one. The musician later described to his young host his method of stretching groundhog skins across a stovepipe to make the head of his homemade fretless banjos.

"As a foreigner, what a great way to learn about America," Feldmann said. "You don't just get the political bullshit, but you go underneath and you find the simple honest and decent people who create this beautiful music and you think 'wow so this is what it means to be an American.'"[172]

WIN STRACKE'S
LAST ACT

The Old Town School's success invigorated Win Stracke, who was often referred to as its "dean," even though he didn't formally teach classes. He was prolific during the school's first decade, writing books, recording music, and almost ten years after being blacklisted, appearing in 1963 on national television as a red-headed giant in "Quillow and the Giant," an adaptation of a James Thurber story for NBC's *Children's Theatre*.[173]

By then he had gained prominence outside Chicago as a singer and folk music scholar who knew how to curate music for children. Golden Records, a New York–based label, matched him with both the Arthur Norman Orchestra and Chorus and Mitch Miller and His Orchestra for a series of singles and albums centered around themes such as railroads, heroes, cowboys, and the Civil War. Even for children, Stracke didn't varnish some of the songs' uncomfortable truths. On "Casey Jones," the early twentieth-century ballad about the heroic death of the mythologized railroad engineer in a 1900 rail crash after trying to stop his speeding train, Stracke includes the controversial coda about Jones's wife, who, until her death in 1958, said it slandered her: "Mrs. Jones sat on her bed a-sighing / Just received a message that Casey was dying / Said go to bed children and hush your crying / You gonna get another papa on the Salt Lake Line."[174]

Stracke recorded *Americana*, his first full-length album for adult listeners in 1957, the year the Old Town School opened its doors, with Richard Pick, his Gate of Horn partner, on guitar. While its title suggests standard wholesome fare, *Americana* is a subversive collection of twelve songs obsessed with hardship, drinking, sex, murder, and heartbreak. As Studs Terkel observes in the liner notes, the songs "pretty much reflect Win Stracke's look at life."[175] Many of the songs were little known at the time. His version of the murder ballad "Duncan and Brady" was the first recorded version since Leadbelly's version ten years earlier; the same is true of "Dink's Song" and "No Irish Need Apply."

As with "Casey Jones," Stracke chose versions of songs that had not yet been sanitized for family audiences by his contemporaries. "Acres of Clams," an 1874 song about a Puget Sound dockworker, is downright morose in its description of toiling with no reward, nearly freezing to death, and suicidal thoughts. While "Big Rock Candy Mountain," a description of paradise as seen through a hobo's eyes, is now mostly recognized as a children's song, Stracke chooses the 1928 version originally recorded by cowboy singer Harry McClintock, which imagines "cigarette trees," "little streams of alcohol," and "a lake of stew" in a place where "the cops have wooden legs / the bulldogs all have rubber teeth" and "they boiled in oil the inventor of toil."[176] Needless to say these are all images that Burl Ives scrubbed from his hit version in 1949.

Alcohol figured heavily. A concoction Stracke titled "Debate—Cold Water Versus Rye Whiskey" is an early mash-up between a Prohibition-era song and a traditional drunkard's lullaby that creates a conversation between stern resolve and natural compulsion. Because of his classical training and fatherly appearance, Stracke was not perceived as someone who was drawn to the seamy and unkempt roots of early folk music. *Americana* not only separated him from his pop-oriented contemporaries, but it foreshadowed the spirit of the coming generation that would turn its back on folk commercialism. At the time, *Billboard* agreed, calling the album "full of pathos, humor and historical significance." Even the cover art, an almost sepia-toned image of a cabin tucked inside dark woods, was noted for lacking "the stamp of the poseur so often found in the folk field."[177]

In 1965, Stracke followed in the footsteps of Alan Lomax, Carl Sandburg, Pete Seeger, and others by publishing his own compendium of folk songs organized by theme, no matter their era or country of origin. As the title suggests, the purpose of *Songs of Man* was to discover musical transcendence, or "the universality of man demonstrated in the universality of the songs he sings."[178] The fifteen chapter titles—including "Men and Women at Work," "Frailties and Foibles," "Well Loved Places," "The Cup That Cheers," and "The Cuckoo"—showed how far Stracke wanted to go in erasing the biographies of individual songs and appreciating them together for their human essence.

To better serve the reader, the nearly four-hundred-page volume was purposely designed for living room amateurs: arrangements are suited to both guitar and piano, strumming is recommended, the keys suit average vocal ranges, and on songs with multiple verses and convoluted lyrics, Stracke and co-author Norman Luboff even marked the strongest beats to stop the singer from getting lost.

Stracke was given a private room at the Newberry Library for a year to research songs. To see how far some songs had traveled, he didn't have to leave the building. "Wren Boy's Song," which he found in an 1841 songbook, originated in the British Isles. One day he walked down the hall and sang the melody to a Newberry guard, a retired Chicago cop born in Ireland. "Why I used to sing that song when I was a youth in County Clare!" he exclaimed. It was the guard's version Stracke chose for the book.[179]

In the late 1960s, while Stracke was embraced by the highest level of government in the state of Illinois, he was still under FBI surveillance. His activities were still being tracked by the agency when the Illinois Sesquicentennial Commission assigned Stracke and Luboff to write an original piece of music to commemorate the state's 150th year in 1968. Illinois governor Otto Kerner even asked Stracke to write new verses to "Illinois," the official state song, which dated back to 1925. Kerner wanted the song updated with an arrangement that "expresses the spirit of the 1960's."[180] Songsheets were printed and distributed throughout the state to prepare people for the fifteen hundred events that would span the year.[181]

Stracke and Luboff were given free rein for their commissioned piece. They came up with a cantata based on the life of Edward Coles, the state's second governor, an abolitionist who eradicated slavery from his state decades before the Civil War. *Freedom Country* was not a simple project; besides the chorus and solo vocal part, it required actors for spoken narration. The *Chicago Tribune* timed its performance at twenty-three minutes. It made its debut February 14, 1968, at Northwestern University.[182]

Stracke kept busy that sesquicentennial year. He performed on *I Remember Illinois*, an hour-long television special broadcast in February on both the local NBC outlet and WGN, in company with other guest luminaries like Jack Benny, Steve Allen, Benny Goodman, Mahalia Jackson, Gene Krupa, and Chicago Mayor Richard J. Daley.[183] He used the exposure to then promote *Songs Bridge the Gap*, a forty-five-minute dinner program he promoted through the Old Town School that cost a booking fee of $150 but was partially underwritten by the sesquicentennial commission.[184]

The commission also funded the release of *Songs of Old Town*, a full-length album that featured songs that Stracke identified with his relationship to Chicago. The songs reflect inherent contradictions. They include a Scottish drinking song ("A Wee Drappie O'T"), a Baptist sermon ("Harp of a Thousand Strings"), traditional songs that remained in his repertoire ("Dink's Song," "Tennessee Stud"), and "The Forty-Third Ward," an original that imagines his beloved Old Town as an oasis for freethinkers. "No one gives a damn what you say or wear / how you make your living or part your hair / you can even grow a beard, we don't care / because this is the home of laissez faire," he sings.[185]

Stracke was enjoying his newfound productivity so much he was willing to subvert his image. In 1970, P.I.P. Records released *The Earthy Side*, a collection of thirty-three playfully obscene folk songs and spoken-word verse written by Thomas Hardy, Abraham Lincoln, Robert Burns, Benjamin Franklin, Rudyard Kipling, and others. Neither the Norman Luboff Choir nor Stracke are credited; instead, they are billed as the Movement to Preserve Scatalogical [*sic*] & Prurient Material in Its Original Form. Thanks to liner notes from Studs Terkel, Stracke's identity was not masked: "The bass-baritone, whose orotundity pervades this album, has for many years been soloist in some of our most distinguished—Shall we say most High?—churches."[186] The songs cover masturbation, flatulence, and sex, but the *Mad* magazine antics strike a profound tenor due to the solemnity of Stracke's voice and the sumptuousness of the classical choir.

A SECOND HOME AND A
NEW GENERATION

Somehow, Stracke also found time to help direct the school's first move. In 1967, the school was asked to relocate because the building's owners had plans to tear it down to build a gas station. The school's board started reaching out to donors to help fund the purchase of the school's own building. Stracke wanted to call it the

Carl Sandburg House and fashion it after the Cecil Sharp House in London, which houses the English Folk Dance and Song Society to this day. The board set goals: the school had to remain in Old Town; it must have an auditorium accommodating four hundred people "with removable seats" so the space could also be used for group dancing and classes; there had to be a library, office space, eight classrooms, and more. Stracke called on anyone to help—former students, political leaders, instrument manufacturers, and civic organizations.[187]

The next year, the North Avenue location closed in July, and on September 16, 1968, the school reopened two miles away at 909 West Armitage, the site of Aldine Hall, a former German social club. The fundraising had been a success: contributions included underwriting from the Newport Folk Festival, the Old Town Triangle Association, and the Illinois Sesquicentennial Commission, as well as money raised by a benefit concert that December featuring Bill Monroe and His Bluegrass Boys. Opening night was similar to the first one on North Avenue. To note the absence of Big Bill, the school named its first-floor performance space Broonzy Hall in his honor.[188]

The move put the school in a predominantly Puerto Rican neighborhood full of people who had already been pushed out of Old Town, which was transforming into a destination playground for young professionals and weekend tourists. Not long after it opened its doors, the school, along with all the other businesses along the Armitage corridor, found its windows smashed by the Young Lords, a Puerto Rican gang lashing out at what they perceived as threats of further displacement. But the school won them over. Right away, it sent donations to a free health clinic and breakfast program for children that the gang operated out of a nearby church. "We just learned they were progressive people. They were into music, they were not gentrifiers," said José "Cha Cha" Jiménez, the Young Lords co-founder. "The folk music people were on our side."[189]

Less than a year after the new location was established, on August 16, 1969, Stracke announced that Dawn Greening had decided to step down. He didn't give a reason. "It's difficult to visualize the school without Dawn's warm, pervasive presence," he said.[190] Writing months later in the school newsletter, he admitted that Greening had wanted to "bow out for some time," but he had convinced her to wait until the Armitage location had opened.[191] She had back problems and was no longer living nearby, having moved from Oak Park to north suburban Glenview. The school had also grown. By its tenth anniversary in late 1967, a total of 6,323 students had attended classes, some staying for just five weeks, the minimum length of a course, and others as long as five years.[192] The personal touch Greening had that drew people to her and then to the school was suddenly out of place. "It didn't need her anymore," said her son Lance.[193]

By this time, the folk revival was winding down nationwide, but the school would survive into the next decade because it had broadened its mission to incorporate dance, ethnic music, and neighborhood outreach, hosting events from book signing parties to holiday plays to folk dances to weekly community sings to even an annual "Los Posadas," a Mexican-themed processional that ran through the neighborhood every Christmas season, and an annual mummers' play, in which Stracke played the role of Father Christmas. The Folklore Center became a major retailer of instruments, accessories, records, and books in Chicago, and if students could not afford to buy their own instruments, the school rented guitars and banjos for $6 a month. The school also obtained funding to provide music in Chicago schools and hospitals, playing for psychiatric patients and sick children.

In late 1969, Stracke started promoting "Project Outreach," a music scholarship program targeting fifty schoolchildren. Stracke campaigned for underwriters, and forty signed up; the top donors were the Illinois Arts Council and Meister Brau beer. That April, the school enrolled fourth and fifth graders from two nearby schools in free guitar classes lasting fourteen weeks with the promise that if they persevered through the entire course, they could keep their instruments. Only four dropped out.[194]

That same month, the school announced another milestone: enrollment hit nearly five hundred students, an all-time high for a single session.[195] The faculty had also increased to nearly twenty instructors, a far cry from the days when Frank Hamilton juggled all the classes. By the early 1960s, Hamilton, who was busy establishing his career as a performer, was burned out. He recorded several albums within a short time, including *Nonesuch and Other Folk Tunes*, a duo album with Pete Seeger, in 1959, the same year Hamilton was invited to play at the inaugural Newport Folk Festival. Although they were twenty years apart in age, and although one was a national folk star and the other far less so, the album presents the two men as equals, trading verses on songs from Africa, the Caribbean, and the American South with the upbeat energy and breezy informality of a nighttime jam session. In the same spirit as the Old Town School, the goal of this mostly instrumental album was to show the full breadth of folk music beyond what might have been considered fashionable at the time. The eclecticism and global ambition of *Nonesuch* makes it wholly different from typical folk fare like the Kingston Trio or even the Weavers.

Three years later, in 1962, Folkways Records released *Frank Hamilton Sings Folk Songs*, Hamilton's true solo debut, featuring just his banjo and twelve-string guitar. Seeger is present in the liner notes, in which he endorses Hamilton as a "genius" and "one of the greatest musicians I've ever met."[196] That same year, when Erik Darling dropped out of the Weavers, Seeger recommended Hamilton as a replacement. Hamilton jumped at the chance and left Chicago for good.

Stracke and Greening had anticipated Hamilton's departure years earlier. He belonged to a small but emerging group of virtuoso banjo instrumentalists, including Erik Darling, Tom Paley, Dick Weissman, Sandy Bull, and Billy Faier, who could play a wide-ranging repertoire with a classical sensibility and acute sensitivity. The same year the Old Town School opened, Hamilton appeared on *The Art of the Five String Banjo* on Riverside Records, a milestone album by Faier from 1957 that was considered essential listening for urban revivalists.[197] In December 1959, Stracke invited Weissman to travel to Chicago, where the school offered him a job as Hamilton's assistant for $75 per week. When he arrived, he performed with Hamilton at the Gate of Horn, but soon realized Hamilton was not aware of his job offer and that he was being used as an "insurance policy" in case Hamilton left Chicago.[198] "The whole situation made me uncomfortable," he said. He declined the offer and returned to New York.[199]

With his fellow founders gone, Stracke was alone. He assigned Ray Tate, a teacher since the mid-1960s, to replace Hamilton. By 1971, Stracke, too, had left the school. That year, he wrote a three-page letter to *Chicago Daily News* writer Marshall Rosenthal, in which he thanks Rosenthal for referring to him as "the father of Chicago folk singers" in a recent article but says he is ready for the new generation to take over.

Just what my contribution to this lovely art in Chicago has been, is a bit more difficult to pinpoint. Perhaps it was the founding of the Old Town School of Folk Music in 1957 and the Old Town Folklore center a few years later. Scores of the now wonderful singers in Chicago like Ed and Fred Holstein, John Prine, Norm Siegel, Steve Goodman, Bonnie Kolok [*sic*], Ginny Clemmens and many others first worked at the center, studied or taught at the school, or were presented in concert at the school early in their development as artists.

I firmly believe that America is having a creative musical explosion unprecedented in our history. I should say literary as well for the outpourings of these young singers and writers begs for comparison with the . . . period of early 19th century Germany which produced such geniuses as Schubert and Heine. It's truly a glorious period and to think that I may have had a part in it is—well, just too much.[200]

Stracke then walks Rosenthal through his past, telling him about his beginnings with the WLS *Barn Dance*, his memories of the Almanac Singers coming to town, his friendship with Big Bill Broonzy, and how "I Come for to Sing" was "probably the first folk song show." He is on a roll, caught up in his memories, until he stops himself. He ends with a declaration: "Listen friend, while I may or may not be 'the father of Chicago folk singers'—I'm not through yet!"[201]

But continuing in that role would prove difficult. Despite surviving the blacklist and ushering the school to unprecedented heights, Stracke suffered deeply from manic depression and was frequently hospitalized during the school's first decade. The first time was in 1959, following the deaths of the three people closest to him: his mother, Big Bill Broonzy, and his best friend, Philip Loeb, a Broadway and television actor from New York City whose career fell victim to the blacklist. Distraught, Loeb died of suicide in 1955. Stracke's daughter Jane said the deaths hit her father "like a ton of bricks."[202] At Michael Reese Hospital, he was diagnosed with bipolar disorder.[203]

The disorder accounted for bouts of manic activity, but also periods when he would simply disappear for weeks. The faculty and staff became accustomed to interacting with two separate people. "He would go into himself. All the sudden Win would not recognize anybody," said Nate Lofton.[204] Stracke would not necessarily hide his condition. "We knew he would go into mental wards on occasions," said Art Thieme. "But he would snap out of it and come back and be part of the school again."[205] As his depression wore on, Stracke would use humor to explain his absences. In a letter to writer Jack Conroy, Stracke struck the tone of a Baptist preacher: "Yes, Brother Jack, for five weeks or more I was ensconced in 15E at the Veterans Research Hospital. Ostensibly I was there because of a depression but to you I confess that my real reason was to have an extended opportunity for meditation and prayer—may I be forgiven for this duplicity."[206]

The depression was worse for his family. Fights with his wife, Genevieve, escalated, after which Stracke would disappear into the basement, where he would live for days or weeks, refusing to let his children see him. Eventually, he was prescribed lithium, and the rest of his life was dedicated to managing his condition. In 1977, ten years after he and Genevieve divorced, he left Chicago altogether and moved by himself to San Miguel de Allende, a city in central Mexico that was a haven for artists and writers. He lived in a hotel for artists. ("This is a perfect place! Gorgeous weather, wonderful people," he wrote the Greening family.)[207] A few years later he moved once more to Fort Collins, Colorado, where the Greenings had retired in 1979 to be near their two daughters. Dawn Greening had not given up on folk music: she spun folk records on a public radio show she hosted for twelve years.[208] Living in the same city once again, she and Win briefly picked up their friendship where it had left off until illness forced him to return to Chicago. He died June 2, 1991, of natural causes.[209] Her death followed two years later, on March 20, 1993.[210]

Stracke's lengthy absence from Chicago compromised the profound stature he had established in the school's first decade. He no longer did anything for newspaper columnists to write about or for radio hosts to promote, and he was not available for concerts, recitals, or acting opportunities. By the time he returned in 1988, Stracke, once championed as Chicago's musicologist and dean of the folk tradition, found that folk music in Chicago had moved to the margins. While his treasured friend Studs Terkel had stayed put and continued to thrive in the years after the folk revival to become a feisty patriarch of the city, Stracke returned to a Chicago that largely didn't recognize him, or he it. Even his beloved Old Town was no longer the soul of the city's bohemian culture, with its coffeehouses, salons, basement theaters, bookstores, trinket shops, art galleries, and folk music school gone. In 1967, the *Chicago Tribune* reported that urban renewal was pushing working families out of the neighborhood and that within twenty years, Old Town would likely "become the residence of the rich."[211]

It wouldn't take even that long. Eight years later, in 1975, developer Rudolph Schwartz announced the pending demolition of nearly five buildings at 1608 North Wells to make way for a $20 million, 54,000-square-foot indoor shopping complex and high-rise.[212] The structure would sit on the footprint of Piper's Alley, an iconic stretch that was home to storefront specialty shops, clubs, and the

Second City, a location that once served as the pulse of the neighborhood's creative community. Today the complex still stands, but is commonly referred to by its former name. Three blocks to the west, the Immigrant State Bank building is now a strip mall.

When Stracke returned to the stage, it was for the rare event outside Old Town, such as the thirtieth-anniversary fundraising concert for the Old Town School at Orchestra Hall in 1987.[213] Time had given him perspective. Watching the bill that included Old Town alumni John Prine, David Bromberg, and Fred Holstein, he was deeply moved. "I'm overwhelmed that something I had a hand in starting should now come to this kind of fruition," he said. Then he joined Studs Terkel in a duet of three songs from *Songs of Old Town*, his album dedicated to the old neighborhood and city he once knew and loved. When they finished, nearly three thousand people stood and applauded.[214]

BOHEMIA IN HYDE PARK

THE UNIVERSITY OF CHICAGO
FOLK FESTIVAL

Mike Fleischer's first exposure to folk music was at a 1948 presidential campaign rally for Progressive Party candidate Henry Wallace at the United Electrical Workers union hall at 37 South Ashland. Fleischer, as a twelve-year-old dragged to the concert by his mother, listened to labor songs sung by the holy trinity of folk music: Woody Guthrie, Pete Seeger, and Cisco Houston.

He was sold. "Music of the people, not crap you get off the radio," is how he summed up the evening decades later.[1]

Folk music had social and political purpose, perfect ingredients for a young man in a hurry. Conformity was not in the cards. "Fleischer said he threw a shoe at his own TV screen eight months ago and doesn't intend to have it fixed," the *Chicago Tribune* reported in 1961. He had grown up to be a cranky and unrepentant twenty-four-year-old only too happy to be portrayed as a contrarian in a generation that fell too easily for good looks. Mass media, he proclaimed, was "murdering tradition and individualism."

> Time was when a youngster who wanted to hear music would learn to play the fiddle. He would keep the old ballads alive and make up new ones. Now he switches on TV or radio and gets commercial junk

with nothing to it but rhythm. . . . Popular music today gives people
no credit for brains. All the songs ever say is "I love you, you love me,
or I don't and you don't and you're a *houn* dawg."[2]

Myron P. "Mike" Fleischer was born in Boston on September 30,
1936, but grew up in Hyde Park, on the South Side of Chicago, where
his father worked at a nearby Chevrolet dealership.[3] Although he
earned a Purple Heart for his Navy service during the Korean
War, that experience also gave him his first opportunity to share
his musical tastes with others by spinning records by the Stanley
Brothers, Bill Monroe, and Hank Williams on naval radio.[4] When he
returned home in 1958 and enrolled in classes at the University of
Chicago, he was already a decorated war veteran with little patience
for artifice. "Like many GI's after World War II, he just wouldn't
take the bullshit," said Josh Dunson, a classmate.[5]

NEWPORT
SETS THE STAGE

Fleischer's return to Chicago coincided with the early stages of the
folk revival in the city. Albert Grossman's Gate of Horn had opened
its doors two years earlier, in 1956, and the Old Town School of Folk
Music had created a home for like-minded enthusiasts on the near
North Side the next year. Fleischer frequented both venues, but
he also attended the first two years of the Newport Folk Festival in
Rhode Island, in 1959 and 1960, also under the direction of Grossman. Fleischer's major may have been cultural anthropology, but
academics were ultimately a distraction from his real passion. It
would take him six years to graduate.

Fleischer became president of the university's Folklore Society,
a position that allowed him to use the connections he had made to
broaden the society's scope beyond organizing hootenannies and
one-off concerts. The society had started in 1953, but had produced
only a handful of concerts to date, most notably by Peggy Seeger,
Odetta, and Bob Gibson, all of whom Fleischer booked to play the
campus in 1958.[6]

In May 1960, Fleischer connected with Mike Seeger, one-third of the New Lost City Ramblers, a pioneering group at the forefront of the folk revival. They popularized Southern roots music recorded prior to 1950 for urban audiences, not just through their own performances but also through workshops and curated performances with regional musicians and singers, many of whom had never performed outside their home regions. That month, the group was in the midst of a Midwestern tour, but when one of the stops was canceled, organizers in Ann Arbor, Michigan, quickly called Fleischer to see if he could arrange a make-up date in Chicago.

Fleischer was probably already familiar with the Ramblers, having attended the first Newport Folk Festival, where they performed two sets on July 11 and 12, 1959. That festival had a distinctive Chicago flavor because programming fell under the direction of co-producer Grossman, who filled both nights with familiar faces from back home—including Bob Gibson, Odetta, and Frank Hamilton, who already held down the Gate of Horn stage. Studs Terkel emceed. The Ramblers benefited from Newport: they received national media attention from outlets like the *Nation* and the *New York Times*, their sets were recorded, and three selections were pulled from those sets for a Newport compilation album released by Vanguard. The album came with a rousing endorsement from Terkel in the liner notes: "The New Lost City Ramblers have set themselves a double task as sprightly performers and as devoted young scholars. . . . Obviously dedicated, these three urban-conditioned musicians have caught the flavor and the fire of another era. Of even happier note is their building of a new audience for this style that is far from dead."[7]

The band members themselves—Mike Seeger, John Cohen, and Tom Paley—recognized their unusual place in the current revival: they were neither a slick commercial act nor had they come up from the South like Uncle Dave Macon, Charlie Poole, Roy Harvey and the North Carolina Ramblers, the Carter Family, and others whose music they admired and revived for urban audiences. Instead, the Ramblers held a new middle ground, representing a new generation that wanted to collect, preserve, and share songs from the pre-electric era, but only if they could use the music as a point of departure for their own creativity.

While they drew attention at Newport, the Ramblers understood their primary audience was university students and others near their age who also saw relevancy in string-band songs composed in an earlier era. Fleischer jumped at the chance to get them to Chicago. Once he received the phone call from Ann Arbor, he organized a concert in three days. On Saturday, May 21, 1960, the group performed two shows in Ida Noyes Hall, a three-hundred-seat auditorium in the heart of campus. The auditorium was so full that lines overflowed into the outside hall.[8] The next night, Fleischer arranged an audition for the group at the Gate of Horn and directed members of the Folklore Society to fill its seats.

"They packed the place," remembered Cohen. "There was such enthusiasm. Then we were hired."[9] The group was awarded its longest commitment to date: a three-week engagement in June. They earned universal accolades in the local media—"They sing none of the old warhorses, they affect none of the standard garb, and their impact is fresh and strong," said the *Chicago Tribune*—which ensured return dates.[10]

CONNECTING TO THE NEW YORK FOLK WORLD

During the Ramblers' first weekend in Chicago, Fleischer cornered Seeger to discuss plans for a folk festival at the university. His connection with the Ramblers gave Fleischer a long arm to reach into the Greenwich Village scene. There, Cohen, Ralph Rinzler of the Greenbriar Boys, and folk music promoter and Folklore Center operator Izzy Young were in the midst of forming Friends of Old-Time Music (FOTM). That organization would present a concert series in New York City featuring many of the artists that would also appear at the Chicago festival.

The interchange between Fleischer and Seeger and, inevitably, Rinzler and the FOTM circle would create the first touring network in the Midwest for Southern musicians like Furry Lewis, Sleepy John Estes, Roscoe Holcomb, and Mississippi John Hurt, whom the concert organizers tracked down and convinced to leave retirement to perform their earlier repertoire. These were the performers Fleischer's generation had first heard on Library of Congress field recordings by John Lomax and his son Alan, and on the three-volume *Anthology of American Folk Music* compiled by ethnomusicologist Harry Smith for Folkways in 1952. Their songs would appeal to a young, largely White and educated, generation of urban listeners who felt disconnected from the growing consumerist society emerging around them, said musicologist Robert Cantwell:

> The younger Lomax wanted to construct an idea of folk music consistent with an activist political program and an idealized populist outlook. Under Moses Asch's Folkways label, the *Anthology* could not have but won acceptance in left-wing culture, which would ultimately appropriate it; but it drew on a body of recorded music from a former generation of entrepreneurs who in the early days of electrical recording had cultivated the ethnic and regional record markets that urbanization, mass marketing, and federal regulation would soon undermine. . . . What had been, to the people who originally recorded it, essentially the music of the poor, the isolated, and the uneducated, the *Anthology* reframed as a kind of avant-garde art.[11]

Organizers in both New York and Chicago wanted to introduce audiences to artists they considered the "original source" of the music heard at Newport. "So much is being made from folk music while almost nothing is being put back into it. There have been millions for exploitation and profit and scarcely a penny for tribute," Cohen, Rinzler, and Young wrote in FOTM's statement of purpose.[12]

Making those introductions meant staging workshops, panel discussions, and seminars, all free and designed to educate audiences about song styles, instrumentation, and even the purpose of folk music in modern life. At the first Chicago festival, held February 3–5, 1961, Seeger and Cohen would lead banjo and guitar workshops; lectures such as "The Value of Tradition in Folk Music," "Growth and Development of 'Bluegrass,'" and "Field Collecting in Folk Music" would round out daytime programming; and an exhibit of "folk toys, instruments, magazines, etc." would be put on display each day in Ida Noyes Hall.[13] Leading folklorists of the day were solicited to introduce performers and talk about their history or current significance. The New Lost City Ramblers, the house band for both the Chicago festival and the first FOTM concert, would accompany many of the performers, or help them organize a repertoire that would appeal to an audience seeking an unvarnished performance.[14]

"The date of the first [FOTM] concert was a week after the first Chicago festival, so there was a lot of communication back and forth," said Cohen.[15] For the New Yorkers, "everything went through" Fleischer, who took charge of organizing every component of the festival, from dealing with the university to arranging hospitality and travel for the performers to securing media attention from campus and neighborhood publications as well as the major dailies. The twenty-four-year-old struck a curmudgeonly tone in explaining to the media that his festival would correct the mistakes of other festivals—presumably Newport—and that the three-day bill would feature only performers who weren't in it just for the money. "It will not be a commercial showcase for folk singers working a night club bill. . . . That's what so-called folk festivals in other cities have turned into, but we've asked only serious singers—and many are coming for expense money," he told the *Chicago Daily Tribune*.[16]

A corresponding photo spread aimed to educate general readers about what was happening in Hyde Park: in one photo, three smiling Folklore Society members gather around an autoharp; in another, a couple relaxes on a couch, a guitar in his hands, her eyes gazing fondly upon him as he strums. "Tuning up for a wing-ding," the caption explains.[17] Anchoring the page is Fleischer, in a profile shot with his Navy-style buzzcut in full view. "Fascinating flipperdinger is one of several 'folk toys' which will be on the display during the festival," reads the caption. Fleischer holds the thin wooden toy in his mouth with his right hand, his cheeks puffed out in full blow. In the accompanying article, he tells readers to get the vocabulary right: "A wing-ding is when people get together with instruments and sing folk songs. . . . A hootenanny is when they get sung to."[18]

ARRANGING
THE FIRST FESTIVAL

In all the coverage leading up to the festival's opening night on February 3, 1961, Fleischer's pitch emphasized the urgency of its purpose. In both the *Chicago Daily Tribune* and the *Hyde Park Herald*, he gives slight variations of the same message: "As many people as possible must be exposed to our folk traditions before they die — before TV reaches into the backwoods of Kentucky."[19]

Besides cultivating an image as "a promoter with a nonprofit purpose . . . in presenting this unusual festival," according to the *Chicago Sun-Times*, Fleischer aimed to give the Chicago festival wider credibility by inviting leading folk-world scholars: University of Illinois folklorist Archie Green, storyteller and folklorist Richard Chase, Canadian folklorist and singer Alan Mills, folk song collector Frank Warner, who was credited with discovering the folk ballad believed to be the source of the recent Kingston Trio hit "Tom Dooley," and his new friends from Greenwich Village: Young, Rinzler, and the New Lost City Ramblers.[20] Also at his disposal were the principals at the Old Town School of Folk Music, who, being much older, had connections on the folk circuit.

"Mike knew exactly what he was doing. He was a hustler. He connected himself with people," said Kit Kollenberg, a Folklore Society member and Fleischer's girlfriend at the time. "He knew the kind of help he needed, so the friends he had met his needs to the greater good. They made it possible to get this incredible folk talent to this concert and to get money in advance to be able to do this. It wasn't inexpensive to run."[21]

Fleischer was not a musician, but considered himself a tastemaker with a gift for promotion: "collaring people and buttonholing them, jawboning" were his specialties, said David Gedalecia, a Folklore Society member and friend. "He could be a little overbearing. Sometimes he could be a little short with you because he was onto his agenda. He was very much wrapped up into what he was doing. In a sense, he did push people along to get things done."[22]

Among his growing circle of prominent university folklorists and new associates in Greenwich Village, Fleischer solicited advice, invited participation, and emphasized the greater good of the festival to their pursuits. One such mentor, George Armstrong, an illustrator from north suburban Wilmette who was at the forefront of the local folk scene as a singer and bagpipe player, took Fleischer's phone calls seeking advice. He wrote Fleischer a four-page letter to provide addresses for Pete Seeger and others. But more importantly, he outlined a kind of mission statement he suggested Fleischer follow:

> In this venture I believe your group has the opportunity to do something truly significant and memorable. Pete Seeger has often said and written that he wishes his audience could hear the songs sung by the people he learned from. Well why not? Why can't some of these traditional singers to whom we all owe so much be brought to a folk festival. Seeger would be thrilled to have the chance to introduce us to Pete Steele one of our great traditional singers and banjo players. Mike Seeger could introduce Elizabeth Cotton [*sic*] that great negro guitarist in Washington D.C. Richard Chase could bring Horton Barker, the blind Virginia ballad singer. . . . What a rich moving experience it would be to bring such people together to have them SHARE their music with us. These traditional singers are the real source of our folk music, but they have been forgotten in the vulgar copywriting payola rat race of commercial folk music.
>
> You mentioned that you had offered $700 to "Lightning" Hopkins to come to Chicago. When Big Bill Broonzy was alive no one around here ever offered him that kind of money and he was the greatest. There's certainly irony here, but now it's too late. Aunt Molly Jackson died a few weeks ago in poverty and obscurity. It's too late for her too. But there are still many of the old timers alive. It

is quite possible that many of them would not be able or willing to participate in a U. of C. Folk Festival. However it seems to me we owe a great debt to these folks and I believe it would be a fine gesture if some of them were invited to your festival. This would at least in some measure serve to recognize the great contribution that these traditional singers both living and dead have made to our heritage. And believe me we would not be doing them a favor, but we ourselves would reap the greatest benefit from their participation. The true tradition of folk music is sharing, not selling and I think one of the prime considerations of your festival should be to create a warm, friendly, and social atmosphere in which the music can be enjoyed at its best.

I would like to urge you to seek the advice and counsel of Pete Seeger and Richard Chase on how to set up your festival. I'm sure if they were convinced that you are interested in a festival that would truly represent genuine folk music, you would get their whole-hearted support.[23]

A few lines later, Armstrong signed the letter, but added a revealing, and capitalized, postscript: "(Our motto: HELP FIGHT FOLKUM—AVOID ANOTHER NEWPORT)."[24]

Through his affiliation with Seeger and Cohen, Fleischer learned he could promote the festival far outside Chicago by tapping into their connections. "He was a fireball," said Cohen. "He was the clearinghouse for all the ideas."[25] As an example, in one letter, Fleischer addressed all three Ramblers with the casual air of a lifelong friend:

Howdy, howdy. Thanks for the free plug at Cornell and I am sure, the free plugs at all of your recent doings, individually and collectively.

I am at a loss as to the mailing of information, letters, and tickets to Roscoe Holcumb [sic] and Elizabeth Cotton [sic]. Shall I send them through you or could you furnish me with addresses.

I have arranged accommodations for them and for Ramblers, wives, and children, Greenbriars, guitars, banjos, and etc. Is this O.K.?

The University legal department, I have concluded, is utterly impossible; so the contracts, deposits, are held up. Sorry . . .

Mike told me about the date you have at Michigan and the one at Wisconsin. I will send a Folklore Society name list as soon as the cotton-pickin' secretary of this Folklore Society gives me the appropriate names.

Very soon now, you will receive several posters about the Folk Festival. You know where to put them. I will also send some mail-order ticket forms. If anyone is interested, give him one.[26]

Letters requesting final confirmation from artists and participants rolled from Fleischer's desk in December, just two months before opening night. Perhaps sensing his need for a swift answer, and also in deference to people he was approaching, Fleischer infused his letters with charm and flattery. In his pitch to Warner, he offered $350 and said the desire to have him participate "is an understatement."[27]

Several of your old friends have been invited to participate in this event, among them Frank Proffitt, Horton Barker, and Richard Chase.

This festival's purpose is not merely entertainment, but is being put into the form of an educational week-end in American traditional folk music. The emphasis is on tradition. In view of this we feel that you would be of definite asset to our undertaking. We look forward to having you come, bringing your old friends with you, not in person but in song. (Of course, please do bring friends in person too.)[28]

Below his signature, Fleischer added a persuasively worded postscript:

I saw you at Newport in 1959 and noticed that you weren't there in 1960. Perhaps you too are fed up with overcomercialization [sic] of folk music.[29]

Working out details for the participants, such as contracts, overnight stays, bus tickets, travel routing, and for Mills in Quebec, visas, was an arduous process that transpired via correspondence that stretched over weeks. As persuasive as he was, Fleischer's workload made him prone to memory lapses—he told Chase that a folk festival without him would be "like a pine forest without needles," but neglected to give him the festival dates, which became Chase's first question in his response a week later.[30]

Contracts needed signing, but their terms were negotiated through the office of the director of student activities, which slowed down the process due to the dean of students' genuine fear of losing money on a risky and overblown venture. Securing Mills, for example, required a total of eight letters passing between Quebec and Chicago over five weeks. On the second round, Mills told Fleischer he was "happy to know, natch, that advance sales for the Festival are going well and that the University is so pleased about it (as they bloody well should be!)."[31] But he still had problems with the contract: travel expenses, estimated by Mills as ranging between $350 and $450 for himself and his wife, Jean, would consume Fleischer's $600 guarantee. "So what's left?" he asked.[32] Mills colored in his problem by describing the reaction of his agent upon learning the figure: "He hit the roof and the 'I-told-you-so's' were flyin' all over the place.... Have you any solution to offer?"[33] And so it continued.

Advocates for performers had serious concerns about their traveling to Chicago, especially during a harsh winter. In correspondence with Fleischer, Chase said he would accompany Frank Proffitt from the singer's home in Reese, North Carolina, by bus. But he worried about "the rather long and, for us old folks, difficult trip." "We're all a bit afraid of the expenses, and possible contingencies.... We would like to have from you some clear and definite kind of written statement, contract.... *I must ask you to do this at once*. There are only 14 days before we are supposed to head up that way," Chase wrote, the second to last sentence boxed in red pen.[34]

The performers themselves tended to express humility, most likely because, for many of them, this was the first time they had been asked to perform to such a large audience. For those located in the most remote pockets of the rural South, it was a rare, if not inaugural, venture into a big city. For Proffitt, the invitation to Chicago came a year before he recorded his first album for Folkways in 1962, two years before his Newport Folk Festival debut in 1963, and almost four years before his death at age fifty-two. It was Proffitt, a banjoist and tobacco and strawberry farmer living in the Beech Mountain region of North Carolina, who taught Frank Warner a variation of "Tom Dooley" (called "Tom Dula") in 1938, and he established an ongoing relationship with the song collector.[35]

In a handwritten note, Proffitt told Fleischer that his invitation to the Chicago festival was "received with appreciation. And I *except* [*sic*] it with gratitude to all concerned," he added.[36] However, Proffitt emphasized his reluctance to perform in an environment that was alien to him and where the expectations of others might be too high:

> I do not rate in any way with professional folk singers or players. It has been my privilege to ad [*sic*] some interest to the traditional folk way of the mountain people. But not in a way that can be called [illegible] on my part. It is only that I have some fears that others may see more in me than is there.
>
> It is a great honor to me to have this invitation and if others think that I am important to the program, I hope I can be able to be of help in a small way.[37]

Proffitt did make it to Chicago, as did others, like the Stanley Brothers, the Clinch Mountain Boys, Elizabeth Cotten, Roscoe Holcomb, Horton Barker, and Jean Carignan. Some artists, however, had to travel only a few blocks, such as Maxwell Street singer-guitarist Arvella Gray, and Memphis Slim and Willie Dixon, who appeared together. Slim, a jump blues bandleader whose 1947 song "Every Day I Have the Blues" was already a standard, had just played piano throughout *Willie's Blues*, the debut album by Dixon, house songwriter and bassist for Chess Records. The duo was just starting to play folk festivals in the United States and Europe.

A welcome tea was held two blocks from Ida Noyes Hall for the performers, many of whom had arrived in wintry Chicago just hours before opening night via Union Station or Midway Airport. Once they stepped into the cold, they were met by students who drove them to campus or otherwise helped them navigate the conditions. "The Stanley Brothers came in the middle of a blizzard. We had sleds and put their instruments on them," Kit Kollenberg remembered.[38] As they warmed up at Ida Noyes Hall, other students poured them tea and coffee in china cups from two large silver samovars.[39]

"A lot of thought was given to hosting because we wanted to make people from rural areas, some who had never seen snow, feel welcomed," said Nina Helstein, a Folklore Society volunteer. "There was an unbelievable excitement."[40]

OPENING
THE FIRST FESTIVAL

When the scene shifted to Mandel Hall for opening night, Fleischer's was the first voice at the microphone. He welcomed the audience, but quickly introduced George Armstrong, who performed the 1793 Scottish anthem "Scots, Wha Hae" on bagpipes, establishing a tradition for the festival's opening for years to come. Three minutes later, Studs Terkel took over as emcee. He announced that the festival was "rather unique," not just because of the variety of performers on the bill, but because they represented what he suggested was a true representation of American song. The festival was a first, "because the kind of music, singing and storytelling here tonight is not beautiful, not pretty in the accepted sense. It is beautiful in a very raw sense," he said, stretching the word "raw" so it roared.[41] "Because many of the singers you will hear are indigenous. In that the music they sing, the stories they tell, are part of the very warp and wound of their very lives," he told the audience. "It was Alan Lomax who said, 'There's no such thing as American national folk music.' There's Virginia folk music, there's New Orleans folk music, there's Kentucky folk music, there's Canadian folk music. And we'll hear singers from all quarters of the country and of our Northern neighbors too"—then, perhaps with a nod to his friend Win Stracke, who was scheduled to perform the next night—"and from places as far off and exotic and distant as the Old Town School of Folk Music." With that, the audience erupted into cheers.[42]

The New Lost City Ramblers took it from there. That night, the festival ran to midnight, long past the allotted time, but the audience didn't leave. They returned Saturday and Sunday, and once again, on both nights, the music went into overtime. Once things wrapped up at Mandel Hall, the party moved to student apartments, where performers played on couches and kitchen chairs until the early morning hours. "That first festival was completely over the top. There were so many performers and the evening performances went on way, way late . . . it went on for hours," remembers Bob Kass, a Folk Society member.[43]

As the weekend progressed, Fleischer—so confident that he announced dates for the next year's festival in the program—didn't hold back his excitement. He had successfully created the nation's most significant folk festival, second only to Newport.[44] "Mike was on the short side and I was always tall," said Josh Dunson. "Mike was so excited, he jumped up to my head and screamed. It was quite an accomplishment."[45]

THE FOLK REVIVAL
IN HYDE PARK

By the time of the festival's launch in 1961, folk music was shedding its association with left-wing politics to become more family-friendly and commercially potent. In Chicago, the music was still in the clubs, but was transitioning into larger, more prestigious venues like Orchestra Hall, home to the Chicago Symphony Orchestra, thanks in part to Frank Fried, the former Chicago steelworker who got his start in the concert business working for Albert Grossman.[46] "What the audiences wanted to listen to was happy, engaging, relatively depoliticized music, and in most cases I had what they wanted," Fried said.

Folk concerts had taken place in Orchestra Hall in the past, and

Fried had produced a successful three-night date for Pete Seeger in 1958 that sold seventy-five hundred tickets. "An incredible turnout," he remembered decades later. "Pete's own manager was surprised. There was no reason for it that he could see. But folk music was booming."[47]

Fried came up with the concept of producing a folk series at Orchestra Hall on Friday nights, when the classical music venue was often dark. For its first season, he booked many of the era's biggest stars—the Chad Mitchell Trio, Miriam Makeba with Chad Mitchell, Josh White, Pete Seeger, the Clancy Brothers, and Ewan MacColl and Peggy Seeger. A success, the series continued a second season and helped Fried establish himself as one of the most prominent folk music promoters in the Midwest.[48] To establish a level of prestige that the clubs could not, Fried took a cue from the classical world and programmed the music as a subscription series. "That quickly gave me a degree of respectability that often eluded the lowly pop promoter," he said. "Many of the artists, not incidentally, liked the way some of that cachet rubbed off on *them*."[49]

Up to that point, folk music in Hyde Park had amounted to occasional concerts in the University of Chicago's Mandel Hall, local clubs, and hootenannies on campus and throughout the neighborhood. The "hoots" grew in popularity in the late 1950s, taking place either in area bars and theaters or at the university, which could bring in a full slate of well-known performers to lead the sing-alongs. "The community commands . . . we comply!" said an advertisement for hootenannies at the Limelight Café Theater, at 1544 East Fifty-Seventh.[50] The University of Chicago's Folklore Society was responsible for the biggest events. More than fifteen performers filled the roster of an April 17, 1959, hootenanny sponsored by the society at International House on campus. The bill foreshadowed the variety of the first Folk Festival: Fleming Brown, Ella Jenkins, Frank Hamilton, Brother John Sellers, and several other local performers were scheduled to perform "blues, ballads, bagpipe music, spirituals, sea chanties, European songs, mountain music, Caribbean songs all for $1.25."[51]

The university was attracting students partly because the Hyde Park neighborhood bordered areas of the South Side that were home to the pioneers of electric blues: Muddy Waters, Howlin' Wolf, Junior Wells, Otis Rush, and others. By 1960, most of Chicago's top blues performers were international stars, while at home they were starting to cross over to White audiences through campus folk festivals. Elvin Bishop, a first-generation White blues guitarist, arrived in Hyde Park in fall 1960 after winning a National Merit Scholarship that guaranteed him enrollment in any university of his choice. For a young man from Tulsa, Oklahoma already enthralled with Chicago blues, that choice was easy.[52] Within his first days on campus, Bishop was talking up Black cafeteria workers for leads on which clubs were best, and soon he was one of the few White faces at Pepper's Lounge, where he could sit just feet away from Waters, pianist Otis Spann, harmonica ace James Cotton, and drummer Willie "Big Eyes" Smith. "How lucky am I?" Bishop remembered thinking at the time.[53]

At the university, students with guitars, banjos, and harmonicas, and some with amplifiers, started showing up not just in formal concert settings, but informally in dorms and student lounges. Central to the activity was the Fret Shop, 1551 East Fifty-Seventh, an instrument sales and repair shop that also offered lessons, records, and a refuge where amateur musicians could meet, exchange information, and play together.[54] The ring of the cash register was not the only music being made. "Lots of jamming happened there," Bishop remembered. "There seemed like a lot of middle-aged women and men in there, leftovers from the forties, radicals, old Communists or Wobblies, playing these old labor songs, Pete Seeger, and all that."[55]

The shop drew visitors from far beyond the neighborhood. Recounting a visit in August 1961, Bill Becker told his fellow students at the University of Illinois that he found John Cohen of the New Lost City Ramblers performing "an impromptu hoot (there always seems to be one in progress)" and praised the shop as ground zero for networking.[56]

Greeting visitors from a large carved chair in the front of the Fret Shop was Paul Durst, a refugee from another era in a flowing white beard. Born in 1868, Durst had seen it all—on site during the Haymarket Riot of 1886 and the Ludlow coal mining massacre of 1914, and as a member of Buffalo Bill's Wild West Show. The shop's owner, Pete Leibundguth, met him on West Madison, Chicago's Skid Row, and offered him a room in the back of the shop. Durst sold instruments for Leibundguth and regaled customers with stories from his early days as a fiddle player. He became a signature draw of the shop for young people.

Leibundguth stocked the store with used instruments collected on trips through the South and elsewhere. One of his earliest customers was University of Chicago student George Gruhn, who in 1970 opened Gruhn Guitars, one of the earliest vintage guitar dealerships and appraisers. Today, Gruhn's collection fills a 13,000-square-foot, four-story showroom that is a fixture in downtown Nashville and a destination for notorious guitar collectors like Eric Clapton, Billy Gibbons of ZZ Top, and Rick Nielsen of Cheap Trick.[57] Gruhn purchased one of his first guitars from Leibundguth in 1963. Hanging out at the Fret Shop taught him the value of early instruments. "Pete was incredibly good at finding stuff from original owners and getting them to part with it for the price they paid for it new," he said.[58]

Leibundguth allowed young guitar fanatics to use his stock to learn their craft, even if they had no intention of buying. Ed Holstein, age thirteen in 1961, remembered meeting teenage guitar prodigy Michael Bloomfield at the store. Bloomfield was "there every day" that summer. One afternoon, he challenged another young guitarist to a duel and, "like gunslingers, they picked guitars off the wall" and walked to Jackson Park. "It was like a scene from 'The Hustler,'" Holstein said. "These guys were such good players, afterwards nobody knew who won. Bloomfield was so competitive that when one of us said that the other guy was pretty good, Bloomfield almost smacked him."[59]

Bloomfield, a high school truant from north suburban Glencoe, spent most of his days in Hyde Park, where he became part of the nucleus of what would later form the Paul Butterfield Blues Band. Except for drummer Sam Lay and bassist Jerome Arnold, the band members—Elvin Bishop, Nick Gravenites, Barry Goldberg, Mark Natfalin, and of course, Butterfield himself—were White university students who used their studies as cover to get close to South Side blues musicians in Black clubs like Smitty's Corner, Frader's Jukebox Lounge, the 708 Club, Theresa's Lounge, and Pepper's.[60]

Gravenites remembered first encountering Bloomfield at the Fret Shop as a "young wise-ass punk" who was steeped in folk music. Bloomfield's virtuosity, especially at such a young age, made him different from the other folk enthusiasts drawn to the shop. Norman Dayron, a University of Chicago student who went on to become a producer at Chess Records, recalled dropping by the shop to pick up banjo strings and suddenly hearing "this fantastic three-finger guitar playing—very fast, very clean."[61]

> I thought it was a record or something. I thought Pete was playing this very hip thing, so I turned around to see where this music was coming from, and I see this guy sitting on a metal chair, bent over one of the guitars that was in the store. . . . He's playing at a whole different level than any of my friends are, or anything I'd ever seen in person. And yet it was very different from anything I'd heard on record. It was just—the music was just dancing out of him.[62]

Like the Fret Shop, the university dormitories doubled as musical incubators where players met one another, exchanged musical knowledge, and learned how to win over an audience. The lounge at the New Dorms, between Fifty-Eighth and Fifty-Ninth on Woodlawn, was the site of countless jam sessions and concerts. There, David Gedalecia played banjo in the Stony Island Boys, a bluegrass trio named after the nearby Chicago thoroughfare, and often shared the bill with ad hoc bands such as Nick and Paul, a duo consisting of Gravenites and Butterfield, who emulated country blues duo Sonny Terry and Brownie McGhee, and the Southside Olympic Blues Team, another group Butterfield played in, with Bishop as his guitar slinger.[63] Later, Bloomfield joined the sessions on electric guitar.[64] Having already logged time in the Greenwich Village folk scene before moving to Chicago in 1960, Gedalecia said the Hyde Park folk scene was distinctive because it was more concentrated and inseparable from urban blues.

The blues beckoned just south of campus along a stretch of clubs and apartment complexes on Sixty-Third, where students could mingle free from the university's eye. "There actually was a party scene there, on the fringes where Hyde Park ended and where the ghetto started," said Bishop. "It was cool for interracial couples to have places together, and it was a place for people who were interested in culturally mixing it up."[65] Regular house parties brought students and Black musicians together. Invitations into the homes of master guitarists like Otis Rush became common. "He was the type of guy every young musician dreamt about. The first thing he did was reach up in a cupboard and get a pint of Old Grand-Dad and pour us a shot and get his guitar out. Nothing not to like about that," Bishop said. "We all knew it was unusual. It was an exceptional thing. They were glad to see the music appreciated by a person like me and I was excited to be accepted by them. It was all win-win."[66]

Back on campus, the young protégés found whatever spot they could to practice their craft. Nina Helstein encountered Bishop tucked atop a high staircase nobody used above the dining hall in the New Dorms. "Elvin had bought himself an old dobro and was teaching himself to play. It was a wonderful place for him because he didn't bother anybody. I would watch on the stairs. There was a nice sound in that stairwell."[67]

BOB DYLAN'S
HYDE PARK

In December 1960, more than a month before the first folk festival, a musician named Robert Zimmerman turned up at the New Dorms. Elvin Bishop recalled the impression he made: "Little chipmunk-faced guy with a flat hat and pea coat on. I said, 'Oh, this poor bastard seems like a nice guy but is never going to make it. Listen to that voice.' His harmonica playing was useless too."[68]

Zimmerman was just a month from landing in New York City, where he would transform into Bob Dylan. His biographers verify that he arrived in Greenwich Village on January 24, 1961, and that his first public performance there was on January 29.[69] But his journey involved a zigzagging trip from Minneapolis to Chicago, back north to Madison, Wisconsin, and finally, to the East Coast by car. According to biographer Clinton Heylin, Dylan initially headed to Chicago upon the invitation of Kevin Krown, a folk singer he had met in Denver that summer. Paul Levy, an undergraduate at the time, said Dylan appeared in the neighborhood just like every other "wannabe folk performer waiting for an opportunity" to audition for the folk festival, but was ultimately rejected. "The poor kid wandered around looking miserable. He was completely alone, without friends or acquaintances. And he didn't have anywhere to stay." The solution for a time was Levy's ground-floor apartment in a house on Fifty-Third. Dylan's sleeping accommodation was "a deep, door-less closet—the only place he could stretch out without being in somebody's way, or getting trodden on by passers-by. He stayed two or three days."[70]

During Dylan's weeks in Hyde Park, eyewitnesses remember encountering him where anyone interested in folk music during that period would be found: in the Fret Shop and in dorm lounges. Kollenberg said that Dylan was such a daily presence at the Fret Shop during those early weeks in January that she assumed he worked there. "He was just another kid hanging out at the guitar shop. We were so surprised a year later when he was that same kid on the album," she said.[71]

Helstein remembered Kevin Krown, whom biographers credit as Dylan's first manager, corralling students into the New Dorms lounge for a special concert: "There's a guy who's going to come play on the steps of the lobby and he's going to go to New York and get famous," Krown declared. "So about 15 or 20 of us just sat there as he sang Woody Guthrie songs," Helstein said. "He was good, but in the way I was accustomed to, because I was already familiar with Woody Guthrie."[72] Memories of Dylan remain for those who saw him during that brief period, but only because of the swift fame that followed. As for his performance? "No big deal," remembered Kass. "He already knew Woody Guthrie's music. But he hadn't shaped his own yet."[73]

By the time the folk festival opened on February 3, Dylan had already arrived in New York City, but he may have returned to Chicago for that weekend. There is plausible evidence that he circled back to Chicago along with Marshall Brickman and Eric Weissberg, two Madison-based folk singers and banjo players who would later be known for performing the "Dueling Banjos" theme for the 1972 film *Deliverance*. Dylan had crashed in their Madison apartment during his brief stay in that city. They returned to their native New York around the same time Dylan arrived there. Brickman and Weissberg then appeared at the University of Chicago Folk Festival, billed as "Marshall Brickman & Co.," to perform two songs on the final night, Sunday, February 5: Guthrie's "This Train Is Bound for Glory" and the spiritual "Oh, What a Beautiful City (Twelve Gates to the City)."[74] Mike Michaels, a Folklore Society member, remembered spotting Dylan at the festival's opening reception, which students took as an opportunity to informally jam with the performers—in this case, the Stanley Brothers:

> I looked over, and there he was—funny hat, pudgy face, harmonica in rack, and a guitar . . . soon I noticed the guy with the funny hat right next to us, bobbing and bouncing to our music. Well, I figured if he liked us he must be OK, so I introduced myself. He told me that his name was Bob Dylan. It turned out that we both loved Woody Guthrie, and we spent a lot of time that weekend playing together in the dorm. Dylan said he was from New Mexico and that his parents were ranchers. I had no reason not to believe him.[75]

David Gedalecia, who also joined in the jamming that night, confirmed Michaels's account. Michaels remembered Dylan "was very upset he didn't get into the folk festival" as a performer, so on the following Monday, Michaels invited the newcomer to join him on the folk music show he hosted on WUCB, the university radio station. They performed Guthrie songs together that night. No recordings of the show survive. "The radio show was probably something where he felt well respected and got something done. I didn't know what his ambitions were at all. I was just interested in what I felt was a wonderful way of doing Guthrie material," Michaels said.[76]

THE FRUITS OF SUCCESS

The inaugural festival helped establish Chicago nationally as a serious home for folk music. Some of the performances in that first year made history. Roscoe Holcomb, for example, a banjo player and singer who labored as a coal miner all his life, had never performed outside the mountains of eastern Kentucky until he met John Cohen in 1959. Cohen coined the term "high, lonesome sound" to describe Holcomb's rendition of "Across the Rocky Mountains," which he recorded. They remained in touch, and Cohen managed to coax the reclusive musician to Chicago to close the festival. It was the first time Holcomb had performed in front of an audience. Cohen never left his side; he accompanied him on the long bus ride to the city and strove to make him feel comfortable onstage:

> I didn't want to tell him how he was supposed to dress or anything. I just wanted him to be what he was comfortable with. There's an old tradition in folk song movements, like to dress Leadbelly in prison stripes and take Big Bill Broonzy and make him wear overalls. Well I wasn't going to do that with Roscoe. And so Roscoe came out in a blue suede suit and a hat, a fedora, and a white shirt and a red, white, and blue tennis sweater. And we went up on the stage together and I said "here's the microphone, just sing into that," and he did and people cheered. And he got excited a little bit, so he put his banjo down and took his jacket off and threw it on the ground and played the next song. After that they were cheering again, so he took his sweater off

and rolled his sleeves up. By the time he was finished, he was playing just in his shirt. He had peeled off the layers of formality in front of the audience. It was beautiful theater, but it wasn't planned, it just came off that way. It was wonderful. He didn't get excited, but you knew he was pleased.[77]

Pete Seeger, who did not attend, liked what he heard about the festival. In a postcard, he persuaded Izzy Young to explain its importance to *Sing Out!* readers and express why it "was so much more important than any of the so-called 'festivals' such as Newport. If you wrote it up in strong enough language and well enough to persuade people you might even start to sound the death knell of the phony festivals and see more festivals like this take place."[78] Young obliged with a rave review in *Sing Out!*, praising it as "the best series of concerts that any Folk Festival in America has yet presented" for the way it presented the traditional musicians in a setting that allowed the music to remain intimate and unvarnished:

> Imagine having tea with Elizabeth Cotten, Roscoe Holcomb, Frank Proffitt, Dick Chase, Horton Barker, along with dozens of your favorite City Singers. And being able to swap anecdotes and experiences in an informal way. . . . That's what happened at the First University of Chicago Folk festival last February. When Horton Barker, only heard on Library of Congress Records, sang his traditional ballads, I felt I had heard my first American Traditional Singer. The Stanley Brothers after a night or two of misunderstandings with the audience as to what homespun humor was—stole the show on the last evening with songs and instrumentals that I'm sure even their audiences down South don't hear. They returned to the older traditional music under the wonderful influence of the Festival and everyone knew it and was happy. Mike Fleischer, the organizer of the Festival, is to be congratulated for a fine and honest job, which should point the way for other interested groups, schools and promoters around the country. It was especially encouraging to know that it was also an economically successful venture.[79]

In the *New York Times*, critic Robert Shelton also approved: "In a period when the popularization of folk music has led to many specious species of dilution and hybridization, the bulk of the music at the festival was as pure and refreshing as a swig of spring water. The key words were tap-roots, tradition, authenticity, and noncommercial. . . . That all these events were as well received by a total of nearly 4,000 persons, and as well conceived by students, is nothing short of remarkable."[80]

Sandy Paton, who appeared that first weekend, later wrote that the Chicago festival proved that traditionalists and urban revivalists could complement one another on the same stage with no fear of cheapening the authentic nature of either:

> The producers of the festival must have known moments of trepidation prior to the first program, for people who were active in the field had long assumed that, in order to get urban audiences to listen to folk music, one had to "interpret" them—That is to say, translate them into a more familiar vocal style, namely that of "art" or "pop" music. That first evening in Chicago proved, without a doubt, that this was no longer true, if, indeed, it had ever been true at all. Urban audiences not only could but most certainly *would* appreciate the opportunity to hear genuine folk artists in live performances.[81]

While the issue of "interpretation" would be debated in the months and years ahead, one thing was certain: the festival had gained instant credibility among tastemakers. "I'll see that more people hear about it," Alan Mills, the Canadian folklorist, wrote Fleischer afterward.[82]

The Chicago dailies, however, were less responsive. The *Chicago Sun-Times*, the only newspaper to make note of the festival, gave it just two slim columns. There, writer Robert Ellis noted the age difference between the traditional musicians and their urban counterparts: "The oldsters had the better of it, of course; their songs, their styles have grown out of their lives," while "the younger generation presented ample evidence it has picked up the feeling of life and music which is folk singing and made it its own." Of particular note was Elizabeth Cotten, who "silenced the hall" with "a gravel voice that belied her age." Her performance, like others that night, prompted Ellis to end with a wish: "Chicago should hope that the Folk Festival becomes a permanent part of the musical scene."[83]

The following year, it did. Now that the festival was established, the student organizers no longer needed to prove its legitimacy and were fielding offers from representatives and advocates for artists rather than having to make their case. Letters arrived that year and the next: John Fahey, the famed guitarist and principal of Takoma Records, pitched Bukka White; Bob Koester of Delmark Records in Chicago pitched Speckled Red, Yank Rachell, and Arvella Gray; and Alan Lomax corresponded with the students in order to help get Hobart Smith and Bessie Jones.

Major record labels solicited the university to release recordings of the festival. A month after the inaugural festival, the university's director of student activities sent its legal department a letter saying that Folkways, Prestige, Vanguard, and Elektra were all clamoring to release the recordings taped by Chicago radio station WFMT. All four labels were the most prominent in the folk music field; many of the performers on the first festival's bill were on Folkways, for example, and it had already released two volumes of music from Newport. Elektra had also released its own Newport compilation in 1960. Folkways apparently was pushing the hardest for the tapes, as it had already invited Fleischer to write the liner notes to its potential album package, and he had recommended that the university move forward with that label because it was partnered with the Library of Congress and was a nonprofit, and therefore most closely aligned with the Folklore Society's mission. The letter states that WFMT's Ray Nordstrand would release the tapes to whomever upon Fleischer's "written consent."[84]

But thorny legal issues remained. The letter asks if WFMT ultimately has full ownership of the tapes since it has handled the artist waivers separately from the university, and therefore controls royalties. There were also the questions of whether the university name should be used, and, if Fleischer were to receive compensation, how that would affect his role with the university. But the letter also reflects how Fleischer understood the benefits of the recordings, especially if the folklore society obtained royalty rights, which would "help to defray costs of future festivals and build up a fund to be used for furthering its educational aims." As for potential money reaped for the artists, the student director is confident in believing the issue is moot: "We have a clean slate on this one since there is no mention of future reproductions of the Festival in the contracts agreed to with the artists."[85]

To date, the recordings have never been released commercially.

The second and third years of the festival brought expanded programming to the already packed weekend, and by the fourth year, a shift from professional to student emcees, as Studs Terkel had irked some students by using what they felt was condescending language to introduce some of the artists.

In the second year, the festival added a Sunday afternoon folk dance and a Saturday morning children's concert, which featured Jack Elliott (not yet known as "Ramblin'") with Ella Jenkins and Win Stracke in its inaugural year. Pouring into Hyde Park that weekend were not just students from universities across the Midwest, but a busload from American University and George Washington University, both in Washington, DC. The neighborhood newspaper trumpeted lectures, dances, and informal jams "with, hopefully, as many as 1,000 instruments playing at one time."[86]

More money was budgeted to accommodate higher-profile artists; by 1963, the society had increased its budget by $1,052 to $5,200 and paid most artists and emcees between $75 and $500.[87] Bill Monroe and the Bluegrass Boys, however, represented the biggest stars the society had booked to date. Their fee for a weekend of performances was $1,200.[88]

TRAVELING SOUTH, MAKING FRIENDS

Booking the festival meant relying on the connections of outside musicologists, but the programming still reflected the intuition of the student organizers. Before their appearances at the Chicago festival, some of the performers had never recorded commercially and were known only by the field recordings they had made decades earlier. To a student like Bob Kass, who became Folklore Society president in the 1962–63 academic year, musicians like Almeda Riddle, a folk ballad and children's singer, or country blues slide guitarist Mississippi Fred McDowell, were only voices on a turntable. "I was going to find these people and ask them to come," he remembered five decades later. "And my father, fool that he was, let me have his car."[89]

Kass and friend Larry Cart headed south in September 1962 for a ten-day trip that started with dropping off fellow student Elvin Bishop at his home in Tulsa, Oklahoma. From there, they steered the car to Arkansas, where they showed up at the farm of Jimmie Driftwood. After knocking on Driftwood's door, they were offered a room to stay in and, the next morning at dawn, enjoyed a farmer's feast of ham and chicken. "It was immediate hospitality. Part of it was natural and part of it was he was intrigued with the idea of the whole festival," Kass said.[90]

Following Driftwood's directions, Kass and Cart showed up unannounced at Riddle's home in Heber Springs, Arkansas, where the sixty-eight-year-old singer was out in the field picking blueberries; when her work was finished, she returned home to find the two students waiting to invite her to Chicago. She agreed only if Driftwood, her neighbor, would be going too. Kass and Cart's visit made such an impression on Riddle that she started a correspondence with them in which she shared small details of her daily life: "Looking forward to your next letter. You boys should feel flattered I guess. I hardly ever get around to writing letters. And by the time you get through trying to read this scrawl, you will probably wish I hadn't this time. But if you can't read it, don't feel bad—I can't either. . . . P.S. am looking forward to seeing you again."[91]

From there, the students traveled to Como, Mississippi, to search for McDowell. Upon entering the town, they immediately sensed they were strangers in a strange land. Como "was old enough to have wooden boardwalks. We asked somebody if they knew where we could find Fred McDowell and the guy gave me instructions and I'm driving out on all these country roads and got lost. So I drove back and said, 'You know, I tried, but I couldn't find him,' and he said, 'Well, you're in luck, because there he is coming out of a store.'"

I walked over and introduced myself and he said, "Follow me." We drove out to where he lived. He was either a sharecropper or a tenant farmer. He lived in a very small building in the middle of the cotton and cornfields. A space for just a bedroom and small kitchen. His wife was there. He went in and got a chair and came out with a guitar and sat down and played for us. His wife came out and they sang a spiritual. She's leaning against the door and he's in front playing and they're singing together. And we gave him the offer of what we could pay to take a train up.

I don't remember if he gave us an answer right away or not. He was nervous. Here's these white guys from the north coming down. It was not a calm time in Mississippi. I think maybe he might have thought we wanted him to play for us. And then maybe he didn't feel comfortable talking to two white people in the town where it would be more visible. So it was tense.[92]

Lomax and assistant Shirley Collins had recorded McDowell for the first time in September 1959. Four years later, on February 3, 1963, at age fifty-nine, McDowell performed at the Chicago festival. It was his first time performing in public, let alone in front of a White audience—all one thousand of them.[93] Kass said the guitarist was so nervous, "he had to have a couple of beers" before he walked onstage.[94] While keeping the beat with a stomping foot, McDowell played "Freight Train Blues," answering his vocals by stinging the slide to his frets.[95] The appearance would be the opening chapter to his remaining nine years, in which he would emerge as a worldwide touring and recording artist, and a direct influence and mentor to Bonnie Raitt and to the Rolling Stones, who recorded their version of McDowell's "You Gotta Move," on their album *Sticky Fingers*, a year before his death in July 1972.

Riddle's performance was similarly bare and powerful. "She did the beat with her hands and sang. Again, one woman. Not a young woman. But she had the audience completely rapt. Not a peep. Singing into the microphone like it's nothing," said Kass. "It was very moving."[96]

CAREERS REIGNITED

In its seven-page cover story on the festival in 1964, *Sing Out!* emphasized its senior artists, particularly Maybelle Carter, the guitarist of the Carter Family, the trio whose dark-themed songs and vocal harmonies, along with Maybelle's guitar style, created the foundation of modern country music. To the magazine, her presence at the festival added not just credibility, but edge:

> No professional promoter would dream of beginning his program with a dozen selections by a female vocalist, but at Chicago, Maybelle Carter held the stage for half-an-hour as the Festival began— and brought her audience along with her to another time and place when the sound of the singing Carter Family was heard on every radio station from Virginia to Texas. . . . For a generation of city folk song fans, it was a new sound and a new experience. Although Maybelle Carter made a passing reference to the Kingston Trio's recording of the old Carter Family favorite, "Worried Man Blues," the world of Peter, Paul and Mary and the "big" sound of modern pop-folk was a long way off.[97]

Maybelle Carter was fifty-four years old when she played the festival in 1964. Her performances that weekend, both solo with guitar and accompanied by the New Lost City Ramblers, bridged her most recent solo recordings with songs from the Carters' historic first recording session on August 1, 1927, for the Victor Talking Machine Company. She had resumed touring with her sister Sara Carter, even though A. P. Carter, Sara's first husband and the third member of the trio, had died four years earlier, in 1960. Maybelle also toured frequently with Johnny Cash, her son-in-law, along with her daughters Anita, June, and Helen, which raised her visibility.

By then, Cash was already established as a major recording star, and his outlaw image was at its height—"Ring of Fire," his biggest hit, had been released a year earlier. While struggling to tune her guitar with the Ramblers, Carter mentioned having similar tuning problems the night before in Peoria, Illinois, on a show she shared with Cash: "He's a little bit low or a little bit high," she said, laughing, unknowingly triggering audience laughter. "I didn't mean for it to sound like that. . . . I mean his instrument is all," she answered. The audience responded with applause.[98]

Carter had met Mike Seeger of the Ramblers a year earlier at the Ash Grove in Los Angeles, where he was tasked with enlisting older traditional artists to perform at the club. She and the Ramblers struck up a friendship and played dates together elsewhere, including road trips to Arizona; they also visited Sara Carter, who at the time was living in a mobile home in Angel's Camp, California, with her second husband. Seeger documented their stories.[99]

> We backed her up with bass and guitar. She hadn't done much of that on her own. She'd been with her daughters and maybe another musician or so. And she wasn't entirely used to it. But she got used to it. And she got used to talking to people about the kind of things that we were interested in, because that's what we were talking with her about backstage. . . . I hesitate to use the word "humble" to describe her because she wasn't humble. She was very solid but understated.[100]

Those traits come across in the recordings of her Chicago appearance, in which she introduces songs by telling the audience they were suggestions of one of the Ramblers, with whom she sounds comfortable after a year of playing together. "I don't play the banjo, but every time I play a show with Mike Seeger, I have to try," she says. Before many songs, she notes how long since she's performed each one: usually twenty years or more.[101]

5

BOHEMIA IN HYDE PARK 265

Before playing the Carter Family song "Sugar Hill," she takes a seat. "Oh, I can't hold these things, they're too heavy," she says of her instrument. "I used to play banjo when I was a little kid, six years old until I was thirteen and got a guitar. This really does look old-timey don't it?" she says laughing. "This is the way we used to play all the time with the Carter Family." Later, the experiment is finished: "My fingers just won't work on that banjo no more. I love the banjo but I just laid it down and never played again. I think I could leave it down there."[102]

Besides guitar and banjo, Carter plays a few songs on her signature autoharp. Audiences shout requests during both her sets, and she obliges: "You Are My Flower," "Keep on the Sunny Side," "The Storms Are On the Ocean," "When I'm Gone," "Diamonds in the Rough," and "Single Girl, Married Girl"[103]—some of the earliest songs in country music, presented unadorned, just as the young audience wanted to hear them.

As it did for Carter, the Chicago festival served as an important stepping stone to new audiences for other artists in their twilight years. Those artists included the originators of bluegrass, a latter offshoot of country that had begun to fade by the early 1960s. This was especially true of Bill Monroe, the fiddler-bandleader who headlined the Chicago festival in 1963, in his first performance at a college. He would rely on the festival circuit thereafter to reach new audiences and establish his place as bluegrass music's reigning patriarch.[104]

By that point in his career, Monroe had slid into relative obscurity, despite having created a modern offshoot of country music defined by breakneck fingerpicking, the instrumental symmetry between banjo, mandolin, and fiddle, and high tenor harmonies that produced a tender, but surging sound. He was the *Grand Ole Opry*'s biggest star by 1947, but ten years later, the music he orchestrated had been eclipsed by rock and roll. Elvis Presley recorded Monroe's "Blue Moon of Kentucky" as a B side to "That's All Right" in 1954, which prompted Monroe to record it again himself.[105] He also faced competitors he had nurtured as sidemen in his Blue Grass Boys, notably his banjo protégé Earl Scruggs and guitarist-singer Lester Flatt, who both quit Monroe's band in 1948 to perform together. The decade before Monroe hit the festival circuit was hard: he played schoolhouses, drive-in theater concession stands, and similar dim bookings. A car accident in 1953 that shattered his collarbone set back his health. Tastes were changing in country music, with an emphasis on jukebox music that would get people to dance. Monroe did not fit.

The folk revival gave bluegrass a new audience, and Scruggs was invited to play the first Newport festival. In 1962, when Monroe was playing an outdoor venue in rural southeastern Pennsylvania, Ralph Rinzler, the FOTM co-founder, approached him for an interview.[106]

Rinzler and Mike Seeger had been following Monroe for years, but hadn't approached him out of fear that the elder statesman, who appeared onstage and off as brittle, would reject their requests to record his performances. What worked was an article Rinzler wrote for *Sing Out!*, titled "Bill Monroe—The Daddy of Bluegrass Music."[107] The designation stuck and would serve Monroe well for the rest of his life.

Rinzler ended up managing Monroe, and his first booking was the 1963 Chicago festival. The night before, Rinzler had handed Monroe the *Sing Out!* issue along with the first album by the Greenbriar Boys, Rinzler's Greenwich Village outfit, which trumpeted Monroe's influence in the liner notes.[108]

> The next day, Rinzler and Seeger saw an amazing transformation. Gone was the haughty and remote Bill Monroe. The man they encountered on this new morning was friendly, forthcoming, even intimate. Monroe spoke of the first time he ever visited Chicago, how his eyes were still crossed, how he had felt "pitiful." He solicited guidance about how to perform for this strange new audience of college students.[109]

"It was all coordinated," remembers John Cohen. "Ralph Rinzler was using all his connections to give credit back to Bill. Bill had never been in a city folk song situation before, so it was very liberating."[110]

Monroe and the Blue Grass Boys performed all three nights. Like Maybelle Carter, they fielded shouted requests, sparing no room between songs for idle chitchat. "A lot of folks wonder why we work the stage, you know, we do one number and we turn right around and do another one right away. You see, we don't get to come up to this part very often and when we get here, we want to play as much as we can and get in every number we can for ya," Monroe told the energetic crowd.[111] The songs he performed suited the audience's craving old-time music: "John Henry," "Soldier's Joy," and "Mule Skinner Blues," the Jimmie Rodgers tune he had used to win an audition for the *Grand Ole Opry* in 1929.[112]

The Stanley Brothers and the Clinch Mountain Boys had preceded Monroe in Chicago at the 1961 festival, where they, too, performed all three nights; it was only their second festival following Newport and their second college appearance ever.[113] Carter and Ralph Stanley were also benefiting from the folk revival after a short period of having to curb their touring due to the declining interest in bluegrass; Carter Stanley even briefly joined Monroe's band when the elder statesman was recovering from his auto accident. The brothers set the stage for their return by hosting a weekly radio show from Live Oak, Florida, that was syndicated across the Southeast in the late 1950s. Soon, their earlier singles were repackaged and reissued in full-length albums for the folk audience.

However, their Chicago appearance also revealed a culture clash. Carter Stanley appeared inebriated the first night, having had to travel through ice and snow to make the date. Their performances steadily improved each time they played, but "the audience sounded unsure of how to respond to bass player Chick Stripling's belligerent brand of country humor."[114] Mike Michaels recounted that the awkward opening night set had less to do with drink than with Fleischer's ambitious programming. Because the bill was so packed, the Stanley Brothers ended up going onstage after eleven o'clock. A few songs into their set, a university custodian "flicked the stage lights off and on in an attempt to hasten the end of the concert."[115]

That didn't sit well with Carter, who responded by turning the show over to Stripling:

> In 1961, the cornpone humor of a country comedian was downright embarrassing to a college audience. . . . It was almost as if Carter was saying, "If you want us to be hillbillies and hicks, you can take our comedy and shove it!"[116]

Mike Seeger later helped calm the nerves of the band, and the brothers returned the next night less agitated. Seeger replaced Stripling on bass due to the musician being "a little bit under the weather," according to Ralph Stanley, when in truth, Stripling had been drinking all afternoon and refused to go on. That night, the brothers felt so comfortable that they showed up after the concert at a party in the dorms, where they borrowed a mandolin and guitar. They performed the old mountain song "East Virginia," forcing the students to lean in to hear their harmonizing, so delicately shaved together. Ralph also taught a banjo workshop the next afternoon. Dave Prine, a young banjoist from suburban Maywood, asked him afterward about the clawhammer style of banjo picking, so Stanley sat him down and gave him personal instruction by playing "Little Birdie" just for him. "Shit, this is something else," Prine told himself as he watched in awe.[117]

By Sunday night, the band had gotten much better acclimated. During "Feast Here Tonight," the song that closed the festival, mandolin player Curly Lambert flubbed a solo, prompting Carter to tell him, "Play it again and play it right!" On cue, Lambert returned to the microphone and hit each note. "It was as if Carter was saying, 'We're all friends here and we can let our hair down,'" Michaels recalled.[118]

The experience stuck with the group. Ralph Stanley, in a handwritten letter sent to the Folklore Society almost two years after their appearance, stressed how much they enjoyed their time in Chicago and wanted to return: "Anytime you could use us for the festival or a concert, we would be proud to visit you folks again."[119]

CHICAGO'S SECOND FOLK BOOM

THE 1970S IN OLD TOWN AND LINCOLN PARK

By 1971, the folk revival had long been over across the United States. Singers with stringed acoustic instruments who mined old songbooks and recordings for traditional songs were no longer in demand on festival stages or television sound stages. Rock and roll had replaced them, and the youth culture had moved on. Folk singers returned to friendly audiences on college campuses or the coffeehouse circuit, which didn't yield to musical trends dictated by the counterculture.

The lone holdout was Chicago. A decade after the folk revival gave way to rock and roll and its multiple strains, Chicago was undergoing a second wave of folk music that in many ways was healthier than the first. "What San Francisco was to acid rock, what Nashville is to country music, this city is to modern day folk music," a Washington journalist declared in a 1974 travelogue.[1] The most obvious reason was Chicago's geographical isolation from both coasts, which allowed artists to cultivate identities without taking commercial trends into account. Folk music had put down deeper roots in Chicago, not only because of the performers, but also because of the audiences that continued to support it, no matter its commercial currency.

A more fundamental reason why folk music remained so relevant up and down Lincoln Avenue is that, thanks to the Gate of Horn and other downtown nightclubs that emerged in the wake of the revival more than a decade earlier, folk music had become part of the firmament of entertainment that dominated North Side nightlife. There was no turning back to the coffeehouses because in Chicago, folk music had spent so little time there to begin with. As a result, folk music fortified the bar scene in Lincoln Park and Old Town. Most of the watering holes were built to showcase live music—specifically, a new crop of local singer-songwriters who, for the moment, were lucky enough to have an actual circuit of venues to play every night of the week. Within those bars emerged a community dedicated to nurturing their work over many late nights and across many different stages. And the scene was young enough that former *Barn Dance* performers like Bob Atcher and Jethro Burns were still around to serve as mentors, as were banjoists Fleming Brown and Bob Gibson, the influential folk revival star. All were energized by the new stock of young people with whom they shared bills around town.

This was the decade when the Old Town School of Folk Music went through a second generation of leadership. The role of the school in galvanizing this second wave is immeasurable. Besides churning out folk singers who inevitably honed their craft on stages not far from its new address in Lincoln Park, it hosted annual all-night parties, fundraisers, and weekly open mikes at the school itself and throughout the North Side. The scene was so robust that in 1975, the school helped launch *Come for to Sing*, a monthly magazine dedicated to profiling artists and debating issues with the same dedication and advocacy as *Sing Out!*, the folk music journal Pete Seeger co-founded out east. The school gave folk music a base where even people from the less stylish quarters of Chicago—including a mail carrier from neighboring Maywood named John Prine—could find a community and see where it might take them.

Pete Seeger admitted he was "damned envious" of what was emerging in Chicago that decade, which he described as "a sort of local patriotism in the Midwest that . . . the cosmopolitan types on the East and West coasts could learn from." "I see this tradition, which I first met in people like Studs Terkel and Win Stracke, being carried on by [*Come for to Sing* editor] Emily Friedman, Fred Holstein, Steve Goodman, and many others. Do you folks in Chicago know how lucky you are to have them?"[2]

Win Stracke, the Old Town School's co-founder, by then sixty-three and in poor health, certainly took notice. He had stood on the front lines watching folk musicians struggle against anti-Communist fever, the ridicule of polite society, the indifference of City Hall, and even betrayal by some of their own who had picked up electric guitars and never looked back. Now, it appeared, the rest of the country was catching up to what the Old Town School had grown. There was hope.

"These are great days for our kind of music," Stracke wrote a colleague in 1971. "I heard John Prine on the David Frost show and last night he was at the [Old Town] School as if nothing had happened. I think that commercial pressures will have met their match with this new crop."[3]

A TEENAGE FOLK SCENE
TAKES HOLD

If the downtown cocktail set made Saturday night plans at the Gate of Horn, the teenagers at home were not left out. By the mid-1960s, doors had opened to all-age audiences through a circuit of coffeehouses and other alternative venues in the city and nearby suburbs. The performers were either locals or up-and-coming touring artists who were on the cusp of national exposure.

The new circuit was for kids, but it wasn't alienation that drove them there. The coffeehouse circuit gave young people their first taste of adulthood. One newspaper writer assessing the scene in 1966 said the clubs represented "a movement among high school and college youngsters . . . to have a place of their own where, first of all, they can express themselves freely, where they can sing, talk, study, play, and learn, without parents breathing down their necks."[4]

Larry Rand was a fifteen-year-old from suburban Skokie in 1961 when he first frequented Scot's Cellar, a coffeehouse in Morton Grove that opened in the basement of Scot's, a popular drive-in restaurant on Dempster. Upstairs were older greasers taking a break from gunning their hot cars on Corvette Night; downstairs were teenagers with guitars. It was where Rand first met Steve Goodman, then a fifteen-year-old from nearby Niles who showed up to play covers he learned from the radio. "The quickest study," Rand said. "You could sing your song once and he could go on the next night and sing your song perfectly."[5]

The bulk of the coffeehouses were located in bedroom communities on the city's fringe. On the South Side, the two underage venues of that period were the 12th of Never, a strip mall storefront in Richton Park, and the Ali Coffee House, 4315 West Sixty-Third. Of the two, the Ali ran the longest. Owner Peter Cora had fought for the Italian resistance in World War II and had survived a German prison camp. He eventually immigrated to the United States, where he rotated through several different careers before opening an espresso shop in 1964. He picked up the harmonica during his POW years and, in Chicago, displayed his musical skills to his passengers from behind the wheel of his cab, a side hustle. "They know they can get a concert as well as a ride to their destination," he explained in 1970.[6] Mike Dunbar, a teenage guitarist who played in a duo called Mike and Michelle, said Cora considered himself a mentor to young musicians from the South Side, where he nurtured talent through annual folk contests and lessons he offered in a music store next door. The Ali, named after Cora's dog, was dimly lit with black lights but "didn't feel hippy." Fifty teenagers were enough to fill the room. Up-and-comers Steve Goodman, Fred Holstein, and other singers on the scene gravitated to the cozy Southwest Side storefront because, like his North Side counterparts, Cora had created a friendly destination for willing ears.[7]

Much farther north was the Why? Coffee House, at 5912 West

Addison, a destination for Wright Junior College students. Evanston had No Exit, at 908 Foster, a Northwestern University club that relocated south to Rogers Park, where it presented folk music under different owners through 1999. In Skokie, the Way Out presented folk music six nights a week.

But the most notorious all-ages venue had to be It's Here, at 6455 North Sheridan in Rogers Park, just steps from Lake Michigan and next door to Loyola University. It's Here was a strict listening room. Audience members were instructed to surrender their shoes at the door before entering a dark area lining the stage, occupied only by pillows and miniature tables. Teenagers called it "the Passion Pit."[8] During the performances, a waitress rotated among the pillows serving ginger ale. The club, which held two hundred people, featured a balcony and coffee bar, and its popularity ran throughout the 1960s into the next decade. The dark and sometimes foreboding decor made it feel like "a slice of the original beatnik scene," said Al Day, an aspiring songwriter who lived in the neighborhood.[9]

Former Old Town School executive director Ray Tate once dubbed the club "Kiddie Big Time" because it was the most professional underage venue on the national folk scene due to its built-in audience of high school and college students living nearby. John Denver, Richie Havens, Joni Mitchell and her husband Chuck, Josh White, Michael Johnson, Jo Mapes, and Buffy Sainte-Marie were among those who played multiple dates there early in their careers. Besides featuring established acts, the club developed local young talent. The Whitsuntide Singers, a group of four young people from Des Plaines, Elmhurst, and Chicago, briefly became its house band in 1966 by re-creating obscure songs from the back catalogs of folk revival stars like Tom Paxton and Peter, Paul and Mary. Michael Johnson, the country singer-songwriter whose career flourished in the 1970s, got his first break at It's Here in 1964 after he won a national talent contest sponsored by WGN. Johnson, then nineteen, signed a ten-week contract to play the club and then joined the roster of Epic Records.[10]

Nothing at It's Here went unnoticed by its owner, Ed Gunger. To those who knew him, Gunger exhibited madman tendencies. He handled every aspect of the business—sound, lights, booking—dealt only in cash, and was known to keep a revolver beside the sound-board at all times.[11] "His whole thing was about control," said Mike Dunbar.[12] Gunger also drank, which made him irascible to anyone blocking his path. Rumors ran for years that he once fired a rifle at a performer onstage, but regardless of whether or not it was true, he was known for finding creative ways to antagonize performers he didn't like. "Whenever somebody onstage was doing something that was not appealing to him, he would get on the mic and yell 'get the hell off my stage,'" said Larry Rand. "Or he would stiff people."[13] A young Joni Mitchell so displeased Gunger that he appeared onstage in the middle of her set with an electric jackhammer to run her off.[14] When Dunbar performed with his duo, Gunger hit the strobe light. After Dunbar complained, Gunger dryly told him to drop in during daytime hours and practice under the strobe to get used to it.[15]

OLD TOWN AND THE
QUIET KNIGHT

For adults, the nucleus of folk music throughout the 1960s and 1970s was Old Town. By the 1950s, Old Town was already garnering comparisons outside the neighborhood to the Left Bank in Paris, the Vieux Carré in New Orleans, or Greenwich Village in New York City. North State Street had long been Chicago's center of bohemian nightlife, with hangouts like coffeehouses Le Montmartre, the Café Oblique, the Yellow Unicorn, and the Fickle Pickle, but gradually rents pushed the scene farther north into Old Town, originally called the Old Town Triangle due to its three bordering streets: Ogden to the west, North Avenue to the south, and Clark to the east. Its narrow streets, brick pavers, and small cottages gave it Old World charm. Artists' galleries, bookshops, and saloons occupied storefronts. But in contrast to the more fabled beatnik enclaves elsewhere, artists and freethinkers were not outsiders in Old Town. "The Triangle was never a Greenwich Village," insisted sculptor Si Gordon in 1957. "It's more permanent, less pseudo, and non-Bohemian. This is a family neighborhood. Here artists are accepted members of the community, and even the beard wearers are good husbands and fathers."[16]

Slim Brundage, who moved his College of Complexes to Wells Street in 1951, said that other cities had similar "off-beat saloons, the same artsy-craftsy shops, the same far-out art, and bookstores." But the difference in Chicago was the irreverent attitude of the young people who populated them. Far-flung bohemian enclaves like New York City and Paris had "real Beats," he explained. However, "Chicago Beats are more insolent than anywhere else in the world. They refuse to put on a show for the kooks from Kenilworth," the affluent North Shore suburb.[17]

That vibe developed because Chicago didn't have the hovering pressure of the recording industry. No careers were being explicitly chased, nor were they the point. The challenge came from winning over the audience you could see from the stage. Along with the folk, jazz, and blues clubs, the improvisational theater Second City added to the radical stagecraft that Wells Street was starting to feed. Comedian George Carlin said that between 1962 and 1964, he often performed free sets at folk clubs like the Earl of Old Town because he found those places more sophisticated than downtown nightclubs:

> I got my first taste of the folk and underground milieu and the feelings that came with it. The freedom of the stage, the people with open-ended and -minded philosophies, who were more than ready for experimentation: they lived for it. . . . The outsider, the rebel in me was being fed by these associations. As a lifelong pot smoker, I fit in that way too. I felt comfortable around them. Already by this time they were beginning to look a little like the hippies they would become. Beginning to affect the free-and-easy physical style that went with their philosophies. I could do material in these places I didn't always trust to a nightclub: about integration, the John Birch Society, the Ku Klux Klan.[18]

Folk music during this period still had elements of the folk revival. Hootenannies, or hoots, took place every night at Le Montmartre, Rising Moon, Club Rue, the Earl of Old Town, and the Fickle

Pickle. Folk singers who signed up to perform ate and drank for free, so "it was entirely possible to stay well-fed and drunk seven nights a week just by singing three songs a night," said folk singer Art Thieme. Enrollment was up at the Old Town School of Folk Music, which churned out singing guitarists at such a high rate that bar owners had no problem finding talent. During the 1960s, these places were incubators of creativity where the unexpected sometimes happened. After a hoot one night at Le Montmartre, as guitars were being retired to their cases, the door swung open and "a towering, wasted drunk" walked in and played "Orange Blossom Special" with only his harmonica keeping the beat. It was Johnny Cash. For that night, the Man in Black was just another Chicago folkie. He spent the remaining three hours of the morning swapping songs with Thieme and Fred Holstein at Holstein's second-floor Wells Street apartment.[19]

"I was in awe," said songwriter John Hiatt of his arrival as a fifteen-year-old on Wells Street after running away from his home in Indianapolis. It was 1967. "The whole folk tradition was there. It was like what I imagined Greenwich Village to be. It just had this vibe. There were people like Phil Ochs and Odetta hanging around. I didn't know who they were necessarily, but I got the sense there were folk singers in Chicago."[20]

For up-and-comers, Chicago was a training ground. David Crosby, later of the Byrds and Crosby, Stills, and Nash, lived on Wells Street just off of North Avenue because that's where the work was. "Musicians who were doing folk music and starting to write their own stuff could get work enough to where they could actually live and that was pretty terrific. I was living right in the middle of it," he said. "It was a very, very, very good scene for a musician to be in."[21]

One of the earliest clubs Crosby played was Mother Blues. The club, located at 1305 North Wells, opened in 1963 and was the first of several music ventures started by a former concrete laborer named Richard Harding.

Harding was born August 3, 1929, and grew up a strict Baptist in Albany Park. There was nothing in his childhood that would suggest he would dedicate his life to music. He was a football player and wrestler at Amundsen High School on the North Side and briefly attended Lake Forest College on a football scholarship before spending about ten years in construction. After a divorce, Harding abandoned the suburban life and returned to the city, where he picked up work as a cabbie and reconnected with former friends. One was Lorraine Blue, also on the heels of a divorce. She was eager to get into the music business and told Harding she had the money to do it. Her favorite club was the Rising Moon on Wells Street, and she suggested they look for a similar space. They didn't have to look far. That year, arson felled the Rising Moon—Harding discovered the buckets of rags and oil underneath the building, by then up on blocks. They took over the site and, relying on Harding's construction experience, rebuilt it as Mother Blues.

Harding was social and ambitious. Customers intimidated by his stocky figure and rough edges discovered he possessed a loud, wicked laugh and a twinkle in his eye. He loved music, but his real interest was discovering new talent. Over the next twenty years he would give up-and-coming acts like Bob Marley, Patti Smith, Talking Heads, and Bruce Springsteen and the E Street Band their first Chicago dates. But his lifelong investment was advancing the careers of singer-songwriters, most notably Leo Kottke, Loudon Wainwright, Jimmy Buffett, Tom Waits, Arlo Guthrie, and Steve Goodman.

Harding knew he wanted to focus on national acts, but his partner disagreed, so he exited Mother Blues after four months and found a bankrupt and newly abandoned folk club called the Sacred Cow at 1363 North Sedgwick, just four blocks west. The building had been an Orthodox Jewish synagogue, and in November 1963 it reopened as Poor Richard's.

A Chicago folk group, the New Wine Singers, opened Poor Richard's, but soon Harding started booking an eclectic roster of national folk and blues artists, including Phil Ochs, Arlo Guthrie, José Feliciano, the Kingston Trio, Jo Mapes, the Paul Butterfield Blues Band, Sleepy John Estes, and Big Joe Williams. The music room operated on the second floor with a balcony; the first floor held a bar and room for pool. The Velvet Underground with Nico took up residency from June 21 through June 26, 1966, as part of Andy Warhol's "Exploding Plastic Inevitable," a multimedia show featuring Warhol films, flashing strobe lights, and characters from his Factory strutting around in fetish wear.[22]

But one year later, in November 1967, Poor Richard's shut down, and Harding returned to Wells Street. Racial tensions had been rising next door at the Old Town Gardens, a multi-unit apartment building that had become racially mixed. The club was also two blocks north of Cabrini-Green, the high-rise development for public housing. More Blacks started frequenting the club, and Harding proudly proclaimed that Poor Richard's represented "the most mixed club in the city." But the police were not pleased, and they started ticketing Harding on unfounded allegations of underage drinking and gambling. "I fought every charge and beat every one in court," he said.[23] That only made the police more determined to close him down.

They had their opportunity when a CTA bus driver, who was Black, pulled a gun on the bartender and, following a struggle, the gun went off and the driver was killed. Poor Richard's shut its doors. The city would not allow a reopening. Rather than fight it, Harding returned to Wells Street in 1968 with a new club, the Quiet Knight. This location was far smaller, with a capacity of only eighty people. That hampered business, but what made things worse was the continuing deterioration of race relations in Chicago. Mayor Richard J. Daley ordered all bars south of North Avenue closed during the 1968 Democratic National Convention, and the streets were not safe from the rioting. "Like an armed insurrection every night," Harding said.[24] He fell into the habit of keeping his German Shepherd Duke nearby, training him to leap over the bar if there was a problem. Singer Bonnie Koloc opened shows for the married folk duo Jim and Jean the week of the convention, and she remembered looking out the window and seeing police beating people with their nightsticks. Harding stopped the show and locked the doors, ushering the three musicians into the protection of a walk-in safe.[25]

The next year, in November 1969, Harding left Old Town for good and moved the Quiet Knight north to 953 West Belmont, in Lake View. The space was formerly home to Havana Madrid, a Hispanic nightclub. The stairs to the second-floor walk-up were steep— "coronary-producing," according to one nightlife writer—but the room at the top was big enough to fit 450 people.[26] Harding would remain there for ten years.

Harding remodeled his new club as a kind of spiritual refuge, installing stained glass windows and pews he had rescued from demolished houses and churches. A gallery in the rear was reserved for young people below drinking age. Harding, who booked the club himself, wanted only artists who were new, at least to Chicago audiences.

When British label Island Records introduced reggae to North America, Harding brought artists like Toots and the Maytals, Jimmy Cliff, and Bob Marley and the Wailers to Chicago for the first time. The Quiet Knight also became one of the first clubs on the North Side to give South Side bluesmen like Muddy Waters and Howlin' Wolf a home base, and the big room was suited for the big bands of Stan Kenton and Sun Ra. A local blues outfit, the Siegel-Schwall Band, took up residency, and other blues acts flowed through, including John Lee Hooker, Taj Mahal, Lightnin' Hopkins, Big Mama Thornton, and Bukka White. Miles Davis debuted his new electrified sound during a three-night stand there in 1971. When country rock took off, Harding booked Gram Parsons with Emmylou Harris, Michael Nesmith, and Linda Ronstadt with her backing band, the Eagles—Bernie Leadon, Randy Meisner, Don Henley, and Glenn Frey.[27] But the folk singers, singer-songwriters, and country outlaws, from Dave Van Ronk, Doc Watson, Randy Newman, Carly Simon, Jackson Browne, Townes Van Zandt, Kris Kristofferson, and Tom Rush to Bobby Bare, Jerry Jeff Walker, Waylon Jennings, and Billy Joe Shaver, remained closest to Harding's heart.

Tom Waits was unknown when he briefly lived in Chicago, at transient hotels near the Quiet Knight, and played sets at the club as the opening act for Sonny Terry and Brownie McGhee, among others. The attraction, he later said, was the barfly characters who populated the place, the most infamous of whom was a one-armed pianist and painter named Eddie Balchowsky.[28]

Older than most of the Quiet Knight patrons by at least twenty years, Balchowsky was the club's janitor who, when his chores were done, climbed onstage and played Chopin flawlessly with only his left hand. He was born in 1916 in Frankfort, a southern Chicago suburb, to Jewish parents who had fled Poland. He later admitted that the ostracizing he endured as the only Jewish student in his school led him to loathe fascists of all stripes. So in 1937, after study-ing music at the University of Illinois, Balchowsky joined the Abra-ham Lincoln Brigade, a group of American volunteers dedicated to fighting General Francisco Franco's army in the Spanish Civil War. "In Spain, I finally found a way to fight back," he told friends years later.[29] Bullets shattered his right hand, and his forearm had to be amputated. Morphine eased the pain, but it also got him hooked. He returned to Chicago with an addiction that would follow him into the late 1960s.

Balchowsky called himself "King of the Back Alleys" because they were his natural terrain. He and Harding were like brothers, according to the Quiet Knight's former general manager Ron Ste-vens, who said Balchowsky's flamboyant spirit lifted Harding out of depressive episodes. It made sense: war stories and songs poured out of Balchowsky, and he was never without a joke or song. "The kind of guy you wouldn't believe really existed. But he was real," said Stevens.[30] Balchowsky was also a painter who dragged his surreal-istic works from tavern to tavern, offering them for sale. He even-tually earned a one-man show at the Art Institute of Chicago, and his work started showing up in Chicago galleries and restaurants, including the Eccentric, co-owned by Oprah Winfrey.[31]

Balchowsky's invincible spirit made him a continued source of wonderment at the Quiet Knight. While cleaning a sheet of glass with his one good hand, he sliced off the tips of two fingers. Once they were grafted back on, he was back at the piano, this time playing Chopin with the remaining three digits.[32] Balchowsky "was Lazarus" who lived "about seven different lives," said Studs Terkel. "A number of times we thought he had died and he'd show up again, usually with younger and younger girls."[33] Naturally, Balchowsky started appearing in songs by many of the songwriters who played the club. Jimmy Buffett based his 1973 ballad "He Went to Paris" on Balchowsky, and Tom Waits, Loudon Wainwright, Utah Phillips, and Dion Di Mucci wrote songs about him.[34] The 1971 Aliotta Haynes Jeremiah ballad "For Eddy" recounted Balchowsky's after-hours performances at the piano ("All stopped once to listen / to the one-armed man play / to their smiles / in an empty saloon"). A few weeks before Christmas in 1989, Balchowsky, age seventy-three, wrote his own ending by falling in front of a CTA train in Wicker Park. Eyewitnesses told police it was not certain if he fell or jumped.[35]

In the same way he gave Balchowsky a creative home, Harding nurtured local talent. "Musicians were like family to him," said Corky Siegel.[36] In 1968, a day or two after taking the midnight train to Chicago from her home in Waterloo, Iowa, singer Bonnie Koloc walked through the Quiet Knight's doors on Wells Street and, minutes later, was auditioning for Harding, who hired her on the spot for the entire summer. The gig not only ensured that she would have the money to stay in town, but the long residency gave her arrival prominence, which helped make her one of the most beloved singers in Chicago over the next decade.

As the Quiet Knight started to gain a national reputation, Harding wanted local up-and-comers to benefit, so he actively hired them as opening acts or advocated for them in front of the right people. "He was the one who made all the national connections for everyone," said songwriter Al Day. His guiding hand was always in motion. When the Rolling Stones were expected to show up over two nights to take in sets by Muddy Waters, Harding told young White blues guitarist Dave Mackenzie to get there early so he could introduce him to Mick Jagger and get his music into Jagger's pocket. And like a good father, he did.[37] Harding hated drug dealers and wanted them out of his club, especially if they started creeping near artists

he knew were vulnerable. He took Bob Gibson under his wing during a period when Gibson was struggling. One night when Gibson's
dealer ascended the Quiet Knight's staircase to check in with his
client, Harding blocked him, and with muscle memory from his
high school wrestling days, threw him down the stairs.[38]

Jimmy Buffett toiled in Nashville for years until 1972, when
Harding invited him to Chicago to open for Neil Sedaka, Dan Hicks
and His Hot Licks, and the Siegel-Schwall Band. "He gave me a
month's work at a time when I really needed it," Buffett later said.
The folk scene he encountered grounded Buffett's act and taught
him how to structure a show. "A renaissance for me," he said. "They
were great storytellers, bullshit artists on stage, and performers. I
gravitated toward that. I found my place."[39]

For Arlo Guthrie, Harding became a pivotal father figure. Guthrie made his Chicago debut February 2–6, 1966, at Poor Richard's.
After each show, Harding took Guthrie to different clubs so he could
meet "everyone even remotely connected to the world of Chicago
folk music," Guthrie later recalled.[40] He returned in January 1971
to play the Quiet Knight, where Harding introduced him to an
unknown singer-songwriter named Steve Goodman, who played
him "City of New Orleans," a song Guthrie would later make the
signature song of his career.

Under Harding's direction, the Quiet Knight not only developed
national artists, but gave them their earliest exposure to Chicago
audiences. As FM radio achieved dominance, major labels had lavish budgets to flood the tour circuit with new singer-songwriters,
and Harding's club became the landmark stop in the heartland. Yet
as golden as those years were, city hall wore blinders. By resisting
attempts to shut down his previous locations, Harding had made
enemies. Under normal circumstances, business owners got out
of Daley's clutches through cash payouts. "Someone sees someone
making money in Chicago, they want part of it. They don't get it,
bad things happen," Harding complained.[41] But Harding, raised a
Baptist, had a stubborn ethical streak that stopped him from pulling out his wallet when the authorities came knocking. "He had a

sense of right and wrong. When he felt he was right, he was going to be very bullheaded about it," said Catherine Harding, his daughter.[42] Unlike Wells Street club owner Earl Pionke, who routinely joked about greasing the palms of city inspectors and the police, Harding "did everything to avoid paying people off." But his stance didn't make sleep easier. "He was scared of what the city would do to him," said Ron Stevens.[43]

The Quiet Knight closed in 1980, and Harding made it no secret why: "The city wanted me out of business." After the tumult of the 1968 convention, Daley's infamous Red Squad had turned its attention away from targeting Communist organizations and toward so-called progressive reform organizations like Operation PUSH, the National Association for the Advancement of Colored People, and the American Civil Liberties Union. The Quiet Knight was friendly to all of them.[44] "Daley wanted to get rid of all opposition. The more he was in office, the more tyrannical he became," said Dick Simpson, a Chicago alderman whose ward office was two doors down from the club.[45] Harding regularly hosted benefits for groups like the North Park Study Center in Old Town, which tutored Black children, or the Universidad Popular, which provided adult literacy classes to Latin American immigrants. If that wasn't bad enough, what was worse were the club's racially mixed crowds, a problem for the gentrified North Side that Daley wanted to create.[46]

City inspections and nighttime visits by the police became so common that Harding had his attorney on call. "These asshole cops were always bugging him. They would walk up the stairs and yell up, 'yeah, we're going to close you down tonight' and he'd have to go off with them with his lawyer," said John Harding, his son.[47] Benefits for Daley's political enemies were the final straw. Each year, Harding opened the bar for Dick Simpson, one of seven aldermen who actively opposed the mayor's agenda. In the eight years Simpson was alderman, between 1971 and 1979, the City Council was a political battlefield where shouting matches erupted whenever anyone challenged the institutional nepotism of the Chicago Machine. In 1971, the Quiet Knight hosted its first annual "Valentine to City

Hall," a political fundraiser for Simpson in the guise of a Sunday afternoon satire revue featuring folk singers Tom Dundee, Fred and Ed Holstein, WFMT's Ray Nordstrand, Dave Prine and Tyler Wilson, and improvisers from the Second City. The show's target was obvious: not only did its poster feature an illustration of Daley clad in a diaper as Cupid, but the performances all lampooned the mayor, from his blustery way of spitting out words to his tyrannical political style.[48]

Daley got revenge. The "Clearview Act," an archaic law that required saloons to give the police a clear view of the barroom from the street, was used against Harding, whose club was on the second floor, its windows far from street view. Harding fought back, and his case was under appeal for seven years. Finally, crippled financially and emotionally, he gave in and closed the Quiet Knight for good. "It wore me down," he said.[49]

He fled briefly to Aspen, Colorado, and in one year opened and closed Richard's at the Jerome, a club at the Jerome Hotel, before moving to San Francisco. Finally, he returned to Chicago and was seen driving a cab. As Lake View had gentrified in his absence, Harding turned to another deteriorating neighborhood poised for an upswing: Wicker Park. On May 8, 1986, he opened Da Vinci's Music Gallery at 2011 West North Avenue, with jazz saxophonist Stan Getz onstage playing ten sets over three nights.[50] Tom Waits flew in for the opening. The 250-seat club was filled with furniture from the old club, and some of the former waitstaff, too. Harding worked the room, a bright pink carnation tucked behind his right ear. "It's the same kind of club as The Quiet Knight," he told a reporter. "And by that, I mean it's a music club! Not a jazz club, but a music club! Not a pop club, but a music club! What's good, you do."[51]

Harding's connections enabled him to get premier talent booked over the club's first few weeks, including Betty Carter, Herbie Mann, Maria Muldaur, Odetta, and Paquito D'Rivera. But six weeks later, it closed. His investment partner was not happy with the returns, and Harding's deteriorating health couldn't handle another fight.

Harding walked away. Over the years, he told his children he would get another club, but it was a passing dream. He died of cancer in 2012.[52]

THE EARL OF OLD TOWN

As Earl J. J. Pionke often told it, Chicago folk music in the mid-1960s was on a death watch. Rock and roll had kidnapped the audience and sent folk's stars to the pricier theater circuit and its traditionalists back to the coffeehouses. For a minute, the Chicago clubs were under the same threats that killed the Greenwich Village scene. "Folk singers have moved into bigger money than they were making in the days when you could hear [Bob] Gibson and Odetta for $2. And they have moved out of the saloons and into Arie Crown theater," complained the *Chicago Tribune* in November 1966. "The one man who thinks folk song has a future," the columnist concluded, was Pionke.[53]

On the first of that month, Pionke started booking live musicians at the club that bore his name: the Earl of Old Town, at 1615 North Wells. The first weekend featured Fred Holstein, Maxine Sellers, and Ginni Clemmens. Crowds were small, so Pionke dared people to come: he boldly installed a seven-night-a-week music schedule with performers booked between 9:00 p.m. and 4:00 a.m. each night. "Chicago couldn't be without at least one folk bar. I figured I wouldn't make a lot of money, but I would keep the folk music and bar alive," he said.[54]

Born in 1933, Pionke was orphaned as a child but, along with his brother and sister, was adopted by a family in suburban Downers Grove in 1937. Eventually they relocated to the city, where he lived the life of an urban Tom Sawyer, always finding ways to hustle money from strangers, whether it was reselling basketball tickets he found for free or agreeing to have his soul saved at a local Christian boys' club just so he could scarf down the free sandwiches and Cokes. At age thirteen he started his first business: a rolling hot dog stand modified from an old horse buggy. To round up customers, he undercut the competition by five cents a dog and added two extra slices of tomato.[55]

After stints as a boxer and nearly ten years operating a liquor packaging house, he and two partners turned a former antique store into the Earl of Old Town. The doors opened on March 14, 1962.[56] Burgers and beer were the main attraction, with classical music and jazz floating from a record player on the bar, a touch of atmosphere he borrowed from the Old Town Ale House, a nearby magnet for artists and writers. Ale House owner E. J. Vangelder "had a great concept," Pionke raved. "He was doing everything he liked to do at home—and he was making money at it!"[57]

The Earl of Old Town had become everyone's home by the time live performers appeared on the schedule in 1966. The room was long and narrow, with tables turned toward the southern brick wall, where in the center Pionke built a stage six inches off the ground. By installing a professional sound system, he transformed the saloon into a true listening room, and performers eventually got used to the accompanying music of the room itself—the banging cash register, ringing phone, slamming back door, and flushing urinals. "The human aspect of rooms like that is a factor that should not be discounted," noted Steve Goodman.[58]

Everything about the Earl demanded attention, starting with Pionke himself. He stood well over six feet, grew a stringy blonde goatee that bore a resemblance to a billy goat's, gave bear hugs like a godfather you both loved and feared, always ate prime rib and drank whiskey with company because he didn't like to dine alone, and had a booming voice that dominated any conversation he was in and all others taking place within earshot. "You'd look at him and think 'what does he know about folk music?' Just this old guy with a Polish last name. But he had the best ear and the most welcoming attitude," said Judy Hauff, a member of the Rotary Connection, a psychedelic soul band from Chicago.[59] Singer Chris Farrell remembered accompanying Pionke to an afternoon White Sox game. The fifteen-minute walk from Halsted to Comiskey Park unfolded like a promenade, with the sidewalk turned into Pionke's red carpet.

Block by block, Pionke knew the locals perched on their stoops or puttering in their front yards, and they updated each other on the details of their lives all the way to the ballpark's front gates, where, once inside, the ushers and security people cajoled him like a prince. Minutes later, he was with his sister Viola, dipping into her cooler full of sandwiches. "He was in his glory," said Farrell. "He had this posture, this strut. It wasn't ego, it was like, 'This is fun.'"[60]

That largess didn't deflate once he was back in his club. Pionke was loyal, but he could be a tyrant. He admitted he knew little about the music, but once his club took off, he became a keen observer of what worked and what didn't on his stage. He dished out advice, whether solicited or not, and it wasn't long before the performers realized he knew something about selling. If the Old Town School emphasized folk music as a vocation, Pionke hounded musicians to make it a career. "If you don't get that copyrighted tomorrow, I'm going to kick your ass," he told Steve Goodman after the songwriter put together "City of New Orleans" in the Earl's dressing room.[61] Goodman called him "the complete good time Charley" and "the best non-musician that I know."[62]

Pionke developed into a father figure because he was a generation older than the performers he booked and because he was so protective. "Our kids" is how he frequently referred to Goodman, John Prine, Bonnie Koloc, Ed and Fred Holstein, and others whose profiles shot up in those early years. When the Ravinia Festival on the North Shore booked Prine, Goodman, and other Earl luminaries for a "Chicago Mini-Festival" on July 21, 1972, Pionke showed up backstage and dismissed the event outright. "They call it mini-Chicago night. I call it Earl of Old Town at Ravinia," he said.[63]

Those managing the door, the bar, and the kitchen were all Pionke's childhood friends from the neighborhood. There was Gus Johns as house manager, Jimmie Johnson and Henry "Duke" Mathaus, who worked the grill and bar, day cook Anton the German, and Pete Karish, the bartender. Unlike the performers, this crew grew up in the Great Depression, had seen their fair share of the world, had already been through marriages, and carried with them a suitcase of stories that were unimaginable if they were not true. In his earlier days, for example, Anton, whose last name is lost to time, traveled the world with the Ringling Brothers as their personal chef; late in his life at the Earl, he served every hamburger like it was chateaubriand. "Bob Dylan didn't mean anything to them. But that's what made them interesting. They took their jobs seriously," said Ed Holstein. Their constant presence—always dressed in a tie and white shirt—made the Earl a place where nonsense died at the door. Everyone, no matter who, came to work.[64]

Discipline was ingrained in the schedule Pionke posted on the wall. He had a rare 4:00 a.m. liquor license (good until 5:00 a.m. on Saturday nights), which meant performers—booked in solid week-long blocks—played marathon seven-hour sets plus a matinee on Sunday afternoon. "At the end of it, if you had six weeks at the Earl, you were physically whipped by that last week," said Larry Rand. "But it was really good for your stagecraft because you were pumping it out, night after night after night."[65] That was the case for John Prine, who said the relentless schedule was "a great way to cut your chops." Charter buses filled with tourists were common during the Sunday matinee, which meant inevitable distractions for the musicians in the midst of a song. "They'd be in a circle [at the door] and going, 'should we look at the menu?' This is while you were doing your show. You had to work with your head turned to look at the audience in the eye," Prine said.[66] The stage was small, about twice the size of a telephone booth, with tables shoved against the edge on all three sides. "People practically in your lap," remembered Dave Prine.[67]

The Earl turned people pro. Herbert Francis Scarpelli grew up obsessed with folk music in Chicago's Little Italy. In 1964, at age nineteen, he joined the Navy to see the world. One day at sea he heard a banjo, guitar, and mandolin from the tail end of his ship. They were played by three fellow seamen, all from Appalachia. He joined in, and by 1970, he returned home serious about playing music for a living. He discovered the Old Town scene and zeroed in on the Earl. "The reputation there was 'you better be good.' And

I didn't feel like I had the chops yet," he said. After returning each week for the open mics, he became the house guitarist for solo touring artists. When he started writing his own songs, Scarpelli became Mick Scott. "You had to write your own originals because you couldn't walk down Wells Street without them. You wore that like a proud coat," he said.[68]

Tom Dundee was born in Chicago, but grew up idolizing cowboy singers like Gene Autry and Tex Ritter. He, too, was tall, handsome, and easygoing. The songs he wrote after he got to the Earl in 1971 were first comparable to John Prine's, mostly because of his similar unassuming vocal style, simple rhyme schemes, and lyrics that were both conversational and abstract. He waited until 1979 to record, and by then, his song catalog was deep. One song, "A Delicate Balance," kept him on the road until his death in a motorcycle accident in 2006. "Expectations we had can lead down that path," he sang, "Where that devil, discouragement, lives."[69]

Dundee was beloved among his peer group. After his death, Michael Smith wrote "Tom Dundee," a comic song about the difficulty of measuring up to him. Smith, however, hardly sounded like anyone else. Born September 7, 1941, he moved to Chicago from Detroit in 1976 at the urging of Bill Redhed, a Pionke friend. Believing that the singer and his wife, Barbara Barrow, needed to be in Old Town's thriving scene, Redhed paid for their move and put them up in one of the apartments he owned around the corner from the Earl. The couple were not novices: in 1970 they formed the psych-folk group Juarez, signed to Decca Records for one album, and spent years touring the United States as a folk duo. Before all of that, Smith had honed his chops in the club scene in South Florida, particularly the Flick in Coral Gables, where he was the house act.

Chicago had been on their tour itineraries for years, so when they arrived in town, every club put them on the schedule. But despite sharing the stage with other songwriters on the scene, Smith was unlike any of them. He sang in a hushed voice, his songs had intricate rhyme schemes, his albums were richly orchestrated, and his lyrics were deeply poetic. Early in his life he was drawn to the mystery of obscure folk songs like "The Bells of Rhymney" by Pete Seeger and "Oh Shenandoah," popularized by Harry Belafonte. He began writing original songs that similarly transported listeners to places they might not clearly recognize but which drew them in on a deeper level.

Two of Smith's songs, "Spoon River" and "The Dutchman," were already known in Chicago before he moved there because Steve Goodman had recorded both. Smith disliked both versions, but nevertheless, he and Goodman became friends and frequent song-writing partners. "I hated the way he played, I hated the way he sang, I hated the way he did my songs, but I couldn't deny the fact that the motherfucker went over like gangbusters. He knew what to do. And he knew how to keep it so you were on the edge of your seat," Smith said. Country artists Jerry Jeff Walker, Suzy Bogguss, David Allan Coe, and many others covered Smith's songs. But Goodman recorded eleven of them, the most of any one songwriter.[70]

One of the few Black folk singer-songwriters to headline the Earl was Terry Callier. Raised in the Cabrini-Green housing project on the near North Side, Callier was immersed in the city's early doo-wop scene due to his childhood friendships with Curtis Mayfield and Jerry Butler. A catalyst for his music was seeing John Coltrane perform live in 1964. "I knew that if I didn't have some of that intensity, some of that commitment, some of that dignity in my own presentation, I might as well find something else to do for a living," he said.[71]

In 1968, Callier released *The New Folk Sound of Terry Callier*, a relatively conventional covers collection. But by the early 1970s, he started recording for Cadet Records, the jazz imprint of Chicago blues powerhouse Chess Records. His three records on Cadet between 1972 and 1974 transcended musical boundaries by incorporating soul, jazz, classical, folk, and social commentary. The nine-minute song "Dancing Girl" begins with a single acoustic guitar but crescendoes with orchestration to tell the story of the title character, who is forced to sell her body to feed her child. Another song, "Trance on Sedgewick Street," addresses racial strife: "Despair will kick your gate in, black and white are hatin' / While the moneymakers havin' fun."[72]

Because the records didn't fit a single genre, they didn't sell well. Nevertheless, Callier's performance style was captivating, especially to folk audiences at the Earl, where he played an unusual mixture of African chant, gentle blues melodies, hushed vocals, and jazz improvisation. "It wasn't very technical, there weren't a lot of chord changes, but whenever he performed you could hear a pin drop because people would get so deeply into it," said saxophonist Rich Corpolongo, who often performed with Callier.[73]

Callier never became nationally known until a few years before his death. He walked away from performing in 1983 to become a computer programmer at the University of Chicago. Unbeknown to him, British acid jazz groups started sampling his earlier records and, as a result, those records were fetching premium prices. Suddenly he had hits in London clubs. The notoriety earned Callier a record contract with Verve. In the late 1990s, he released six more albums, and he collaborated with iconoclastic British songwriters Paul Weller and Beth Orton and the techno group Massive Attack. Of the first time he took a break from his job to play to an adoring audience in London, Callier said, "It was like a dream. A couple of times I had to stop the show because it was just too over the top emotionally for me to continue. People knew all the words to my songs."[74]

The Earl's reputation grew too. Mike Seeger with Elizabeth Cotten, Odetta, Bob Gibson, Utah Phillips, Jo Mapes, Dave Van Ronk, and newcomers like Gordon Lightfoot, Townes Van Zandt, Gamble Rogers, John Denver, Liz Corrigan, James Lee Stanley, and Kris Kristofferson all played its stage. Besides tourists and other musicians, the room filled with local journalists and Second City improvisers, and it was common to stumble upon notable celebrities in town. On the eve of his 1974 comeback tour with The Band, Bob Dylan and three members of The Band showed up at the Earl to take in the scene. Nashville songwriters Mickey Clark and Mickey White were on the stage, with Fred Holstein to follow. After the first song, the door opened, and the four musicians walked in, wearing sunglasses. They sat front and center and watched a full set, but left right before it ended. Dylan was all over the national media because his show at the Chicago Stadium the following night would open his first tour in eight years. Later that month, when talking about artists he was considering for a new label he was forming, Dylan mentioned to *Rolling Stone* he liked what he saw at the Earl and named both Mickeys as potential signees. Back at the Earl, Gus Johns announced he had been able to rescue only three of the glasses that Dylan and The Band had used.[75]

Because the Earl had a 4:00 a.m. liquor license, the club turned into an informal incubator where songwriters could listen to one another. Most bars went dark at 2:00 a.m., allowing musicians to gather at the Earl for the final two hours of the night. Hamburgers hit the grill and songwriters tested new material in front of their peers. "You'd get the most amazing audience then," remembered songwriter Claudia Schmidt, who moved to Chicago from outside Detroit in 1974 and became a mainstay at the Earl. "I used to describe it as the bar scene from *Star Wars* because you just never knew who would show up. It was a great place to work on stage presence and craft because you had to be thinking on your feet all the time. It was almost like vaudeville."[76]

Improvisers from the Second City, located across the street, inevitably walked through the door between their sets. John and Jim Belushi were regulars, as was their mentor, actor and director Del Close, who at one point used the bar phone as his permanent number.[77] Riffing off the energy, improvisers often landed on the Earl's stage, as when John Belushi, invited up by folk singer Ed Holstein, hopped onstage in 1972 to perform his Marlon Brando impression during a 3:00 a.m. set.[78] The Brando impression also stuck with John Prine, who remembered the improviser often appearing at the Earl to mumble Prine originals like "Angel From Montgomery" as Don Vito Corleone from *The Godfather*.[79]

Most nights the party moved to the Sneak Joint, a club located directly behind the Earl on the first floor of a coach house. The operation was run by Sylvester Klish, Pionke's nephew, and was designed to be louder and wilder than was allowed or expected at the Earl. The club was open to the public but never publicized, so it always felt like a clubhouse for insiders. Klish avoided the need for a Chicago liquor license by selling alcohol, purchased at the Walgreen's next door, by ticket, which meant the club could stay open through sunrise. Nights burned long with the help of alcohol, marijuana, and cocaine, all in ready supply, along with a jukebox and a pinball machine that never went silent. When John Belushi and Dan Ackroyd camped out in Chicago during the filming of *The Blues Brothers*, the Sneak Joint went private, open to insiders only. "It was the hoi polloi of the entertainment people in Chicago or anybody like that who was in town because it was truly nudge-nudge, wink-wink," said Skip Haynes, who lived above the Earl.[80]

After the Earl closed in 1984, Pionke remained a touchstone for the songwriters who created careers on his stage. Nearly two dozen of them returned to Chicago in June 2012 to pay tribute when Pionke turned eighty. The night was as epic as the man. Four hundred people crammed inside FitzGerald's in Berwyn, and another four hundred and fifty people stood outside watching on television monitors. Over twenty performers—including John Prine, Bonnie Koloc, Ed Holstein, Jim Post, Claudia Schmidt, and Corky Siegel—serenaded Pionke during a show that stretched over six hours. "The folk reunion of the century," Pionke said from his seat, too weakened by health issues to make it to the stage and too choked up to say more. Toward the end of the evening, he had one request—that Prine sing "Hello in There," his ballad about the loneliness of senior citizens, forgotten by everyone except one another.[81] Less than a year later, in April 2013, Pionke died of pancreatic cancer.[82]

FRED HOLSTEIN:
FOLK TROUBADOUR OF CHICAGO

When Pionke planned the Earl of Old Town, he had one performer in mind who defined the kind of music that would cement his club's reputation: Fred Holstein.

Holstein did not write songs, but like his hero Pete Seeger, he considered old songs the gateway to illuminating the troubles of modern life and provoking change. But unlike Seeger, Holstein believed the stranglehold that concert halls and college stages had on the music was a contradiction of its community roots. He held that folk music was meant to thrive in the setting where it had thrived for centuries: "Why do artists in the folk idiom shy away from saloons?" he asked in 1981. "I have been playing bars since I was about 18 or 19, and most of the really special audiences—the ones who have given me my most precious moments as a performing artist—have been in bars. They will give you their attention if you give them yours."[83]

Holstein was born December 9, 1942, the eldest of three brothers, in Chicago's South Shore neighborhood.[84] Their parents ran Holstein's, a pharmacy and small goods store in Chatham, three miles from their house. It was a social center for the neighborhood where kids hung out to buy, read, or trade baseball cards or comics. When she wasn't on tour, gospel star Mahalia Jackson, a neighbor, would stop by for ice cream. After Fred and his brother Eddie attended a Pete Seeger concert at Orchestra Hall in 1959, Sally Holstein, their mother, bought Fred his first guitar, a Martin, at Lyon and Healy downtown.[85] "I was trying to grow up and *be* Pete," he said. Four years later, Fred was out of high school, playing at the clubs in Old Town and selling records and songbooks at the Old Town School of Folk Music's Folklore Center. His inauguration into his new life was the evening Dawn Greening drove him to her house in Oak Park, where she was hosting a dinner party; the guests included Studs Terkel, Win Stracke, and Pete Seeger. Holstein, not yet twenty, sat on the Greenings' floor and just listened. "I was flabbergasted. . . . I had not known her long at all. But she knew how much it meant to me," he recalled.[86]

From the very beginning, Holstein knew he didn't want to write songs, as his brother Ed would do. "He was ashamed of his writing," said Emily Friedman, the editor of *Come for to Sing*, which Holstein helped start in 1975. "He didn't have a lot of the usual skills of daily living. But what he had was an ability: he could interpret songs to the point where he could get insurance executives to sing along with him. Or make them cry."[87] He became a totem of traditional folk music and a mentor to young players making their way. Onstage, he introduced songs found in songbooks or on the archival Folkways and Folk-Legacy labels that spoke directly to current headlines involving the Nixon and Daley administrations. The songs he knew best were written by "anonymous mountain people, Delta bluesmen, whores, hoboes, and cowboys," Friedman wrote in the inaugural issue of her magazine. "How does a city kid from Chicago get away with singing these people's songs? Because he is one of them . . . he's honest."[88] Holstein derided the folk purists of his day and refused to treat the songs he dusted off as museum artifacts. "I don't ever want to see folk songs kept underground because a few people see it as their personal property," he said. At the same time, he grimaced at contemporary retreads "garbaged up by overproduction" that were "totally devoid of human emotion."[89] When it came to exploiting the music, the academics and the record moguls represented two sides of the same coin. To Holstein, the music was alive only if it was performed in front of people seeking shelter from the street. That's where Earl Pionke stepped in.

Pionke had run into Holstein over many years, having seen the teenager playing guitar and singing while perched atop the pinball machine at the Old Town Ale House or, a few years later, tending bar at Poor Richard's.[90] In 1966, Pionke dropped in during one of Holstein's bartending shifts, declared he was his "number one favorite Chicago singer," and said he wanted him to lead the new direction of his club. Holstein was unconvinced. Old Town clubs were starting to book bands like the Jefferson Airplane and the Velvet Underground, and it wasn't clear there was still an audience for traditional folk music. To Pionke, that wasn't an answer. "I'm gonna do it," he fired back. Holstein, Pionke later said, was the one who "built the Earl of Old Town as a folk club."[91]

Holstein commanded a stage because he refused to make folk songs background music. "As flexible as a ramrod," in Friedman's words, he could quiet a room by command, and then bring everyone together to sing a chorus.[92] Even though he revered Pete Seeger and all he represented, not everything from his mentor translated. His barrel-chested physique, his sturdy voice, his swagger, and his full commitment to his performance made him a purely Chicago creation. "Pete Seeger was the same person onstage or off. Fred, on the other hand, was like Dr. Jekyll and Mr. Hyde. He smoked Lucky Strikes, loved to shoot pool, and drank like a fish. He was James Dean and Pete Seeger all in one," said his brother Alan Holstein.[93]

Because he pre-dated the scene that emerged in the early 1970s, he served as a mentor to the rotating crop of younger folk singers who arrived in the Earl's doorway to scope out the stage. His column in *Come for to Sing* spoke of the performer's purpose and the music's history, but it also offered practical tips. To Chris Farrell, who showed up in Chicago in January 1975 from Wilkes-Barre, Pennsylvania, Holstein gave no quarter. After listening to every one of Farrell's songs during an open mic, Holstein waved Farrell over to sit with him. He was complimentary at first, but when he learned that a few songs in the set were originals, he blasted Farrell for dismissing "the American canon." Holstein often worried out loud that his own generation was one step away from ditching the old songs, and with them, the struggles that created them. The continuum mattered because, in the right hands at least, the songs still had relevance.

"Fred had this great saying, 'You always have to remember, the song is more important than you,'" Farrell said. "Meaning, it's still gotta be about the song. He never pushed it or used phony dramatics. He just understood what the song meant and what it should be communicating. When he did a song, for three or four minutes, it was the most important thing in the world."[94]

Diplomacy disappeared when Holstein talked music. "Oh, I heard your new song and I think it really sucks," wouldn't be uncommon. "But he would also say, 'I really like that other stuff.' He would give you honest feedback," said Larry Rand.[95] With others, Holstein's assistance was more tangible. After Stephen Wade, an aspiring banjoist, revealed how much he pined for a 1925 No. 9 Tubaphone banjo,

Holstein dug into his pockets and handed over $500 in cash. The banjo became the first professional instrument Wade owned, and he used it to launch his career. Holstein "never lost his patience with the meager payments I sometimes had to offer him," Wade said. "He comfortably straddled the worlds of folk music idealism and late-night, Chicago saloon revelry."[96]

Despite accepting invitations to play East Coast festivals, Holstein realized early on that he didn't like touring. He also started turning down advertising work, which was unheard of at a time when Chicago was one of the centers of the commercial jingle industry. Fred and his brother Ed once relocated to San Francisco, but returned to Chicago after a year. The reason was simple: they missed the prime rib and martinis. Comfortable at home, Holstein rarely ventured outside Chicago. During one stint on the East Coast, he wrote Pionke to tell him he was having a rough time and needed gas money to get home. Pionke rounded up a handful of Earl regulars and hopped on a plane to New York, where the group snuck into the balcony of Kenny's Castaways, the Bleecker Street club in Greenwich Village where Holstein was performing that night. Midway through his set, Holstein heard a familiar voice bellow from above, "Hey Fred, I brought you the money!" His tribe had arrived.[97]

Holstein died during stomach surgery on January 12, 2004, but he had left the music industry years earlier. As the Old Town scene faded in the 1980s, there were fewer clubs to play and even fewer singers coming up who knew the old songs. Holstein went back to tending bar and withdrew from the scene. He left behind two albums he recorded in 1977 and 1983. *Chicago and Other Ports*, his only studio album, is a testament to his strengths and life interests. True to its title, the album connects Holstein's hometown to European port cities through songs like "Streets of London," the Ralph McTell ballad, to "Maggie May," the Liverpool folk song about a thieving dockside prostitute, to "Down by the River," a traditional that catches fire due to Holstein's frenetic banjo playing. Union songs also populate the album, but the highlight is a cover of Jacques Brel's "Amsterdam," which tells of the desperation of sailors on leave. The midnight atmosphere, summoned slowly by Holstein's twelve-string guitar, builds into a full crescendo in a performance that illustrates his commitment to delivering a song's dark essence, and to arranging his vocals and guitar so that combined, they sound like a mini–chamber group. *For All the Good People*, recorded before a live audience at WFMT, documents Holstein's connection to Pete Seeger. On several songs, Holstein makes the audience his backing chorus. The title song had been Holstein's signature for years. Again on twelve-string guitar, he leads the audience through a waltz that also served as a recitation of his life: "This is a song for all the good travelers / Who passed through my life as they moved along / The ramblers, the thinkers, the just-one-more-drinkers / Each took the time to sing me a song."[98]

BONNIE KOLOC:
PURITY OF VOICE, ANXIETY OF HEART

The night should have been a big one for Bonnie Koloc. It was November 1969, and she was about to kick off a four-week stand at the Earl of Old Town after being out of town for months. So many people packed the room that the tables had to be removed, making the bar resemble "a Loop subway stop at rush hour," according to one critic.

Five minutes before she went onstage, Koloc couldn't take it anymore. When a nearby reporter asked her how she was feeling, she grabbed his notebook and pencil and wrote a one-word answer: "HELP!"[99]

That's how fast things were moving for the twenty-two-year-old singer from Waterloo, Iowa, who had arrived in Chicago a year earlier with nothing but a guitar and some underwear stuffed into its case. That summer, Koloc knew only one person in Chicago: her friend Gib Foster, who let her sleep on his floor in a sleeping bag. In the first month, she was offered a weekly job singing at the Quiet Knight, but the Earl was where she found a permanent home.

A woman in the male-dominated folk scene, especially in a boy's club like the Earl, was not common. But nothing about Koloc was routine. In Waterloo, she bypassed local folk clubs and played show lounges, following the go-go dancers, where she learned to lift her alto voice above the crowds of traveling salesmen double her age. Moonlighting to pay tuition at the University of Northern Iowa, she performed over five years at local colleges, the Ramada Inn, the Holiday Inn, a PTA Council meeting, the Kiwanis Ladies Night, an IBM Christmas party—any gig she could get. Those early years were her training. She was an operatic mezzo-soprano working the cocktail crowd. "I know how to get people to listen," she said.[100]

Waterloo was not a happy place for her. Born February 6, 1946, she grew up in a cinder block house, where her parents argued and then divorced. The family was poor and life was unstable. For a time, she thought only successful people had indoor plumbing and that her future meant marrying a factory worker like her father. "I want more than this," she thought. So she bought a midnight ticket on the Illinois Central to Chicago.[101]

Work was abundant in that first year. After six months in Chicago, Earl Pionke booked her for almost a month. Skip Haynes, who opened each night, was astounded by her audience's instant devotion. She "was so popular that she demanded that the audience not smoke and they didn't. That's how much power she had," he said.[102]

Pionke wanted to keep booking her, but she refused, worried that she would outstay her welcome. The tactic worked: when news later broke that she was returning to the Earl after a hiatus, her shows sold out. Jim Tullio, her bassist from those days, remembers parking his car during a harsh February snowstorm and fighting his way to the Earl through six feet of snow and subzero temperatures. Getting close, he was astonished to discover a line of people stretched four blocks down Wells waiting to get in. "She was very, very well-loved," he said.[103]

For Koloc, the attention was both thrilling and anxiety-inducing. Eventually record companies came calling. In 1971, Glenview-based Ovation Records released *After All This Time*, a set of mostly original songs that are completely unlike the standard folk-rock fare of the time. Ruminative and moody, the songs are heavily textural, built around Koloc's crystalline vocals, which slide through octaves effortlessly while her band, which included Chess Records session guitarist Phil Upchurch on bass and guitarists Ron Scroggin and Stu Heiss, summons a midnight groove. Koloc is a mixture of Cass Elliot and Joni Mitchell: "Devil's Nine Questions," an original, has the mystery of an Irish folk ballad, in contrast to the country funk of Ed Holstein's "Jazzman" and "Another New Morn." *After All This Time* defines her strengths both as a pitch-perfect singer who traversed folk, jazz, and blues and as a serious experimentalist who disguised her insurgent intentions with Midwestern ordinariness.

After All This Time sold sixty thousand copies in its first year, a respectable number for an independent label with little promotional experience. Within two years, Koloc released two more records on Ovation, and she appeared on *The Dick Cavett Show*, *The Merv Griffin Show*, and the BBC.[104] Prominent faces soon appeared in her audience and backstage: B. B. King, Bob Dylan, John Denver, and Kris Kristofferson at the Earl, Astrud Gilberto in Cincinnati, and John Lennon and Yoko Ono at Mr. Kelly's in Chicago's Rush Street district, where the couple made a beeline to meet her once the set was over. Paul Simon called her apartment to ask if she could show him around the Chicago folk clubs as part of his research for *One-Trick Pony*, his film debut as an actor. She did, and before his last night in town she invited him to the Earl, where she would be performing. Simon showed up, but Gus Johns, the doorman, turned him away because the room was beyond packed and Simon was just another fan.[105] "Famous people were always streaming through to see her," said Ron Scroggin, the guitarist on Koloc's first three albums. "Bonnie's following was just monumental."[106]

In 1973, Ovation sent her to Nashville to record at Quadraphonic Sound Studios, where Joan Baez had just recorded a cover of The Band's "The Night They Drove Old Dixie Down," which became a career-reviving hit. Quad was run by Norbert Putnam and David Briggs, two members of the original Muscle Shoals rhythm section, who had recorded with Elvis Presley, Harry Mancini, and Roy Orbison a decade earlier. When Koloc arrived, Quad was in its prime.

Besides Baez, Neil Young had recorded his landmark *Harvest* album there nearly two years earlier, and folk-rockers Dobie Gray, Linda Ronstadt, Dan Fogelberg, Steve Goodman, and Jimmy Buffett were there creating career-defining work. Koloc was perceived to be among those ranks by the Nashville crew. "Very similar to Joan Baez but more pure," Briggs said of her voice.[107]

Koloc was desperate for a hit, but was turned off by the songs Ovation pushed on her—"real schmaltzy, awful"—in lieu of her own songs, which were the standouts of her first three albums.[108] She turned to Briggs for relief. In Nashville, Briggs had access to some of the city's greatest working songwriters; one of them was "Funky" Donnie Fritts, another Muscle Shoals original. While his job playing keyboards for Kris Kristofferson paid the bills, Fritts also penned hits for Willie Nelson, Dusty Springfield, and Waylon Jennings, among many others. Briggs decided that one of his songs, "You're Gonna Love Yourself (In the Morning)," would be just the commercial hit Koloc needed. A companion song, "I Have to Say I Love You in a Song" by Jim Croce, was targeted as the first single. Briggs changed some parts and added strings and a French horn.

Briggs was especially encouraged because Koloc was unusually prepared. Little overdubbing was needed to fix the vocals. "She was such a great singer, she had her parts nailed. It was just easy with her," he said—so easy that the entire album took just a little over a week to complete.[109] Like Putnam and Briggs, the other session musicians were among Nashville's finest, including drummer Larry London, guitarist Pete Wade, and Ginger and Mary Holladay, all of whom had worked with Elvis Presley. The album is an overlooked benchmark of the country-soul era. The Koloc-penned "Children's Blues" uses snapshots from her childhood ("they may send you off to school / in old hand-me-down clothes / you got your holes in your soul / you think the whole world knows") to create a devastating portrait, while "Roll Me on the Water," another original, is a grand soul gesture; like most of the album, it pushes Koloc to heights she sounds comfortable commanding.[110]

But bad luck intervened. Briggs made the mistake of telling Croce's widow that Koloc's cover would be pushed to radio, and in response, she rushed out an unreleased version by her husband, which quickly became a posthumous Top 10 hit. "That killed our record," Briggs said. The Fritts song became the fallback, but Ovation only had the promotional budget to get it briefly to the Top 20 before it tumbled back down. The lack of planning was inexcusable. Briggs begged Ovation to buy more ads, but his plea fell on deaf ears. He said that in the interim he was fielding interest in Koloc from Columbia Records president Clive Davis, a Quad client. It became clear that in more established hands Koloc would have had the breakthrough hit she sought. "I could have produced her with Columbia and it would have been a much bigger record. They had that machine," he said.[111]

The experience devastated Koloc, and she broke the Ovation contract. Besides Columbia, Epic Records was now interested. Brokering the deal was Irving Azoff, the powerhouse rock manager whose main clients were the Eagles and Dan Fogelberg. Azoff and Eagles guitarist Joe Walsh showed up to meet Koloc after she played the famed Troubadour in Los Angeles. Azoff carried a suitcase stuffed with money to show her he was serious.[112] She signed, and Epic released two albums under its Full Moon subsidiary, run by Azoff. Recorded in Los Angeles, *Close-Up*, released in 1976, was filled with country-rock royalty, including Mike Campbell (guitarist with Tom Petty), David Lindley (with Jackson Browne), T Bone Burnett, and Chicago's Corky Siegel.

But depression prevented her from taking full advantage of the opportunities the record opened up. She was perpetually unhappy and besieged by perfectionism. Tullio remembered Koloc hurling her guitar across the room after he suggested she listen to a recent Laura Nyro version of "Up on the Roof," a Gerry Goffin and Carole King song they were rehearsing, just to get pointers on the arrangement.[113] She complained about the sound of her records. "I went from knowing who I was to totally giving it up to somebody else," she said.[114] Worsening her emotional pain was a fractured relationship with an early producer and the deaths of her brother Jim and her boyfriend, Curt Cole Burkhart, a professional photographer who died of a heart attack in 1975, at age thirty-four. Burkhart had been fishing on the Tippecanoe River in Northwest Indiana, near where they shared a cottage. Koloc found his body in the boat, which was lodged in a sandbar and had filled three-fourths of the way with water.[115] She fell into an emotional tailspin and, for a while, found performing difficult. Burkhart's death "really did a number on Bonnie's head," said Ira Kart, her keyboardist during the Earl days. "She felt so out of control that she very much felt she needed to be in total control of any situation that she could find."[116] *Close-Up* is dedicated to Burkhart, and his photographs dominate the cover and inside art. He is present throughout the lyrics: "The moon glows faded yellow out over the Tippecanoe / When the string breaks and it should fall, I'll still be missing you," she sings on the ending song, her voice alone, then doubled on the final three syllables in haunting harmony.[117]

Seven years later, in 1982, Koloc moved to New York City, where another pathway opened: Broadway. Koloc worked in musical theater and, later, visual art. Her musical career never waned, and she continued to perform and release music, but without the pressure of making hits. "I always felt like an outsider. But my singing saved me in my life. It saved me from my childhood. So I put all that feeling into it," she said. "When I sang, I sang from a place in me."[118]

STEVE GOODMAN:
LIVING AGAINST THE CLOCK

Keyboardist Donnie Fritts knew little about Chicago when he played the Quiet Knight with Kris Kristofferson for five nights in 1971. Normally Fritts would skip out on the local opener, but a short, cherubic, bearded fellow named Steve Goodman caught his eye on opening night. "The guitar was about as big as he was. He was a little bitty cat," Fritts recalled. When Goodman started playing, however, he seemed to grow in size. "One of the best guitar players I had ever heard in my life. All the songs were great and he was funny," Fritts said. He and guitarist Stephen Bruton stood in the back of the club, mesmerized. Between songs, Fritts ran backstage to fetch his boss. "Come out and listen to this kid," he told him. Kristofferson followed, and all three watched Goodman go through his setlist: "City of New Orleans," a train song he had just written, "Would You Like to Learn to Dance?," a ballad, and "Sam Stone," an antiwar song fresh off the page by Goodman's friend John Prine. The three songs were different from one another, but as a group, they were timely and completely unexpected.

"He owned the damn stage," Fritts said. "We couldn't get back on it."[119]

The story is now a show business fairy tale. Kristofferson and his band saddled up to Goodman all week. By Saturday, May 1, their final night, they had hooked in Paul Anka, the teenage heartthrob from the 1950s ("Puppy Love," "Put Your Head On My Shoulder"), who by 1971 was a pop statesman, having written signature songs like "My Way" for Frank Sinatra. Before Kristofferson ended the night, Anka bounced up the club's stairs wearing a tuxedo, fresh from his engagement headlining the Palmer House's Empire Room with a twenty-seven-piece orchestra. Earlier that week, the two men had bumped into each other at the airport, where Anka had told Kristofferson that he was incorporating Kristofferson's "Help Me Make It through the Night" into his act.

After a rowdy rendition of "My Way" at the Quiet Knight, Anka coaxed the group, including Goodman, back to his penthouse suite at the Palmer House. They feasted, and at Kristofferson's request, Goodman performed "Would You Like to Learn to Dance?" After the last note, Anka was the first to speak: Could he fly Goodman to New York to get a record contract? Goodman's answer was yes, but on one condition: Would they follow Goodman to the Earl the following night? Prine, his friend, was playing, and he was good, if not better, than what they had just heard. By sunrise on May 3, Prine had earned his ticket to New York too.

The graciousness Goodman showed toward Prine was an outgrowth of a scene that was familial before it was competitive. "What it is, is that we have the kind of respect for each other," Goodman said a year later. "I guess it's not found in some other situations. . . . Everybody in New York respects the guy who works at the other record company, but we actually live together. Fred [Holstein], Ed [Holstein] and I go out to dinner when we're in town. John [Prine] comes in from Melrose Park and we'll go out. That's it. We're actually friends." More than others, Goodman also understood why that bond was necessary. "Doing this for a living can get very lonely. You feel like you really don't have a real worth at times unless there's a certain amount of audience acceptance and your career's rolling along all right. You see your friends getting out of school, getting established, going into practice if they're doctors, being lawyers, or starting a business, starting raising families. . . . And folk singers for the most part don't do that. They're the lonely ones."[120]

In private, Goodman was prone to rumination because, unlike other young men in their prime, he knew he was dying. In January 1969, he was diagnosed with leukemia, a disease poorly understood at the time. It was before stem cell transplants and other state-of-the-art treatments that would extend the lives of adults and produce cure rates in the high double digits. When he got the news, Goodman was a student at Lake Forest College, a postal worker in suburban Park Ridge, and a regular performer at the Earl, where he often opened shows for Bonnie Koloc. He was twenty. Life ahead was nothing but "a time bomb." The disease set his compass. "I said, 'What do I *really* like to do?' I decided it was to play music, write songs and listen to other people play and sing. I just liked music and wanted to be a part of it somehow."[121]

Goodman quit school and the post office, and between 1971 and 1984, the year he finally succumbed to the disease, he recorded nine albums, played up to two hundred dates a year, got married, and raised three daughters.[122] "The grit it took for him to marshal on in the face of this constant death was just crazy. He wasn't about to do what anyone else had in mind. And he had more justification. He knew what he was careening toward," said Michael Smith.[123]

Goodman was determined to entertain. Onstage, he was magnetic, prone to bridge songs with storytelling, and so at ease in front of audiences he could improvise a new set of lyrics on the spot or replace a broken guitar string mid-song with sleight of hand worthy of a parlor magician. As someone who knew he was sick but largely kept it a secret, he burned energy faster than most, which led to larger-than-life performances that could never be choreographed twice. Goodman was a natural storyteller, but he also came from the tradition of his hometown, where folk music was less sanctified than in the Greenwich Village coffeehouses. As a twelve-year-old, he was taken by an uncle to the Gate of Horn to see Bob Gibson, the influential folk star who embodied that nightclub's approach. "It all goes back to the Gate," Goodman said years later. "I picked this up by osmosis."[124]

There was no other songwriter of his time who was so deeply rooted in Chicago. The lore of the city, its characters and intersections, populated his songs. His setlists over the years included "Daley's Gone" (1977), a lament for former Chicago mayor Richard J. Daley, and "Lincoln Park Pirates" (1972), which imagined the operators of Lincoln Towing Service, a notorious towing company on the city's North Side, as jolly scourges who terrorized parking lots "from Wilmette to Gary."

One year before his death, Goodman wrote "A Dying Cub Fan's Last Request." A lifelong Chicago Cubs fan, he debuted the song on March 16, 1983, on WGN radio, accompanied by Jethro Burns on mandolin. The song is constructed like a Christmas story: partly comic, partly ominous, and packed with metaphors. The narrator knows wishing for his favorite team's victory is foolish, so verse by verse, he realizes Wrigley Field is not a field of dreams, but a graveyard. "Build a big fire on home plate out of your Louisville Slugger baseball bats / And toss my coffin in / Let my ashes blow in a beautiful snow / From the prevailing thirty-mile-an-hour southwest wind," he sings.[125] Radio host Roy Leonard said Goodman had not told him about the song beforehand, but the moment he and Burns finished, "phones rang off the hook." The song's narrative structure and dark humor made it accessible. "Steve approached songwriting as a craft, not an art. I don't know anybody who worked at it as hard," he said.[126]

Goodman, of course, went far beyond Chicago in his music, but like Prine, he developed his own voice on the Old Town circuit. Before he met Kristofferson, the means *were* the end, as far as he was concerned.

> None of us thought that much about what we were doing. Sort of like that second city thing, that inferiority thing that Chicago has, right? We all sort of sat around and we knew that we were having a good time and that audiences were coming out to hear us. . . . I knew I could get by. I never did think I'd get to make an album or get to travel around the country and actually get paid for singing, but I knew I could make twenty or twenty-five a night at the Earl of Old Town doing it. . . . That was the extent of our motivation. We just basically liked the music.[127]

Goodman had tried New York. He was born July 25, 1948, and lived in different neighborhoods throughout the North Side until his family settled in suburban Niles. As early as fourteen, he enrolled in an advanced guitar class at the Old Town School of Folk Music and started playing teen clubs in the area. In 1967, he withdrew from the University of Illinois and told his parents he was headed to Greenwich Village. Five months of unstable living as a busker in Washington Square Park and the potential of a draft notice arriving at his doorstep sent him back to Chicago to reenroll in school. That fall, he began playing at the Earl of Old Town.[128] If it meant making a comfortable living by singing his own songs in a city where he could also raise a family, staying in Chicago was an easy choice.

"City of New Orleans" came soon after that. The song connects to deep threads within the folk tradition, particularly Woody Guthrie's expansive telling of America's story as a travelogue, and the metaphorical train ride of Jimmie Rodgers, who adopted the railroad persona of "the Singing Brakeman." Goodman admitted that his song would not have existed without Rodgers.[129] Besides writing some of country music's fundamental songs between 1927 and 1933, Rodgers had been an early twentieth-century pop star with a sound that was freewheeling and cosmopolitan, not rigid and rural. That sound held great appeal to a middle-class kid from the suburbs who discovered he liked to entertain, but who didn't come from Appalachia.

The song was also true to itself. Goodman sketched it out while riding the Illinois Central with his wife, then debuted it at the Earl and recorded it for WFMT's *Midnight Special*. In other words, the song was just a local product. Richard Harding, the Quiet Knight owner, changed that when he approached Arlo Guthrie in January 1971, when Guthrie was playing a weekend engagement at his club.[130] Would Guthrie take a song he knew Johnny Cash would love to the Man in Black himself? Guthrie ignored his pleas. Then, after the last show, as Guthrie headed back to his hotel, Harding stopped him and asked a final time.

"Oh, c'mon, man, I don't want to hear no songs. I don't like songs. I don't even like *my* songs!" Guthrie told him. But Harding had already summoned Goodman. Sizing him up, Guthrie made him an offer: "Buy me a beer and I'll sit here and drink it and as long as it lasts, you do whatever you want." When Goodman finished playing "City of New Orleans," Guthrie put his guitar case down. The two songwriters played songs for each other through the night. Come morning, Goodman handed Guthrie tapes and lead sheets to take home with him.[131] The next year, Guthrie's version of "City of New Orleans" became the only *Billboard* Top 40 hit of his career; the song made Guthrie's *Hobo's Lullaby* the fourth-best-selling record of all time for Warner Bros./Reprise and kept it on the charts for thirty-two weeks.[132] Versions of the song by Willie Nelson, John Denver, Judy Collins, and, yes, Johnny Cash followed.[133]

The song changed Goodman's life—"the greatest thing that ever happened to me," he said of Guthrie's version.[134] But he freely admitted he summoned his true power when performing in front of an audience. On his first national tour, he opened sixty-two dates for comedian Steve Martin, a run that included a twenty-five-night

stand in Las Vegas.[135] Despite the constant churn of spending a
third or more of the year on the road, Goodman didn't retreat when
he returned to Chicago. Most late nights, he showed up at the Earl
or other clubs to watch younger songwriters, mingle with friends,
or woodshed new songs. All this time, he was weakened by constant
chemotherapy treatments but never let it show. "Backstage, the guy
was a pale shade of gray and sweating and it looked like he's going to
die in five minutes. He goes out onstage and Christ, he's bouncing
off the walls! I think he had a nuclear power plant in him," said Dave
Prine.[136] Goodman and John Prine also stayed connected, not just
by playing together, but by co-writing songs, including "The 20th
Century Is Almost Over," which featured Pete Seeger on vocals and
banjo, "How Much Tequila (Did I Drink Last Night)," and "If She
Were You." Before outlaw country singer David Allan Coe had a 1975
hit with "You Never Even Call Me by My Name," the duo's lampoon of
country music, Prine didn't want his name listed because he feared
it was needlessly insulting.

Goodman's first two albums, *Steve Goodman* and *Somebody
Else's Troubles*, both on New York's Buddah label, set him apart from
the standard-bearers of the singer-songwriter era. His eponymous
debut from 1971, co-produced by Kristofferson and Norbert Putnam, reflects the eclectic mix of his live shows: besides including
New Orleans jazz, country rock, classic honky-tonk, and baroque
folk, its setlist was evenly split among originals (including "City
of New Orleans") and covers from his Chicago tribe (John Prine,
Ed Holstein), new collaborators (Dan Penn and Donnie Fritts) and
longtime influences (Hank Williams, Johnny Otis). Goodman's sly
humor and the adroit performances of the most renowned Nashville session men of the period—Ben Keith, Bucky Wilkin, Stephen
Bruton, Billy Sanford, and Pete Wade on guitars, Kenny Buttrey on
drums, Charlie McCoy on harmonica, David Briggs on piano, Fritts
on organ, and Putnam on bass—contribute tenderness and color
without overstatement. Goodman's minimal, almost talkative,
vocals add to the music's intimacy. Even though *Steve Goodman*
was released in a time when one-hit troubadours were running up

the pop charts with orchestrated love songs, Goodman's debut was distinctive for its stylish detail and charming ordinariness.

Somebody Else's Troubles, the follow-up from 1972, is far more confident. Apart from a few covers, including Michael Smith's "The Dutchman," the album consists of Goodman originals. They are songs with wearier themes, including "The Ballad of Penny Evans," sung a cappella from the perspective of a Vietnam War widow. The title song is pure Goodman: set to a banjo and fiddle, with Bob Dylan plunking a piano and shouting the chorus in the background, Goodman lists life's cruelties but then comically finds a sliver of hope: "Just as long as fate is out there bustin' somebody else's bubbles / Everything is gonna be alright."[137]

Even though *Somebody Else's Troubles* was recorded in both Hollywood and New York City, most of the album is pure country. Arif Mardin of Atlantic Records produced, fresh from working on *Dusty in Memphis*, Dusty Springfield's breakthrough, and producing and arranging hits for Aretha Franklin that transformed her from a gospel singer into the Queen of Soul. Maria Muldaur layered Goodman's vocal with harmonies. David Bromberg played lead guitar, accompanied by tenor saxophonist David "Fathead" Newman as well as Dylan. While Goodman had already proved he could captivate an audience by himself, *Somebody Else's Troubles* showed he was a serious recording artist with the songs to back him up.

The album art was designed to reaffirm Goodman's Chicago roots to the outside world. Goodman told photographer Gib Foster he wanted the cover photo to emulate the down-home feel of *Déjà Vu*, the 1970 album by Crosby, Stills, Nash, and Young, whose cover shows all four musicians gathered against a tree in Civil War garb.[138] The cover photo for *Somebody Else's Troubles*, also in black and white, is proudly clannish: staged in Goodman's apartment at 3759 North Wayne, it features all the essential people in his life— Earl Pionke, John Prine, Jimmy Buffett, Goodman's wife Nancy, and Fred and Ed Holstein—surrounding him as he sits in a rocking chair, bouncing his daughter on his lap.

But Chicago was not Goodman's final resting place. In 1980, he moved his family to Seal Beach, California, south of Los Angeles. Considering that Goodman was such a totem of the Chicago scene, the decision alarmed some of his closest friends. After Jim Tullio asked for an explanation, Goodman answered, "I just want to be on the beach with my kids." "He didn't say, 'I'm gonna die in a few years and I want to experience this with my kids.' The only reason why he went out there was to experience living on the beach before he died. It had nothing to do with turning his back on Chicago," Tullio said.[139]

Three years after his move, Goodman went public with his disease. He had undergone chemotherapy for nearly nine years, but when he started missing tour dates and losing his hair, he figured he had no choice. "I didn't want any favors," he said, explaining why he had kept it a secret. "Everybody has a set of special circumstances. There are musicians on the road who have diabetes. I know a couple of musicians who are epileptics. Yet you never hear about those things. . . . I couldn't see my dragging it around as part of my press kit."[140] At a Seattle hospital the next year, on September 20, 1984, he died of complications from a bone marrow transplant.[141]

THE PRINE FAMILY
OF MAYWOOD

When the limousine from the Palmer House pulled up to the Earl of Old Town around 3:00 a.m. on Monday, May 3, 1971, John Prine was asleep in the club. Chairs rested atop tables, and Fred Holstein was cleaning the bar. Prine had performed four separate shows at the Earl since the previous day and was waiting to get paid. But once the door opened, he woke up, and minutes later, he was back onstage, standing in front of an audience of fewer than ten people. They included Paul Anka, Kris Kristofferson, and Prine's friend Steve Goodman, who had phoned the bar earlier and instructed Holstein to make sure Prine didn't leave.

The original songs Prine performed that night were so unexpectedly good that when he finished, Kristofferson asked him to perform the entire set a second time, as if making sure he wasn't deluded by what he had just heard. Among the songs: "Sam Stone," a harrowing first-person account from the child of a heroin addict just returned from Vietnam; "Paradise," an obituary for Prine's ancestral Kentucky home obliterated by a corporate coal giant; "Hello in There," a portrait of two senior citizens watching the world pass by; and "Donald and Lydia," a dispatch from two long-distance lovers seeing their dreams quietly vanish inside the dead space between them. They were songs that Prine would play for the rest of his life, but in that early morning hour, he was a scrawny and unknown twenty-four-year-old who, despite having just woken up, demonstrated the lyrical weight and craftsmanship of someone older than everyone else in the room combined.

"Absolutely destroyed us," Kristofferson said of what he heard that night. "One after another. It was the most incredible thing. I get chills thinking about it."[142]

Prine's intuitive understanding of the inner lives of ordinary people can be traced back to the two-story frame house at 1110 South First Avenue in Maywood where William Nathan Prine and Verna Valentine Prine raised four sons: Dave, Doug, John, and Billy. Maywood might be a suburb of Chicago, but thirteen miles west of Lake Michigan was far enough from the city to be isolating. Prine's friends, he said, "could count on one hand how many times they'd come down to downtown Chicago. They acted like it was going to New York."[143]

The Des Plaines River bordered his hometown; on its east side were River Forest and Oak Park, two wealthier suburbs lined with Victorian homes and legendary for luminaries in literature (Ernest Hemingway), architecture (Frank Lloyd Wright), and the Chicago Outfit (bosses Tony Accardo and Sam Giancana both lived there during their respective reigns). Maywood stood on the river's western edge. North and to the west was Melrose Park, a predominantly Italian suburb.

Class and race separated Maywood from its neighbors on both sides of the river, probably because it was home to three major employers: American Can Company, Western Electric, and Illinois Bell. According to the US census, Maywood was majority White in

1960, but Black residents represented 20 percent of the population, an astonishing 624 percent increase from 1930.[144] This diversity was unique in the Chicago area and gave the Prine brothers an atypical suburban childhood compared with those of their peers.

The Maywood of Prine's childhood was "a melting pot." "There were Mexicans and people from the South and Blacks, compared to just the Italians in Melrose," he said. It took getting drafted into the US Army in 1966 for him to realize his childhood was an outlier. At basic training outside Leesville, Louisiana, "you're meeting guys your own age from all around the country. They were really shocked. They had never been with Mexicans or Black people, you know? I always thought, 'Well, geez, I must have come from a good place because I went to school with everybody.'"[145]

Empson Scobie Prine moved to Maywood from Muhlenberg County, Kentucky, in 1924 with his family, which included William Nathan Prine, a nine-year-old everyone called Bill. Empson was an itinerant carpenter who worked on crews that raised new public buildings, including those at the 1933 Chicago World's Fair.[146] One summer, his son Bill met and courted Verna Valentine Hamm from back home, and they kept up a long-distance relationship until they married in 1936, when she was sixteen and he was twenty-one. She moved to Maywood and took to Chicago fast. Dave Prine, their oldest, was born the next year on November 2, 1937.[147]

Bill Prine was a tool and die maker. His trade kept him employed for thirty-five years at American Can Company, which guaranteed security for his growing family.[148] Their home was a Southern one: Verna's cooking included steak and gravy, fried chicken, and pot roast, and the living room turntable spun 78 rpm records by people like the Carter Family, Roy Acuff, and Bill's favorite, Hank Williams. The country playlist of WJJD flowed nonstop, and on Saturday nights, Bill went into the basement to fiddle with Dave's ham radio kit to catch the *Grand Ole Opry*. On summer vacations, the family headed back to Kentucky in their 1939 DeSoto to fish and attend the annual family reunion. It was common for the Prines to take in cousins and other close family members as they, too, tried to establish a foothold in Chicago, where there was honest work. "Anything to get out of western Kentucky, which was a barren landscape ripe for the strip mining. And my family didn't want to coal mine," John said.[149]

Maywood had few Southerners. To feel at home, Bill periodically visited bars in Uptown or straddled a stool at Flippo's, at 2200 St. Charles Road in nearby Bellwood, a country bar he considered his hangout because its jukebox was stacked with classic country. When country stars started playing downtown theaters in the 1960s, the Prines bought tickets and took their boys on pilgrimages to see Buck Owens and Loretta Lynn with opener Charley Pride at the Medinah Temple; Ernest Tubb and Flatt & Scruggs at the Arie Crown; and Johnny Cash at the Civic Center in Hammond. Maybe it was because he was bullied at school about his accent, but Bill was insistent that his sons never forsake where they came from. Dave Prine recalled a grade school assignment that required him to research his European ancestry. But first he needed to understand what that was.

> So I came home and the old man was sitting at the table with his quart of Old Style, and I said, "What's my nationality?" And he said, "You're a Kentuckian, by damn!" That was good enough for me. And so I go back to school the next day, and the teacher is going through the class pointing out this kid's from Poland and this one's from Ireland and this one's from Italy. And she comes to me and I said, "I'm a Kentuckian!" Hell, I thought it was totally legitimate! As far as I was concerned, Kentucky was as far away from here as Russia.[150]

Neither parent played an instrument. The first of their sons to bring one home was Dave, a restless and largely self-taught musician who would become a central figure in Chicago's old-time music revival of the 1970s. It took his mother buying him a guitar, in 1962, for him to get serious. He took lessons from Ray Tate at the Old Town School of Folk Music. Another instrument switch got him to the banjo, and that stuck. Fleming Brown enlisted him in his class, and between 1963 and 1966, Brown became Prine's mentor until Prine taught the class himself into the next decade.

By trade, Dave Prine was an electrical engineer, a career that gave him the lifelong stability to support his musical pursuits. He learned fiddle and started playing with Tyler Wilson, a friend from Evanston, also an engineer. It was 1966, and the folk revival was dimming. Years earlier, in 1961, the Friends of Old-Time Music in New York had formed to promote early blues, country, and gospel performers in urban settings, and their efforts had creatively fed the University of Chicago Folk Festival that launched that same year. Prine's greatest influence, the New Lost City Ramblers, served as the house band for both. Every year he attended the festival and their workshops. As the majority of Old Town School students were abandoning their Folkways records in favor of writing original songs, a "renegade element" at the school was organizing to keep the traditional songs alive.

The obvious outlet for their efforts, Prine figured, would be a Friends of Old-Time Music chapter in Chicago. "We just said 'hell, we're as good as they are, let's do it,'" Prine recalled. The first meeting was in the living room of a Victorian house Prine and his wife rented in Maywood. Over the years, the number of people attending the weekly picking jams grew, and they became a place to trade tapes, share songs, and occasionally hop in cars together to travel to folk festivals in the South.[151] Prine and Wilson eventually formed a duo, the National Recovery Act, which performed over the next decade throughout the Midwest. At the time, they were the only band playing old-time music on a local scene dominated by singer-songwriters. They played a variety of instruments—guitar, mandolin, banjo, dobro, autoharp, fiddle, even a crow call—and stocked their setlists with songs that could be too raw for modern ears. When they opened for Odetta at Evanston's Amazingrace folk club, some in the audience were repelled by a performance of "Pretty Polly," a traditional murder ballad that ends with the killing of a woman in the woods. A fight broke out, and the band stopped to cool things down. "It made us think a lot about the type of thing we were doing and that there might be people out there who would take offense," Wilson said. From then on, note-for-note renditions of the original recordings became less important to them, and they felt freer to interpret.[152]

Dave Prine's influence on at least two of his three younger brothers was profound. He was nine years older than John, born October 10, 1946, and sixteen years older than Billy, born Sept. 20, 1953. (Doug Prine, the second oldest brother, liked Chicago blues, but opted for a career as a lieutenant in the Chicago Police Department on the city's West Side.) For John, Christmas 1960 produced a Silvertone guitar. He wanted to dabble in early rock and roll like Little Richard and Buddy Holly. Dave taught him three chords to start, but he didn't stop there. "Dave's big thing was 'you gotta learn a song.' A lot of kids learn riffs, like 'Satisfaction' [by the Rolling Stones]. But Dave told us you really need to sit down and learn how to sing a song," Billy Prine said. So Dave introduced John to Ray Tate at the Old Town School, and he started lessons. Sensing his brother was a daydreamer, he fed him records by the Carter Family, Jimmie Rodgers, and Hank Williams. There were also field trips to the University of Chicago Folk Festival, where the Prines saw some of the artists on those old records, like Elizabeth Cotten, Doc Watson, and the Stanley Brothers. The mentoring was casual, but it took hold. One night, as the brothers were playing tunes by Charlie and Bill Monroe, John mentioned that he'd been dabbling in songwriting.

"Oh, that's interesting. Will you play a couple for me?" asked his brother. It turned out that two or three of the songs would later end up on his first album. "And he was writing this stuff as a teenager. It blew my mind," Dave said. "My little brother!" he thought, holding his fiddle. "Where did this come from?"[153]

The truth was, John started writing songs before his Army service in West Germany, but it was when he returned home in 1968 that he got serious about it. He had seen more of life, and how Vietnam was affecting his friends and community. Newly married to Ann Carole Menaloscino, his high school sweetheart, and settled in a Melrose Park apartment at 902 North Nineteenth, John resumed a job he had taken before his time in Germany as a mail carrier for the US Postal Service in Maywood, Broadview, and Westchester. The next year, on February 13, 1969, he returned to class at the Old Town School of Folk Music.[154]

Neither his wife nor his family knew that John was writing songs prodigiously. That was revealed one night at the Fifth Peg at 858 West Armitage, a club located across the street and down a block from the Old Town School. Ray Tate and fellow Old Town School teacher John Carbo opened its doors in May 1969, and part of the club's schedule was a weekly amateur night for Old Town students.[155] John showed up and hung in the rear of the room to watch the local talent. "They were pretty bad. I had a couple of beers too many so I said so, like loudly," he recalled. Eventually, someone at a nearby table dared him to do better. Prine stepped onstage and played three songs: "Sam Stone," "Hello in There," and "Paradise."[156] He was nervous about his voice and didn't think he could sing. But before he headed out the door, both owners asked him to return every Thursday to play three sets. "How long do you have to sing?" Prine asked. "When they told me, I went home and wrote enough songs to fill up an hour."[157]

That fall, the Fifth Peg moved Prine to Fridays and Saturdays, and his crowds grew. "We've got a genius on our hands," Fleming Brown told the *Chicago Tribune*.[158] In October 1970, the word of mouth drove *Chicago Sun-Times* film critic Roger Ebert to stop in and check out Prine, who by then had "one of the hottest underground reputations in Chicago." In the story that followed, titled "Singing Mailman Who Delivers a Powerful Message in a Few Words," Ebert hailed Prine as a storyteller in league with greatness. His songs are "nothing like the work of most young composers these days, who seem to specialize in narcissistic tributes to themselves. He's closer to Hank Williams than to Roger Williams, closer to [Bob] Dylan than to [Phil] Ochs."

Prine is good. He appears on stage with such modesty he almost seems to be backing into the spotlight. He sings rather quietly, and

his guitar work is good, but he doesn't show off. He starts slow. But
after a song or two, even the drunks in the room begin to listen to his
lyrics. And then he has you.[159]

The story appeared a day before Prine's twenty-fourth birthday.
The following year, Atlantic Records released *John Prine*, a debut
album that featured songs already familiar to Chicago audiences.
Most of the album was written in that Nineteenth Avenue apartment,[160] and its songs had roots in those streets. "Far From Me"
came from the memory of his first girlfriend, a waitress in downtown Maywood. "Your Flag Decal Won't Get You into Heaven Anymore," a protest song of the Vietnam era, has proved applicable to
wars ever since because of its lampooning of right-wing nation-
alism. Prine became all too familiar with the US flag decals that
came from *Reader's Digest* after lugging them on his mail route.
The heroin addict in "Sam Stone" came directly from the Vietnam
veterans he saw on the streets. "Grandpa Was a Carpenter" shared
memories of his Grandpa Empson, and "Fish and Whistle" came
from his first job: cleaning the parking lot of Skip's Fiesta Drive-In,
a hamburger joint on North Avenue. Atlantic understandably tried
to market Prine as a new country poet in the mold of Kris Kristofferson or even Bob Dylan, who had already left New York City and was
in the midst of his own reinvention, playing laid-back country rock
with Nashville studio musicians. The cover of *John Prine* showed
Prine in denim resting on hay bales. Later, he said his more natural
habitat was a city bus: "I had never sat on a bale of hay in my life."[161]
  Despite his family's roots, Prine's songs are not entangled in
the gothic drama or the religiosity of his Southern peers. Instead,
through their wry humor and newspaperman detail, the songs exem-
plify how empathy and ordinary language can produce the weight of
an entire novel. "Six O'clock News," from *John Prine*, transcribes
the trajectory of James Lewis, a "kid with two first names," in four
verses. In the beginning, he is born to a single mother and running
in a schoolyard, and by the end, "his brains were on the sidewalk
and blood was on his shoes"—a fate delivered with matter-of-fact

resignation, the worst kind of horror. The slivers of description—
"'God bless this kitchen' said the knick-knack shelf'"—offer neither
answers nor consolation, only a glimpse of familiarity.[162] The song,
like so many of his others, is as bleak and as beautiful as a Chicago
winter morning.

"I don't feel I could write songs about being a Southerner," Prine
acknowledged. "I still got that Midwestern mentality. That's where
I go back there as a touchstone with my writing. . . . They get me in
Wisconsin and Iowa."[163]

Those early songs were built with images. "There's a hole in
daddy's arm where all the money goes" is the lyric that has kept
"Sam Stone" relevant over generations. The song's protagonist even
earned kinship with Pink, the drug-addled hero of Pink Floyd's
rock opus *The Wall*, after co-founder Roger Waters started adding
Prine's song to his setlists. The song originated from Prine's cartoon
image of "a rainbow of money falling down" into a human arm. "If
the image is strong enough, the rest of the song develops out of it,"
he told Studs Terkel in 1970. "I don't want to get too far from the
original thought."[164]

Every character has a name—Donald, Lydia, Fred, Loretta,
Rudy—which compounds the feeling their stories were caught from
runaway newspapers scattered by the wind. The names anchor the
writing with the sense that the songs are dealing with real humans
confronting true human mysteries, a practice that pushes against
the craftmanship side of songwriting that demands order and purpose. "As long as I've been writing, I have no idea what I'm doing. I'm
always starting out brand new. I couldn't say to anybody 'this is what
you do to write a song.' I don't know where they come from and I don't
know where they don't come from—*that* even more so," Prine said.
"I do know when I'm not writing I'm just making up something. It
might come out well crafted, but it wouldn't come from my heart.
I gotta trust my instinct when it comes to that. Because it always
served me really well."[165]

Prine remained in the Chicago area throughout his Atlantic
years, releasing three more albums for the label. Like his debut,

the next two were made with house producer Arif Mardin, who by then was best known for his landmark collaborations with Aretha Franklin. To produce *Common Sense*, his fourth, Prine picked Steve Cropper, the famed house guitarist for Stax Records, who added horns and backup singers and turned Prine into a houserocker. But critics blasted *Common Sense* for sounding too slick and its songs as too dark, and Atlantic, preoccupied with mega-selling acts like the Rolling Stones and Led Zeppelin, was upset that Prine chose Cropper over Mardin so didn't give the album the marketing support it deserved. The experience led Prine to a crossroads. "I just felt lost," he said. His response was to exit Atlantic and make a record in Chicago.

Bruised Orange remains the only album Prine recorded in his hometown. Newly signed to Asylum, he first hired musical raconteur "Cowboy" Jack Clement to make a rockabilly album in Nashville. But after recording over the summer of 1977 with no results, Prine turned to Steve Goodman for help. Goodman instructed him to "just show up with your guitar and sing the songs however you want to sing them."[166] Goodman ended up producing *Bruised Orange* at the Chicago Recording Company in 1978.

Unlike those for *Common Sense*, the Chicago sessions were filled with familiar faces to make Prine comfortable: Jethro Burns on mandolin, his son Johnny Burns on guitar, progressive bluegrass mandolinist Sam Bush, Corky Siegal on harmonica, and Dave Prine and Tyler Wilson on background vocals, along with others from Prine's Earl of Old Town days, including Bonnie Koloc, Ed and Fred Holstein, Harry Waller, and Earl Pionke himself. But Goodman wouldn't allow Prine to make the slapdash record he aimed for in Nashville with Clement; instead, the sessions were balanced between hard-charging rockabilly ("Iron Ore Betty"), dark, foreboding tales ("Bruised Orange [Chain of Sorrow]"), psychedelic folk ("Sabu Visits the Twin Cities Alone"), and songs related to his more whimsical early days ("Fish and Whistle," "That's the Way That the World Goes 'Round"). "He was like Edward G. Robinson," Prine said of Goodman in the studio. "He wouldn't mind if I argued every day, but I didn't have it in me. We made a deal we'd go in and do this, though, so I listened to him."[167]

Goodman's instincts turned out to be right: *Bruised Orange* won back the critics. Prine felt so recharged that he hit the road with some of the Chicago players—John Burns, harmonica player Howard Levy, bassist Tom Piekarski, and drummer Angie Varias— who were later dubbed the Famous Potatoes, after a 1978 cult novel. Two years later, in 1980, Prine relocated to Nashville for good, but the Famous Potatoes served as his band for his next two albums. Together, they gave Prine what he was searching for: a hell-bent bar band that could play country, R&B, and rockabilly with the stage flash of his teenage musical heroes. "Eventually John got even crazier than us. I remember us doing a show with Emmylou Harris where at the end of a song he took his guitar and just tossed it into the air and off the stage.... We really loosened him up," said Burns.[168]

Despite his move to Nashville, Prine's family was never far from his songwriting. On "When I Get to Heaven," from *The Tree of Forgiveness* (2018), he imagines his second life inside the pearly gates, swigging cocktails, smoking outrageously long cigarettes, and looking up his parents—"and good old brother Doug." "I want to see all my momma's sisters because that's where all the love starts," he says during a pause in the music. "I miss them all like crazy."[169]

But the song that articulated the Prine family's emotional journey from Kentucky to Chicago was from his debut album. "Paradise" is sung from the perspective of a second-generation Kentuckian removed from the ancestral home in those mountains and returning to see how a coal giant—in this case, the Peabody Energy Corporation—has stripped the land of its people and, ultimately, its soul. The narrator is Prine, and his audience is his father. "Daddy won't you take me back to Muhlenberg County / Down by the Green River where Paradise lay," Prine sings. "Well, I'm sorry my son, but you're too late in asking / Mister Peabody's coal train has hauled it away."[170]

The version Prine cut in New York had a session musician play country fiddle, but when Bill Prine heard it, he said it sounded wrong. He insisted that brother Dave play fiddle on the recording, making it as close to a family affair as possible. John agreed, and flew Dave to New York to overdub the signature part. To hear the final version, their father sat in a dark room pretending he was listening to a jukebox. He cried.[171] Two months before the album came out, on August 16, 1971, Bill Prine died of a heart attack at age fifty-six. His family moved his body to a family cemetery in Muhlenberg County, next to where Paradise once stood.[172]

"Paradise" closed Prine's shows until the end. For dates in Chicago, brother Dave often joined him to play fiddle, and Billy helped sing the chorus. The song earned a second life as a bluegrass standard due to versions by John Denver; the Country Gentlemen, which featured young Kentucky native Ricky Skaggs on fiddle; West Virginia bluegrass duo Jim & Jesse; and even the Everly Brothers, whose family also had deep roots in Muhlenberg County. The song also became a tool for environmental activists who sued Peabody Energy in 2015 for violating their civil rights when they were arrested outside the company's shareholder meeting two years earlier. Their legal brief quoted the song, which caused the company to call the lyrics inflammatory and worthy of being thrown out.[173] Its request was denied. The precedent had been set by US Chief Justice John Roberts, the judge explained, who once quoted Bob Dylan in his legal writing.

The next year, Prine performed the entirety of his debut album for the first and only time. It was at the Station Inn, a small bluegrass club in Nashville, before about two hundred people. In his hands all night was the same guitar that appeared on the album's front cover. Forty-one years later, his voice, deepened by a bout with throat cancer, filled the songs with the natural ache of age, giving them deeper weight than the nasally twang of his younger self. "Paradise," he told the audience, "wasn't a protest song, but when Peabody heard it, they went ape shit. That's what started the war between us."[174]

The war ended in April 2016. Plunging coal prices forced Peabody, saddled with $10 billion in debt, to declare bankruptcy.[175]

Three years later, on April 7, 2020, Prine died in Nashville from complications of COVID-19.[176]

Music moved north of Fullerton starting in 1969 with Orphans, 2462 North Lincoln, a club known for folk and jazz. In the following years, other music clubs opened their doors on North Lincoln: Wise Fools Pub, 2270 North Lincoln (1970), Ratso's, 2464 North Lincoln (1971), and Clearwater Saloon, 3447 North Lincoln (1976), and later, Déjà Vu, 2624 North Lincoln, and Irish Eyes, 2518 North Lincoln, among many others. If the Old Town scene kept folk music from dying in the 1960s, the Lincoln Avenue strip extended its life well into the 1980s.

"You could park your car right around Fullerton and Lincoln and walk almost a mile north and it was club after club after club. You could walk past one club and hear blues and another one you could hear country music, and another one folk music and bluegrass music and across the street, Celtic music, and jazz. It was fabulous," said Greg Cahill, the founder of the bluegrass band Special Consensus.[177]

Kingston Mines, Chicago's longest-running blues club, opened in 1969 as the Kingston Mines Theatre Company, which produced experimental plays at 2356 North Lincoln, a cavernous space that was once a machine shop. In 1971, the theater launched the world premiere of *Grease*, its original musical. For entertainment during intermission, the company hired Dave Prine and Tyler Wilson's old-time folk duo, the National Recovery Act. When the theater shuttered, the duo stayed for almost a decade to build an audience for the space's new owner. The new Kingston Mines hosted folk and bluegrass until 1982, when it moved to Halsted for a rebranding as a blues club.[178]

One late night in 1974, Earl Pionke, stumbling out of Orphans into the early morning, noticed a rental sign for a storefront on the same block. "Should we take a shot?" he asked his friend. Within months he had bought into the strip by opening Somebody Else's Troubles, a satellite of the Earl at 2470 North Lincoln, named after a Steve Goodman song. His business partners were a ragtag group of musicians and friends: Goodman, Fred and Ed Holstein, Henry "Duke" Nathaus, and Bill Redhed, a college professor who lived in Old Town and considered Pionke "like a father."[179] With the Earl booking more touring artists, Troubles would focus on local folk acts. Pionke wanted a "living room party atmosphere," so he kept drink prices low to encourage musicians to hang out.[180] Every month, the club hosted a "Cook and Sing," a Sunday night event that featured a favorite dinner prepared by the headlining act. For his month, Steve Goodman served 1,352 shrimp in garlic and butter sauce and twenty-four pounds of green noodles. In another month, John Prine handed out two hundred White Castle hamburgers.[181]

Like the Earl, Troubles was long and thin, with booths against one wall and the bar on the opposite side. One row of tables ran down the middle. Antique mirrors, copper cookware, and paintings lined the walls. Fred Holstein was the house act, which suited him since he lived around the corner and could come and go between sets. Ed Holstein managed the booking. To musicians, a club booked by one of their own was welcome. "Under their mustaches, there was always this happy smirk. Not a snarky smirk, but a joyous one. They were larger than life," said keyboardist Ira Kart.[182]

Born February 4, 1947, Ed Holstein was by then a beloved figure on the Chicago folk scene. Unlike his older brother Fred, Ed was a songwriter. "Jazzman," his best-known composition, had already been covered by artists like Bette Midler, Tom Rush, Steve Goodman, Bonnie Koloc, and Martin Simpson. If Fred Holstein stirred up audiences with songs about the struggles of dockworkers or immigrants, Ed Holstein was a master of understatement. He told comic stories, covered Bob Dylan and Gene Autry, and generally peppered his sets with the nonsensical humor and comic timing of an old-time vaudevillian. He was the closest Chicago had to a Second City improviser on a folk stage. For that reason alone, John Belushi was a fan.

FIG. 20 Singer-songwriter Steve Goodman (*left*) developed a friendship and musical affinity with bluegrass humorist and mandolinist Jethro Burns (*right*), who settled in suburban Evanston during the glory days of Homer and Jethro. After his partner's death, Burns taught a new generation of bluegrass musicians from his basement, and during his last decade of life, performed relentlessly throughout Chicago. PHOTOGRAPH BY PAUL NATKIN.

FIG. 21 Two years before he moved to Nashville in 1980, Maywood native John Prine formed the Famous Potatoes, a Chicago-based band that backed him up over three albums, including *Bruised Orange*, produced by Steve Goodman. Here, Prine, guitarist Johnny Burns, and Goodman tear up the stage.

PHOTOGRAPH BY PAUL NATKIN.

FIG. 22 Fred Holstein, waiting to play ChicagoFest at Navy Pier, August 2, 1980. Holstein considered himself a saloon singer in the purest sense: he didn't write songs, but sold them to audiences with both swagger and sensitivity. "He was James Dean and Pete Seeger all in one," said his brother Alan. Because he pre-dated the scene that emerged in the early 1970s, Holstein served as a mentor to the folk singers arriving in Old Town eager to learn the old songs. PHOTOGRAPH BY STEVE KAGAN.

FIG. 23 Bonnie Koloc arrived in Chicago from her native Iowa in 1968 and almost immediately became a sensation in Old Town clubs. A succession of albums in the 1970s reflected a singer who blended avant-garde sensibilities with blue-eyed soul PHOTOGRAPH BY PAUL NATKIN.

FIG. 24 *From left*, Marc Edelstein and Greg Cahill of Special Consensus. The band would be the first from outside the South to crack the bluegrass circuit, influencing dozens of bands in its wake. PHOTOGRAPH COURTESY OF GREG CAHILL.

FIG. 25 The Clearwater Saloon, 3447 North Lincoln Avenue, pictured in 1979. The North Side club featured progressive bluegrass bands in the late 1970s and 1980s, including Special Consensus, which held a weekly residency. PHOTOGRAPH BY CHARLES CHERNEY.

FIG. 26 Folk singer Andrew Calhoun helped move Chicago's folk scene into the 1990s with the launch of Waterbug, a record label that released about 130 albums between 1992 and 2019 and documented a national scene of folk singer-songwriters PHOTOGRAPH BY NOEL NEUBERGER.

FIG. 27 *From left*, Kelly Kessler and Jane Baxter Miller. As the Texas Rubies, the duo played an unorthodox mix of Appalachian music and early blues in Chicago subways, art galleries, and punk-rock clubs because there were few other places for the music at the time. They pre-dated the alternative-country boom that would explode in the late 1990s. PHOTOGRAPH BY DEBRA RAE STEWARD.

FIG. 28 *From left*, Jay Farrar, Mike Heidorn, and Jeff Tweedy of Uncle Tupelo, at Lounge Ax, October 1991. The downstate Illinois band was one of a few at the time starting to fuse early country music covers with punk rock. PHOTOGRAPH BY MARTY PEREZ.

FIG. 29 The Waco Brothers at Lounge Ax. *From left*, Tracey Dear, Dean Schlabowske, Jon Langford, Alan Doughty, Steve Goulding, and Mark Durante. The Wacos helped establish punk-country as a genre with its strident blue-collar anthems and raucous stage shows. When Langford moved to Chicago from England, he became a patron saint of the emerging scene through his many collaborations and his artwork. PHOTOGRAPH BY PAUL NATKIN.

FIG. 30 The best songwriter to come out of Chicago since John Prine, Robbie Fulks quickly established himself as a fundamental talent with his songs, musicianship, showmanship, and collaborative instinct. Like Jeff Tweedy, he helped establish the alt-country genre, but then transcended it through albums that combined power-pop, bluegrass, noise rock, and traditional singer-songwriter fare.

PHOTOGRAPH BY PETER ERIKSSON.

FIG. 31 The Blacks at the Hideout, December 1999. *From left*: Gina Black, James Emmenegger, Danny Black, and Nora O'Connor. An alt-country band that drew from elements of vaudeville, gospel, and country music fatalism, the Blacks could never have happened anywhere but in Chicago. "Nobody thought they were going to make a living playing it," said Danny Black. "That freed you up to just enjoy playing music for the sake of the music." PHOTOGRAPH BY PAUL NATKIN.

FIG. 32 Brett and Rennie Sparks of the Handsome Family at Metro, July 1998. The married couple came from the Lounge Ax scene as surrealists who filtered Appalachian ballads, country spirituals, and acoustic blues traditions through their own postmodern lens using electronic distortion and beats as well as poetic details.

PHOTOGRAPH BY MARTY PEREZ.

FIG. 33 *From left*, Jay Bennett, Ken Coomer (partially blocked by the guitar neck), Jeff Tweedy, and John Stirratt of Wilco, Lounge Ax, January 2000. The band's breakthrough success helped draw national attention to the restless underground scene in Chicago featuring musicians steeped in the country and folk traditions but eager to experiment. PHOTOGRAPH BY MARTY PEREZ.

FIG. 34 *From left*, Julia Adams and Sue Miller, co-owners of Lounge Ax, a rock club in Lincoln Park that served as a clubhouse for Chicago's eclectic independent music scene in the 1990s. Lounge Ax also actively promoted alt-country touring artists like Jimmie Dale Gilmore, Joe Ely, and Bad Livers. PHOTOGRAPH BY MARTY PEREZ.

FIG. 35 Wilco's Jeff Tweedy and Roger McGuinn of the Byrds, backstage at the Auditorium Theatre, December 1, 2007. The evening was a celebration of the Old Town School of Folk Music's fiftieth anniversary, but the bill also served as a cross-generational presentation of folk and country music's deep roots in Chicago. PHOTOGRAPH BY PAUL NATKIN.

Open stages were held Mondays and Tuesdays. Songwriters would get three songs or fifteen minutes, and if the Holstein brothers liked you, you'd move to a weekend slot. If Pionke took notice, you had a chance to move to the Earl and open for a national headliner. It was a farm system that forced songwriters to develop their craft. Other clubs, like Orphans, the Earl, Kingston Mines, and the Barbarossa on Dearborn, had similar nights for newcomers on the scene. In total, songwriters on their way up could hone their craft before a paying audience nearly every night of the week. "That was your way in," said Chris Farrell.[183]

Bolstering the scene was the grassroots media that developed around it. WFMT's weekly *Midnight Special* brought artists into the studio, played new releases by local artists, or broadcast directly from the clubs. The magazine *Come for to Sing* was launched in 1975 by Emily Friedman, who moved to Chicago in 1969 and was immediately captivated by Fred Holstein and the scene at the Earl. She had worked as an editor for *Encyclopedia Britannica*, and had noticed the absence of the Chicago scene in the pages of Pete Seeger's *Sing Out!* magazine. "I just finally decided somebody had to chronicle this. Nobody knows what's happening here," she said.[184] The Old Town School gave Friedman and her volunteer staff space and helped subsidize the costs. The staff did thorough work: between 1975 and 1987, the magazine reviewed albums and concerts; published songs, interviews, and an annual guide to Midwestern clubs and festivals; and ran lengthy stories that explored every component of the Chicago folk scene. Besides managing the magazine, Friedman started Aural Tradition, a folk music society that brought international artists like Jean Redpath (Scotland), John Allan Cameron (Canada), and Stan Rogers (Canada) to Chicago at a time when they struggled to get bookings. The society also booked domestic artists like Piedmont blues guitarists John Jackson and Carl Martin.[185]

In March 1981, the Holstein brothers, along with younger brother Alan Holstein, left Troubles to open their own club. Holsteins, at 2464 North Lincoln, was designed as a listening room strictly for folk music. Unlike the Earl and Troubles, it had a music room separate from the bar, a decision made to direct attention to the stage and cut down on noise. The club had a no-talking policy it enforced through announcements on the stage and at the door. If people wanted a place to drink and talk, they were directed to other bars down the street. "You have to protect your audience," Ed Holstein said.[186]

The brothers' commitment to running a seven-night-a-week folk club made Holsteins unique. Like the Gate of Horn decades earlier, it was a singular destination for roots-based musicians across the country, including Loudon Wainwright, Jonathan Richman, Sonny Terry and Brownie McGhee, Eric Anderson, Utah Phillips, Dave Van Ronk, New Grass Revival, Ramblin' Jack Elliott, Doc Watson, John Hartford, Greg Brown, Tom Paxton, John Gorka, and Ewan Mac-Coll and Peggy Seeger. Van Ronk often drove from New York just to play Holsteins because the club offered a guaranteed packed house, something the influential folk singer struggled to find at home in Greenwich Village. "He was convinced they must have put amphetamine in the water in Chicago because everyone partied and played music all night," said Andrea Vuocolo Van Ronk, his wife. "He said there's a lot more going on in Chicago than on any given night in New York, especially in the 1980s when there was nothing."[187]

Holsteins helped extend folk music into the late 1980s, mostly because it gave the brothers an opportunity to do things their way. "For the first time, we were able to run a folk music setting the way we saw fit. And we learned that some of our ideas were appreciated," said Ed Holstein. "There was no elitism. The performers were always accessible to members of the audience. The performers were mature and giving, and the audiences were the same way. This didn't feel like a 'scene,' it felt like a family."[188]

But once its seven-year lease was up and the rent doubled, Holsteins closed its doors. The near North Side was gentrifying quickly, and Troubles, Orphans, the Earl of Old Town, and other clubs had already vanished. The Holstein brothers had carried folk music as far as they could, and splitting the work among just the three of them had taken its toll. "I don't feel sad, this place has been great to us," Ed Holstein said before locking the doors for good. "And I'm looking forward to not having to work so hard."[189]

A FOLK BOOM POSTSCRIPT:
WATERBUG RECORDS

As a young man, Andrew Calhoun largely missed the folk boom of the 1970s, and he didn't regret it. "The Chicago folk scene was sort of folk entertainment after a while," he said. "I didn't fit."[190]

The scene that flourished in the bars along Lincoln Avenue and elsewhere on the North Side faded as more clubs shuttered. The economics of owning a club started favoring dance clubs and singles bars, not live music, particularly the kind played with guitars and fiddles. The folk boom was over, but as the new decade opened, the music did not disappear.

Folk music migrated from bars to quieter rooms, returning to its early roots when performers didn't have to fight to be heard and the strongest drink served was espresso. With folk series taking root in coffeehouses, community halls, churches, and other venues in the city and suburbs, folk music quietly developed a larger and more committed audience. Helping things along were its affordability—admission was usually cheap or free—and accessibility for families. Two Way Street, at 1047 Curtiss in suburban Downers Grove, and No Exit Café, at 6670 North Glenwood in the city, became destinations for both touring artists and locals. Classical station WFMT continued to promote the music and, in 1984, partnered with the city to launch an annual folk festival in Grant Park that became part of the city's Taste of Chicago celebration.

This time around, it was the community itself that was leading the scene, not bar owners. Folk music societies like Aural Tradition used membership dues and volunteers to book and operate festivals, barn dances, and concerts by prominent artists passing through town. The most prominent, and longest lasting, was the Fox Valley Folklore Society, formed in 1975, which hosted concerts, workshops, and barn dances throughout the year, including an annual two-day festival along the banks of the Fox River in Geneva, a western suburb. The society was so central in supporting the music, and the scene so big, that it maintained a twenty-four-hour hotline (TGI-FOLK, or "Thank Goodness It's Folk") to promote two weeks' worth of upcoming concerts and events.[191]

Calhoun was born November 30, 1957, in New Jersey but grew up in Glen Ellyn, a western suburb of Chicago. In 1970, after reading a rave review in the *Chicago Sun-Times* by Roger Ebert, his mother orchestrated a family field trip to the Fifth Peg, an Old Town folk club, to hear John Prine. "The radical voice of love," Calhoun remembered of Prine. "Like being in heaven. It completely lit me up. I knew what I wanted to do with my life." He started writing songs right away, and two years later enrolled in classes at the Old Town School of Folk Music. At sixteen, he was driving into the city to play open mics.[192]

When Calhoun started performing, he noticed Chicago was lacking songwriters who mixed traditional songs with original ones. In places like Iowa City, a scene dominated by singer-songwriter Greg Brown, and at annual songwriter summits like the Kerrville Folk Festival in Texas, Calhoun found his tribe: poets who approached songwriting as a literary art in the tradition of the old songs. Inspired by return trips to Kerrville, Calhoun found a purpose: "to get America's real singing poets on the airwaves." Later, he founded a record label that would do just that.

Between 1992 and 2019, Calhoun's label, Waterbug, released about 130 albums, documenting a national scene of songwriters who were pushing back against the commercial charts. The title of his first compilation served as a mission statement for the kind of sound that would fill his new label: *American Impressionist Songwriters*. Over time, Waterbug would be home to some of folk music's most literary-minded songwriters: James McCandless, Anaïs Mitchell, Sloan Wainwright, Art Thieme, Erin McKeown, Rose Polenzani, Dan Bern, Cosy Sheridan, Dar Williams, Kate MacLeod, Mark Dvorak, Annie Gallup, Kat Eggleston, Gina Forsyth, Sons of the Never Wrong, and Calhoun himself.

Through Waterbug, Calhoun would create a home for songwriters who were detached from the saloon scene of the earlier era and who approached their craft with diligence, but without industry backing. "There isn't any commercial avenue for the song as art. I wanted to change the climate, to find an audience that was not about personality, but about the work," he said. The mission, he said, was solely to present "songwriting as an art form" from songwriters who, much like fiction writers and poets, produced unique work while supporting themselves with other jobs and touring only sporadically.[193] Calhoun ran the recording studio from his apartment, and his agreements with artists were generous: Waterbug promised radio publicity and national distribution, while the artists promised to finance their own recordings but were allowed to retain all rights to their music, including all profits earned from the stage.

As Waterbug developed prestige in the folk market, artists starting their careers sought the label out to be associated with its roster. For others, like Dar Williams, Waterbug served to launch larger careers. At the label's height, Calhoun was orchestrating release campaigns for a new record every month. The projects became so consuming that Calhoun eventually withdrew to focus on his own work. He shuttered Waterbug in 2019, the same year that Anaïs Mitchell, who had launched her career on Waterbug in 2004, swept the Tony Awards when her musical *Hadestown* won Best Musical and Best Original Score. The accolades reflected the care that Calhoun had put into building a community of songwriters, most unknown at the time, and giving them a platform when they needed it most. "I'm trying to do work that lasts," he said, "that will be relevant in two hundred years."[194]

COUNTRY MUSIC
SURGES AND BLUEGRASS
ARRIVES

By the time the Lincoln Park folk scene was drying up, country music was becoming chic. The hillbilly image associated with the music for decades had finally been shed due to a sophisticated urban audience that didn't relate to it and a homogenized sound from Nashville that trended toward country rock and soft pop.

Sleek dance halls in the suburbs serving up food and a family atmosphere were new alternatives to the rough bars in Uptown and elsewhere. People could now read about the latest country stars in the Chicago dailies, which started covering country music seriously in their Arts sections. In 1976, two local newspapers were launched that exclusively covered both the national and local country scenes: *CountryStyle*, a biweekly tabloid produced in suburban Niles, and *Country Rambler*, out of Franklin Park. Each had circulations topping four hundred thousand.[1] Even the Portage Theater, a former Northwest Side movie palace, went country for a short period in 1975 when it was renamed the Portage Palace and featured Conway Twitty, Loretta Lynn, and George Jones in its opening month.[2]

Chicago also boasted the largest and most important radio market for country music outside Nashville, largely due to powerhouse WMAQ, which became Chicago's second full-time country music station in 1974. Because of its 50,000-watt signal, capable of reaching thirty-eight states at night, WMAQ had greater reach than WJJD, which in 1977 switched its call letters to WJEZ and began operating with a reduced signal strength. WUSN, a third station, also went country that decade. All three stations promoted a polished brand of country designed to bring in pop fans. "It has to have an 'uptown' feel to it that will not be an irritant" to listeners, said WMAQ general manager Lee Davis, "but hopefully will satisfy the same taste that enjoys an Olivia Newton-John."[3] Similarly, on the week it changed call letters, WJEZ branded itself "Beautiful Country," a format it defined by "softer" country artists like Eddy Arnold and Charlie Rich, who would share airtime with pop crooners like Perry Como. "It's country music for people who like easy listening," explained general manager George Dubinetz.[4]

The benchmark moment of country's crossover was the 1980 hit film *Urban Cowboy*. The film was an outlier in the disco era, and suddenly the hedonism of the urban club scene vanished, replaced by dancers in Wranglers, Stetsons, and cowboy boots. The film's soundtrack redefined modern country through hit singles by Johnny Lee, Mickey Gilley, Boz Scaggs, Anne Murray, and Kenny Rogers. The backlash from traditionally minded artists like George Strait, Lyle Lovett, Vince Gill, and Suzy Bogguss was still around the corner. For the time being, it was *Urban Cowboy* star John Travolta who was setting trends.

The Chicago area did not have any venues the size of Gilley's Club, the Houston area honky-tonk featured in the film. The most comparable were Nashville North, 101 East Irving Park Road, in suburban Bensenville, the Country Music Inn, Milwaukee Avenue and Aptakisic Road in Prairie View, the Lake N' Park Inn, 108th Street and Roberts Road in Palos Hills, and line dancing clubs like Cadillac Ranch, 1175 West Lake Street in Bartlett, and White Horse Country, 152 West Higgins Road in Hoffman Estates. In the late 1970s, all the clubs' house bands would get together for Sunday jam sessions at one of the clubs in an effort to promote the overall scene. Music started at 1:00 p.m. and ran until midnight. Each band got a seventy-five-minute set. "You could see all the Chicago bands at once," said TC Furlong, a pedal steel player. "These places were packed all day."[5]

Nashville North, located about ten miles west of Chicago, was particularly grandiose when it opened in October 1975. Archie Drury wanted to "class up country a little bit," so he installed carpeting and chandeliers in a former pizza restaurant and hired a doorman to make sure his customers were in proper attire.[6] Drury, along with his wife, Marlene, added a shop that claimed to carry the biggest collection of western wear east of the Mississippi, including boots, jeans, shirts, hats, and accessories. The restaurant served New York strip steak, catfish, and ribs. "It was not your gutbucket honky-tonk," said Dallas Wayne, a Nashville musician the Drurys hired to book talent and lead the house band. The show floor held three hundred and fifty people, who could dance to "a constant stream of acts coming in from Nashville," Wayne said.[7] Besides booking *Grand Ole Opry* stars Ernest Tubb and Faron Young, the club became the first Chicago area venue for up-and-comers Lorrie Morgan, Clint Black, and Garth Brooks. Brooks played Nashville North in 1989, not long before the release of *No Fences*, the breakthrough album that sent his career into stadiums.

The suburban country scene was active because that's where people were moving. The migration from the South to Chicago's North Side had largely ended by 1980, and the exodus to the suburbs was in full flight. Suburban collar counties boomed, driven by the expansion of corporate headquarters, commercial developments, and economic conditions that grew professional service jobs. Between 1960 and 1990, the population of DuPage County grew 149 percent, according to US census data. Other nearby counties took similar leaps: Lake (76 percent), McHenry (118 percent), and Kane (52 percent). Growth in Cook County, home to Chicago, was zero.[8]

The group that made it farthest out of the suburbs was Jump 'N the Saddle Band, through a song that, most improbably, was a tribute to the early film shorts of the Three Stooges. Born April 15, 1955, TC Furlong was a teenager in Northfield who, at age seventeen, taught himself the pedal steel guitar for no reason other than its sound, which illuminated every record he heard. Before graduating from high school he was touring as the youngest member of Rio Grande, a country band that played three nights a week throughout the Midwest starting in 1975.

Three years later, half of Rio Grande formed Jump, which, through originals and covers, paid tribute to the music of Texas swing maestro Bob Wills and his Texas Playboys. Jump didn't have the elaborate horn section Wills did, so they created arrangements to make a saxophone, a fiddle, and Furlong's pedal steel sound like one. "Our challenge was to make it sound big. And we did," said Furlong.[9]

Jump recorded a first album in Nashville in 1981, but it was a fluke single that put the band in front of Atlantic Records. Written in one night and recorded immediately afterward, "The Curly Shuffle" was a one-hit wonder with both twang and wise-guy humor. Lead singer Peter Quinn came up with it after noticing audiences responding to a backward dance step bit he did onstage that was inspired by Curly Howard, the bald foil of the comic trio. In August 1983, the band self-released the single and sold about seventy thousand copies on their own. Once local radio started playing it in Chicago and elsewhere, Atlantic Records came calling. The label rushed out a re-pressed single the following February, and then a video that made it the first novelty song in rotation on MTV. The song reached number fifteen on the *Billboard* Hot 100 chart. Atlantic told the band the single sold four hundred thousand copies, but an independent auditor the band hired reported they sold about a million.

Jump followed up with an album for Atlantic, but soon realized they'd rather be strictly a working band. "We were an excellent bar band, but not an excellent studio band. We only wanted to do what Bob Wills had done—play dance halls," Furlong said.[10]

FLYING FISH RECORDS AND
THE REBIRTH OF ROOTS MUSIC

While smaller record labels came and went, powerhouse independent labels Alligator and Delmark dominated Chicago's recording scene, each with global distribution and beloved by blues and jazz listeners around the world. Country and folk music labels during the 1960s and 1970s were more sporadic. Birch Records, for example, based in the Wilmette home of founder Dave Wylie, focused primarily on reissuing or making new recordings of prewar country artists like former *Barn Dance* stars Patsy Montana and the blind mandolin-and-guitar duo Mac and Bob.[11] In 1972, Birch recorded the only album by Blind Arvella Gray, who had been a fixture on Maxwell Street since 1946, but was becoming known after appearing on opening night at the first University of Chicago Folk Festival in 1961.[12] Little is known about Gray, who was born in Texas in 1906 and who lost his vision in his thirties following a shotgun blast to the face during a botched holdup or a vicious fight with a woman—the story was never clear. And his left hand lacked two fingers, leaving the majority of his interpretive work on his National resonator guitar to the slide work of his right. He was a survivor and defiant. "I is proud of my life 'cause I come through it with my skin on. And if I had to live it over, I wouldn't change nothing 'cause I growed into this," he told *Rolling Stone*.[13] On street corners in front of the Jazz Record Mart or Englewood Station, among other places, he played blues and spirituals as well as country and western standards, especially the folk standard "John Henry," his signature song. He was 66 when Cary Baker, a Winnetka teenager and blues enthusiast, recorded him during an all-night session at Sound Unlimited, a studio in the southern suburb of Harvey. "Arvella, the mic is live—go for it!" Baker told the singer. They cut nearly fifteen songs, working until dawn in a comfortable setting for a singer who primarily performed outside on the pavement. Only a thousand copies of *The Singing Drifter* were pressed.[14]

Ovation Records emerged as the only Chicago area label with a serious presence in Nashville, despite its label president knowing little to nothing about country music. Dick Schory was born December 13, 1931, in Chicago. Raised in Iowa, he returned to the area to attend Northwestern University to study percussion.[15] Eventually, he became a session musician around town and signed to RCA Victor, where he released a series of well-received instrumental albums with the Percussion Pops Orchestra, a twenty-two-member ensemble he used to create a "stereophonic" experience by designing where they sat onstage and in the studio. The group earned Grammy nominations and toured for more than a decade.

By 1971, Schory had purchased a colonial-style bungalow at 1249 Waukegan Road in Glenview, a northwestern suburb, and turned it into the headquarters of Ovation Records. There were few genres Schory didn't try recording—in its early years, Ovation released folk, pop, and novelty. There were also blues records from Chicago veterans Willie Dixon, Howlin' Wolf, and Mighty Joe Young, and jazz and soul through two subsidiary labels bearing the odious titles Black Jazz and Grit Records. Ovation didn't gain traction, however, until Schory hired Brien Fisher, a record producer from Kyles Ford, Tennessee, to scout country artists for him in Nashville.

Fisher was a sharpshooter during the Korean War who had pursued record producing when he returned home.[16] He earned his standing at Ovation when he signed the Kendalls, a father-daughter duo from St. Louis. Under Fisher's direction, they recorded "Heaven's Just a Sin Away," a cheating song with a touch of sanctimonious dread, as their Ovation debut. It became a number one hit on the country charts in 1977 and crossed over into the Top 40. Grammy and CMA awards followed. Ovation was now a Nashville player.

That year alone, Ovation released nine country albums. "We're in the country field to stay and we're backing Brien with all our available resources," Schory announced.[17] The label purchased a building on Nashville's Music Row and staffed up. "Dick was very deferential to Brien. He considered that he really struck gold with the Nashville office and he was willing to listen to anything Brien recommended," said Cary Baker, who worked in publicity for Ovation at the time.[18] Under Fisher's direction, Ovation released records by Vern Gosdin, Max D. Barnes, country comedian David "Stringbean" Akeman, and the bluegrass group Tennessee Valley Authority. Joe Sun, who worked in promotions for the label, convinced Fisher to consider putting him in the studio. Fisher did, and "Old Flames (Can't Hold a Candle to You)" became another Ovation hit in 1978, reaching number fourteen on *Billboard*'s country chart. Two years later, Dolly Parton pushed the song to number one. Ovation's run up the country charts ended when Fisher left the label in 1983 to form his own company.[19]

Churchill Records was another Chicago area label that made an initial splash with country. Founded in suburban Des Plaines by talent agents Tommy Martin and Herb Gronauer, the label launched in 1977 with Don Drumm, a Massachusetts native who had been singing country music in downtown lounges. Through Churchill, Drumm had a *Billboard* Top 20 hit with the ballad "Bedroom Eyes," written by Ray Hillburn, a relocated Tennessean active in Chicago's bluegrass scene. The two men met at Pam's Playhouse, an Uptown club, when Drumm walked in and found Hillburn singing the song onstage. Drumm heard a hit and took it to Nashville to record.[20] The song was Churchill's first release to chart. Martin sent Drumm back to Nashville to complete a full-length album, which Churchill released the next year. Martin continued his country streak by signing artists such as Mac Wiseman and Hank Thompson. Hillburn recorded for Churchill too, but his main job was as an in-house songwriter for Drumm and others. "I thought you had to go to Nashville to find country songwriters," said Martin in 1978. "But the Chicago audience is probably as good as a country audience as anywhere, and that's where the songwriters come from."[21]

Until Bloodshot Records opened its doors in 1994, Flying Fish Records served as Chicago's longest-running label for roots music. Starting in 1974 with an album of boogie-woogie duets from pianists Jimmy Walker and Erwin Helfer, Flying Fish released more than five hundred titles that spanned blues, reggae, gospel, Afro-pop, jazz, bluegrass, country, and its main focus: traditional and contemporary folk music. It gave a home to singer-songwriters Claudia Schmidt, Tom Paxton, Si Kahn, John Gorka, Chris Smither, Andrew Calhoun, Eric Bogle, Michael Smith, Anne Hills, Gamble Rogers, Robin and Linda Williams, and Guy Carawan; traditional folk and bluegrass instrumentalist-composers like Norman Blake, Vassar Clements, Bryan Bowers, Doc and Merle Watson, and John

Hartford; and neo-traditionalist bluegrass acts like the New Grass Revival, Tim O'Brien, and the Red Clay Ramblers. Before the revival of roots music that emerged in the 1990s, Flying Fish was one of just a few independent labels with global distribution. Founder Bruce Kaplan, a trained musicologist, operated through handshake deals, but he pursued artists who were committed to a professional touring life, which he supported with albums that, unlike those from most niche labels at the time, were professionally designed and packaged to compete with major labels in the record bins. By the end of its run in 1995, when Cambridge-based Rounder Records purchased its catalog, Flying Fish had done its part to push Americana music from the fringes toward the commercial center.

Kaplan, born February 27, 1945, grew up in a third-floor apartment at 30 North Central in Austin, on Chicago's westernmost edge. Before he started high school, his family crossed the border into Oak Park, a middle-class suburb.[22] His father, Samuel Kaplan, was the embodiment of the American dream: he had gone from working on the assembly line of the Zenith Radio Corporation to being named president of the company.[23] A similar discipline was embedded in his son, as well as a thirst for knowledge. Librarians at the Oak Park Public Library told him that the books he wanted to check out were beyond his age, which he resented. His response: leaving high school and enrolling in college a year early.

Oak Park was parochial, and racial prejudice was evident whenever Kaplan ventured out with Black friends. He was interested in music and had grown close to Maggie, his nanny, who exposed him to Black gospel music. When he was old enough to take the North Avenue bus, he found refuge Saturday mornings at the Old Town School of Folk Music, an experience that went beyond just learning the guitar. "Those bus rides and those classes and those visits with the wonderful, visionary old men of the proletarian party who would sit on the park benches across the street, living out their last years but still living their dream, dazzled at least one bourgeois teen," he later recalled.[24]

Accepted to both Harvard University and the University of

Chicago, Kaplan chose the latter for one reason: the University of Chicago Folk Festival. He became president of the Folklore Society in 1965 and remained involved with the student organization throughout his adult years by helping to book artists and by promoting the festival in a folklore column he wrote in *Come for to Sing*. His drive connected to an early interest in cultures far beyond western borders. After earning a doctorate in South Asian languages and spending two years in India, Kaplan joined Rounder Records as a production assistant when the label was a collective. The job was a free pass to explore music that was strange, raw, and marginalized.

Kaplan admitted early that he had no interest in competing with major labels. Flying Fish didn't release singles, only albums, and in the heyday of FM radio, it refused to campaign for hits. "I have no desire to try for artists in the Top 40 mass market. I've already spent too much of my life selling things I don't like," he said. By 1979, the label had twenty-five artists, annual sales of $1 million, and a Grammy for a John Hartford album.[25] Six years later, the label's catalog had grown to more than 250 titles, and it had earned fifteen Grammy nominations. Kaplan told friends that he was happy releasing albums that might sell fewer than fifteen thousand units, unlike best-selling acts like Hartford, Doc Watson, and Sweet Honey in the Rock, who tended to sell more than twenty thousand units apiece.[26] Those hits allowed him to release albums by artists he considered worthy of attention—like Martin Jack Rosenblum, a biker poet known as "Holy Ranger" who performed at Harley-Davidson gatherings; a twenty-seven-song collection called *In Country* featuring Vietnam veterans singing folk songs from the war; or a range of Hebrew, Latin American, Celtic, Russian, Indonesian, and African ethnic music.

Flying Fish was ultimately Kaplan's archival project, and he considered its catalog his body of work. Si Kahn, a songwriter-activist on the label, once asked Kaplan why he released his records when he knew they wouldn't be big sellers. Kaplan replied that he wasn't in the business "to put out individual records." "John Hartford and others make enough money that I can use to put out music I believe in or is politically important. I don't say 'this one made money or this one didn't make money.' I put out music I think should be heard."[27]

Flying Fish got ahead of the progressive bluegrass trend by releasing titles by some of the movement's most important artists. Folk and bluegrass dominated the label because Kaplan felt they represented music that was communal. Folk music is "about people who have something beautiful, and who keep it and polish it and make it better and share it with others," he wrote in 1980.[28] But unlike most folk purists, he didn't like the idea that folk music should be only one thing. "The term folk carries a lot of negative connotations . . . images of insipid aggregations of ersatz ruralists, or self-indulgent and incompetent singer-songwriters either bemoaning their fate incomprehensibly, or failing to recognize the difference between a pamphlet and a song," he said.[29] He considered rock and roll folk music as well, which is why he signed two rock bands with country roots: Killbilly, a punk band from Dallas, and the Farmers, a Chicago trio self-described as a cross between the Carter Family and the Ramones.[30]

Kaplan ran his business with a do-it-yourself aesthetic later associated with underground rock. He preferred handshake deals and he calculated budgets in his head or on scraps of paper. The label headquarters was a two-unit frame house at 1304 North Schubert in Lincoln Park that had once been the site of a murder and had been taken over by gangs. As the neighborhood gentrified, Kaplan kept the graffiti on the inside walls as a source of pride. The stock was kept in the basement, staff worked on the first floor, and he reigned upstairs. Kaplan's personal dress code was a T-shirt and jeans, and the office atmosphere was just as casual. Bongs, dogs, loud music—all were allowed at work. "Bruce kept it funky. It was matter of pride for him that the place was a dump," said Seymour Guenther, a Folklore Society member whom Kaplan hired to work in promotion.[31]

Just as the label represented his musical passions, Kaplan personified the label. At about three hundred pounds and with a temper just as large, he became known as the "Big Fish." When a female model failed to show up for a photo shoot to promote the company's T-shirt line, Kaplan stepped in and became the public face of the label. In 1982, he declared his candidacy for the Illinois state legislature on the Citizens Party ticket. "There's always been a link between folk music and politics," he explained.[32]

The label courted artists without pretense. Singer-songwriter Claudia Schmidt had made a name for herself over five years of playing clubs around town after she relocated to Chicago from rural Michigan. One day, while sitting on a rocking chair on the Schubert building's front porch, she mentioned to Kaplan that she was thinking of recording her own album. "When do you want to start?" Kaplan responded. "That was the extent of our discussion," she later said.[33]

As Flying Fish entered the 1990s, it was one of the largest roots music labels in the world. That ended in December 1992, when Kaplan left work and walked through the alley to his house on the opposite block. He had an ear infection and wanted to stretch out on his bed. Every day that week, he had gone home in the middle of the day, until one morning his wife, Sandra Shifrin, found him unconscious. Banjoist Stephen Wade played music at his hospital bedside, but it was futile. Three days later, he died of viral meningitis. "There was no goodbye," said Shifrin.[34] In November 1995, she sold Flying Fish to Rounder Records. During negotiations, Rounder executives promised to keep the label running, she said. But "they were not honest." Two months later, on Christmas Eve, a fax machine spit out termination letters to each of Flying Fish's remaining ten staff members. The label would exist in name only, its catalog folded into Rounder's. For the Flying Fish staffers, the label's blunt end left a bitter aftertaste because they knew Kaplan had considered Rounder too corporate since its early collective days in the 1970s, when he served as its in-house producer. "They were always the big brother that looked down their nose at us," said Guenther.[35]

But Kaplan's legacy went beyond the music. He may not have known it at the time, but he was quietly influencing a new generation of punk rockers with big label dreams. Nan Warshaw, Killbilly's publicist, said the band chose Flying Fish because, like the reigning underground rock labels at the time, "it was making music for all the right reasons."[36] In 1993, one year after Kaplan's death, she formed the Chicago label Bloodshot Records with Eric Babcock, a former Flying Fish employee, and Rob Miller. Bloodshot would document the Chicago bands that were forming at the intersection of punk rock and country, the ripples of which would reach far beyond the city in the decades to come.

SPECIAL CONSENSUS BRINGS BLUEGRASS NORTH

To purists, a bluegrass musician in Chicago in the mid-1970s was akin to a surfer in Dubuque. The very idea was anathema to a tradition that could see itself only within strict geographical borders around the South.

Then came Greg Cahill, and boundaries disappeared. Bluegrass could no longer be restricted by geography. Only skill and passion were required.

The market for bluegrass in the United States had shrunk by the early 1960s. But then came a revival, courtesy of two pop-culture phenomena: "The Ballad of Jed Clampett," the theme of television's *Beverly Hillbillies*, recorded in 1962 by Lester Flatt and Earl Scruggs, and the soundtrack of the 1972 film *Deliverance*, which introduced the world to "Dueling Banjos," a traditional tune performed by Marshall Brickman and Eric Weissberg. In the years between, "Foggy Mountain Breakdown," recorded in 1949 by Flatt & Scruggs, entered the *Billboard* Hot 100 in 1967 after it underscored car chase scenes in the film *Bonnie and Clyde*, and the folk revival gave Bill Monroe, Ralph Stanley, and Flatt & Scruggs new opportunities to play college campuses and the festival circuit.

The subgenre "newgrass" emerged in the 1970s to describe the next generation of bluegrass musicians who mixed in elements of rock and pop. In Chicago, bluegrass bands sprang up along the Lincoln Avenue corridor, most notably at the Clearwater Saloon, 3447

North Lincoln Avenue, where Special Consensus, the first bluegrass band from Chicago to gain national prominence, held court every Wednesday night and on weekends.

The band formed through informal jams held in different pockets of the city—in the hallways of the University of Chicago during the Folk Festival; at afternoon sessions at Jimmy's Woodlawn Tap, a local watering hole in Hyde Park; and at North Side blues clubs like Wise Fools Pub on off nights. Leader Greg Cahill was a child of the folk revival. The banjo playing of Kingston Trio co-founder Dave Guard led Cahill to pick up the longneck instrument himself while living at home in south suburban Oak Lawn. He slowed 33⅓ rpm bluegrass records down to 16 rpm so he could learn all the notes. Cahill earned a master's degree and found a stable job as a social worker, but he quit that life in 1974 to pursue music full-time. Special Consensus, named after a phrase in a Carlos Castaneda novel, became his vocation one year later.

Bluegrass could be heard at most North Side clubs, but the audiences wanted high volume, which meant that in the early days, Special Consensus incorporated covers of the Grateful Dead or Creedence Clearwater Revival to get people on their feet. In its first year, the band landed a Monday night residency at Minstrels, at 6465 North Sheridan Road. Over seven years, the weekly shows gave the band, which then included co-founder and bassist Marc Edelstein, time to hone stage skills, write original songs, and learn the tradition. For the rest of the week, they rotated through other clubs until they were playing nearly seven nights around town. By then, it was time to head South.

Crossing over wasn't easy. No bluegrass band from Chicago had achieved success in the South, and bluegrass promoters still considered any band from Chicago a novelty. Cahill found himself forced into the role of ambassador for his city, telling people that all the seminal bluegrass recordings by Monroe, Flatt & Scruggs, and others were recorded in Chicago, and that the blueprint for the *Grand Ole Opry* came directly from WLS, a Chicago radio station. "I was constantly reminding people it wasn't outside the realm of possibility that you would have an audience of country and bluegrass music here," he said. "But it took a lot of years to really be well accepted."[37]

Cahill's experience was common among that first generation of bluegrass musicians from the Midwest, who weren't taken seriously by the tight-knit world of bluegrass promoters or by purist audiences in Kentucky or Tennessee. If a booking came through, it was not unheard of for emcees to mock them for playing "our music." "There was prejudice," said Don Stiernberg, a mandolinist who occasionally toured with Special Consensus. "You could hear all the lawn chairs snapping shut when we got onstage." Over time, it became clear the pushback wasn't personal. "It's not that people had it out for Special Consensus, they had it out for Chicago," he said. It was considered a win any time the music moved the audience to forget about geography: "You really felt like you were breaking down a barrier."[38]

One important benchmark for Special Consensus was the time the group headlined the Station Inn, Nashville's storied bluegrass club. Bill Monroe himself sat in the audience, decked out in a powder-blue suit and white cowboy hat. "I want to hear how you play my music in Chicago," he told Cahill before they started. Monroe was on a date with Dee Presley, the former stepmother of Elvis himself, and so he informed the boys the couple's investment was probably just in the first set.

They stayed for three. Between breaks, Monroe visited with the band, and soon Special Consensus was Monroe's opener whenever he came through town. "We were finally acceptable," Cahill said.[39]

The band's debut album, which appeared in 1975, was the first of nearly twenty albums spanning forty years, making Special Consensus one of the longest-running groups of the genre. Like Monroe, Cahill structured his band specifically to groom young talent. The lineup mostly stuck to banjo, guitar, mandolin, and upright bass, but in some years electric instruments were added and then dropped, and even drums made a few rounds. More than forty musicians passed through its ranks, including Robbie Fulks between 1988 and 1990, when he was new to Chicago and years before he became a piv-

otal figure in the alternative country scene. Other notable alumni
include singers and guitarists Dallas Wayne (1989–1991) and Chris
Jones (1981–1985), mandolinist Ron Spears (2004–2007), and fiddler Al Murphy (1990–1991). By the band's third decade, Cahill had
not only gained industry credibility, but had evolved into an elder
statesman of the genre. One of his students was Noam Pikelny of the
Punch Brothers, who as a teenager bicycled from Skokie to Cahill's
home in Evanston to take lessons. "I was in disbelief that the greatest bluegrass banjo player in this part of the country could be in
this same little suburb," Pikelny said.[40] Fast-forward to the 2013
Grammy Awards, and both men were nominated separately for Best
Bluegrass Album.[41]

Cahill's unorthodox trajectory culminated in 2007 when he was
named president of the Nashville-based International Bluegrass
Music Association, the bluegrass community's trade organization.
He was struck by the accomplishment. "The head of the IBMA is a
guy from Chicago," he thought. "It is a far cry for a guy who people
said can't really play that music."[42]

By the late 1970s, a bluegrass scene was flourishing in Chicago.
Grass Clippings, a monthly magazine launched in 1978 to cover the
bluegrass festivals, jams, club dates, and bands in town. The Chicago Area Bluegrass Music and Pickin' Society, which ran the magazine for six years, was based at 1437 West Howard, in a three-unit
apartment building that also housed Tin Ear, a recording studio and
label dedicated to bluegrass and folk music. Ralph Stanley recorded
there after a concert at the Old Town School of Folk Music, on sessions that ended up on *Smarter Than the Average Idiot*, the 1984
album by West Virginia fiddler and longtime Stanley sideman Curly
Ray Kline. Special Consensus, singer and guitarist Larry Sparks,
the Greater Chicago Bluegrass Band, North Carolina banjoist Don
Reno, and other artists recorded albums there, and the studio also
held sessions for Steve Goodman and Bob Gibson. The operation
was a labor of love for Bill and Claudia Landow. Coming out of DeVry
University, Bill was a recording engineer who said his life "took a
paradigm shift" after he attended classes at the Old Town School

of Folk Music. "Bluegrass was not on the radio," he said. Tin Ear "tried to promote the music and let people know what was going on. We were a hub."[43]

The hub was growing. Bluegrass festivals in the city and suburbs boomed. The Old Town School partnered with the city to host a bluegrass festival on Navy Pier in 1979 that featured local acts plus *Grand Ole Opry* stars Jim & Jesse and banjo innovator Bill Keith. In 1978, at the first annual Illinois Bluegrass Festival in south suburban Crete, two thousand people showed up.[44] Besides Special Consensus, the local scene was crowded with bands: the Greater Chicago Bluegrass Band, Bucks Stove & Range Company, and Prairie Union all served as antidotes to the disco scene that dominated the downtown nightclubs.

The bands included the Wildwood Pickers, an all-woman quartet featuring guitar virtuoso Muriel Anderson, a native of suburban Downers Grove who later became the first woman to win the National Fingerstyle Guitar Championship. She also collaborated with Chet Atkins and Les Paul. Anderson, Kim Koskela (banjo), sister Robin Koskela (vocals), and Kathy Jones (fiddle) were teenagers when they started the band in 1977 and, in tribute to the Carter sisters, dressed in checkered blouses and red scarves. Cory Koskela, mother to the two sisters, later joined on bass. Her roots in the Allegheny Mountains of western Pennsylvania had brought traditional music into the family home.[45] Outside Special Consensus, the Pickers went the farthest from Chicago, becoming the house band at Dollywood, Dolly Parton's theme park in Pigeon Forge, Tennessee; playing festivals across the United States and overseas tours for the US Department of Defense; and in 1981, becoming the first all-woman group to play traditional bluegrass on the *Grand Ole Opry*.[46]

Jim Lauderdale was also passing through Chicago around that time, just a few years before he started down the path to becoming one of country music's most prolific songwriters for hire (George Strait, Dixie Chicks) as well as an acclaimed and Grammy-winning solo artist. Lauderdale grew up in North Carolina, but moved to Chicago in 1984 to perform in *Pump Boys and Dinettes*, a hit Broadway musical with original country songs. The show gave him steady work, but Lauderdale wished he had original material. On off nights he performed up and down Lincoln Avenue with the West River Boys, a bluegrass trio he formed with two Chicagoans he met in town: multi-instrumentalist John Rice and country fiddler Ollie O'Shea, both of whom became lifelong collaborators. Besides playing bluegrass standards, the group woodshedded originals that Lauderdale started writing while holed up in his room at the Belmont Hotel. "I really dug into my writing during the day and after the shows at night," he said. "It was a really great creative time for me to be there. There was something too with the winter times. It can get pretty cold and that really gets you cocooned in your dwelling to create. I got almost two hundred songs over a course of a few years."[47]

THE SECOND ACT OF
JETHRO BURNS

A lynchpin of the Chicago bluegrass scene was Jethro Burns, a mandolin player and humorist from a much earlier era who, late in his life, gave lessons in his basement at 1338 Main Street in Evanston. Burns was fifty-one in 1971 when his lifelong musical partner, Henry "Homer" Haynes, died. For the next eighteen years, until his own death in 1989, Burns taught a steady stream of young and hungry mandolinists how to play. He then joined them, playing on their records, opening their shows, and enjoying a revival as an elder statesman surrounded by admirers who looked up to him as the master of the instrument and of the musician's life.

With a career spanning country music's evolution from radio barn dances to Las Vegas footlights, Burns was a connector to another time. Born March 10, 1920, in Conasauga, Tennessee, Kenneth "Jethro" Burns was one half of Homer & Jethro, a harmony and comedy team that started in 1932.[48] After transitioning to radio, including a stint on the WLS *Barn Dance* in Chicago, Homer & Jethro became one of the most successful acts in country music history, scoring hits on *Billboard*'s country charts and premier bookings on network television variety shows, the urban nightclub circuit, and large halls overseas. Despite their renown as a comedy act, Burns was a deeply sophisticated mandolinist, incorporating jazz harmonies and improvisation into the music that make him more comparable to jazz guitarist Django Reinhardt than to Bill Monroe. His mastery was compounded by his light touch and breezy humor, attributes that made his musicianship accessible to pop audiences. For local teenagers, whose interest in bluegrass was peaking in the early 1970s, discovering that Burns lived in their backyard was a revelation. Homer & Jethro were household names who had played for US presidents, pitched corn flakes on television, and made albums that sold in the millions. "I wanted to be him," said jazz mandolinist Don Stiernberg, who was sixteen years old in 1972 when he started traveling to Evanston for weekly lessons. "From the very first lesson with him, I had my direction. He was the coolest guy I ever met."[49]

Haynes's death left Burns flummoxed. To get him out of the house after a year of mourning, his wife, Gussie, convinced him to try teaching. "Do anything, get moving," she told him. Gussie was the reason why Burns had relocated to Chicago; they met in 1949 when Homer & Jethro headlined the Chicago Theater for a month while pulling double duty with a stint on the WLS *Barn Dance*. Taking his wife's advice, Burns advertised lessons at Main Music, a storefront in Skokie, but not long afterward, he redirected new students to a location with an easier commute: the basement of his townhouse. One-hour lessons cost $10, or in some cases, just a six-pack of beer.

The basement was, in modern vernacular, a man cave. Visitors descending the stairs from the kitchen came upon a record collection, pictures on the wall spanning Homer & Jethro's career, and in the room by the laundry machines, his instrument collection and a couch. A dart board featuring Bill Monroe's face hung on one wall, a poster of Barbara Eden, then the star of *I Dream of Jeannie*, on the other. Lessons required minimal setup: a chair for Burns, a stool for his student, and a record player within reach. As austere as the setting was, it was a magnet for musicians, from teenagers learning from scratch to John Prine and Steve Goodman to New

Grass Revival mandolinist Sam Bush and even Paul McCartney, who made a point of dropping by the basement during a Chicago tour stop with Wings.

"People would say to him, 'Oh, I hear so-and-so took lessons.' He would jokingly say, 'Yeah, everybody has.' It was true. It was nationwide. People would make the journey to sit with Jethro for a lesson, or many lessons," said Stiernberg.[50]

Renowned Nashville guitarist Chet Atkins married Gussie's sister Leona, so the basement became a retreat for both men when Atkins was in town. Peter Nye, then a teenager from nearby Deerfield, did not expect he'd be performing "Lady Be Good" with one of the inventors of the Nashville Sound during his Saturday morning lesson, but stepping off the bottom landing, he encountered Burns and Atkins, both in their underwear and socks, waiting for their laundry to dry before taking in a Chicago Cubs game that afternoon. Atkins cradled a guitar in one hand and an Orange Crush in another. "Pete, this is my brother-in-law Chet," Burns drawled. "Then it dawned on me: The first time I'm meeting Chet Atkins I get to perform with him," Nye said.[51]

For Muriel Anderson, another teenager at the time, the Atkins connection went further. She too met him through mandolin lessons with Burns when she was a student at DePaul University. Atkins became her mentor in Nashville and helped introduce her around town, where she eventually became a world-class classical guitarist. "I was real knocked out," he said of the first time he heard her play. "I've learned a lot of things from Muriel. She has the right-hand technique I wish I'd learned when I was younger. She's the hardest worker I've ever known. Those are the people who make it."[52]

Besides musicianship, Burns offered his students hard-earned wisdom. Because of his lengthy career, he had friendships with luminaries like Hank Williams, a fishing buddy. He often told the story of the time Homer & Jethro shared a 1953 New Year's Day bill with Williams in Canton, Ohio, and had to stretch their forty-minute set because Williams was a no-show. Offstage, they learned their friend had been found dead in the back seat of his Cadillac.

Burns shared practical tips about performing, about the record business, and everything in between. After New Grass Revival signed to Capitol/EMI in 1986, Burns told Bush to get to know the major label's receptionist "and the boy in the mailroom because they'll run the place someday." About life on the road, he told Bush: "The first thing you do is introduce yourself to the bartender and waitress, get to know them a little bit because they work there every day and they want to have a good day too. If they like you they'll tell everybody you're good before you hit the first note and if they don't like you they'll tell everybody you suck before you hit the first note." "He always emphasized the little things. Getting along with people. How to better deal with people at the clubs," said Bush. "Because, he said, we're all working under the same roof."[53]

His teaching style was similarly homespun. Students were expected to bring blank cassette tapes to record each lesson. Nothing would be written down. He taught by locking eyes with the student throughout the hour while he discussed chords and fret positions for songs culled from the Great American Songbook. The method seared his words into their brains; the cassettes served as a later reference. "When a grown man looks at you in the eye like that, it gets your attention. You get an adrenaline flow, and your ears respond at the same time," said Stiernberg.[54] In the decades since his death, former students have digitized their cassettes to share for free on various websites, making it possible for Burns to keep teaching generations he'd never know.

His presence lent legitimacy to the local scene. Once word spread, Burns was solicited to play on records by John Prine, Steve Goodman, Special Consensus, and others, and he often found himself onstage with his protégés. Cahill said it was Burns's appearance on his record in 1980 that helped Special Consensus turn heads in the South. "The fact that I was friends with Jethro, that gave me credibility," he said.[55] The Jethro Burns Quartet was born when Burns accepted an invitation to host a Sunday open stage at Durty Nellies, a suburban club, and solicited Stiernberg to form a backing band.

In the last decade of his life, there wasn't a stage in Chicago Burns didn't play, usually with former students and often with Goodman, who met Burns after the elder introduced himself at the Earl of Old Town and told him, "If you ever need a mandolin player, give me a call." They hit the road as a duo driven by fast licks and humor. Burns clearly enjoyed his newfound notoriety and used it to his advantage to win over audiences who were more often than not half his age or younger. "Jethro was exposed to an entirely new generation of fans through Goodman. It brought him back to life," Stiernberg said.[56]

As an opening act, Burns took joy in poking fun at his young admirers. One night before New Grass Revival took the stage at Holsteins, Burns told the audience that Bush hoped to play "Rocky Top," the bluegrass standard, except there was a problem: "The poor kid can't play the bridge," Burns said. "So yell out the song and somehow maybe the young kid can get through it." Once the band heard what Burns was up to, they quickly worked up the song in the club's basement specifically to make the music collapse at the bridge. "Jethro sold it so well, you could hear people in the audience go 'aww,'" Bush said. No matter the headliner, Burns always returned during the encore to claim the stage as his own. "The man would jam our ass under the table all night," Bush said.[57]

Burns received a diagnosis of prostate cancer three years before his death in 1989. The news drove him to immerse himself in the songs and stories of his long musical life through a series of recordings he made both in his basement and in Stiernberg's living room. He was offered a studio, but chose one-on-one sessions, with himself on mandolin and Stiernberg on rhythm guitar. Between September 1987 and January 1988, they recorded a total of sixty-two songs. These recordings would eventually become *The Jethro Burns Legacy Project*, released in three separate volumes by Acoustic Disc, the label owned by mandolinist David Grisman, another Burns devotee. The songs were those that held important memories for him—Hank Williams's "You Win Again" to commemorate his lost friend, "Up a Lazy River," a favorite from childhood, and blues and jazz standards ("Body and Soul," "Fly Me to the Moon," "Corrina, Corrina,"

"Swing Low, Sweet Chariot"). Burns had recorded albums for Flying Fish and other labels in recent years, but these sessions were intimate and tracked informally, with no goal but to share what he had learned. For someone who knew what lay ahead, Burns's playing was surprisingly quick, clean, and full of joy. "It was his gift to all of us," said Stiernberg. "He was trying to tell us how much he loved being alive."[58]

"INSURGENT COUNTRY"

LOOKING BACKWARD
TO GO FORWARD

Before Jethro Burns turned to teaching, he first thought Homer &
Jethro might continue if he had a new partner. Curt Delaney was
the obvious choice. Delaney, a fellow Southerner who grew up in
Moultrie, Georgia, had been playing country guitar in Chicago since
he was hired as a staff musician for *Don McNeill's Breakfast Club* in
1952. One night at the Old Town School of Folk Music, Burns asked
if he'd consider the job, but Delaney turned him down. He already
had a band.[1]

That band, the Sundowners, never achieved the fame of
Homer & Jethro or any other national country and western act
because they chose to have the world come to them. Between 1959
and 1989, the trio—Delaney, Don Walls, and Bob Boyd—played every
Wednesday through Sunday night in a subterranean club located
in Chicago's Loop district that over time served as a hangout for a
cross-section of nightlife—pimps, prostitutes, drug pushers, bar-
flies, but also conventioneers; celebrities like Robert Duvall, Fats
Domino, and John Entwistle of the Who; country singers like Webb
Pierce, Gene Autry, Mel Tillis, and Faron Young; newspapermen
like columnist Mike Royko; middle-class suburbanites on a night
out; and, near the end, young punks from the indie-rock scene, who

saw all three musicians as icons of country authenticity. "Growing up in the suburbs, I thought, 'Hey, this is great, everything they warned me about,'" said musician Kent Rose.[2] The allure was not just in the rough setting, but in the trio's magnetic vocal harmonies, craftsmanship, and commitment to weaving a wide range of music together without showing the stitching—a skill made possible by thousands of hours logged on the bandstand over decades.

Like Burns, they too were displaced Southerners who headed to Chicago seeking a better life. Walls, the son of a coal miner, was born in Rita, West Virginia, on December 4, 1930. He picked up the guitar at a young age.[3] As early as 1949, he was roaming the country playing county fairs, festivals, nightclubs, VFW halls, and radio barn dances as a member of the Circle C Boys, a guitar-bass-accordion trio fronted by a colorful leader named Curly Coldiron, a North Carolina native who played the upright bass and shot blanks from a pistol when leaping onstage.[4] The group appeared on the WLS *Barn Dance* and joined bills with Homer & Jethro, Rex Allen, and Lulu Belle and Scotty, among others, as part of the packaged tours the station sent around the Midwest. Boyd, from Chattanooga, Tennessee, had moved to Chicago as a boy and ended up working the Madison Street honky-tonks. Eventually he, too, joined the Circle C Boys. When Coldiron retired in 1959, Delaney was hired to replace him.[5]

The Sundowners took their name from the title of a 1960 Robert Mitchum movie. Their home club could have floated in from the back lot of a Hollywood western. The Ringside Ranch opened in 1948 at 5 North Clark and featured country bands until the building was torn down in 1959 to create a parking lot. Co-owner Michael Scheid was convinced country music needed to remain in the Loop. "They told him he was crazy and that it would never make it. But he had been in the service and had met a lot of country boys, and he figured they would be coming to Chicago," said his wife, Barbara. Three years later, in 1962, Scheid reopened his bar around the corner in the basement of 56 West Madison and called it the Bar R-R Ranch. When that location also fell to the wrecking ball in 1977, he moved one more time to 56 West Randolph, between the city's Greyhound station and the Woods Theatre, a dilapidated 1922 movie palace showing kung fu and horror fare.[6]

In the heart of the financial district, the Ranch provided a quick escape into another time and place. A nondescript doorway led visitors down a short flight of stairs into a saloon decorated with wall-mounted animal heads, horns, barbed wire, a leather-encrusted map of Texas, and a glass display case of antique pistols. Arranged on the floor were small wooden tables, their round tops carved with graffiti by knives. A sign advertised the "world's best chili" in thirty varieties. If things got out of hand, the cook, a former professional wrestler named Little Bill, stepped out of the kitchen and intervened. "When the parties get a little wild, you might find someone who wants to pull a little strip show and I've got to stop them," he explained.[7]

The band drew from a repertoire of more than fifteen thousand songs. Everything was fair game—Hawaiian guitar, jazz, early rock and roll, novelty, western swing, and of course, every flavor of country, from cowboy songs to disco steppers. Four books of songs were always close by, but all three musicians mainly played by ear, bending the familiar songs into versions that were unmistakably their own. "It takes a lot longer to learn it the other way and then you're playing somebody else's feelings. But if you play by ear you play it how *you* feel it," Delaney once explained. The hallmark of their sound was three-part vocal harmonies, polished by Walls's falsetto and the flash of his steel guitar. "Watching those guys perform was like watching someone fill a glass of water—effortless, smooth, and perfect," said musician Peter Nye.[8]

For young musicians in the audience, the band's seven half-hour sets were night school. "They may have been on automatic pilot but their automatic pilot was such a high caliber, they were an absolute model for what it was to be a musician," said musician Roger Bellow, the nephew of novelist Saul Bellow.[9] All three Sundowners recognized that younger faces were coming to see them, and their response was to widen the stage to invite them up to play and, in the true folk tradition, teach them what they needed to learn. Despite needing to be at his post office job in the suburbs by sunup, Kent Rose spent nights at the Ranch, first observing the band from the bar, then sitting in with them, and eventually being hired to perform solo during breaks. He had already spent more than a decade playing in country bands, one of which had backed Tanya Tucker for nearly a year on the road, but playing with the Sundowners had forced greater sophistication in his playing. "One night they called [the early jazz standard] 'Limehouse Blues,' which I never heard of. I asked Curt what it was like. He said 'a circle of fifths,' but I didn't know what that was either. So he said 'Just chunk along on rhythm' and I did until I learned it," he said.[10]

One band that descended the Ranch stairs in 1987 was the Mekons, a British art-punk band that one year earlier had released *Fear and Whiskey*, considered one of the first alternative country records for its barroom fiddle, steel guitar, and honky-tonk piano cover of Leon Payne's "Lost Highway" as well as songs that raged against the inequities of capitalism and social engineering. During a Chicago stop on a tour of the United States, the band, enamored with Americana, bought cowboy shirts at a local western wear shop and were then directed to the Loop to see the Sundowners in action. "It was somewhere I had dreamed of being, but yet when it actually happened, it was totally terrifying," said Jon Langford, a Mekons co-founder. By the end of the night the Mekons, too, were onstage, playing covers of songs by Buck Owens, Merle Haggard, and Johnny Cash. "The only way I was able to play any of that music in the states was because I had that experience," said Langford.[11]

The Sundowners recorded only two studio albums over their three decades at the Ranch, one produced by Lloyd Maines, a Grammy-winning producer and steel guitarist who is also the father of Dixie Chicks singer Natalie Maines.[12] But in 1994, they were invited to contribute two songs to *For a Life of Sin: A Compilation of Insurgent Chicago Country*, a record that ended up serving as a mission statement for a new record label in town: Bloodshot Records. Operated by three twentysomethings, the label was formed to document a new scene that referenced an older form of country. The Sundowners served as a local touchstone for this eclectic generation, which included Langford, the Bottle Rockets, Robbie Fulks, and the Handsome Family. By that point, in 1989, the Sundowners had moved out of the Loop. They briefly operated the Sundowners Ranch, a restaurant and lounge in Franklin Park, a western suburb. They also started playing rock clubs like Lower Links and Lounge Ax, where the indie-rock audience sought them out.

Eventually their new audience reciprocated: On December 1, 1993, at Bub City, a North Side bar, a roster of bands as eclectic as the Mekons and the Texas Rubies paid them tribute. The attention even motivated Chicago mayor Richard M. Daley to issue a special proclamation to name the day in their honor. Four years later, Delaney died, followed by Boyd in 1999 and Walls in 2011. For a band so wired to the glories of country's past, standing on the stage that day with a new generation let them glimpse the future. To Delaney, the adulation that came so late in his life was a revelation: "I never thought it would come to this."[13]

THE COUNTRY OF
ALTERNATIVE COUNTRY

In 1990, a band named Uncle Tupelo from Belleville, Illinois, located across the Mississippi River from St. Louis, released *No Depression*, a debut album that featured a collection of rock songs and ballads played with the speed, volume, and angst of Black Flag, but with the timeworn soul of country and folk music. The title song is a reimagining of "No Depression in Heaven," recorded in 1936 by the Carter Family.[14] With an electric bass bouncing underneath, the guitar feverishly strums at the tempo of the original. But in this version, the band omits A. P. Carter's verse that imagines the future bounty of an afterlife where "there'll be no hunger / no orphan children crying for bread." Instead, in the reading of Jay Farrar, the song is far gruffer and more urgent, sounding like it's being sung on an empty street corner in a dusty region of the Midwest where the lessons from the Great Depression are not distant history.

The song and album are both fundamental to the origin story

of alternative country, an underground genre that emerged in the 1990s as a reaction to the commercial mainstream, but by the following decade had come to influence its direction. Although Uncle Tupelo is often credited with inventing the genre, many bands with similar sensibilities—such as Jason and the Scorchers and Rank and File in Austin, Lone Justice and X in Los Angeles, and Dash Rip Rock in New Orleans—preceded them. What gave Uncle Tupelo such singular stature was not only that the two bands that rose from its demise—Son Volt and Wilco—achieved far greater notoriety, but that, in retrospect, the band appeared at exactly the time when commercial country music was branching furthest from its honky-tonk and string-band roots.

The year 1990 also happened to be the year of *No Fences*, the breakthrough album by an Oklahoma-born country singer named Garth Brooks. Brooks, along with new stars Tim McGraw, Shania Twain, and Faith Hill, quickly became the face of "New Country," an inaugural commercial radio format that represented the next phase of pop country by incorporating rock guitars and drums, synthesizers, sleek videos, line dancing, and stage spectacle defined by pyrotechnics, dancers, and other elements of arena rock long established by bands like KISS and Def Leppard. While those elements appealed to disenfranchised pop listeners turned off by the angst of grunge rock, it created fractures among some longtime country fans. New Country itself was partly a reaction against the so-called new traditionalists of the 1980s—George Strait, Ricky Skaggs, Keith Whitley, Reba McEntire, John Anderson, Marty Stuart, Alan Jackson, and Dwight Yoakam are just a few—who sought to preserve and broaden traditional styles, whether honky-tonk, western swing, or bluegrass. New Country didn't end any careers, but it did help splinter country music into more subgenres. As its name suggests, alternative country was the subgenre that positioned itself as a counterweight to the slick commercialism that New Country represented.

From the beginning, "alternative country" (sometimes rendered as "alt-country" or "alt.country") identified an eclectic mix of artists who could be easily identified by their connection to traditional American roots genres, starting with country, folk, and blues but including Cajun, zydeco, bluegrass, and western swing. The genre also adopted artists midway through or late in their careers who had found themselves stonewalled from mainstream radio and major-label marketing dollars. For example, Loretta Lynn, Johnny Cash, George Jones, Dolly Parton, Tom Petty, and Elvis Costello all attracted alt-country audiences.

The burgeoning alternative music media—magazines such as *No Depression*, *Paste*, *Harp*, and *Blender*, independent radio shows, and early Internet groups—that emerged during the 1990s was pivotal in promoting the genre. The origin of *No Depression* was particularly organic: the bimonthly magazine developed from an AOL online discussion folder and daily email digest where fans shared information about their local scenes and favorite artists. Sensing an underserved market, three posters—Peter Blackstock, Grant Alden, and Kyla Fairchild—pooled resources and launched a print magazine in September 1995, with Son Volt on its first cover. Unlike *Rolling Stone* and *Spin*, whose editorial decisions were dictated from a perch in New York City, *No Depression* had no centralized office. While it hired professional music writers to contribute, it developed a community of readers who reported on nascent music scenes in areas of the country that were often ignored by national media: Atlanta, Dallas, North Carolina's Triangle (Raleigh, Durham, Chapel Hill), Minneapolis, Portland, and Chicago. The regionalism in its coverage was matched by in-depth features that promoted contemporary artists who were mostly unknown to wider audiences. By the time it folded in May 2008, after a seventy-five-issue run, *No Depression* had become the bible of the genre.

Alternative country was also the last musical genre that benefited from the heyday of daily-newspaper music critics. Before digital delivery forced the decline of print, it was routine for daily newsrooms throughout the United States to include full-time music critics. That investment in local tastemakers guaranteed exposure of local music scenes to a large general-interest audience, and it also helped introduce readers to touring artists rotating through town.[15]

The music industry also came around to accepting alternative country as a legitimate musical genre, beginning in 1995 when the trade magazine *The Gavin Report* released its first Americana chart. The Americana Music Association, a not-for-profit trade association based in Nashville, was formed in 1999. The organization was responsible for helping the Recording Academy establish three Grammy categories for Americana artists—Best Album, Best Roots Performance, and Best Roots Song—in 2009. Another achievement came in 2011, when it convinced the Merriam-Webster dictionary to include "Americana" as a legitimate musical term. (The official definition is now "a genre of American music having roots in early folk and country music.") By 2016, the genre was so mainstream that *Billboard* announced it was changing the name of its folk chart to "Americana/Folk" in order to count the weekly sales of break-through artists like Jason Isbell and Margo Price.[16]

EARLY FLICKERING OF A SCENE: CLUB LOWER LINKS AND THE TEXAS RUBIES

If the beginning of alternative country in Chicago could be traced to a single place, it would be an unlikely one: Club Lower Links, a performance art club located in a Lake View basement. The space originally opened as an alternative to the blocks of drinking establishments surrounding neighboring Wrigley Field. Unlike non-profit galleries that also had music, Club Lower Links became one of the few commercial venues in the city that, between 1988 and 1992, booked poets, performance artists, and free jazz musicians—including national figures Henry Rollins, Linda Mancini, Nancy Reilly, Paula Killen, Richard Hell, David Sedaris, saxophonist Ken Vandermark, multi-instrumentalist Hal Russell, and the NRG Ensemble—seven nights a week. Founder Leigh Jones grew up on her family's ranch in Buffalo, Wyoming, but moved to Chicago in 1980 seeking "adventure." After waitressing at the nearby Park West, she wanted to try opening her own place where she could foster a scene she knew needed a home. "I just wanted it to matter," she said.[17]

It took $50,000 in 1988 to purchase Club Lower Links, at 945 West Newport, which Jones transformed into a European cabaret from another era. Tables, mismatched chairs, and frayed red sofas populated the T-shaped room, dimly lit against black walls. Nearby clubs like Exit, Neo, and Smart Bar all spun the latest house, punk, or New Wave, but Jones, in a nod to her Wyoming roots, decided to title her club's DJ night "Dark Country" and feature only vintage country songs. And she stocked Lone Star beer. The juxtaposition of School of the Art Institute students, experimental jazz improvisers, and punk rockers listening to George Jones and Conway Twitty was deliberate. "It was a discovery thing," said Jones. "There were a whole bunch of people who hadn't heard that music before because nobody was doing that music in town at that time." When the Bar R-R Ranch closed and the Sundowners were temporarily without a home, she invited them to play. Their shows were particularly memorable, with Ranch regulars mixing it up with the younger crowd. "Their people didn't know what they were coming into, but everybody—the audience and the band—were really kind with each other and happy we booked them," she said.[18]

Then she met the Texas Rubies. When Kelly Kessler moved back to Chicago in 1983 after attending Berea College in eastern Kentucky, she wanted to sing the old songs. Berea had given Kessler, who grew up in Lincoln Park, a chance to reconnect with her family's Appalachian roots. There she met singers off the mountain who had learned ballads through the oral tradition, and she even met former WLS *Barn Dance* star and Berea alumnus Bradley Kincaid, who, though nearing ninety, regularly returned to the area to attend the college's annual Celebration of Traditional Music festival.

In Chicago, Kessler felt she was without musical peers. At the time, "you couldn't pick a more unpopular music than country music," she said. "It's hard to describe how unhip it was."[19] While working as a potter at Lillstreet Art Center, Kessler started a Sunday morning sing in her apartment with a small group of like-minded women. A mutual friend brought along a native Kentuckian who had moved to Chicago just a year earlier to find work as an actress: Jane Baxter Miller.

Miller grew up in Pikeville, Kentucky, in the heart of the Appalachian Mountains. Her family harmonized at home and in the car, and her grandfather played banjo. But the music didn't take. It was only at West Virginia University in Morgantown that Miller connected with bluegrass—not in the classroom, but at parties, where it was common for instruments to come out. "It was the first time I had experienced how music can transcend," she said. "How voices coming together can transport you to another place. There was something there that resonated so hard and deep in me that I never let go."[20]

In June 1991, Kessler and Miller descended the subway stairs with their guitars. Trackside below Chicago Avenue and State Street, they performed a short set of songs that no rush-hour commuters in Chicago were likely to know—but they soon would. Kessler and Miller were determined to represent Hazel Dickens and Alice Wheeler, two pioneering female bluegrass singers from decades earlier. When they sang the Hazel and Alice tune "Working Girl Blues," people got quiet and heads turned. "They listened," remembered Kessler. "I did not know what to expect, but I did not expect that."[21]

That experience energized the duo to play more. Without an obvious country audience, they instead approached coffee shops, art galleries, and rock clubs. Club Lower Links soon became their home. Without even hearing them, Jones told Miller she had eight dates available, and Miller responded by taking them all. Two months after their first subway appearance, the Texas Rubies were on the bill of Milly's Orchid Show, a cabaret at the Park West, a thousand-seat club. The rapid acceptance of their music took them by surprise. "Our expectation for being roundly hated was not quite what we encountered," Kessler said.[22] In their three years together, from playing the downtown city country festival to opening shows for Guy Clark and Joe Ely, the Rubies represented the appealing duality of country music: heartbreaking harmonies on songs that sounded ripped from the gut, interspersed with goofball humor. For Kessler and Miller, both came naturally.

The Rubies also played an unorthodox repertoire, including "James Alley Blues" by early twentieth-century blues guitarist Richard "Rabbit" Brown, "Blue Diamond Mines" by Appalachian songwriter Jean Ritchie, and "Hank Drank" by obscure Montana songwriter Bobby Lee Springfield, as well as originals. Like Emmylou Harris, an obvious touchtone, the Rubies connected to darker themes like humiliation and loss. *Working Girl Blues*, their 1993 debut album, embodied that fatalism. Preceding the era of online streaming, these songs were not easily discoverable, so for the Rubies' audience of free jazz musicians and performance artists, "it was their introduction to that music," Kessler said.[23]

FREAKWATER MINES
KENTUCKY ROOTS

Another Kentucky-Chicago connection made during this time was the one between Janet Beveridge Bean and Catherine Irwin. They met in 1982 as teenagers attending a punk show in their hometown of Louisville, but as the years went by they discovered an organic bond between their voices—Irwin's lead vocal twang, sounding boozy and broken-down, and Bean's alto, only a shade away from Emmylou Harris, reverberating with classic vulnerability. The Carter Family loomed large for both, not just in the uncanny connection in their vocal harmonies, but in their fascination with the trio's early songs that treated death with eerie beauty. By 1988, Bean had relocated to Chicago and emerged as a drummer with the rock band Eleventh Dream Day. But in the next year, Freakwater, the band she and Irwin formed with upright bassist David Gay, would release its debut album. Freakwater, like Uncle Tupelo, the Texas Rubies, and others, showed that early country music could be source material for a different way of talking about contemporary life.

Although the band recorded covers (Bill Monroe, Conway Twitty, Merle Travis, Black Sabbath), Irwin was its primary songwriter. The bleakness of her vision was matched by her natural gift as a storyteller. Her songs explored timeless themes like infidelity, the toll of whiskey, and unrequited love, but she didn't consider what she did recycling. The themes of her songs "don't seem that different to me than the themes in any popular music," she said. "Maybe it's because [country music] lyrics are so much more prominent, and so much easier to understand. . . . But a lot of Black Sabbath songs, aren't they talking about death? It's all grim."[24]

Freakwater found a home not with a country label, but with Thrill Jockey, a Chicago-based label with an eclectic roster that included underground artists Tortoise, The Sea and Cake, and Bobby Conn. By the mid-1990s, the band started touring Europe, and attracted the attention of Steve Earle, who wanted to sign them to E-Squared, his boutique label connected to Warner Bros. According to Earle, he wanted to record the band in Nashville with esteemed veteran bluegrass and country players Peter Rowan, Norman Blake, and Roy Huskey Jr. in order to "reach an entirely different and much larger audience."[25] The band said no. Instead, it continued to record with Thrill Jockey. The 1999 album *End Time* introduced chamber strings to its traditional country sound. Irwin temporarily moved to Chicago to record *Thinking of You*, released in 2005, which featured Califone as the backing band, with contributions from Chicago multi-instrumentalist Jim Becker and Jim Elkington of the Zincs on electric guitar.

Despite those inflections, Freakwater rarely strayed from the timeless setting of acoustic guitars, fiddle, pedal steel, and piano. On "My Old Drunk Friend," which opens the 1993 album *Feels Like the Third Time*—the band's finest hour—Irwin and Bean harmonize as the steel guitar shimmers. The street reunion is first empathetic: "You're lookin' kinda thin / I won't ask where you've been, you never want to say," Irwin sings. But by the end, Irwin's narrator joins her friend at the bar because she realizes she too is lost: "I should have moved to New York City but I never was that cool," she sings. "I just languished in the Midwest like some old romantic fool."[26] The song could be sung on any corner of any Illinois town invisible from the interstate because of the cornfields.

So, too, could "Lullaby," which closes the album. Featuring only

Bean and Irwin with Irwin's acoustic guitar, its lyrics are quietly sung from the perspective of a father to a small child: "The land-lord's comin' down the hall / He wants the rent, but I spent it all." But the twist to Irwin's lyrics is that this isn't another drunkard's lament. Instead, he explains: "The heat goes off on Monday, 'twas a letter sent / I took that money to pay the rent / The food is all gone now, there's nothing to eat / I took that money to pay the heat."[27] Pick a recession from any decade, and these are the words of anyone stuck in the quicksand of poverty. Brad Wood, who produced three Freakwater albums, observed that songs like that would be "number one if Dolly Parton sang them" because they fit the definition of clas-sic country. "The best country songs combine tragedy and a wicked sense of humor and self-deprecation and bitterness all at once," he said. "And Janet and Catherine are masters of that."[28]

THE TRANCE-ROOTS OF SOULED AMERICAN

Across town in Wicker Park, Souled American was likely playing Phyllis' Musical Inn, a corner dive on Division. The band formed in 1987 and, like the Texas Rubies and Freakwater, was drawn to the fatalism and soul of early twentieth-century string-band music. Unlike the Rubies, the foursome didn't stick to the American song-book, but instead played mostly originals. Souled American's sound was droning and polyrhythmic, and Chris Grigoroff sang with a deep Southern twang that came naturally to someone who had grown up in Charleston, in southern Illinois. "I feel like I'm always country when I sing. With our rhythm section, though, we'll do something completely non-country. I think more of our tunes show a country side now, but I hate to label things," he said.[29]

Soon enough, the band drew fans among critics and other musi-cians. Gary Louris, the leader of the Minneapolis group the Jay-hawks, remembered meeting two Illinois bands at South by South-west in Austin, Texas, in 1988: Uncle Tupelo and Souled American. He formed a connection with both. Souled American, he said, "had that twisted kind of folk music that I liked. It was art folk, weird.

They had a lead bass player. And the drummer was really bizarre in a Thelonious Monk kind of way, playing these crazy time signatures. I absolutely loved them."[30]

Souled American's sound was appealing enough to garner a record deal with Rough Trade, the London-based label that was home to the Smiths. *Fe*, the band's Rough Trade debut, became an instant benchmark for a genre that had yet to be defined. Souled American grew more psychedelic on *Flubber* (1989) and *Around the Horn* (1990), the band's remaining Rough Trade records. Those albums included covers of Lowell George, John Fahey, A. P. Carter, and the Louvin Brothers, all influences from Grigoroff's and bassist Joe Adducci's shared childhood in Charleston. Neither man knew the other growing up, but they met in 1982 when both played the bar band circuit around Bloomington. Country music dominated Adducci's household thanks to his mother, Vicki, who was herself a country singer and a prolific songwriter. Souled American's first album included "I Keep Holding Back the Tears," a Vicki original. Grigoroff had earned his chops playing old-time string music at local bluegrass festivals. His collaboration with Adducci connected to themes of poverty and mortality. Over the course of the band's albums, it's difficult to distinguish early traditionals like "Soldier's Joy" and "Buck Dancer's Choice" or the Carter Family's "Rise Above It" from band originals "Magic Bullets" and "Mar'boro Man."

Souled American served as a brief pivot point that foreshadowed trance-roots artists like Richard Buckner, Sun Kil Moon, and Will Oldham. As alternative country gained more traction, the band itself faded. Rough Trade's US division folded, drummer Jamey Barnard left, and Grigoroff and Adducci moved to a farmhouse in Kansas, Illinois. (Guitarist Scott Tuma, a Naperville native, remained in Chicago.) They released two albums, *Frozen* and *Notes Campfire*, on Moll, a label in Hamburg, Germany. Their sound was denser, droning, with a glacial pace, all of which contrasted with the beauty of Grigoroff's vocals. Grigoroff said withdrawing allowed them to make the music sound more organic. "We didn't try to control life. We just let the songs take over," he said.[31]

The Texas Rubies, Freakwater, and Souled American playing mountain tunes and country spirituals to performance artists in cellar clubs and corner bars are early examples of Chicago musicians deliberately inverting the country genre. They freely rejected commercial trends from Nashville, but they also dismissed the exaggerated stereotypes of country music held by people who knew little about it in the first place. In a way, early alternative country bands like these were outsiders playing to other outsiders, a dynamic that created fertile ground for future experimentation by a coming generation of musicians who were slowly discovering that going backward was the most sensible way to move forward.

COUNTRY IN PUNK BARS AND ALTERNATIVE ART SPACES

Alternative country emerged in Chicago in the late 1980s and early 1990s in spaces such as rock clubs, art galleries, performance art theaters, and punk bars: besides Club Lower Links, there was Cabaret Metro, the Rainbo Club, the Beat Kitchen, Crash Palace, Déjà Vu, the West End, the Artful Dodger, the Augenblick, and Club Dreamerz, 1516 North Milwaukee Avenue in Wicker Park, considered the city's first punk bar, where Nirvana played its first Chicago show. Country bands also played the Main Street Pub, 1572 North Milwaukee Avenue, which became the Double Door, a rock club, in 1994. The Lunar Cabaret, at 2827 North Lincoln, home to the experimental theater company the Curious Theater Branch, also opened in 1994. The intimate seventy-five-seat space featured outer-fringe folk, jazz, and performance art, including Texas songwriter Townes Van Zandt in December 1994.[32] Preceding all these venues was FitzGerald's, a spacious roadhouse at 6615 West Roosevelt in neighboring Berwyn, which opened in 1980 and became the central spot in Chicago for American roots music from Texas, Louisiana, and beyond.

A series of annual shows also played roles in the music's emergence. Schubas, a corner saloon with a rear music room at 3159 North Southport, actively promoted alternative country, most notably a birthday-party tribute to Buck Owens, architect of Bakersfield-style honky-tonk. These annual shows, which ran between 1995 and 1999, defined the freestyle collaboration that was becoming a hallmark of the underground country scene. The lineups featured a dizzying range of artists: Jim Lauderdale; soul greats Otis Clay, Tyrone Davis, and Mavis Staples; lounge singer Tony Ocean; Robbie Fulks, Jon Langford, Steve Dawson, and Jane Baxter Miller; polka bandleader Eddie Blazonczyk Sr.; and even the folk ensemble Sones de Mexico, all introducing audiences to Owens's rich catalog of hits like "Act Naturally," "Crying Time," and "I've Got a Tiger by the Tail."

Chicago performance artist Brigid Murphy became a chief instigator of the scene with "Milly's Orchid Show," a surreal vaudeville show she developed after visiting Nashville in 1987 and envisioning the character of Milly May Smithy, a sassy, fame-obsessed cowgirl dressed in denim hot pants, gaudy makeup, giant eyelashes, and a tower of hair. The character served as the emcee of the country variety show—"a cross between Ed Sullivan and the *Grand Ole Opry*"— which, in its first year at Lounge Ax, a Lincoln Park rock club, featured oddball actors, cartoonists, comedians, musicians, dancers, and performance artists with names like Monk the Wanderin' Wizard and Samantha and Her Trained Rats.[33] The show was such a hit that Murphy moved it to the Park West, a thousand-seat club at 322 West Armitage, and briefly to New York City. She not only created early opportunities for performance artists, poets, and monologists like David Sedaris, Eric Bogosian, Marc Smith, and the Blue Man Group, but blended them with musical performances by country artists such as Jim Lauderdale, the Texas Rubies, Syd Straw, and Robbie Fulks. Murphy, as Smithy, also sang originals, including her theme song that crowned her "Queen of Country." Like the Owens tribute, the Orchid Show illustrated the tight bonds between Chicago's country musicians and the wider creative community. It showed that the scene didn't operate in a silo, but was open to collaboration, often from far and wide.

One of the more unexpected incubators of the scene was a thrift shop: the Record Roundup, operated by Heather McAdams and

Chris Ligon, a married couple who promoted art, fashion, film, and records that all coalesced around country. Both Southerners, she originally from Virginia and he from southern Illinois, they met at Lower Links soon after Ligon moved to Chicago in 1991. "She played a Hank Snow song to me over the telephone a week after we met. I go, 'oh my god, this is the girl I want to be with,'" Ligon said.[34] They married two years later, and in 1997 opened the shop at 2034 West Montrose. Hanging out there was like an archaeological dig for Americana oddities: vintage photograph collections, films, games, toys, novelties, clothing, and thousands of records spanning genres of outsider music and hardcore country. The couple's passion for the *Grand Ole Opry*'s glory years sent them on frequent road trips to Nashville to seek out appearances by its remaining elders. It also fueled their interest in becoming presenters of their own shows back home.

Until it shuttered in 2001, the Record Roundup hosted variety nights with performances by a rotating band of locals, including Neko Case, the Handsome Family, Sally Timms and Jon Langford, Kelly Hogan, and Robbie Fulks. But the couple's longest-running project remained the Country Calendar, which featured original McAdams cartoons of American country, blues, jazz, and other roots music stars as well as other pop-culture dignitaries. A long-time veteran of Chicago's comics scene, with artwork published in *Mademoiselle* and the *Village Voice*, McAdams focused on her childhood in her earliest work as a graduate student at the School of the Art Institute. Her cartoon self—adorned in a tiny red cowboy hat, boots, and western shirt with fringe—was not unlike the real version seen around town. Eventually, she and Ligon organized special shows every December to promote the calendar, and solicited luminaries from the city's country scene to portray each year's featured personalities. The variety shows and the calendar series were never framed as just kitsch. For the growing audience that was becoming aware of country music's fading past, they also served as homegrown history lessons.

Ligon topped the bill as emcee for the shows for more than

twenty years. He also wrote and performed deceptively simple but subversive songs, recording a series of mostly self-released albums over thirty years. Like Harry Nilsson, Ligon easily navigated among musical styles—rockabilly, dreamy pop, piano ballads, doo-wop, comedy bits—making even dire subjects tuneful, with an ingenuous sense of wonder. On "Great State of Texas," a death-row inmate sings of all the things he'll miss in life while his cellmate joins him in harmony. In another stark song, "The World Missed Out," the narrator says farewell after a life of being invisible to others: "Old and gray / one fine day / I climbed to the top of that St. Louis arch / And pushed myself out on the sunny, sunny first of March," he sings. "The world missed out on me."

Ligon's work got a boost when the Flat Five used a collection of his songs as the template for their 2016 debut album, *It's a World of Love and Hope*. The Flat Five could be best described as Chicago's answer to the Wrecking Crew: its musicians had individually and collectively backed up Mavis Staples, NRBQ, the Decemberists, Neko Case, and Andrew Bird, among others. As the songs reached a wider audience, Ligon acknowledged his own limitations as a musician: "My only piano skills are to such a degree that I can write my own songs and that's about it," he said. "But having limitations can really inspire you to go into directions you would have never tried if you were a virtuoso. I figured if I were to do anything interesting, it better be personal."[35]

LOUNGE AX
COALESCES A SCENE

In 1993, Chicago became the center of the music universe. That year, the Smashing Pumpkins released the epic guitar symphony *Siamese Dream*, a platinum seller, and Urge Overkill and Liz Phair released *Saturation* and *Exile in Guyville*, respectively, which catapulted them to national prominence. Just as Nirvana's major-label debut *Nevermind* had put Seattle on the map two years earlier, these three albums turned the recording industry's attention to Chicago, particularly Wicker Park, a low-key neighborhood that was home to coffee shops, diners, Polish bars, hangouts like Urbis Orbis, Ear Wax, the Busy Bee, and Czar Bar, and most importantly, cheap rents and rehearsal spaces. The Empty Bottle and the Double Door emerged as ground zero for area rock bands. The attention peaked in August, when *Billboard* published a cover story declaring Chicago "Cutting Edge's New Capital."[36] A few months later, the *New York Times* followed up, announcing things were "Edgy in Chicago."[37] It was the first time since the golden era of blues that Chicago was recognized nationally for its overall music scene, despite the fact that so many record labels (Pravda, Touch and Go, Wax Trax, Drag City, Thrill Jockey), studios, and clubs had already made it possible for influential bands like the Jesus Lizard, Ministry, Naked Raygun, Big Black, Royal Trux, Material Issue, and Red Red Meat to establish themselves in years prior. Thanks to the commercial success of the Pumpkins, Phair, and Urge, major-label scouts descended upon the city, and it wasn't long until a legion of Chicago rock bands— Veruca Salt, Loud Lucy, Local H, Fig Dish, the Smoking Popes, Triplefastaction—also got major-label contracts.

As the Chicago scene became a golden ticket, some musicians swerved left. Early roots music became a truer alternative to the two commercial trends that dominated the 1990s: the music branded "alternative" rock by the recording industry, and New Country. "At a certain point when all your friends have all the right records in their collection, like the Ramones, you want to get a Hank Snow record, and that's more punk rock because it's not punk rock," said musician Mark Greenberg.[38] "A lot of these people dove deep into country because no one in their scene was digging into it."

Heather McAdams said that she remembered knowing little about country music, but was drawn to its traditional forms because they "sounded more authentic" than what she recognized from country radio. "There was a lifestyle that people in the punk community had, where they were interested in art, performance, film and junk shopping, digging through records and rediscovering people like George Jones. It wasn't going to be hot new country music radio formats that were going to promote those kinds of rediscoveries. It had to come out of something that was completely the opposite," she said.[39]

Musicians also found the country crowd more collaborative than the local rock scene, where "there was no community," said Danny Black, co-founder of the Blacks, an alternative country band that drew from elements of vaudeville and rockabilly. Black had played in rock bands, but left unsatisfied because the primary focus was getting signed to a major label. Country music was more creatively appealing because "nobody thought they were going to make a living playing it." "That freed you up to just enjoy playing music for the sake of the music. And that comes through when you're not trying to do anything mainstream," he said.[40]

Dean Schlabowske had already recorded albums with the noise band Wreck before he co-founded the Waco Brothers, a punk-country band that became emblematic of the scene. For him, stepping out of the rock scene was a relief, since it wasn't a natural outlet for the songs he wanted to write. "The post-punk attitude was so cynical you couldn't imagine yourself showing up at rehearsal with a heartfelt sad song," he said. The alternative country scene, he discovered, was the opposite: "Everybody was anxious to collaborate. Everyone was open to playing on everyone else's records. Whereas the scene I came out of, everyone's instinct was to diss on every other band. I did not miss being part of that world at all once I left it."[41]

Chicago's isolation from both coasts created not only a sense of artistic freedom but also a strong work ethic, according to singer Sally Timms of the Mekons, who moved to the city in 1997. "It's always been a little unfashionable to be here. So we benefit from that. People aren't super aware of how they're perceived anywhere else. They just get on with the work and hope for the best. That creates a lot of really strong networks," she said.[42]

Nineteen ninety-three was also the year that Uncle Tupelo released *Anodyne*, its major-label debut. The downstate band broke up soon afterward, but not until Jeff Tweedy, the band's co-founder and bassist, moved to Chicago. Wilco, his next band, would be at the heart of a roots music scene that was developing that decade.

If that scene had an unofficial headquarters, it was Lounge Ax.

Lounge Ax, at 2438 North Lincoln, was not the longest-running rock club in Chicago, nor the largest, but it became the most influential in creating a community for the underground music scene, which spanned experimental jazz, indie rock, alternative country, and everything in between. Jennifer Fischer and Julia Adams opened the doors in September 1987. Their original plan was a blues club, but after a few weeks they discovered the North Side market for blues was saturated. From there, the club's focus became "predominantly rock, some country," said Fischer.[43]

Both women had worked for ten years managing different bars in the neighborhood, but none had featured live music. Their main competition for bookings was the nearby Cubby Bear, located across from Wrigley Field on Clark Street. "We realized that if we were going to survive, we couldn't compete," said Adams. Upon learning that Susan Miller, the Cubby Bear talent buyer, was growing unhappy at her job, Fischer brought her to Lounge Ax. In 1989, Miller became a partner.

Miller had years of promotion experience at music clubs like the Cubby Bear. Lounge Ax gave her the opportunity to play a larger role in a space designed specifically for music. Fischer and Adams had already stripped away the wood paneling and knocked down a wall to make the club into one narrow room designed for sound, with the stage at one end and the bar at the other. Miller's policy for booking bands was simple: she pledged to listen to every cassette and CD demo that came across the transom. Instead of being asked who they knew or how many people they'd draw, bands had to meet one requirement to get a show: "not sucking."[44] That policy made the club instrumental in fostering creativity and experimentation, especially for local bands that were in the midst of developing a sound.

In 1991, Fischer left to go to graduate school, leaving Adams to handle bar management and Miller the booking. Together, they earned a reputation for making bands feel comfortable enough to want to drop in even if they weren't playing that night. It wasn't unusual for the partners to throw surprise birthday celebrations for musicians or to invite touring bands to crash at their apartments after a show. "They'd instantly make you part of the family. It wasn't fake, it was real," said Greenberg.[45] Lounge Ax developed a clubhouse atmosphere. Adams and Miller were always present, and the staff had little turnover, so both the bands and the audiences were greeted with familiar faces every time they walked through the door. "It meant a friendly environment for women to come and play in what is often a macho environment. They always treated people with respect unlike other pig-like club personalities in Chicago," said Steve Albini, a Chicago-based producer and musician. The vibe extended to security: "We never hired the big, burly, nonecks. Julia and I would do [security]. We would be their mom to get [drunks] to calm down. I think people respected that," Miller said.[46] Adams agreed: "We used it to our advantage. Women most often are perceived as being kinder. And we would act like mothers more than anything. It was a lot more effective if I went up to some kid and said 'Why are you acting like such an asshole?' than if a guy did it."[47]

Lounge Ax became a national destination for touring artists: the long list includes Guided by Voices, Bad Livers, Superchunk, Joe Ely, Jimmie Dale Gilmore, the Jesus Lizard, Sleater-Kinney, Elliott Smith, John Hiatt, Pavement, Meat Puppets, Built to Spill, Alex Chilton, Stereolab, Phish, and Jim Carroll. Its reputation was strong enough for Matt Berninger, the lead singer of the National, to drive from his house in Cincinnati to Chicago to check out shows before he formed a band of his own. "It was one of those places where you found your identity," he said. "It was one of those churches where you learned how to be in a band."[48]

Adams, who grew up in Rockford, had spent more than a few nights under the low ceiling of the Bar R-R Ranch listening to the Sundowners. Her taste for country music leaned traditional. As the alternative country scene grew, Lounge Ax served as a place where bands both played and went to watch one another. Once Miller brought the Mekons from the Cubby Bear to Lounge Ax, other

bands with similar sensibilities followed: the Old 97's, Whiskey-
town, the Palace Brothers, Freakwater, the Handsome Family, the
Bottle Rockets, Grant Lee Buffalo, Moonshine Willy, Smog, Pinetop
Seven, Calexico, Johnny Dowd, Neko Case, Will Oldham, Kelly
Hogan, Diane Izzo, Edith Frost, Blue Mountain, Meat Purveyors,
Lambchop, Scroat Belly, Dolly Varden, the Waco Brothers, and the
Blacks all appeared on the calendar.

Wilco grew up in the club. Once Tweedy launched the band in
1994, Lounge Ax served as his home base for solo shows, secret
band shows, or side projects like Golden Smog, a supergroup that
included members of Soul Asylum and the Jayhawks. Between 1995
and 2000, the year Lounge Ax closed, Wilco released three albums,
and its sound developed from countrified garage rock to the psychedelic pop of *Summerteeth*, the band's artistic breakthrough. Later
that decade, Wilco collaborated with British singer-songwriter Billy
Bragg on two volumes of *Mermaid Avenue*, a project that introduced
new music to unused lyrics written by Woody Guthrie. The presence
of Wilco during this short but fertile period drew attention to other
Chicago bands, but more importantly, it helped frame a hometown
scene that was collaborative, was interested in pushing boundaries, had a sense of humor about itself, and ignored popular trends
on either coast. The Loft, Wilco's recording studio and all-around
headquarters in Albany Park, became an example of Chicagoan
self-sufficiency. Tweedy opened the doors for other artists on the
scene to record there while demonstrating that they didn't need
to chase a career on the coasts to grow artistically. In fact, Chicago
represented an incubator of the sort that might be found in smaller
towns, but, as a major city, also gave musicians access to the studios,
clubs, record labels, and creative talent those towns lacked.

Like many music clubs before it, including the Gate of Horn
and the Quiet Knight, Lounge Ax was doomed by gentrification. A
condo development that rose behind the club led to repeated noise
complaints to the city by a single tenant starting in 1995. A court
battle followed once the city's liquor commissioner discovered the
club didn't have a Public Place of Amusement license. Then, in

1999, a twenty-six-year-old mortgage broker bought the building in the hope of turning the club into a "sophisticated bar with character." He gave Miller and Adams two months to leave.[49] By then, both women were burned out from fighting the city. The club's final two weeks featured familiar faces: Wilco and the Minus Five, a solo Jeff Tweedy show, Tortoise, Shellac, and a closing night show by the house band, the Coctails.[50] Also on the calendar was an all-star tribute to outsider country songwriter Doug Sahm from Texas that featured Andrew Bird, Robbie Fulks, and Jay Bennett and John Stirratt of Wilco. The community that Lounge Ax created would disperse far and wide from Lincoln Avenue after the club shut its doors. But in those final days at least, the circle was unbroken.

BLOODSHOT RECORDS:
INSURGENT COUNTRY AND DEFIANT ROOTS

The line at the Split Rail in Austin, Texas, was around the block. It was March 1996, and Bloodshot Records, a Chicago label that had existed for a mere two years, suddenly had every music industry tastemaker at the South by Southwest Music Conference clawing to get inside the room where the core of Bloodshot's artist roster was about to play: Moonshine Willy, the Waco Brothers, Whiskeytown, and the Old 97's. "We were sneaking in writers like Greil Marcus through the back door," said label co-founder Nan Warshaw. In the bathroom that night, her business partner Rob Miller overheard two reps from a major label discussing ways they could buy Bloodshot that night and get its bands wholesale. Miller said nothing while running his hands under the faucet.[51]

The excitement that Bloodshot generated almost from the moment it started showed that the label had defined a movement represented by bands that placed high value on songwriting, irreverent attitudes, and exciting live shows. "Right place at the right time doing the right thing," said Miller of the label's success.[52] The malaise on the mid-1990s musical landscape didn't hurt. Nirvana bandleader Kurt Cobain had died by suicide two years earlier, a grim end to the once-promising wave of underground bands filtering into the mainstream. The "alternative rock" era was proving it was an alternative to nothing. The looming digital revolution would democratize the way people discovered music, creating greater exposure for independent artists shut out of corporate radio.

Everything about Bloodshot's early days was about speed. In late 1993, Warshaw, Miller, and co-founder Eric Babcock sat on barstools sketching out ideas on cocktail napkins. Their initial idea was not to launch a label, but simply to put out a compilation CD to document the scene that was growing around them. That impulse would spread, as Bloodshot would be the first label to document similar scenes throughout the United States.

Like the founders of the Old Town School of Folk Music, Warshaw, Miller, and Babcock had little in common, but they struck up a friendship around the music they loved. Warshaw, born November 2, 1962, grew up in Old Town until her parents relocated to Evanston so she could start first grade there. They were folkies who brought her to Amazingrace in Evanston to see John Prine, John Hartford, and Steve Goodman. She discovered punk rock in high school. At Columbia College, she immersed herself in that scene. She went out to the clubs five nights a week and, in a community that relied on do-it-yourself ingenuity, started helping bands by serving as a booking agent and publicist, and eventually as a talent buyer for various bars. The scene was small but staunch. The music's appeal was its unpredictability and raw power, but by the late 1980s, Warshaw and her circle of friends noticed that their excitement was starting to fade as major labels started co-opting the scene. Dwight Yoakam, the Cramps, and the Knitters—a country side project by members of the punk band X—served as gateways to country music for such dissatisfied punk fans because they played covers of older, more traditional artists that those listeners didn't necessarily know. Warshaw, who had been DJ-ing at clubs around town since 1986, started pushing country. She turned Wednesdays into country night at Crash Palace, and the slot became so popular it ran for eighteen years. For the first six weeks, she alternated with an unlikely partner: Al Jourgensen, leader of the pioneering industrial rock band Ministry, who was also an unabashed country fan.

"I was seeking out something where the lyrics were three chords and the truth," Warshaw said. "Where it was everyday themes of working-class people. And the lyrics weren't sugarcoated and the stories were true and dark and often twisted. In that way, country tracked well with punk rock."[53]

One of Warshaw's many jobs was publicist for Killbilly, a Dallas punk-country band that had just signed to Chicago's Flying Fish label. Through that work, she met Eric Babcock, a Flying Fish employee who was already an industry veteran, having logged years at Chicago's Alligator Records and the Chicago office of Blind Pig, a San Francisco blues label. Babcock, born October 20, 1963, grew up in Kalamazoo, Michigan, and moved to Chicago to attend Northwestern University. He needed no introduction to country music, as he had grown up with it in Michigan and had already done his homework on the music's outlaw wing. At a backyard cookout, Warshaw approached Babcock about the idea of creating a CD to record other country bands in town.[54] Babcock was interested, but before the idea went anywhere, Warshaw brought in a third partner: Rob Miller.

Miller moved to Chicago in 1991. Born May 22, 1965, he grew up outside Detroit. While attending the University of Michigan, he started working in production for a local concert promoter and hosted music shows on the local radio station. During a road trip to Chicago to see Dwight Yoakam and Buck Owens at the Chicago Theatre, he and a friend descended the stairs of the Bar R-R Ranch afterward to see the Sundowners. The band played until sunrise. "Okay, I can move here," he told himself while walking back to his car. He applied and was accepted for a master's degree program in English literature at DePaul University and relocated the next year.[55]

Like Warshaw, Miller was losing interest in punk rock because it had breached commercial radio playlists and felt stale. His bridge to roots music was artists like the Meat Puppets, Bad Livers, and the Knitters, all of whom were rotating through Lounge Ax, just steps from DePaul's Lincoln Park campus. "It was this weird stew

of something a lot of people my age were reacting to because it had
an immediacy that was very similar to the punk scene," he said of
the music.[56] Eventually he started showing up at Crash Palace on
Wednesday nights to hear Warshaw spin country 45s. It was a subculture he felt comfortable in, so he started bringing in his own
records to play. The two hit it off, and Warshaw invited him to meet
Babcock.

Warshaw, Miller, and Babcock agreed that the bands they were
seeing deserved wider attention, and drawing that attention became
their passion project. "We were bored. We didn't know what we were
doing," Miller said. They met to finalize a list of bands they wanted
to include on the CD, but also to create critical language to brand
the sound those bands shared. They chose "insurgent country," a
phrase that would soon become larger than Bloodshot itself in how
it defined the national alternative country movement. But at the
time, "insurgent country" did the job: "It had a good underground
punk-rock feel to it and it tempered the 'C' word. We were never
pretending to be a country label," Miller said.[57]

In December 1993, at the Empty Bottle, a local rock club, the
three were cobbling together plans when Miller spotted Jon Langford entering the room. Babcock and Miller, both Mekons fans,
were too awestruck to approach him to ask if he'd like to be involved.
So Warshaw, who knew little about the band, walked over and introduced herself. Langford had just moved to Chicago from Leeds a year
earlier. "I was sitting around wondering what to do with my life," he
said.[58] Not only did Langford agree to participate, but he invited all
three partners to his apartment that night so they could view slides
of his artwork—skeletons dressed up in cowboy suits, angels rising
from the ashes of forgotten country stars, and a despondent Hank
Williams, arrows protruding from his chest, penetrated by fame
and struck down by both the music industry and his own demons.
Langford's vision of the ghosts of country's past neglected by the
same forces now promoting New Country struck the perfect tone
for the statement Bloodshot planned to make.

For a Life of Sin, released in June 1994, defined the early Blood-

shot sound. The Chicago bands on the compilation spanned generations, genders, and approaches to country music: besides Langford,
Freakwater, the Texas Rubies, Brigid Murphy, and the rockabilly
band the Riptones, it included two tracks from the Sundowners and
the first solo recording by a former member of Special Consensus
named Robbie Fulks. The recording adopted punk's lo-fi aesthetic:
most songs were recorded live to capture the natural performances
in the room with very little overdubbing, reverb, or compression.
Intentionally or not, the sound of *For a Life of Sin* was that of a red-
hot barroom floor late on a Saturday night. The spirit of the songs
themselves was similarly rebellious. "Success on someone else's
terms / don't mean a fucking thing," is the resounding lyric of Langford's "Over the Cliff."[59] The album's statement was bold enough that
Bill Friskics-Warren, the music critic for the *Nashville Scene*, wrote
a full-page review that championed the release, calling Bloodshot
"a label that hopes to establish itself as a vital source for alternative country music [that] combines the best of both of these eras."[60]

Only a thousand copies of the CD were manufactured, but half
were sold within months. There was no plan for a follow-up until
Bloodshot started receiving letters and faxes from music writers,
musicians, and fans throughout the United States describing the
local alt-country scene in their city and suggesting it was deserving
of the same treatment. The world of Bloodshot was now revealing
itself. "What we were doing in Chicago was sending up that signal flare and declaring 'here's what we like and here's some other
people who like it too,'" Babcock said.[61] Connections were quickly
established in other cities "with people who were passionate about
the same music," Warshaw said.[62] Their attempt to document an
underground scene special to Chicago ended up exposing a national
scene that was previously ignored or underappreciated. In the following years, Bloodshot produced *Hell-Bent* (1995), a survey of
alt-country bands from across the United States; *Nashville: The
Other Side of the Alley* (1996), a collection of alt-country bands in
Music City itself; and *Straight Outta Boone County* (1997), another
national compilation of bands performing nearly century-old cow-

boy, mountain, and folk songs. In addition to the collections, debut albums by groups like Moonshine Willy, the Waco Brothers, and the Old 97's established a new genre that the greater recording industry was forced to reckon with.

Forming a record label in the early 1990s did not require heavy lifting. Manufacturing CDs was fairly cheap, there were numerous media outlets to pitch for reviews, Chicago had multiple college radio stations with dedicated listeners, and online file sharing had yet to strike a blow to sales. Early on, Bloodshot operated lean, with an eye on the long game rather than immediate gains. None of the co-founders drew a salary in the first three years, and they all worked full-time jobs. Kelly Hogan, a country-soul singer from Atlanta who resettled in Chicago, was the only paid employee, receiving $500 a month. The label operated out of a bedroom in Warshaw's apartment, and most of the company's business was performed in neighborhood bars. Taking a cue from longtime indie labels in Chicago like Touch and Go, Bloodshot sealed artist deals with handshakes. It didn't seek outside investors, but instead paid for each album from the proceeds of the previous album. This frugality extended to routine expenses: Warshaw used her connections at Elektra Records, a major label where she once had an internship, to recycle jewel cases from overstock CDs for Bloodshot promo copies. Then there was the friend at a local Kinko's who gave the label free copies in exchange for free music. "It was completely DIY," she said of the operation at the time. "That's why it was affordable."[63]

The label's creative turning point came in 1996 with the release of *Country Love Songs* by Robbie Fulks, an unknown country singer from North Carolina. Now living in Chicago, Fulks was the most traditional country artist yet on the label, and he knew the genre so well that he could freely invert it without sacrificing the integrity of the music. The punk energy of his live shows, combined with his lyrical wit, nimble musicianship, and crooning vocals, made him a standout artist for the genre. But because Bloodshot refused to spend money on advertising and instead relied on media publicity and word of mouth, *Country Love Songs* became such a sleeper hit that by 1998, Fulks had signed to Geffen Records.

By 1997, alt-country had hit the mainstream, partially due to the success of recent albums from Wilco and Son Volt. Major labels subsequently signed away some artists on the Bloodshot roster (including Whiskeytown, the Old 97's, and Neko Case). One label offered the Waco Brothers $75,000 to sign, but the band turned it down. "Our answer was, 'We want a million dollars and total artistic freedom,'" said guitarist Dean Schlabowske.[64] During this same period, new labels—Yep Roc (1997), New West (1998), Anti- (1999), ATO (2000), Lost Highway (2000)—popped up to chase the trend with their own rosters of alt-country artists. All were either subsidiaries of major parent companies or flush with investor money.

As the 1990s ended, Bloodshot expanded its staff and moved to a permanent storefront at 3039 West Irving Park. In 1998, the label began to look beyond Chicago by signing veteran Texas singer-songwriter Alejandro Escovedo. He already had a twenty-year career in punk and roots rock, but was in a lull without a label. Bloodshot reintroduced him to a new generation of listeners, and by the end of the 1990s, his three albums with Bloodshot earned him *No Depression*'s "Artist of the Decade" status. "I never had the connection with Chicago until the solo records came out. Once that relationship developed it's more of a home for me than Austin has been," Escovedo said.[65] Having him on the roster gave Bloodshot prestige. Over the years, the label would attract similarly revered icons such as Graham Parker, Dex Romweber of Flat Duo Jets, and Exene Cervenka of X.

One artist moved to Chicago from Tacoma, Washington, just to record for Bloodshot. When she arrived in April 1998, Neko Case tended bar at the Hideout, lived in the extra bedroom in Rob Miller's coach house, and was getting to know local musicians like bassist Tom Ray, pedal-steel guitarist Jon Rauhouse, and singer Kelly Hogan, who would later form the nucleus of her band. She found the creative environment in Chicago to be relaxed and open. "It's very community based," she said. "It's very encouraging and doesn't feel as competitive as it does in other places."[66] It was Hogan who had first heard Case's 1997 album *The Virginian*, produced by Mint Records in Toronto. "I just had this crazy feeling about it," she said. She played it repeatedly in the Bloodshot office for months and finally convinced Warshaw and Miller to go to the CMJ Music Marathon in New York City, in September 1997, to see Case perform. They, too, fell under her spell. By springtime the next year, Blood-shot had licensed *The Virginian* in the United States, and Case had moved to Chicago in April to record for her new label.[67]

It was easy to see why Case was a good fit for Bloodshot. Her music is based in traditional country, but is confident in all its strains: torch ballads, R&B, and experimental pop. *Furnace Room Lullaby*, her 2000 Bloodshot album, elevated her strengths as a singer who can breeze through the octaves but still touch every necessary emotional detail along the way. There is a toughness in her approach, reminiscent of Kitty Wells and Loretta Lynn, and as a writer, she too leans into the dark side of each story. Wandering is a recurrent theme. On "South Tacoma Way," a waltz, she regrets missing a funeral in her hometown: "I couldn't pay respects to a dead man / your life was much more to me / And I chased away with sticks and stones / but that rage kept following me," she and Hogan sing together quietly as if outside under stars. Miller said it wasn't until that album that he realized Case's unique gifts. "Here's somebody with not only this voice, but something to say and a way to say it," he said.[68]

After *Blacklisted*, her second Bloodshot release, Case signed to Anti-, which broke her through to a bigger audience. But while Nash-ville would appear to be a natural home for her gifts, Case remained in Chicago. "Everybody should be completely thrilled about what we're doing in Chicago, how the music we play is completely acces-sible to people and still at a grassroots level," she said. "I don't give a moment's thought to Nashville."[69]

The release that bankrolled the label's second decade was *Heart-breaker*, a solo album by Whiskeytown front man Ryan Adams. Because of the success of his former band, Adams was promised a major-label career with Lost Highway, a subsidiary of the Universal Music Group. He had just recorded *Heartbreaker*, a set of minimal-ist songs recorded in Nashville that featured harmony singing with

Gillian Welch and Emmylou Harris. His management decided it was best to rush it out on an indie label before releasing a second record that was more geared toward commercial radio. Although they suggested Rounder Records, Adams insisted on Bloodshot. "It was mainly because I really liked the people . . . and felt we had a kinship," he said.[70]

Bloodshot would have to pay $30,000 to license the record—cheap for a major label, but a steep price for an indie whose records up to that point had never cost more than $3,000 to produce.[71] And Adams was a gamble. His name was unknown outside Whiskeytown, and he had a reputation for being unreliable. *Heartbreaker* also fit no category—it was too edgy to be folk, not exactly country, and definitely not rock. "They were expecting a much more lively and rabble-rousing kind of album, but I think maybe they were kind of nervous because of the initial investment that they were going to make to secure it, and I handed in this thing that's kind of gloomy and dark and slow and cerebral," Adams said.[72]

Neither Miller nor Warshaw wanted to put the label at risk, so each took out a personal loan to secure the licensing. They created a campaign that would let the album circulate slowly through specialty radio shows, print media, and word of mouth. Eight weeks later, *Billboard* editor in chief Timothy White called *Heartbreaker* "an intuitive document destined to be a prized, restorative possession for anyone fortunate enough to encounter it" on the second page of the industry bible.[73] Similar praise, no less effusive, followed from all quarters of the music press.

Heartbreaker sold more than three hundred thousand copies in the United States, an additional hundred thousand copies overseas, and would outsell every Adams album since except 2001's *Gold*.[74] "Ryan allowed us to not be teetering on the edge of financial oblivion," Miller said.[75] A steady earner for the label over the next decade until Adams bought back the record in 2016, *Heartbreaker* gave Bloodshot a cushion that allowed it to experiment with more fringe artists it wanted to support.

Then came the Great Recession of 2008. By that time, alt-country was no longer underground due to cultural phenomena like the Grammy-winning soundtrack to the film *O Brother, Where Art Thou?* and subsequent tours and albums featuring the soundtrack stars. The success of *O Brother* helped introduce traditional roots music to a wider audience, as did breakthrough folk-based acts like the Lumineers and Mumford and Sons. Suddenly, Bloodshot realized it needed to expand its identity to stand out from the crowded field it helped create. "'Insurgent country' became a noose around our necks," Warshaw said.[76] The new bottom line was that new Bloodshot artists had to be exceptional on the live stage and commit to a life of hard touring in order to build word of mouth and sell music. Country was no longer a signifier either. "We didn't want to put out the same Old 97's record again, and neither did they. We had to keep ourselves interested," Miller said.[77] The label also needed to follow what younger buyers wanted to hear, so "a conscious decision was made to inject new talent," said label manager Scott Schaefer. "And when that new talent came in, we needed to find that critical mass."[78]

Over the years, Bloodshot added neo-soul (JC Brooks and the Uptown Sound), garage (The Detroit Cobras, Gore Gore Girls), and indie rock (The Yawpers, Banditos, Ha Ha Tonka) artists to its roster alongside younger singer-songwriters like Justin Townes Earle, Luke Winslow-King, Laura Jane Grace, Sarah Shook, and Lydia Loveless. "Defiant roots" replaced "insurgent country" as the label's descriptor.

To acknowledge the label's twenty-fifth year in 2019, Bloodshot followed the original blueprint of 1994's *For A Life of Sin* and, once again, documented Chicago's underground country scene. *Too Late to Pray: Defiant Chicago Roots*, a two-record set, features familiar names (Freakwater, Robbie Fulks, Handsome Family) but is largely dominated by new ones: folk artist Half Gringa, country-rock singer-songwriter David Quinn, and honky-tonkers the Lawrence Peters Outfit, the Family Gold, the Hoyle Brothers, the Western Elstons, and Wild Earp. Sequenced together, the past and present blur together to reveal a family tree with roots that keep growing deeper.[79]

JON LANGFORD:
PATRON SAINT OF CHICAGO ALTERNATIVE COUNTRY

Alejandro Escovedo, the acclaimed Texas songwriter, once held the informal title of "the mayor of Austin," not just because his music coalesces all the strains of music that represent the Texas capital, but also because he was a generous collaborator and his presence on the scene was constant. Everywhere, from grand halls to taco stands, Escovedo brought the music to the people. In Jon Langford, he recognized a peer. "He is very influential in keeping the musical community in Chicago together. He's kind of like the ringleader, mentor, and resident genius," Escovedo said.[80]

Langford was an unlikely candidate for any of these three roles. He was born in Leeds, a city in northern England, on October 11, 1957, and moved to Chicago in 1992. Very soon, he became a driver of the city's music scene: besides forming the Waco Brothers, a punk band immersed in country honky-tonk, Langford became the central figure in collaborations with musicians in every pocket of town as a producer, musician, songwriter, or illustrator. "Jon just works, he doesn't sleep," said singer-songwriter Richard Buckner, who recorded an album with Langford. "He's like a bat."[81] His other musical projects, Skull Orchard, Pine Valley Cosmonauts, and Four Lost Souls, resulted in a prolific output of music that spanned Southern soul, western swing, rock, electronic, and folk. The socialist principles that inspired his earliest work in Leeds with the Mekons continued to inspire the music he made in Chicago. But over time, the driving theme running throughout most of Langford's output is profound disappointment in the perversions of truth that perpetuate the ongoing rewriting of his adopted country's story. More literary-minded than most, Langford's lyrics skewer American mythology, but with the wit and good humor of someone exposed to it from the outside. While his peers in Leeds were turning to acid house music in the mid-1980s, the only music that interested him was country music, the most American popular music and the most mythologized.

All it took was a cassette of honky-tonk classics mailed to him by Terry Nelson, a Chicago radio DJ who befriended the Mekons and became their stateside advocate. The mixed tape was one of several Nelson sent Langford in 1983. Nelson drew the line directly from the Leeds punk band to people like Merle Haggard, Johnny Cash, and Ernest Tubb. "All your songs are two, three chords and they're about drinking in bars and failed sexual relationships," he told Langford. "You're like a country band." As a twenty-six-year-old who felt he had already lived his share of life, Langford realized that the music "suddenly made perfect sense."[82]

At that time, the Mekons had paused. Formed in 1977 as one of the first British post-punk bands, they were a collective of University of Leeds art students who originally used music as the vehicle for their ideas about social theory and removing the separation between audience and performer. Over their time together, which included a brief stint on major label A&M Records, the Mekons developed into a working band that could write straightforward rock anthems, folk songs, conceptual art-pop, and punk revelry. The British miners strike of 1984–85 gave the band new purpose. The result: the 1985 album *Fear and Whiskey*, considered one of the earliest alt-country records for its honky-tonk piano, fiddle, and acoustic guitars that together articulated working class despondency.

The Mekons would continue to chase American idioms into the next decade. But in 1988, Langford helped to lay the groundwork for the eventual return of country music's greatest icon: Johnny Cash.

That year, Langford and Marc Riley, of the Fall, co-produced *'Til Things Are Brighter*, a Cash tribute album that featured a group of indie, electronic, and punk artists, including the Mekons, Michelle Shocked, Pete Shelley of the Buzzcocks, Marc Almond of Soft Cell, and Stephen Mallinder of Café Voltaire, who each recorded irreverent covers of Cash touchstones. Their interpretations of songs like "Ring of Fire" and "Straight 'A's in Love," placed Cash in a wildly new context: one that was subversive, confrontational, and fun.

At that point, Cash was struggling. Columbia Records, his label since 1958, had dropped him a year earlier, and he hadn't had a Top 10 solo hit since 1981. His audience had aged. Riley recalled seeing Cash at the Manchester Apollo in his twenties and being one of a few young people in the audience. Cash "was probably at his lowest point of cool. . . . He wasn't courted at all by anyone under the age of 45, which at that time seemed very old."[83] It became evident Nashville had forgotten him. Cash was, by all accounts, depressed.

The tribute album gave him the best press in recent years. Articles in *NME* and *Melody Maker* in England recast Cash as a serious artist, while reviews ran in most alternative music magazines, which would otherwise ignore an artist of Cash's age. College radio stations picked up the album and added it to their playlists. Cash had met up with Riley and Langford that May at a local tour stop and posed with them for a photo, which appears on the album's back cover. Cash enthusiastically talked up the album during a television appearance on the BBC.

As time went by, Cash and Langford stayed in touch. Rosanne Cash, his daughter, said her father "felt a real connection with those musicians, he felt very validated." "It was very good for him," she said of the album. "He absolutely understood what they were tapping into and loved it. It was reenergizing."[84] While it would take six years for rock producer Rick Rubin to fully launch Cash's comeback, which lasted until the singer's 2003 death, *'Til Things Are Brighter* paved the way by affirming Cash's stature as the ultimate alternative artist, no matter the genre and no matter the year.

The tribute reinforced Langford's obsession with Americana. In Leeds, he formed a duo with fellow Mekon Rico Bell dedicated to performing Buck Owens songs in local pubs using an electric guitar, accordion, and drum machine. But it was clear they were outcasts. Each Mekons tour in the United States ended with a return home clad in cowboy suits, boots, and bolo ties. "People looked at us like we were insane," Langford said.[85] By 1992, Langford's relocation to Chicago seemed preordained: he had already gotten to know the Sundowners and was set to be married to his longtime girlfriend there. The city meant freedom from the creative restrictions he felt living in England. "I was cooped up for such a long time," he said.

"Moving to Chicago, I felt liberated. I can do things here I could have never have dreamed of doing back home."[86]

To Langford, country music was about the things that modern country had long drifted away from: the radical politics of the working class, outlaw heroes, and hardscrabble living, all conveyed through eloquent language and storytelling. He would make those themes touchpoints for his new band, the Waco Brothers, alongside songwriters Tracey Dear and Dean Schlabowske. The earlier generation of country stars "were working class stiffs trying to get by and make it," said Dear. "I can relate."[87]

The Wacos originated from punk rock. In 1990, Langford was still living in Leeds, but making frequent trips to Chicago and getting to know the local scene. During one of those trips, Schlabowske hired Langford to produce an album by Wreck, Schlabowske's noise rock band. Born August 17, 1965, Schlabowske had moved to Chicago in 1987 from his native Milwaukee so he could get deeper into the city's rock scene. Realizing they shared a love of vintage honky-tonk, Langford and Schlabowske started playing around town as a duo. In 1994, they were joined by another Englishman, Tracey Dear, who had been living in Chicago since 1986. Dear, born August 29, 1965, grew up in the countryside along the southern coast of England, where he attended square dances at local village halls. Although he played in punk bands as a teenager, he had grown up listening to Johnny Cash and Glen Campbell. He had known of Langford, but met him properly only in Chicago. By 1994, all three stood on the bar of the Rainbo Club in Wicker Park—two guitars and a mandolin among them—and played their first show together.[88] Two shows later, the trio added a rhythm section—Tom Ray on bass and Steve Goulding on drums. Goulding, another Englishman who had moved to Chicago in 1988, had the most prominent resumé.[89] Besides serving as the drummer for the Mekons, Goulding had been a founding member of Graham Parker and the Rumour and had also played on singles by Elvis Costello, Nick Lowe, and the Cure.

At first, the Wacos avoided clubs in favor of small neighborhood taverns that normally didn't have music. Dear worked for Jam Productions, a local concert promoter, so he had access to professional equipment, which became key to the band's early sound: "I would have the sound guys load in a much bigger PA than we needed, and we'd do a commando-style sound attack at these unsuspecting bars and blow the doors off," he said.[90] At that point, the band didn't have a name and played only for beer money, but they developed enough notoriety around town that rooms filled up fast whenever word spread they were playing.

They became a proper band in 1995 after Bloodshot released "Bad Times Are Coming 'Round Again," a Langford original with "The Harder They Come," a Jimmy Cliff cover, on the B side. Bloodshot requested a full-length album after that. Starting with *To the Last Dead Cowboy*, in 1995, the Wacos drew from the disillusionment of the Clinton and Bush years to channel songs that didn't just rage at the rapidly growing inequities suffered by working people, but mourned them as well. "What if our history means nothing at all?" Schlabowske cries out in one of many songs rebuking the postindustrial age, while Langford portrays marginalized workers as ghosts dragging their own tombstones, or prisoners "walking on hell's roof looking at the flowers." Over three decades, the Wacos successfully moved beyond the drinking and cheating clichés of country music to create bar anthems that, like those of Merle Haggard, reflected empathy for the toil of the forgotten class. The fact that they managed to sound more like a gang than a band—with three lead singers, group vocals, and turbulent stage energy—compounded the urgency.

Outside the Wacos, Langford launched other projects. The Pine Valley Cosmonauts became a vehicle to pay tribute to past icons, like Johnny Cash and Bob Wills, using a core band and special guests. The most impactful project was *The Executioner's Last Songs*, an album in three separate volumes dedicated to songs about death, murder, and execution, made with a wide range of guest artists, including soul music great Otis Clay, David Yow of the Jesus Lizard, Neko Case, Steve Earle, and Jimmie Dale Gilmore. All three volumes benefited the Illinois Death Penalty Moratorium Project,

an advocacy group that played a central role in abolishing execu-
tions in the state.

At the same time, Langford's artwork had grown from portraiture of forgotten country stars of the past to dreamscapes of desolate western plains, skeletons, and cowboys on horses with skulls
for heads. In his vision, the erosion of country music into banal
pop music was a metaphor for America itself, a place where collective memory of the cultural past was becoming extinct. His prolific
output eventually expanded to books, albums, magazine covers, and
gallery showings.

His biggest commission came when the Country Music Hall of
Fame and Museum in Nashville hired him to create the artwork to
accompany *Dylan, Cash and the Nashville Cats: A New Music City*,
a major exhibition that opened in March 2015. The exhibition ran
for nearly two years and to date is considered the most popular show
in the museum's history. Langford's portraits of unsung Nashville
session players of the 1960s and 1970s lined the hallway leading
into the exhibition and adorned the accompanying poster art and
book. Langford's first attempt at portraiture, and his first portrait
of Cash, had served as the cover art of *'Til Things Are Brighter*. That
painting later ended up Cash's hands and was hung in the singer's
home in Jamaica. Twenty-seven years later, Langford's interpretation of Cash covered almost the entire wall of the massive downtown museum, making it impossible for tourists several levels below
not to look up. Langford's Cash emerges as a faded memory high
above Nashville, but more than a decade after the singer's death,
the Man in Black is quintessentially alive in a new Music City that
has become better at embracing outsiders, great and small.

ROBBIE FULKS:
EVERY KIND OF MUSIC PLUS COUNTRY

Before Robbie Fulks cut an album in Nashville in the late 1990s, he
was often in that town playing in songwriter showcases attended by
music industry types scouting for new songs for their country stars.
One such showcase was the Western Beat Barn Dance, a weekly

event at the Exit/In hosted by Billy Block, a music champion known around town as "Mr. Nashville," who was credited with supporting left-of-center country artists like Buddy Miller, Lucinda Williams, and Jim Lauderdale.

It was there one night that Fulks's performance was suddenly interrupted onstage by Claire Mullally, an actress playing a frustrated artists' manager who complained that his songs weren't commercial enough. Again and again, she kept tweaking Fulks to change his act, until finally she transformed him into another singer entirely—topped with a cowboy hat, tucked into cowboy boots, his upper lip slapped with a mustache, and playing versions of his songs "in a horrible radio style—like, with Garth Brooks kind of arrangements," he said, a single bland guitar lick driving every song, every intro, every guitar solo. Before the sketch was over, Fulks closed his set with a new song that summed up his feelings about trying to become a songwriter for hire in Nashville: "Fuck This Town."[91]

Seated at the bar with their mouths open were Nashville songwriters Tom Thady and Dallas Wayne. "We were blown away," said Wayne.[92]

For anyone else, a satirical take on the music business might be seen as biting the hand that could potentially feed a comfortable lifestyle for years. But this was on-brand behavior for Fulks. "Nobody was surprised Robbie Fulks would do something like that. Not at all. Robbie Fulks was always doing something like that," said musician Fats Kaplin, who was also in the audience that night.[93] Because his songs were so respected by insiders in Nashville, his gonzo humor was not just tolerated, but cheered. Many in the audience were just like him: musicians who went to Nashville with expectations of making records like the ones they had grown up with, but who found themselves in the absurd situation of trying to operate within an industry system that appraised creative quality with formulaic standards—and found the formula dominating 1990s country radio to be the most banal of all.

Fulks had emerged from his Nashville experience as a singular artist who followed his own instincts, forcing fans to keep up.

Those instincts led to many things, both familiar and not: albums that drew from honky-tonk country of a past era, others consisting of serious singer-songwriter fare, still others with collaborators from post-punk's Steve Albini to rockabilly's Linda Gail Lewis, and album-length reimaginings of Michael Jackson and Bob Dylan. "He's so well-versed, musically," said New Grass Revival's Sam Bush. "If you want a great rock and roller, he is. If you want a great bluegrass guitar player, he is. If you want old-time country, he can do that."[94] It's the kind of versatility that isn't flashy, but organic to each form. As such, Fulks transcended the alt-country era and, over time, showed he is a restless experimentalist working within strict genre traditions. The tension inherent in that dynamic is what makes him so different from most in the singer-songwriter field. Fulks is not only about showing off his full powers as a musician, a songwriter, or even a music encyclopedia. Instead, there is the sense that he is reaching for different ways to erase expectations so that the songs, no matter their vintage, live fully in the modern day.

Fulks was born March 25, 1963, in York, Pennsylvania, but spent his teenage years in Creedmoor, North Carolina, a small town about thirty miles northeast of Raleigh. His parents, both bluegrass fans, brought him to festivals where he got to hear Doc Watson, New Grass Revival, and the Osborne Brothers. The father of a childhood friend happened to be Tommy Thompson, the late banjoist with the Red Clay Ramblers, a long-running string band revival group. Absorbing all that music at such a young age led him to pursue the music full-time. He was playing banjo before he turned ten, and his earliest idol was banjoist John Hartford. But by the time Fulks enrolled at Columbia University in New York City in 1980, he was committed to the guitar. He headed to downtown clubs to catch the fumes of the old Greenwich Village folk scene. But in 1983, he left school and the city to move to Chicago, following a girlfriend.

In Chicago, he too descended the stairs of the Bar R-R Ranch to listen to, and eventually sit in with, the Sundowners. "I fell in love with it right away," he said.[95] Not long after, the band recorded "Cigarette State," Fulks's send-up of North Carolina. His chance to play in a bluegrass band finally came when he won an audition to join Special Consensus in 1988. Fulks "brought a lot of joy to the band," said leader Greg Cahill, not just through his musicianship, but also his stage presence.[96] "His wit was so quick that you always had to stay on your toes just to figure out where he was going. But his wild behavior, frankly, would make us nervous in some certain bluegrass situations," remembered bassist Dallas Wayne. On the steps of a library in Ohio, for example, Fulks ended the final song by diving into a reflecting pool, located directly in front of the stage. He emerged thoroughly soaked but just in time to play "Black Mountain Rag" as the encore. "Half the people were horrified and half the people were delighted," said Wayne. "But at least 100 percent of the people were paying attention."[97]

Special Consensus, and especially Iowa fiddler Al Murphy, who was nearly twenty years older than Fulks, expanded his musical vocabulary. Murphy's knowledge of country music ran subterranean and he started exposing Fulks to eclectic artists like Hank Thompson, Bob Black, Skeets McDonald, Carl Butler, and Ira and Charlie Louvin. "He was a great role model for me as far as dedication to the music and also breaking down the wall between country music and bluegrass," Fulks said. They spent overnights together traveling between tour stops, listening to cassette after cassette in Murphy's car. For Fulks, "just quietly listening in the company of a Zen master who is showing you all of these pathways into other, deeper places was a really vivid experience."[98]

That experience helped cultivate Fulks's appreciation of country music from the late 1940s through the early 1960s, a period when the recording industry was smaller, the recordings less technical, the performances more intense, and the performers less averse to risk. The musicianship during that time is also renowned because musicians were forced to be correct, lively, and fast within short recording time slots, as opposed to the limitless possibilities that computers allowed years later. Fulks wrote songs evoking that era, in strong allegiance with British New Wavers like Elvis Costello, Nick Lowe, and Dave Edmunds who found similar inspiration in older music. The same impulse also drove Fulks to host *Secret Country*, an hour-long XM satellite radio show that shed light on country legends from the fringes, like Connie Smith and Jean Shepard. On *13 Hillbilly Giants*, a 2001 album, Fulks covered other outsider songwriters from country music's past, like Hank Cochran, Jimmy Logsdon, and Hillous Butrum, all denied fame for writing some of the genre's strangest and darkest tunes.

For a time, his impulses ran in direct opposition to his daily pursuits as a staff songwriter on Music Row in Nashville. Music Row, a district located southwest of downtown Nashville, is widely considered home to the country music industry because within its perimeters are many of the recording studios, music licensing agencies, record labels, and publishing houses that work in tandem to service the commercial side of the industry. Between 1993 and 1998, Fulks worked for publishing companies in the hope of writing songs for the hitmakers of the day. For the majority of that time he was contracted to Affiliated Publishers, a company run by veteran songwriter Johnny Slate that had hits with singers Tim McGraw and Joe Diffie. Despite some interest, Fulks did not sell a single song. "I was a total failure. I was really dismayed by that," he said.[99]

Dallas Wayne, who co-wrote songs with Fulks during this period, said Fulks was in Nashville at the wrong time. "Nashville loved Robbie Fulks but just didn't know what to do with him. The kind of stuff Robbie wanted to write was at a kind of lull in Nashville. Your Mickey Newburys and Willie Nelsons and Shel Silversteins and Guy Clarks and all those magical writers had all moved on from that scene," he said. "He missed the renaissance of songwriting that would have welcomed him with open arms."[100]

The experience made Fulks even more determined to cut his own record. He came to Bloodshot's attention through "Cigarette State," which the Sundowners had recorded for the label's first compilation. He told Bloodshot he had recorded his own version of that song, among others, with Steve Albini. In a proposal, he asked Bloodshot for $3,000 to record the rest of the songs for what would be a full-length record. The plan, he said, was to make it sound like vintage country except with "lyrics that sounded like a modern, urban person." Also, he added, its tone would run counter to the modern country of that decade, which he found too "message-oriented and relentlessly cheery and moralistic."

To make that kind of statement meant recording the album, *Country Love Songs*, not in Nashville, but in Chicago and in Springfield, Missouri, where he had "access to a lot of great musicians but hardly any specifically country musicians." The choice was "a positive" for the sound he wanted. "I had always loved the idea of mongrelized music. That somebody outside an idiom could bring a fresh feel to it, and fresh ideas," he said.[101] Fulks had also developed a friendship with Steve Albini, a producer who by then was best known for recording underground rock bands, including breakthrough albums by the Pixies and Nirvana. Albini worked quickly and liked to capture performances rather than laboring over endless takes.

Country Love Songs and *South Mouth*, the Fulks albums released by Bloodshot in 1996 and 1997, respectively, represent a barnstorming of ballads, honky-tonk country, waltzes, and sophisticated pop tunes that tell bleak tales of hardship, suicide, and heartbreak. With "The Buck Starts Here," a tribute to the Bakersfield sound of Buck Owens, there is romance in the redemptive power of country music itself. The wry humor in the lyrics stands confidently alongside the wit of Owens, Roger Miller, and Harlan Howard. On "Let's Live Together," a tribute to bad love, Fulks's protagonist makes the argument that "these ain't the cave times / I'm not a hunter-gatherer / or a backwater Baptist / I want your loving / I don't want babies / so let's live together sweetheart." The one cover Fulks includes is apt: Nashville songwriter Tim Carroll's "Every Kind of Music but Country," about a girlfriend who isn't impressed by her partner's music until the night she hears his band.

But mostly, both albums play it straight on songs that, in just under three minutes, reflect efficient and tuneful songcraft. With a steel guitar throughout, "Tears Only Run One Way" is a bouncy shuffle about the inevitability of the blues, and "I Push Right Over," about the inevitability of falling in love; both have the sweetness of Buddy Holly. Other songs, like the vocal duet "Heart, I Wish You Were Here," the stark "I Was Just Leaving," and "Forgotten But Not Gone," are tense with the drama of good storytelling. The two albums not only serve as a commentary on what modern country lacks, but also contribute to the canon of songs, and the spirit, the genre was built upon.

Country Love Songs was Bloodshot's first legitimate country release. Fulks's roots were in country music and bluegrass, not punk rock. But that didn't mean the album was accepted in any of those worlds. Bloodshot's punk-rock audience didn't get it, and traditional bluegrass and country people were turned off by the lyrics. "We were getting flak from both sides," Nan Warshaw said.[102] Nevertheless, Bloodshot saw Fulks as the embodiment of what the label strove to establish: an artist with a singular vision, lyrical wit and depth, and who sounded modern despite playing with traditional idioms. It took time for the album to catch on, but eventually, through word of mouth and underground radio, sales built in its second and third years. Country music media wanted nothing to do with it, so all the praise came from the local press and rock zines. In Rob Miller's view, that showed the extent to which corporate labels had defined the boundaries of country music. "Early on, people like Robbie and Jon [Langford] and Neko [Case] and the Old 97's were not permitted to be considered country artists. So many of the conversations we had early on was who is allowed to be country. I found that to be utterly tedious horseshit," he said.[103]

Even so, recording industry insiders recognized the strength of the material and saw Fulks as a promising star. Six weeks after the release of *Country Love Songs*, Fulks started fielding offers from four major labels: Geffen, DreamWorks, Columbia, and Elektra. "Jesus Christ, the record's out there, it hasn't sold anything, nothing has changed except there's this semi-hysteric pile-up of buzz," he thought.[104] Fulks quit his job teaching guitar at the Old Town School of Folk Music, and in 1997 he signed to Geffen Records, the namesake label of mogul David Geffen and a subsidiary of Seagram's

Universal Music Group. *Let's Kill Saturday Night*, his Geffen debut, was released in September 1998. Produced by Rick Will, who had worked with everyone from AC/DC to Gillian Welch, the album reflected an astonishing versatility: power pop, folk-rock, stadium rock, honky-tonkers, Byrds-style ballads, Celtic-tinged folk, and a lusty harmony duet with Lucinda Williams. Tying them together were big melodic hooks and storytelling, often bleak or morose, that pushed against the often manic energy of the songs. Fulks recorded the album in Nashville, but it became apparent that he had little interest in playing by industry expectations. Before one session, Fulks pulled aside Sam Bush, who played fiddle and mandolin on the record, to tell him, "This one for sure is going to get me on the country radio." "And the song is called 'God Isn't Real,'" Bush said. "That cracked me up."[105]

Earlier that year, Fulks hit the theater circuit, opening shows for the pop band Ben Folds Five. But promoting the album was short-lived. In December, Universal Music Group finalized its $10 billion acquisition of Polygram. As a result, Geffen was collapsed into Interscope, the hip-hop and industrial rock label, two hundred artists were dropped, and three thousand Universal and Polygram employees were fired. For new artists like Fulks who were barely out of the gate, the reorganization was devastating. Fulks lost all financial, administrative, and tactical support, which meant *Let's Kill Saturday Night* was effectively dead. "Secretaries over there [are] giving me the impression that it's like Dresden after the war," he told the *New York Times* that month.[106]

But the situation would give Fulks time to recalibrate. The freedom of not having a label meant he could let his idiosyncrasies fly. For an annual year's-end show at FitzGerald's, he roasted newsmakers and trends from the previous twelve months and performed "Rap of the Dead," a free-flow memorial to the year's fallen, both famous and pitifully obscure. He released *50-Vc. Doberman*, a package of fifty new songs available exclusively as downloads. He built shows around loose concepts such as fusing the songs of Thelonious Monk and the Monkees. He self-funded a 2010 album, *Happy*, a tribute to Michael Jackson that deconstructed the King of Pop's canon into country soul, bluegrass, and power balladry. The songs included "Privacy," now a speed-metal collage featuring Albini's noisy post-punk band Shellac. Every turn was not a casual flight of fancy: Fulks executed each one with rabid attention to detail. By not trying to conform to a single sound, he inevitably attracted a larger audience that valued contradiction, especially within Americana, a genre where tradition tended to trump experimentalism.

Things started to turn around once he slowed his touring and settled into a Monday night residency at the Hideout, a music room in the back of a former factory workers' bar located across from where the city's streets and sanitation department parked the garbage trucks. There, in a room resembling a Wisconsin supper club, between 2009 and 2017, Fulks held court, bringing in different performers to experiment with. He wanted to lower the volume so that he, and his audience, could pay attention to both the songs and the interplay among the musicians. "I want to pick smaller things and then delve deeper into them," he said. Most sessions did not include drums. Their highlights were improvisational exchanges involving Fulks, Brooklyn fiddler Jenny Scheinman, multi-instrumentalists Robbie Gjersoe and Chris Scruggs, singer Nora O'Connor, Chicago mandolinist Don Stiernberg, and Redd Volkaert, the former lead guitarist with Merle Haggard. Much of the reason for the new direction was burnout: Fulks was starting to feel the ache of fifteen years of being on the road. "It was starting to be like *Groundhog Day*, singing in the same clubs and going out with the same guys," he said. He briefly considered leaving music entirely, but the new setting—and playing acoustically with different ensembles of players—offered renewal. "I was interested in music again. I just had to change some of the procedural details to really still do it with passion and love," he said.

The music deepened as a result. A series of albums—*Couples in Trouble* (2001), *Georgia Hard* (2005), *Gone Away Backward* (2013), and *Upland Stories* (2016)—represent the evolution of his second act. The albums are less commentaries on country music itself than they are a deepening of its storytelling traditions. Their songs feature characters caught in private moments, as if the listener is eavesdropping from the other side of the door. With no grand resolutions or comic payoffs, just explorations into the psychological realities of everyday people, they hark back to the earliest folk traditions.

The new direction was possible because Fulks opened himself up more as a writer. Up to that point, he said, he had "avoided depth and wisdom for a long time." "There are all these great songwriters like Ira Louvin or Buck Owens who don't have deep songs. They skid along with a happy, shiny surface and avoid a certain type of poetry. I love that kind of song. But for a long time I was senselessly skirting a lot of areas I had strengths in. I love words and I love books and I love ideas and a lot of that didn't come into play with the music I was doing in the '90s."[107]

On *Couples in Trouble*, his first album of the new century, the songs are in the voices of distinctly different characters. On "Real Money," the album's standout track, there is a sinister undercurrent of kidnapping, young lust, and violence atop a sly soul groove. *Georgia Hard* and *Gone Away Backward* evoke singer-songwriter country records from the prime era of the 1960s and 1970s. "Georgia Hard," in particular, follows a familiar theme: the homesickness of the Southern transplant in Chicago. Working in a mailroom and living in an apartment facing an alley, the song's protagonist could be living in Uptown. "There's no Carolina moon over Chicago / no bluegrass growing out in my backyard / no fields of sugarcane / no soft Virginia rain / but damned if this livin' ain't Georgia hard," he sings. By the song's end, he's on the phone calling home hustling for work on a pecan farm.[108]

Upland Stories borrows images from short story masters Anton Chekhov and Flannery O'Connor. With three songs inspired by James Agee's Great Depression opus, *Let Us Now Praise Famous Men*, the album takes the rural route into marginalized America, where standing still and breaking away are at odds. In other hands that theme might sound bleak, but the album is lively, a direct result of the small ensemble of players who gathered at Electrical Audio, Albini's studio, and learned their way inside the songs by playing them together on the spot. The sound of *Upland Stories* is quiet, tender, and mysterious, but at times also harsh and ominous. "America Is a Hard Religion" could be a field recording of an apocalyptic-minded preacher, with Fulks, accompanied by banjo, firing off dire proclamations ("Paid by thanks nor praise, yet we soldier on / Trials to test our hearts, doubts to make us strong") just before a fiddle swoops in to dance. Storytelling is the heart of country music, but here the narratives are circular. In "A Miracle," a Tennessee boy finds himself out of his element, in a train running along the Hudson River, until he recognizes "the pines, poplars, and the hickories" from back home. The music is warm but grows eerier from deeper recognition that "the land at his feet is steeped in wild blood."[109]

If Fulks's second act emerged from abandoning the need for industry approval, he coincidentally got some: he received his first Grammy nominations—for Best Folk Album and Best American Roots Song—for *Upland Stories* in 2017. They show that staking a claim on country music's map, instead of waiting for an invitation, is not just a possibility but can also be a career.

THE OLD, WEIRD CHICAGO

By the time Lounge Ax closed its doors, a new club had emerged to take its place. The Hideout was originally a shanty constructed by Irish factory workers for housing in 1865 and was later moved across the street to 1354 West Wabansia in 1881. The first floor, built shotgun style, was first a boarding house and, after Prohibition, a bar called the Hideout Inn, serving factory workers along the North Branch of the Chicago River. In 1996, it was turned into a music club by new owners: brothers Mike and Jim Hinchsliff, their childhood friend Tim Tuten, and Tuten's wife, Katie, whose father had been a regular at the Inn decades earlier. From the start, the club focused on alternative country, but with the demise of Lounge Ax, the bookings expanded to include experimental jazz, country blues, and indie rock. Musicians became the primary workforce, both onstage and off, including Neko Case, who took bartending shifts. Chicago soul great Mavis Staples recorded a live album there, and a chance meeting between Staples and Wilco's Jeff Tweedy in the club's upstairs room led to Tweedy producing her next three records.[1]

Along with Schubas and FitzGerald's, the Hideout served as an important incubator where musicians could informally network, strike up collaborations, and experiment with new ideas on the stage. All three clubs were vital in the development of Chicago artists like singer-songwriter Andrew Bird, a violin prodigy from suburban Lake Bluff who tried out every one of his new band projects

at the Hideout, including his first, the swing-jazz ensemble Bowl of
Fire. Psych-folk songwriter Edith Frost, country-soul songwriter
and bandleader Steve Dawson, Southern soul singer Kelly Hogan,
singer-songwriter Chris Mills, and country singer Anna Fermin and
her band Trigger Gospel, among others, circulated through these
stages as they developed new work.

One of the first signs that the underground scene had bubbled
to the top came in late 2002, when Billy Corgan, having recently
disbanded the Smashing Pumpkins—the most successful rock
band Chicago would produce—decided to host a ten-week Monday
night residency at the Hideout. The shows started after midnight
when Corgan, walking onstage to a crowd of fewer than a hundred
people, played new songs and covers; introduced jugglers, poets,
and comedians; and brought Hideout regulars like Freakwater,
Neko Case, and Kelly Hogan onstage sing with him.[2] The following
year, he revealed what he had been working on: a series of original
folk songs all focused on Chicago lore. Among their subjects were
the 1893 World's Columbian Exposition, the Black Sox scandal, the
state's prairie landscape, White City, a park on the South Side from
the early 1900s, and Bobby Franks, the kidnapped teenager mur-
dered by Leopold and Loeb in 1924. In 2004, Corgan performed at
Metro on a theater set designed to look like a living room, complete
with floor lamps, an easy chair, a side table, a birdcage, and stars
twinkling in the background. There were moments of stunning
intimacy, particularly "Riverview," a creeping nocturnal blues song
that imagined the long-forgotten North Side amusement park as a
spooky late-night meeting spot.[3]

The resurgence of interest in vintage Americana was fed, in part,
by a stream of major CD reissue campaigns in the 1990s and early
2000s that exposed a mass audience to lost or forgotten sounds from
more than a half century earlier. The decade started with *Robert
Johnson: The Complete Recordings*, a thorough reexamination of
the Delta blues guitarist that thrust his name back into the limelight in 1990. It was followed by other seminal collections such as
the *Anthology of American Folk Music* (1997), a Smithsonian reis-

sue of Harry Smith's 1952 compilation of country, folk, and blues recorded between 1926 and 1933; *Country Blues: Complete Early Recordings (1927–29)* (1997), a definitive collection of Dock Boggs's music on guitarist John Fahey's Revenant label; *The Asch Recordings*, a Smithsonian collection of 105 of Woody Guthrie's best-known original and traditional songs recorded between 1944 and 1945; *The Complete Hank Williams* (1998), a Grammy-winning ten-disc collection containing every recording of the famed singer and songwriter between 1947 and 1953; *In the Shadow of Clinch Mountain* (2000), which contained every recording of the Carter Family; *Screamin' and Hollerin' the Blues: The Worlds of Charley Patton* (2001), also on Revenant, a seven-disc set of remastered recordings of the blues singer plus interviews with his contemporaries; and *Goodbye, Babylon* (2003), a collection of White and Black gospel from the mid-1920s to the mid-1950s. All these sets, and others, received national media attention, made the music readily accessible to a new generation, and served as source material for musicians seeking inspiration.

Country and folk stars from earlier eras also got a second look through collaborations with younger musicians. In addition to Rick Rubin's reengineering of Johnny Cash's career in his later years, these included albums that paired Ralph Stanley with Jim Lauderdale, Porter Wagoner with Marty Stuart, and Loretta Lynn with Jack White. Woody Guthrie was the focus of *Mermaid Avenue*, a three-volume series of albums by Wilco and British singer-songwriter Billy Bragg, who together wrote music to newly unearthed and unused Guthrie lyrics. The project successfully recast Guthrie not as the familiar troubadour of the labor movement, but as a playful poet whose repertoire of romantic love ballads and nonsense songs sounded contemporary.

All this vintage music served as a refuge from transformations in digital technology that were allowing contemporary artists to indulge more in studio artifice. Just as Wilco and Bragg introduced Guthrie as a contemporary man in all his fleshy glory, the reissues presented real people, unadorned before the microphone, with no tricks performed behind the studio glass to smooth the crevices caused by fingers or tongues. Yet the recordings themselves felt incomplete, not just because of the antiquated sound production, but because the people themselves left so little behind for biographers—in contrast to the present day, when no detail of any public figure's life is left unexposed. Instead, these recordings served the listener as open doors to open spaces, with plenty of room inside to sit and look around. In his 1997 book *Invisible Republic*, critic Greil Marcus called these songs a reflection of "the old, weird America" brimming under the surface of commercial culture.[4] Although he was comparing the songs that surfaced in the folk revival with the heft of new ones Bob Dylan and The Band made in upstate New York in 1967, the description was readily applied in the 1990s to describe anything analog, obscure, and raw.

The mystery seared into the songs of Dock Boggs, Furry Lewis, Richard "Rabbit" Brown, Uncle Dave Macon, the Carter Family, and Charlie Poole gave other musicians room to make their own contributions, to join a community of voices they had never met or known, but with whom they shared a fascination. In Chicago, bands like Freakwater and Souled American were among the earliest to experiment with the old and weird songs of murder and lost love. As the 1990s wore on, other bands on the scene burnished their credentials as country rockers, but only a few—the Handsome Family, Califone, and the Blacks among them—detoured to follow the path in the forest that led back to those vintage recordings. In ways indistinguishable from one another, they articulated the tenets of country and folk music in surrealist terms, but remained bound to core truths that any of those artists in the black-and-white photos would recognize.

THE POSTMODERN FOLK MUSIC
OF THE HANDSOME FAMILY

When Rennie Sparks and her husband Brett lived in Chicago, their home was a third-floor loft space in Wicker Park, long before the neighborhood gentrified and became lined with condo high-rises and boutiques. At night, through their wall of windows facing Milwaukee Avenue, Rennie could observe all manner of nightlife: scurrying rats, the alley underneath the L tracks, a dimly lit corner that pointed to a dark side street, and, if you craned your neck and looked southeast, the downtown skyline. The concrete jungle that produced the boom of industrial rock bands playing down the street evoked a different kind of habitat for the lyric writer.

"I was always thinking about dense forests while in Chicago," she said. "So I built a forest in my head and started populating it with stories."[5]

Underneath the pavement of this world lives the wilder world of the Handsome Family: the couple emerged from the Lounge Ax scene as surrealists who filtered Appalachian ballads, country spirituals, and acoustic blues traditions through their own postmodern lens using electronic distortion and beats and lyrical details from the present day.

The couple met in a New York City bar and relocated to Ann Arbor, Michigan, where Rennie, who grew up on Long Island, earned her master's degree in creative writing. Chicago was the next stop; what they found was a city that "was so Nelson Algren—gray and hulking and grotesque," Brett said. For Rennie, Chicago in the early 1990s "was kind of like being in a black-and-white movie."[6] In other words, perfect. They had no awareness of the city's growing alternative country scene until they arrived. Within a year, they were invited to appear on *For a Life of Sin*, Bloodshot Records' inaugural compilation.

Jon Langford became an early advocate for the duo, opening doors for them until eventually the Handsome Family found a drummer and landed on local label Carrot Top. Their early sound was closer to the dissonance of rock's outer limits at the time, but by *Through the Trees*, their third album, a sound had formed: Rennie played keyboards and bass and adopted the autoharp—the harp-like instrument of Maybelle Carter—while Brett strummed banjo and guitar. The minimal setup served the songs—tragicomic stories of insanity, despair, and murder told with needle-perfect detail in the lyrics. The couple's working relationship was technically simple—lyrics, her; music, him. But when together, their dynamic became so natural that it was impossible to separate one from the other. Rennie explained that the mystery of her lyrics is never revealed, even to herself, until she hears how Brett, a baritone, phrases each line. "It surprises me," she said. "He brings things out in the song that didn't even occur to me." To Brett, who grew up singing in a Baptist church and tried opera for a few years while studying music at the University of New Mexico, singing is about trying "to paint every word," even though he might not know how those words connect together. "The best songs I've written with her are lyrics I feel most ambiguous about," he said. "It's actually really liberating. They could be nonsense syllables."[7]

That ambiguity, which invites the listener to participate in the duo's imagination, is key to their music, giving honeyed undertones to images that may appear disconnected until the music reveals their thread. Forests, logs, moats, spiders, and woodland creatures populate the lyrics. Brett's sturdy voice is part preacher, part Johnny Cash, with a twang native to Odessa, Texas, his hometown. On "Weightless Again," the protagonist stops for coffee in the Redwoods, where there are "giant dripping leaves, spoons of powdered cream" and, in the forest, a sense of the final days of Native American tribes: "Most died of TB, the rest went insane." His partner tells him she felt like she was floating the first time they had sex. The remark, no matter how lovely its intent, makes him think of this country's lineage of despair, from "those poor lost Indians" to people who "OD on pills and jump from the Golden Gate Bridge. . . . Anything to feel weightless again."

The duo's adopted hometown, long a source for pulp fiction writers, gave them natural source material. On "The Woman Downstairs," a tuba puffs out the beat, sticks rattle, and a banjo strums. As a portrait of summer in the city, the song has it all: rats on the fire escape, old men sucking down boiled eggs in corner bars, a lonely neighbor dead in her apartment, and thoughts of suicide by L train. "Lake Michigan rose and fell like a bird," Brett sings. "The wind screamed up Ashland Avenue."

The success of *Through the Trees* allowed the couple to quit their jobs and tour for long stretches of time. Unexpectedly, they discovered loyal audiences in Europe, where they established a touring schedule that sent them there for several months every year. "Americans focus more on the morbidity" of their songs, Brett said. "In Ireland, they just think it's a reflection of everyday life." In 2014, the couple's profile was raised further when their song "Far From Any Road" became the opening theme for *True Detective*, a hit HBO series, and Andrew Bird chose to dedicate an entire tribute album to their songs. He stated his goal was "that people would look at these songs as being up there with the best of Townes Van Zandt or Leonard Cohen."[8]

A touchstone for the duo is Dock Boggs, the banjoist from southern Appalachia who made his first records in Chicago in September 1929 for Lonesome Ace Records. The stock market crash the next month drove the label out of business, and the sides weren't heard widely until Revenant reissued them on CD in 1997. Boggs, a coal miner for most of his life, is known for his powerful singing and interpretations of dark fare like "Pretty Polly" and "Lost Love Blues," which achieve serenity despite the supernatural doom of the lyrics.

The Handsome Family are steeped in that tradition. Their finest moment is "Giant of Illinois," influenced by the story of Robert Pershing Wadlow of Alton, Illinois, who earned that title because of his height of nearly nine feet. Born in 1918, Wadlow lived only twenty-two years. In his later life he signed a contract with Ringling Bros. and earned worldwide fame by appearing in the circus's center ring at Madison Square Garden and other venues. Eventually, he became a spokesman for a shoe company in exchange for free shoes, which otherwise cost him $100 a pair. An awkwardly fitted leg brace led to his demise when a blister caused a deadly infection that spread.[9]

In the Handsome Family's telling, the giant befriends "a boy with a club foot" who walks with him in the woods. The two boys spot a creature weaker than they—a swan sleeping in a stream—and they kill it with rocks. The violence is unsettling and, lying on the grass afterward, the giant looks to the sky for redemption. "Delirious with pain" as his shoe fills with blood, he feels his body "soaring up through fallen snow."

"The sky was a woman's arms," Brett sings tenderly, harmonizing with Wilco's Jeff Tweedy. "The sky was a woman's arms."

THE COUNTRY DREAMSCAPES OF CALIFONE, JIM BECKER, AND DIANE IZZO

As the leader of Red Red Meat, Tim Rutili had had his slice of Chicago's rock explosion in the 1990s. He had toured with the Smashing Pumpkins, recorded three albums for influential indie label Sub Pop, and seen the world. "We got sick of it," he said.[10] It was time to do something quieter.

Califone, named after a brand of schoolroom turntable, evolved as a solo project until his former bandmates joined in to help shape a sound from their current influences: trip-hop pioneer Tricky, rapper-producer J Dilla, and early country music pioneers the Carter Family and Dock Boggs. Rutili heard a connection between artists born at opposite ends of the recording technology spectrum. "There's something loose and human with what those guys can do with machines that really, really goes with what Dock Boggs can do with this weird, angry banjo," he said. With studio computers now making it easier to create loops and electronic beats, "making collages" was possible.[11] Rutili would take those capabilities further than any of his contemporaries in taking early Appalachian melodies and incorporating them with modern elements like feedback, electronics, and unorthodox instruments.

Rutili already knew about country music despite growing up in the suburbs on a steady diet of classic rock. Born August 3, 1966, in Addison, west of Chicago, he escaped into the city as a teenager to attend Monday open mics at the Townhall Pub, a Halsted Avenue bar where he met "stragglers from the Lincoln Avenue scene" who were three times his age. They bought drinks for him and his friends, taught him John Prine and Steve Goodman chestnuts and how to harmonize, and occasionally invited him home to their tiny apartments nearby to comb through their record collections. Robert Johnson, Charlie Patton, Mississippi John Hurt, the names were all new. "It stayed with me," he said. A few years later, he spent long nights at the Bar R-R Ranch to listen to the Sundowners play. "They weren't afraid," he said of the three musicians. "I couldn't talk with them. I was afraid to talk with anybody who could play like that."[12]

Red Red Meat developed from the rock scenes at the Empty Bottle and Lounge Ax, but behind the scenes the musicians he met were delving into music they weren't necessarily playing themselves. He formed a friendship with James Iha, the Smashing Pumpkins guitarist, who lent him tapes of Hank Williams and Jimmie Rodgers. "He knew all about that stuff," Rutili said.[13] By the time of Califone's second album, the Harry Smith anthology had just been reissued by the Smithsonian, and Rutili wanted to get deeper inside the haunting folk music he was listening to, but he didn't know anyone who could play that music without making it sound overly precious or historical—that is, until he got to know Jim Becker.

Burly, bearded, and with a husk of a voice, Becker could have easily risen from swampland fog, but the landscape he knew was unincorporated Melrose Park, a factory town near Chicago known for its numerous Italian beef stands and mafia lieutenants. Becker, born July 14, 1965, was the son of a factory worker whose neighbors, all workers at the same punch press, were mostly Southerners who listened to the country music they brought with them to Chicago. Becker's future at the same punch press, where he worked summers, seemed cast in stone, but the sound of acoustic guitars on Rolling Stones and Led Zeppelin albums was enough to inspire him to buy one of his own when he turned ten. Over the next few years, he discovered Chet Atkins, Django Reinhardt, Bill Monroe, and the Carter Family. Moving into the city in 1986 was the next step. He rounded out the decade learning the banjo, fiddle, and mandolin and traveling to old-time music festivals in the South.[14]

Becker became so proficient that he stayed at the Old Town School for eighteen years, teaching classes and, in the meantime, becoming a conduit between the folk world there that treated the music with reverence and the indie-rock world that sought to use it as inspiration. His old-time band, the Paulina Hollers, rotated Old Town School players through its roster; it played rock clubs on bills with Neko Case, Freakwater, Andrew Bird, and the Handsome Family. Rutili was a fan. The two musicians did a tour of Europe as a duo to get comfortable with each other; when they returned, Becker joined Califone to help push it in a new direction. Attracted to his new bandmate's ability to "play Black Sabbath and then know these crazy Appalachian old-time songs on the banjo and fiddle," Rutili admitted that Becker "had a lot to do with Califone getting more real."[15]

In establishing a more static group of players—Becker on banjo, guitar, and fiddle; Ben Massarella on percussion; and Joe Adamik on drums—Califone achieved a sound that is futuristic and heavy on the groove, but tuned to the past. *Heron King Blues*, released in 2004 on Chicago's Thrill Jockey label, is a sensory mix of funk guitars, loops, squawks, and percussion, as well as the textures of banjo and other folk instruments. In 2006, the band followed it up with *Roots and Crowns*, a more accessible collection of tunes that, minimally arranged, draw from elements like fiddle, banjo, and Cajun accordion that seamlessly integrate with loops, feedback, African polyrhythms, horns, field recordings, and other modern accoutrements. The music is not a straightforward revival of its influences; instead, the mixture of organic and synthesized is warm, inviting, but eerie. It is the reinvention of the dirty but sweet, raw but pretty textures of those Smithsonian recordings that Rutili and Becker shared an obsession for. "The world those songs inhabit is beautiful and scary," Rutili said. "Not in the way people think scary is now. The scariest rap guy who's rapping about killing people is not as scary as Dock Boggs singing about the rent."[16]

In addition to his work with Califone, Becker became an in-demand sideman, touring the world with Iron & Wine, and became known as a restless improviser with a natural gift for establishing mesmerizing moods. "I like raw," he said of his approach. "Pick up a guitar and right away hit a string. There's an aggressiveness to it. It comes from being fucked over so many times in life, like everybody else. It's channeling all that anger, exorcising the demons in a peaceful way."[17]

One of Becker's collaborators was Diane Izzo. She recorded just one album and slugged it out as an unknown for many years, but the impression she made reverberated throughout the Chicago scene. Born May 13, 1967, Izzo grew up in River Forest and didn't start writing songs until she was in her early twenties, when she handed out cassettes of her music to friends. She developed a command of language, using it to communicate multiple meanings; that, combined with a husky voice, led to comparisons with Patti Smith. "She could bend a lyric when she sang in a way that brought out the physical and the inexplicable feeling that can only be expressed with music. I haven't heard many people that can do that. That feeling poured out of her," said Rutili.[18]

Early on, Izzo found a home with Chicago's storefront theater scene. She regularly played the Lunar Cabaret, home to the Curious Theater Branch, the city's leading experimental theater company, which regularly incorporated musical performances. She met Becker there, and from that moment, he considered her a muse. "Her voice was beautiful, she was mesmerizing onstage," he said. She also had the wicked humor of a homegrown Chicagoan. Her songs, however, "were just dark."[19]

Becker built the foundation of *One*, Izzo's 1999 album, using banjo, mandolin, organ, and guitar. They recorded with producer Brad Wood, best known for producing Liz Phair's first three albums and others by Red Red Meat, Veruca Salt, the Jesus Lizard, and the Smashing Pumpkins. Wood got to know Izzo over a series of coffee shop meetings and said he considered Izzo and Phair "practically equals" because they both excelled at writing lyrics. "I fell in love with Liz's lyrics and Diane was right up there," he said. "It was amazing to work with two such talented women writers in the same city." His approach to recording *One* was identical to the one he chose for *Exile in Guyville*, Phair's 1993 breakthrough album: record Izzo's guitar and voice together and later layer in instruments and loops. At that point in their careers, both women were most comfortable recording by themselves at home and had never played in a band setting. "The idea was to have that kernel of her, so if you muted all the other instruments, you would still have her guitar and voice," he said.[20]

Wood's experience guiding some of Chicago's most successful rock bands was put to good use on more traditional songs like "Wicked Spell," with its churning rock guitars and Izzo's singing spun between a whisper and a wail. The unsettling sound perfectly fit its subject: "If you were to say is there some sort of theme, or narrative that runs through that song, it would be mental illness," Izzo said. "That's something that I've had to, in the realm of my life, deal with [concerning] different people. I think it's a song that people take as a rock song and I feel kind of funny playing it because I don't know if anyone is listening [to the words]."[21]

What was transfixing about Izzo is what the best country singers share: the ability to bring characters to life with convincing ease through a voice that makes every syllable, every tick, every yodel, build the story. The winding verses of "Horse of Diana," which concludes *One*, flow for nearly six minutes without losing momentum. One of her finest moments is her cover of "O Death," the Appalachian traditional song recorded with the Pine Valley Cosmonauts. Backed by John Rice on banjo, she begins the song as a summoning of the reaper, then moves into a conversation with him, her voice trembling as if trapped in a trance. There is no escaping, she tells us, only the regret, the most terrible betrayal, of giving in.

It was something she came to know well. Twelve years after she played a triumphant release show at Metro, supported by Andrew Bird and Jon Langford; after touring with kindred spirits Mercury Rev and Sparklehorse; after moving to Taos, New Mexico; after being diagnosed with a cancerous brain tumor; after surgery, after radiation, and after chemotherapy, Izzo died in February 2011 of cancer that had spread to her spine. Her husband, the multimedia artist Marcos Zas, organized a memorial concert at the Hideout months later that featured Califone, Souled American, and Becker. Years before her death, Izzo had recorded at least two albums' worth of music with members of Califone and Wilco, and Zas had pledged to use the funds raised by the concert to bring them to the public. But then, in late 2015, he died of kidney failure. The music survives only on a hard drive Zas mailed to Wood.

"Diane had a lot more music in her," Wood said. "She was a force of nature. And it just seemed really unfair."[22]

THE BLACKS:
PUTTING GLAM INTO COUNTRY

One night in 1995, Dan McDonough went with his brother to Lounge Ax to see a band, but instead he met the next chapter of his life. Gina Black, a DePaul University freshman classical music student, told him she played upright acoustic bass. "And that was exactly what I was looking for," he said.[23] Within weeks of meeting McDonough, Black dropped out of school to form a band with him. Years of playing bass in an orchestra "was pretty frustrating," she admitted. "I was determined to be heard."[24]

McDonough had already grown tired of playing in conventional rock bands and, having discovered Hank Williams, envisioned creating a band that emulated Williams's doom-laden storytelling, but with the volume of AC/DC, the group harmonies of the Mills Brothers, and in the cabaret style of Tom Waits. The sound remained parked in his head as he spent more than a year trying out drummers. Then, in September 2017, he met James Emmenegger, a rock drummer with swagger in his body and a natural ability to play behind the beat. A few months later came Nora O'Connor, a rhythm guitarist and singer who McDonough considered a "human overdub" for her shining harmonies.[25]

The group clicked. Several labels scouted the Black Family within their first year, but the band wanted Bloodshot, not just for its established name, but because they felt they fit well with the raw country sound the label championed. Two weeks before Bloodshot released *Dolly Horrorshow* in September 1998, the Irish group the Black Family contacted the label to say it claimed the name. So, in a late-hour fix, McDonough trimmed it to the Blacks. He had already adopted the stage name Danny Black.

Years before, McDonough had removed himself from West

Lawn, a Southwest Side neighborhood near Midway Airport dominated by city workers like his parents, who were both Chicago police
officers. "Music was a way to escape it," he said. He started traveling to the North Side to catch shows at Metro or Lounge Ax, and
when he turned nineteen he moved there permanently. At the time,
McDonough was writing songs privately outside the cover bands he
played with. He didn't start singing until he turned twenty-four.
By then he had taught himself banjo and trumpet, was listening to
krautrock bands like Faust, and became immersed in Tom Waits
and Hank Williams. The Blacks became the band to tie all those
strings together. In doing so, they created a sound that was like no
other band in Chicago.[26]

The Blacks capitalized on the queasy tension between
McDonough and Black, by then a couple. On many songs, their
call-and-response vocals are scorching, as on "Horrorshow,"
which becomes unhinged via Black's witchy shrieks, or "Head on
a String," where she sounds like she's calling from deep inside a
well. The band's unshackled sound makes those switches in tone
sound natural, but it also presents the music in the realm of early
field recordings or an imagined juke joint somewhere beside the
Illinois Central tracks. Their boozy cover of Bill Monroe's "I'll Meet
You in Church Sunday Morning" teeters back to midnight on Saturday with its stomping waltz beat and fuzztone guitar. McDonough's
vocals are romantic but restrained: he's delivering the song like the
news without a hint of self-pity or pathos. Black's bass bow, which
leads many instrumental breaks, deepens the sense of eeriness, as
on "Dear Little Girl," the traditional murder ballad that McDonough
sings as a sweet love song.

The Blacks show their authority in howling blues and White
gospel throughout their limited output (two albums and an EP),
but their music is most directly connected to early country and its
songs of lost hope and weird visions. Their song "New New Waltzing
Blues" channels Hank Williams's visions of doom, but is lined with
a funeral trumpet. "Crazy" is sung from the perspective of someone with the title affliction. "A thousand of devils are screaming

at me," Black sings before imitating what she hears: a chorus of yodeling. Connecting "Foggy Minded Breakdown" with the blue-grass instrumental "Foggy Mountain Breakdown" is McDonough's clucking banjo as Black pushes her bow deeper down the strings. It's a jail song of madness sung by someone looking back at his mis-deeds and then forward because "that old-time religion calls." The trumpet that groans between verses strains to make the song sound comedic, but with few laughs.

Unlike other bands, the Blacks didn't wear their street clothes onstage or raid western wear stores for cowboy shirts and boots. Instead, they chose wigs, sparkly dresses, and for McDonough, a white preacher's suit. The thrift store look was initially "to mask being scared shitless," but it was effective in unintentionally plac-ing the music in no time period whatsoever. In their short time together, the Blacks had successfully shaken the museum dust from their influences and made them live in the present day.[27]

But as quickly as the band hit their stride, it was over. Alcohol and more had heightened the tension between Black and McDonough that originally fed the music. Emmenegger moved to Los Angeles. A short-lived reunion came and went in 2007. Despite packed shows for his band and a standing deal with Bloodshot, Danny Black even-tually started working solo on the storytelling circuit. Then, a few weeks before Christmas in late 2019, he and O'Connor appeared at the Montrose Saloon, a cozy corner bar. They played new songs, and some old ones, like the traditional murder ballad "Down in the Willow Garden" and the Blacks' own "Foggy Minded Breakdown." No costumes, no drums, just harmonies and two acoustic guitars. The hushed crowd had heard some of this before. But now, the old and the new sounded cut from the same root.

A NEW CENTURY, A NEW CULTURAL MOVEMENT

Time in the music business ran in a straight line in the first cen-tury of its existence. As one trend appeared, flourished, and died, another trend rose from its remains and was modernized, whatever that meant in that particular moment. Louis Armstrong, Bill Monroe, Miles Davis, Grandmaster Flash, Kurt Cobain—these benchmark figures, among others, became easier to recognize and laud as the century wore on because the music traveled forward and not in reverse.

The emergence of file sharing in the late 1990s, and of streaming media in the new century, changed that pattern forever. Evolution now ran sideways, backward, up, and down, but hardly forward. The new media gave audiences access to any voice, instrument, or genre they wanted to hear with a single click. Now, what was old and buried for one generation could easily become new to the next. Time periods blended, and the prejudice against discarded trends became irrelevant.

For Chicago's country and folk scenes, the new century brought an overlapping of eras in various ways. The Sundowners, all dead by 2011, were renewed in spirit at the Hideout, which honored the influential trio not only at a 2004 tribute night when Bloodshot Records released a collection of their recordings, but when John Rice, the band's archivist, donated several tables to the Hideout from the Bar R-R Ranch, their tops etched with names and dates by the knives of Ranch goers decades ago.

Awareness of the WLS *Barn Dance* grew as well, partly due to surviving musicians like violinist Johnny Frigo, who played in the postwar years of the show, and partly due to Jon Langford's enthusiastic rebranding of the show as a forgotten history deserving of attention. In 2004, he and sculptor Rob Lentz opened an art show—"The Rise & Fall of the National Barn Dance"—at the Chicago Cultural Center, which featured portraits, dioramas, and installation work dedicated to the show's stars. That same year, Langford's side project, the Pine Valley Cosmonauts, featuring Frigo, released a full-length album (*Barn Dance Favorites*, on Bloodshot) of hits associated with the show. In 2020, Special Consensus honored its forty-fifth year by releasing its own WLS *Barn Dance* tribute: *Chicago Barn Dance* was loaded with special guests, including Robbie Fulks, who sang "East Chicago Blues," an original telling of Bill Monroe's oil refinery days across the Indiana border. The title song is a primer on the broadcast, complete with the sound of square dancers raising a ruckus on the outro. Other musicians explored *Barn Dance* lore as well. One duo, the Girls of the Golden West, resurrected the name of the former sister group with legitimacy: Marydee Reynolds, who had previously recorded with industrial rock groups Pigface and Die Warzau, happened to be the great-niece of original Golden West sister Millie Good.

Musicians who played the club scene in the 1990s were now earning Grammy recognition and other accolades. The theater and festival circuits opened up to them, as did late-night television. Thanks to the reach of online media, mainstream outlets, ranging from the *New York Times* to *Pitchfork* to NPR, started paying attention. Wilco, Neko Case, Andrew Bird, Robbie Fulks, Ryan Adams, and the Handsome Family, among others, became legacy artists with staying power far outside the boundaries of Chicago.

At home was a growing stable of bands like the Hoyle Brothers, the Cairo Gang, Wild Earp, and the Henhouse Prowlers that spanned the spectrum of bluegrass and country music. By the 2010s, a barn dance revival was also under way, driven mostly by an "old-time square-and-contra-dance community of younger people," said Al Scorch, a member of Old Lazarus' Harp, a collective of string-band players who have organized annual events like Midwest Sing & Stomp and the Maypole Folk Festival at bars like the Hideout, the Inner Town Pub, and the Beat Kitchen. The scene, Scorch said, was a reaction against folk music purists. "People are definitely tired of the non-inclusive, 'folk music is a religion and if you don't follow the tenets of it you should be expelled and excommunicated' [attitude]," he said.[28] Another collective, the Golden Horse Ranch Band, formed to host an annual all-night square dance called the Barn Dance Apocalypse; by 2019, its fifteenth year, the event had moved to Thalia Hall, a theater in Pilsen with a capacity of about fifteen hundred people.

The Old Town School of Folk Music was also on the move. The school expanded north from its Armitage Avenue location to Lin-

coln Square in 1997. Executive director Jim Hirsch, who took over
in 1982, spearheaded the expansion. His vision of the school was
to make it reflect the changing demographics of Chicago. "Within
my first year, it occurred to me we had to rebrand this organization
so the tent could be made much, much bigger," he said.[29] Programming included more ethnic dance and music from all around the
world, such as flamenco, Senegalese drumming, and jazz singing,
all taught by preeminent musicians in the city.

The city sold the school the new facility, a 40,000-square-foot
1929 Art Deco public library building at 4544 North Lincoln, for
one dollar, but it took $10 million to turn the stacks into a 425-
seat auditorium. Joni Mitchell performed on opening night. Nine
years later, in 2006, the school purchased a bakery across the
street for $2 million, razed it, and in 2011 broke ground on a third,
27,000-square-foot facility. In this new phase, the school once again
became a nucleus for an emerging generation of singer-songwriters
and performers. One familiar face in the classroom was Ed Holstein, who returned to the school after decades to teach guitar and
songs plumbed from the 1970s folk scene in Chicago.

This was Win Stracke's vision: his imagined utopia where ordinary people met outside the demands of their lives' routines to
make music together, in one spot, for no reason but to strengthen
a connection otherwise unattainable amid the noise from the other
side of the door. The longevity of the Old Town School, the longest-
running institution of its kind in the United States, made it a vehicle for country and folk music in Chicago as the music grew and
transformed over decades and through generations.

No single night illustrated that better than December 1, 2007.
It was a three-hour evening at the Auditorium Theatre, the crown
jewel of downtown Chicago designed by architects Dankmar Adler
and Louis Sullivan. The Auditorium had hosted every significant
world-class city arts institution since 1889: the Chicago Symphony
Orchestra, the Chicago Civic Opera, the Joffrey Ballet, and other
hometown groups from the Impressions featuring Curtis Mayfield

to Wilco. Theodore Roosevelt, Franklin D. Roosevelt, and Booker T. Washington all spoke, John Philip Sousa conducted his band, and Pete Townshend spun windmills across his guitar with the Who on its stage. It was an audacious choice by the Old Town School of Folk Music for its fiftieth anniversary celebration. The evening, however, was a primer on what might be considered indigenous Chicago music. Setting it in a physical testament to Chicago design and engineering just seemed right.

The night had a theme, observed Jeff Tweedy: "continuum."

"I'm really glad Frank [Hamilton] taught Roger McGuinn the guitar because I wouldn't be here," he said from the stage.[30] Indeed, Hamilton, the school's last surviving co-founder, who taught the school's first lesson on November 29, 1957, stood onstage with McGuinn, his former protégé and later auteur of the Byrds. Holding his twelve-string guitar, McGuinn took in the moment before both men performed. "I was sitting down just 50 years ago and you were teaching me how to play this thing," he told his former mentor.[31] They embraced afterward, and the four thousand people in the seats could see how far that continuum stretched, not just into the 1960s but to the present moment.

The audience watched the Stetson-topped Lonnie Brooks playing electric blues, and Bonnie Koloc, accompanied by guitarist David Bromberg, who shrunk the stage to the size of the Earl of Old Town. Then it morphed into the Hideout when Robbie Fulks, Sally Timms, Kelly Hogan, and Jon Langford—dubbed the Bloodshot Family Band—covered songs by Alejandro Escovedo, their labelmate, and the Carter Family. Woody Guthrie entered the room via Sones de Mexico, a nine-member group that performed "This Land Is Your Land," in Spanish first and then in English so the crowd could join the hootenanny.

The night was coming to an end. Tweedy, alone with his guitar, walked out. He brought back Guthrie through "Remember the Mountain Bed" and the ghost of Hank Williams through "Acuff-Rose." But it was a song of his own that articulated why everyone was there in the first place. Around the microphone with him were five Old Town School students currently learning Wilco songs. Together they sang:

> *If you feel like singing a song*
> *And you want other people to sing along*
> *Just sing what you feel*
> *Don't let anyone say it's wrong*

Win Stracke was onstage in those words. "If the whole world's singing your songs," Tweedy sang, "Just remember what was yours is everyone's from now on."[32]

Acknowledgments

I've read enough books to know the single author theory is false. This book, in particular, came together over ten years thanks to the people, some strangers at first, who lent a hand, pointed me in right directions, read drafts, or shared photographs, recordings, news clippings, or their stories, the most valuable resource of all. Several hundred people were interviewed for this book. I hope they see the end product, a first on the subject, as a work of gratitude and respect. Their contribution to Chicago history lives on here.

Thank you Nina Helstein, the first person I interviewed for this book. Nina was involved in the University of Chicago Folklore Society in its first year and still remains active in the annual folk festival. Besides sharing her memories, she lent me her collection of recordings from the festival's earliest years. Those headphone hours placed me in Mandel Hall in 1961 and every year thereafter, so I can't thank her enough for the time machine.

Thank you to the University of Chicago Folk Festival for lending me letters, some handwritten and some not, contracts, and other material from the earliest years, all of which were unavailable to any researcher up to now.

Thank you John Rice, an ace Chicago multi-instrumentalist involved in the country and bluegrass scene for five decades. John is also a sound archivist who lent me recordings, made introductions, and shared his personal insight into the Sundowners, a group he championed and archived. Without John's diligence, much of what we know about that group and that time would have been lost.

Thank you Mark Dvorak, another Chicago musician who today

embodies the original spirit of the Old Town School of Folk Music. Now a cherished teacher, he was a student in 1979 when he first walked through the school's doors. Mark lent me his interviews with Win Stracke. His is the longest and most complete set of recordings of this important Chicago figure, and for that we all owe Mark gratitude.

Thank you Ted Johnson and Marcia Johnson, who were among the first students at the Old Town School. Both shared recordings, helped clarify facts, and made introductions. Stephen Wade, too, was a big help, so I thank him for sharing his recordings and articles related to important Old Town School figures like Fleming Brown.

Thank you Colby Maddox for opening the doors to the Old Town School of Folk Music Resource Center and for his work in archiving the bounty of historical material there which will help scholars for decades to come.

If you're feeling down about the world, I highly recommend an afternoon with the perennially upbeat Eddie Holstein, not only a master storyteller, but also a walking encyclopedia of Chicago folk history, from street names to song titles. Thank you, Eddie, for your insight into many of these chapters. Thanks also to Marina Jason for feedback and introductions to people involved in Chicago's second wave of folk music. Sadly, Marina died just weeks before I turned this book in. She is one of more than a few dozen people I interviewed over the course of many years who have since passed. I am grateful to have captured their stories, yet regret they are not here to see how they contributed to this wider story.

Research took me to Tennessee and Kentucky. I am in debt to the vast archives at the Country Music Hall of Fame and Museum in Nashville, where I spent hours going through about a dozen oral histories, long-forgotten country music magazines, and other materials pertaining to the WLS *Barn Dance*. Thank you Senior Historian John Rumble and Associate Librarian Becky Miley for your help. I also thank Sharyn Mitchell, research services specialist at the Special Collections and Archives Department of Berea College in Kentucky, who helped me dig through materials related to John

Lair, Bradley Kincaid, and the many other Kentuckians who formed the strong link between the Appalachians and Chicago.

I had help chasing down information, both arcane and obvious, from two accomplished writers: Ben van Loon and Jessica Mlinaric. Thank you both. I am humbled by your own passion for Chicago history and how you explore it through your own excellent work.

This book also benefited from the scholarship and feedback of Chicago music journalists Bob Riesman, Bob Marovich, Aaron Cohen, James Porter, and the late Chrissie Dickinson. I thank them for answering my periodic questions and for general help. This book also benefits from their past scholarship as well as that of Ronald D. Cohen, the nation's top historian of the folk revival, and journalist Dave Hoekstra, who documented the story of the Sundowners in both the *Chicago Sun-Times* and the *Chicago Reader*.

Thank you to Jonathan Gourlay for reading drafts, and to Angela Bowman for help on my early proposal. I also express deepest thanks to Lara Weber for her encouragement and enthusiasm at times when I had neither.

Thanks to Robert Devens, now at the University of Texas Press, who encouraged me to pursue this project and carried it through to the acceptance stage before leaving Chicago for Austin. And thanks to Alan Thomas, editorial director at the University of Chicago Press, and the entire Press staff.

I thank Jean and Victor Guarino, my parents, for showing me early on that books matter. So why not write a few?

Finally, I pay a great spiritual debt to Val Camilletti (1939–2018). Every creative scene needs someone whose role is connector, booster, and reality checker. Val was all three. As a teenager, I bought my first record from Val's Halla, the store in Oak Park she operated for nearly fifty years. As an adult, I stopped in frequently to pick up the latest *No Depression*, scour the bins, and listen to her stories of attending the University of Chicago Folk Festival, hanging at the Earl of Old Town, and working in the Capitol Records promotions department preparing Chicagoans for a new British group called the Beatles. She was a child of the folk revival and, in recent years, fed me stories for this book. She kept at me to finish because she wanted to make it her summer read. Val, I regret missing your deadline. Your life is in these pages.

Appendix A: Chicago in Song

Nothing about Chicago makes it an obvious subject for a song. As the center of the United States, the city has represented many things to different people over different time periods: harsh weather, beautiful architecture, good food, persistent public corruption, persistent street violence, and beloved sports franchises. While it is true that many songwriters have turned to that checklist of tangibles for musical inspiration, other songwriters have used Chicago as a metaphor for isolation, heartache, and loneliness—all qualities that make a good country song.

For your next mixtape, here is a brief, but incomplete, list of country and folk songs sourced from the City That Works.

"A Dying Cub Fan's Last Request"—Steve Goodman
"Ain't Hurtin' Nobody"—John Prine
"Asphalt Cowboy"—Blake Shelton
"Ballad of Elizabeth Dark"—Michael Smith
"Blue Chicago Moon"—Songs: Ohia
"Chicago"—Stephen Wade
"Chicago"—Tom Waits
"Chicago Barn Dance"—Special Consensus
"Chicago Cops"—Bob Gibson and Hamilton Camp
"Chicago River Blues"—Hayden Thompson
"Chicago Wind"—Merle Haggard
"City of Chicago"—Luka Bloom
"City of New Orleans"—Steve Goodman
"Cold Irons Bound"—Bob Dylan
"Dear Chicago"—Ryan Adams

"El-A-Noy"—Win Stracke

"Far, Far Away"—Wilco

"43rd Ward"—Win Stracke

"Fox River"—The Waco Brothers

"Gate of Horn"—Roger McGuinn

"Georgia Hard"—Robbie Fulks

"Golden Ring"—Tammy Wynette and George Jones

"Goodnight Chicago"—Lucy Wainwright Roche

"Harm's Way"—The Waco Brothers

"Heaven Only Knows"—David Allan Coe

"Hey Chicago"—Low

"I Ain't Already There"—Toby Keith

"I Take a Lot of Pride in What I Am"—Merle Haggard

"Lake Marie"—John Prine

"Lincoln Park Pirates"—Steve Goodman

"Mama Chicago"—Bonnie Koloc

"(Margie's at the) Lincoln Park Inn"—Tom T. Hall

"My Home Is in Chicago (But My Heart's in Tennessee)"—The Possum
    Hollow Boys

"North to Chicago"—Hank Snow

"Old Chicago"—Fred Holstein

"On the South Side of Chicago"—Ray Price

"Pulaski at Night"—Andrew Bird

"Red Leaves of October"—Michael Smith

"Rogers Park"—Justin Townes Earle

"Sidewalks of Chicago"—Porter Wagoner

"Star Witness"—Neko Case

"Streets of Old Chicago"—Mark Dvorak

"Sunshine in Chicago"—Sun Kil Moon

"The Chicago Story"—Tom T. Hall

"The El"—Rhett Miller

"The Flame That Killed John Wayne"—The Mekons

"The Giant of Illinois"—The Handsome Family

"The Last Honky-Tonk in Chicago"—Wild Earp & The Free For Alls

"The Woman Downstairs"—The Handsome Family

"Trance on Sedgewick Street"—Terry Callier

"Via Chicago"—Wilco

"When the Fire Comes Down from Heaven"—Hank Williams

"William Butler Yeats Visits Lincoln Park and Escapes Unscathed"—
  Phil Ochs

"Windy City Anne"—Tom T. Hall

"Windy City Rag"—Alison Krauss and Union Station

Appendix B: Essential Chicago Country and Folk Albums

The catalog encompassing all the country and folk music connected to Chicago is vast. I myself have several boxes of vinyl records, 45 rpm singles, and CDs that claim Chicago as their origin or their influence, or both. The following list of albums is intended as a companion to this book. Note that this is a selective list, and that for some essential artists, like John Prine or Robbie Fulks, a deeper discography is needed to tell the full story.

The reader should also be warned that many albums on this list are out of print and some are not available even via streaming services like Spotify. If you search for these, your local used record store, Discogs, and eBay are your friends. If you're seeking early transcriptions of the WLS *Barn Dance*, or music from many of its performers, check YouTube, Spotify, or the many compilation records that have been released over the years.

Andrew Bird, *Things Are Really Great Here, Sort Of . . .* (Wegawam), 2014

Andrew Calhoun, *Where Blue Meets Blue* (Waterbug), 1999

Angel Olsen, *Half Way Home* (Bathetic), 2012

Art Thieme, *The Older I Get, the Better I Was* (Waterbug), 1998

Big Bill Broonzy and Pete Seeger, *In Concert* (Verve Folkways), 1965

Bob Gibson, *Offbeat Folksongs* (Riverside), 1956

Bob Gibson and Hamilton Camp, *Gibson and Camp at the Gate of Horn* (Elektra), 1961

Bonnie Koloc, *After All This Time* (Ovation), 1971

Bonnie Koloc, *You're Gonna Love Yourself in the Morning* (Ovation), 1974

Cal Starr, *Cal Starr and Guitar in Nashville* (Fraternity), n.d.

Califone, *Heron King Blues* (Thrill Jockey), 2004

Califone, *Roots and Crowns* (Thrill Jockey), 2006

Carl Sandburg, *Sings His American Songbag* (TC), 1960

Catherine Irwin, *Cut Yourself a Switch* (Thrill Jockey), 2002

Chicago Farmer, *Flyover Country* (self-release), 2020

Chris Ligon, *Crazy Dazy* (Record Roundup), 2001

Dean Schlabowske, *Ramblin' Deano and Ice Cold Singles* (self-release), 2019

Dennis J. Leise, *State of Fairs* (self-release), 2019

DeZurik Sisters, *Yodel and Sing Their Greatest Hits* (Mississippi Records), 2014

Diane Izzo, *One* (Sugar Free), 1998

Dolly Varden, *The Dumbest Magnets* (Evil Teen), 2000

Eddie Holstein, *Eddie Holstein* (Holstein), 2008

Ella Jenkins, *You'll Sing a Song and I'll Sing a Song* (Folkways), 1966

Fleming Brown, *Fleming Brown* (Folk-Legacy), 1962

Frank Hamilton, *Frank Hamilton Sings Folk Songs* (Folkways), 1962

Frank Hamilton and Pete Seeger, *Nonesuch and Other Folk Tunes* (Folkways), 1959

Freakwater, *Feels Like the Third Time* (Thrill Jockey), 1993

Fred Holstein, *Chicago and Other Ports* (Philo), 1977

Fred Holstein, *Live at the Earl of Old Town* (Holstein), 2007

Ginni Clemmens, *Sing a Rainbow and Other Children's Songs* (Folkways), 1965

Jane Baxter-Miller, *Harm among the Willows* (Durga), 2010

Jeff & Janet (Jeff Lescher and Janet Beveridge Bean), *Jesus Built a Ship to Sing a Song To* (Kokopop), 1993

Jerry Butler, *Folk Songs* (Vee Jay), 1963

John Prine, *John Prine* (Atlantic), 1971

John Prine, *Bruised Orange* (Asylum), 1978

Jon Langford, *All the Fame of Lofty Deeds* (Bloodshot), 2004

Jump 'N the Saddle Band, *Jump 'N the Saddle Band* (Acme), 1981

Katie Lee, *Katie Lee Sings Spicy Songs for Cool Knights* (Specialty), 1956

Kelly Hogan, *I Like to Keep Myself in Pain* (Anti-), 2013

Kelly Kessler, *The Salt of Your Skin* (Melungeon), 2002

Lulu Belle and Scotty, *Early and Great* (Old Homestead), 1985

Michael McDermott, *620 W. Surf* (Giant), 1991

Michael Smith, *Michael Smith* (Flying Fish), 1986

Michael Smith, *Love Stories* (Flying Fish), 1987

Neko Case, *Blacklisted* (Bloodshot), 2002

Nora O'Connor, *My Heart* (Pravda), 2022

Odetta, *Odetta at the Gate of Horn* (Tradition), 1957

Patsy Montana, *The Cowboy's Sweetheart* (Flying Fish), 1988

Robbie Fulks, *Country Love Songs* (Bloodshot), 1996

Robbie Fulks, *Upland Stories* (Bloodshot), 2016

Sally Timms, *Cowboy Sally's Twilight Laments for Lost Buckaroos* (Bloodshot), 1999

Scott Lucas & the Married Men, *Blood Half Moon* (The End), 2012

Souled American, *Fe* (Rough Trade), 1988

Souled American, *Flubber* (Rough Trade), 1989

Special Consensus, *Special Consensus* (Tin Ear), 1979

Special Consensus, *Long I Ride* (Compass), 2016

Special Consensus, *Chicago Barn Dance* (Compass), 2020

Steve Goodman, *Somebody Else's Troubles* (Buddah), 1972

Steve Goodman, *Live at the Earl of Old Town* (Red Pajamas), 2006

Stephen Wade, *A Storyteller's Story: Sources of Banjo Dancing* (CD Baby), 2019

Stu Ramsay, *Stu Ramsay Loves Dobro, Banjo, Guitar and Harmonica* (Mercury), 1963

Terry Callier, *The New Folk Sound of Terry Callier* (Prestige), 1965

Terry Callier, *Occasional Rain* (Cadet), 1971

Texas Rubies, *Working Girl Blues* (Texas Rubies), 1993

The Blacks, *Just Like Home* (Bloodshot), 2000

The Greater Chicago Bluegrass Band, *The Greater Chicago Bluegrass Band* (Fargo), 1980

The Handsome Family, *Through the Trees* (Carrot Top), 1998

The Handsome Family, *In the Air* (Carrot Top), 2000

The Lawrence Peters Outfit, *What You Been Missin'*, 2011

The Pine Valley Cosmonauts, *The Executioner's Last Songs*, Volume One (Bloodshot), 2002

The Pine Valley Cosmonauts, *The Executioner's Last Songs*, Volumes Two & Three (Bloodshot), 2003

The Pine Valley Cosmonauts, *Barn Dance Favorites* (Bloodshot), 2004

The Stanley Brothers, *Folk Festival* (StanleyTone), 2001 (contains all three sets of the Stanley Brothers at the 1961 University of Chicago Folk Festival, and one set from the 1965 festival)

The Sundowners, *The Sundowners* (EJ Records), 1980

The Sundowners, *Chicago Country Legends* (Bloodshot), 2004

The Waco Brothers, *To the Last Dead Cowboy* (Bloodshot), 1995

Tom Dundee, *A Delicate Balance* (Freckle), 1979

Various Artists, *Golden Ring* (Folk-Legacy Records), 1964

Various Artists, *Gathering at the Earl of Old Town* (Dunwich), 1976

Various Artists, *For a Life of Sin: A Compilation of Insurgent Chicago Country* (Bloodshot), 1994

Wilco, *Being There* (Reprise), 1996

Wilco, *Cruel Country* (dBpm), 2022

Willie Wright, *I Sing Folk Songs* (Concert-Disc), 1958

Win Stracke, *Americana* (Bally), 1957

Win Stracke, *Songs of Old Town* (Flair), 1968

Notes

INTRODUCTION

1   Howard Grafman and B. T. Manning, *Folk Music USA* (New York: Citadel Press, 1962), 121–24.

2   Ronnie Pugh, *Ernest Tubb: The Texas Troubadour* (Durham: Duke University Press, 1996), 133.

3   "Dave Kapp, Open for Orchestra and Song Arrangement," classified advertisement, *Chicago Tribune*, October 7, 1924, 36.

4   William Howland Kenney, *Recorded Music in American Life: The Phonograph and Popular Memory, 1890–1945* (Oxford: Oxford University Press, 1999), 161.

5   Tweedy and Staples met when Staples recorded a live album at the Hideout in 2008, an event that sent her career in an entirely new direction.

6   Colin Escott, with George Merritt and William MacEwen, *I Saw the Light: The Story of Hank Williams* (New York: Back Bay Books/Little, Brown, 2004), 51–52.

CHAPTER ONE

1   Bob Greene, "Tribute to Karl Davis for His Gift of Song," *Chicago Tribune*, June 4, 1979, section 2, 1.

2   "The Old-Fashioned Barn Dance: Radio's Hardiest Perennial," *Sponsor* 12, no. 31 (August 2, 1958): 27.

3   Paul L. Tyler, "The Rise of Rural Rhythm," in *The Hayloft Gang: The Story of the National Barn Dance*, ed. Chad Berry (Chicago: University of Illinois Press, 2013), 19.

4   Karl and Jean Davis, interview by Douglas B. Green, June 8, 1974 (OH41), Country Music Foundation Oral History Project, Country Music Hall of Fame® and Museum, Nashville, Tennessee.

5   George P. Stone, "Radio Has Gripped Chicago: The Ears of the Entire Middle West Were in the Auditorium Opera House Last Winter, and Boys Are Building Thousands of Sets," *Radio Broadcast* 1 (May 1922–October 1922): 503–5.

6   Stone, "Radio Has Gripped Chicago," 503.

7   Erik Barnouw, *A History of Broadcasting in the United States*, vol. 1, *A Tower in Babel–To 1933* (New York: Oxford University Press, 1966), 88–90.

8   "Radio Diverts Big Rotary Meeting," *Radio Age* 2, no. 3 (April 1923): 26.

9   Stone, "Radio Has Gripped Chicago," 506–7.

10   James F. Evans, *"Prairie Farmer" and WLS: The Burridge D. Butler Years* (Chicago: University of Illinois Press, 1969), 155.

11   The *Chicago Tribune* purchased WDAP in 1923 and changed its call letters to WGN (World's Greatest Newspaper). Terry Clifford, "The Glory Days of Chicago Radio," *Chicago Tribune*, March 4, 1979, F28.

12   Stone, "Radio Has Gripped Chicago," 506.

13   J. Farrell, "Farm Radio Making Rapid Progress," *Radio News*, January 1925, 1143.

14   Evans, *"Prairie Farmer" and WLS*, 157.

15   Evans, *"Prairie Farmer" and WLS*, 158.

16   Evans, *"Prairie Farmer" and WLS*, 160.

17   Scott Childers, *Chicago's WLS Radio* (Arcadia Publishing, 2008), 13.

18   Evans, *"Prairie Farmer" and WLS*, 161.

19   "WLS, Chicago, Opens with Music 'Feast,'" *Radio Digest* 9, no. 3 (April 26, 1924): 4.

20   Evans, *"Prairie Farmer" and WLS*, 162–63.

21   Wayne Daniel, "National Barn Dance," in *The Encyclopedia of Country Music*, ed. Paul Kingsbury (New York: Oxford University Press, 1998), 372.

22   George C. Biggar, "The WLS National Barn Dance: The Early Years," in *Exploring Roots Music: Twenty Years of the JEMF Quarterly*, ed. Nolan Porterfield (Lanham, Maryland: Scarecrow Press, 2004), 36. The station was not the first in the country to offer fiddle music or even to follow the barn dance format. Both can be traced to stations in Texas, Iowa, and Georgia as early as 1922. Even the term "barn dance" appears as early as 1908 to describe square dancing, "the latest society craze" in Chicago. The dance is characterized as a fad among young people because "it gives them a chance to romp." As with most spectacles embraced by young people, the older generation disapproved. Dance instructors refused to teach it, and two society clubs, the Ravenswood Club and Edgewater Country Club, did not permit the dance in their ballrooms because their floors and walls could little support "when so many couples hop at the same time." "The barn dance is all right for an informal little party at home, but for the ballroom it is entirely too inelegant," one instructor sniffed. "Barn Dance: The Latest Society Craze," *Chicago Daily Tribune*, May 25, 1908, F6.

23   "Barn Dance," *Chicago Daily Tribune*, May 25, 1908.

24   "National Barn Dance Tonight," *Chicago Herald and Examiner*, April 19, 1924.

25   George C. Biggar to Sarah Gertrude Knott, May 11, 1937, series 2, box 7,

John Lair Papers 1930–1984, Southern Appalachian Archives, Berea College, Berea, Kentucky; George C. Biggar, "When the Cowbells Ring Out on Saturday Night: It's National Barn Dance Time," in *100 WLS Barn Dance Favorites* (Chicago: M. M. Cole, 1935), 96.

26 Paul L. Tyler, "Fiddling," in *The American Midwest: An Interpretive Encyclopedia*, ed. Andrew R. L. Cayton, Richard Sisson, and Chris Zacher (Bloomington: Indiana University Press, 2006), 384–86.

27 Biggar, "WLS National Barn Dance."

28 Biggar, "WLS National Barn Dance."

29 Charles K. Wolfe, "George D. Hay," in Kingsbury, *Encyclopedia of Country Music*, 233.

30 Charles K. Wolfe, *A Good-Natured Riot: The Birth of the Grand Ole Opry* (Nashville: Country Music Foundation Press and Vanderbilt University Press, 1999), 7–8.

31 "New Chicago Records Coming," *Talking Machine World* 50, no. 2 (February 15, 1925): 146.

32 "George Hay Winner of Gold Cup: "Solemn Old Judge Takes Highly Contested Trophy," *Radio Digest* 10, no. 11 (September 20, 1924): 3.

33 Wolfe, *Good-Natured Riot*, 9.

34 Craig Havighurst, *Air Castle of the South: WSM and the Making of Music City* (Chicago: University of Illinois Press, 2007), 25.

35 Charles K. Wolfe, *Tennessee Strings: The Story of Country Music in Tennessee* (Knoxville: University of Tennessee Press, 1977), 56.

36 Paul M. Gifford, "Henry Ford's Dance Revival and Fiddle Contests: Myth and Reality," *Journal of the Society for American Music* 4, no. 3 (2010): 324.

37 Gifford, "Henry Ford's Dance Revival," 325–27.

38 Paul L. Tyler, "Hillbilly Music Re-imagined: Folk and Country Music in the Midwest," *Journal of American Folklore* 127, no. 504 (Spring 2014): 172.

39 Tyler, "Hillbilly Music Re-imagined," 173.

40 Tyler, "Hillbilly Music Re-imagined," 179.

41 Evans, *"Prairie Farmer" and WLS*, 165.

42 Chubby was born Frederick R. Parker. He recorded "King Kong Kitchie Kitchie Ki-Me-O" three times for three different labels, first in 1928 and then in 1930 and 1931; it was also included in the 1952 *Anthology of American Folk Music*. Tony Russell, *County Music Records: A Discography, 1921–1942* (New York: Oxford University Press, 2004), 676–77.

43 Bradley Kincaid, interview by Douglas B. Green, July 10, 1974 (OH83), Country Music Foundation Oral History Project, Country Music Hall of Fame® and Museum, Nashville, Tennessee.

44 Bradley Kincaid, interview by Douglas B. Green, July 10, 1974 (OH83), Country Music Foundation Oral History Project, Country Music Hall of Fame® and Museum, Nashville, Tennessee.

45   *Chicago "Y" College Glee Club Touring, The Young Men's Christian Association College*, pamphlet, series 1, box 1, Bradley Kincaid Collection, Southern Appalachian Archives, Berea College, Berea, Kentucky.

46   Bradley Kincaid, interview by Dorothy Gable, November 2, 1967 (OH332), Country Music Foundation Oral History Project, Country Music Hall of Fame® and Museum, Nashville, Tennessee. In 1968, Kincaid donated his original "Houn' Dog" guitar to the Country Music Hall of Fame. "Artifacts Continue to Come In to the Country Music Hall of Fame and Museum," *Billboard*, January 6, 1968, 28.

47   Michael Wright, "Bradley Kincaid Houn' Dog," *Vintage Guitar Magazine*, January 2003, http://www.vintageguitar.com/3271/bradley-kincaid-houn -dog/.

48   Wright, "Bradley Kincaid Houn' Dog."

49   Wright, "Bradley Kincaid Houn' Dog."

50   Archie Green, "Bradley Kincaid's Folios," *JEMF Quarterly* 13, no. 45 (Summer 1977): 21.

51   Kincaid, *My Favorite Mountain Ballads and Old-Time Songs* (Chicago: self-published, 1928), 15; Russell, *County Music Records*, 67.

52   Green, "Bradley Kincaid's Folios," 27.

53   Loyal Jones, "Bradley Kincaid," in Kingsbury, *Encyclopedia of Country Music*, 283.

54   Jack Hurst, "Barn Dance Days: Remembering the Stars of a Pioneering Chicago Radio Show," *Chicago Tribune*, August 5, 1984, J10.

55   Bradley Kincaid, interview by Douglas B. Green, July 10, 1974 (OH83), Country Music Foundation Oral History Project, Country Music Hall of Fame® and Museum, Nashville, Tennessee.

56   Russell, *County Music Records*, 482–85.

57   Green, "Bradley Kincaid's Folios," 27.

58   "Bradley Kincaid: The Man Who's Called Country Music's Pioneer," *Berea Alumnus*, January–February 1975, 6.

59   Jones, "Bradley Kincaid," 283.

60   Evans, *"Prairie Farmer" and WLS*, 89, 85.

61   Evans, *"Prairie Farmer" and WLS*, 173.

62   Evans, *"Prairie Farmer" and WLS*, 175.

63   Evans, *"Prairie Farmer" and WLS*, 13–16.

64   Evans, *"Prairie Farmer" and WLS*, 17.

65   Evans, *"Prairie Farmer" and WLS*, 89.

66   Burridge D. Butler, "Greetings to Our Friends," *The 1930 WLS Family Album*, 5.

67   Bob and Maggie Atcher, interview by John W. Rumble, May 2, 1987 (OHC18), Country Music Foundation Oral History Project, Country Music Hall of Fame® and Museum, Nashville, Tennessee.

68   Karl and Jean Davis, interview by Douglas B. Green, June 8, 1974 (OH41),

Country Music Foundation Oral History Project, Country Music Hall of
Fame® and Museum, Nashville, Tennessee.

69 "It's National Barn Dance Time at WLS," *The 1930 WLS Family Album*, 17.

70 Evans, *"Prairie Farmer" and WLS*, 202.

71 Timothy A. Patterson, "Hillbilly Music among the Flatlanders: Early Midwestern Radio Barn Dances," *Journal of Country Music* 6, no. 1 (Spring
1975): 12.

72 Evans, *"Prairie Farmer" and WLS*, 222.

73 Biggar, "WLS National Barn Dance," 41.

74 Biggar, "WLS National Barn Dance," 41.

75 Evans, *"Prairie Farmer" and WLS*, 223–24.

76 John Lair and Bradley Kincaid, interview by Loyal Jones, November 20,
1971 (AC-OR-002-013), Berea College Appalachian Sound Archive, Berea,
Kentucky.

77 John Rumble, "John Lair," in Kingsbury, *Encyclopedia of Country Music*,
288.

78 Michael Ann Williams, *Staging Tradition: John Lair and Sarah Gertrude
Knott* (Chicago: University of Illinois Press, 2006), 7.

79 John Lair and Bradley Kincaid, interview by Loyal Jones, November 20,
1971.

80 John Lair, WLS interview, series 6, box 31, John Lair Papers 1930–1984,
Southern Appalachian Archives, Berea College, Berea, Kentucky.

81 National Folk Festival script, series 6, box 31, John Lair Papers 1930–1984,
Southern Appalachian Archives, Berea College, Berea, Kentucky.

82 John Lair to Ernest Hodge, October 22, 1930, series2, box 7, John Lair
Papers 1930–1984, Southern Appalachian Archives, Berea College, Berea,
Kentucky. Because he mentioned Gene Ruppe, the group Lair was assembling was probably the Cumberland Ridge Runners. Ruppe was the group's
fiddler.

83 Ernest Hodge to John Lair, October 28, 1930, series 2, box 7, John Lair
Papers 1930–1984, Southern Appalachian Archives, Berea College, Berea,
Kentucky.

84 John Lair to Ernest Hodge, November 2, 1930, series 2, box 7, John Lair
Papers 1930–1984, Southern Appalachian Archives, Berea College, Berea,
Kentucky.

85 Contract between Karl V. Davis and John L. Lair, January 3, 1931, series 2,
box 7, John Lair Papers 1930–1984, Southern Appalachian Archives, Berea
College, Berea, Kentucky.

86 John Lair to Bernard F. Henson, May 29, 1934, series 2, box 7, John Lair
Papers 1930–1984, Southern Appalachian Archives, Berea College, Berea,
Kentucky.

87 Karl and Jean Davis, interview by Douglas B. Green, June 8, 1974 (OH41),
Country Music Foundation Oral History Project, Country Music Hall of

Fame® and Museum, Nashville, Tennessee.

88 Dave Samuelson, "Karl & Harty," in Kingsbury, *Encyclopedia of Country Music*, 275.

89 Karl and Jean Davis, interview by Douglas B. Green, June 8, 1974 (OH41), Country Music Foundation Oral History Project, Country Music Hall of Fame® and Museum, Nashville, Tennessee.

90 Charles K. Wolfe, *Classic Country: Legends of Country Music* (New York: Routledge, 2001), 121–22.

91 Karl and Jean Davis, interview by Douglas B. Green, June 8, 1974 (OH41), Country Music Foundation Oral History Project, Country Music Hall of Fame® and Museum, Nashville, Tennessee.

92 Russell, *County Music Records*, 470–71.

93 C. Eric Banister, *Johnny Cash FAQ: All That's Left to Know about the Man in Black* (Milwaukee: Backbeat Books, 2014).

94 Even though Davis agreed to credit their songs to "Karl and Harty," he was the primary songwriter. His name alone appears under "Kentucky." However, early pressings of *Songs Our Daddy Taught Us* by the Everly Brothers incorrectly credit the song to "H. Prichard," or Henry Prichard, who published another song of the same name. The mix-up prevented Davis from receiving royalties in his lifetime, his family said. "I want those records correctly identifying my father. It's his song. It is indisputable," said daughter Susan Dunahoo. Susan Dunahoo, telephone interview by author, October 29, 2015.

95 Dick Spottswood, "Mandolin," in Kingsbury, *Encyclopedia of Country Music*, 323.

96 Jeffrey J. Lange, *Smile When You Call Me a Hillbilly: Country Music's Struggle for Respectability 1939–1954* (Athens: University of Georgia Press, 2004), 58.

97 Charles K. Wolfe, *Kentucky Country: Folk and Country Music of Kentucky* (Lexington: University of Kentucky Press, 1982), 55.

98 Bill Monroe, interview by John W. Rumble and Chris Skinker, November 11, 1993 (OHC191), Country Music Foundation Oral History Project, Country Music Hall of Fame® and Museum, Nashville, Tennessee.

99 John Rumble, "Bill Monroe," in Kingsbury, *Encyclopedia of Country Music*, 351.

100 Richard D. Smith, *Can't You Hear Me Callin': The Life of Bill Monroe, Father of Bluegrass* (Cambridge: Da Capo Press, 2000), 25–30.

101 Bill Monroe, interview by John W. Rumble and Chris Skinker, November 11, 1993 (OHC191), Country Music Foundation Oral History Project, Country Music Hall of Fame® and Museum, Nashville, Tennessee.

102 Charlie Monroe, interview by Douglas B. Green and Fred Bartenstein, September 1, 1972 (OHC501), Country Music Foundation Oral History Project, Country Music Hall of Fame® and Museum, Nashville, Tennessee.

103 Smith, *Can't You Hear Me Callin'*, 33–34.

104 Bill Monroe, interview by John W. Rumble and Chris Skinker, November 18, 1993 (OHC192), Country Music Foundation Oral History Project, Country Music Hall of Fame® and Museum, Nashville, Tennessee.

105 Charlie Monroe, interview by Douglas B. Green and Fred Bartenstein, September 1, 1972 (OHC501), Country Music Foundation Oral History Project, Country Music Hall of Fame® and Museum, Nashville, Tennessee.

106 Charlie Monroe, interview by Douglas B. Green and Fred Bartenstein, September 1, 1972 (OHC501), Country Music Foundation Oral History Project, Country Music Hall of Fame® and Museum, Nashville, Tennessee.

107 Karl Davis, interview by Douglas B. Green, June 9, 1974 (OH42), Country Music Foundation Oral History Project, Country Music Hall of Fame® and Museum, Nashville, Tennessee.

108 Neil V. Rosenberg and Charles K. Wolfe, *The Music of Bill Monroe* (Chicago: University of Illinois, 2007), 57.

109 Rosenberg and Wolfe, *Music of Bill Monroe*.

110 Dave Tianen, "The Wizard of Waukesha," *Milwaukee Journal Sentinel*, April 17, 2003, http://archive.jsonline.com/entertainment/53148927.html.

111 Steve King and Johnnie Putnam, *A Little More Les* (Chicago: Bantry Bay Books, 2015), 236.

112 "The Ridge Runners and Linda," *WLS Family Album 1935*, 42.

113 "John Lair," *WLS Family Album 1933*, 21.

114 "No Hill Billies in Radio: Ballads Are Still Written, Says John Lair," *WLS Weekly*, March 10, 1936, 7.

115 John Lair 1933 World's Fair script, series 6, box 31, John Lair Papers 1930–1984, Southern Appalachian Archives, Berea College, Berea, Kentucky.

116 Dave Samuelson, "Linda Parker: WLS's Sunbonnet Girl," *Journal of the American Academy for the Preservation of Old-Time Country Music* 30 (1995): 17.

117 Dave Samuelson, "Linda Parker," in Kingsbury, *Encyclopedia of Country Music*, 404.

118 Samuelson, "Linda Parker: WLS's Sunbonnet Girl," 17.

119 Contract between Jeanne Muenich and John L. Lair, n.d., series 2, box 7, John Lair Papers 1930–1984, Southern Appalachian Archives, Berea College, Berea, Kentucky.

120 "Linda Parker," *Behind the Scenes at WLS*, 1932, 27.

121 John Lair, "Single Girl" notation, in *100 WLS Barn Dance Favorites* (Chicago: M. M. Cole, 1935), 45.

122 Archibald McKinlay, "Calumet Roots: Linda Parker Made Her Mark in Country Music," *Northwest Indiana Times*, December 11, 1994, http://www.nwitimes.com/uncategorized/calumet-roots-linda-parker-made-her

-mark-in-country-music/article_abb75bb3-846f-59d3-b93f-0d6940841b3f
.html.

123 "Sunbonnet Girl," *Stand By!* 1, no. 28 (August 24, 1935): 11.

124 John Lair, "Notes from the Music Library," *Stand By!* 1, no. 30 (September 7, 1935): 12.

125 John Lair, *100 WLS Barn Dance Favorites* (Chicago: M. M. Cole, 1935), 2.

126 John Rumble, "Red Foley," in Kingsbury, *Encyclopedia of Country Music*, 176.

127 John Lair to Clyde Foley, February 24, 1931, series 2, box 7, John Lair Papers 1930–1984, Southern Appalachian Archives, Berea College, Berea, Kentucky.

128 Arnold Gingrich, "Springfield, Mo.: Radio City of Country Music," *Coronet* 41 (April 1957): 154.

129 Lange, *Smile When You Call Me A Hillbilly*, 215.

130 Scott Wiseman, interview by Dorothy Gable, October 19, 1967 (OH390), Country Music Foundation Oral History Project, Country Music Hall of Fame® and Museum, Nashville, Tennessee.

131 William E. Lightfoot, "Lulu Belle & Scotty," in Kingsbury, *Encyclopedia of Country Music*, 308.

132 Kristine M. McCusker, *Lonesome Cowgirls and Honky-Tonk Angels: The Women of Barn Dance Radio* (Chicago: University of Illinois Press, 2008), 52.

133 Scott Wiseman, interview by Dorothy Gable, October 19, 1967 (OH390), Country Music Foundation Oral History Project, Country Music Hall of Fame® and Museum, Nashville, Tennessee.

134 Lorraine Thomas, "Lulu Belle Goes to Town," *Radio Guide*, May 23, 1936, 7.

135 "Hail, the Queen!," *Radio Guide*, November 7, 1936, 3.

136 Stephen Parry, "Afterword," in Berry, *Hayloft Gang*, 202. After leaving the *Barn Dance* in 1958, the Wisemans sold their house in Oak Park, Illinois, a Chicago suburb, and returned to North Carolina. Myrtle Wiseman then got involved in state politics, becoming the first woman to enter the North Carolina House of Representatives in 1975. In 1977, she gave a speech to protest a proposal to abolish the death penalty for cases of murder and rape. She said she had been raped ten years earlier by a paroled convict who forced her with a pistol. The House killed the proposal that day. "Legislator Tells Own Rape to Sway Death-Penalty Vote," *Chicago Tribune*, May 5, 1977, B15.

137 Lucia Lewis, "Home, Home on the Ranch: When the Dudes and the Cowboys Play," *Chicagoan* 13, no. 10 (May 1, 1933): 48–49.

138 "Town Talk: Cowboy," *Chicagoan* 8, no. 2 (October 12, 1929): 19.

139 "Occasions," *Chicagoan* 5, no. 9 (July 28, 1928): 2.

140 Liam T. A. Ford, *Soldier Field: A Stadium and Its City* (Chicago: University of Chicago Press, 2009), 166–70.

141 Douglas Bukowski, *Big Bill Thompson, Chicago, and the Politics of Image* (Chicago: University of Illinois Press, 1998), 11.

142 "Mayor Thompson Proposes Cowboy Method to Sweep Chicago Clean," *Los Angeles Herald*, December 22, 1915, no. 44, 4.

143 Ron Grossman, "'Big Bill' Thompson: Chicago's Unfiltered Mayor," *Chicago Tribune*, February 6, 2016, http://www.chicagotribune.com/news /opinion/commentary/ct-big-bill-thompson-trump-flashback-perspec -0207-jm-20160205-story.html.

144 James Doherty, "I Remember Prohibition: Big Bill Thompson," *Chicago Tribune Magazine*, April 29, 1951, 7.

145 Arthur Evans, "Big Bill Cowboys to Whoop It Up on River Voyage," *Chicago Tribune*, April 10, 1927, part 1, 5.

146 Gene Autry with Mickey Herskowitz, *Back in the Saddle Again* (Garden City, New York: Doubleday, 1978), 3.

147 Autry, *Back in the Saddle Again*, 9.

148 Autry, *Back in the Saddle Again*, 1.

149 Autry, *Back in the Saddle Again*, 32.

150 Holly George-Warren, *Public Cowboy No. 1: The Life and Times of Gene Autry* (New York: Oxford University Press, 2007), 107.

151 Russell, *County Music Records*, 77.

152 "Gene Autry," *Behind the Scenes at WLS*, 1932, 21.

153 Russell, *County Music Records*, 78–79.

154 George-Warren, *Public Cowboy No. 1*, 81.

155 Autry, *Back in the Saddle Again*, 5.

156 Autry, *Back in the Saddle Again*, 31.

157 Betty Johnson, telephone interview by author, August 25, 2015.

158 George-Warren, *Public Cowboy No. 1*, 123.

159 Autry, *Back in the Saddle Again*, 33.

160 "Tumble Weed," *WLS Family Album 1936*, 42.

161 Marjorie Gibson, "Smilin' Cowboy Bill," *Rural Radio* 2, no. 1 (February 1939): 8.

162 "Pokey Martin," *WLS Family Album 1938*, 28.

163 "Radio No Secret for Hoyt Allen," *Sooner Magazine* 21, no. 3 (November 1948): 10.

164 Don Finlayson, "Park Avenue, R.F.D.," *Rural Radio* 2, no. 4 (May 1939): 11.

165 "Wind in the Pines," *Stand By!* 2, no. 11 (April 25, 1936): 9.

166 "Searching the Dial," *Stand By!* 1, no. 41 (November 23, 1935): 2.

167 George Biggar, "Minstrels in the Hayloft," *WLS Weekly*, March 23, 1935, 5.

168 "Girls of the Golden West, *WLS Family Album 1937*, 28.

169 Charles Wolfe, "The Girls of the Golden West," in Kingsbury, *Encyclopedia of Country Music*, 204.

170 Robert K. Oermann, "Louise Massey & The Westerners," in Kingsbury, *Encyclopedia of Country Music*, 329.

171 "Girl on the Cover," *WLS Weekly*, February 23, 1935, 7.

172 "Louise Massey Mabie," *WLS Family Album 1935*, 12.

173 Russell, *County Music Records*, 608–13.

174 Don Cusic, "Cowboys in Chicago," in Berry, *Hayloft Gang*, 179.

175 Burt A. Folkart, "Curt Massey; Musician and Broadcaster," *Los Angeles Times*, October 23, 1991.

176 Douglas B. Green, "Rex Allen," in Kingsbury, *Encyclopedia of Country Music*, 10.

177 Bob Atcher tells a different story about why Allen left: he broke the jaw of a station producer who criticized his singing. "Rex just hit him. He was wound up pretty tight, I guess, in those days," Atcher recalled. The producers' union demanded the station fire their biggest star, which they did. Bob and Maggie Atcher, interview by John W. Rumble, May 1, 1987 (OHC17), Country Music Foundation Oral History Project, Country Music Hall of Fame® and Museum, Nashville, Tennessee.

178 Edward Morris, "Singer/Cowboy Actor Rex Allen Sr. Dies at 78," CMT.com, June 20, 2003.

179 Bob Atcher, interview by Douglas B. Green, June 11, 1974 (OH122-LC), Country Music Foundation Oral History Project, Country Music Hall of Fame® and Museum, Nashville, Tennessee.

180 Wolfe, *Kentucky Country*, 137.

181 Atcher had to rewrite the melody of the song, which Roy Acuff would later borrow for the Kitty Wells hit "It Wasn't God Who Made Honky Tonk Angels." Wolfe, *Kentucky Country*, 138.

182 "Bob and Marguerite Atcher," *WLS Family Album 1950*, 43.

183 Wolfe, Kentucky Country, 138.

184 Bob Atcher, interview by Douglas B. Green, June 11, 1974 (OH122-LC), Country Music Foundation Oral History Project, Country Music Hall of Fame® and Museum, Nashville, Tennessee.

185 Jessica Seigel, "Job Done, Schaumburg's Atcher Rides Into Sunset," *Chicago Tribune*, February 14, 1989.

186 Mary A. Bufwack, "Patsy Montana," in Kingsbury, *Encyclopedia of Country Music*, 353.

187 Patsy Montana with Jane Frost, *Patsy Montana: The Cowboy's Sweetheart* (Jefferson, North Carolina: McFarland, 2002), 34.

188 Montana, *Patsy Montana*, 37–38.

189 Montana, *Patsy Montana*, 45–46.

190 "Girl on the Cover," *Stand By!* 1, no. 42 (November 30, 1935): 11.

191 Cathy Fink, "Patsy Montana and the WLS Barn Dance," *Come for to Sing* 9, no. 1 (Winter 1983): 22.

192 Patsy Montana with Jane Frost, *Patsy Montana: The Cowboy's Sweetheart*, 47–48.

193 Montana, *Patsy Montana*, 51.

194 Montana, *Patsy Montana*, 52.

195 Montana, *Patsy Montana*, 53.

196 Bob Atcher, interview by Douglas B. Green, June 11, 1974 (OH122-LC), Country Music Foundation Oral History Project, Country Music Hall of Fame® and Museum, Nashville, Tennessee.

197 Patsy Montana, interview by Douglas B. Green, October 16, 1974 (OH7-LC), Country Music Foundation Oral History Project, Country Music Hall of Fame® and Museum, Nashville, Tennessee.

198 Montana, *Patsy Montana*, 68.

199 Cyndi Lauper, telephone interview by author, April 21, 2016.

200 Fink, "Patsy Montana and the WLS Barn Dance," 23.

201 "Patsy Montana," *WLS Family Album 1936*, 22.

202 Fink, "Patsy Montana and the WLS Barn Dance," 24.

203 Jim Klein, telephone interview by author, November 3, 2015.

204 John Biguenet, "The DeZurik Sisters: Two Farm Girls Who Yodeled Their Way to the Grand Ole Opry," in *The Best Music Writing 2006*, ed. Mary Gaitskill (Cambridge, Massachusetts: Da Capo, 2006), 96.

205 *Barnyard Follies*, posted by Paramount Vault, YouTube video, November 12, 2015, https://www.youtube.com/watch?v=LzhZKIQM9fY.

206 Lily May Ledford, *Coon Creek Girl* (Berea, Kentucky: Berea College Appalachian Center, 1980), 5.

207 Ledford, *Coon Creek Girl*, 10.

208 H. Lisle Krieghbaum to Howard Chamberlain, November 21, 1935, series 1, box 1, The Lily May Ledford Collection 1917–1985, Southern Appalachian Archives, Berea College, Berea, Kentucky.

209 Albert Skidmore to John Lair, February 28, 1936, series 2, box 7, John Lair Papers 1930–1984, Southern Appalachian Archives, Berea College, Berea, Kentucky.

210 Ledford, *Coon Creek Girl*, 11.

211 Ledford, *Coon Creek Girl*, 11.

212 Ledford, *Coon Creek Girl*, 14–16.

213 Ledford, *Coon Creek Girl*, 16.

214 Lily May Ledford, interview by Cathy Fink, "Lily May Ledford Program Outtake," 57:19, posted by Jeff Kaplan, April 15, 2013, Internet Archive, https://archive.org/details/0264LilyMayLedford.

215 Ledford, *Coon Creek Girl*, 16–17.

216 Loyal Jones, "Coon Creek Girls," in Kingsbury, *Encyclopedia of Country Music*, 109.

217 "A Program of American Music," show program, June 8, 1939. series2, box 7, John Lair Papers 1930–1984, Southern Appalachian Archives, Berea College, Berea, Kentucky.

218 Loyal Jones, *Minstrel of the Appalachians: The Story of Bascom Lamar Lunsford* (Lexington: University of Kentucky Press, 2015), 73.

219 Jones, Minstrel of the Appalachians.

220 "Happy Days!" *WLS Family Album 1933*, 26–27.

221 "Flashes," *WLS Weekly*, February 23, 1935, 3.

222 *WLS at the Fair*, pamphlet (Chicago: Prairie Farmer Publishing, 1933), 6–16.

223 "Illinois State Fair Barn Dance," *WLS Family Album 1936*, 24–25.

224 Edythe Dixon, "Chicago's Birthday Jamboree!," *Stand By!* 3, no. 30 (September 4, 1937): 3.

225 Fourth Annual National Folk Festival May 22–28, 1937, Orchestra Hall, Chicago, Auspices Adult Education Council of Chicago, program, series 2, box 7, John Lair Papers 1930–1984, Southern Appalachian Archives, Berea College, Berea, Kentucky.

226 Robert Marovich, "'Lift Up Your Heads': J. Wesley Jones and Chicago's Metropolitan Community Church Choir," *Chicago History* (Fall 2016).

227 "U.S. Folklore Traced, Says Festival Director," *Chicago Daily News*, April 9, 1937.

228 At the time, Dandurand lived at 3142 North Kedzie Avenue, Biggar said, adding he "has not been doing radio work for several years." He also suggested George A. Halstead of 5535 Ellis Avenue, and two harmonica players, Floyd Holmes from Kentucky and Check Stafford, a veteran of the dance circuit in Indiana and Illinois. George C. Biggar to Sarah Gertrude Knott, May 11, 1937, series 2, box 7, John Lair Papers 1930–1984, Southern Appalachian Archives, Berea College, Berea, Kentucky.

229 When the royalty checks started rolling in, Wiseman contacted Lunsford and gave him co-writer credit. Jones, *Minstrel of the Appalachians*, 36.

230 "Radio in the Barn," *Stand By!* 3, no. 29 (August 28, 1937): 2.

231 "Tribute," *Stand By!* 3, no. 8 (April 3, 1937): 2.

232 "These Modern Children," *Stand By!* 3, no. 45 (December 18, 1937): 2.

233 "Misses Home Town," *Stand By!* 1, no. 42 (November 30, 1935): 2.

234 Lair didn't cut ties completely with WLS, apparently. In 1942, *Billboard* reported that he commuted to Chicago two days a week "to assist in production" of the *Barn Dance*. Nat Green, "Chicago," *Billboard*, August 8, 1942, 8.

235 Williams, *Staging Tradition*, 51.

236 The complex still operates today as the Renfro Valley Entertainment Center, with shows running March through December. Williams, *Staging Tradition*, 74.

237 Bob Atcher, interview by Douglas B. Green, June 11, 1974 (OH122-LC), Country Music Foundation Oral History Project, Country Music Hall of Fame® and Museum, Nashville, Tennessee.

238 Bob Atcher, interview by Douglas B. Green, June 11, 1974 (OH122-LC), Country Music Foundation Oral History Project, Country Music Hall of Fame® and Museum, Nashville, Tennessee.

239 Patsy Montana, interview by John W. Rumble, September 2, 1985 (OH197-

LC), Country Music Foundation Oral History Project, Country Music Hall of Fame® and Museum, Nashville, Tennessee. Ironically, Petrillo and the Italian dictator exchanged messages in 1931 when the union leader cabled Mussolini to complain that his consul in Chicago did not hire union musicians for a Jubilee performance. The response he received "was not favorable." Robert D. Leiter, *The Musicians and Petrillo* (New York: Bookman Associates, 1953), 46.

240 James C. Thomson, *The "Prairie Farmer" Story 1950 to 1980* (self-published, 1987), 119.

241 Bob and Maggie Atcher, interview by John W. Rumble, May 1, 1987 (OHC17), Country Music Foundation Oral History Project, Country Music Hall of Fame® and Museum, Nashville, Tennessee. One of those musicians was Johnny Frigo, a South Side bassist who later switched to fiddle and became a world-acclaimed jazz artist. He played on the *Barn Dance* for thirteen years starting in 1951. Adam Bernstein, "Johnny Frigo, 90; Jazz Violinist and Bassist," *Washington Post*, July 6, 2007, http://www.washingtonpost.com/wp-dyn/content/article/2007/07/05/AR2007070501899_pf.html.

242 Casey Bukro, "City Boy Goes to the Grand Ole Opry," *Chicago Tribune*, June 18, 1989, 29.

243 Greg Kot, "When Country Was King," *Chicago Tribune*, January 16, 2000, http://articles.chicagotribune.com/2000-01-16/news/0001160406_1_country-music-national-barn-dance-chicago.

244 John C. Drake, "On Spontaneity," *Sponsor* 3, no. 15 (June 20, 1949), 4 and 6.

245 Fred Rose, "Open Letter," *Billboard*, August 3, 1946, 123.

246 Bob and Maggie Atcher, interview by John W. Rumble, May 2, 1987 (OHC18), Country Music Foundation Oral History Project, Country Music Hall of Fame® and Museum, Nashville, Tennessee.

247 Wayne W. Daniel, "Music of the Postwar Era," in Berry, *Hayloft Gang*, 89.

248 Eric Zorn, "National Barn Dance Reunion: A Hoedown with History," *Chicago Tribune*, June 30, 1983, 6.

249 Thomson, *"Prairie Farmer" Story*, 123.

250 Daniel, "Music of the Postwar Era," 93–94.

251 Childers, *Chicago's WLS Radio*, 57.

252 Thomson, *"Prairie Farmer" Story*, 104–5.

253 Daniel, "Music of the Postwar Era," 96.

254 Bill Taylor, telephone interview by author, November 6, 2015.

255 Jim Klein, telephone interview by author, November 3, 2015.

256 Bill Taylor, telephone interview by author, November 6, 2015.

257 Patsy Montana to John Lair, March 29, 1967, series 2, box 7, John Lair Papers 1930–1984, Southern Appalachian Archives, Berea College, Berea, Kentucky.

CHAPTER TWO

1   Ernest Fuller, "Dedicate New Prudential 41 Story Building," *Chicago Daily Tribune*, December 9, 1955, 13.

2   Arnold R. Hirsch, "Urban Renewal," in *The Encyclopedia of Chicago*, ed. Janice L. Reiff, Ann Durkin Keating, and James R. Grossman (Chicago: The Chicago Historical Society, 2005), http://www.encyclopedia .chicagohistory.org/pages/1295.html.

3   Todd DePastino, *Citizen Hobo: How a Century of Homelessness Shaped America* (Chicago: University of Chicago Press, 2003), 72.

4   John Elmer, "Propose Skid Row's End," *Chicago Tribune*, November 28, 1965, 5.

5   Dominic A. Pacyga, *Chicago: A Biography* (Chicago: University of Chicago Press, 2009), 342.

6   William Mullen, "West Side Story: From Skid Row's Ashes, Hope Rekindles for America's Cities," *Chicago Tribune*, February 16, 1986, 10.

7   *Annual Report of the City Clerk of the City of Chicago*, February 1917; "Check Ordered on 1,900 Women Tavern Owners," *Chicago Daily Tribune*, December 31, 1948.

8   Joan Delaney, face-to-face interview with John Rice, 1999. Recording courtesy of John Rice.

9   Charlie Musselwhite, telephone interview by author, May 25, 2016.

10   John Prine, face-to-face interview by author, November 4, 2016.

11   "Tells Jurors He Gained $20 in Bar Fraud," *Chicago Daily Tribune*, March 17, 1960, A11.

12   "Nab 9 in Strip Joint Raid; Free Two Preachers," *Chicago Daily Tribune*, March 30, 1953, B11.

13   "Story of Girl Causes Mayor to Shut 4 Bars," *Chicago Daily Tribune*, November 1, 1961, 18.

14   "8 Toughs Held in Bar Brawl; 1 Shot in Foot," *Chicago Daily Tribune*, January 12, 1958, 29.

15   Dale Watson, telephone interview by author, August 3, 2016.

16   Johnny Pitts, face-to-face interview by author, July 16, 2013.

17   "Gang Smashes a Stench Bomb, Fires on Tavern," *Chicago Daily Tribune*, November 14, 1950, 11.

18   "20 Shots Fired as 50 Fight in Bar with Chairs, Bottles," *Chicago Daily Tribune*, November 9, 1956, 3.

19   Bruce H. Klauber, *World of Gene Krupa: That Legendary Drummin' Man* (Ventura: Pathfinder, 1990), 8, 83.

20   Johnny Pitts, face-to-face interview by author, July 16, 2013.

21   "20 Shots Fired," 3.

22   Greg Gibson, face-to-face interview by author, January 30, 2017; Jeff Stevens, "Hartford Shop Owner Composed Country Classics," *Hartford*

Times-Press, December 27, 1984, 18.

23 Greg Gibson, face-to-face interview by author, January 30, 2017.

24 "The Song Hasn't Ended for Arbie Gibson," *Hartford Booster*, July 21, 1987, 14.

25 Peggy Constantine, "The C&W Sound—What Is it?," *Chicago Sun-Times Midwest Magazine*, August 8, 1965, 8.

26 Hayden Thompson, face-to-face interview by author, November 5, 2005.

27 Hayden Thompson, face-to-face interview by author, November 5, 2005.

28 Dan Kening, "Blue Suede Blues: In Europe, Hayden Thompson Drives the Fans Wild; Here, He Drives a Limo," *Chicago Tribune*, November 25, 1990, 24.

29 Jan Mark Wolkin and Bill Keenom, *Michael Bloomfield: If You Love These Blues; An Oral History* (San Francisco: Miller Freeman Books, 2000), 26.

30 Hayden Thompson, face-to-face interview by author, November 5, 2005.

31 Roger Guy, *From Diversity to Unity: Southern and Appalachian Migrants in Uptown Chicago, 1950–1970* (Lanham, Maryland: Lexington Books, 2007), 28.

32 Guy, *From Diversity to Unity*, 33–34.

33 Guy, *From Diversity to Unity*, 35.

34 *The Invisible Minority: Urban Appalachians*, ed. William W. Philliber and Clyde B. McCoy with Harry C. Dillingham (Berea: University Press of Kentucky, 1981), 2.

35 Clarus Backes, "Uptown: The Promised Land," *Chicago Tribune*, September 22, 1968, F24.

36 Roger Guy, "Down Home: Perception and Reality among Southern White Migrants in Post World War II Chicago," *Oral History Review* 24, no. 2 (Winter 1997): 43.

37 Backes, "Uptown: The Promised Land."

38 Holly George-Warren, *Public Cowboy No. 1: The Life and Times of Gene Autry* (New York: Oxford University Press, 2007), 94.

39 Gabe Ward, interview by Douglas B. Green, March 31, 1975 (OH91), Country Music Foundation Oral History Project, Country Music Hall of Fame® and Museum, Nashville, Tennessee.

40 Todd Gitlin and Nanci Hollander, *Uptown: Poor Whites in Chicago* (New York: Harper & Row, 1970), xix.

41 Gitlin and Hollander, *Uptown*, xix.

42 Robert Rehak, telephone interview by author, November 2, 2013.

43 "Hill Folk Strum New Note into Volunteer Tutoring," *Human Relations News of Chicago* 7, no. 4 (June 1965): 2.

44 Lynn Van Matre, "'Un-Ravinia': The Hull Thing," *Chicago Tribune*, July 14, 1972, B1.

45 James N. Gregory, *The Southern Diaspora: How the Great Migration of Black and White Southerners Transformed America* (Chapel Hill: Univer-

sity of North Carolina Press, 2005), 161.

46   Henry Bushnell, "Uptown Aids Newcomers: Motivation Class Helps Southerners," *Chicago Tribune*, July 30, 1964, 2.

47   Roger Bellow, telephone interview by author, November 13, 2017.

48   Norma Lee Browning, "Girl Reporter Visits Jungles of Hillbillies," *Chicago Daily Tribune*, March 3, 1957, 1.

49   Browning, "Girl Reporter Visits Jungles of Hillbillies," 1.

50   Browning, "Girl Reporter Visits Jungles of Hillbillies," 9.

51   "Of Hillbillies," *Chicago Daily Tribune*, March 8, 1957, 16.

52   "Who Said Hillbillies Are Illiterate?," *Chicago Daily Tribune*, March 7, 1957, 14.

53   "Of Hillbillies," 16.

54   Norma Lee Browning, "Charges Upset Feudin' Brand of Hillbillies," *Chicago Daily Tribune*, March 10, 1957, 1.

55   Norma Lee Browning, "Is 'Hillbilly' Fighting Word or a Kind One?," *Chicago Daily Tribune*, March 16, 1957, 14.

56   Norma Lee Browning, "Virginia Couple Finds Chicago a Cold and Lonesome Place," *Chicago Daily Tribune*, March 12, 1957, 5.

57   Norma Lee Browning, "The Hillbilly: Writer Looks at His Haunts," *Chicago Daily Tribune*, May 4, 1957, 1.

58   Albert N. Votaw, "The Hillbillies Invade Chicago," *Harper's Magazine*, February 1958, 67.

59   "Dixie Hillbillies Invade Chicago," *Pittsburgh Courier*, February 8, 1958, B5.

60   The tension between the Chicago Police and Appalachians even became the subject of a 1989 Warner Bros. film starring Patrick Swayze and Liam Neeson as brothers from Carbon Glow, Kentucky, avenging the murder of their youngest brother by the Chicago Outfit. Shot in Uptown, *Next of Kin* continually contrasts the community bonds of the brothers' Kentucky homestead with the vice and corruption of Chicago. This is best illustrated by the opening sequence, which features a lively fiddle playing over an image of the family holler. Soon that dissolves into a rainy night in Uptown. Electric guitar, police sirens, and pounding rain are the soundtrack as the camera pans to two Chicago detectives sitting in a car outside a flophouse. "Uptown, Saturday night. A helluva place," says one. The second cop's reply: "Fucking hillbilly heaven is what it is."

61   Hy Thurman, face-to-face interview by author, March 20, 2016.

62   Charlie Musselwhite, telephone interview by author, May 25, 2016.

63   Hy Thurman, face-to-face interview by author, March 20, 2016.

64   Guy, *From Diversity to Unity*, 37–38.

65   Amy Sonnie and James Tracy, *Hillbilly Nationalists, Urban Race Rebels, and Black Power: Community Organizing in Radical Times* (Brooklyn: Melville House, 2011).

66 James Tracy, "Revolutionary Hillbilly: An Interview with Hy Thurman of the Young Patriots Organization," https://www.redneckrevolt.org/single -post/2016/09/24/revolutionary-hillbilly-an-interview-with-hy-thurman -of-the-young-patriots-organization.

67 Tracy, "Revolutionary Hillbilly."

68 Jakobi Williams, *From the Bullet to the Ballot: The Illinois Chapter of the Black Panther Party and Racial Coalition Politics in Chicago* (Chapel Hill: University of North Carolina Press, 2013), 135.

69 Tracy, "Revolutionary Hillbilly."

70 Paul Siegel, face-to-face interview by author, June 14, 2017; "Disabled Miners in Chicago Tell Their Own Story," pamphlet, Chicago Area Black Lung Association, revised edition October 1978, author's collection.

71 Carol Coronado, telephone interview by author, June 3, 2017.

72 Studs Terkel, *Hard Times: An Oral History of the Great Depression* (New York: New Press, 1986), 50.

73 Clarus Backes, "Poor People's Power in Uptown," *Chicago Tribune Magazine*, September 29, 1968, 52.

74 Carol Coronado, telephone interview by author, June 3, 2017.

75 Guy and Candie Carawan, *Voices from the Mountains: The People of Appalachia—Their Faces, Their Words, Their Songs* (Athens: University of Georgia Press, 1996), 72.

76 *Against the Picture Window: A Time of the Phoenix Compendium*, ed. Mary Austin Speaker, Chris Martin, and Sam Gould (Minneapolis: Wooden Leg Print & Press, 2016).

77 Carol Coronado, telephone interview by author, June 3, 2017.

78 Speaker, Martin, and Gould, *Against the Picture Window*.

79 Speaker, Martin, and Gould, *Against the Picture Window*.

80 Speaker, Martin, and Gould, *Against the Picture Window*.

81 Speaker, Martin, and Gould, *Against the Picture Window*.

82 Speaker, Martin, and Gould, *Against the Picture Window*.

83 José "Cha Cha" Jiménez, telephone interview by author, July 29, 2017.

84 Bob Gibson and Marion Fischer, "The Ballad of Fred and Mark," on *Bob Gibson*, Capitol Records, ST-742, 1970, 33⅓ rpm.

85 José "Cha Cha" Jiménez, telephone interview by author, July 29, 2017.

86 "Dawning of a Brand New Day," lyrics, courtesy of José "Cha Cha" Jiménez, author's private collection.

87 Marisol V. Rivera and Judson L. Jeffries, "From Radicalism to Representation: Jose 'Cha Cha' Jimenez's Journey into Electoral Politics, *Journal of African American Studies*, October 25, 2019, 308. https:// crossculturalsolidarity.com/wp-content/uploads/2021/03/Cha-Cha-and -Electoral-Politics.pdf.

88 Gitlin and Hollander, *Uptown*, xix.

89 Carawan and Carawan, *Voices from the Mountains*, 71.

90   Hy Thurman, face-to-face interview by author, March 20, 2016.

91   "ABC Music Service Occupies Own New Quarters This Week," *Billboard*, February 2, 1946, 86.

92   "Perpetual Inventory Key to Efficient Record System," *Billboard 1952 Juke Box Special*, March 15, 1952, 84.

93   Roger Bellow, telephone interview by author, November 17, 2017.

94   Robert Rehak, telephone interview by author, November 2, 2013.

95   Greg Cahill, telephone interview by author, December 5, 2017.

96   Chad Berry, *Southern Migrants, Northern Exiles* (Chicago: University of Illinois Press, 2000), 158.

97   Greg Gibson, telephone interview by author, November 14, 2016.

98   Greg Gibson, telephone interview by author, November 14, 2016.

99   Johnny Pitts, face-to-face interview by author, July 16, 2013.

100 Johnny Pitts, face-to-face interview by author, July 16, 2013.

101 Johnny Pitts, face-to-face interview by author, July 16, 2013.

102 Classified ad, *Chicago Tribune*, November 3, 1968, A27.

103 Johnny Pitts, face-to-face interview by author, July 16, 2013.

104 Greg Gibson, face-to-face interview by author, November 14, 2016. The connection between the Pitts and Williams families went deep. Johnny's mother, Rose Etta Pitts, was the Williams family babysitter back in Alabama.

105 Johnny Pitts, face-to-face interview by author, July 16, 2013.

106 Johnny Pitts, face-to-face interview by author, March 28, 2014.

107 Johnny Pitts, face-to-face interview by author, March 28, 2014; Greg Gibson, telephone interview by author, November 14, 2016.

108 Illinois Legislative Investigating Commission, "A Report to the Illinois General Assembly," May 1978, NCJRS, June 5, 1978, 9–14.

109 Roger Guy, "We Shall Not Be Moved: Hank Williams Village and the Legacy of Advocacy Planning," *Humanity & Society* 37, no. 2 (May 2013): 169.

110 Paul Siegel, face-to-face interview by author, June 14, 2017.

111 John Harding, face-to-face interview by author, February 16, 2017.

112 Hy Thurman, telephone interview by author, June 28, 2017.

113 Roger M. Williams, *Sing a Sad Song: The Life of Hank Williams* (Chicago: University of Illinois Press, 1981), 69.

114 John Rumble, "Fred Rose," in *The Encyclopedia of Country Music*, ed. Paul Kingsbury (New York: Oxford University Press, 1998), 459.

115 Bradley Kincaid, interview by Douglas B. Green, July 10, 1974 (OH83), Country Music Foundation Oral History Project, Country Music Hall of Fame® and Museum, Nashville, Tennessee.

116 "Fred Rose: A Pioneer Song Writer and a Discoverer of Artists," *Billboard*, February 26, 1972, 26.

117 Tony Russell, *County Music Records: A Discography, 1921–1942* (New York: Oxford University Press, 2004), 48.

118 Elizabeth Schlappi, *Roy Acuff: The Smoky Mountain Boy* (Gretna, Louisiana: Pelican, 1997), 29.

119 "MOA Sets Sights on '61 Meet: Say Org Now Reps on National Level," *Billboard*, March 25, 1950, 112.

120 Johnny Sippel, "Folk Talent and Tunes," *Billboard*, March 18, 1950, 29.

121 Whet Moser, "Hank Williams Village: Chicago's Best Urban Plan That Never Happened," *Chicago Magazine*, June 20, 2013, http://www.chicagomag.com/Chicago-Magazine/The-312/June-2013/Hank-Williams-Village-Chicagos-Best-Urban-Planning-Idea-that-Never-Happened/.

122 Roger Guy, "We Shall Not Be Moved: Hank Williams Village and the Legacy of Advocacy Planning," *Sociology in Action*, April 18, 2013, 165.

123 Robert Svejcara, "Junior College Site Hailed as Asset for Uptown Area," *Chicago Tribune*, March 21, 1968, 1-3A.

124 Edith Herman, "Propose Village in Uptown: DUR Gets Plans from Community Group," *Chicago Tribune*, June 30, 1968, N-A1.

125 Guy, "We Shall Not Be Moved," 167.

126 Svejcara, "Junior College Site Hailed as Asset," 1-3A.

127 Hy Thurman, face-to-face interview by author, March 20, 2016.

128 Guy, *From Diversity to Unity*, 119.

129 Guy, "We Shall Not Be Moved," 169.

130 Guy, "We Shall Not Be Moved," 169.

131 Guy, *From Diversity to Unity*, 119.

132 John Hurst, "Hillbillies Form Chicago's Almost Invisible Minority," *Los Angeles Times*, December 16, 1979, 27.

133 Rob Miller, face-to-face interview by author, September 6, 2019.

134 Bill Daley, "Carol's Pub Could Reopen if Go Fund Me Campaign Successful," *Chicago Tribune*, October 4, 2016, http://www.chicagotribune.com/dining/ct-carols-pub-go-fund-me-drive-donations-to-reopen-story.html.

135 Mark Guarino, "Longtime Carol's House Band Diamondback Brings New Fans and Old Regulars to the Resuscitated Country Bar," *Chicago Reader*, December 24, 2018, https://www.chicagoreader.com/Bleader/archives/2018/12/24/longtime-carols-house-band-diamondback-brings-new-fans-and-old-regulars-to-the-resuscitated-country-bar.

136 "WJJD Soundcheck," *Chicago Country 1965* (blog), https://chicagocountry1965.wordpress.com/2014/11/10/project-intro-and-one-hour-of-vintage-country-music-radio/. WJJD stands for James J. Davis, the founder of Mooseheart, the childcare community established by the Loyal Order of Moose. Mooseheart established the radio station in 1924, but over the years it would go through several owners, including Marshall Field III and Plough Pharmaceuticals.

137 Ray Brack, "WJJD Format Boosts Country," *Billboard*, October 16, 1965, 3, 60; Clarence Peterson, "The Big New Sound of Country Music," *Chicago Tribune*, May 29, 1966, 22.

138 George G. Dubinetz, "Is Country Music Golden Key?," *Billboard*, April 8, 1967, 32.

139 Diane Pecknold, *The Selling Sound: The Rise of the Country Music Industry* (Durham: Duke University Press, 2007), 161.

140 "WJJD-Chicago: Chicago's Contemporary Country," *Cash Box*, August 9, 1969, 52.

141 Pecknold, *The Selling Sound*, 161.

142 Peterson, "Big New Sound of Country Music," 22–23.

143 Jon Hartley Fox, "Suppertime Frolic," in Kingsbury, *Encyclopedia of Country Music*, 519–20; "Randy Blake," http://www.hillbilly-music.com /artists/story/index.php?id=14769. Penny Winston Blake Stein, Blake's daughter, recalls her father, raised in an Orthodox Jewish home, asking his rabbi if it was okay to sing Christian hymns on the radio. "You don't have to believe the words because you're bringing joy to other people," Blake was told. He eventually recorded a full album of hymns for Capitol Records in the 1940s. Penny Winston Blake Stein, telephone interview by author, April 5, 2020.

144 Jonny Whiteside, "Ken Nelson," in Kingsbury, *Encyclopedia of Country Music*, 373–74; Paul Wadey, "Ken Nelson: Shaper of Post-War Country Music," *The Independent*, January 10, 2008, http://www.independent.co.uk /news/obituaries/ken-nelson-shaper-of-post-war-country-music-769267 .html.

145 Hugh Cherry, "Country DJs Carry Music to the People," *Music City News* 18, no. 4 (October 1980).

146 Penny Winston Blake Stein, telephone interview by author, April 5, 2020.

147 Matt Brennan, *When Genres Collide: DownBeat, Rolling Stone, and the Struggle Between Jazz and Rock* (New York: Bloomsbury Publishing, 2017), 69.

148 Randy Blake, interview by Douglas B. Green, June 12, 1974 (OH11), Country Music Foundation Oral History Project, Country Music Hall of Fame® and Museum, Nashville, Tennessee.

149 Dubinetz, "Is Country Music Golden Key?," 32.

150 Nick Biro, "WJJD Spurred to Success," *Billboard*, June 12, 1965, 37.

151 Pecknold, *Selling Sound*, 153.

152 Nick Biro, "Country Hits on All Fours, Advertising Seminar Told," *Billboard*, July 24, 1965, 8.

153 Biro, "Country Hits on All Fours," 8.

154 Pecknold, *Selling Sound*, 162.

155 "Country and Western Jamboree Today," *Chicago Tribune*, February 14, 1965, section 5, 11.

156 "Shower of Stars Shows Over the Years," in *Chicago Country: The Good Times 1965 to 1972*, booklet (Chicago: Arlington Place Songs, 1972).

157 Biro, "WJJD Spurred to Success," 37.

158 These acts included Johnny Cash with the Tennessee Three, the Carter Family with Mother Maybelle, Carl Perkins, Kitty Wells, Dolly Parton and Porter Wagoner with the Wagonmasters, Charley Pride, Bill Anderson, Waylon Jennings, Hank Snow, George Jones, Jerry Lee Lewis, off and on with his sister Linda Gail Lewis, Loretta Lynn, Tom T. Hall, Merle Haggard and the Strangers, Connie Smith, Chet Atkins, Floyd Cramer, and Chicago's Hayden Thompson. "Shower of Stars Shows Over the Years."

159 Will Leonard, "An Oyster Bar, a Lobster Tank—and Swahili," *Chicago Tribune*, February 14, 1965, section 5, 12.

160 Ray Brack, "Promoter Rounding Up Backing for Yearly Chi Country Fest," *Billboard*, December 4, 1965, 3.

161 "Study Group Backs Country Fest Plans," *Billboard*, January 1, 1966, 3.

162 "Large C&W Club Success in Chicago," *Billboard*, January 15, 1966, 15.

163 Brack, "Promoter Rounding Up Backing," 44.

164 Brack, "Promoter Rounding Up Backing," 44.

165 "Shower of Stars Shows Over the Years."

166 Hayden Thompson, face-to-face interview by author, November 5, 2005.

167 Cal Starr, face-to-face interview by author, July 17, 2014.

168 Cal Starr, face-to-face interview by author, July 17, 2014.

169 Cal Starr, face-to-face interview by author, July 17, 2014.

CHAPTER THREE

1 Will Leonard, On the Town, *Chicago Tribune*, July 31, 1955, F12.

2 Bob Riesman, *I Feel So Good: The Life and Times of Big Bill Broonzy* (Chicago: University of Chicago Press, 2011), 163.

3 Pat Philips, face-to-face interview by author, August 29, 2013.

4 Riesman, *I Feel So Good*, 213.

5 Pat Philips, face-to-face interview by author, August 29, 2013.

6 Pat Philips, face-to-face interview by author, August 29, 2013.

7 Slim Brundage, "Is It True What They Say about Wells Street?," *Chicago Tribune*, March 21, 1965, 126.

8 Jimmy Savage, Tower Ticker, *Chicago Daily Tribune*, March 20, 1951, A7.

9 Pat Philips, face-to-face interview by author, August 29, 2013.

10 Ella Jenkins, face-to-face interview by author, October 14, 2013.

11 Ella Jenkins, face-to-face interview by author, October 14, 2013.

12 "Biography of Slim Brundage," Inventory of the Slim Brundage Papers, 1955–1991, bulk 1964–1972, Newberry Library, Chicago.

13 Bob Hughes, "Raising Issues [and Ire] at the '20s Pungent Dill Pickle," *Chicago Tribune*, January 12, 1986, H7.

14 William Leonard, "The College of Cut-ups!," *Chicago Daily Tribune*, May 13, 1956, H26.

15 Hughes, "Raising Issues."

16   Hughes, "Raising Issues."

17   "Mystery Angel Plots $250,000 Dill Pickle Club," *Chicago Daily Tribune*, March 7, 1920, A6.

18   Slim Brundage, "Step High, Stoop Low and Leave Your Dignity Outside," in *The Rise & Fall of the Dil Pickle Club: Chicago's Wild '20s!*, ed. Franklin Rosemont (Chicago: Charles H. Kerr, 2013), 89.

19   Ben Reitman, "Chicago's Intellectual and Literary Center," in *The Rise & Fall of the Dil Pickle Club: Chicago's Wild '20s!*, ed. Franklin Rosemont (Chicago: Charles H. Kerr, 2013), 64–65.

20   "Biography of Slim Brundage," Inventory of the Slim Brundage Papers, 1955–1991, bulk 1964–1972, Newberry Library, Chicago.

21   Alexander Ebin, "A Hobo Jungle of Ideas," in *The Rise & Fall of the Dil Pickle Club: Chicago's Wild '20s!*, ed. Franklin Rosemont (Chicago: Charles H. Kerr, 2013), 176.

22   Slim Brundage, *From Bughouse Square to the Beat Generation: Selected Ravings of Slim Brundage, Founder & Janitor of the College of Complexes*, ed. Franklin Rosemont (Chicago: Charles H. Kerr, 1997), 20; Slim Brundage, "Prolegomena to the Complex History of the College of Complexes," in Brundage, *From Bughouse Square to the Beat Generation*, 107.

23   Brundage, *From Bughouse Square to the Beat Generation*, 106.

24   Terri Schultz, Our Town, "King of Failures Clings to His 'College' Presidency," *Chicago Tribune*, n.d.

25   Schultz, "King of Failures Clings to His 'College' Presidency"; Leonard, "The College of Cut-ups!" *Chicago Daily Tribune*; *From Bughouse Square to the Beat Generation*, 136.

26   Brundage, *From Bughouse Square to the Beat Generation*, 116.

27   Brundage, *From Bughouse Square to the Beat Generation*, 117; "Grant Liquor License Denied by Kennelly," *Chicago Daily Tribune*, April 15, 1955, 18.

28   Fanny Butcher, The Literary Spotlight, *Chicago Daily Tribune*, June 3, 1956, C6; Brundage, *From Bughouse Square to the Beat Generation*, 27.

29   Brundage, *From Bughouse Square to the Beat Generation*, 36.

30   Slim Brundage, "Lessons from History?," *Chicago Tribune*, October 6, 1967, section 1, 20.

31   Kenan Heise, "Off-beat Myron 'Slim' Brundage," *Chicago Tribune*, October 30, 1990; Brundage, *From Bughouse Square to the Beat Generation*, 38.

32   Brundage, *From Bughouse Square to the Beat Generation*, 135.

33   Dan Caine, "Blue Note Memories," *Chicago Reader*, August 17, 1989.

34   Bob Gibson and Carole Bender, *I Come for to Sing: The Stops along the Way of a Folk Music Legend* (Gretna, Louisiana: Pelican, 1999), 30–33; "Waitress Wanted by Ken Nordine," classified advertisement 11, *Chicago Daily Tribune*, October 13, 1955, C15.

35   The *Chicago Tribune* hailed it as "the offbeatiest place" in town, not just

for the spoken-word performances and dimly lit atmosphere, but because it was designed to guide attention to the stage: "The place is packed, the atmosphere is as cozy as it is arty, and Nordine's readings, once you and your table mates learn to stop talking and start listening, can be highly interesting." Will Leonard, On the Town, *Chicago Daily Tribune*, October 23, 1955, F15.

36 Will Leonard, On the Town, *Chicago Daily Tribune*, October 23, 1955, F15.

37 Ronald D. Cohen, *Rainbow Quest: The Folk Music Revival & American Society, 1940–1970* (Amherst: University of Massachusetts Press, 2002), 114.

38 Herb Lyon, Tower Ticker, *Chicago Daily Tribune*, February 23, 1956.

39 Katie Lee, "Katie's Historical Discography," http://www.katydoodit.com/pages/Katies_Music_NEW.shtml.

40 Katie Lee, telephone interview by author, September 30, 2014.

41 Katie Lee, *Spicy Songs for Cool Knights*, Specialty Records, SP 5000, 1956, 33⅓ rpm.

42 Katie Lee, *Songs of Couch and Consultation*, Commentary Records, CNT-01, 1957, 33⅓ rpm.

43 Katie Lee, telephone interview by author, September 30, 2014.

44 Herb Lyon, Tower Ticker, *Chicago Daily Tribune*, February 20, 1956.

45 Rau, Review Digest, *Billboard*, April 16, 1955, 11.

46 Pat Philips, face-to-face interview by author, August 29, 2013.

47 Katie Lee, telephone interview by author, September 30, 2014.

48 Will Leonard, On the Town, *Chicago Tribune*, March 11, 1956.

49 Ray Allen, *Gone to the Country: The New Lost City Ramblers and the Folk Music Revival* (Urbana: University of Illinois Press, 2010), 82.

50 John Cohen, telephone interview by author, September 18, 2013.

51 "Honor Roll of Hits," *Billboard*, November 17, 1958, 50; William J. Bush, *Greenback Dollar: The Incredible Rise of the Kingston Trio* (Lanham, Maryland: Scarecrow Press, 2013), 97, 177.

52 Jac Holzman, telephone interview by author, April 23, 2014.

53 Jac Holzman, telephone interview by author, April 23, 2014.

54 Peggy Seeger, telephone interview by author, February 10, 2014.

55 Peggy Seeger, telephone interview by author, February 10, 2014.

56 Peggy Seeger, telephone interview by author, February 10, 2014.

57 Joan Baez, *And a Voice to Sing With: A Memoir* (New York: Summit Books, 1987), 59.

58 Baez, *And a Voice to Sing With*, 59.

59 June Sawyers, "Folk Was King at Chicago's Gate of Horn," *Chicago Tribune*, March 15, 1987.

60 Frank Hamilton, telephone interview by author, May 26, 2013.

61 Frank Hamilton, telephone interview by author, May 26, 2013.

62 Cohen, *Rainbow Quest*, 114–15.

63 Bob Spitz, *Dylan: A Biography* (New York: W. W. Norton, 1989) 178.

64 Andrea Vuocolo Van Ronk, telephone interview by author, November 26, 2013.

65 Dave Van Ronk with Elijah Wald, *The Mayor of MacDougal Street: A Memoir* (Cambridge, Massachusetts: Da Capo Press, 2005), 57–58.

66 Andrea Vuocolo Van Ronk, telephone interview by author, November 26, 2013.

67 Tony Weffzel, The Town Crier, *Chicago Daily News*, February 29, 1956, 50.

68 Jac Holzman, telephone interview by author, April 23, 2014.

69 Rory O'Conner, "Albert Grossman's Ghost," *Musician Magazine*, June 1987, http://theband.hiof.no/articles/agg_musician_june_1987.html.

70 Spitz, *Dylan: A Biography*, 178–79.

71 Michael Goldberg, "Albert Grossman: 1926–1986," *Rolling Stone*, no. 469, March 1986.

72 Bob Dylan, *Chronicles*, vol. 1 (New York: Simon & Schuster, 2004), 97.

73 Robert Shelton, *No Direction Home: The Life and Music of Bob Dylan* (Milwaukee: Hal Leonard Corporation, 2011), 108.

74 Shelton, *No Direction Home*, 109.

75 Baez, *And a Voice to Sing With*, 58.

76 Baez, *And a Voice to Sing With*, 58.

77 William Grimes, "Mary Travers of Peter, Paul and Mary Dies at 72," *New York Times*, September 17, 2009.

78 Cohen, *Rainbow Quest*, 190.

79 Cohen, *Rainbow Quest*, 190–91.

80 Izzy Young, *The Conscience of the Folk Revival: The Writings of Israel "Izzy" Young*, ed. Scott Barretta (Lanham, Maryland: Scarecrow Press, 2013), 185.

81 Jan Mark Wolkin and Bill Keenom, *Michael Bloomfield: If You Love These Blues; An Oral History* (San Francisco: Miller Freeman Books, 2000), 143–44.

82 Ella Jenkins, face-to-face interview by author, October 14, 2013.

83 Judy Collins, *Sweet Judy Blue Eyes: My Life in Music* (New York: Crown Archetype, 2011), 107.

84 Frank Hamilton, telephone interview by author, May 26, 2013.

85 Frank Fried, "Martha Schlamme," *From Lenin to Lennon* (blog), April 16, 2011, http://www.showbizred.com/?tag=martha-schlamme.

86 Frank Fried would soon become one of the biggest concert promoters in Chicago. In 1964 he booked the Beatles at the International Amphitheater, which was the first Chicago appearance by the British group. Fried also booked the first appearance by Barbra Streisand. Besides a long-running folk series at Orchestra Hall that included the Weavers, Josh White, Pete Seeger, Odetta, Bob Dylan, and many others, he dominated theater bookings in Chicago for performers like Johnny Carson, Liberace, Buddy Hackett, and the Rolling Stones. "Johnny Carson Show Opens Triangle

Productions Season," *Chicago Tribune*, September 26, 1965, F11; "Triangle Adds Music Bookings," *Chicago Tribune*, November 3, 1963, F8; "Beatles Are Coming Sept. 4," *Chicago Tribune*, April 14, 1964, B4.

87 Cohen, *Rainbow Quest*, 151.

88 Cohen, *Rainbow Quest*, 146.

89 George Wein, *Myself among Others: A Life in Music*, with Nate Chinen (Cambridge, Massachusetts: Da Capo Press, 2003), 313.

90 Wein, *Myself among Others*, 313.

91 Wein, *Myself among Others*, 313.

92 Israel "Izzy" Young, "Newport Folk Festival," *Caravan* 18 (August–September 1959): 25–27.

93 Wein, *Myself among Others*, 205.

94 Wein, *Myself among Others*, 212.

95 Wein, *Myself among Others*, 214–15.

96 Cohen, *Rainbow Quest*, 151.

97 Mike Thomas, *Second City Unscripted: Revolution and Revelation at the World-Famous Comedy Theater* (Evanston, Illinois: Northwestern University Press, 2012), 3.

98 Anthony Scaduto, *Bob Dylan: A Biography* (London: Helter Skelter, 1997), 142; "Shelley Unveils His New 'Image' at Mister Kelly's," *Chicago Tribune*, May 5, 1963, E12. Display ads and newspaper items from throughout the restaurant's history highlighted music performed there, particularly female singers who went by single names: Lois, Evelyn, or Genevieve. It is described as a "victual Valhalla." Will Davidson, "A Busy Week of Openings for Chicago Cafes," *Chicago Daily Tribune*, November 9, 1941, G2.

99 Gordon Quinn, telephone interview by author, October 8, 2014.

100 This was Dylan's first professional appearance in Chicago. The *Chicago Tribune* noted he was "a highly interesting 21-year-old folk singer who writes his own songs, admits he's influenced by Woody Guthrie and sounds like it. . . . He's gone now but let's hope he'll be back." "Shelley Unveils His New 'Image' at Mister Kelly's," *Chicago Tribune*, May 5, 1963, E12.

101 "1963 Concerts and Recording Sessions," *Still on the Road* (Bjorner.com), entry #430, #450, #460, http://www.bjorner.com/DSN00340%201963.htm #DSN00450.

102 The Dylan appearance would be the "soft" opening for the Bear, presumably because the liquor license was not granted in time. However, when the club opened May 1, 1963, the license was still late. "The new Bear, with top stars ringside including Bette Davis, could serve no booze and all the food was free," the *Chicago Tribune* reported. The city finally granted the club the license two days later. Herb Lyon, Tower Ticker, *Chicago Tribune*, May 3, 1963, 18.

103 Marcia Johnson, face-to-face interview by author, June 6, 2014; Jo Razowki, face-to-face interview by author, June 6, 2014.

104 Marcia Johnson, face-to-face interview by author, June 6, 2014.

105 Jo Razowki, face-to-face interview by author, June 6, 2014.

106 Clinton Heylin, *Bob Dylan: Behind the Shades Revisited* (New York: Harper Collins Publishers, 2001), 119.

107 Dylan told *Rolling Stone* in 2009 that Bloomfield was his favorite guitarist: "The guy that I always miss, and I think he'd still be around if he stayed with me, actually, was Mike Bloomfield. He could just flat-out play. He had so much soul. And he knew all the styles, and he could play them so incredibly well. He was an expert player and a real prodigy, too. Started playing early. . . . He could play like Willie Brown or Charlie Patton. He could play like Robert Johnson way back then in the Sixties. The only other guy who could do that in those days was Brian Jones, who played in the Rolling Stones. He could also do the same thing. Fingerpicking rhythms that hardly anyone could do. Those are the only two guys I've ever met who could . . . from back then . . . the only two guys who could play the pure style of country blues authentically." Douglas Brinkley, "Bob Dylan's Late-Era, Old-Style American Individualism," *Rolling Stone*, RS1078, May 14, 2009, http://www.rollingstone.com/music/news/bob-dylans-america-20090514.

108 Jann S. Wenner, "The Rolling Stone Interview: Mike Bloomfield," part 1, *Rolling Stone*, April 6, 1968, https://www.rollingstone.com/music/music-news/the-rolling-stone-interview-mike-bloomfield-228277/.

109 The 1963 Bear appearance would be the last time Dylan played a small club in Chicago until 1997, when he headlined Metro, the North Side rock club. Dylan returned to the Chicago area the next year, on June 17, 1964, to make his debut at the Ravinia Festival in Highland Park, on a bill he would share with Miriam Makeba. It would be his only appearance at the summer outdoor festival, which that year was in its twenty-ninth season. "He played '"Mr. Tambourine Man' for that Chicago audience and it had not been recorded yet," remembers Ed Holstein, who was there that night. "There were three thousand people there and you could hear every single word; there was no affectation in his voice yet. . . . I could not believe that song and nobody in that audience could and that audience was old, young, everybody." Dylan would wait forty-eight years before returning to Ravinia on June 24, 2016. "Tonight's Program at Ravinia," *Chicago Tribune*, June 17, 1964, B1; "Ravinia Opens Festival Season Tuesday," *Chicago Tribune*, June 14, 1964, E10; Ed Holstein, face-to-face interview by author, May 3, 2013.

110 Howard Sounes, *Down the Highway: The Life of Bob Dylan* (New York: Grove Press, 2001).

111 Sounes, *Down the Highway*.

112 "Old Grey Whistle Test," 1977 Bearsville Picnic, YouTube video, https://www.youtube.com/watch?v=VNK4wRc4O8U.

113 Paul Smart, "Bearsville's Baron: Remembering Albert Grossman, 25 Years Later," *Ulster Publishing*, February 24, 2011.

114 Michael Goldberg, "Albert Grossman: 1926–1986," *Rolling Stone*, no. 469, March 1986.

115 Gibson and Bender, *I Come for to Sing*, 67–68.

116 John Cohen, telephone interview by author, October 17, 2014.

117 David Crosby, telephone interview by author, October 6, 2016.

118 Lynn Van Matre, "Guitar Man: Bob Gibson Benefit to Help the Folk Legend Fight Parkinson's Disease," *Chicago Tribune*, September 22, 1994.

119 Gibson and Bender, *I Come for to Sing*, 5–6.

120 Gibson and Bender, *I Come for to Sing*, 14.

121 Gibson and Bender, *I Come for to Sing*, 3.

122 Gibson and Bender, *I Come for to Sing*, 3.

123 Will Leonard, "Act? He Lets Audience Do It," *Chicago Tribune*, November 21, 1971, 13.

124 Paul Galloway, "Folk Singer Bob Gibson Pays 'Overdue' Tribute to Sandburg's Early Years," *Chicago Tribune*, October 8, 1984, section 5, 1–2.

125 Galloway, "Folk Singer Bob Gibson Pay Tribute," 1–2.

126 Emily Friedman, "Bob Gibson: Folksinger," *Come for to Sing* 5, no. 2 (Spring 1979): 8.

127 Friedman, "Bob Gibson: Folksinger," 9.

128 Jac Holzman, telephone interview by author, April 23, 2014.

129 Lisa Rogak, *A Boy Named Shel: The Life and Times of Shel Silverstein* (New York: Thomas Dunne Books, 2007), 32.

130 Dylan, *Chronicles*, vol. 1, 253.

131 Collins, *Sweet Judy Blue Eyes*, 56.

132 Collins, *Sweet Judy Blue Eyes*, 57–58.

133 Collins, *Sweet Judy Blue Eyes*, 58–59.

134 Baez, *And a Voice to Sing With*, 58–59.

135 Baez, *And a Voice to Sing With*, 61.

136 Mick Houghton, *Becoming Elektra: The True Story of Jac Holzman's Visionary Record Label* (London: Jawbone Press, 2010), 90.

137 Richie Unterberger, *Turn! Turn! Turn!: The '60s Folk-Rock Revolution* (San Francisco: Backbeat Books, 2002), 55.

138 Art Thieme, telephone interview by author, February 8, 2014.

139 Simon & Garfunkel recorded the Gibson and Camp song "You Can Tell the World" to kick off their 1964 debut album, *Wednesday Morning, 3 AM*, on Columbia. Playing bass on that album is Bill Lee, also the house bassist at the Gate of Horn and the father of film director Spike Lee. Simon & Garfunkel, *Wednesday Morning, 3 AM*, Columbia, CL 2249, 1964, 33⅓ rpm.

140 By March 1961, Camp had joined the Second City as a troupe member and first appeared in the revue "Animal Fair." "Talent Topics," *Billboard*, March 27, 1961, 41.

141 Bob Gibson and Hamilton Camp, *Gibson and Camp at the Gate of Horn*, Elektra, EKL-207, 1961, 33⅓ rpm.

142 "Faye Asks 500G for Ditty Damage," *Billboard*, January 27, 1962, 5.

143 Shel Silverstein, liner notes, Bob Gibson and Hamilton Camp, *Gibson and Camp at the Gate of Horn*, Elektra, EKL-207, 1961, 33⅓ rpm.

144 Collins, *Sweet Judy Blue Eyes*, 102–3.

145 Gibson and Bender, *I Come for to Sing*, 90.

146 Gibson and Bender, *I Come for to Sing*, 92. Frank Hamilton, Gibson's original partner, said heroin in the folk music world was indicative of its downward spiral: "It was when folk music became show business. There turned out to be a lot of slick operations and shady dealings and there were drugs involved and it was crummy lifestyle, with people going out on road and beating their brains out with unscrupulous managers. When folk music first started, it was not like that. It was a rebellion against that. But it became enveloped by the music business." Hamilton, telephone interview by author, May 26, 2013.

147 Frank Hamilton, telephone interview by author, May 26, 2013. Ed Holstein notes that another problem Gibson had in the 1960s was that "he was never a hippie. . . . He was too old. Gibson represented a different generation." Holstein, face-to-face interview by author, May 3, 2013.

148 Skip Haynes, telephone interview by author, May 7, 2017.

149 Jac Holzman, telephone interview by author, April 23, 2014.

150 Gibson and Bender, *I Come for to Sing*, 95.

151 "Folk Singer Gibson Faces Drug Charge," *Chicago Tribune*, August 15, 1969, A1.

152 Late-night jams were common after the clubs closed during that period. Nashville songwriter Mickey Clark recounts that he opened the show for Linda Ronstadt at the Quiet Knight. Afterward, he met Bernie Leaden, whom he already knew through a mutual friend. According to Clark: "We were going to have a picking session and Bernie was coming with us and he said, 'Do you mind if we pick up a friend of mine who is playing another club? He was playing Mr. Kelly's.' I said, 'No, that's no problem.' So we go to Mr. Kelly's and there was a guy standing in front with a banjo. He gets in the car with us and we go back and have this picking session and the banjo player said very little the whole night. He was like an introvert. It turns out it was Steve Martin." Mickey Clark, telephone interview by author, May 20, 2017.

153 Accounts vary as to whether Prine was aware Gibson recorded his song; in his autobiography, Gibson says Prine knew, but Ed Holstein says he was the one who told Prine of the song's inclusion after Gibson's album was released, which set the wheels in motion for Atlantic to take legal action. Gibson and Bender, *I Come for to Sing*, 107; Ed Holstein, face-to-face interview by author, August 29, 2013.

154 Tom Paxton, telephone interview by author, February 20, 2015.

155 Lawrence Rand, "Old Folkies: A Gathering of the Gate of Horn Crowd," *Chicago Reader*, October 6, 1994.

156 Dan Kening, "Friends Star at Benefit to Aid Bob Gibson," *Chicago Tribune*, September 29, 1994.

157 Gibson and Bender, *I Come for to Sing*, 239, 249.

158 Gibson and Bender, *I Come for to Sing*, 239.

159 Gibson and Bender, *I Come for to Sing*, 244.

160 Will Leonard, "'Monday Omnibus'—New and Exciting Potpourri," *Chicago Tribune*, June 18, 1961.

161 "A Gasser," *Time*, November 24, 1958.

162 "White Blues Singer: Blonde Keeps Blues Alive," *Ebony*, November 1959, 149.

163 "White Blues Singer," 150.

164 "Gate of Horn Shows to Aid Scholarships," *Chicago Tribune*, July 9, 1960.

165 "Chicago Jazz Spots Stage CORE Night," *Jet*, November 23, 1961, 60.

166 Bill Cosby, "The Julliard School, 2002," in *Take This Advice: The Most Nakedly Honest Graduation Speeches Ever Given*, ed. Sandra Bark (New York: Simon Spotlight Entertainment, 2005), 24.

167 Cosby, "The Julliard School, 2002," 24.

168 Maya Angelou, *The Collected Autobiographies of Maya Angelou* (New York: Random House, 2012), 688.

169 Angelou, *Collected Autobiographies*, 690.

170 Angelou, *Collected Autobiographies*, 691.

171 Angelou, *Collected Autobiographies*, 693.

172 Robert Pruter, *Chicago Soul* (Urbana: University of Illinois Press, 1992), 34.

173 "Arson Squad Opens Quiz in Hotel Blaze," *Chicago Daily Tribune*, April 9, 1959, 15.

174 Will Leonard, "Folk Song Famine Over—Gate's Open and Swinging," *Chicago Daily Tribune*, June 21, 1959, 11.

175 Will Leonard, "Salute to a Glittering Gate of Horn, 'Odyssey' Style," *Chicago Tribune*, April 23, 1961.

176 Will Leonard, "Lenny Reminds You This Isn't a Walt Disney World," *Chicago Tribune*, November 18, 1962.

177 "Comedian to Face Charges of Indecency," *Chicago Tribune*, December 6, 1962.

178 Soundcloud, "Audio of Lenny Bruce Show Raided by Chicago Police," recording, https://soundcloud.com/sheckygrey/audio-of-lenny-bruce-show.

179 "2 Take Stand in Night Club Obscenity Case," *Chicago Tribune*, January 30, 1963, A7.

180 Soundcloud, "Audio of Lenny Bruce Show Raided by Chicago Police." https://soundcloud.com/sheckygrey/audio-of-lenny-bruce-show.

181 "2 Take Stand in Night Club Obscenity Case," A7.

182 "Set Trial Date for Lenny Bruce, 2 Others," *Chicago Tribune*, December 13, 1962, 14.

183 George Carlin, *Last Words* (New York: Free Press, 2009), 106–7.

184 Carlin, *Last Words*, 106–7.

185 Kenan Heise, "Moses Moon, Owned the Gate of Horn," *Chicago Tribune*, August 31, 1993.

186 Lenny Bruce, *How to Talk Dirty and Influence People* (New York: Fireside, 1992), 146.

187 "Gate of Horn's Liquor License Up to Mayor," *Chicago Tribune*, January 31, 1963, D2.

188 "2 Take Stand in Night Club Obscenity Case," A7.

189 "Gate of Horn Loses Permit for 15 Days," *Chicago Tribune*, February 9, 1963, S7.

190 "Bailes Espanoles: Channel 9 Today At 9," *Chicago Daily Tribune*, August 11, 1962, A6.

191 Larry Wolters, "Folk Music Show Brightens TV Scene," *Chicago Tribune*, July 15, 1963, B12.

192 Folkfest, episode with Martin Yarborough, TV_09893, Museum of Broadcast Communications, https://museumtv.pastperfectonline.com/archive/37354375-4EB5-400D-AB45-394034258069.

193 Rudy Orisek, interview by Cary O'Dell, Museum of Broadcast Communications, Chicago, http://chicagotelevision.com/RUDY.htm.

194 David Somerville, telephone interview by author, November 4, 2014.

195 Will Leonard, "2 'Discoveries' Have the Gate Swingin'," *Chicago Tribune*, March 17, 1963.

196 "Gate of Horn Club Assets Will Be Sold," *Chicago Tribune*, February 13, 1964.

197 "Henry E. Norton, 64, Chicago Chop House Owner," *Chicago Sun-Times*, April 28, 1994.

198 "'Sunshine' Brightens Gate of Horn," *Chicago Defender*, November 25, 1972.

199 Roger McGuinn, "Gate of Horn," on *Peace on You*, Columbia Records, KC-32956, 1974, 33⅓ rpm.

200 William Leonard, "Stracke, Pick Quit Concerts for Night Club," *Chicago Daily Tribune*, May 26, 1957, E8.

CHAPTER FOUR

1 Mark Dvorak, face-to-face interview by author, November 4, 2013.

2 Mark Dvorak, face-to-face interview by author, November 4, 2013.

3 Terry Galanoy, "Folk Music Is for All God's Children," *Chicago Tribune*, December 7, 1969, D4.

4 "Win Stracke," promotional pamphlet, n.d., subseries 4, box 18, Old Town School of Folk Music Collection, Chicago.

5 Win Stracke, "The Joyous Noise of Old Town Past," *Chicago Tribune*, December 26, 1971, G20.

6 Marshall Rosenthal, "The Six Decades of Win Stracke: Singing Out for the

Joy of It," *Chicago Daily News*, September 25–26, 1971, 4.

7   Stracke never became a household name on the *Barn Dance* like so many others at the time. However, in 1932, he was featured in "Embarrassing Moments," a feature of *Behind the Scenes at WLS*, a promotional magazine WLS published each year. As "Winfred Stracke, the bottomless bass of the Melody Men," he recounted that while "stretched out on the sand," he decided to ask a passerby holding a basket for a bag of the popcorn he must be selling. After the man exclaimed that the basket was holding "a dimpled, sleeping baby" and none of "the tasty stuff," "Win turned the color of beets, sheepishly deciding he didn't want any popcorn in the first place!" "Embarrassing Moments," *Behind the Scenes at WLS*, 1932, 20.

8   Rosenthal, "The Six Decades of Win Stracke," 4.

9   Win Stracke, interview by Mark Dvorak, June 14, 1990.

10 Rosenthal, "Six Decades of Win Stracke," 4.

11 Studs Terkel, *Touch and Go: A Memoir* (New York: The New Press, 2007), 95.

12 Rosenthal, "Six Decades of Win Stracke," 4.

13 Win Stracke, interview by Mark Dvorak, July 26, 1990.

14 Rick Kogan, "Actress Beverly Younger Podewell, 83," *Chicago Tribune*, July 29, 1999.

15 *Studs' Place*, "Bowling," video, 27:31, Media Burn Independent Video Archive, http://mediaburn.org/video/studs-place-bowling/.

16 Federal Bureau of Investigation (FBI), file 100-7848, 14.

17 FBI, file 100-16487-1, John Edgar Hoover to Special Agent in Charge, Chicago, Illinois, April 7, 1941, FOIA case no. 46804, doc. ID 32512444, declassified June 22, 2015.

18 FBI, file 100-2655, WINFRED STRACKE, July 1, 1941, FOIA case no. 46804, doc. ID 32512444, declassified June 22, 2015, 1.

19 FBI, file 100-2655, WINFRED STRACKE, July 1, 1941, FOIA case no. 46804, doc. ID 32512444, declassified June 22, 2015, 2–3.

20 FBI, file 100-2655, WINFRED STRACKE, October 8, 1941, FOIA case no. 46804, doc. ID 32512444, declassified June 22, 2015, 1–2.

21 FBI, file 100-2655, WINFRED STRACKE, October 8, 1941, FOIA case no. 46804, doc. ID 32512444, declassified June 22, 2015, 2.

22 FBI, file 100-116487-17, "CHANGED" WINFRED STRACKE, December 11, 1953, FOIA case no. 46804, doc. ID 32512444, declassified June 22, 2015, 1.

23 FBI, file 100-116487-17, "CHANGED" WINFRED STRACKE, December 11, 1953, FOIA case no. 46804, doc. ID 32512444, declassified June 22, 2015, 7.

24 Studs Terkel, *Hard Times: An Oral History of the Great Depression* (New York: New Press, 1970), 166–67.

25 Rosenthal, "Six Decades of Win Stracke," 4.

26 Rosenthal, "Six Decades of Win Stracke," 2.

27 Ted Okuda and Jack Mulqueen, *The Golden Age of Chicago Children's Television* (Chicago: Lake Claremont Press, 2004), 229.

28 FBI, file 100-16487-13, WINFRED JOHN STRACKE, February 24, 1956, FOIA case no. 46804, doc. ID 32512444, declassified June 22, 2015.

29 Rosenthal, "Six Decades of Win Stracke," 4.

30 "Win Stracke," promotional pamphlet, n.d.

31 Jane Bradbury, face-to-face interview by author, June 1, 2013.

32 William Leonard, "Stracke, Pick Quit Concerts for Night Club," *Chicago Daily Tribune*, May 26, 1957, E8.

33 Win Stracke, interview by Mark Dvorak, July 26, 1990.

34 Frank Hamilton, email exchange with author, June 11, 2015.

35 Ray Flerlage, "Booklet Part II (Biographical)," on *Frank Hamilton Sings Folk Songs*, Folkways Records, FA 2437, 1962, 33⅓ rpm.

36 Will Kaufman, *Woody Guthrie, American Radical* (Urbana: University of Illinois Press, 2011), 19, 34–35.

37 Joe Klein, *Woody Guthrie, A Life* (London: Faber & Faber, 1981), 402.

38 Frank Hamilton, telephone interview by author, July 6, 2013.

39 Bess Lomax Hawes, "But I Can't Carry a Tune . . . ," *Sing Out!* 11, no. 2 (April–May 1961): 26–27.

40 Frank Hamilton, telephone interview by author, July 6, 2013.

41 Frank Hamilton, telephone interview by author, July 6, 2013.

42 Ronald D. Cohen, *Rainbow Quest: The Folk Music Revival & American Society, 1940–1970* (Amherst: University of Massachusetts Press, 2002), 5–6.

43 Frank Hamilton, telephone interview by author, July 6, 2013.

44 Cohen, *Rainbow Quest*, 6.

45 David Gedalecia, telephone interview by author, February 28, 2013. Another student who went to Hamilton's house for lessons was Michael Bloomfield. Jan Mark Wolkin and Bill Keenom, *Michael Bloomfield: If You Love These Blues; An Oral History* (San Francisco: Miller Freeman Books, 2000), 32.

46 FBI, letter to Benjamin Van Loon, June 1, 2016, regarding FOIPA Request No. 1339273-001 STRAWN-HAMILTON, FRANK.

47 FBI, file 100-22181, DAWN GREENING, January 1, 1951, FOIA case no. 15329, doc. ID 70001323, declassified June 22, 2015, 49.

48 Lance Greening, face-to-face interview by author, August 19, 2013.

49 "Arson Fails at Home of a Negro Scientist," *New York Times*, November 23, 1950, 29.

50 "Negro's Suburban Home Bombed," *New York Times*, June 14, 1951, 20.

51 Lance Greening, face-to-face interview by author, August 19, 2013.

52 Ramblin' Jack Elliott, telephone interview by author, August 15, 2014.

53 Lance Greening, face-to-face interview by author, August 19, 2013.

54 Peggy Seeger, telephone interview by author, February 10, 2014.

55 FBI, file 100-22181, DAWN GREENING, August 2, 1950, FOIA case no. 15329, doc. ID 70001323, declassified June 22, 2015, 1.

56 FBI, file 100-22181, DAWN GREENING, August 2, 1950, FOIA case no. 15329,

doc. ID 70001323, declassified June 22, 2015, 1–2.

57 FBI, file 1022181, DAWN GREENING, August 2, 1950, FOIA case no. 15329, doc. ID 70001323, declassified June 22, 2015, 2.

58 FBI, file 1022181-5, DAWN GREENING, January 1, 1951, FOIA case no. 15329, doc. ID 70001323, declassified June 22, 2015, 50.

59 FBI, file 100-393127, DAWN GREENING, February 11, 1953, FOIA case no. 15329, doc. ID 70001323, declassified June 22, 2015, 23.

60 FBI, file 100-393127, DAWN GREENING, February 11, 1953, FOIA case no. 15329, doc. ID 70001323, declassified June 22, 2015, 24; FBI, file 100-393127, DAWN GREENING, March 12, 1953, FOIA case no. 15329, doc. ID 70001323, declassified June 22, 2015, 1.

61 FBI, file 100-393127, DAWN GREENING, March 12, 1953, FOIA case no. 15329, doc. ID 70001323, declassified June 22, 2015, 3.

62 FBI, file 100-22165 DAWN GREENING, November 15, 1953, FOIA case no. 15329, doc. ID 70001323, declassified June 22, 2015, 11.

63 FBI, file 100-22165 DAWN GREENING, November 15, 1953, FOIA case no. 15329, doc. ID 70001323, declassified June 22, 2015, 11.

64 Brother John Sellers to Dawn Greening, June 29, 1968, subseries 3, box 14, Old Town School of Folk Music Collection, Chicago.

65 Billy Chips to Dawn Greening, 1965, subseries 3, box 14, Old Town School of Folk Music Collection, Chicago.

66 Lance Greening, face-to-face interview by author, August 19, 2013.

67 Lance Greening, face-to-face interview by author, August 19, 2013.

68 Lance Greening, face-to-face interview by author, August 19, 2013.

69 Frank Hamilton, talk, Old Town School of Folk Music, Chicago, April 19, 2015.

70 Win Stracke, interview by Mark Dvorak, July 26, 1990.

71 R. M. Lawless, *Folksingers and Folksongs in America: A Handbook of Biography* (New York: Duell, Sloan and Pierce, 1960), 108.

72 Hamilton, talk, Old Town School. of Folk Music.

73 Steve Romanoski, "Dawn Greening: The Mother of Us All," *Come for to Sing* 6, no. 1 (Winter 1980): 7–8.

74 Ted Johnson, face-to-face interview by author, June 30, 2013.

75 Win Stracke, interview by Mark Dvorak, July 26, 1990.

76 Will Leonard, "Art for Art's Sale? Not in Evanston," *Chicago Tribune*, July 27, 1968, section 1, 6.

77 Win Stracke, essay, in *The Old Town School of Folk Music: The First Ten Years or The Biography of a Hunch*, pamphlet, 1967, subseries 4, box 18, Old Town School of Folk Music Collection, Chicago, 2.

78 Ted Johnson, face-to-face interview by author, June 30, 2013. In 1952, Baulcr moved his hybrid office-taproom one block west to 401 West North Avenue and kept the De Luxe Gardens name. Will Leonard, *Chicago Daily Tribune*, May 7, 1952, section 3, 9. See also Win Stracke, interview by Mark

Dvorak, July 26, 1990; Leonard, "Art for Art's Sale? Not in Evanston," 6.

79   Edward Schreiber, "2 in Lead for Paddy Bauler's Seat," *Chicago Tribune*, February 12, 1967, 10-2, 3.

80   Jane Bradbury, face-to-face interview by author, June 1, 2013.

81   Win Stracke, "Paddy's Song," song sheet, n.d., subseries 4, box 18, Old Town School of Folk Music Collection, Chicago.

82   Art Thieme, telephone interview by author, February 8, 2014.

83   Win Stracke to Jack and Gladys Conroy, November 27, 1957, box 30, file 1518, Jack Conroy Papers, Newberry Library, Chicago.

84   Stracke, essay, in *Old Town School of Folk Music*, 2.

85   Stracke to Jack and Gladys Conroy, November 27, 1957, box 30, file 1518, Jack Conroy Papers.

86   Ted Johnson, face-to-face interview by author, June 30, 2013.

87   Bob Riesman, *I Feel So Good: The Life and Times of Big Bill Broonzy* (Chicago: University of Chicago Press, 2011), 226.

88   Riesman, *I Feel So Good*, 238–44.

89   Soltker is responsible for preserving much of the Chicago Repertory Group's history. She donated a collection of scripts, scrapbooks, programs, publicity photos, and mimeograph copies of 267 plays, songs, and sketches to the Special Collections Research Center of the University of Chicago Library in June 1958. https://www.lib.uchicago.edu/e/scrc/findingaids/view.php?eadid=ICU.SPCL.CRG&q=Soltker.

90   The company started in 1933 at the Marshall Field Apartments at 1450 North Sedgwick Street, which opened four years earlier. It moved to a renovated church at 1718 North North Park, less than three blocks away from the Old Town School. Robert Blau, "Workshop's Last Act to Be Legacy," *Chicago Tribune*, April 3, 1986.

91   Nate Lofton, face-to-face interview by author, October 22, 2014.

92   FBI, file 175-7-19, January 3, 1973, FOIA case no. 1338029-0, declassified March 15, 2016, 1.

93   FBI, file 175-7-27, February 7, 1973, FOIA case no. 1338029-0, declassified March 15, 2016, 1.

94   Stracke, essay, in *Old Town School of Folk Music*, 4–5.

95   Lance Greening, face-to-face interview by author, August 19, 2013.

96   Stracke, essay, in *Old Town School of Folk Music*, 3.

97   Old Town School of Folk Music, "1961–62 Schedule," pamphlet, box 50, folder 2008, Inventory of Jack Conroy Papers, 1864–1991, Newberry Library, Chicago.

98   Hamilton, talk, Old Town School of Folk Music.

99   Norma Lee Browning, "Are You a Folknik in a Hootenanny? Then You're Having Fun in Music Craze," *Chicago Daily Tribune*, June 24, 1960, 13.

100 Norma Lee Browning, "Mountain Music Goes to Town: City Slickers Are Whoopin' and Whompin' Gee-tars Fit to Kill. Only They Call It Art,"

Chicago Daily Tribune, April 20, 1968, C32. Stracke later added to the list. In an appeal to donors, he wrote that the occupations of students were as random as "office workers, engineers, psychiatrists, high school and college students, housewives, elementary, high school and college teachers, artists, priests and Protestant clergymen, nuns . . . salesmen, doctors, lawyers, social workers, firemen, photographers, a great number of advertising men, and recently several professional hockey players and their wives." Stracke, essay, in *Old Town School of Folk Music*, 3.

101 Norma Lee Browning, "Are You a Folknik in a Hootenanny?," 13.

102 Hamilton, talk, Old Town School of Folk Music.

103 Izzy Young, *The Conscience of the Folk Revival: The Writings of Israel "Izzy" Young*, ed. Scott Barretta (Lanham, Maryland: Scarecrow Press, 2013), 50. In an interview, Weissman denied he was part of the New York school, but he did say he borrowed the Old Town School's model of teaching for the banjo and guitar classes he taught in Denver with Harry Tuft, who later founded the Denver Folklore Center in March 1962. Richard Weissman, telephone interview by author, June 25, 2015.

104 Mike Boehm, "He's Tied to the Strings: Teaching Guitar Techniques via Audio and Videocassettes Has Been the Dominant Theme in Happy Traum's Folk-Music Career," *Los Angeles Times*, January 23, 1992, http://articles.latimes.com/1992-01-23/entertainment/ca-1066_1_folk-music.

105 Harry Tuft, telephone interview by author, July 15, 2015.

106 Advertisement, *Chicago Tribune*, September 29, 1963, G2.

107 "Folk Singer Heads Performers at Booth House Second 'Hootenanny,'" *Chicago Defender*, July 22, 1959.

108 Norma Lee Browning, "Are You a Folknik in a Hootenanny?," 13; Stracke, essay, in *Old Town School of Folk Music*, 5–6.

109 *Studs Terkel's Almanac*, WFMT-FM, recording, 1963.

110 Stu Ramsay, face-to-face interview by author, November 4, 2014.

111 Stu Ramsay, face-to-face interview by author, November 4, 2014.

112 Stu Ramsay, face-to-face interview by author, November 4, 2014.

113 Stu Ramsay, face-to-face interview by author, November 4, 2014.

114 Stu Ramsay, face-to-face interview by author, November 4, 2014.

115 Stu Ramsay, *Stu Ramsay Loves Dobro, Banjo, Guitar and Harmonica*, Mercury, SR-60775, 1963, 33⅓ rpm. The wall belonged to Gene Segal Antiques at 431 North Wells Street in Old Town. The artwork served as a kind of early guerilla marketing campaign. The *Chicago Tribune*'s Will Leonard noted that people were "mystified" for months about what the message could mean: "Strange kind of valentine, we mused." Will Leonard, "'No Tip' Coin Fails in Its Mission," *Chicago Tribune*, May 18, 1963, 13.

116 Chad Mitchell, liner notes, Stu Ramsay, *Stu Ramsay Loves Dobro, Banjo, Guitar and Harmonica*, Mercury, SR-60775, 1963, 33⅓ rpm.

117 Herb Lyon, "Tower Ticker," *Chicago Tribune*, May 15, 1963, section 1, 14.

118 Lyon, "Tower Ticker," *Chicago Tribune*, May 15, 1963, section 1, 14.

119 Stu Ramsay, face-to-face interview by author, November 4, 2014. Ramsay made one more album: *Scufflin' with Stu Ramsay and Chicago Slim*, on Capitol Records, in 1969. The producer was Nick Venet, known for signing the Beach Boys to Capitol and producing their early hits, as well as for producing other Capitol stars like Glen Campbell, Bobby Darin, and Ricky Nelson. ("A lot of teenage cats are playing and singing the blues in layers. They're O.K., but this one's real," he writes in the liner notes.) Slim was a harmonica player named Noel Schiff who briefly played with Michael Bloomfield. "He had connections to Maxwell Street. He knew Johnny Young, Big Walter. He was like a son to Howlin' Wolf, they hung together all the time. His father was on Mayor Daley's commission. They were all connected. He could drive his car all over the city and he would never be bothered. He loved the blues," Ramsay said. Ramsay's opinion of this record is the same as his opinion of the first: "It sounded like crap." He ordered Capitol not to release it, and they pulled it from the shelves. James B. Murphy, *Becoming the Beach Boys, 1961–1963* (Jefferson, North Carolina: McFarland, 2015), 72; Stu Ramsay and Chicago Slim, *Scufflin' with Stu Ramsay and Chicago Slim*, Mercury, ST-344, 1969, 33⅓ rpm.

120 Tim Spannaus, "Dr. King Appeals for Non-violence," *Elmhurst Press*, July 14, 1966.

121 Stu Ramsay, face-to-face interview by author, November 4, 2014.

122 *Studs Terkel's Almanac*, WFMT-FM, recording, 1963.

123 Emily Friedman and Fred Holstein, "Interview with Fleming Brown," *Come for to Sing* 1, no. 2 (April 1975): 6.

124 Stephen Wade, "The Conduit," *Journal of Country Music* 17, no. 3 (1995): 10.

125 Kenan Heise, "Fleming Brown, 58, Banjo Player, Singer," *Chicago Tribune*, December 7, 1984, D14.

126 Wade, "The Conduit," 10.

127 George Armstrong, liner notes, *Fleming Brown*, Folk-Legacy Records, FS1-1, 1962, 33⅓ rpm.

128 Lucy Key Miller, "Front Views & Profiles," *Chicago Tribune*, January 29, 1952, part 2, 1.

129 Emily Friedman and Fred Holstein, "Fleming Brown: Earlier Days," *Come for to Sing* 1, no. 3 (Summer 1975): 17.

130 Brown played a major role in starting *The Midnight Special*, the long-running folk music show on WFMT-FM. In 1956, Mike Nichols, the famed film and Broadway director, was an announcer on the station and a member of the Compass Players, which evolved into the Second City improv troupe. Nichols asked Brown to organize a folk music show for the station. Nichols explained that he knew little about folk music and had tried bringing in a few University of Chicago students, but they "just went berserk" in

front of the live microphone by playing dirty songs. Brown agreed to help and organized a small band of players who performed live at the Orrington Hotel in Oak Park. They performed for a full year under Nichols's direction. Brown also gave the show its title because it was the time the show started. "We'd go until we couldn't stand the heat anymore or ran out of six packs of beer, whichever came first," he said. Friedman and Holstein, "Fleming Brown: Earlier Days," 16.

131 Friedman and Holstein, "Interview with Fleming Brown," 7.

132 Friedman and Holstein, "Interview with Fleming Brown," 7.

133 Friedman and Holstein, "Interview with Fleming Brown," 7.

134 George Armstrong, liner notes, *Fleming Brown*, Folk-Legacy Records, FS1-1, 1962, 33⅓ rpm.

135 Friedman and Holstein, "Fleming Brown: Earlier Days," 20.

136 Friedman and Holstein, "Interview with Fleming Brown," 8.

137 Stephen Wade, telephone interview by author, August 8, 2013.

138 Heise, "Fleming Brown, 58, Banjo Player, Singer."

139 "De Castro, Valucha," *Chicago Tribune*, March 18, 2007.

140 *Studs Terkel's Almanac*, WFMT-FM, recording, 1963.

141 Buffington adopted her maiden name, De Castro, after her divorce. She stayed with the school into the 1970s but kept performing throughout the Midwest afterward. She died February 12, 2007, of liver cancer. "De Castro, Valucha," *Chicago Tribune*, March 18, 2007.

142 Nate Lofton, face-to-face interview by author, October 22, 2014.

143 Paul Collins, telephone interview by author, June 5, 2015.

144 Liam T. A. Ford, *Soldier Field: A Stadium and Its City* (Chicago: University of Chicago Press, 2009), 143–44.

145 Monica C. Reed, "Music Festivals and the Formation of Chicago Culture," *Journal of the Illinois State Historical Society* 103, no. 1 (Spring 2010): 67.

146 "Rural Dances Get Place at Music Festival," *Chicago Sunday Tribune*, June 25, 1939, 1.

147 "1,000 Barn Dance Fans to Swing in Soldiers Field," *Chicago Daily Tribune*, July 30, 1939, SW2.

148 "Do-Ci-Do! City Folks Round Up in Square Dance," *Chicago Tribune*, November 19, 1950, NW6.

149 Lloyd Wendt, "Something Afoot in Dancing," *Chicago Sunday Tribune*, January 5, 1947.

150 "Square Dances Draw North Side Groups to Parks," *Chicago Tribune*, December 13, 1942, N2.

151 Johnny Sippel, "Folk Talent and Tunes," *Billboard*, November 4, 1950, 35.

152 Ruth Moss, "10,000 Square Dancers Hoof Away 15 Hours," *Chicago Daily Tribune*, October 25, 1953, 7.

153 Leslie Monypenny, "2 Great Mass Attractions at Music Festival," *Chicago Daily Tribune*, August 22, 1951, part 1, 4.

154 Paul DeBeaubien, "Do-Se-Do with John Dolce," *Daytona Beach Morning Journal*, July 18, 1976, 6.

155 Laurie Goering, "Roll Out the Barrel: State Chooses Square Dance Over Polka," *Chicago Tribune*, August 18, 1990, S1.

156 Paul Collins, telephone interview by author, June 5, 2015.

157 Paul Collins, telephone interview by author, June 5, 2015.

158 *Studs Terkel's Almanac*, WFMT-FM, recording, 1963.

159 Ella Jenkins, face-to-face interview by author, October 13, 2013.

160 Louise Dimiceli, "Ella Jenkins: Chicago's Magical Pied Piper," *Come for to Sing* 4, no. 2 (Spring 1978): 5.

161 Ella Jenkins, face-to-face interview by author, October 13, 2013.

162 Mara Tapp, "Ella Jenkins: Singer Charms Children with Her Folk Songs," *City Talk*, June 22–29, 2001.

163 Ella Jenkins, *Call-and-Response: Rhythmic Group Singing*, Smithsonian Folkways Recordings, 1998, CD.

164 Anthony Seeger, "Curator's Introduction to the 50th Anniversary Reissue of *Call-and-Response*," *Call-and-Response: Rhythmic Group Singing*, Smithsonian Folkways Recordings 1998, CD.

165 Ella Jenkins, *You'll Sing a Song and I'll Sing a Song*, Folkways, Smithsonian Folkways Recordings, 1992, http://www.folkways.si.edu/ella -jenkins/youll-sing-a-song-and-ill-sing-a-song/childrens/music/album /smithsonian.

166 Shia Kapos, "Ginni Clemmens, 66: Popular Chicago Folk, Blues Singer," *Chicago Tribune*, March 9, 2003.

167 Old Town School of Folk Music Newsletter no. 2, December 1960, 4.

168 In 1980, Clemmens produced *Gay and Straight Together* for Folkways, a compilation meant to unite all sexual orientations and provide an album that was considered an important forerunner in queer folk music. The album was a live recording at an open mic night at His 'N Hers, a lesbian bar on Addison Street. The album resulted in international attention for the bar, and its open mic became a popular stop for European tourists. Clemmens produced more music that advocated for gay rights up until her death on February 15, 2003, from injuries sustained from a car crash in Hawaii, where she had been living for her last fifteen years. Jorjet Harper, "A 'Cheers' for Chicago: His 'N Hers," in *Out and Proud in Chicago: An Overview of the City's Gay Community*, ed. Tracy Baim (Chicago: Surrey Books, 2008) 172; Kapos, "Ginni Clemmens, 66."

169 Emily Friedman, "Ginni Clemmens: Music Is More Than a Song," *Come for to Sing* 5, no. 2 (Summer 1979): 5.

170 Stracke, essay, in *Old Town School of Folk Music*, 5–6.

171 Peter Feldmann, telephone interview by author, September 15, 2015.

172 Peter Feldmann, telephone interview by author, September 15, 2015.

173 The blacklist was not mentioned in his return to the airwaves. However,

Stracke said the story, which pits a single giant against a village of little people, appealed to him because it was a twentieth-century parable against violence "that could very well be performed before the U.N." The show aired November 3, 1963. "Children's Theatre Color Show Premieres Sunday," *Southeast Missourian*, November 1, 1963, 2B.

174 Other versions of "The Ballad of Casey Jones"—the Stracke version is titled just "Casey Jones"—suggest Janie Jones tells her children their real father is on the Salt Lake Line, making it even more hurtful. The Grateful Dead later rewrote the song to suggest Jones was "high on cocaine." Janie Jones spent much of her life litigating against magazines and film studios that used the original version. "The Casey Jones song has haunted my whole life. . . . My Casey, husband Casey, meant the world to me," she said the year of her death. Lily Rothman, "The Other Half of the Casey Jones Legend: His Wife," *Time*, April 30, 2015, http://time.com/3828342/casey -jones-wife/.

175 Win Stracke, *Americana*, Bally Records, BAL 12013, 1957, 33⅓ rpm.

176 Win Stracke, *Americana*.

177 "Folk Albums—Americana by Win Stracke," *Billboard*, May 16, 1957, 28. One reason why *Americana* was not widely appreciated was its limited distribution. It was released on Bally Records, a Chicago-based subsidiary of the slot machine and pinball game manufacturer, but the label lasted just two years, 1955–1957.

178 Norman Luboff and Win Stracke, *Songs of Man* (New York: Bonanza Books, 1965), 10.

179 Joseph Haas, "Find Old Folk Song Still Being Used," *Chicago Daily News*, December 9, 1964, 91.

180 Otto Kerner, "Illinois Sesquicentennial: Celebrating 150 Years of Statehood," song sheet, n.d., author collection.

181 "On the Cover," TV Mailbag, *Chicago Tribune*, February 17–23, 1968, 1–2.

182 Ann Plunkett, "Stracke, Luboff Write Sesquicentennial Song," *Chicago Tribune*, November 9, 1957, S6.

183 "On the Cover," TV Mailbag, 1–2.

184 "Win Stracke: The Voice of the Sesquicentennial," promotional pamphlet, date unknown n.d., subseries 4, box 18, Old Town School of Folk Music Collection, Chicago.

185 Win Stracke, *Song of Old Town*, Flair Records, FLAIR S-912, 1968, 33⅓ rpm.

186 The album was recorded in 1968. The Movement to Preserve Scatalogical [*sic*] & Prurient Material in Its Original Form, *The Earthy Side*, P.I.P. Records, PIP 6804-A, 1970, 33⅓ rpm.

187 Win Stracke, "An Appeal," pamphlet, n.d., subseries 4, box 18, Old Town School of Folk Music Collection, Chicago.

188 Lisa Grayson, *Biography of a Hunch: The History of Chicago's Legendary*

Old Town School of Folk Music, booklet (Chicago: Old Town School of Folk Music, 1992), 22.

189 José "Cha Cha" Jiménez, telephone interview by author, July 29, 2017.

190 Win Stracke, letter, August 16, 1969, subseries 4, box 18, Old Town School of Folk Music Collection, Chicago.

191 Win Stracke, "Dawn Steps Down," Old Town School of Folk Music Newsletter 2, no. 1 (April 1970): 2.

192 Stracke, essay, in *Old Town School of Folk Music*, 9.

193 Lance Greening, face-to-face interview by author, August 19, 2013.

194 Bob Cromie, "Small but Bright Project," *Chicago Tribune*, July 20, 1970, 26; "Project Upbeat," Old Town School of Folk Music Newsletter 2, no. 1 (April 1970): 2.

195 "Enrollment Hits New High," Old Town School of Folk Music Newsletter 2, no. 1 (April 1970): 1.

196 Pete Seeger, liner notes, *Frank Hamilton Sings Folk Songs*, Folkways Records, FA 2437, 1962, 33⅓ rpm.

197 The catalyst for that album was Bob Gibson, who introduced Faier to Riverside when both were regulars in Greenwich Village jam sessions.

198 Hamilton would return to the Old Town School over the following decades to perform and visit classes. In 2015, at the age of 81, he returned to full-time teaching when he helped open the Frank Hamilton School of Folk Music in Atlanta at the Epworth United Methodist Church near his home. The school is sponsored by the Atlanta Area Friends of Folk Music and is patterned after the Old Town School. Mark Gresham, "Review: Roots Music Legend Frank Hamilton Performs, New Atlanta Folk Music School Announced," ArtsATL.com, August 18, 2015, https://www.artsatl.org /review-roots-music-legend-frank-hamilton-performs-folk-music-school -announced/.

199 Richard Weissman, telephone interview by author, June 25, 2015.

200 Win Stracke to Marshall Rosenthal, August 19, 1971, subseries 4, box 18, Old Town School of Folk Music Collection, Chicago.

201 Stracke to Rosenthal, August 19, 1971.

202 Jane Bradbury, face-to-face interview by author, June 1, 2013.

203 Jane Bradbury, telephone interview by author, September 1, 2015.

204 Nate Lofton, face-to-face interview by author, October 22, 2014.

205 Art Thieme, telephone interview by author, February 8, 2014.

206 He went on to write he was looking forward to attending an Oktoberfest in "the beer-washed precincts of Munich" with Paddy Bauler. "Pray for the success of our mission," he wrote. Win Stracke to Jack Conroy, June 8, 1965, box 30, folder 1518, Inventory of Jack Conroy Papers, 1864–1991, Newberry Library, Chicago.

207 Win Stracke to the Greenings, postcard, January 2, 1969, subseries 3, box 14, Old Town School of Folk Music Collection, Chicago.

208 According to Joe Spease, who was KCSU-FM's general manager at the
time, Dawn Greening's immediate popularity among listeners caused listener donations to "quadruple" during the four years she hosted her show
on Saturday nights, where it bookended *A Prairie Home Companion* for an
hour at each end. Upon moving to the area, Greening noticed that the station was weighted heavily toward classical and jazz. Sensing an opening,
she convinced the station to give her a show. Greening tapped her Rolodex,
and pretty soon all the major folk stars of the day, including Pete Seeger
and Odetta, were swinging through Fort Collins, sitting down for interviews with the station, playing shows, and later appearing in the Greenings' living room for potluck hootenannies. "She was a terrific interviewer
and she had such a history. It kept audiences mesmerized," Spease said.
Stracke moved to town at the urging of Greening, and soon enough, he was
a regular guest on her show as well. Learning of his long history onstage
and in the antiwar movement, the locals took to him as well. Soon he was
coaching vocal students on Mozart, holding court among young people
every Friday afternoon at a local pizza parlor, and even starring in a local
production of *Carmen*. Wherever he went during his short time there, he
was beloved. "He had a chance to live affordably with people who cared for
him and still allowed him to take care of that agitator side of his mind that
really needed an outlet," Spease said. Joe Spease, telephone interview by
author, July 24, 2017.
209 "Win Stracke Is Dead; Folk Singer Was 83," *New York Times*, July 3, 1991,
D19.
210 Kenan Heise, "Dawn Greening: Helped Start Folk Music School," *Chicago
Tribune*, March 24, 1993.
211 Donna Gill, "Some See Old Town Becoming Rich Man's Quarter," *Chicago
Tribune*, December 8, 1967, B1.
212 Robert Davis, "Many-Sided Old Town Comes of Age," *Chicago Tribune*,
February 27, 1975, W6.
213 Margaret Carroll, "Old Folkies Come Home," *Chicago Tribune*, January 28,
1987, F3.
214 Margaret Carroll, "Old Folkies Come Home," F3.

CHAPTER FIVE

1   Ronald D. Cohen, *Rainbow Quest: The Folk Music Revival & American
Society, 1940–1970* (Amherst: University of Massachusetts Press, 2002),
65–66.
2   Mary Pakenham, "U. of C. Group Opens Folk Music Fest," *Chicago Daily
Tribune*, January 22, 1961.
3   Obituary, *Daily Herald* (Arlington Heights, Illinois), May 21, 2004.
4   Cohen, *Rainbow Quest*, 169.

5   Josh Dunson, telephone interview by author, February 3, 2014.

6   Ronald D. Cohen, *A History of Folk Music Festivals in the United States* (Lanham, Maryland: Scarecrow Press, 2008), 71.

7   Studs Terkel, liner notes, *Folk Festival at Newport*, vol. 2, Vanguard, VSD-2054, 1959, 33⅓ rpm.

8   Ray Allen, *Gone to the Country: The New Lost City Ramblers and the Folk Music Revival* (Urbana: University of Illinois Press, 2010), 82.

9   John Cohen, telephone interview by author, September 18, 2013.

10   Allen, *Gone to the Country*, 83.

11   Robert Cantwell, *When We Were Good: The Folk Revival* (Cambridge, Massachusetts: Harvard University Press, 1996), 189–90.

12   John Cohen, Israel Young, and Ralph Rinzler, "The Friends of Old Time Music," *Sing Out!*, February–March 1961, 63.

13   1st Annual University of Chicago Folk Festival, program, 1961, University of Chicago Special Collections.

14   Izzy Young, *The Conscience of the Folk Revival: The Writings of Israel "Izzy" Young*, ed. Scott Barretta (Lanham, Maryland: Scarecrow Press, 2013), xxvi.

15   John Cohen, telephone interview by author, September 18, 2013. The first FOTM concert was held February 11, 1961, at Public School 61 in New York City.

16   Pakenham, "U. of C. Group Opens Folk Music Fest."

17   Pakenham, "U. of C. Group Opens Folk Music Fest."

18   Pakenham, "U. of C. Group Opens Folk Music Fest."

19   "U of C to Sponsor First Public Folklore Festival," *Hyde Park Herald* (Chicago), January 18, 1961.

20   "Folk Music Rings Out at U. of C.," *Chicago Sun-Times*, n.d.; Allen, *Gone to the Country*, 90.

21   Kit Kollenberg, telephone interview by author, February 28, 2013.

22   David Gedalecia, telephone interview by author, February 28, 2013.

23   George Armstrong to Mike Fleischer, September 29, 1960, University of Chicago Folklore Society.

24   Armstrong to Fleischer, September 29, 1960.

25   John Cohen, telephone interview by author, September 18, 2013.

26   Mike Fleischer to John Cohen, Mike Seeger, and Tom Paley, December 4, 1960, University of Chicago Folklore Society.

27   Mike Fleischer to Frank Warner, December 3, 1960, University of Chicago Folklore Society.

28   Fleischer to Warner, December 3, 1960.

29   Fleischer to Warner, December 3, 1960.

30   Mike Fleischer to Richard Chase, December 3, 1960, University of Chicago Folklore Society; Richard Chase to Mike Fleischer, December 8, 1960, University of Chicago Folklore Society.

31 Alan Mills to Mike Fleischer, December 28, 1960, University of Chicago Folklore Society.

32 Mills to Fleischer, December 28, 1960.

33 Mills to Fleischer, December 28, 1960.

34 Richard Chase to Mike Fleischer, January 17, 1961, University of Chicago Folklore Society.

35 Frank Proffitt, *Frank Proffitt Sings Folk Songs*, Folkways, FA 2360, 1962, 33⅓ rpm.

36 Frank Proffitt to Mike Fleischer, n.d., University of Chicago Folklore Society.

37 Proffitt to Fleischer, n.d.

38 Kit Kollenberg, telephone interview by author, February 28, 2013.

39 Nina Helstein, face-to-face interview by author, February 2, 2013.

40 Nina Helstein, face-to-face interview by author, February 2, 2013.

41 University of Chicago Folk Festival, February 3, 1961, CD, Nina Helstein collection.

42 University of Chicago Folk Festival, February 3, 1961, CD, Nina Helstein collection.

43 Bob Kass, face-to-face interview by author, October 17, 2013.

44 Dick Weissman, *Which Side Are You On? An Inside History of the Folk Music Revival in America* (The New York: Continuum International Publishing Group, 2005), 125.

45 Josh Dunson, telephone interview by author, February 3, 2014.

46 Cohen, *Rainbow Quest*, 151.

47 Frank Fried, "Little Boxes," *From Lenin to Lennon* (blog), October 30, 2010, http://www.showbizred.com/?p=67.

48 Cohen, *Rainbow Quest*, 172.

49 Frank Fried, "Orchestra Hall," *From Lenin to Lennon* (blog), July 24, 2012, http://www.showbizred.com/?p=119.

50 Limelight Café Theater, advertisement, *Hyde Park Herald* 30, October 18, 1961, 10.

51 Folklore Society for the Festival of the Arts, advertisement, *Hyde Park Herald* 77, April 15, 1959, 5.

52 Elvin Bishop, telephone interview by author, March 6, 2013.

53 Elvin Bishop, telephone interview by author, March 6, 2013.

54 Advertisement, *Hyde Park Herald* 80, June 21, 1961, 7.

55 Elvin Bishop, telephone interview by author, March 6, 2013.

56 Bill Becker, "The Fret Shop," *Autoharp* 2, no. 3 (February 2, 1962).

57 Alan di Perna, "George Gruhn: Nashville's Vintage Guru," *Guitar Aficionado*, Winter 2011.

58 Jeff Makos, "Buying and Selling Vintage Instruments Is More Than a Business for George Gruhn AB'67," *University of Chicago Magazine*, August 1996.

59   Ed Holstein, face-to-face interview by author, February 25, 2013.

60   Jan Mark Wolkin and Bill Keenom, *Michael Bloomfield: If You Love These Blues; An Oral History* (San Francisco: Miller Freeman Books, 2000), 39.

61   Wolkin and Keenom, *Michael Bloomfield*, 39. Bloomfield told Jann Wenner of *Rolling Stone*: "I fucking love country music. . . . I like it all, I like even the most insipid period of country music, country swing. Are you hip to that? . . . Spade Cooley and Bob Willis and the Country Playboys whatever or Texas Playboys. I dig walks, chicken walks, stuff like that. I could play almost every song, man, I know country music up the ass on the guitar. I could play about every country style guitar there is: old Flatt, picking, Travis picking, Chet Atkins, right on down to chicken picking. I have played a lot of country music, I have played it for years. I could put it into my guitar playing, but I don't want to. I won't play country music." Jann S. Wenner, "The Rolling Stone Interview: Mike Bloomfield," part 1, *Rolling Stone*, April 6, 1968, https://www.rollingstone.com/music/music-news/the-rolling-stone-interview-mike-bloomfield-228277/.

62   Wenner, "The Rolling Stone Interview: Mike Bloomfield," part 1.

63   Wenner, "The Rolling Stone Interview: Mike Bloomfield," part 1, 42.

64   Bloomfield also accompanied the blues singer Reverend Gary Davis at the second University of Chicago Folk Festival in 1962. Ed Ward, *Michael Bloomfield: The Rise and Fall of an American Guitar Hero* (Chicago: Chicago Review Press, 2016), 29.

65   Elvin Bishop, telephone interview by author, March 6, 2013.

66   Elvin Bishop, telephone interview by author, March 6, 2013.

67   Nina Helstein, face-to-face interview by author, February 2, 2013.

68   Elvin Bishop, telephone interview by author, March 6, 2013.

69   Clinton Heylin, *Bob Dylan: A Life in Stolen Moments; Day by Day, 1941–1995* (New York: Schirmer Books, 1996), 13.

70   Paul Levy, "My Flatmate Bob," *The Guardian*, May 11, 2011, http://www.theguardian.com/friday_review/story/0,3605,488665,00.html.

71   Kit Kollenberg, telephone interview by author, February 28, 2013.

72   Nina Helstein, face-to-face interview by author, February 2, 2013.

73   Bob Kass, face-to-face interview by author, October 17, 2013.

74   1st Annual University of Chicago Folk Festival, program, 1961, University of Chicago Special Collections.

75   Mike Michaels, "Dylan, Bloomfield, and Me," *University of Chicago Magazine*, July–August 2012, https://mag.uchicago.edu/arts-humanities/dylan-bloomfield-and-me.

76   Mike Michaels, telephone interview by author, February 21, 2013.

77   John Cohen, telephone interview by author, October 17, 2014.

78   Cohen, *Rainbow Quest*, 170.

79   Young, *Conscience of the Folk Revival*, 56–57.

80   Robert Shelton, "Students Import Folk Art to Chicago," *New York Times*, February 12, 1961.

81 Allen, *Gone to the Country*, 91.

82 Alan Mills to Mike Fleischer, February 10, 1961, University of Chicago Folklore Society.

83 Robert Ellis, "Two Generations Join in U. of C. Folk Songfest," *Chicago Sun-Times*, February 5, 1961.

84 Perry A. Constas, Director, Student Activities, to Mr. Susch, Legal, March 15, 1961, University of Chicago Special Collections.

85 Constas to Susch, March 15, 1961.

86 "Folklore Society to Hold Festival," *Hyde Park Herald* 31, January 31, 1962, 7.

87 James E. Newman to Thomas O'Keefe, memo, January 7, 1963, University of Chicago Folklore Society.

88 Bob Kass to Bill Monroe, August 6, 1962, University of Chicago Folklore Society.

89 Bob Kass, face-to-face interview by author, October 17, 2013.

90 Bob Kass, face-to-face interview by author, October 17, 2013.

91 Almeda Riddle to Bob Kass and Larry Cart, October 16, 1962, University of Chicago Folklore Society.

92 Bob Kass, face-to-face interview by author, October 17, 2013.

93 Bob Kass, face-to-face interview by author, October 17, 2013.

94 Bob Kass, face-to-face interview by author, October 17, 2013.

95 University of Chicago Folk Festival, February 3, 1963, CD, Nina Helstein collection.

96 Bob Kass, face-to-face interview by author, October 17, 2013.

97 Irwin Silber, "Traditional Folk Artists Capture the Campus," *Sing Out!*, April–May 1964, 10–11.

98 University of Chicago Folk Festival, January 31, 1964, CD, Nina Helstein collection.

99 Bill C. Malone, *Music from the True Vine: Mike Seeger's Life & Musical Journey* (Chapel Hill: University of North Carolina Press, 2011), 122.

100 Beth Harrington, *The Winding Stream: An Oral History of the Carter & Cash Family* (Georgetown, MA: PFP, 2014) 126.

101 University of Chicago Folk Festival, January 31, 1964, CD, Nina Helstein collection.

102 University of Chicago Folk Festival, January 31, 1964, CD, Nina Helstein collection.

103 University of Chicago Folk Festival, January 31, 1964, CD, Nina Helstein collection.

104 Richard D. Smith, *Can't You Hear Me Callin': The Life of Bill Monroe, Father of Bluegrass* (Cambridge: Da Capo Press, 2000), 173.

105 Smith, *Can't You Hear Me Callin'*, 132.

106 Smith, *Can't You Hear Me Callin'*, 163–64.

107 Smith, *Can't You Hear Me Callin'*, 171.

108 Smith, *Can't You Hear Me Callin'*, 173.

109 Smith, *Can't You Hear Me Callin'*, 173.

110 John Cohen, telephone interview by author, October 17, 2014.

111 University of Chicago Folk Festival, February 2, 1963, CD, Nina Helstein collection.

112 Smith, *Can't You Hear Me Callin'*, 60.

113 Neil V. Rosenberg, *Bluegrass: A History, Twentieth Anniversary Edition* (Chicago: University of Illinois Press, 2003), 175.

114 David W. Johnson, *Lonesome Melodies: The Lives and Music of the Stanley Brothers* (Jackson: University Press of Mississippi, 2013), 185.

115 Mike Michaels, *A Springtime of Bluegrass*, self-published, author's collection.

116 Michaels, *A Springtime of Bluegrass*.

117 Dave Prine, face-to-face interview by author, December 3, 2016.

118 Mike Michaels, *The Stanley Brothers and the First University of Chicago Folk Festival*, self-published, author's collection.

119 Ralph Stanley to University of Chicago Folklore Society, January 18, 1963, University of Chicago Folklore Society.

CHAPTER SIX

1   Boris Weintraub, "Chicago Is Still Home to Many Folk Musicians," *Washington Star-News*, January 9, 1974, C-4.

2   Pete Seeger, "A Note on Studs, Chicago, and City Folk," *Come for to Sing* 6, no. 2 (Spring 1980): 10.

3   Win Stracke to Marshall Rosenthal, October 1, 1971, subseries 4, box 18, Old Town School of Folk Music Collection, Chicago.

4   Kay Loring, "Coffee Houses for Young People Gaining Popularity," *Chicago Tribune*, May 22, 1966, 5.

5   Larry Rand, telephone interview by author, July 31, 2017.

6   "Cabbie Gives Patrons Earful with Harmonica," *Chicago Tribune*, January 1, 1970, 3A, 2.

7   Mike Dunbar, telephone interview by author, July 29, 2017.

8   Mike Dunbar, telephone interview by author, July 29, 2017.

9   Al Day, telephone interview by author, August 19, 2017.

10   Philip Maxwell, "Coffee-House Singer to Star at Luncheon," *Chicago Tribune*, July 6, 1964, section 1, 12.

11   Tom Barrett, telephone interview by author, May 13, 2017.

12   Mike Dunbar, telephone interview by author, July 29, 2017.

13   Larry Rand, telephone interview by author, July 31, 2017.

14   Skip Haynes, telephone interview by author, May 7, 2017.

15   Mike Dunbar, telephone interview by author, July 29, 2017.

16   Norma Lee Browning, "Let's Tour Old Town," *Chicago Tribune*, December 1, 1957, G10.

17 Slim Brundage, "Is It True What They Say about Wells Street?," *Chicago Tribune*, March 21, 1965, 126.

18 George Carlin, *Last Words* (New York: Simon & Schuster, 2009).

19 Art Thieme, "Chicago Folk Clubs, Past and Future," *Come for to Sing* 6, no. 1 (Autumn 1980): 15.

20 John Hiatt, telephone interview by author, June 12, 2014.

21 David Crosby, telephone interview by author, October 6, 2016.

22 The Warhol show tour ran between 1966 and 1967, but the Poor Richard's residency was without Lou Reed, who was hospitalized with hepatitis, leaving Velvets John Cale and Sterling Morrison to handle lead vocals. The folk audience didn't know what to make of Warhol's multimedia tools like strobes and tinfoil. "No one knew what the fuck they were doing," remembered Skip Haynes, who ran the Sunday night hootenanny. "Just crazy shit." Skip Haynes, telephone interview by author, May 7, 2017.

23 Peter Coclanis, "The Business of the Blues," *Living Blues*, March/April 2002, 49.

24 Coclanis, "Business of the Blues," 49.

25 Bonnie Koloc, telephone interview by author, February 24, 2013.

26 Les Bridges, "A New, Blue Folk Knight," *Chicago Tribune*, November 14, 1969, B21.

27 Chicago songwriter Michael Smith opened for the Parsons shows, February 28–March 4, 1973. He remembered Parsons looking "like heaven's version of Hank Williams." "He would do a fifth of bourbon a night. But he was a nice man. Charming. But just loaded to the gills all the time. I don't know how he managed to keep it up. Always high but beautiful. When he talked to me, I felt it was a little audience with the Pope. It's not that he was musically that great, but just the physicality of his presence was just so extraordinary." Parsons would die later that year, on September 19, 1973. Michael P. Smith, face-to-face interview by author, April 20, 2018.

28 Mark Richardson, "Tom Waits: The One-of-a-Kind Singer-Songwriter on His New LP, *Bad as Me*," *Pitchfork*, October 18, 2011, https://pitchfork.com/features/interview/8691-tom-waits/.

29 Jon Anderson, "R.I.P. for a Chicago Musician-Artist-Raconteur-Freedom Fighter," *Chicago Tribune*, November 7, 2000, section 2, 90.

30 Ron Stevens, face-to-face interview by author, February 23, 2014.

31 Ron Grossman, "Maestro of the Streets," *Chicago Tribune*, December 15, 1989, 80.

32 Ron Stevens, face-to-face interview by author, February 23, 2014.

33 Associated Press, "Services Set for One-Armed Pianist Eddie Balchowsky," December 4, 1989.

34 Dave Hoekstra, "Owner of the Former Quiet Knight Club Dies," *Chicago Sun-Times*, May 15, 2012.

35 Associated Press, "Services Set for One-Armed Pianist Eddie Balchowsky,"

December 4, 1989.

36 Hoekstra, "Owner of the Former Quiet Knight Club Dies."

37 Al Day, telephone interview by author, August 19, 2017.

38 Ron Stevens, face-to-face interview by author, February 23, 2014.

39 Dave Hoekstra, "Jimmy Buffett Remembers Time He Hung with Chicago's Folk Heroes," *Chicago Sun-Times*, July 18, 2011.

40 Hoekstra, "Owner of the Former Quiet Knight Club Dies."

41 Coclanis, "Business of the Blues," 48.

42 Catherine Harding and John Harding, face-to-face interview by author, February 16, 2017.

43 Ron Stevens, face-to-face interview by author, February 23, 2014.

44 Coclanis, "Business of the Blues," 50.

45 Dick Simpson, telephone interview by author, November 17, 2017.

46 Coclanis, "Business of the Blues," 50.

47 Catherine Harding and John Harding, face-to-face interview by author, February 16, 2017.

48 Dick Simpson, *The Good Fight: Life Lessons from a Chicago Progressive* (Emmaus, Pennsylvania: Golden Alley Press, 2018), 237–38.

49 Coclanis, "Business of the Blues," 50.

50 Even though Da Vinci's only lasted a month, it left a legacy into the next decade. Harding and his son John helped gut the two-story space, where they created a balcony on the second floor to look down on the stage. Ten years after Harding closed his doors, the rock club Subterranean took over the space in 1996 and continues to operate.

51 Rick Kogan, "Quiet Knight to DaVinci's: Can a Legend Strike Twice?," *Chicago Tribune*, May 9, 1986, WC, A2.

52 Hoekstra, "Owner of the Former Quiet Knight Club Dies."

53 Will Leonard, "Fading Folk Singing in Pubs Having a Revival," *Chicago Tribune*, November 13, 1966, G14.

54 Howard Reich, "At 20, the Earl of Old Town Is Down—but Far from Out," *Chicago Tribune*, June 13, 1982, G6.

55 Les Bridges, "The Earl Is Just Folks," *Chicago Tribune*, April 29, 1973, I26.

56 Dave Hoekstra, "Earl Pionke: The Man, the Pub," *Chicago Sun-Times*, June 15, 2012.

57 Bridges, "The Earl Is Just Folks," I26.

58 Steve Goodman, interview by Win Stracke, box 1, folder 1, The Win Stracke Collection, Special Collections and University Archives, University of Illinois at Chicago.

59 Judy Hauff, telephone interview by author, March 16, 2017.

60 Chris Farrell, telephone interview by author, July 22, 2017.

61 Emily Friedman, "Earl Pionke: The Earl of Old Town," *Come for to Sing* 3, no. 3 (Summer 1977): 6.

62 Steve Goodman, interview by Win Stracke, box 1, folder 1, The Win

Stracke Collection, Special Collections and University Archives, University of Illinois at Chicago.

63 Listings, *Daily Herald*, July 21, 1972, section 4, 41; Win Stracke and Earl Pionke, CD, box 1, folder 1, The Win Stracke Collection, Special Collections and University Archives, University of Illinois at Chicago.

64 Ed Holstein, telephone interview by author, January 4, 2018.

65 Larry Rand, telephone interview by author, July 31, 2017.

66 Hoekstra, "Earl Pionke: The Man, the Pub."

67 Dave Prine, face-to-face interview by author, December 3, 2016.

68 Mick Scott, face-to-face interview by author, February 17, 2016.

69 Tom Dundee, "A Delicate Balance," on *A Delicate Balance*, Freckle Records, FR-01901, 1979, 33⅓ rpm.

70 In the 1980s, Smith transitioned to Broadway after he was hired to write the music for Steppenwolf Theatre's Tony Award-winning production of *The Grapes of Wrath*. Michael P. Smith, face-to-face interview by author, April 20, 2018.

71 Ben Sisario, "Fame Calls Back and a Programmer Gets a Gig," *New York Times*, December 2, 1998, section E, 3.

72 Terry Callier, "Dancing Girl," on *What Color Is Love*, Cadet Records, CA-50019, 1972, 33⅓ rpm.

73 Howard Reich, "After 15 Years, A Second Chance," *Chicago Tribune*, January 25, 1998, 12.

74 Ben Sisario, "Terry Callier, Singer and Songwriter, Dies at 67."

75 Ben Fong-Torres, "Transcript of the Interview with Bob Dylan," in *Knockin' on Dylan's Door*, by the editors of *Rolling Stone* (London: Straight Arrow Publishers, 1974), 109; Mickey Clark, telephone interview by author, May 20, 2017.

76 Claudia Schmidt, telephone interview by author, July 7, 2014.

77 Kim Howard Johnson, *The Funniest One in the Room: The Lives and Legends of Del Close* (Chicago: Chicago Review Press, 2008), 226.

78 Bob Woodward, *Wired: The Short Life & Fast Times of John Belushi* (New York: Simon & Schuster, 2012), 57.

79 "John Prine and Ramblin' Jack Elliott," *Bobby Bare and Friends*, Nashville Network, 1985, YouTube video, https://www.youtube.com/watch?v=iI9AfsIsu4E.

80 Skip Haynes, telephone interview by author, May 7, 2017.

81 Dave Hoekstra, "Earl Pionke's Birthday Journey," *Chicago Sun-Times*, June 25, 2012.

82 Peter Nickeas, "Owner of Earl of Old Town Folk Club Dies," *Chicago Tribune*, April 27, 2013.

83 Fred Holstein, "Rambling 'Round . . . Booze and Folk Music Do Indeed Mix," *Come for to Sing* 2, no. 1 (Winter 1981): 17.

84 Ed Holstein, telephone interview by author, February 28, 2018.

85   Steve Schmadeke, "Sally Holstein: 1918–2008," *Chicago Tribune*, May 19, 2008, section 2, 6.

86   Fred Holstein, "My Friend Dawn," *Come for to Sing* 6, no. 1 (Autumn 1980): 10.

87   Emily Friedman, telephone interview by author, November 19, 2013.

88   Emily Friedman, "Fred Holstein: Your Friendly Neighborhood Troubador" [*sic*], *Come for to Sing* 1, no. 1 (January 1975): 8.

89   Fred Holstein, "Focus on Chicago," *Come for to Sing* 1, no. 4 (Autumn 1975): 11.

90   Emily Friedman, face-to-face interview by author, December 28, 2013.

91   Friedman, "Earl Pionke," 4–5.

92   Friedman, "Fred Holstein," 9.

93   Alan Holstein, face-to-face interview by author, June 27, 2017.

94   Chris Farrell, telephone interview by author, July 22, 2017.

95   Larry Rand, telephone interview by author, July 31, 2017.

96   Stephen Wade, "For All the Good People," *Chicago Tribune*, January 25, 2004, section 2, 1.

97   Chris Farrell, telephone interview by author, July 22, 2017.

98   Ken Hicks, "For All the Good People," on Fred Holstein, *For All the Good People*, Holstein, 001, 1983, 33⅓ rpm.

99   Bridges, "A New, Blue Folk Knight," B21.

100 Bonnie Koloc, face-to-face interview by author, July 28, 2017.

101 June Sawyers, "Bonnie Koloc Comes to Terms with Fame," *Chicago Tribune*, November 27, 1987, 14.

102 Skip Haynes, telephone interview by author, May 7, 2017.

103 Jim Tullio, face-to-face interview by author, April 14, 2018.

104 "Ovation in Reorganization; Bonnie Koloc Prime Promotion," *Billboard*, April 15, 1972, 2.

105 Bonnie Koloc, face-to-face interview by author, July 28, 2017.

106 Ron Scroggin, telephone interview by author, May 18, 2018.

107 David Briggs, telephone interview by author, February 1, 2018.

108 Bonnie Koloc, face-to-face interview by author, July 28, 2017.

109 David Briggs, telephone interview by author, February 1, 2018.

110 Bonnie Koloc, "Children's Blues," on *You're Gonna Love Yourself in the Morning*, Ovation Records, OVQD 14-38, 1974, 33⅓ rpm.

111 According to Koloc, Columbia walked away from signing her because Ovation Records president Dick Schorr demanded the label also buy his entire roster of artists, none of whom were of great significance. Bonnie Koloc, face-to-face interview by author, July 28, 2017.

112 Bonnie Koloc, face-to-face interview by author, July 28, 2017.

113 Jim Tullio, face-to-face interview by author, April 14, 2018.

114 Bonnie Koloc, telephone interview by author, February 24, 2013.

115 "Curt C. Burkhart Obituary," *Rochester Sentinel*, April 22, 1975.

116 Ira Kart, telephone interview by author, August 28, 2013.

117 Bonnie Koloc, "I'll Still Be Loving You," on *Close-Up*, Epic/Full Moon Records, no. 34184, 1976, 33⅓ rpm.

118 Bonnie Koloc, telephone interview by author, February 24, 2013.

119 Donnie Fritts, telephone interview by author, August 2, 2017.

120 Steve Goodman, interview by Win Stracke, box 1, folder 1, The Win Stracke Collection, Special Collections and University Archives, University of Illinois at Chicago.

121 Jack Hurst, "Steve Goodman: Singing, Smiling through His Battle with Leukemia," *Chicago Tribune*, May 15, 1983, 111.

122 Lynn Van Matre, "At 27, Steve Goodman Has 'Got It Made,'" *Chicago Tribune*, July 20, 1976, B1.

123 Michael P. Smith, face-to-face interview by author, April 20, 2018.

124 Steve Goodman, interview by Win Stracke, box 1, folder 1, The Win Stracke Collection, Special Collections and University Archives, University of Illinois at Chicago.

125 Steve Goodman, "A Dying Cub Fan's Last Request," on *Abstract Art*, Red Pajamas Records, no. RPJ-002, 1983, 33⅓ rpm.

126 Roy Leonard, telephone interview by author, May 28, 2013. In 1984, WGN hired Goodman to write "Go Cubs Go," a jingle they aired during Cubs games. The song was revived at Wrigley Field years later and became a postgame tradition after Cubs wins. When the Cubs won the World Series in 2016, the team's first title since 1908, the song became an unexpected hit, landing at no. 21 on *Billboard*'s Pop Digital Song Sales chart that November. However, the Goodman family had sold the publishing rights to his song catalog just months earlier. "At this point it's solidified as this team's anthem. For me, that's the ultimate. I think my dad would have been incredibly honored," said Rosanna Goodman, his daughter. But in a way, Goodman was part of the celebration. Years earlier, David Goodman, his brother, had sprinkled a vial of Goodman's ashes on Wrigley Field. Andy Grimm, "Family: 'Go Cubs Go' Success a Fitting Memorial to Steve Goodman," *Chicago Sun-Times*, November 13, 2016, https://chicago .suntimes.com/sports/family-go-cubs-go-success-a-fitting-memorial-to -steve-goodman/.

127 Steve Goodman, interview by Win Stracke, box 1, folder 1, The Win Stracke Collection, Special Collections and University Archives, University of Illinois at Chicago.

128 Clay Eals, *Steve Goodman: Facing the Music* (Toronto: ECW Press, 2012), 30, 68, 118.

129 Steve Goodman, interview by Win Stracke, box 1, folder 1, The Win Stracke Collection, Special Collections and University Archives, University of Illinois at Chicago.

130 Hank Reineke, *Arlo Guthrie: The Warner/Reprise Years* (Lanham, Maryland: Scarecrow Press, 2012), 127.

131 "John, Arlo, Kris and Others Discuss Steve Goodman," YouTube video,

March 16, 2011, https://www.youtube.com/watch?v=yZx7xCK6yfo.

132 Reineke, *Arlo Guthrie*, 147.

133 On September 3, 2005, Goodman's friend Jimmy Buffett turned the song into an elegy for New Orleans just days after Hurricane Katrina by playing an acoustic version in the bleachers of Wrigley Field on the first night of a two-night stand at the ballpark.

134 Steve Goodman, interview by John Platt of WXRT-FM, April 1975, YouTube video, https://www.youtube.com/watch?v=kjxMZruZ2iM.

135 Cliff Radel, "No, Goodman Isn't Going Straight . . . Not Yet," *Cincinnati Enquirer*, April 17, 1979, 9.

136 Dave Prine, face-to-face interview by author, December 3, 2016.

137 Steve Goodman, "The Ballad of Penny Evans," on *Somebody Else's Troubles*, Buddah Records, no. BDS 5121, 1972, 33⅓ rpm.

138 Hoekstra, "Jimmy Buffett Remembers."

139 Jim Tullio, face-to-face interview by author, April 14, 2018.

140 Hurst, "Steve Goodman," 111.

141 "Steve Goodman, Composer and Folk Singer, Dies at 36," *New York Times*, September 22, 1984, 100.

142 "John, Arlo, Kris and Others Discuss Steve Goodman," YouTube video, March 16, 2001, https://www.youtube.com/watch?v=yZx7xCK6yfo.

143 John Prine, face-to-face interview by author, November 4, 2016.

144 Jean Louise Guarino, "Maywood, IL," in *Encyclopedia of Chicago*, ed. Janice L. Reiff, Ann Durkin Keating, and James R. Grossman (Chicago: The Chicago Historical Society, 2005), http://www.encyclopedia.chicagohistory.org/pages/796.html.

145 John Prine, telephone interview by author, November 19, 1999.

146 Billy Prine, telephone interview by author, November 13, 2016.

147 Dave Prine, face-to-face interview by author, December 3, 2016.

148 The Maywood location of American Can is in the history books for producing the first beer can in 1935. Once covering 18 acres, the plant had a 4,500-person workforce, which made it one of the region's biggest employers. The plant closed in 1975. Joseph Sjostrom, "Once-Bustling Land to Yield Jobs Again," *Chicago Tribune*, May 31, 2005, http://www.chicagotribune.com/news/ct-xpm-2005-05-31-0505310097-story.html.

149 John Prine, face-to-face interview by author, November 4, 2016.

150 Dave Prine, face-to-face interview by author, December 3, 2016.

151 Dave Prine, face-to-face interview by author, December 3, 2016.

152 Lawrence Rand, "Dave Prine and Tyler Wilson: The National Recovery Act," *Come for to Sing* 4, no. 4 (Autumn 1978): 7. Wilson also contributed to the old-time scene by helping open Hogeye Music in Evanston. In 1978, he and his wife, Joan Wilson, along with Anne Hills and Jan Burda, opened the music store at 1920 Central, which sold vintage instruments and records, and held a folk concert series for decades. Victoria Scott, "Still

Fiddlin' Around . . . Hogeye Folk Arts Marks 30th Anniversary," *Evanston Roundtable*, September 14, 2010, https://evanstonroundtable.com/2010/09/14/still-fiddlin-around-hogeye-folk-arts-marks-30th-anniversary/.

153 Dave Prine, face-to-face interview by author, December 3, 2016; Billy Prine, telephone interview by author, November 13, 2016.

154 John Prine, *Beyond Words* (Nashville: Oh Boy Records, 2016), 15.

155 Irene Powers, "Mount Sinai Club Names Co-Presidents," *Chicago Tribune*, May 27, 1969, section 2, 6.

156 "John Prine and Ramblin' Jack Elliott," *Bobby Bare and Friends*, Nashville Network, 1985, YouTube video, 1985, https://www.youtube.com/watch?v=iI9AfsIsu4E.

157 John Prine, telephone interview by author, November 19, 1999.

158 Will Leonard, "Franz Fiddles toward Record in the Consort," *Chicago Tribune*, October 4, 1970, section 5, 6.

159 Roger Ebert, "Singing Mailman Who Delivers a Powerful Message in a Few Words," *Chicago Sun-Times*, October 9, 1970.

160 John Prine, face-to-face interview by author, November 4, 2016.

161 Lloyd Sachs, "To Believe in This Living," *No Depression*, May–June 2005, no. 57, 78.

162 John Prine, "Six O'clock News," on *John Prine*, Atlantic Records, SD-8296, 1971, 33⅓ rpm.

163 John Prine, face-to-face interview by author, November 4, 2016.

164 Studs Terkel Interviews John Prine, WFMT-FM, January 7, 1970, https://open.spotify.com/track/2XqfOOKmBryme3UJHjUamb.

165 John Prine, face-to-face interview by author, November 4, 2016.

166 Sachs, "To Believe in This Living," 81.

167 Sachs, "To Believe in This Living," 81.

168 Dan Kening, "Famous Potatoes," *Chicago Tribune*, May 28, 1990, section 4, 3.

169 John Prine, "When I Get to Heaven," on *The Tree of Forgiveness*, Atlantic Records, OBR-046, 2018, 33⅓ rpm.

170 John Prine, "Paradise," on *John Prine*, Atlantic Records, SD-8296, 01971, 33⅓ rpm.

171 Billy Prine, telephone interview by author, November 13, 2016.

172 Eddie Huffman, *John Prine: In Spite of Himself* (Austin: University of Texas Press, 2015), 59.

173 Ben Neary, "Coal Protestors, Peabody Energy Still Battle over Song Lyrics in Suit," Associated Press, August 6, 2015, https://www.stltoday.com/business/local/coal-protesters-peabody-energy-still-battle-over-song-lyrics-in-article_9eb8d238-51b1-5825-8469-65dc65c0c37d.html.

174 Mark Guarino, "Legendary Songwriter Looks Back to the Beginning," *The Guardian*, September 25, 2016, https://www.theguardian.com/music/2016/sep/24/john-prine-songs-music-review-nashville-first-album-concert.

175 Reuters, "Peabody Energy Emerges from Bankruptcy Protection," April 3, 2017, https://www.reuters.com/article/us-peabody-energy-bankruptcy /peabody-energy-emerges-from-bankruptcy-protection-idUSKBN1752EZ.

176 Mark Guarino, "Did John Prine Die for Donald Trump's Sins?," *Chicago Reader*, April 8, 2020. https://chicagoreader.com/music/did-john-prine -die-for-donald-trumps-sins/.

177 Greg Cahill, telephone interview by author, December 5, 2017.

178 Dave Prine, face-to-face interview by author, December 3, 2016.

179 Kathy Boyce, "Where Folk Music's Served with Drinks," *Wheeling Herald*, May 17, 1974, 33. Legendary Texas songwriter Blaze Foley was briefly a regular at Somebody Else's Troubles after moving with a girlfriend for a short time to Chicago in 1977. Foley was introduced to the club through musician Betsey Redhed, co-owner Bill Redhed's daughter. Foley also frequently played sets at Mr. Kiley's, a West Lakeview bar at 1200 West Belmont. That gig ended abruptly when Foley stormed off the stage after he complained about noise and the bartender told him to "shut up and sing." Before Foley left Chicago for good, he wrote two of his signature songs, "Cold, Cold World" and "If I Could Only Fly." Sybil Rosen, *Living in the Woods in a Tree: Remembering Blaze Foley* (Denton: University of North Texas Press, 2008), 162–66.

180 Les Bridges, "What? No 'Chicago Cordon Blues' to eat?," *Chicago Tribune*, March 15, 1974, section 2, 1.

181 Dave Hoekstra, "Obit: Martha Redhed," *Chicago Sun-Times*, January 18, 2006. Pat Colander, "Deals by the Mouthful, on Wine, Food, Song," *Chicago Tribune*, January 10, 1975, section 3, 1.

182 Ira Kart, telephone interview by author, August 28, 2013.

183 Chris Farrell, telephone interview by author, July 22, 2017.

184 Emily Friedman, telephone interview by author, November 19, 2013.

185 Emily Friedman, face-to-face interview by author, December 28, 2013.

186 Emily Friedman, "How to Survive as a Club Manager," *Come for to Sing* 2, no. 2 (Spring 1981): 21.

187 Andrea Vuocolo Van Ronk, telephone interview by author, November 26, 2013.

188 Emily Friedman, "Ed Holstein's Changing Times," supplement, *Come for to Sing* 2 (1987): 9.

189 John Voland, "Chicago's Most Famous Folk Music Club Closed the Doors for Good," *Los Angeles Times*, January 4, 1988.

190 Andrew Calhoun, face-to-face interview by author, March 24, 2019.

191 Lynn Van Matre, "Summer Nirvana for Fans of Folk," *Chicago Tribune*, June 16, 1988, section 5, 12.

192 Andrew Calhoun, face-to-face interview by author, March 24, 2019.

193 Bill Mahin, "Folk Tales," *Chicago Reader*, July 22, 1999, https://www .chicagoreader.com/chicago/folk-tales/Content?oid=899759.

194 Andrew Calhoun, face-to-face interview by author, March 24, 2019.

CHAPTER SEVEN

1　Jack Hurst, "Country Music Tabs Stand by Their Fans," *Chicago Tribune*, September 23, 1976, section 2, 1.

2　Jack Hafferkamp, "The Portage Goes Country," *Chicago Daily News*, April 28, 1975. Twangy fare could still be found throughout the city at lounges that advertised country bands all week, including the Te Pe Lounge, 5805 West 87th Street in Oak Lawn, and the Lake N' Park Inn, 10800 South Roberts Road in Palos Hills, then all the way north to the Society Lounge, 7100 North Clark Street; Fuddpuckers, 1134 West Argyle Street; Moose's Lounge, 4553 North Pulaski Road; Governor's Lounge, 2000 West Roscoe Street; Blue Star Lounge, 3109 West Irving Park Road; and Mr. Kiley's, 1125 West Belmont Avenue, a landing point for outlaw country direct from Austin, Texas.

3　Gary Deeb, "WMAQ Radio Heading Down a Country Path," *Chicago Tribune*, September 5, 1974, B12.

4　Gary Deeb, "'Code R' Surely Won't Rescue CBS from a Near-Fatal Attack of Ratings," *Chicago Tribune*, January 28, 1977, section 2, 10.

5　TC Furlong, telephone interview by author, December 14, 2019.

6　Shaun-Michele Golden, "Nashville North: One of a Kind," *Country Connection* 2, no. 4 (October 10, 1993): 36.

7　Dallas Wayne, telephone interview by author, October 2, 2019.

8　"Population of States and Counties of the United States: 1790 to 1990," compiled by Richard L. Forstall, Population Division, U.S. Bureau of the Census, March, 1996, https://www2.census.gov/library/publications /decennial/1990/population-of-states-and-counties-us-1790-1990 /population-of-states-and-counties-of-the-united-states-1790-1990.pdf.

9　TC Furlong, telephone interview by author, December 14, 2019.

10　Furlong recalled that Atlantic president Doug Morris initially wanted Jump to follow up "The Curly Shuffle" by writing a song about the Marx Brothers. When they hesitated, he then suggested they cover "Shaving Cream," a 1946 novelty song by Benny Bell. The band agreed. Furlong, as a lark, added an extra lyric to the demo: "We rewrote the song for Atlantic / They wanted us to give them a hit / Instead we put together this ditty / And sent them a big pile of—Shaving Cream!" Morris was not happy. "He dropped us. Because he didn't have a sense of humor," Furlong said. TC Furlong, telephone interview by author, December 14, 2019.

11　Lester McFarland (Mac) and Robert Gardner (Bob), both of whom were blind, met at the Kentucky School for the Blind in 1915. They were stars on the WLS *Barn Dance* throughout the 1930s and 1940s, until Gardner became a missionary and McFarland became a music therapist at Chicago State Hospital, a psychiatric facility on the Northwest Side, in 1950. They made over two hundred recordings. Their Birch record consisted primarily of reissued recordings with two new recordings by McFarland, accompanied by Ray Tate of the Old Town School. Dave Wylie, liner notes, *Mac and Bob*, Birch Records, no. 1944, n.d., 33⅓ rpm.

12   1st Annual University of Chicago Folk Festival, program, 1961, University of Chicago Special Collections.

13   Jas Obrecht, "Arvella Gray 1906–1980," *Rolling Stone*, November 13, 1980, 26.

14   Cary Baker, telephone interview with author, December 23, 2017. Baker, who later became an LA-based publicist for IRS Records, where he promoted groups like R.E.M., re-released the record on CD in 2005. By then, Gray had been dead twenty-five years.

15   Joel Whitburn, *The Billboard Book of Top 40 Albums* (New York: Billboard Books, 1991), 234.

16   Robert K. Oermann, "Country Producer Brien Fisher Dies at 82," *Music Row*, April 11, 2016, https://musicrow.com/2016/04/lifenotes-country -producer-brien-fisher-dies-at-82/.

17   "Ovation Installs Fisher in Nashville," *Billboard*, April 23, 1977, 37.

18   Cary Baker, telephone interview with author, December 23, 2017.

19   A highlight of Fisher's career was producing the 1998 debut of Old Dogs, a country music supergroup featuring Waylon Jennings, Bobby Bare, Mel Tillis, and Jerry Reed performing the songs of former Chicagoan Shel Silverstein.

20   Drumm had been a jazz pianist in New York City before relocating to Chicago. In 1960, he had a regional hit with "Shortnin' Bread," a jazz treatment of the folk traditional that featured Johnny Frigo on bass. Jack Hurst, "Country Music Getting 'Hit Men' from Chicago," *Chicago Tribune*, May 25, 1978, 22.

21   Churchill didn't last long, as it quickly expanded its roster into other genres, including jazz and novelty, with artists that included Frank Sinatra Jr. and, improbably, Chicago Cubs announcer Harry Caray, who recorded "Take Me Out to the Ball Game" for the label. Howard Mandel, "Don Drumm Sets Beat at Churchill," *Billboard*, January 14, 1978, 11.

22   Sandra Shifrin, face-to-face interview by author, August 31, 2013.

23   Peter Gorner, "Orchestra Leaders Given Facts, Music," *Chicago Tribune*, September 17, 1968, 38.

24   Dan Kening, "Bruce Kaplan of Flying Fish Records," *Chicago Tribune*, December 17, 1992.

25   Kip Kirby, "Flying Fish Label Bucking Tide," *Billboard*, May 19, 1979, 43.

26   Moira McCormick, "Flying Fish Flies Folk Flag," *Billboard*, January 26, 1985, 84.

27   Si Kahn, telephone interview by author, February 14, 2014.

28   Bruce Kaplan, "The A Capella Singing Convention," *Come for to Sing* 6, no. 1 (Autumn 1980): 20.

29   Bruce Kaplan, "Folk Recording, Fragmentation, and 'Flashdance' . . .

Whither Alternative Recording?," *Come for to Sing* 10, no. 1 (Winter 1984): 18.

30   "The Farmers," *Chicago Tribune*, September 14, 1990, http://articles .chicagotribune.com/1990-09-14/entertainment/9003170383_1_guitar -hard-rock-beatles.

31   Seymour Guenther, telephone interview by author, September 28, 2013.

32   Moira McCormick, "Bruce Kaplan Flies into Politics," *Billboard*, October 9, 1982, 51.

33   Claudia Schmidt, telephone interview by author, July 7, 2014.

34   Sandra Shifrin, face-to-face interview by author, August 31, 2013.

35   Seymour Guenther, telephone interview by author, September 28, 2013.

36   Nan Warshaw, telephone interview by author, March 2, 2018.

37   Greg Cahill, telephone interview by author, December 5, 2017.

38   Don Stiernberg, face-to-face interview by author, January 25, 2018.

39   Greg Cahill, telephone interview by author, December 5, 2017.

40   Chrissie Dickinson, "Take Your Picker: Student and Teacher Vying for Bluegrass Album Grammy," *Chicago Tribune*, January 23, 2013, https:// www.chicagotribune.com/entertainment/ct-xpm-2013-01-23-ct-ent-0124 -pikelny-cahill-20130123-story.html.

41   The Steep Canyon Rangers picked up the award: https://www.grammy.com /search/steep-canyon-rangers.

42   Greg Cahill, telephone interview by author, December 5, 2017.

43   The label name Tin Ear was meant as a wry joke. But when Don Reno said he would never record for a label with that name, Landow rebranded it to Acoustic Revival. Bill Landow, telephone interview by author, January 11, 2018.

44   Jack Hurst, "Bluegrass," *Chicago Tribune*, May 18, 1979, section 3, 1.

45   Lucille Thomas, "Jayland Bluegrass: Wildwood Pickers Will Be Feature Attraction at Annual Festival," *Muncie Star*, June 19, 1983, section B, 8.

46   Murphy Hicks Henry, *Pretty Good for a Girl: Women in Bluegrass* (Chicago: University of Illinois Press, 2013) 307–8.

47   Jim Lauderdale, telephone interview by author, October 4, 2016.

48   Dave Samuelson, "Homer & Jethro," in *The Encyclopedia of Country Music*, ed. Paul Kingsbury (New York: Oxford University Press, 1998), 244–45.

49   Don Stiernberg, face-to-face interview by author, January 25, 2018.

50   Don Stiernberg, face-to-face interview by author, January 25, 2018.

51   Peter Nye, telephone interview by author, November 3, 2017.

52   Vicky Edwards Gehrt, "A Guitar Picker's Guitar Picker: When Muriel Anderson Plays, Nashville Listens," *Chicago Tribune*, September 4, 1993, section 18, 6.

53   Sam Bush, telephone interview by author, March 22, 2019.

54   Don Stiernberg, face-to-face interview by author, January 25, 2018.

55 Greg Cahill, telephone interview by author, December 5, 2017.

56 Don Stiernberg, face-to-face interview by author, January 25, 2018.

57 Sam Bush, telephone interview by author, March 22, 2019.

58 Don Stiernberg, face-to-face interview by author, January 25, 2018.

CHAPTER EIGHT

1   Dave Hoekstra, "Trio Grande," *Chicago Reader*, August 14, 2003, https://www.chicagoreader.com/chicago/trio-grande/Content?oid=912938.

2   Kent Rose, telephone interview by author, July 26, 2018.

3   Obituary, "Donald Clinton Walls Sr.," *Chicago Tribune*, August 1, 2011.

4   Dressed in cowboy gear, the Circle C Boys were so convincing that during the 1952 Democratic National Convention in Chicago, Robert Kerr, a senator from Oklahoma, hired them to stand in the lobby of the Hilton Hotel every day and insert his name in western songs. "They wore levis and ten-gallon hats and looked as if they had just stepped off the plains of Oklahoma," a writer from New Jersey exclaimed. "You could imagine they were next door neighbors and that when they heard Mr. Kerr had decided to seek the presidency, they just grabbed their gee-tars and their accordions and rushed out to Chicago to do their bit for 'Old Bob.'" Ed Reardon, "Passing By with Ed Reardon—It Happened in Chicago," *Herald-News*, August 1, 1952, 6.

5   Hoekstra, "Trio Grande."

6   Kenan Heise, "Michael Scheid, Loop's Country Music Impresario," *Chicago Tribune*, March 11, 1989, 7.

7   "A Little Bit of Country Leaves Chicago," *Daily Chronicle*, January 12, 1989, 13.

8   Peter Nye, telephone interview by author, November 3, 2017.

9   Roger Bellow, telephone interview by author, November 13, 2017.

10 Kent Rose, telephone interview by author, July 26, 2018.

11 Jon Langford, face-to-face interview by author, December 10, 2019.

12 In 2003, Bloodshot Records released *Chicago Country Legends*, a collection of live recordings of Sundowners shows between 1960 and 1971.

13 Dan Kening, "Sundowners Still on Top with Fans," *Chicago Tribune*, December 3, 1993, SW, 28.

14 Although "No Depression in Heaven" is widely credited to the Carter Family, it was actually written by White gospel composer James David Vaughan in 1932; the song was subsequently recorded by Charlie Monroe and the New Lost City Ramblers.

15 However, deep newsroom cutbacks starting the following decade largely eliminated those positions; since 2000, 80 percent of all arts writer positions in print media have been eliminated. Jerome Weeks and Hady Mawajdeh, "Newspapers Are Banishing All Their Arts Writers. Wait, Is

That the Good News?," *Art + Seek*, October 27, 2017.

16 Americana Music Association, "The History of the Americana Music Association," web page, https://americanamusic.org/node/495.

17 Leigh Jones, telephone interview by author, May 25, 2018.

18 Leigh Jones, telephone interview by author, May 25, 2018.

19 Kelly Kessler, telephone interview by author, December 27, 2017.

20 Jane Baxter Miller, telephone interview by author, December 28, 2017.

21 Kelly Kessler, telephone interview by author, December 27, 2017.

22 Kelly Kessler, telephone interview by author, December 27, 2017.

23 Kelly Kessler, telephone interview by author, December 27, 2017.

24 Neil deMause, "Louisville Lip: An Interview with Catherine Irwin," *Here*, http://demause.net/heremagazine/irwin.html.

25 Steve Earle, Jack Emerson and Kelly Walker, "Dealing with Freakwater," *Chicago Reader*, December 19, 1996. https://chicagoreader.com/news -politics/dealing-with-freakwater/.

26 Freakwater, "My Old Drunk Friend," on *Feels Like the Third Time*, Thrill Jockey Records, THRILL-010, 1993, 33⅓ rpm.

27 Freakwater, "Lullaby," on *Feels Like the Third Time*, Thrill Jockey Records, THRILL-010, 1993, 33⅓ rpm.

28 Brad Wood, telephone interview by author, March 12, 2020.

29 Tom Popson, "You Never Know: The Texas Trip That Paid Off for Souled American," *Chicago Tribune*, October 14, 1988, F1.

30 Gary Louris, telephone interview by author, April 25, 2016.

31 Mark Guarino, "Unknown Legends Souled American Rise Again," Time Out, *Daily Herald*, July 16, 1994.

32 Van Zandt's frailty due to alcohol addiction was evident, according to Jim Becker, the Chicago multi-instrumentalist who opened the show with songwriter Diane Izzo. "Both nights he broke down crying. He was just fucked up," Becker said. Van Zandt would die less than three years later. Jim Becker, face-to-face interview by author, January 15, 2019.

33 Rick Kogan, "'Orchid Show' Is Back: We've Missed You but Never Forgotten, Milly," *Chicago Tribune*, July 14, 2017, section 4, 2.

34 Chris Ligon, telephone interview by author, October 15, 2014.

35 Chris Ligon, telephone interview by author, October 15, 2014.

36 Eric Boehlert, "Chicago: Cutting Edge's New Capital," *Billboard*, August 21, 1991, 1.

37 Margy Rochlin, "Edgy in Chicago," *New York Times*, March 13, 1994, section 9, 1.

38 Mark Greenberg, face-to-face interview by author, March 5, 2018.

39 Greg Kot, "McAdams' and Ligon's Homage to the Greats," *Chicago Tribune*, December 12, 2003, section 7, 3.

40 Danny Black, face-to-face interview by author, July 17, 2019.

41 Dean Schlabowske, telephone interview by author, July 17, 2019.

42 Sally Timms, telephone interview by author, August 24, 2019.

43 June Sawyers, "Lounge Ax: A Rock Club where Women Run the Show," *Chicago Tribune*, June 16, 1989, CN, A14.

44 Mark Guarino, "Lounge Ax: Axed Home for Indie Rock Gets Edged Out by Plans for 'Sophisticated Bar,'" Time Out, *Daily Herald*, December 10, 1999, 4.

45 Greenberg, who ended up assisting Miller in booking shows at Lounge Ax, had his first taste of the club's commitment to local bands when he and his band, the Coctails, showed up one day in 1990 to see if they could get a show. Because the club didn't have a turntable, Adams and Miller suggested walking the band's record across the street to listen to it at Wax Trax, the record store. "So without knowing us from anybody, they walked with us across the street and asked the guy to put it on. After a side was over, they both said, 'Yeah, let's get you a show.' It blew our minds," Greenberg said. Mark Greenberg, face-to-face interview by author, March 5, 2018.

46 Guarino, "Lounge Ax," 4.

47 Julia Adams, face-to-face interview by author, February 25, 2016.

48 Matt Berninger, telephone interview by author, March 21, 2014.

49 Guarino, "Lounge Ax," 4.

50 The final night of Lounge Ax extended past 3:00 a.m. Near the end, Coctails drummer Mark Greenberg thrust open the back doors of the club and dragged his microphone into the alley. "For some reason, they have an idea they want to move into a condo behind night life and not hear night life!" he shouted, egging on the crowd. Mark Guarino, "One Last Primal Screen Echoes from Lounge Ax," *Daily Herald*, January 17, 2000, 86.

51 Nan Warshaw, telephone interview by author, August 18, 2019.

52 Rob Miller, face-to-face interview by author, September 6, 2019.

53 Nan Warshaw, telephone interview by author, August 18, 2019.

54 Eric Babcock, telephone interview by author, November 11, 2018.

55 Rob Miller, face-to-face interview by author, September 6, 2019.

56 Rob Miller, face-to-face interview by author, September 6, 2019.

57 Rob Miller, face-to-face interview by author, September 6, 2019.

58 Jon Langford, face-to-face interview by author, December 10, 2019.

59 "Over the Cliff" was written quickly as a response to the suicide of Nirvana's Kurt Cobain. It is based on Langford's memory of seeing Nirvana at Chicago's Aragon Ballroom and witnessing the disconnect between Cobain and the crowd "of hairy guys stripped to the waist screaming" who had no interest in the softer songs with strings that Cobain wanted to play. "At the end you could see he was despondent. He just jumped into the crowd and they swallowed him up. It wasn't a triumphant leap. He was drowning," Langford said. Jon Langford, face-to-face interview by author, December 10, 2019.

60 Bill Friskics-Warren, "City Twang," *Nashville Scene*, January 19, 1995.

61 Eric Babcock, telephone interview by author, November 11, 2018.

62 Nan Warshaw, telephone interview by author, August 18, 2019.

63 Babcock left Bloodshot in 1997. He eventually moved to Nashville and became a primary-school teacher. In Bloodshot's early days he moonlighted by running Checkered Past Records in Chicago. Smaller than Bloodshot, but funded by an investor, Checkered Past released albums by Johnny Dowd, Paul Burch, the Silos, and other artists considered fundamental to the alt-country scene at the time. Babcock later created Catamount, another label, and released music by Souled American.

64 Dean Schlabowske, telephone interview by author, July 17, 2019.

65 Alejandro Escovedo, telephone interview by author, April 13, 2001.

66 Neko Case, telephone interview by author, February 2, 2009.

67 Kelly Hogan, telephone interview by author, February 11, 2009.

68 Rob Miller, face-to-face interview by author, September 6, 2019.

69 Greg Kot, "Why Country-Soul Singer Neko Case Has Settled in Chicago," *Chicago Tribune*, January 26, 2001, 44.

70 Mike Greenhaus, "Interview: Ryan Adams Reflects on 'Heartbreaker,'" *Relix*, https://relix.com/articles/detail/interview_ryan_adams_reflects _on_heartbreaker/.

71 Nan Warshaw, telephone interview by author, August 18, 2019.

72 Simon Harper, "Heartbreaker: Ryan Adams on His Desolate Debut," *Clash*, April 5, 2016, https://www.clashmusic.com/features/heartbreaker -ryan-adams-on-his-desolate-debut.

73 Timothy White, "Ryan Adams' Healing 'Heartbreaker,'" *Billboard*, November 4, 2000, 2.

74 David Menconi, *Ryan Adams: Losering; A Story of Whiskeytown* (Austin: University of Texas Press, 2012), 135.

75 Rob Miller, face-to-face interview by author, September 6, 2019.

76 Nan Warshaw, telephone interview by author, August 18, 2019.

77 Rob Miller, face-to-face interview by author, September 6, 2019.

78 Scott Schaefer, telephone interview by author, July 26, 2019.

79 The music didn't stop, but the label did. In October 2021, Warshaw and Miller sold Bloodshot to Exceleration Music, a newly formed company that said it planned to manage and monetize its catalog, not make new recordings. The relationship between the two founders had fractured in 2019 after Bloodshot artist Lydia Loveless accused Warshaw's domestic partner of sexual harassment. Loveless never pressed criminal charges. The decision to sell resulted from a stalemate between Warshaw and Miller once it became public that Bloodshot owed at least $500,000 in unpaid royalties and other related earnings to its artists and songwriters. An external valuation set the company's worth at $3.2 million. Warshaw characterized Exceleration as "indie leaders who will honor Bloodshot's history and are ideally suited to carry Bloodshot's artistically rich legacy forward." Mark

Guarino, "Bloodshot Records Is Bought by Exceleration Music," *Chicago Reader*, October 22, 2021. https://chicagoreader.com/music/bloodshot -records-is-bought-by-exceleration-music/.

80   Alejandro Escovedo, telephone interview by author, April 13, 2001.

81   Richard Buckner, telephone interview by author, April 7, 2015.

82   Jon Langford, face-to-face interview by author, December 10, 2019.

83   Graeme Thomson, *The Resurrection of Johnny Cash: Hurt, Redemption and American Recordings* (London: Jawbone Press, 2011), 115.

84   Thomson, *Resurrection of Johnny Cash*, 119.

85   Jon Langford, face-to-face interview by author, December 10, 2019.

86   Jon Langford, face-to-face interview by author, 2004.

87   Tracey Dear, telephone interview by author, August 6, 2019.

88   Dean Schlabowske, telephone interview by author, July 17, 2019; Tracey Dear, telephone interview by author, August 6, 2019.

89   When Ray left to join Neko Case's band, he was replaced by Alan Doughty, an Englishman who had played in British hitmakers Jesus Jones. His manic stage energy helped steer the Wacos in a rock direction.

90   Tracey Dear, telephone interview by author, August 6, 2019.

91   Robbie Fulks, telephone interview by author, January 3, 2020.

92   Dallas Wayne, telephone interview by author, October 2, 2019.

93   Fats Kaplin, telephone interview by author, January 21, 2020.

94   Sam Bush, telephone interview by author, March 22, 2019.

95   Robbie Fulks, telephone interview by author, January 3, 2020.

96   Greg Cahill, telephone interview by author, December 5, 2017.

97   Dallas Wayne, telephone interview by author, October 2, 2019.

98   Robbie Fulks, telephone interview by author, January 3, 2020.

99   Robbie Fulks, telephone interview by author, January 3, 2020.

100 Dallas Wayne, telephone interview by author, October 2, 2019.

101 Robbie Fulks, telephone interview by author, January 3, 2020.

102 Nan Warshaw, telephone interview by author, August 18, 2019.

103 Rob Miller, face-to-face interview by author, September 6, 2019.

104 Robbie Fulks, telephone interview by author, January 3, 2020.

105 Sam Bush, telephone interview by author, March 22, 2019.

106 Neil Strauss, "A Major Merger Shakes Up the World of Rock," *New York Times*, December 21, 1998, 62.

107 Robbie Fulks, telephone interview by author, January 3, 2020.

108 Robbie Fulks, "Georgia Hard," on *Georgia Hard*, Yep Roc, 2101, 2005, 33⅓ rpm.

109 Robbie Fulks, "America Is a Hard Religion" and "A Miracle," on *Upland Stories*, Bloodshot, BS242, 2016, 33⅓ rpm.

CHAPTER NINE

1. Members of Wilco often camped out at the Hideout with side projects such as the Autumn Defense, featuring John Stirratt and Pat Sansone. Leroy Bach and downstate songwriter Edward Burch had a long-running Monday night residency as Wilco was recording *Yankee Hotel Foxtrot*, and Jeff Tweedy and Jay Bennett also performed there as a duo. The full band showed up unexpectedly in 2002 when the club held an after-party for the launch of *I Am Trying to Break Your Heart*, a film documentary about the band. For entertainment, the club hired students from a "Wilco Ensemble" class at the Old Town School of Folk Music to perform the band's songs. As the night went on, the real Wilco climbed onstage and joined them, which became a very Chicago moment in the band's history.

2. Mark Guarino, "Billy Corgan and the Two-Drink Minimum," *Spin*, January 2003, 24.

3. Mark Guarino, "Billy Corgan at the Metro," *Daily Herald*, April 2004. When Corgan resurrected the Smashing Pumpkins name seven years later, he delved more deeply into traditional folk instruments. His 2019 solo album *Cotillions* goes the furthest in that direction, using pedal steel, fiddle, and banjo; recorded partly in Nashville, it was inspired by a month-long road trip through Middle America and by listening to classic artists like Bill Monroe. Corgan returned to Nashville in 2020 to record a new Pumpkins album there. He said he came to country late because of the stigma it had in his childhood. "In Chicago, growing up [country] had the classic [stigma of] 'Oh, it's redneck music.' And now I realize how incredible that world was. I didn't know it growing up because of the way people talked about it. So now I'm a fan and I love that music." Dave Paulson, "Billy Corgan Has Been Making an Epic New Smashing Pumpkins Album in Nashville," *Tennessean*, January 31, 2020.

4. Greil Marcus, *Invisible Republic: Bob Dylan's Basement Tapes* (New York: Henry Holt, 1997), 85.

5. Rennie Sparks, Skype interview by author, August 13, 2014.

6. Mark Guarino, "Family Values: Chicago's Handsome Family Mines Beauty from Grime," *Daily Herald*, February 11, 2000, 4.

7. Brett Sparks, Skype interview by author, August 13, 2014.

8. Greg Kot, "Andrew Bird Shares Handsome Family Obsession," *Chicago Tribune*, August 8, 2014, C8.

9. "Robert Pershing Wadlow (1918–1940)," Living History of Illinois and Chicago, website, http://livinghistoryofillinois.com/pdf_files/Robert%20Pershing%20Wadlow%20Worlds%20Tallest%20Man,%20Alton,%20IL.pdf.

10. Tim Rutili, telephone interview by author, November 10, 2018.

11. Tim Rutili, telephone interview by author, November 10, 2018.

12. Tim Rutili, telephone interview by author, November 10, 2018.

13. Tim Rutili, telephone interview by author, November 10, 2018.

14   Jim Becker, face-to-face interview by author, January 15, 2019.

15   Tim Rutili, telephone interview by author, November 10, 2018.

16   Tim Rutili, telephone interview by author, November 10, 2018.

17   Jim Becker, face-to-face interview by author, January 15, 2019.

18   Jessica Hopper and J. R. Nelson, "Gossip Wolf: The Scoop on Pitchfork Headliners," *Chicago Reader*, March 2, 2011, https://www.chicagoreader.com/chicago/gossip-wolf-pitchfork-superchunk/Content?oid=3349416.

19   Jim Becker, face-to-face interview by author, January 15, 2019.

20   Brad Wood, telephone interview by author, March 12, 2020.

21   Gail Worley, "Diane Izzo: She's the One," *Ink* 19, August 6, 1999, https://ink19.com/1999/08/magazine/interviews/diane-izzo. Sugar Free, a Chicago indie, released *One*, but went out of business two years later. Wood said the label lacked the money to fully market the record, but it may not have mattered, since 1999 was a watershed moment in the recording industry due to its battle with illegal file sharing and the subsequent major-label consolidation that led to the wave of teen-pop stars like Britney Spears. "It was a really crappy time for an artist like [Izzo] to put a record like that out. Napster was ripping at the throat of the music industry and gutting it, leaving it for dead, and nobody had time to nurture an artist like Diane," he said. Brad Wood, telephone interview by author, March 12, 2020.

22   Brad Wood, telephone interview by author, March 12, 2020.

23   Danny Black, face-to-face interview by author, July 17, 2019.

24   Greg Kot, "Kindred, Queasy Spirits: The Blacks Invent an Odd, Potent Place," *Chicago Tribune*, March 10, 2000, 48.

25   Danny Black, face-to-face interview by author, July 17, 2019.

26   Danny Black, face-to-face interview by author, July 17, 2019.

27   Danny Black, face-to-face interview by author, July 17, 2019.

28   Leor Galil, "Strap On Your Dancing Shoes for the Chicago Square Dance Summit," *Chicago Reader*, October 15, 2015, https://www.chicagoreader.com/Bleader/archives/2015/10/16/strap-on-your-dancing-shoes-for-the-chicago-square-dance-summit.

29   Jim Hirsch, telephone interview by author, May 15, 2013.

30   Mark Guarino, "Old Town School of Folk Music's 50th Anniversary Celebration," *No Depression*, no. 73, January–February 2008.

31   Greg Kot, "Warm Memory for a Stormy Night," *Chicago Tribune*, December 3, 2007, 2-1.

32   Wilco, "What Light," on *Sky Blue Sky*, Nonesuch, 131388-2, 2007, 33⅓ rpm.

Index